How to
ORGANIZE and OPERATE
a SMALL BUSINESS

fifth edition

CLIFFORD M. BAUMBACK, Ph.D.

Professor of Management
University of Iowa

KENNETH LAWYER, Ph.D.

Professor Emeritus of Marketing
Case Western Reserve University

The late PEARCE C. KELLEY, Ph.D.

Professor of Marketing
University of Oklahoma

Prentice-Hall, Inc., *Englewood Cliffs, New Jersey*

Library of Congress Cataloging in Publication Data

Baumback, Clifford Mason,
    How to organize and operate a small business.

    First-3d editions by P. C. Kelley and K. Lawyer;
4th ed. by P. C. Kelley, K. Lawyer and C. M. Baumback.
    Bibliography: p.
    1. Small business — Management.   I. Lawyer, Kenneth,
joint author.   II. Kelley, Pearce Clement. How to
organize and operate a small business.   III. Title.
HD69.S6B38 1973   658'.022   72-10876
ISBN   0-13-425736-7

Printed in the United States of America

10   9   8

Prentice-Hall International, Inc., *London*
Prentice-Hall of Australia, Pty. Ltd., *Sydney*
Prentice-Hall of Canada, Ltd., *Toronto*
Prentice-Hall of India Private Limited, *New Delhi*
Prentice-Hall of Japan, Inc., *Tokyo*

Dedicated to the memory of Pearce C. Kelley,
a pioneer in education for small business management

Contents

Business Origins – Big and Small, 4 · What Is Small Business? 4 · Trends in the Number of Self-Employed, 6 · Where Small Business Predominates, 7 · Economic Contributions of Small Business, 11 · Advantages of Being Small, 15 · Summary and Conclusions, 16 · Review Questions, 17 · Discussion Questions, 17 · Supplementary Readings, 17

Why Does a Business Fail? 20 · Personal Obstacles to Effective Small Business Management, 22 · Disadvantages of Being Small, 23 · Education for Small Business, 32 · Government Assistance to Small Business, 33 · Organized Voices for Small Business, 35 · Summary and Conclusions, 36 · Review Questions, 37 · Discussion Questions, 38 · Supplementary Readings, 38

Genuine Business Opportunity, 41 · Managenement – What Does It Require? 46 · The Way It Is Done, 49 · Some Homely Maxims for the Small-Business Owner, 53 · Summary and Conclusions, 55 · Review Questions, 56 · Discussion Questions, 56 · Supplementary Readings, 57

4 The decision for self-employment   58

Working for Others, 59 · Why "Go It Alone"? 60 · Small Business as a Part-Time Venture, 61 · Disadvantages of Business Ownership, 62 · Making the Decision, 63 · Preparing for Business Ownership, 71 · Pre-Ownership Experience "On Location", 75 · Summary and Conclusions, 77 · Review Questions, 78 · Discussion Questions, 79 · Supplementary Readings, 79

PART TWO: Getting Started   81

5 Buying a going concern   83

Profits, 85 · Tangible Assets, 87 · Intangibles, 89 · Estimates, 90 · Why Is the Business Being Sold? 91 · Setting the Price, 92 · Advice to the Novice, 95 · Summary and Conclusions, 97 · Review Questions, 98 · Discussion Questions, 99 · Supplementary Readings, 99

6 Justifying a new business   101

Sources of Information, 102 · Room for Another Similar Business? 102 · Introducing a Unique Idea, 104 · Discovering Business Opportunities, 109 · Choosing a Name for the New Business, 112 · Summary and Conclusions, 113 · Review Questions, 113 · Discussion Questions, 114 · Supplementary Readings, 114

7 Acquiring a franchise   116

Franchising Defined, 116 · Growth of the Franchising Concept, 118 · Franchising Systems, 119 · Pros and Cons of Acquiring a Franchise, 127 · Franchising Abuses, 128 · Minority Franchisees, 133 · Summary and Conclusions, 134 · Review Questions, 134 · Discussion Questions, 135 · Supplementary Readings, 135

8 Selecting the merchandising or service location   137

Selecting the Town, 138 · Selecting the Site, 145 · The Retail Location, 152 · Location of Service Establishments, 156 · The Small Wholesaler's Location, 157 · Summary and Conclusions, 160 · Review Questions, 161 · Discussion Questions, 162 · Supplementary Readings, 163

19 Advertising and sales promotion   349

Public Relations, 349 · Special Aspects of Sales Promotion, 351 · Advertising, 354 · Sales Promotion in Retailing, 362 · Sales Promotion in Wholesaling, 366 · Sales Promotion in Manufacturing Establishments, 367 · Sales Promotion in Service Businesses, 369 · Summary and Conclusions, 370 · Review Questions, 371 · Discussion Questions, 372 · Supplementary Readings, 372

20 Credit — a sales tool   374

Types of Credit, 374 · When to Extend Credit, 377 · Credit as a Sales Tool, 379 · Collections, 380 · Regulation of Consumer Credit Terms, 381 · Credit in Retailing, 385 · Credit in Wholesaling, 395 · Credit in the Small Factory, 397 · Credit in the Service Business, 400 · Summary and Conclusions, 400 · Review Questions, 401 · Discussion Questions, 402 · Supplementary Reading, 402

21 Inventory control   404

Inventory Control in Merchandising, 408 · Stock Control in Wholesaling, 417 · Inventory Control in the Small Factory, 421 · Inventory Control in the Service Establishment, 431 · Summary and Conclusions, 432 · Review Questions, 432 · Discussion Questions, 433 · Supplementary Readings, 433

22 Production control in the small plant   434

Production Order Planning, 434 · Production Order Control, 443 · Flow Control, 449 · Summary and Conclusions, 450 · Review Questions, 451 · Discussion Questions, 452 · Supplementary Readings, 452

23 Profit planning and cost control   453

Profit Planning, 453 · Financial Statements and Their Interpretation, 461 · Expense Control in Retailing, 469 · Expense Control in Wholesaling, 477 · Expense Control in the Small Factory, 478 · Service Establishment Expenses, 480 · Demand Forecasting, 481 · Summary and Conclusions, 481 · Review Questions, 482 · Discussion Questions, 482 · Supplementary Readings, 483

Preface

This book is written for all persons with an interest in small-business management. It may be used for independent reading or as a basis for a college or adult extension course for students who plan to go into business for themselves, as well as for owner-managers who desire to increase their knowledge of modern small-business operation. The authors aspire to show a person how he can succeed as an independent entrepreneur.

The book will also be of value to those who are not themselves entrepreneurs, or who do not contemplate small-business ownership, but who are nonetheless concerned about the "welfare" of small business. Many large businesses, for example, are greatly dependent on smaller enterprises for either the distribution of their products or for the supply of many of their materials. The poor quality of management is frequently cited as the primary cause for the high mortality of these businesses. The economic costs of their failure are borne by the business community in general, but the dislocations and trouble frequently come home with great force on the larger companies. The present temper of government is to view with alarm both vertical and horizontal integrations in large companies, and this only adds to the necessity for keeping the smaller companies alive and healthy. Economists, bankers, and career counselors, among many others, also are concerned with the problems and opportunities of small business.

The book follows the same general organization of chapters as in the preceding editions. The importance of small business, its status, problems, and requirements for success, are discussed. Then topics are considered in the order they would ordinarily occur to the reader. The first question considered is whether or not to go into business for oneself. Next the preparation needed and the methods of launching an enterprise on a sound basis and keeping it operating profitably are discussed. Separate chapters are then devoted to each important management function involved in operating the enterprise. In all cases attention is given to the relatively greater importance of personal factors in small, as compared to big, business. A comprehensive checklist for organizing and operating a business is presented in Appendix B.

Also provided are sources of information on the starting and managing of specific types of business. Listed in Appendix A are data sources for over sixty kinds of small-business enterprise.

The text discusses the organization and operation of small enterprises in each of four different types of business: retailing, wholesaling, manufacturing, and the service trades. In most chapters, following a general treatment of the topic, special applications to each of these four fields of small business are considered in turn. This organization helps to stress the fundamentals basic to small business management in all types of business operation while recognizing variations in application suited to particular needs.

Though the general organization of the book has been retained, the text material of the three preceding editions has been updated and rewritten and much new material has been added. The many changes and improvements made in this new fifth edition include the following:

1) Three new chapters have been added — "Acquiring a Franchise" (Chapter 7); "Insurance and Risk Management" (Chapter 15); and "Small Business International" (Chapter 27). The expanded coverage extends the usefulness of the text.

2) Chapter 3 ("Factors in Small Business Success") has been thoroughly rewritten to include many illustrative examples of successful new business ventures. The revised chapter also discusses recent market and social trends and how a review of these trends will suggest many business opportunities for the smaller enterpriser. Among the trends analyzed are antimaterialism (or the "counterculture") and the increasing concern for the quality of our environment (or ecology).

3) Into the overview of small-business management has been inserted a variety of new developments, such as stricter credit regulations (the Truth-in-Lending Law and the Fair Credit Reporting Act), the Federal crime insurance program for small business, the professional consumer movement (and its implications for small business), and the variety of private and governmental programs to stimulate minority business enterprise.

4) Review questions at the end of each chapter have been rewritten, and are sequenced to follow the discussion in the text. These questions are intended to test the students' understanding of the material presented in the chapter.

5) Discussion questions, not readily answerable from the text, have also been added at the end of each chapter. Also new, in an added part of the book, is a set of 21 short cases. Unlike the review questions, the discussion questions and cases are intended to test the students' ability to analyze, reason, and appraise.

Some of the materials included in this volume are based on the authors' research. However, much valuable information was also received from trade and professional journals, publications of the U.S. Department of Commerce and the Small Business Administration, former students who are now independent businessmen, many owners and managers of small businesses, and other sources too numerous to mention here. References to them are cited throughout the text. The authors wish to acknowledge indebtedness to each of these sources of information and ideas.

The authors wish also to recognize the assistance given by various colleagues and associates who reviewed various portions of the manuscript related to their specialized academic interests — in particular, Professors Irving Kovarsky and Chester A. Morgan (labor legislation), and Professor Emmett J. Vaughan (insurance), all from the University of Iowa; and Professors Albert R. Mitchell and Victor Tidwell (income tax accounting), of West Texas State University and Arizona State University respectively. Each has advised and corrected us on many matters, and for this we are most grateful.

Clifford M. Baumback

Kenneth Lawyer

PART ONE
Small Business:
Free Enterprise

- ROLE OF SMALL BUSINESS IN THE ECONOMY

- THE WELFARE OF SMALL BUSINESS

- FACTORS IN SMALL BUSINESS SUCCESS

- THE DECISION FOR SELF-EMPLOYMENT

1

Role of small business
in the economy

The American economy consists of over 210 million people whose material needs and wants are satisfied by approximately 10 million business enterprises.[1] Many of these are internationally famous businesses. Our roster of multibillion-dollar corporations, including such names as General Motors, Standard Oil, United States Steel, General Electric, and du Pont, is the envy of the world. Even the smallest firm on *Fortune's* list of the 500 largest industrial corporations had an annual sales volume in 1971 of over $176 million.[2] The world thinks of the United States as a land of industrial giants; as a nation of "big operators." We are regarded as a people who, characteristically, "do things on a grand scale."

Yet these grand-scale operations, these giant corporations, are the exceptions, not the rule. In the manufacturing industries only slightly more than $\frac{1}{10}$ of 1 percent of the total number of firms employ more than 2,500 people. Of all manufacturing establishments, 89 percent employ fewer than 100 people and 65 percent have fewer than 20 employees. The employment-size proportions are even greater in nonmanufacturing industries. Of the total number of business firms of all kinds it is estimated that 98 percent employ fewer than 50 people! In other words, most American businesses are small independently owned and operated establishments.

This situation differs little from the characteristics of business anywhere else in the world. Though the giant corporations and "mass production" firms loom important in terms of total productivity, it is small business that actually constitutes the backbone of the world's economy.

[1] Unless otherwise indicated, the statistics cited in this chapter are taken from, or derived from, the most recent data compiled by the U.S. Department of Commerce, as reported in the various volumes of the Bureau of the Census and in the monthly *Survey of Current Business.*

[2] *The Fortune Directory: The 500 Largest U.S. Industrial Corporations, 1971* (New York: Time, Inc., May, 1972).

3

BUSINESS ORIGINS – BIG AND SMALL

Big business in the United States is less than a century old, but small business antedates the Union itself. In 1858, R. H. Macy was still trying to start a successful retail store and Henry Ford was struggling to build his first "gas buggy" by hand. Few would have predicted at the turn of the century the present-day mass production and big business that the name "Ford" now symbolizes throughout the world. As late as 1900, the steel industry consisted of numerous small firms, and only after 1900 did department stores come to be identified by their present designation. Chain stores were "syndicates" in 1911–1912 when the first study of their growth was made by the staff of *Printers' Ink*. And the newly developed monopolistic tactics of the large concerns in steel and similar industries did not receive public attention until 1914, when the Federal Trade Commission Act and the Clayton Anti-Trust Act became law.

Without exception, every one of our present-day examples of big business started in a small way. The firms listed in *Fortune*'s directory, as well as our largest and best known department stores, chain stores, and mail-order houses were all launched by individuals with an idea and not much else. Often these businesses were begun under the shadow of considerable public opposition and ridicule. But this is not unusual. The resistance faced by the innovator of business methods from those whose domain he invades is the natural reaction to change. Each successful innovator goes through a period of experimentation and adjustment. This is followed by emulation by others, including, eventually, the injured and resentful competitors. Then comes acceptance by the public and the industry of the new product or method. The development of an idea into a business, the exploitation of a patent into an industry – these typify many successful products now familiar to all of us. Such significant innovations almost invariably have been pioneered by self-employed, small-scale enterprisers.

Thus the origins of many large concerns are explained. Yet the implication may be that the idea behind starting a new firm must have novelty or a unique product or service as its distinguishing feature. That this is not so is shown by the fact that the typical beginning small business simply represents an effort to provide commonly used merchandise to a new or growing market or to serve an old established market better than, or at least as well as, the firms now located there. The premium is usually greater on improved quality, better service, and possibly lower prices in offering commonly used products and services, than on the novelty or innovation, important as this is. The apathy, inefficiency, and slow reaction time of many existing businesses ease the task for the alert and efficient opportunist, particularly in the older industries. In addition, the possibilities of failure and the needs for starting capital (to offset early trial-and-error costs) are lower, since the pattern of operation has been established and the entrepreneur is more likely to possess the appropriate experience.

WHAT IS SMALL BUSINESS?

If 98 percent of American firms have fewer than 50 employees, then almost all businesses are "small." What are the measures of business size? Are they the same in all industries? The most widely used measures of size are those considered thus far in this discussion: (1) number of employees, and (2) dollar sales volume. The Small Business Administration, for example, classifies a manufacturing enterprise as "small" if it has 250 employees or less. But in some industries even a plant twice this size must be regarded as small when compared with the larger plants *in that industry*. Recognizing that labor requirements in manufacturing activity vary widely, the SBA imposes employment-size guidelines that differ from one type of industry to another. Thus, a firm in the household appliances industry is small if it employs no more than 500 people, whereas a steel-rolling mill is small so long as its employment does not exceed 2,500.

In each of the nonmanufacturing industries, the measure of relative size is dollar sales volume. Retail stores and service establishments with annual net sales or receipts of less than $1 million, and wholesale houses with net sales of less than $5 million per year, are small businesses by SBA standards.

A disadvantage in applying numerical standards is that they must be revised from time to time. As large firms grow larger, and small firms become relatively smaller, the Small Business Administration has found it necessary periodically to raise the maximum employment-size limits in identifying "small' firms in certain industries. Similarly, as inflation has continued to reduce the value of the dollar, sales volume standards expressed in monetary terms have also been raised from time to time.

Qualitative criteria can also be used in defining or identifying a small business. Probably the most fundamental definition of a small business is the one proposed by the Committee for Economic Development. According to the CED, a business enterprise is small if it possesses two or more of the following characteristics:[3]

1. Independent management (usually the managers are also owners)
2. Owner-supplied capital
3. Mainly local area of operations
4. Relatively small size within the industry

However one defines a small business — whether by qualitative or quantitative standards — depends largely on the problem at hand or the purpose of the analysis. The number of employees, for example, has a direct bearing on labor relations and the establishment of personnel policies and practices; similarly, in the provision of physical facilities and the establishment of operating procedures the dollar volume of sales is a more relevant criterion. On the other hand, for the purpose of analyzing the impact of taxation on small business, qualitative considerations are more appropriate. Taxes may bear more heavily on a firm not because it has fewer than 250 employees, or has an annual sales volume of less than $1 million, but because it is largely dependent upon internal sources of capital to finance its growth.

In the opinion of the authors, a qualitative definition such as that of the Committee for Economic Development is the most satisfactory. It is the four attributes therein cited — independent management, owner capital, local area of operations, and relative size within the industry — that give rise to most of the problems and special needs of the small, as compared to the large, business unit.

"Small business," "entrepreneur" or "independent enterpriser," and "self-employed" are terms which will be used throughout this book. Each expression

[3] *Meeting the Special Problems of Small Business* (Report of the Committee for Economic Development, New York, June 1947), p. 14.

implies some aspect of the institution with which we are concerned. Typically, small business units possess the following characteristics in common:

1. *Independence.*   By accepted definitions, independence – or no outside control – is a feature of all small business. It leads to many problems when carried to excess, but it is also a highly valued, desirable attribute. It needs qualification in some cases because many small ventures are not entirely independent of some control by supporting family members or close associates, and at times by outside creditors or franchises.

2. *Enterprise.*   Every type of self-employment demonstrates some degree of enterprise, risk-taking, or pioneering, even though it may be forced in some cases because of the absence of acceptable alternatives. For example, during hard times a large company might cut salaries drastically. Two employees in such a situation may react quite differently: one, lacking enterprise accepts the salary reduction meekly; the other resigns and strikes out on his own even though he would have preferred to remain employed, and may later return to dependent employment when salaries return to near their former level. Our primary concern is with small business where enterprise appears in a more positive or voluntary form, such as a desire to put one's own ideas and abilities to effective use.

3. *Personal touch.*   The independent enterpriser often knows personally all of his employees, and may know many of his customers, some on a first-name basis.

TRENDS IN THE NUMBER OF SELF—EMPLOYED

A century ago, 80 percent of our labor force was self-employed. Today, however, only about 20 percent are so employed. This dramatic shift in the nature of employment has caused some Jeremiahs to moan that small, independent enterprise is doomed. Senator William Proxmire, for example, has prefaced his book on small business by asserting that "If you're a small businessman . . . you may soon be as extinct as the village blacksmith."[4] Nothing could be further from the truth. The independent enterpriser is as important today as he has been at any time in history. Though the number of self-employed has declined considerably, in relative terms, the economy is as dependent upon the *functions* performed by small business as it ever was. The decline in the relative numbers of the self-employed is largely accounted for by the decline in farming opportunities. There are more small businesses now (22 firms per 1,000 population) than there were in 1900 (18 firms per 1,000 population).

Applications of power machinery and modern technology to agriculture have reduced the importance of family labor on the farm. The result also has been an increase in the optimal (or average) size of farm; since the total amount of farmland has remained fairly constant over the years, there has been a concommitant decrease in the number of farms, and hence in the number of farm owners and operators.

Although a major factor that accounts for the reverse in the ratio of those in self- or dependent-employment is the decrease in the number of people who are

[4] William Proxmire, *Can Small Business Survive?* (Chicago: Henry Regnery Co., 1964), p. v.

self-employed in small-scale farming, another factor is the great increase in the number of wage earners in large-scale industry that has accompanied the rise of mass production and industrial concentration. The increase in large-scale industrial employment has more than compensated for the decline in agricultural workers.

WHERE SMALL BUSINESS PREDOMINATES

Opportunities exist for small business in all private sectors of the economy. The relative importance of the small firm, however, differs considerably from one type of business to another. We shall consider only the major areas of business activity – the manufacture of products; the distribution of products of all kinds (whether manufactured or not); and the rendering of services (which may, in some cases, involve the use of a product).[5]

Manufacturing

Any business may be considered a manufacturing enterprise if it is engaged primarily in receiving materials in one form and, after working on them, distributing them in an altered form. This would include processors of farm products, local craftsmen or artisans, bottling plants, and similar enterprises.

It is the growing concentration of power in manufacturing which has led to the belief of some that small business is "on the way out." In a study by economists at Robert R. Nathan Associates for the Small Business Administration, it was found that although 70 percent of the companies in manufacturing employ fewer than 20 employees, about 70 percent of the total manufacturing employment is concentrated in only 3 percent of the companies.[6] The figures cited in this study are for the year 1958. Since then, there has been a progressive *decrease* in the proportion of firms employing fewer than 20 workers – to 68 and 65 percent in census years 1963 and 1967, respectively. Obviously, there has been a corresponding increase in the size of the larger plants. The Nathan study also indicated that between 1947 and 1962 the 200 largest manufacturers increased their share of "value added" from 30 percent to 40 percent.

Another indication of this growing concentration of power is that manufacturing is the only nonagricultural sector of the economy in which the number of business enterprises has declined in recent years – from 306,650 in 1963 to 305,680 in 1967. During this same period, value added by manufacture in *constant* dollars

---

[5] Excluded from this discussion are farming; the extractive industries (mining, forestry, and fisheries), which account for less than 3.2 percent of the total number of business enterprises in the U.S.; and contract construction. Contract construction is an important sector of the small business economy, 90 percent of the firms employing fewer than 20 workers. However, this type of economic activity has characteristics akin to both manufacturing and the service trades, in varying degrees depending upon the type of construction. The problems of large building contractors, for example, are more nearly like those of manufacturers, whereas the service aspect of their work looms larger for plumbers, electricians, and carpenters.

[6] Richard D. Hollander, et al., *The Future of Small Business,* prepared by Robert R. Nathan Associates, Inc. (New York: Frederick A. Praeger, 1967), p. 9.

(that is, after allowing for changes in the price level) increased by more that 26 percent.

Although big business is predominant in manufacturing, there is still much room in which the small firm can maneuver. That there are still abundant opportunities for the small enterpriser can be surmised from the observation that thousands of new small manufacturing firms are launched each year. Not insignificant is the fact that between 1963 and 1967, despite the overall decline in the number of manufacturing establishments, there was an *increase* in the number of enterprises employing from one to four workers!

Big business is most effective in well-established industries where large markets for low-unit-cost products exist; where technology and mechanization have been developed to a high degree of efficiency, but where huge capital investments are required; and where standardization and simplification (limitation of variety) are desirable policies. However, the mass-production system is often dependent on the small production plant. It is the very existence of the large manufacturer that provides the smaller manufacturer with many of his opportunities.

Some observers comment that our large mass-production industries are essentially assemblers of the products of thousands of small specialized manufacturers. Mass-produced goods such as motor vehicles, planes, refrigerators, radios, and so on have from a few hundred to several thousand component parts, indicating that, on the average each large concern buys materials and parts from small firms in hundreds of different kinds of business. One big producer may use the products of a score of manufacturers. Probably not over 500 firms in the mass-production industries employ as many as 1,000 workers each. Over 300,000 firms have fewer than 500 employees, or a crude ratio of 600 small manufacturers to one in large-scale production.

Thus it is the manufacture of producers' goods (products made for other manufacturers) wherein most of the opportunities exist for the small, independent enterpriser. As big business grows, so does small business.

But opportunities exist also for the small manufacturer in local consumer markets. Some of the more common examples of "local" manufacturing are printing shops, bakeries, bottling plants, and processed dairy products. These are the ubiquitous industries present in every community to provide needed products for local consumption. As a community grows, so also do the opportunities for the small local manufacturer.

Merchandising

Merchandisers are middlemen in the channel of distribution who actually sell products to the final consumers (retailers), or who buy goods for resale to retailers (wholesalers).

There are more retail stores than any other kind of business enterprise; in 1967 they accounted for more than 40 percent of the total number of firms of all kinds. Furthermore, most of them are small; some of them can even be described as tiny. In 1967, about 71 percent of them had fewer than four paid employees, and 95 percent employed fewer than 20 workers. Despite the deep incursions into the market made in recent years by large department stores, chain stores, and mail-order houses, retailing remains largely the "bailiwick" of the small, independent enterpriser.

Small firms also predominate in wholesaling, though to a lesser degree. A smaller proportion of them employ fewer than 20 persons (slightly more than 87 percent). However, over 20 percent of the firms employ only one person, and over 65 percent have fewer than eight employees!

Though the number of independent, small-scale wholesalers is increasing, this increase is not keeping pace with the growth in population. Opportunities for the small businessman in this field are not as great as they once were, owing principally to the absorption of the wholesaling function by franchising organizations, manufacturer's representatives, and large-scale integrated retailers like chain stores, department stores, and mail-order houses.

Just as the mass production system is dependent on the small specialized manufacturing plant, so also is it dependent on the small merchant. As previously noted, 95 percent or about 1,100,000 of our retail establishments are small-scale independents. Each store handles from a few thousand to well over 20,000 different items (over 600,000 in a very large department store). These small, independent retailers distribute the products of thousands of small manufacturers and about 6,000 large manufacturers (500 employees or more). A conclusion that at least 500 different suppliers and several thousand retail dealers serve each large manufacturer is probably very conservative. In addition, most consumer goods go through wholesale establishments, the majority of which are small businesses, and each large producer buys services from numerous small and mostly local establishments. Obviously, the small merchant plays a major role in gathering together and making available for use America's wealth of production.

Service Establishments

The service businesses offer literally hundreds of different kinds of services to consumers, to governmental agencies and nonprofit organizations, and to other businesses. They are staffed by technicians and professionally trained people with skills for hire. Most of the common types of service establishments perform work on goods owned by the customer or upon the person of the client. Many others perform services of a different kind, such as instruction or counselling. A "service" may be defined as an intangible economic good, nonreversible or nonreturnable, whose value does not depend primarily upon some material article that may or may not accompany the rendering of the service.

In its *Census of Business* the U.S. Bureau of the Census reports data only for "selected" types of service — professional services and those commonly defined as service "trades." Data are provided in this census category for the following kinds of business:

Hotels, motels, tourist courts, and camps;

Personal services, such as laundries, dry cleaning plants, barber and beauty shops, shoe repair shops, mortuaries, etc.;

Business services, such as advertising agencies, public accounting firms, credit bureaus and collection agencies, management consulting firms, equipment rental, sign painting shops, etc.;

Automobile repair and other types of repair services, garages, parking lots, etc.;

Amusement and recreational services, such as motion picture theaters, dance halls and studios, billiard parlors and bowling alleys, boat and canoe rentals, etc.;

Medical and other health services;

Educational services; and

Legal services.

The above are the predominant types of service businesses, accounting for well over 90 percent of the total number of service establishments.

Other types of service business include: banking and other financial services; insurance and real estate; and transportation, communications, and public utilities.

Except for some notable exceptions in the transportation, communications, and public utilities field (embracing the railroads, airlines, telephone and telegraph companies, light and power companies, and other "natural monopolies"), the dominant characteristic of the service businesses is their small size. Most of them require only a small initial investment and depend heavily on close personal supervision. The barber shop, for example, has never achieved mass production, nor has the watchmaker or the lawnmower repairman. Neither the finisher of antique furniture nor the restorer of metal objects can do his work mechanically beyond certain preparatory steps. Nor can the lawyer, physician, or accountant automate his services.

The role played by "service industries" in the economy is becoming increasingly larger. The number of service establishments rose from 1,180,000 in 1963 to 1,320,000 in 1967. Not only has there been a gain in the number of service establishments, but the *proportion* of such establishments has been rising as well. Between these two census years, the proportion of service businesses to the total number of businesses of all kinds rose from 10.3 to 11.6 percent.

An important factor contributing to this growth is that the purchase of services is taking an increasingly larger proportion of the consumers' dollar. Higher incomes and the increased purchasing power available to the average consumer has provided him with funds "to hire someone else" to perform personal and business services. Ironically, this is coupled with increased personal leisure time and the "do it yourself" trend. These may be related; as people have more money, they have more possessions and wider interests which call for an increasing number of services. Perhaps a boat motor will require repair, a frame may be needed for a newly painted picture, or a hand-knit sweater will have to be blocked.

The growth of the service "industry" can also be attributed to the fact that, since most services are difficult if not impossible to mechanize or automate, productivity per worker is not increasing as rapidly in this industry as in most other sectors of the economy. Consequently, a given increase in the amount of services rendered generates more new service enterprises (as well as more employment) than a similar increase in agricultural output or manufacturing output. This is particularly evident in business services, repair services, personal services, amusements and recreational services, and in professional services. Almost all of these new service establishments can be classed as small businesses.

To a lesser but nonetheless significant degree, the growth of the service-trade industry in agricultural areas is also due to the increased purchases of business and repair services by farmers, such as the repair of farm equipment, the grinding and mixing of feeds, and the like.

Thus the service trades provide some of the finest opportunities for an independent enterpriser. Working wives, increased incomes and increased sales of household appliances, automobiles, gardening devices, and recreational equipment have provided a natural market for specialized services of various kinds. Many of these do expertly for consumer those things which he had previously done for himself. Markets also exist for the repair, maintenance, or storage of certain products such as skiis, boats, power mowers, or camping equipment. Increased automobile ownership and usage has called for broadened service facilities in that field, many of them highly specialized.

The service industries offer at least two advantages as business opportunities: (1) They permit greater self-expression and personal contacts, and (2) the investment requirements are usually relatively low. The insurance counselor's work with his clients, the golf instructor's training efforts, or the window cleaner's functions constitute constantly changing person-to-person relationships. They can be limited as to geographical area, and can sometimes be started in the home.

ECONOMIC CONTRIBUTIONS OF SMALL BUSINESS

Small business is important to our economy for the following reasons:

1. All businesses are interdependent.
2. It is desirable to preserve competition and our system of free enterprise.
3. Small business units and prospective entrepreneurs provide the major fund of new ideas and inventions.

Interdependence of Business

If any one conclusion can be drawn from the preceding discussion, it is this: A basic reality of modern economic life is the interdependence of all business. This is as true today as it was when the Committee for Economic Development arrived at the same conclusion 25 years ago.[7] No modern business is an entity in itself. It must buy from other firms and sell either to different businessmen or to consumers in competition with a great many other businesses. This means that there is a place for everyone, if he has something worthwhile to offer and if he offers it in an effective, efficient way. Furthermore, numerous small enterprises are essential to enable a few large ones to concentrate on those activities where their efforts are most effective.

The prophets of doom notwithstanding, small business is not facing extinction. The fact that our economy, with so much mass production, requires great numbers of small wholesalers, retailers, industrial distributors, and other middlemen must be emphasized. The products of our great business "names" are equally available in Gila Bend, Arizona; Chugwater, Wyoming; and Coon Hollow, West Virginia. They are available in thousands of such remote locations only through the invaluable services provided by small independent merchants, gas station operators, and owners of crossroad general stores. Without these middlemen, these regional merchant-sales representatives and their warehouses, mass distribution of our mass production would be impossible.

[7] *Meeting the Special Problems of Small Business.*

It is also apparent that the mass producers of automobiles, farm machinery, TV sets, and other electromechanical products of our increasingly affluent society are dependent on thousands of small, independent service establishments for the repair, upkeep, and maintenance of these products. Small enterprises also perform a wide variety of professional, technical, and clerical services for big business itself, just as they do for any of their other customers in need of their specialized skills and knowledge.

Even in manufacturing, big business and little business work hand in hand. Not only do small firms make most of the component parts which feed our huge assembly lines, as well as a wide variety of industrial supplies (such as corrugated boxes and other shipping containers), they are also important users of many of the large firms' products.

The automobile industry provides one of the best illustrations of the basic and far-reaching interdependence of business. When one thinks of this industry there is a tendency to think only of the "Big Four" — General Motors, Ford, Chrysler, and American Motors. Yet according to the latest count there are more than 2,700 firms classified in this industry. Most of them are parts producers, rather than assemblers, and employ fewer than 50 people. Only 14 percent of them (including the Big Four) employ in excess of 250 workers.

Small businesses are even smaller in the automobile-*related* industries. Of the approximately 110,000 automobile repair shops in the U.S., for example, 70 percent have only one to three employees; and of the more than 215,000 service stations, three-quarters of them are in this size range. Of the 62,000 new-car dealers, 60 percent employ fewer than 50 people.[8]

A. W. Hartig, Director of Purchasing for the Chrysler Corporation, states that in 1971 his company purchased goods and services from over 20,000 companies, 70 percent of whom employ fewer than 100 workers. These companies provide job and business opportunities for thousands of people in over 4,500 communities in all 50 states. Mr. Hartig estimates that one business in six is related in one way or another to the automobile industry and that these predominantly small businesses employ over 12 million workers, or approximately 15 percent of the nation's employed labor force. These figures clearly indicate, he writes, that "small, independently-operated businesses remain a keystone of our economic way of life."

Maintenance of Competition

In the preceding paragraphs we have stressed the *noncompetitive* aspects of business enterprise, that is, the interdependent or *complementary* nature of the functions and activities of large and small firms. But big and small business also compete with each other in many areas, and it is equally important (if not more so) to preserve competition and our system of free, independent enterprise.

The nation first became concerned about the growing concentration of business power more than 80 years ago — in 1890, when Congress enacted the Sherman Act. Subsequent *anti*-trust legislation includes the Clayton Act of 1914 and the Wheeler-Lea Act of 1938. In 1953, however, a new, *positive* approach to the problem of growing monopoly power was taken with passage of the Small Business Act; here the purpose is to avert monopoly not by dissolving the giant firms or

[8] Employment-size data cited by A. W. Hartig of the Chrysler Corporation.

trusts, but by *aiding the smaller businesses.* In passing this act the Congress reaffirmed the principle that "the essence of the American system of private enterprise is free competition." "Only through full and free markets, free entry into business, and opportunities for the expression and growth of personal initiative," the preamble to the act continues, "can individual judgment be assured. Indeed, such security and well-being cannot be realized unless the actual and potential capacity of small business is encouraged and developed."

Among other things, the act set up a new department of government – the Small Business Administration. The importance that the Federal government attaches to small business and the maintenance of our system of free enterprise is further evidenced by the creation of the White House Committee on Small Business and the two Congressional committees – the House Small Business Committee and the Senate Select Committee on Small Business. Each year, also, the President proclaims the third week in May as National Small Business Week, and the Small Business Administration selects the "Small Businessman of the Year."

The importance of competition in our economy cannot be gainsaid. In an age of rapid change, competition can be the vehicle of change, through innovation or through improvement. Modern competition appears in many forms: in price, credit terms, service, product improvement, interindustry struggles concerning substitution and replacement, innovations as to method, and so forth. Basically, it is rivalry for consumer patronage. If a truly free competitive economy is the desired goal of a nation, the continued existence of independent enterprises is imperative. Competitive capitalism insures freedom of enterprise and provides an outlet for individual creative impulses and abilities, as well as a livelihood for a large segment of the population. It is the best insurance that our economy will remain dynamic and provide a continuous stream of innovations, new ideas, experiments, and pioneering efforts.

Innovation

Individuals and small business units provide the major fund of new ideas and inventions. Records of the U.S. Patent Office show that from 1946 to 1970, 31 percent of the patents were issued to individuals, and 26 percent to small- and medium-sized business establishments. Many patents, however, are never put to effective use, and the Department of Commerce has found it necessary to encourage enterprisers to exploit thousands of patents on a free or minimal royalty basis.

The small, independent enterpriser will always be important in pioneering some innovation and proving its worth on a small scale until the growth stage, if there is to be one, is reached. At this point the small enterprise may adopt large-scale techniques if the necessary capital can be secured, or sell out to a larger firm better able to finance the larger operation.

Small business often serves as the proving ground for new ideas and products, patented or unpatented. Many of these never achieve public acceptance, but they must be given a trial before it is possible to know their future. Big business tends toward conservatism in this respect, and some of our cherished products of today would still be in the "science fiction" stage but for the daring pioneer efforts of small businessmen with confidence in a new idea.

Many innovations originated because (1) alert and sympathetic individuals realized a need for them when unusual conditions were encountered, and (2) individuals sought relief from some problem formerly accepted as inescapable. A few illustrations of each type will prove interesting as well as suggestive of other opportunities for innovation.

In 1851, Gail Borden on a transatlantic trip observed that the milk supply was not refrigerated and that many babies aboard ship died; this led him to develop canned condensed milk, which did not require low temperatures for preservation. A mild winter in 1890 reduced the supply of natural winter-cut ice upon which families and industries dealing in perishable products, such as meats, had formerly depended; this prompted efforts to manufacture ice by mechanical means. The Hygeia nursing bottle was invented by a physician in general practice to help curb the infant cholera that often resulted from the use of unsterilized containers for babies' milk. Quick freezing of perishable foods was developed by Clarence Birdseye in the early 1920s to preserve the natural flavor of fresh foods that were out of season or were shipped great distances from their points of origin. Once ice cream was a luxury served only at the most elaborate functions of royalty. In 1846 Nancy Johnson, a housewife, contrived a simple hand-cranked freezer which she considered to be too obvious to patent and in 1851 a Baltimore milkman started quantity production and marketing of ice cream at popular prices.

Our second group of illustrations shows how innovations originate in efforts to solve personal problems and later become the bases for business enterprises. For centuries, mothers had been laboriously squeezing or straining vegetables and fruits and extracting juices from meats to feed their infants before they had teeth. In one of the typical family scenes more than a generation ago, Dan Gerber was prodding his wife to hurry or they would be late for an engagement. In desperation she said, "Here, smarty, *you* strain the baby's peas!" Dan's first attempt did not set any speed record, but it did lead to the first factory production of prepared baby foods in his cannery in Fremont, Michigan. Thus our current multimillion-dollar baby food industry was launched more than 35 years ago.

In the 1930s, Mrs. Margaret Rudkin provided another outstanding example of the development of a traditionally "home-cooked" product into a national brand. Her Pepperidge Farms, Inc., established in Fairfield, Connecticut, baked and sold whole-wheat bread. Mrs. Rudkin originally prepared this bread to alleviate her son's asthma, and it was produced according to an old family recipe. The business is now nationwide and markets 57 different bakery products, with annual sales exceeding $50 million.

Many major inventions of the past, such as the steam engine, automobile, flying machine, and telephone, were at first considered worthless. It was not until their economic value was proved by their pioneers that they became "worth" anything. The same is true of many innovations in marketing — the chain store, department store, vending machines, and other ideas widely accepted today.

In any discussion of product innovation, of invention of a new device, or the use of a new business method, several facts must always be borne in mind: (1) the inventor's evaluation of his idea may not be supported by the reality of the marketplace; (2) a market study to determine the potential of the project and the details of a marketing plan must be carefully prepared; and (3) capital requirements for launching the project, particularly allowing for costs of experimentation in the market, can be substantial, as will be noted later in this text. New products rarely "get off the ground" without adequate initial financing. Ideas are often no better than the plan which will make them profitable.

The history of the typewriter illustrates the latter point, as well as the genius of the American businessman. During the 154 years prior to 1868, seven men in foreign countries had invented "writing machines," but not one was marketed. Christopher Sholes, an American, perfected a typewriter in 1868 and produced and marketed his product so successfully that before long it was in use throughout much of the civilized world.

ADVANTAGES OF BEING SMALL

The small business remains so because it has functions to perform that are impossible for most large organizations. Frequently it operates in a limited market, serving as supplier to local household consumers or to other firms. Some firms are small by choice, seeking to retain strong personal control. Some are small because they are specialists in a greatly limited field.

Some businesses, by their very nature, can never become large – the many small repair shops, for example. Others start small in order to introduce a new idea or a new product or service. They may grow as the idea, product, or service grows, or they may fail. Many, however, are small-scale operations in industries where the size range, as well as the efficiency of operation, varies greatly.

In competing with large concerns, the small firm has at least two important factors working to its advantage: (1) closer contact with customers and employees; and (2) flexibility in production, marketing, and service. These competitive advantages were repeatedly cited by 173 small business owners and executives in a recent survey by the National Industrial Conference Board.[9] How these factors contribute to the strength of small business can be no better stated than in the words of the small businessmen themselves.

"Basically," said one respondent to the NICB survey, "the smaller company has the advantage of being managed customarily by long-time residents of the community, resulting in a more intimate knowledge of the community's needs, peculiarities and relationships. Normally such management has a large circle of friends and acquaintances that are a definite plus in the acquisition of business. There is also generally a desire on the part of inhabitants of a community to do business with a concern closely identified with that particular community."

The importance of flexibility or adaptability was stressed by all respondents. In the words of one of them, "The small company generally has a closely knit organization that operates on an informal basis and, generally, has excellent communications. This allows a small company to react to changes and problems arising in any area and take corrective action quickly." This same idea was expressed in a different way by another respondent, who replied: "Our decisions are often made very close to the point of customer contact, and our people dealing with customers usually have more authority than those in larger corporations." One

[9] As summarized by Sorrell M. Mathes, "Competing with the Big Fellows," *Conference Board Record* 4 (April 1967):13–14.

respondent spoke of the corresponding disadvantages of a big company. "It would seem apparent from our experience," he commented, "that the systems and procedures utilized in larger corporations impose a penalty in the time required for such a concern to respond to a customer's [request for information or service]."

In addition to flexibility and "personal touch," Professor Alfred Gross cites *greater motivation* as a third factor which possibly contributes to small business strength: "In small companies the top executive is often the owner or a major stockholder. He usually works harder, longer, and with more personal involvement than do executives of larger corporations."[10]

In general, the small enterprise has inherent advantages, or is otherwise the more appropriate, under such conditions as the following:

1. For new ventures, because: (a) the soundness of the idea and the ability of the management require proof before much capital is invested; or (b) efficient machinery and a body of technology must be developed before a large volume of output is feasible.

2. Where a high degree of flexibility is required because of: (a) frequent demand changes; (b) demand for small quantities in a wide variety of styles; or (c) rapidly developing techniques of production.

3. Where manual labor and personal attention to details by the owner-manager are of dominant importance. This criterion embraces the professional fields and most semi- and nonprofessional services, such as interior decorating, repair services, and personal services such as beauty and barber shops.

4. Where demand is strictly local because of (a) the nature of the product or service, such as custom tailoring and the sale of residential real estate; (b) high transportation charges, such as for concrete blocks; or (c) customer convenience, such as neighborhood grocery stores and drug stores.

5. Where both raw materials and finished products are perishable, such as cut flowers and most dairy products.

SUMMARY AND CONCLUSIONS

The small enterprise is of special interest to us because (1) the great majority of businesses must be classified as small; hence (2) small businesses characterize our modern economy; (3) successful enterprises that start in a small way tend to expand and grow into big businesses; and (4) the new enterprise pioneering some innovation has occupied a unique and extremely valuable place in the development of our economy.

Interest in small business has increased in recent years also because of a growing fear of concentration of economic power and a recognition by big business of its dependence upon many small firms.

That big business has made enormous contributions to our high standard of living is obvious, but that small business is equally essential we have endeavored to make similarly obvious.

[10] Alfred Gross, "Meeting the Competition of Giants," *Harvard Business Review* 45 (May-June 1967):175.

REVIEW QUESTIONS

1. How significant is small business in the American economy today? Is small business more or less significant in the economy than in the past? Why?

2. How do you explain the relative decline in the number of self-employed?

3. Do most new firms have a unique product or service as its distinguishing feature? Explain.

4. How does one define a "small" business?

5. What is the disadvantage in using numerical standards of size, such as dollar sales volume or number of employees?

6. For what purposes might quantitative criteria be preferred as a measure of size? Qualitative criteria?

7. What characteristics do all small businesses have in common?

8. In what types of business is the small enterprise predominant? In each instance, what accounts for the dominant position of the small firm?

9. Do you agree or disagree with the contention that in manufacturing, at least, small business is "doomed"? Explain.

10. How do you account for the increasing importance of the "service industries" in our economy?

11. In what ways is small business important to our economy?

12. What is meant by the "interdependence of all business"? Give some examples, other than those cited in the text.

13. How has small business helped big business to achieve such a high level of efficiency?

14. Contrast the Sherman (or Clayton) Act and the Small Business Act, so far as their approach to the problem of growing monopoly power is concerned.

15. Why is competition so important in our economy?

16. What are the advantages, if any, of being "small"?

17. What conditions or factors suggest the appropriateness of small (as opposed to large) business units?

DISCUSSION QUESTIONS

1. Can you think of any exceptions to the statement by the authors that "every one of our present-day examples of big business started in a small way"? Is there reason to believe that in the future some new firms will be launched as very large corporations? Why do you think so?

2. Would you classify the American Motors Corporation as a "small" company? Why or why not?

SUPPLEMENTARY READINGS

Gort, Michael. *The Pattern of Changes in the Size Structure of Business Firms.* Small Business Management Research Report prepared for the Small Business Administration. Chicago: University of Chicago, 1964. Explores the implications of changes in the size structure of firms to determine the role of small business in various industries.

Gross, Alfred. "Meeting the Competition of Giants." *Harvard Business Review* 45 (May-June 1967):173–84. Discusses the decline in the relative position of small business in many industries. Analyzes the problem and proposes a program of action.

Petrof, J. V., and J. E. McDavid. "Big Business is the Small Businessman's Best Friend." *Marquette Business Review* 14 (Spring 1970): 18–23. Discusses the complementary roles of big and small business in the American economy, or the symbiotic nature of all business.

2

The welfare
of small business

It is difficult to be dispassionate and objective about "small business," whether considering it as a contributing and important segment of the economy or as an expression of "The American Way of Life," of free enterprise and capitalism. Because there are strong human considerations involved, various individuals and groups, either genuinely or ostensibly interested, often exhibit great concern. These include (1) the small businessman himself; (2) his suppliers, who depend on him for existence; (3) various trade associations; (4) economists and other students of "the problems"; and (5) politicians. All are properly concerned with "the little fellow's" current welfare, his future progress and often, with his reciprocal support, be it economic or political. This concern manifests itself in various studies of small business's problems, in philosophic and patriotic essays, and in "aid" programs at all governmental levels. In recent years, the "unfortunate small businessman" has eclipsed "the downtrodden farmer" as a focal point for such interest and activities. Much of this concern is highly influenced by sentiment, whether it be true or pretended.

It is our view that in general, (1) the problems of small business are those of all business, and (2) small business, as a human activity has the problems of any field of personalized human endeavor. Trade associations are formed largely for the collective protection and improvement of their members. Suppliers are interested in keeping their customers alive and prosperous. The scholars are simply behaving as scholars, often coming up with valuable conclusions and suggestions. The politicians are naturally interested in any possibilities for improving the lot of their constituents.

Making a fetish of small business, as such, serves no useful purpose. Most business is small business and most of it is likely here to stay. The poorly operated will fail, the well-managed will succeed. There will always be elephants and lions and tigers in the economic jungle, yet through the years the balance of nature has somehow been preserved, except where governmental and other outside influences have interfered. The individual business, if it is knowledgeable of its environment, alert, resourceful and flexible, can adjust to the constant changes of our dynamic economy and can survive. Unless, of course, these outside influences do seriously change the nature of our constantly changing environment – to the end that only the massive operator can succeed in it. This, we believe, is highly unlikely.

WHY DOES A BUSINESS FAIL?

American business methods have been effective and successful. They have been tested and proven over the years, have been developed through trial and error and constant experimentation in the vast laboratory of applied economics. Participation has been voluntary, the new business or the going business contributing an innovation in product, service, or method with a full knowledge of the risks involved. The resultant successes or failures were taken in stride, the loss or gain shared by those who provided the financial or other backing.

The causes of business failures include (1) certain highly personal factors, as well as (2) general business conditions, (3) inadequate financing, (4) inadequate or unused records, and (5) unwillingness or inability to keep abreast of, or ahead of, change. However, these causes may be classified in numerous ways, and great overlapping occurs no matter which classification is used.

Two groups of reasons for failure always appear: the owner's explanation, and that of outside agencies. These are two of several possible classifications, including the apparent reasons and the actual ones. What may be described by the person who fails as "excessive competition" might instead be ineffectual sales effort. What may have been called "bad debts" may in reality have been careless extension of credit, and "inadequate capital" could mean anything from too expensive fixtures to too many relatives on the payroll or spending inventory capital for a Christmas trip to Florida. All of these have been actual causes, but not all were so listed or known to the public or even to creditors.

Obviously failure means a situation where available capital is insufficient to pay all the obligations of a business. No matter how large or how small initial capital may have been, incompetent management has not only exhausted it but incurred debts beyond ability to pay. To the failing entrepreneur the most obvious reason is lack of capital, regardless of how inefficiently he has managed what capital he had.

A recent study of small business failures in Philadelphia comments on this defensive tendency: the unsuccessful businessman does not see himself in the same way as others do, and he attributes his failure to many causes, rarely personal defects. The basic difficulty in small business is bad management, and few businessmen will admit that they are bad managers. The owner generally attributes his failure to other reasons, such as poor location, excessive competition, difficulties relating to receivables and inventory, and, for whatever reason, inadequate sales.[1]

Two other classifications of operating problems or reasons for failure may be considered: (1) those peculiar to small business as opposed to those affecting all business, and (2) those caused by external factors as against those having their

[1] *A Further Analysis of Little Business and the Little Businessmen in Philadelphia* (Philadelphia: Drexel Institute of Technology, College of Business Administration, 1965), pp. 7–8. The term "little" was appropriately used in this study to indicate very small enterprises, such as restaurants, service stations, and beauty shops.

sources within the firm. To repeat, our observation is that in any effort to classify the causes of business failure, there are so many functional interrelationships that a clearcut breakdown is very difficult. The following list will illustrate this point. The question arises, for example, as to whether "lack of knowledge" should be called a personal factor or an educational shortcoming. Also, might not using obsolete methods be due to lack of knowledge? This list, therefore, is submitted as being more comprehensive than clearly categorized.

Personal factors
 Lack of knowledge of the business
 Unwillingness to accept advice
 Unwillingness to work long hours
 Contentment with things as they are, inflexibility, resistance to change
 Excessive expenditures in flush periods
 Expenditure of operating capital for other things

Inadequate planning
 Lack of knowledge or foresight regarding location
 Failure to anticipate emergency financial needs
 Failure to foresee one major beginning error
 Failure to understand relationships between income, sales, and expenses

Inadequate financing
 Not enough to afford proper location
 Not enough to weather that "one major error"
 Not enough to buy merchandise independently at best price, in adequate quantities or varieties

Obsolete methods
 Lack of adequate expense controls
 Lack of adequate inventory controls
 Lack of adequate personnel controls
 Lack of modern equipment

Multiplicity of duties
 The "one-man band" problem — inability to perform a wide variety of business functions equally well

Competitive factors
 Patent advantages of competitors
 Superior managerial ability of competitors
 Inability to attract best product lines

Poorly qualified personnel — resulting from:
 Inability to pay competitive wages
 Unwillingness to delegate responsibility

Lack of technical research
 Not large enough to utilize competent research personnel or facilities economically

Decline of the industry
 Entrance into an industry which is no longer an essential one, because of (1) changing social and economic needs, or (2) change in buying habits

Legal restrictions
 Legislation and regulations — licensing, zoning, health

Taxation
 Difficulty of building up capital for expansion

Lack of need for the business in the area selected

Lack of patent protection

Business is a hard competitive struggle, and the mortality rate among the newer, smaller enterprises is high. In normal times more than 1,000 new concerns open their doors each business day, and almost as many (approximately 800) close. The mortality rate is particularly high during the first year of operation. In retailing, one out of three new stores does not survive the first year and two out of three close their doors within 6 years. In wholesaling and manufacturing, one out of five concerns discontinues in the first year and two out of three close within 9 years.

Many and varied reasons are given for small business failure. Many are inherent in the small size of the business, but most result from personal inadequacies and ineffectual management.

PERSONAL OBSTACLES TO EFFECTIVE SMALL BUSINESS MANAGEMENT

It is poor management that is at the root of most of the operating problems of small business. Many small businessmen are either ill prepared or not prepared at all for operating their enterprises, and the great demands on their time make it difficult for even the competent enterprisers to manage their businesses effectively.

The Unprepared

Two major reasons have prompted many unqualified persons to undertake business ownership too hastily: a sudden desire for independence, and the appearance of an unexpected business opportunity that would be lost if not taken advantage of at once. The usual result in either case is that the would-be businessman realizes too late the amount of managerial ability required for success.

Often problems related to incompetence can be traced to the fact that small business ownership for many is an unplanned occurrence. In other words, these individuals are in business as a result of inheriting a going concern, because of some event that left them with a business to salvage, or owing to the necessity of making a living to support the family when an attractive job was not to be had.

The inheritance of a business does not necessarily mean poor management will result. Of several small business owners interviewed by the authors four had taken over a family enterprise. In each case the individual had grown up with the business. One had worked in the family enterprise for several years before recognizing his need for college training. All four planned their college courses to be of greatest benefit to them later as managers of their particular businesses. In another case a former student married into a business partnership, and he reports his college training as invaluable. Several cases not included in the survey, known personally to the authors, include: (1) former students who majored in marketing and business management so as to be better prepared to take over a family business, which they have since been operating successfully; and (2) cases where students purchased businesses with parental assistance while still in college and then planned the balance of their courses with this owner-manager objective as a goal. (The incentive of ownership has resulted in a noticeable increase in students' interest in courses relating directly to their future business.)

To compensate for the natural tendency toward overemphasis on self-reliance by the small businessman, the following suggestions deserve consideration:

1. No one can be expected to know all things about buying a business. Therefore, it is well to hire a competent lawyer, or to discuss your problem with the local bank or other "knowing" individuals or concerns to help determine the true value of the property you are about to purchase.

2. If you know that some day you will inherit a going business, begin now to learn the business by actual work in the establishment and by supplementary training related to that business.

3. Make a *habit* of seeking advice and discussing your ideas with others. Talk particularly with successful alumni enterprisers and seek their advice.

4. Practice organizing your work (job, studies, and so forth) so as to have "free" time for self-improvement activities and participation in community projects.

5. If you are a college student, emphasize such courses as accounting, business law, oral and written communication, statistics, economics, management theory, consumer behavior, and — if available — courses in small business management or entrepreneurship.

Finding the Time

A major problem characteristic of small business is the importance of *time* to the owner-manager. With so many essential duties to perform, or to supervise, and only the same amount of time available as is used by each of a number of persons in big business, the number of hours in a day is usually the most serious problem of the typical small businessman.

The great demands made on the owner-manager lead to the problem of lack of free time, once the business is in operation, in which to study and improve his business methods through self-development. If he does take the time after attending to all essential business duties, he is likely to be so tired and worried as to experience difficulty in learning effectively. The solution, at least for the prospective small businessman, is adequate preparation in advance or a willingness to get outside assistance.

It has often been said that the chief problem of the independent businessman is his independence. Small business ownership does attract an independent, self-reliant type of person — one less likely to seek advice and assistance from those of greater experience and know-how. Often the biggest problem is to get the independent to appreciate his need for outside assistance, and then to be willing and able to take the time to profit by it.

DISADVANTAGES OF BEING SMALL

Many problems of small business are inherent in the small size of the enterprise, rather than in the enterpriser himself. Some of the more important of these problems are discussed below.

The "One-Man Band" Problem

In small business there are limited opportunities to specialize management. Thus a shortage of capable management personnel permeates most small enterprises; this, in turn, creates unique problems in providing for management in the small firm. In the beginning of a very small concern one man is likely to bear all managerial responsibility without an understudy or assistant manager. With increased size, some opportunity appears to share responsibility and to specialize the management functions, and the company is able to attract qualified personnel.

Any discussion of the versatility required of the owner-manager of a small business calls to mind the "one-man band." Those small business operators who have seen this musical phenomenon in operation will agree that they and the musician have a common problem. With a bass drum at one foot, snare drum at the other, a cymbal on each knee, a harmonica on a frame in front of his mouth, a guitar hung over his chest, the musician is an amazing sight. Any veteran of small business will agree that his own need to coordinate and to keep things running smoothly and profitably according to plan are eclipsed only by the efforts of the musician in a one-man band who achieves harmony while following the melody outlined in the score. Both men are very busy fellows. Yet this versatility and the ability to plan, to concentrate, and to coordinate are the measures of one-man managerial success.

Acquiring Manpower

Small businessmen during post–World War II years have frequently mentioned the near-impossibility of securing satisfactory employees as one of their major problems. With business conditions unusually favorable for the little concern, the employee problem goes deeper than the inability to pay the high wages of big employers. Certainly the relative wage-paying ability did not decline for the small independent as compared to prewar years. Three conditions appear to be primarily responsible for the small businessman's difficulty in acquiring satisfactory personnel: (1) the general decline by most employees in a willingness to do a fair day's work when jobs are plentiful; (2) big business attracting the more energetic and ambitious employees; and (3) others willing and able to work hard choosing self-employment. During a tight labor market normal competition between big and little business for competent employees is intensified – particularly for college graduates and certain types of skilled workers.

Federal minimum-wage legislation also works a hardship on the smaller businesses, which rely more heavily on teenage and student employment. In April 1971, for example, when the national unemployment rate for the labor force as a whole was 6.1 percent, the Department of Labor reported that the rate of unemployment among teenage workers was 17.2 percent! Thus it is the unskilled, teenage workers, and the smaller businesses which would normally hire them as apprentices and trainees, who are most seriously affected when statutory hourly minimum-wage rates are increased. Efforts to exempt teenage workers from the requirements of the minimum-wage law, or at least to lower the minimum rate for such workers, has met with steadfast resistance on the part of organized labor.

The smaller business likewise finds it increasingly difficult to recruit managerial employees. Our expanding economy is creating the greatest competition between big and little business for future executive material the country has so far experienced. College recruiting has been stepped up, executive training programs streamlined, almost fabulous beginning salaries plus numerous fringe benefits offered, and new inducements devised such as postgraduate training at company expense.

The competition seemingly has been too great for the small employer to meet, although most have never been sufficiently aggressive in their recruiting activities. It has, however, had little effect upon the determination of many graduates to become self-employed, other than causing some to defer launching their own enterprise for a few years. This interval is expected to furnish an opportunity to obtain experience and some additional capital, but in particular to result in launching their own venture at a time when qualified employees should be more abundant on reasonably competitive terms.

A well-managed small firm can often turn the disadvantage it may face in acquiring managerial employees into an advantage. This may be accomplished by "selling" desirable prospects on experience to be gained in the small concern as preparation for entrepreneurship or for preferred executive employment in big business. Since World War II several large corporations in various fields both at home and abroad have established small subsidiaries for the primary purpose of testing and training future executives for the parent company. Experience has taught them all too often that promising executive material becomes submerged in the complex specialized duties of the large concern. In the past big business has often employed men trained in small firms, and still does so. The well-managed independent business affords an ideal opportunity for the ambitious man or woman to learn all the functions of management and to develop managerial ability more rapidly than could be done in a large organization.

The beginning small enterprise is also at a disadvantage in paying the high wages characteristic of most big business and rarely can it guarantee employment as a few big corporations do. This problem has been met successfully by many small enterprisers through profit sharing, closer employee relations, and even partnership plans. While these techniques have little appeal to the employee interested mainly in the highest possible immediate and assured income, they do attract the more desirable men who want their incomes to be in proportion to their contributions and ability, and those anxious to become business owners. In other cases the small independent has obtained dependable employees by selecting the physically handicapped and older workers. Both groups are not generally sought by large firms, although recent experience indicates that in many ways they are superior to other employees. For years the small-scale employer was unable to compete with big business on many employee services and fringe benefits. In postwar years several agencies have developed programs suited to the needs of the small enterprise, such as group life and disability insurance, retirement funds, and hospital and medical care plans. Progress is being made.

Obtaining Capital

In at least three respects small business has a serious financial problem: (1) in securing long-term equity capital, in contrast to short-term working capital loans; (2) in obtaining greater protection from the calling of loans or stoppage of credit during trying times when outside financial aid is most direly needed; and (3) in securing funds in small amounts at lower rates.

It costs just about as much for a banker or other lender to investigate and evaluate a loan application for $1,000 as one for $1,000,000. The former may cost more because the applicant for the large loan is often more helpful in providing significant information. So long as the failure rate is higher for small than for big business, the risk of financing and the resulting costs will be higher.

A lender or investor insists on a greater degree of control of the enterprise when financing a small business. This often hampers the management of the small firm and keeps many independents who are unwilling to share control from obtaining the financing they need. When accompanied by high taxes, it becomes a serious matter for the little fellow.

Whether or not adequate facilities have been available for financing small business in recent decades is a moot question. Numerous investigations seeking the facts have been conducted by government committees, the Federal Reserve Banks, and the Chamber of Commerce of the United States. Their results are not conclusive. In general, studies by bankers reach the conclusion that ample financing is available for all "creditworthy" enterprises. The creditworthiness is, of course, decided by the bankers, so this conclusion is understandable.

Bankers also call attention to relatively new devices, such as floor-plan financing and installment loans to small concerns, as further evidence that the financial needs of small business are better provided for now than in former years. They claim that providing equity capital has never been a function of commercial banks, although in practice many banks in small communities did so until the practice was stopped by government regulation.

Taxation and Regulations

Because of the greater reliance upon the resources of the entrepreneur and that of his family and friends as a source of capital, taxation has a greater impact on the small firm than it does on the larger business. High personal income taxes, for example, make it difficult for prospective or incumbent small-business men to acquire initial capital or funds for expansion. On the average, the initial capital required to start a small concern has doubled since World War II. The result is that employees (contemplating going into business for themselves) have found it increasingly difficult to accumulate sufficient venture capital.

Similarly, friends and relatives and other potential private investors are unwilling to furnish funds on an "all risk and no gain" basis — taking all the usual risks of financing a new enterprise but paying practically all of any possible gains to the government in taxes. For example, a 10 percent return on $25,000 invested by a single person would leave after taxes only 2.5 percent for the individual with a $50,000 income, or only 3.5 percent with an income of $25,000. All losses have to be absorbed by the investor; so many play safe by putting their funds into tax-exempt government securities.

Since the vast majority, probably well over 90 percent, of all new enterprises are not incorporated at first, their owner-managers also find it difficult to build up capital for expansion. Even those started as small corporations have had heavy tax burdens and such legislation as the excess profits tax to contend with. Even after paying high federal income taxes, the corporation risks a tax penalty if it fails to pay out as dividends a large portion of its profit after taxes. What the government agents consider a reasonable amount to retain in the business without penalty is usually thought by the management to be inadequate. An "accumulated earnings credit" or amount retained for reasonable needs of the business may be excluded from the taxable base for that year. In 1958 this amount was raised from $60,000 to $100,000.

The smaller business is also handicapped by existing inheritance and gift tax laws. Such taxes, combined with high personal income taxes, have given considerable impetus to the merger movement. Many small business owners sell out to larger firms in anticipation of death taxes. They have found in mergers an opportunity not only to increase the liquidity of their estates, but also to realize, in the form of capital gains, income which they had reinvested in their businesses over the years. Records of the Federal Trade Commission indicate that many of these small firms were earning rates of return in excess of 10 percent on net worth at the time of their merger with large competitors; thus the effect of the merger movement is often to reduce competition by reducing the number of successful small enterprises.

Added to the problems of taxation of small enterprise are those of greatly increased government regulation — both direct regulations imposed on business and the indirect restrictions which come from laws passed to assist labor and others. Some wage and hour laws blanket supervisory and technical personnel. There are numerous records to keep and reports to make, such as Social Security records and tax reports, and then there is the responsibility of abiding by agreements made by labor unions with big business on an industrywide basis.

In addition to the taxes levied directly against the firm (if incorporated) or against the entrepreneur (if a proprietor or partner), the business firm is obligated by law to collect sales taxes from customers and income and Social Security taxes from employees. The burden of serving as a free tax-collecting agent for the government is greater on the small firm than on the large firm. In a recent study it was found that the time required to compute withholding for federal income and F.I.C.A. taxes, to post employee records and general ledger accounts, prepare W-2 and W-3 forms, and prepare quarterly and annual reports ranged from 1.5 to 11.2 hours per year for each employee — the firms with the largest number of employees tending to require the least amount of time per employee. The reason for this was attributed to "better training, organization, and bookkeeping equipment."[2] Simplification of the tax laws would effectively decrease this burden on the small firm.

Promoting Industrial Research

Because of the lack of both the funds and the specialized personnel required, most small businesses are at a disadvantage in promoting research on new products, materials, and methods. However, following suggestions made at the 1958 White

[2] Fred J. Mueller, "Burden of Tax Compliance Keeps Mounting for Small Business Firms," *Journal of Taxation* 21 (Dec. 1964): 378–81.

House Conference on Technical and Distribution Research for the Benefit of Small Business, many small firms have pooled their resources and in this way are making satisfactory progress in meeting their common research needs. In some cases the research facilities of governmental agencies are utilized; in others, by pooling research efforts the facilities of private research agencies have been employed; and in a few cases large companies have made their research departments available to small firms.

Patent Abuses

The young imaginative enterpriser (or prospective enterpriser) faces problems in introducing new ideas once they are developed in the laboratory. Some of these obstacles can be removed only by a simplified and modernized patent system. When an early patent, granted before later discoveries were made, covers a broad enough area to hamper new ideas, or when patents on minor changes in the original basic patent idea are granted almost continuously, the situation approaches hopelessness. The inadequacy of our present patent system is one of the most serious problems facing small businessmen.

At least three alternative solutions are available in many cases. One is to employ a patent attorney (possibly one recommended by the inventor's local attorney or some fellow inventor), secure the patent if possible, and go ahead with production and marketing hoping for the best. If capital and experience are limited, the inventor might do better to team up with a reliable organization specializing in the financing of new businesses; the added protection might be worth the sacrifice of sharing future profits, at least for the first invention.[3] A third alternative is to take up the proposition with a large manufacturer likely to be interested. This last alternative would be more logical if the invention consists of a product superior to one already produced by a large company, but serving the same purpose. Either this company or a likely but equally strong competitor could be consulted. If the invention represents a major improvement on an already patented article, but the existing patent prevents production of the new one without serious danger of infringement, there is no apparent alternative for the little fellow other than to sell out to the present patent holder — if he can. When an invention is discussed with other companies before a patent has been secured — or, if patented, before production begins — the inventor's attorney should be able to advise on reasonable safeguards to be taken.

According to the late Professor Floyd L. Vaughan, well-known authority on patent history, an increasing number of patents have been assigned to big business by outsiders and employees in recent decades. The small businessman lacks the funds needed to carry his patent through to successful production and marketing. It is so much easier for him to sell to the big company for a few thousand dollars cash and a royalty on production. Employees often have no choice but to assign their patents since this has become part of many employment contracts.

The holder of a patent also has difficulty in preventing infringement of his patent, primarily because of the high cost of litigation. The casualty rate among patents submitted for court adjudication is very high. Senator McClellan recently

[3] See p. 218 for a detailed discussion of small business investment companies.

reported that over a two-and-one-half-year period, 72 percent of all patent suits were found invalid. The high cost of litigation and the difficulty of enforcing patent rights prompted Mr. Lewis Evans, a member of the Board of Trustees of the National Small Business Association, to remark that "a patent today is only worth the money that one is willing to put behind it."

Taking the Risks

In many fields big business concentrates on products with a steady or predictable demand, leaving to the small operator the slower sellers and more risky items. This makes effective use of advertising harder for the small enterprise. For many small concerns it also raises the problem of obtaining adequate volume to justify the business. The question of inadequate sales ranks high as a cause of discontinuance among many small firms, but such a statement is likely to be misleading. The beginning enterprise pioneering a new idea naturally does not have a product or service of proven demand; neither would big business if small firms had not done the pioneering. The difficulty of building adequate sales for something new is so universally underestimated, in terms of the time and expense required, that frequently several pioneers go bankrupt in the process before one finally succeeds. Thus this problem distills to (1) lack of knowledge by the beginner, and (2) inadequate finances. Big business, though possessing both knowledge and developmental funds, conservatively holds back until small independent enterprise has developed a proven market for the innovation. An example of this is the development and marketing of a cornstarch pudding which requires no cooking. The first "instant pudding" was produced by a small manufacturer on the West Coast. It was a superb product, but marketed only in the Pacific Northwest. Many vacationers who sampled it traveled east with several packages in their suitcases. After a few years a major company produced a similar product (though not nearly so tasty). Their product was introduced with a national advertising campaign. Those who had been buying the original pudding were sorry to discover that it was moved to a bottom shelf and ultimately discontinued.

Vendor Relationships

A recent problem has been "the right to buy" — the refusal by primary producers to sell to certain potential buyers, especially fabricators and independent contractors. It is often associated with vertical integration where the primary producer owns or controls fabricating plants or particular distribution channels or outlets. Thus it is within the law that recognizes a vendor's right to select his vendees, and avoids prohibitions of the Robinson-Patman Act against price discrimination among buyers. However, even when the product is one enjoying patent monopoly privileges, there are valid questions regarding the desirability of excluding able and willing buyers from participation in efforts to bring the benefits to consumers. When an integrated producer sells to independents as long as they do not compete with his own outlets but cuts off their supply when they do, or during periods of supply shortage, the practice is open to serious question and public concern.

Another aspect of this problem is that of producers imposing undue burdens on their dealer outlets — often shifting the results of erroneous producer forecasts to the shoulders of dealers. This problem became so acute among automobile dealers during the late 1950s that they were able to secure some relief only through federal action.

Discriminatory Practices

Small business is weak in coping with vested interests or monopolistic practices, even though some of the latter may be illegal. Also, it is harder for the little fellow to deal satisfactorily with representatives of organized labor or even with his own local government. It is more difficult for the small businessman to secure the best brands and exclusive agencies. Selective selling policies of vendors plus the fact that established dealers often have already secured the favored lines make this a serious problem in starting a new retail store. A small firm may encounter greater problems than its big brother if it becomes involved in some controversy over its product. Also, the little fellow often has trouble presenting a convincing case when seeking assistance from state agricultural and industrial commissions accustomed to dealing mainly with large industries.

Problems related to monopolistic practices have been the main reason for our early antitrust laws, and the maintenance of fair competition is still a major concern of government. Probably in most cases the small independent having problems in coping with unfair business practices should discuss them first with his local Better Business Bureau. The latter will know what action to take.

Controlled Shopping Centers

Controlled shopping centers are a fairly recent development. One organization owns and controls the center with its parking facilities and other services and screens tenants to be admitted or granted leases. Controlled centers are of the community or regional type, in contrast to downtown and neighborhood retail districts. They are larger than earlier shopping centers or retail districts where land ownership tended to be multiple, with each landowner selecting his own tenants. Thus controlled centers require a large capital investment of the type sought by the big insurance companies. Stringent government regulation aside, insurance companies usually seek long-time investments in enterprises of *proven* financial stability. Small merchants for certain lines of merchandise, notably drugs, food, variety, and shoes, are often kept out of such developments. Each of these fields, in particular, is plagued by problems arising from chain-store domination of these prime locations. While the policies established by the financiers of shopping centers are understandable, they represent a real obstacle to the small merchant. Credit ratings figure strongly in acceptance for shopping center occupancy. The existing formula for shopping center financing is based on steady income provided by tenants with top credit rating occupying approximately 70 percent of the total space. Applicants with less attractive credit ratings have more difficulty obtaining shopping center locations. A proper "merchant mix," essential to successful shopping center operations, is sometimes difficult to attain because retailers whose occupancy is otherwise desired do not have the required credit rating.[4] Ways should be found to meet the valid needs of controlled shopping center promoters and financiers that also permit qualified independents to locate there.

Price Competition

In every type of business, and in every aspect of business operation, the small firm's unit costs are higher than those of his larger competitors. In manufacturing, for example, more efficient use of labor results from the large firm's ability to subdivide work for greater specialization. The specialization or simplification of work tasks, in turn, has led naturally to the development and use of machine methods. For both these reasons labor productivity has increased tremendously in the mass-production industries.

In addition, the large manufacturer's enormous purchasing power makes it easier for him to buy and use materials more efficiently, usually through purchase according to specification and often on an extended-contract basis. Such materials may be carefully engineered to the machine processes to be performed and to requirements of the finished product, which constitutes another advantage.

In the merchandising field, chain stores often secure lower prices from their suppliers for one or more of the following reasons: expert buyers; larger volume of purchases; and integration, that is, performing for themselves most of the functions performed for the independent retailer by the wholesaler.

The "New Consumerism"

Since its launching in 1965 by Ralph Nader, the modern consumer movement has been making an impression in many areas of business practice. The impact of the "new consumerism" is particularly felt at the retail level, the functional business area in which most small enterprises are engaged. Nader-inspired changes such as *unit pricing* and *open code dating,* for example, are bothersome and tend to increase the retailers' costs.[5] The small retailer and distributor is also intimately affected by recent safety and quality-control requirements imposed on manufacturers, and by the closer scrutiny of their advertising claims by the Federal Trade Commission; he is obviously much concerned with how consumer protection and the common law affect his legal as well as his moral responsibilities to consumers in the sale of goods and services.

Mr. Rufus W. Gosnell, past president of the National Small Business Association, believes that small business will suffer most heavily — and disproportionately — from the enactment of the many consumer bills now before Congress. He aptly

---

[4] Thomas Lea Davidson, *Some Effects of the Growth of Planned and Controlled Shopping Centers on Small Retailers,* Small Business Management Research Report, prepared by the University of Connecticut under a grant by the Small Business Administration (Washington, D.C.: G.P.O., 1963).

[5] *Unit pricing* is the practice of listing the price of an item in terms of a common unit of measurement, such as an ounce or a foot. *Open code dating* is a method of informing the consumer how long an item has been on the shelf.

describes small business as a shuttlecock between the warring factions of the professional consumer movement and big business.

That "One Serious Early Error"

Another problem is the strong probability, almost a certainty, that the beginning independent will make one serious error in judgment during his first year, which usually leads to costs exceeding income. The following case is illustrative. An acquaintance of the authors, after 25 years of successful experience as buyer and merchandising manager for a department store chain, decided to have a business of his own. He spent two years in making a careful market analysis and preparing the prospectus for his enterprise. His family living expenses would not need to be drawn from his business capital for the three years estimated to have his enterprise self-supporting. He waited nearly two years for the right location. He built up proper bank "connections." He erred in only one respect: he concentrated on the "in-between" markets of big business. A bad combination of unseasonable weather and advance buying would have put him into bankruptcy in nine months if his bank connections had been "typical." His former employer weathered the freak season easily because of diversified markets and ample finances, but failure to recognize that *most beginners make one serious error during their first year* almost resulted in disaster.

The large firm has greater latitude in its capacity to make some major errors in judgment from which it can recover, but the smaller firm cannot afford to make many bad decisions. As Professor Watson has expressed it, "Big business has a momentum. Success can continue based upon decisions which are right 51 per cent of the time. But small business can fail on one wrong decision."[6]

EDUCATION FOR SMALL BUSINESS

Most of the problems of small business are amenable to solution, particularly the internal ones resulting from bad management, as well as the adverse environmental or external conditions, most of which can only be corrected by governmental or legislative action. The former are the more easily corrected. Prebusiness and continuing education in economics and business management will better equip the small businessman to cope with the problems of operating his enterprise.

An increasing number of college graduates today are showing an interest in independent enterprising, especially those from our university schools of business. During the 1930s, many graduates became self-employed because no other employment was available. Some found such ventures to their liking and remained independents. Since then, courses in colleges and schools of business have paid increasing attention to the advantages of independent enterprising. Many college graduates planning to take over family enterprises have called for appropriate course offerings. More recently, the "new individualism" on the nation's campuses has led many college graduates to foresake large corporations for entrepreneurship or employment in smaller firms, where there is greater freedom of action.

[6] Frank Watson, *An Analysis of the Business Curriculum,* Monograph C-14 (Cincinnati: South-Western Publishing Co., 1966), pp. 58–59.

Courses in small business operation are being offered in an increasingly larger number of colleges and universities. Additional evidence of the interest of colleges and universities in training and education for small business are the many conferences, institutes, and seminars sponsored by these institutions in recent years. Some of these, covering specific topical areas, have been attended by specific trade or industrial groups; others have been general in nature. Many have been sponsored or encouraged by the Management Assistance Division of the Small Business Administration.

Surveys conducted by the National Council for Small Business Management Development and other organizations continue to reveal this greatly increased attention by schools of business to preparation for entrepreneurship and assistance to existing entrepreneurs, in contrast to what some have considered to be an emphasis on training for big business employment. Many of the titles of university and college courses indicate that their primary concern has been with the problems of high-level finance, mass production, mass communications within massive plants, and mass employment.

The beginning businessman, with his restricted scope of activities, has definite limits as to the sophistication of the operating methods he can employ. One objective of this book is to compensate for the failure of many business texts to recognize the importance of small business. This text emphasizes some of the special skills and techniques particularly needed for the smaller organization.

GOVERNMENT ASSISTANCE TO SMALL BUSINESS

As noted in Chapter 1, the federal government in 1953 took a new, positive approach to the problem of growing business power with the passage of the Small Business Act. The purpose of this act is to slow down the growing concentration of business power not by dissolving the giant firms but by *aiding* the smaller ones. It was with the passage of this legislation, which created the Small Business Administration, that the government first became actively concerned about the "welfare" of small business.

Three major areas of assistance to the small businessman are provided by the SBA: (1) financial assistance, (2) management and technical assistance, and (3) assistance in processing government contracts. Governmental and other financial assistance to small business firms is discussed in detail in Chapter 11, and management and technical assistance in Chapter 14; this section describes only the SBA's subcontracting program and the government's efforts to increase the number of prime contracts awarded to small firms.

Several ingenious devices have been developed by the SBA to assist small firms that want to obtain government prime contracts and related subcontracts, such as the *joint determination or "set aside" program* and the *production pool.* Under the joint-determination program, certain government procurement orders may be earmarked for competitive bidding exclusively by small firms. Under the production pool arrangement, several small firms may merge their facilities to bid on orders too large or complicated for any one of the firms to handle alone. An inventory or register of the capabilities of small manufacturers (and other types of small firms) is also maintained.

SBA works closely with the largest contract-awarding government agencies, such as the Department of Defense, General Services Administration, National Aeronautics and Space Agency, and others. Under regulations established by these agencies, prime contractors must give small concerns an adequate opportunity to compete for their subcontracts. SBA maintains close contact with prime contractors and refers qualified small firms to them. In the case of minority enterprises, SBA assists *directly* in the procurement of subcontracts. Under section 8(a) of the Small Business Act the SBA has authority to negotiate procurement contracts from other federal agencies on a noncompetitive basis and to award subcontracts for the performance of these contracts to minority-owned businesses.

In recent years the federal government has endeavored to mobilize public and private leadership, funds, and other resources to support the development and growth of minority-owned businesses; for this purpose, the Office of Minority Business Enterprise (OMBE) was established within the Department of Commerce in March 1969. At the federal level it has organized a number of interagency "task forces." The Task Force on Procurement for Minority Businessmen, for example, is comprised of representatives of specific governmental offices engaged in procurement and fund-granting activities. Another coordinating group is the Task Force on Minority Business Concessions, comprised of representatives of federal departments and agencies that operate facilities using concession-type businesses.[7] The OMBE also identifies and catalogues private sources of managerial, technical, and financial support necessary to successful small business operation.[8]

To insure that resources get to the individual businessman at the local level, OMBE has adopted two approaches: (1) the organization of a Minority Business Opportunity Committee (MBOC) in each city in which various federal agencies have field offices; and (2) the development of an "affiliate" system.

The purposes of the MBOC program are (1) to coordinate over 80 programs administered by 16 different federal agencies which affect minority business enterprise in one way or another; (2) to promote or develop business opportunities for present or prospective minority entrepreneurs; and (3) to provide information on sources of venture capital. MBOC membership depends upon which federal agencies are located in the city in question. In general, the Departments of Commerce, Labor, Agriculture, Defense, Treasury, Justice, Interior, Transportation, Housing and Urban Development, and Health, Education, and Welfare, as well as the Small Business Administration, General Services Administration, Veterans Administration, Postal Service, National Aeronautics and Space Administration, and the Atomic Energy Commission are represented. In addition, at least one minority business organization is a member, together with representatives of the local government and private resource groups.

Prior to the establishment of MBOCs, difficulty was often experienced by minority businessmen in identifying and fully utilizing all the federal assistance programs that were available to them. These local committees have also made several other important contributions. The first comprehensive listing of minority businesses has been prepared in several cities, and a plan to assist with

[7] Such as the Department of Defense, which leases space in a large shopping concourse to serve Pentagon employees.

[8] This section is concerned primarily with nonfinancial assistance to minority business; see pages 218-220 for a discussion of financial aid under the OMBE program.

tax-delinquency problems has been developed. MBOCs have also moved to increase small purchase awards (under $2,500) and SBA 8(a) subcontract awards to minority entrepreneurs.

The coordination of management and technical assistance programs at the local level is achieved by OMBE by means of its "affiliate" system. Business-development organizations in selected cities with large concentrations of minority population have been chosen to work with OMBE in assisting minority business and developing effective methods of meeting local needs. To be designated an OMBE affiliate, an organization must have an established reputation and be capable of providing a full range of management or technical assistance to existing or prospective minority-owned businesses. Among the private agencies participating in the OMBE program as affiliates are selected universities,[9] human rights commissions, human resources divisions of Chambers of Commerce, Urban Leagues, Business and Professional Men's Associations, and various black economic groups. OMBE affiliates serve as the focal point for information, business and technical assistance, and follow-up services. They also sponsor workshops, seminars, and short courses in small business management.[10] Many of them are funded by the Economic Development Administration.

In 1971 the first *Census of Minority-Owned Businesses* (containing data for the year 1969) was published by the Bureau of the Census. The basic purpose of this survey, conducted in cooperation with the Office of Minority Business Enterprise, is to fill an existing gap in economic data about minority participation in business. Information is provided on the number and kind of businesses, employment, receipts, legal form of ownership, and geographic location of businesses by black, American Indian, Mexican-American, Puerto Rican, Cuban, Chinese, and other minority-group members. This information will be used as source material for measuring the impact and efficiency of SBA, OMBE, and other federal programs designed to stimulate minority participation in the national economy.

ORGANIZED VOICES FOR SMALL BUSINESS

There is no bigger organization in the world than the government in Washington. And since the passage of the Wagner Act in 1935 organized labor has been a most potent lobbying force.[11] Large business firms also aggressively promote and protect their interests in Washington and the various state capitals. Yet until very recently the nation's largest economic force — small business — has had no organized voice to compete with that of Big Business and Big Labor in the legislative halls of Big Government.

Small businessmen have been notoriously hard to organize, perhaps because of their individualism. Prior to the '30s, various attempts to get them to work together failed. The first successfully organized "voice" for small business — the National Small Business Association — was organized by the Junior Chamber of Commerce

[9] For example, Howard University's Institute for Minority Business Education (IMBE).

[10] Management and technical assistance and other forms of nonfinancial aid available to all small business firms (not merely minority firms) is discussed in detail in Chapter 14.

[11] Over 60 labor unions have located their national headquarters in Washington.

in 1937 with headquarters in Washington. Another effective organization of small businesses is the National Federation of Independent Business, formed in 1943 and now located at San Mateo, California.

Though these groups differ in organization and mode of operation, they have basically the same purposes or objectives: to inform their members on what is going on in Washington and to carry the "message" of the small business community back to the legislative policymakers. The activities of the National Small Business Association, as stated in their membership brochure, are typical:

1. Helping the small businessman become aware of his potential loss of freedom by unnecessary governmental authority.
2. Encouraging constructive revision of the tax structure, adoption of a sound fiscal and economic policy, and the establishment of an equitable management-labor policy to insure an environment wherein small business can remain competitive.
3. Opposing policies, actions, and activities that discourage and defeat initiative.
4. Curtailing the growth of governmental regulations, reports, and all unnecessary burdens on the limited resources of small business.
5. Promoting governmental procurement policies that permit small business to obtain its fair share of government business.
6. Opposing unfair and monopolistic practices of big business and organized labor.
7. Limiting and reducing areas where government is in unnecessary competition with private enterprise.

SUMMARY AND CONCLUSIONS

Every year thousands of men and women, most of them already employed by existing concerns, venture forth with their accumulated job know-how, capital, and judgment in search of the income and independence they believe to be associated with going into business for one's self. And the number of enterprises thus begun increases annually. However, statistics show that a large number of these fledgling small businesses are relatively short-lived. The question is, why? The authors assert that it is their weaknesses as businesses, rather than their small size or lack of maturity, that cause these undertakings to fail. In the highly competitive arena in which all businesses contend, poor judgment, careless handling of detail, or other incompetencies in management can readily bring failure. The trouble usually lies in the new owner-managers' limited preparation, lack of administrative experience, and failure to apply the easily understandable principles and methods of business operation which have always characterized the successful firm.

The fact that many of these businesses which failed were founded by persons possessing unusual mechanical aptitudes, manual skills, and artistic or other talents is significant. The cost of failure is increased by their loss of capital, investment, and of hard-won status in their previous occupations, as well as attendant injuries to their personal pride. The problem is this: they had never encountered, as employees, the particular responsibilities and difficulties they encountered as owner-managers of their own businesses. The point here is that business *management* calls for a wide variety of talents far beyond those of the person performing – or in charge of – any single business function. Many persons who know their jobs do not know the businesses of which those jobs are a part. These sobering restrictions need not be feared, but they must be observed. They are intelligible to those who seek to understand them.

Although it is growing increasingly important, formal education has never been a prime requisite of the successful entrepreneur. Yet recognition of the many facets of business – of the importance of each as a functional part of business operation – and a willingness to respect each enough to master it, either personally or with the help of associates, has ever been a requisite. This book is written with emphasis on that respect, with an assumption that the reader is willing to learn, and with a deep conviction that, under normal circumstances, basic principles combined with modern methods, serving as rules, can aid in assuring success.

REVIEW QUESTIONS

1. Why is there so much concern expressed about the "welfare" of small business? Who are those most concerned?

2. What are the five general reasons for business failure cited in the text? What other classifications of business failure can you suggest?

3. Why are the causes of business failure sometimes hard to identify?

4. What are some of the personal obstacles to effective management of the small enterprise?

5. How can problems relating to the limited time available to the small businessman be solved?

6. What problems of small business are inherent in the small size of the enterprise rather than in the enterpriser himself?

7. Why does federal minimum-wage legislation work a greater hardship on the small business than on the larger firm?

8. How can the small firm turn the disadvantage it faces in acquiring competent managerial employees into an advantage?

9. In what respects does a small business have a serious problem in obtaining the capital it needs?

10. Why is the cost of capital greater for the small firm than for the larger firm?

11. Are adequate facilities available today for financing small business? Discuss.

12. How do high personal income taxes make it difficult for prospective or incumbent small businessmen to acquire initial capital or funds for expansion?

13. How have the inheritance and gift tax laws contributed to the increasing number of mergers of small firms with larger firms?

14. Why is the burden of serving as a free tax-collecting agent for the government greater on the small firm than on the larger firm?

15. Why do most small businesses find it difficult to engage in industrial research?

16. What are the major problems relating to patents faced by the individual inventor? Suggest solutions for each.

17. Why are the risks of operating a small enterprise greater than those of a larger business?

18. What kinds of problems do some small business firms have with their large suppliers and vendors?

19. What kinds of problems arise for the small business in coping with vested interests and monopolistic practices?

20. What criteria are generally used in determining who may lease space in controlled shopping centers?

21. Why are the small firm's unit costs of production and distribution higher than those of its larger competitors?

22. What implications does the modern consumer movement have for small business?

23. Discuss the probabilities of success in small business as compared with big business.

24. Which problems of small business are most amenable to solution?

25. What is the justification, if any, for separate courses in small business management at the college level?

26. What are the major areas of assistance to the small businessman provided by the Small Business Administration? Describe SBA's procurement assistance program.

27. For what purpose was the Office of Minority Business Enterprise established? Describe the ways in which OMBE hopes to achieve this objective.

28. What are the purposes and activities of such organizations as the National Small Business Association and the National Federation of Independent Business?

DISCUSSION QUESTIONS

1. Business-failure statistics reported each year by Dun & Bradstreet indicate that less than 1 percent of all businesses "fail." Are such statistics a true reflection of business "failure"? Why or why not?

2. Classify the problems or reasons for failure enumerated on pp. 21-22, using each of the classification schemes suggested in this chapter.

3. Which is basically a more important cause of the demise of small firms: lack of capital or lack of managerial ability? Explain.

SUPPLEMENTARY READINGS

Kuehn, W. H. *The Pitfalls in Managing a Small Business.* New York: Dun & Bradstreet, Inc., 1969. Discusses the major pitfalls in managing a small business as reported to Dun & Bradstreet by people who are actually in business, and offers some suggestions as to how the pitfalls may be avoided.

Mayer, Kurt B., and Sidney Goldstein. *The First Two Years: Problems of Small Firm Growth and Survival.* Small Business Research Series no. 2. Washington, D.C.: G.P.O., Small Business Administration, 1961. Analyzes the causes of failure and the reasons why some firms survive.

Proxmire, William. *Can Small Business Survive?* Chicago: Henry Regnery Company, 1964. Though feeling that independent enterprise is heading toward extinction, Senator Proxmire feels that the "economic illness" of small business is "curable." Offers suggestions to the small businessman as to how he may improve his economic and competitive position, and where he can get practical advice and assistance from private and public agencies.

3

Factors in
small business success

Most studies of small business seek causes of failure. These are generally enumerated as lack of know-how, inadequate capital, and poor accounting. Believing that it is just as important to know why a firm succeeds as to know why it fails, some of the authors' research has been in that direction — determining what is *the right way* to do things.

Let's start out with some "currently useful generalizations," which could be defined as statements of conviction. These generalizations were developed from a Western Reserve University study of 120 successful small metalworking plants.[1]

1. In most industries, there are enough marginal operators with inferior quality, high prices, and poor service to permit success to a competent and determined beginner.

2. Certain patterns prevail in the different industries in terms of product needs, locations, and timing which can have significant effects on the beginner's chances of success.

3. Most successful small businesses were founded by men who were successful but unhappy working for someone else, and who were willing to gamble their futures on their own talents.

4. Most successful small operators in production plants are experts, talented perfectionists — recognized specialists in some mechanical, fabricating, or technical skill.

5. Most of these men are competent in a variety of business functions, or smart enough to know where to go for help if they need it.

6. The successful small manufacturer usually knows exactly what is happening in his operation — who is doing what, how, and with what results.

7. One of the greatest strengths of the typical small businessman is his effectiveness in communications, of getting "the word" out, where it counts.

8. Most successful small business operators are happy with the size of their businesses as they are — not wishing to lose many of the benefits they cherish so much.

[1] Kenneth Lawyer, et al., *Small Business Success: Operating and Executive Characteristics*, Small Business Management Research Report, prepared by Bureau of Business Research, Western Reserve University, under a grant by the Small Business Administration (Washington, D.C.: G.P.O., 1963).

Now let's consider the source of some of these generalizations and arrive at some additional conclusions.

Existence of a genuine business opportunity.   The successful small metalworking plants in Ohio have been alert, responsive, and flexible in serving a specialized and well-defined market with unique talents of production and service. Out of the whole research experience a central theme emerged: the successful management focused its limited, but highly competent facilities on a restricted but unique production and marketing objective. Success was most probable in the offering of an apparently much needed service or a product of such nature that larger firms were not interested in it for technical reasons, or because it was needed only in small amounts.

The founder of each metalworking firm knew the detailed technology of his prospective market well enough to select a product, or service, which in his opinion (*a*) had been persistently troublesome, costly, and/or neglected in the market; (*b*) was not likely to be corrected by anything known to be under technical study, and (*c*) could be solved by an original and attractive method known to him. *Financial adequacy was of course essential.*

Managerial ability.   From the beginning of the study it was felt by its designers that the management skills and personality traits of the chief executive of the small plant might often be more important than the sophistication of the operating methods employed. "Wearing many hats" and working long hours, the successful small plant's owner-manager apparently has strong personal motivation; a talent for motivating and controlling others; a broad awareness of varied factors, including a balanced flow of work; and the ability to make speedy decisions and thus to maintain great flexibility.

The man whose background is production tends to assume that goods well made are half sold. The reverse is more likely to be true. It is usually easier to find someone who can make a good product than it is to find someone who will buy it, or one who can sell it. That fact has been hard to accept by many small manufacturers.

The successful industrial plant operator of the past century was primarily a production man. Even fifty years ago, the successful manufacturer was one who would get the most out of a group of workers at machines in a shop. Now the premium (especially since World War II) is on the one who can find out what most customers want, and who sells it to them at a profit. He is still a production man, but market-oriented and market-competent. He works in terms of marketing goals and marketing efficiency. He must achieve not only an adequate product, but satisfied customers, through good service.

Summary.   In summary, the small metalworking plant succeeds in direct proportion to its highly motivated owner's possession of certain essential talents of modern business operation. These include: (1) alertness to change; (2) ability to adjust or to create change oneself; (3) ability to attract and hold competent workers; (4) $180°$ vision with respect to operating details; and (5) a knowledge of the market – his customers and their needs. First and foremost, of course, there must be a genuine business opportunity, for. if there is none, no amount of managerial talent can overcome this lack.

These factors – a genuine business opportunity coupled with managerial ability – are as important to the success of a merchandising or service establishment as to a manufacturer.

GENUINE BUSINESS OPPORTUNITY

Before an enterprise is launched with reasonable prospects for success, a genuine business opportunity must be discovered and its possibilities appraised. Too often an idea plus ambition are mistaken for a business opportunity, or maybe a vacant store is so interpreted. A genuine business opportunity means a need for the proposed good or service in sufficient volume and at a high enough price to operate at a profit. Often, however, a demand will have to be stimulated or developed. Especially will this be true when the embryo businessman has something new to offer.

An indefinite but very large number of businesses fail because they never should have been started. There is no justification for their existence. Notice how thoroughly big business goes about launching a new product. Laboratory experiments, product analysis, market surveys, and pilot operations are often conducted for several years before the newcomer is announced to the public. Although big business could afford to make a few mistakes, it seldom does; but small business, where a single major error is fatal, makes many.

Prosperous times attract many entrants into small business ownership who misinterpret the easy going as a harbinger of success. Many do not understand economic trends and are unable to make accurate forecasts. When the inevitable readjustment comes, the casualties are heavy. Even a few years of experience may not equip the entrepreneur to meet the problems which develop when the going gets tough. Further aggravating the problem is that many have paid inflated prices for goodwill, leaseholds, fixtures, and merchandise.

Emotional decisions to become one's own boss also occur more frequently during prosperous times. An employee with some savings becomes angry at his boss and decides to become independent. The first vacant building looks like his opportunity, and he learns only too late that it is easy to enter small business but difficult to get out without a loss of some sort.

Business opportunities may be uncovered in a variety of ways. Most common is the situation where an expanding market justifies the establishment of additional businesses of the same type. Another situation creating a favorable opportunity for a new business of an existing kind is where the market is not being adequately served because of the inefficient management of existing concerns. A third type of business opportunity arises from the introduction of a new product or service which meets the needs of the market the prospective entrepreneur proposes to serve. Opportunities such as these exist for large as well as small businesses and are discussed in some detail in Chapter 6.

Our concern here, however, is with the *unique* opportunities of the smaller firm and how small business can compete successfully with big business. The question is: What is the key to *small* business "opportunity"? Professor Gross suggests that it lies in the exploitation of the inherent advantages of the smaller enterprise, particularly its flexibility, its ability to adjust rapidly to change. "With few exceptions," he says,

> the giant is geared to "big business," to large volume, to large orders, to large numbers of customers. The giant designs products to satisfy large segments of the market. Products are engineered for "average" consumers because they account for the bulk of sales. In this way it is possible to maximize production efficiency. Marketing tactics follow a similar pattern; advertising and sales promotion campaigns are geared to the "average" customer, not to the unusual one.
>
> But large numbers of customers are not "average." When we study consumers, we quickly observe an important fact. Markets are segmented, not homogeneous, and consumer demand varies widely for most products. . . .
>
> The giant with his "average" product fits the general market well enough, but he leaves plenty of room for the small businessman to maneuver, to move in with fresh styles, new packaging, new product ideas, and new services that appeal to sizable market segments.[2]

Thus small business is particularly suited for satisfying the demands of a segmented market. A review of market trends will suggest many genuine business opportunities for the smaller enterpriser. Following are some of the more important trends:

1. *Increasing consumer affluence.*   Higher incomes and increased purchasing power have increased the demand for luxury items and discretionary services, and for products and services which are "cultural" in nature — as evidenced by the growth of boutiques and specialty stores of all types, such as dress shops, bookstores, record stores, gift shops, card and stationery shops, antique shops, and art goods stores. Following are two representative success stories — one in the retailing field, the other in the service trades:

> [For many years, Maxine Casey dreamed of operating a dress shop in Cleveland, Ohio. Last year [1970] this dream came true. Though at last report she had been in business less than a year, her small boutique already is showing a profit. With personal service, personality and special styles she has competed successfully with the large Cleveland department stores.]
>
> Maxine's dress shop is exclusively midi. [Though nationwide the outcome of the mini-midi battle is still in question, Maxine feels she knows her customers.] "They're between 25 and 45 years old, middle and upper-middle class, wives of professional men, suburbanites, socialites," she says. In short, the kind of people who both want and can afford to be "very fashion-aware." . . .
>
> [To serve her clientele she chose a location on Shaker Square], a fashionable address with many other smart shops, and a gateway to Shaker Heights, the wealthy suburb whose women regularly shop on the square.[3]

[2] Alfred Gross, "Meeting the Competition of Giants," *Harvard Business Review* 45 (May-June 1967):176, 178.

[3] William Wong, in the *Wall Street Journal,* September 9, 1970, p. 36 (abridged).

Even more impressive is the success story of Earl Gragosian, president of a small chain of perhaps the most expensive motels in the country:

[Earl Gragosian opened the first of his Royal Inns in 1965; by 1970, he had opened 39 others. In the first half of 1970, a relatively bad year for the motel industry, the profits from his motor inns tripled. Though nationwide room occupancy was down 7 percent, occupancy at his motels was up 6.7 percent.]

The secret behind the success of his venture is expensive, self-indulgent luxury. Behind gold-and-white facades are elegantly designed rooms, [with] white satin bedspreads, deep-pile carpeting, antique-white furniture and a full wall-size mural. Some rooms are equipped with bars, refrigerators and log-burning fireplaces. Each of his motels also has a swimming pool and sauna bath. The prices charged, of course, are compatible with the luxuriousness of the services provided. Earl Gragosian's motel enterprise is successful because he dared move away from the industry's tradition of offering the traveler not much more than shelter.[4]

A related trend of significance for the prospective small businessman is the growth of the convenience or "bantam" food store. Such stores are not to be confused with the small neighborhood grocery stores which have been largely supplanted by the large supermarkets. Bantam stores are conveniently located in shopping centers or on arterial streets and highways with drive-in facilities, are open long hours (often around the clock in metropolitan areas), and provide rapid checkout service. Between 1969 and 1970 the number of convenience food stores increased 14 percent, their volume of sales increasing 24 percent.[5]

Increased consumer affluence accounts largely for this growth; the lower prices and limited service of the supermarket no longer have the same attraction for some consumers. Many consumers today are placing a greater value on convenience, service, and quality.

2. *Increased leisure time.* Increased leisure time, together with higher consumer incomes, has resulted in a dramatic increase in the amount spent for recreation and other services. Not only has this increased demand provided growing opportunities in the "traditional" small-scale, recreation- or amusement-oriented businesses (bowling alleys, sporting goods stores, and hobby shops, for example), but it has also given rise to many types of new small businesses, such as scuba shops, vehicle distributorships (snowmobiles, campers, etc.), and trailer or camper parks.

3. *The "do-it-yourself" trend.* There has also been a recent surge in home sewing, furniture refinishing, and other types of handcraft hobbies, at least partly the result of increased leisure time and affluence. This trend likewise has led to many small business opportunities. Take home sewing, for example:

Back in 1880, Iowa housewives were providing a major part of their family wardrobes by their own sewing efforts. That was the year Falk Brody formed a wholesale clothing firm [in Des Moines].

The company prospered because it was ready when the tide turned to "ready mades." . . .

[4] *Time,* November 16, 1970, p. 87.

[5] According to statistics furnished by the *Progressive Grocer.*

If Falk Brody were alive today he would probably be amazed at the changing trend of his business because now the firm's warehouse is jammed with bolts of cloth ready to be shipped to retailers who will sell the fabrics to the "sewing housewives of the 70's."

"Fabric sales have jumped from a quarter to better than half of our volume in the last few years," says Julian Brody, grandson of Falk. . . .

The company still supplies a wide line of men's and boys' furnishings for wholesale distribution, but a combination of new fabric development, increased costs of manufactured clothes, improved home sewing equipment, and increased leisure time have "really boomed home sewing in the last ten years," Brody says.[6]

Many women, however, dislike or have trouble using sewing patterns. Now a solution to their problem is the precut packaged garment, produced by some enterprising manufacturers:

[Some stores are] now showing good-looking clothes — from dresses to pantsuits to bikinis — which can be put together easily from parts already cut, marked and ready to sew. [Savings amount to] 40 to 70 percent of the cost of comparable ready-made clothes. Moreover, when the home-sewer does it herself she can make sure the seams are well-stitched, the length is what she wants, and the measurements taken in or let out to suit her need.

So far, these pre-cut packaged garments have been shown only by the small specialty shops. But some large department stores are farsighted enough to see that this could develop into an important consumer demand.[7]

4. *Antimaterialism, or the "counterculture."*   In recent years many young people have reacted strongly against the older generation's preoccupation with "status" and the acquisition of material wealth, and have made a fetish of living with a bare minimum of possessions. Protesting bureaucracy, or the "Establishment," they have stressed their individualism — in thought and action, and in their appearance. Take clothes, for example:

It's a badge of the "counter culture" [of the] young people to wear clothes that look almost worn out. As the fad caught on, youths started dipping their brand-new Levis into bleach and fraying the cuffs so they would look old. Some even sewed patches where there were no holes.

This activity did not long escape the attention of enterprisers like E. A. Morris who owns the controlling interest in Blue Bell, Inc., a small blue jeans manufacturer. . . . [Morris] quickly figured out how to bleach and tatter jeans before they even left the factory.

Clothing makers have capitalized on the counterculture in other ways, too. . . . Denim, [for example], has blossomed as a raw material for high fashion, and many expensive clothes for both men and women now are styled to vaguely resemble work clothes. . . .

Army surplus shirts and jackets, rugged work boots, and sandals are also prized by the ["now"] generation, for very practical reasons: They are cheap, comfortable and durable. Because of their durability, in fact, they tend to remain useful long after they have become faded and frayed around the edges.[8]

[6] James Lawless, in the *Des Moines Register*, June 27, 1971, p. 3-F (abridged).

[7] Margaret Dana, in the *Des Moines Register*, April 18, 1971, p. 1-T (abridged), © 1971 United Features Syndicate, Inc.

[8] Barry Newman, in the *Wall Street Journal*, April 27, 1971, pp. 1, 18 (abridged). For another example of products aimed at the "counterculture" market, see p. 64, ref. footnote 3.

Also indicative of the counterculture is modern youths' scorn of the mass-produced products of our industrial society and their preference for the handcrafted goods of artisans who share their aversion to mass production. Other preferences of the "turned-on" generation are such products as incense, Eldridge Cleaver "wanted" posters, peace-symbol pendants and posters, men's hair spray to provide the "natural" or "dry" look (as opposed to that greasy kid's stuff and similar hair-grooming aids), and cosmetics that don't make a woman look made-up. These and many other products bought by young people today are found in hip boutiques and "head shops," often located adjacent to college campuses.

5. *Environmental concern, or ecology.*   Most citizens today, of all age groups, are interested in improving the quality of the environment in which they live. Concerned about air pollution, as well as their physical well-being, for example, many people have turned to bicycles as a means of transportation, with the result that the sales of these vehicles have skyrocketed. In response to this specialized demand, there has been a proportionate increase in the number of cycle shops.

Similarly, because of the growing concern about the effects of chemical additives, fertilizers, and pesticides on the quality of food, many "organic"- or "natural"-food shops have also sprung up in recent years. The existence of this new type of food store is in response also (though perhaps to a less extent) to the public's concern about water pollution and the effect of chemicals on the balance of nature.

Other new products offered by the enterprising small businessman — largely to the youth market — include ecology flags, posters, and decals and "ecology pants" (white jeans with green-and-white ecology flags sewed on as patch pockets).

6. *Technological development.*   It was noted in the introductory chapter that small business serves as the proving ground for many new ideas and products — proving their commercial worth on a small scale until the growth stage, if there is to be one, is reached.

Large manufacturers put a much greater effort into the development of new products and processing techniques than do smaller companies because they have the specialized personnel to do it and can better afford the required research facilities. However, many of their new-product ideas do not have sufficient market potential to justify large-scale production, at least initially. Hence, many of the large companies license small concerns to produce and market them. The following case is typical:

> A portable device for testing integrated electronic circuits was designed by quality-control engineers at the General Electric Co. for use in their own work: to facilitate trouble-shooting on the production line. . . . The company, however, was not interested in exploiting this device commercially. . . . For rights to the product, Emcee Electronics, Inc., a small manufacturer in New Castle, Del., offered to pay G.E. an initial licensing fee plus a slice of all future tester sales. Then it set about to modify the unit to test a broader range of electronic circuits. . . . Before long, Emcee was profitably marketing the tester for use in servicing computers and other electronic gear.[9]

[9] Scott R. Schmedel, in the *Wall Street Journal*, September 25, 1970, p. 28 (abridged).

Thus it can be expected that many kinds of new small businesses will evolve from our rapidly changing technology.

7. *Industrial decentralization.* Increasing industrial decentralization provides a new opportunity for small business assistance to large organizations. The new community must provide not only adequate auxiliary services to the big industry, but also maintain attractive stores and additional personnel and amusement services for the employees of the large concern. The large firm moving to a smaller town, or opening a branch there, needs assistance which small independent enterprisers are best able to render. Alert communities today recognize this fact. If local people are unable to establish and operate modern service establishments, retail stores, and places of amusement, there always seem to be plenty of "camp followers" anxious to do so — a fact that slower moving local businessmen may learn to their sorrow.

Satellite concerns function in four main areas: (1) as suppliers of materials and parts — often as subcontractors in defense work, (2) as service agencies to the large firm and its employees, (3) as dealers or distributors, and (4) as customers who use, rather than distribute, products of the large corporation.

MANAGEMENT — WHAT DOES IT REQUIRE?

Among the factors that contribute to the successful management of a small business are training and experience and business-mindedness. Most important, however, are the personal elements.

Personal Factors

"The purpose of the economy is to satisfy the wants of people." This phrase or its equivalent is near the opening of most economics textbooks. It says that every business function, every business institution, every person engaged in performing these functions in or for a business institution, is seeking to satisfy human wants and needs. To the extent that consumer wants and needs are satisfied effectively, economically, and therefore profitably, these businesses are successful and remain in existence. If any one of them is deficient in this regard, it soon ceases as an economic institution. Such are the realities of public preferences and of competition.

Business operation, management, and personnel recruitment are equally involved in human considerations. The ability to direct, to lead, even to inspire others, is a human attribute, obviously, as is the ability to accept and execute assignments of responsibility from another. The ability to gain and maintain confidence — as reflected in securing financial backing, credit extensions, loyal employees — is a personal characteristic of vital importance in business.

Probably most important, the continued ability to satisfy the needs of a clientele comes only through a satisfaction of these needs in terms of quality, price, and service. These are usually inseparable from the customers' attitudes toward the purveyor. Hence, the personal attitudes of individual customers are of major importance in business success.

The beginning small business, particularly, is a projection of the entrepreneur's own ideas as to how he wants to go about making his economic contribution and gaining the related satisfactions. His policies are the way he visualizes how a business should be operated – in terms not only of quality, service, and price, but also appearance, atmosphere, and attitudes. Thus his business philosophies become his business practices, which are an extension of his own personality and thus of himself.

This inseparability of the owner's personality from his policies reflects itself in many ways, not all of them always in the interests of the firm. The owner's knowledge of business methods may constitute the firm's knowledge of them. His competence in the various functional areas will be the firm's competence. His open-mindedness to the need for change, his willingness to ask for and accept advice, to take proper action, or to adjust in time of emergency – these are purely personal characteristics, which can make or break a business. Business is indeed a personal thing, and the smaller the business the more personal it is.

The impact of personal factors on business success cannot be overemphasized. Dun & Bradstreet has kept records of business failures over many years. In the opinion of *creditors and others who had dealt with the demised firms,* ineffectual management was listed as a contributing factor in 91 percent of the business fatalities recorded in 1971.[10] It is poor management that is at the root of most of the operating problems of small business.

Training and Experience

Selection of the best location, determination of initial capital requirements, and even the wise choice of an appropriate kind of business to enter are difficult for persons lacking adequate training and balanced experience. Personal preferences, likes and dislikes, influences of family members or close friends, and limited perspective often lead to unwise business ventures. If outside capital is required even for a sound undertaking, it is difficult for such enterprisers to present a convincing case to possible lenders. If the basis of their project is something new, no matter how sound it may be, the idea is hard to sell for one lacking training and experience in marketing. By the same token, former salesmen may encounter unexpected difficulties in production and other functions. And in all cases where an employee shifts to self-employment without a balanced background, the big surprise is likely to come in achieving self-discipline, time management, and similar directions formerly provided by his employer.

The extent to which trade experience must be acquired by the slow, laborious process of first-hand personal experience depends on the individual. The modern trend, for college graduates at least, is to shorten the time spent acquiring personal experience and devote much more attention to learning from the experience of others. A properly trained analyst can learn much more from the experience of numerous other successful operators in one month than he can in two years or more of normal personal experience. The most successful operator of the largest

[10] *The Failure Record Through 1971* (New York: Dun & Bradstreet, 1972).

supermarket in one city opened his own grocery store without any personal experience in the field. He has pioneered more new methods and launched more innovations in his store than have the other five supermarkets in town combined, and one of these is owned by the second largest chain in the country. Before every new move this man has spent from two to six weeks making an intensive study of the latest and best methods in various parts of the country. What he could not have learned from years of personal experience he has mastered in a few short weeks devoted to absorbing the years of experience of others.

Experience alone, however, is not enough; it must be combined with business acumen. No better illustration of this can be found than in the problems encountered by small businessmen of the old school and the plight of retail stores and other formerly prosperous businesses located in the small towns of the country. There is no doubt that lack of progressiveness and lack of good management on the part of most small-town merchants provided the opportunity for the mail-order houses and many chain stores to get their start. Decades later, when good roads, automobiles, and busses made it easy for small-town residents and farmers to shop in the larger towns and cities, most small-town merchants were unable to stop this trend. In a few cases where new and well-trained managers took over the old stores and modernized them in all respects, they *have* been quite successful. Usually such success has occurred where other conditions have also been favorable, which reflects the good judgment of the new management in selecting these locations. While on the one hand the continuous decline in economic importance of rural areas and movement to the cities has lessened the importance of small towns, on the other hand the trek to the suburbs and industrial decentralization have increased the importance of small towns. Thus it behooves the small-town merchant to be alert to new and better ways to serve his customers.

Obviously if it were contended that personal experience in the actual trade is indispensable, then no novel or unique businesses would ever be created. Many businesses have been successfully started and successfully operated by novices, with little capital and without apparent proof of business acumen. But these are indeed exceptions, for the paths of commerce are strewn with the bones of businesses that started out thus ill equipped.

Since perhaps no one knows what a beginner's problems will be, he cannot be expected to know them. His ability to anticipate them, to surmount them, to make the best decisions, to "do the right thing at the right time" will depend on his general business experience and how closely this is related to the new business.

In beginning a business in a well-known field, one in which many others are already engaged, the need for experience in the trade is apparent. In retailing, for example, the grocery business has certain well-established practices that make for efficiency in handling goods, reducing expenses, and building goodwill. In the service occupations there have been developed — for example, in the gasoline business, the laundry or dry cleaning trades, and repair shops of most kinds — certain ways of "cutting corners," improving service, and protecting materials and equipment. These would be unknown to the beginner. In small manufacturing establishments certain organizational routines, order-or-work patterns of production flow, and methods of buying and of caring for materials are essential to success and profit.

Business-Mindedness

Every individual is more or less business-minded, but most of us are less so. In everyday living as consumers, only a few seem naturally to take a businesslike approach to matters of shopping, banking, property management, and the buying of services.

Bankers are of necessity good judges of business aptitude. When reviewing the possibilities of extending a loan to an operating or prospective businessman, the banker will frequently inquire as to his client's personal business habits. He will find it significant, perhaps, that overdrafts are frequent in the applicant's checking account record.

A sure way to ruin the business is for the short-funded owner to draw from the business more than it is earning; that is, to draw from operating capital rather than from income.

The man or woman who has no standards of dollar-for-dollar values in goods, services, or manpower will also be a hazardous business operator. The person who is continually being sold "gold bricks" in the form of unneeded frills and useless gadgets cannot be expected to exercise sound judgment in the markets of his trade.

The little business may some day be a big business. Until it is larger, it had best copy its progressive elders as to behavior. Its elders are successful, or else they would not be in existence. They have followed successful ways of operation and have proven them to be successful. The fledgling should carefully study these proven successful methods.

THE WAY IT IS DONE

The principles of business have been developed over the years in terms of plain common sense and therefore are not difficult to understand. Their practice, however, is another matter. Knowing what to do is far different from knowing how to do it. Still harder is to do it the best way. The farmer who wrote to the Department of Agriculture, "Please quit sending me more bulletins, I'm not farming half as well as I know how now," is a case in point.

Granted that the small business operator has experience, capital, business acumen, and judgment, he should be able to organize and establish his business with some degree of success. Keeping it going will depend on how well he conducts it. The following principles and practices may be applied to large and small businesses alike. They were developed largely by bigger concerns and have served as vehicles for their progress.

1. Careful study of markets
2. Wise planning of activities
3. Vigilant control of investment, merchandise, personnel, equipment, and buildings to insure maximum use for production
4. Adequate expense records
5. Thoughtful selection of goods

6. Strategic location with particular reference to the market, but also bearing in mind resources and transportation of goods

7. Sound policies, unalterable in general objective, but flexible and adjustable to meet obvious business expediencies

8. Strong working relationships with suppliers

9. Judiciously controlled credit

10. Customer selection and market concentration

11. Skillfully selected personnel

12. A well-planned sales promotion program

The above list represents a very general set of modern operating rules. If the operating problems and discussions of the reasons for business failure considered in the preceding chapter are reviewed, it will be observed that they stem from violations of these basic guidelines.

There are no pat formulas or trade secrets of significance to provide the key to successful business operation. Rather, there are principles which suggest rules and these rules suggest methods.

Business is essentially based on logic – on logical assumptions and logical procedures. Few methods employed by successful operators are lacking in common-sense justification. The difficulty is in discovering the most logical, sensible thing to do.

If the small businessman will liken his firm to a motorcar, he may see this point more clearly. A smooth-running automobile, one which gives its driver comfortable, dependable, and economical performance mile after mile, is a well-balanced mechanism. The engine has just the right compression ratio and spark timing. The chassis has just the right strength and resiliency, the body is the right size. Wheels and tires are engineered to coordinate with engine power and speed and with road conditions.

Most poorly designed, unsatisfactory cars lack this balance, this coordination of mechanical elements and effort. An oversized engine or undersized tires will immediately cause trouble, as will insufficient battery power or a malfunctioning distributor. These facts are familiar to all of us. An automobile fails because its engineers did not provide for balanced elements and effort.

This homely parallel seeks to reemphasize the need for balanced facilities and effort in the operation of a business. Offerings to the community, to the market, must be in proportion to its needs. The money supply must be adequate to carry it safely over the early rough roads. The advertising appropriation must be one which will give the most "mileage," one where the results will justify the cost. The payroll must be paid to people who are achieving results, who are not a drag on the firm's progress. So on and on, the parallels are seemingly endless.

The successful small business operator first knows where he wants to go and how he wants to get there – and in what condition. In the first place, he must have decided that for both emotional and financial reasons he wanted to go into business. Then came the planning of a business that could justify itself in terms of profit and thus income, over a long enough period for him to get a good return on his investment. He must have chosen a good location.

The entrepreneur must have recognized the importance of human relationships in business — with suppliers, with employees, and with customers. Surely he must have adequate capital, good merchandise resources, and a competent labor supply. He must know his costs and to what degree he is achieving his original goals. He must be a marketer, a salesman, and a sales promoter, for the lifeblood of a business is its sales volume.

All independent businessmen start with the same hopes, the same goals — a decent income acquired in a personally satisfying manner. Essentially, they have the usual seven *m*'s of management to work with — men, money, materials, machines, methods, markets, and minutes. The problem is: (1) to be sure the supply of each of these is in balance with the others, (2) to plan a program that, logically, will achieve the desired goal, and (3) to develop and execute controls that will keep the venture on the road, running smoothly.

Modern Methods in Merchandising

Perhaps the small retailer, more than any other businessman, can profitably bring his methods up to date and get in step with modern business. Manufacturing generally had made greater progress than distribution in streamlining operations and thus reducing costs. Although this movement has been led by the large manufacturers, their competitive price challenges have entered the markets of all productive enterprises, no matter how small. In contrast, many small stores have never felt genuine competition, owing to their locations in spots lacking attractiveness to chains and other large operators. Yet efficient methods would have prevented many of their failures, would have insured greater profits for small store owners, and would bolster them against the day when stiff competition becomes a reality.

A typical example was the neighborhood grocer whose business boomed after an arterial highway was routed past his door. But the new class of cash-and-carry trade interfered with service to his old customers. Soon a modern supermarket opened up across the street and most of his newly acquired customers shifted their patronage. Old customers used his charge and delivery service during bad weather but took the more profitable cash business to the supermarket. An effort to offset lost sales by remaining open nights after the competitor had closed helped somewhat, but involved excessively long hours.

When the situation looked hopeless, a wholesaler's representative suggested a plan of modernization and concentration of purchases with his house under agreements typical of the voluntary chain plan. Shortly after putting the new cash-and-carry, semi-self-service plan into operation in an enlarged, modernized building, the grocer was making a profit again. His intimate knowledge of customers' needs and preferences was put to good use. Close cooperation with the wholesaler in buying and merchandising proved advantageous to both.

This case is only one of many examples of how the merchant or shop owner must adjust himself to the times. Although new ideas are not always successful, the world thrives on change. It may be sound judgment to play safe and go slowly, but when the public clearly indicates its preferences, it is the alert merchant's duty to provide services or goods as required. Otherwise he cannot long exist.

Retailers in small towns often fail to appreciate the need to keep up to date, and many are less well informed about new merchandise and materials than are their customers. The radio and national magazines keep customers alert to new developments and create new wants which, if not satisfied by their home-town merchants, are taken care of by mail-order or out-of-town shopping trips.

In many cases it takes outside competition to jar the local merchants out of their lethargy. Retail history is replete with examples of how innovators forced change. Less familiar are examples such as the following:

An independent merchant in the Southwest opened a branch store, thirty miles from where he lived, in a town of 3,000 population. Although opened in an old building, the new store had an all-glass front, an attractive interior, and air-conditioning. Within six months five other stores modernized and seven installed air-conditioning — the first changes made in the business district by local merchants in a quarter of a century. All merchants who modernized are well pleased with the results, and two who failed to do so went out of business within less than a year after the new pacesetter opened for business.

Modern Methods in the Service Business

The same principle, of using the proven methods of successful operation as demonstrated over the years by the big operators, applies in all branches of business; the service trades are no exception. The difficulty is that so few small operators will admit their weaknesses and seek the needed information. A laundry owner in a small midwestern community was an exception.

The owner had inherited a successful laundry business from his father, who had built it up over a period of 30 years in a town of 6,000. When the young man took over, the business was paying no great profit, supposedly owing to a general depression. As business conditions improved the laundry did not. After his son had studied the situation carefully it dawned upon him that perhaps he was doing things too much as his father had done.

He joined the laundrymen's trade association, from which he gained figures on operating expense that differed so greatly from his own that he was alarmed. He visited a fellow member who was known as a successful operator. After seeing his neighbor's business and restudying his own situation he started making changes.

Within three months he had reduced his operating cost 22 percent, while his production potentials were increased 18 percent. He found that he had had poor management controls in different operations; no standards of performance; no idea of relative costs; that accounting for bundles was outmoded; equipment was behind the time; and his handling of customer accounts was inefficient and costly. The business is now thriving. The son combined open-mindedness and a willingness to change with the integrity and industry he had learned from his father.

Modern Methods in a Small Factory

Opportunities for the most efficient division of labor and use of machinery tend to vary directly with the size of the establishment. Modern methods of management in the small firm have been developed, however, that overcome many disadvantages. The major problem lies with management that is unable or unwilling to learn and apply new techniques. Methods analysis, work organization, and scheduling so as to take maximum advantage of the basic principles of specialization can be applied to the smallest enterprise. But planning and system are required. Small jobs can often be accumulated and done in larger batches. Even the railroads use this system when they delay less-than-carload shipments until a carload is accumulated. Automobile manufacturers run all of one variety through before shifting to another. Department stores do not send their trucks out to deliver each sale as it is made but carefully route and schedule deliveries. In the small concern with ten employees and 40 tasks it is often possible to have each employee specialize in four duties and shift operations to secure a major portion of the advantages of labor subdivision. In the use of machinery the small firm is less able to use highly efficient single-purpose machines, which may be as much of an advantage as a disadvantage under capable management. Greater flexibility and more efficient use of capital investment are advantages, provided multipurpose machines are carefully selected and used most effectively.

Technology, know-how, or science applied to industry and business may be more highly or more rapidly developed in big organizations, but the little fellow can profit by progress, too. Only certain very restricted phases of technology are appropriate exclusively to the giant enterprise. In most cases the basic problem is, again, the attitude and training of the small business owner-manager. Business college students contemplating self-employment are exposed to the same technical training received by future executives of big business. Those who have imagination and initiative and an opportunity to take small business or independent enterpriser courses have no reason to be at a disadvantage when they become entrepreneurs. It is the man rather than the size of the establishment that makes technology a problem in some cases but not in others.

SOME HOMELY MAXIMS FOR THE SMALL-BUSINESS OWNER

Interpreted by the authors, with apologies to their various sources (and to those who prompted them)

The strength of a building is as great as that of its base, and even the highest buildings begin from the ground.

What you want and what the customer wants may not be the same — but unless you give him what he wants, you won't get what you want!

As you enter business, bear in mind the bad practices you complained about as a customer — and watch that you don't repeat them.

Don't depend on business through friends — they're fickle, and they're scarcer than you think. Get your friends through business!

Today's customers cannot be neglected as we seek tomorrow's. A dozen loyal customers are worth a gross of possible ones.

If you are out to buy, there are many anxious to sell — and with cash, buying is easy. But to *sell* — that's what takes drive, enthusiasm, courage!

Don't hire relatives, especially "in-laws" — and don't hire close friends — you know each other too well.

It is sometimes hard to realize that bankers, like policemen, are really nice people, trying to protect us. The trouble is that they are so realistic.

Do what needs to be done now, when you ought to do it, whether you want to or not — this is a measure of your will power, of your business success.

Experience *is* an excellent school, but the tuition is very high, and most of its graduates are too old to go to work.

Most people can stand adversity better than prosperity. It takes less courage to suffer than it does to restrain oneself when things go well.

Some people sell out and retire from their businesses; others retire with their businesses — but sometimes the business retires first!

The well-known radio commentator Earl Nightingale has also prepared a set of basic rules for the small businessman which he first introduced on his program, "Our Changing World":

Do you have good business sense? Well — let's see: More than 200 successful businessmen were asked: "What advice can you offer to someone who wants to get into business and stay there?"

From their composite answers here are the ten basic rules that topped the list:

1. Be more concerned with the accumulation of money than with what money can buy. Most people are never able to go into business for themselves simply because they lack the self-discipline to acquire the necessary capital. And thousands fail because they started on a shoestring that was too short. To succeed in business takes time; prepare for twice the time you think it will take you.

2. Keep your markup higher than your overhead. The No. 1 cause of business failure is a matter of buying for too much or selling too low. This can lead to that terrible treadmill where every day is a frantic attempt to keep your chin above water. A few bad days . . . and . . . you're under. But the quality of your product or service must fully justify your prices. When a sale is made properly, it's not a game where somebody wins and somebody loses. Everybody wins. The product must be worth more in use value . . . than its cost.

3. Be liberal in your standards of friendship. Winning business and keeping it depends to a great extent on cordial personal relationships. I know of a case where the wife of the businessman thought he was far too lenient with his employees. Finally, after years of heckling, he let her become personnel manager. Before long, all the employees quit. This is a two way street.

4. Stay with it. Long hours are an inevitable part of the job. You can forget the eight-hour day and the five-day week.

5. Be prepared for the unexpected. Don't leave yourself financially unprotected against emergencies. This applies to the family as well as the business. But a good backlog of operating capital has saved many thousands of businesses from going under. It's insurance against mistakes . . . and bad times.

6. Be ruthless with people who would cash in on your success. Prosperity always draws parasites. Tell those relatives and old friends who would love to go on a permanent vacation on your payroll that you're just not hiring this year.

7. Become an expert on the items or the service you sell.

8. Be selective in your advertising. Pick your spots. Make your ad dollars count.

9. Deal primarily in fast-moving items. Look at your stock from the customer's point of view. And make sure there's a sufficient market for what you're selling.

10. Don't expand too quickly. Other things being equal, you'll do well to wait on that second location or branch store until you can afford to gamble at least twice the sum spent on your original location.

So there you have them: Ten tips that are a part of the good business sense of the successful businessman or woman.

Whether you plan to go into business for yourself or not, here's some advice you'll never go wrong to heed. See that you have at least one year's income in savings of some kind. It will give you a comfortable feeling, and it could save your neck.[11]

SUMMARY AND CONCLUSIONS

The following are generally accepted as prerequisite to success in any small business:

1. A genuine business opportunity
2. Managerial ability
3. Adequate capital

These factors in small business success are listed in their order of importance. First and foremost there must be a genuine business opportunity, for if there is none no amount of money or managerial talent can overcome this lack. On the other hand, capital and the other factors of production must be efficiently managed if a business opportunity is to be fully exploited, or if further competition is to be discouraged.

The following conclusions can be drawn from the discussion of these factors in this chapter: (1) competition and changing conditions set standards that the small businessman must and can meet; (2) larger businesses usually have developed methods that can be successfully adopted and adapted by the small operator; and (3) basically, requirements for business success are the same in all fields regardless of the position held or the size of the firm in that field.

Although many reasons are given for business failures, they usually represent the *occasions* for the failure rather than the *causes*. Had the management been efficient, it would have anticipated and controlled them. Businesses fail for very simple, readily understandable reasons — largely failure to do the logical, sensible thing.

Yet these *logical, sensible* things are not always easily done or done with equal ease by any two people. They call for a variety of skills that few people possess in balanced amounts, and this constitutes the "one-man band" problem.

That there is need for knowledge of the market and the customer is obvious. Planning in business is an absolute *must* — if "having the right goods at the right place at the right time and price" is the accepted goal of any business. Controls are indispensable; these include financial controls as well as good records. Adequate capital, a good location, a needed product or service — the need for these is

[11] "How's Your Business Sense?" program 1302. Reproduced by courtesy of the Nightingale-Conant Corporation.

obvious. Remember also that the business is a projection of management's personality. In general, the individual has what it takes or he doesn't, and "having it," he does a good job willfully or he fails. These points cannot be overstressed, for business success is a philosophy, a point of view, an approach which must permeate the entrepreneur's mind thoroughly if he is to have mastery of his enterprise.

REVIEW QUESTIONS

1. What are some of the "principles of success" enumerated in the results of the Western Reserve study of successful small metalworking plants?
2. What are the prerequisites for success in small business? Which is the most important? Discuss.
3. What is the basis of a genuine business opportunity?
4. Why do some prospective entreprenuers tend to misjudge the existence of a genuine business opportunity?
5. How can small business compete successfully with large business? What is "market segmentation"? Why do Professor Gross and the authors regard this as the "key" to small business opportunity?
6. What are some of the more important market trends, suggested in the text, which can be exploited by the small businessman? Discuss each of the success stories presented in the text, and cite other examples.
7. In what ways does the trend toward industrial decentralization provide new opportunities for small business?
8. What are "satellite" firms?
9. What factors contribute to the successful management of the small business?
10. Why is prior experience in the trade or industry helpful when establishing a small business? Is it a necessary prerequisite for success?
11. What are the seven basic elements which any successful businessman must manage? Why must they be kept in balance?
12. Give several examples of how big business sets the pace for small business in the same field.
13. Distinguish carefully between the occasions for business failure as opposed to the causes.
14. What general conclusions can be drawn from the discussion in this chapter?

DISCUSSION QUESTIONS

1. Discuss the importance of each of the "operating rules" for a small business listed in the text on pp. 49-50.
2. Comment upon each of the "maxims for the small business owner" suggested by the authors and by Earl Nightingale on pp. 53-55.
3. Identify and discuss the nature of the small business opportunities which prompted the establishment of two or three new enterprises in your community within the past three years.

SUPPLEMENTARY READINGS

Lawyer, Kenneth. "Characteristics of Small Business Success (or How to Succeed in Small Business by Really Trying)." *Journal of Small Business Management 2,* (July 1964):3-9. An examination of operating methods and management practices in small metalworking plants, and the factors which contribute to small business success.

Patterns for Success in Managing a Business. Business Series no. 2. New York: Business Education Division, Dun & Bradstreet, 1967. Discusses guidelines or patterns for success in the management of any business. Outlined are the attitudes and strengths shared by those who are successful in business.

4

The decision
for self-employment

Our lives are molded by our needs, our desires, and our preferences; so the way we live and what we achieve (within the limits of our ability or our particular circumstance) are the products of these feelings. Successful, happy people know what they want and are willing to work for it. They set goals which are realistic, recognizing their personal strengths and weaknesses, then decide how these goals can best be achieved and what training and experience will be necessary.

Basic human needs such as the need for security, self-expression, recognition, and affection provide the motivation for all we do. The relative importance of these needs varies from person to person. To one, security may be most necessary; to another, it may be self-expression. Some accept life as it comes, while others seek change or opportunity. These individual differences affect the way each of us determines to earn his living, whether to accept dependent employment or to be independent.

The successful "go-it-aloner" prefers self-expression to security, at least in his early undertakings. The independent operator's goal may be to prove himself or pattern himself after someone he admires or envies. He may feel that as an employee there are restrictions which are undesirable, it not unbearable to him.

The person who is content to work for another may cherish security, may prefer to be told what to do and how to do it, and possibly may even wish to avoid making decisions. This person may be a conformist, a follower. Certainly he is no gambler, unless he repeatedly changes jobs. Of course, the great bulk of humanity lies somewhere between these two poles.

The material in this chapter does not seek to idealize the independent businessman. Instead, it concerns the decision each of us must make in choosing the nature of his employment. What factors should be considered? What are the personality characteristics of those who are known to have been successful as independents? Nor is it the purpose of this book to convert the reader to the idea of self-employment. Some are simply not fitted for it; some would not enjoy it; and others would not succeed.

WORKING FOR OTHERS

The final decision as to the manner in which one makes his living resides with the individual. Before making it he must consider many factors, mostly of an intangible nature requiring many value judgments. Let's first consider the advantages and disadvantages of working for someone else.

Advantages of Dependent Employment

Some individuals are better suited to be employees; others would *rather* be employees, especially with large, well-established concerns. Some of the advantages are: security, the prestige that goes with working for a well-known company, the receipt of unemployment insurance and other benefits, greater regularity of income, a more limited area in which knowledge and ability are expected, and less worry outside of business hours.

Other advantages of dependent employment are: no risk of personal savings or other capital; shorter hours, regular vacations, and pay for overtime; larger initial income; more limited responsibility; less planning of tomorrow's work; and in general a more regular routine.

Disadvantages of Dependent Employment

That salaries and wages paid by big business are good, and that even beginnning salaries for college graduates in recent years have risen very highly, are well known. However, independent enterprisers are able to take business deductions not allowable for professional management employees, and to reinvest a resonable proportion of their earnings for business expansion. Of course, big business has also devised many ways of rewarding their better-paid men so that their incomes are not subject to as heavy a tax. In general, these plans involve stock options or the deferment of raises or bonuses until after retirement.

But changes in top management are frequent in many big firms. Such changes often initiate a chain reaction involving the security of numerous other executives down the line. Some positions seem to be highly volatile, such as those of department store buyers, sales managers, and general managers of large corporations. Mergers also tend to disturb the security of many executives.

Many employers want "organization men" who can fit nicely into any niche and be content not to overstep its predetermined boundaries. This is a dissappointment to someone who would like an opportunity to exercise all the faculties of a well-trained graduate from a collegiate school of business.

Criticism of the usual policy of big business to claim prior rights on all innovations made by employees has been growing. The subject is highly controversial. To the person with a creative mind a condition of employment that forces him to relinquish his constitutional right to seek and exploit a patent on his own ideas must be quite distasteful. No doubt some employees have taken unfair advantage of their position which gave them access to information belonging to their employers, and others may have failed to reveal discoveries made on the job which they were being paid to seek. But the exact origin of ideas that lead to inventions and other innovations is often obscure, and employment contracts that give the employer prior claim to these may at times be unfair.

WHY "GO IT ALONE"?

If an individual has ideas and wants to try them out, he can do so as his own boss to a far greater extent than as an employee. If he likes to pioneer, small business is a natural for him; if he likes to carry through to successful completion a job once started even if it means working overtime, he should enter business for himself. If he enjoys a line of useful work, is good at it, and is not afraid of hard work, he will probably make much more in this type of business working for himself, and will be happier than he would be working for the other fellow. If he wants to secure all the profits from his efforts and will take the risk of loss, if he wants to do something differently from the way it is being done, or if he is unhappy working for others and feels restrained from the opportunity for self-expression, he should make sure first and then start on his own business. If an individual really wants to go into business for himself but is afraid to start because of the many risks involved, he should plan definitely to do so anyway, waiting only until he has an even chance for success.

Self-expression

Business ownership gives a person a chance to exercise all of his abilities, skill, knowledge, energy, and his desire for pioneering and adventure. This fact is not only especially important for the college graduate in capitalizing fully on his investment in a broad education, but also emotionally in providing expression for the entire personality.

As his own boss, the individual has fewer restraints on his actions, is able to express himself more fully, and can develop any creative idea he has to the limit of his ability and resources, no matter how "harebrained" it may seem to others. He is not restrained by precedent, regulations, or limitations of the past, or by the conservatism characteristic of big business employment.

The desire to experiment, to test one's strength, to prove one's ability to master a situation and thus to gain all the emotional and material benefits to be derived therefrom, is inherent in most of us. The entrepreneur, by nature, is more willing than others to take a risk to provide such benefits to himself. The existence of opportunities for such fulfillment is a characteristic of democracy, a free society, and the free world. One speaker has expressed it as follows:

> Freedom of enterprise is more than the freedom to succeed. At the core, it is the freedom to fail. This country owes its greatness to men who are free to take chances and who dare. We can stick our chins out, we can take risks . . . and we get the reward for doing it if we are right. Our cold war opponents have no such latitude.[1]

The desire to start a small business is a common one, for the entrepreneur seeks to provide for his material needs through self-expression and with independence. In

---

[1] Ray R. Eppert, President, Burroughs Corporation, in an address before the Boston Conference on Distribution.

this way, the purely economic needs of the individual are supplied in a manner emotionally pleasing to him. To be an independent business operator is the inherent ambition of millions of men and women in every land, of all ages, and of varying backgrounds, intentions, and qualifications. When an employee can observe that "the boss" is reaping substantial profits from the special talents of the employee, the idea often occurs that those benefits could or should belong to the employee instead. Under such circumstances, with a little capital and a lot of courage, an independent businessman may be born.

For the development of self-reliance, for making men as well as money, small business excels. Operating a small business suits the personality and independent attitude of many.

Security and Income

Once established, a small business offers to the owner security comparable to employment, and for a much longer period of time. There is also the satisfaction of being known in the community as an independent businessman and not as merely an employee who takes his orders from others. Employment opportunities and inducements offered by large companies fluctuate according to economic conditions fully as much as the prospects for success in independent enterprising.

If a person owns his own business, he cannot be fired, except by customers – his real bosses. He need have little fear of petty jealousies, factions, internal politics, or favoritism; instead, he has the forces of competition to be met successfully. This may not always be easy, but at least it is usually above board, ethical, and available to all competitors equally or according to their ability.

The small business owner and independent professional man are not subject to the same time limitations on their earning power as are employees who must accept retirement at a certain age because of company policy. Some prefer to get the entire profit from their own efforts, ideas, judgment, and skill, saving or investing as they choose and retiring when they please.

Freedom of action is greater. If an owner wants to slow down a bit or take a vacation, that is his business. The proprietors of many small businesses admit that they could make more money if they would work harder, but they do not want to. From one point of view this is a weakness of small business, since many proprietors, in the absence of any prodding from higher-ups, show a tendency to loaf. From another standpoint, however, this is really a good thing, for life certainly should have a meaning other than continual hard work under pressure.

SMALL BUSINESS AS A PART-TIME VENTURE

While ownership of a firm obligates most operators to devote their full attention to it – at least until it is well established – there may be circumstances under which a business can be begun as a sideline. Sometimes an employee of a large company buys or launches a small enterprise that he can supervise or operate without encroaching upon his employment duties. Similarly, members of professions such as accounting or teaching, as well as employees of business concerns, often establish sideline enterprises. These may add as much net income as the primary "bread-and-butter" job, furnish legitimate income tax advantages under current legislation and regulations, provide a hedge in case of unsatisfactory developments with the enterpriser's employer, and lead to a postemployment occupation of well-established and proven value.

Several other groups have found small businesses a welcome source of supplemental income. This includes retired people who wish to continue working – but at a more leisurely pace; schoolteachers, college professors, and some political officeholders often have a small venture of their own which they operate three or four months each year. Not infrequently undergraduate business students operate their own enterprises in lieu of taking part-time jobs to earn their expenses.

DISADVANTAGES OF BUSINESS OWNERSHIP

Attractive as owning your own business may seem, the attractiveness is not without its limitations. Risk is probably the greatest of these – risk of financial loss, of the loss of your business reputation, and of personal prestige. Actually, loss of business reputation is not great, as most small businesses that do not succeed fold up quietly with plausible excuses given to the public. In a surprisingly large number of cases one or two failures are followed by success that eventually leads to an outstanding business. Woolworth and Macy may be cited as examples, although the number is legion.

The person who fails to grasp opportunity fails in business; and the person who characteristically permits others to overrule, override, and overrun him will just as characteristically be ridden, ruled, and run out of the business world. Business is not unethical, but some businessmen are. The fact of the existence of such business hazards, plus the fact that business is, above all, sometimes cruelly practical, will soon be evident to the naive beginner.

The following list summarizes frequently given disadvantages of business ownership:

1. Greater risks, financial and personal; certain risks may be covered by insurance but others cannot. Among the latter group are: errors in forecasting demand and price changes, obsolescence, changes in government policy, changes in the international situation, inventions, new ideas launched by competitors, and changes in traffic routing or freight rates.
2. Longer hours and, sometimes, more worry.
3. Entire responsibility for all decisions and for meeting payroll and other expenses.
4. Irregular income since all business is subject to continuous ups and downs.
5. Responsibilities to employees and creditors.
6. Too many people to please: the public, customers, creditors, the government, and other social groups.
7. Income is usually small at the beginning.
8. Many agencies, in addition to those already mentioned, will regulate activities and reduce independence, such as the minimum standards required by insurance companies, the local fire and police departments, health authorities, labor unions, and quite possibly others – depending on the type of business.
9. The burden of numerous government reports makes heavy demands on the owner's time and resources.
10. Taxation bears heavily on the beginning small enterprise.

MAKING THE DECISION

Innumerable studies and surveys indicate that the desire for independence is the most frequently cited reason for "going it alone" rather than working for others. The next most important reason is to enter a family business. Another compelling reason is the desire for higher income.[2]

While a superior income and prestige may come to the successful small businessman, these factors should not be the primary reasons for making the decision for self-employment. If operating a small business is first of all a personally satisfying activity, financial rewards are more likely to result.

Thousands of individuals who would chafe under the restrictions of salaried employment find business ownership to their liking. Small business offers the opportunity for self-employment to hundreds of thousands — some with technical and professional training, others with business experience, and large numbers who are outside the employable standards set by many concerns, especially big business. Men past middle age, those with physical handicaps, and others who for various reasons are not attractive as employees find self-employment the best road to living a productive life. Widows lacking previous business training or experience, housewives desiring to supplement the wage earner's income, and young married couples often find small business ventures attractive and profitable.

Upon retirement, many people prefer to remain in their home towns; others find it necessary to do so because of family or other obligations. When the town is fairly small or nonindustrialized, opportunities to secure well-paying jobs or to expand an independent enterprise may be limited. The flexibility of free enterprise has solved this dilemma for many small-town and home-town people by allowing multiple enterprises. Thus a physician in a small southern town owns and operates a service station, drug store, and grocery store, and a practicing attorney in the Southwest is the owner-operator of a self-service automatic laundry and a maintenance and repair service (he also sells reconditioned automatic washers, and plans to expand into the automobile service station, grocery, and enough other fields to give him control over ten separate small enterprises — all within his home town of about 30,000 population).

Women with managerial or merchandising ability often operate small establishments of their own and make more money than they could as employees under our double-wage standard. In addition, they have greater flexibility and more control over their own time and responsibilities than they would have as employees. Conceivably this development may help to reduce or even eliminate the double-wage standard — at least for the better qualified women.

Increasingly in recent years, young people and members of minority groups have also looked upon business ownership as a means of self-fulfillment or increased economic well-being. The reaction of young people to bureaucracy, as symbolized in part by big business, was noted in the preceding chapter. This reaction against bigness and conformity has resulted in a strong individualistic spirit among the nation's youth, many of whom find self-employment attractive because it offers an opportunity for economic self-expression. Small business has traditionally been the stronghold of economic individualism; among young people today it is known as

[2] See, for example, Kurt B. Mayer and Sidney Goldstein, *The First Two Years: Problems of Small Firm Growth and Survival*, Small Business Research Series no. 2 (Washington, D.C.: G.P.O., Small Business Administration, 1961), pp. 28 ff.

the "alternative" capitalism, or by some as "hip" capitalism. The following case is illustrative:

> Two young Iowans . . . have combined their college majors in art and economics with a funny name and have come up with a thriving shirt-manufacturing business [in Iowa City.]
>
> Grace Bible and Banana Co. (a name chosen because it "sings") started operations a year ago when Dean Samuels and Cindy Luthey began making shirts for a local boutique shop. The shirts sold well in Iowa City where the vast University of Iowa student population creates a market for unusual and novelty fashion items. Soon, Samuels . . . wondered if there was room in the national boutique market for his company's shirts. After a trip to the 1970 National Boutique Show in New York City, he discovered there was. . . . [An expansion program was begun, and now the company makes unique men's and women's shirts for boutique shops and large department stores across the country.] Customers include Bloomingdale's and Macy's in New York and some of San Francisco's smartest shops. . . .
>
> Miss Luthey designs the clothing and supervises the production line; [Samuels keeps the business books and does all the buying and sales promotion.]
>
> Taught by her mother to sew, Miss Luthey was an art major in college specializing in printmaking. She uses her creative talents to come up with unusual shirt designs. . . . One of the most unusual — and successful — is a skimpy women's blouse made out of four common, everyday household dish rags. . . . A new spring shirt to be introduced will be called the "Feed Sack," appropriately featuring a front panel consisting of a feed sack. The company also makes a selection of men's sports shirts — the puffy-sleeved kind that men wear when they want to be especially "in" these days. . . .
>
> "This is what I've always wanted to do," Samuels said. "I didn't want to work for someone else. It's more fun when you're responsible for the success or failure [of a business]. It's also a lot harder."[3]

Members of minority groups have looked upon self-employment as desirable for quite a different reason: as one of the ways of bringing themselves into the economic mainstream of American life. However, their opportunities for business ownership have long been severely restricted. Though comprising approximately 17 percent of the population, minorities own fewer than 3 percent of the nation's businesses; furthermore, these minority-owned enterprises represent less than 0.5 percent of the nation's industrial and business capital. If we are to have a strong, healthy national economy, the incorporation of minority groups into the business structure is essential. National attention has been focused on this problem for the past several years. In an effort to create viable opportunities and sources of venture capital for potential minority entrepreneurs, President Nixon in March 1969 established the Office of Minority Business Enterprise (OMBE) as an agency of the Department of Commerce.[4] It is hoped that this program will generate economic opportunities for disadvantaged minority groups on a par with those available to the general population.

Regardless of emotional, social, or economic considerations, however, the person contemplating going into business for himself should be aware of the personality

---

[3] Larry Eckholt, in the *Des Moines Register*, August 15, 1971, p. 7-F (abridged).

[4] Financial aid under this program is discussed in Chapter 11; managerial and other types of nonfinancial assistance are discussed in Chapter 14. The OMBE is also a cosponsor, with the SBA, of the "25×2" franchise program, described on p. 133.

characteristics required for success as an entrepreneur, and then to rate himself objectively in terms of those traits.

The Entrepreneurial Ego

A young businessman entered his home one evening after a hard day and was beseeched by his four-year-old son: "Daddy, play with me." After reluctant refusal and continued complaint while he was trying to read from a newly arrived magazine, the parent finally conceived an idea. On the magazine page before him was the picture of an industrial plant. This he pointed out to his son; then, reviewing the principle of the jigsaw puzzle, he tore the sheet into several pieces and challenged the boy to put it together again, thus to grant himself some minutes respite.

Surprisingly, the boy was quickly finished with his task, entirely too quickly to suit the father, despite his natural pride. Yet he complimented the son and asked him how he did the job so fast. The boy replied: "Well, Daddy, it's like this. I saw that magazine earlier today – and I saw the picture of the plant, too. It looks like where you work. But I was more interested in the picture of a man which was on the other side of the page. I remembered him better. So, Daddy, I just put the man together – and when the man was right, the plant was right."

"When the man was right, the plant was right," might well be the quickest and simplest statement of what it takes to be a success in small business.

In terms of temperament and motivations, there are as many varieties of small firm operators as there are varieties of employees. However, numerous studies suggest that there are certain personality characteristics which successful small businessmen seem to have in common. A team of psychologists at Western Reserve University, using tests, questionnaires, and depth interviews, studied the chief executive officers of several successful small businesses and prepared the composite profile presented below:

1. The successful small businessman is a *gambler*, or if you prefer, an adventurer, but with a combination of daring and caution. His motivation for independence of action is stronger than his need for security. He shows an exceptional willingness to expend more than ordinary effort to achieve. Financial gain is not his driving power. His gamble is not for the sake of "the fast buck." His desire for acquisition is not as high as his passion for achievement. It is a deeper, more elemental, creative urge to leave his mark on something he alone brought from an idea to reality. His satisfaction is not in plaudits or rewards. He finds it in accomplishment. To achieve, he will lay security on the line.

2. The successful small businessman is *decisive*. He expects and covets the part of decision maker. Most of the chief executive officers tested and interviewed kept a tight grip on the reins of all phases of management, though not, by any means, in a tyrannical way. His sense of responsibility for the business is so overpowering he feels that important decisions of policy and day-to-day operations should be made by him or referred to him for discussion. Curiously enough, though the popular concept of an efficient executive is a willingness to delegate authority, little resentment was found among subordinates interveiwed. This is probably because in a small, closely-knit operation teamwork is not a slogan on a poster, but a natural outgrowth of limited size. Thus subordinates, thrown into daily close contact with the "boss" on a multiplicity of problems, feel a sense of participation in the exercise of authority. The point is, however, the man who runs a successful small firm is not a

vacillator or a "referrer to committee." He faces problems as they come, is not afraid to make decisions, in fact, prefers to do so. After all, his first decision — to risk security for independence — is indicative of the kind of man who expects to make the decisions.

3. The successful small businessman is *versatile.* In business matters, rather than being confined in his scope of activities to one area of the business, he constantly strives to become competent in all areas. In many instances if his background had been in sales, marketing, production or engineering, he took courses in other phases of business operation in which he felt he lacked adequate knowledge. Unless a man is interested in not only the planning function, but also the business details, the technical aspects of marketing and production, and is genuinely concerned for the quality of his product or service leading to the reputation of his firm, he might think twice before launching his own venture, for he is not typical of successful small businessmen who were studied. Studies of causes of failure consistently point to three things: inadequate capital, poor accounting, and *lack of know-how.*

4. The successful small businessman is a *"finisher."* Many people start a project with wild enthusiasm, high hopes and banners waving. To a man, the group studied had not only strong motives to achieve, but equally strong motives to endure, to finish the task at hand. When this is accompanied by a need to dominate, things get done. We were often told by the subordinates of these men, whom we interviewed to get their appraisal of their chief, "If we're in a bind on a job the boss rolls up his sleeves and slugs it out right with us, evenings, Sundays, holidays if necessary, until the job is complete."

5. The successful small businessman is *self-confident.* Rated on fifteen psychological needs the executives scored lowest on "abasement" (admitting error or defeat) and "deference" (following suggestions or instructions from others). This indicates a person with a strong belief in his own capabilities, with unpleasantly aggressive tendencies. Yet our table showed that "aggression" (or hostility) scored thirteenth, just above "abasement" and "deference." Thus a mature belief in one's self is a requisite to head up a small business operation successfully, but it must not be teamed with an overbearing or hostile manner.

6. The successful small businessman is a *benevolent despot.* The chief executive officers who were studied viewed themselves as versatile, energetic workers whose primary concern was the success and continuity of the business. Giving freely of his time and energy, the small business owner-manager expects subordinates to do likewise. His subordinates view him as generally friendly, willing to listen to suggestions but not always accepting them, not insisting on standard ways of doing things or over-concerned with the details of their work, not expecting rigid conformity. His expectations are for productivity and competence; he is flexible as to the method of doing a job. He is more interested in getting it done and done right.[5]

Another study of the personality characteristics that lead to success in small business was made by Dr. H. B. Pickle, of Southwest Texas State College, who identifies five characteristics which he considers significant: (*a*) *drive,* comprised of responsibility, vigor, initiative, persistence, and health; (*b*) *thinking ability,* com-

---

[5] Kenneth Lawyer et al., *Small Business Success: Operating and Executive Characteristics,* Small Business Management Research Report, prepared by Bureau of Business Research, Western Reserve University, under a grant by the Small Business Administration (Washington, D.C.: G.P.O., 1963).

prised of original (creative) and critical (analytical) thinking; (*c*) *human relations ability,* comprised of ascendancy, emotional stability, sociability, cautiousness, consideration, cheerfulness, cooperation, and tact; (*d*) *communications ability,* both oral and written; and (*e*) *technical knowledge.*[6]

Objective Self-analysis

As has been shown in the studies cited above, the successful independent in business or professional practice exhibits many traits in addition to those generally conceded to be important for success as an employee. Stated another way, these are (1) enterprise — a self-reliant attitude supported by confidence in one's ability to take risks, to make decisions, to assume responsibility, and to pioneer; (2) determination — a driving urge for success as an independent and persistence and stamina enough to carry through in spite of obstacles; (3) balance and control in self- and time management; (4) ingenuity or creative imagination — constantly seeking new and better ways to do things, to outdo competition, to determine and control one's own progress; and (5) honest self-evaluation and constant efforts to improve. Notice that these are all stimuli often provided for employees in varying degrees by the employer, if and when they are wanted or needed. However, they must originate with the individual himself when he is on his own.

It's a big order. Can *you* fill it? Sit down and honestly analyze yourself. What are your likes and dislikes? What did you do as a boy — deliver groceries after school for regular pay or run your own lemonade stand or a similar independent business venture? When did you consider starting your own business? What gave you the idea in the first place? Was it some friend's unexpected success as his own boss? Was it a reaction to taking orders with no chance to talk back, such as many veterans experience during and after military service? What are your goals? Your family's attitude toward the undertaking, as well as your financial responsibilities to your family, may have a bearing on the decision.

Rating scales are often used by employers in evaluating prospective new employees. Consider that you are employing yourself to manage your own capital, reputation, and future. Be honest with yourself. How would you rate?

The rating scale in Figure 4–1 may help the reader in deciding whether he should be his own boss.

Another type of self-test was developed for use in the Western Reserve study by the team of psychologists headed by Dr. Jay L. Otis. Following are 21 of the original 140 test statements used in appraising the chief executives of successful small business firms.[7] Try them on yourself; ask your wife or a friend to check you for objectivity. The rating scale follows on page 71.

---

[6] Hal B. Pickle, *Personality and Success: An Evaluation of Personal Characteristics of Successful Small Business Managers,* Small Business Research Series no. 4 (Washington, D.C.: G.P.O., Small Business Administration, 1964).

[7] Prepared by Charles M. Davis, "Solving the Riddle of Business Success," *The Rotarian* (March 1966); p. 21; based on Dr. Jay L. Otis's "Personal Description Inventory" used in the Western Reserve study, op. cit.

Figure 4-1.   Rating Scale for Evaluating Personal Traits of Small Business Owner-Managers

1	2	3	4	5
Poor — not acceptable at all; failure to measure up	*Fair — barely acceptable, must improve; between 1 and 3*	*Good — acceptable; only average; can improve*	*Very Good — better than average; between 3 and 5*	*Excellent — top quality; commendable performance*

1. PERSONALITY, ENTHUSIASM

1	2	3	4	5
Not an agreeable person; apparently does not like *people*, as employees or as customers		Lukewarm; agreeable but not very friendly; acceptable behavior in most situations		Pleasing and congenial personality; contagious enthusiasm and inspirational manner

2. ACCEPTANCE OF CRITICISM

1	2	3	4	5
Resents any criticism as personal; does not welcome suggestions or advice		Accepts advice casually; reacts slowly to suggestions		Welcomes constructive help of any kind; anxious to learn from any likely source

3. ABILITY TO LEARN

1	2	3	4	5
Slow to change his thinking — "set in his ways" or lacking in ability to understand and adjust to training and experience		Able to adjust to change within reasonable time; not particularly aggressive in thinking or in grasping new concepts and procedures; learns slowly but retains well		Grasps ideas and methods readily; analytical of situations and alert to changes; retains and uses what he learns

4. INDUSTRY

1	2	3	4	5
Puts in minimum of time and effort, avoids responsibility of extra work; lays off frequently, arrives late, etc.		Performs adequately and well the routine functions of management, but not an aggressive manager		Works early and late as needed to keep business at maximum efficiency; a conscientious and hard worker

5. INITIATIVE

1	2	3	4	5
Does little thinking for himself; no originality, little resourcefulness or imagination; not a creative person		Occasionally has a good idea, but may not try it, until encouraged; follows line of least resistance		Resourceful, inventive and self-reliant; can usually work himself out of difficulties without assistance, gets good ideas, puts them into action

6. DECISION

1	2	3	4	5
Hesitant, ultraconservative		Prompt, confident, usually sound decisions. "plays the percentages"		Prompt, courageous, yet not reckless

7. RESPONSIBILITY

1	2	3	4	5
Avoided whenever possible		Accepted without protest or complaint; handles major responsibilities effectively		Sought and welcomed

Figure 4-1. (continued)

1	2	3	4	5
Poor – not acceptable at all; failure to measure up	*Fair–barely acceptable, must improve; between 1 and 3*	*Good – acceptable; only average; can improve*	*Very Good – better than average; between 3 and 5*	*Excellent – top quality; commendable performance*

8. PERSEVERANCE

1	2	3	4	5
Little or none		Average determination and persistence		Steadfast in purpose; not easily discouraged

9. PLANNING ABILITY

1	2	3	4	5
Poor planner and organizer		Does generally fair job of planning – acceptable		Good organizer; planning is farsighted

10. LEADERSHIP

1	2	3	4	5
Tolerated by employees but not respected as leader		Diplomatic and tactful order giver; may not delegate well		Obtains top performance from all employees; inspires loyalty to company and self; can delegate authority

Poorest ratings are at the left, the best at the right. Please note that while there are descriptions for only three scores, the horizontal line is divided into five parts and can be scored accordingly.

1. If the statement is only rarely or slightly descriptive of your behavior, SCORE 1.
2. If the statement is applicable under some circumstances, but only partially true, SCORE 2.
3. If the statement describes you perfectly, SCORE 3.

Score

1. I relish competing with others. . . . . ————
2. I compete intensely to win regardless of the rewards. . . . . ————
3. I compete with some caution, but will often "bluff." . . . . ————
4. I do not hesitate to take a calculated risk for future gain. . . . . ————
5. I do a job so effectively that I get a definite feeling of accomplishment. ————
6. I want to be "tops" in whatever I elect to do. . . . . ————
7. I am not bound by tradition. . . . . ————
8. I am inclined to forge ahead and discuss later. . . . . ————
9. Reward or praise means less to me than a job well done. . . . . ————
10. I usually go my own way regardless of others' opinions. . . . . ————
11. I find it difficult to admit error or defeat. . . . . ————
12. I am a self-starter — I need little urging from others. . . . . ————
13. I am not easily discouraged. . . . . ————
14. I work out my own answers to problems. . . . . ————
15. I am inquisitive. . . . . ————
16. I am not patient with interference from others . . . . . ————
17. I have an aversion to taking orders from others. . . . . ————
18. I can take criticism without hurt feelings. . . . . ————
19. I insist on seeing a job through to the finish. . . . . ————
20. I expect associates to work as hard as I do. . . . . ————
21. I read to improve my knowledge in all business activities. . . . . ————
    TOTAL . . . . ————

A score of 63 is "perfect"; 52 to 62 is "good"; 42 to 51 is "fair"; and under 42, "poor." Obviously, scoring high here is no guarantee of becoming a successful small businessman, since many other personal qualities must also be rated. But it should encourage you to pursue the matter further.

PREPARING FOR BUSINESS OWNERSHIP

If the decision is made to undertake business ownership, careful preparation should follow. Personal qualities, genuine business opportunity, business know-how, and the ability to make a plan and execute it are essential components contributing to the success of a business. The initial step, however, is adequate preparation and planning. First one must acquire the necessary knowledge and then learn how to apply it.

The unwillingness of some to spend the time and effort necessary to prepare adequately is one of the chief causes of business failure; for success involves sufficient knowledge of business and industry to recognize the essential factors in good planning, such as how to use capital and the need for adequate control systems.

Formal Education

Preparation for business ownership should involve both education and business experience. Though a university education by no means assures business success, and though many successful businessmen have little formal education, study and training in a college of business is one of the best ways of laying a sound foundation. Courses are also being offered for small businessmen in some community colleges, junior colleges, and adult-education programs. The nature of the business will to some extent determine the degree and kind of training needed. To operate a business, the entrepreneur needs a knowledge of accounting, business law, economics, management, and marketing. In addition he must have special knowledge applicable to his particular field, such as manufacturing techniques, merchandise lines, or the skills necessary to perform a service.

Those who plan to operate a service enterprise will usually be applying skills or professional knowledge learned in a formal education or training program. The architect, pharmacist, or accountant first acquires professional training. The teaching of business skills necessary for independent enterprise is usually considered secondary. The same may be true of the plumber, the metalworker, the barber, or the commercial artist; yet without the knowledge of how to organize and operate a business he is quite unprepared for self-employment. Some professional and trade schools include courses on small business operation. Others do not.

In fact, it is shortsighted for any college student, regardless of major or any other factors, to neglect at least a minimum of preparation for self-employment. Our society has become highly complex, interdependent in all spheres, and definitely a pecuniary market-economy. We buy our living in the marketplace. While in college the engineer, education major, home economist, physical education major, journalist, fine arts student, and all others should enroll in several business courses, including one or more dealing specifically with the independent enterpriser.

The future is uncertain at best. Extensive experience shows that many college graduates do not remain with their major subject throughout their careers. Individuals and economic conditions change; some occupations decline in importance and new ones appear. Unpredictable events may indicate the desirability of changing occupations or of shifting from salaried employment to self-employment, or vice versa. One way of being better prepared for such developments is for the nonbusiness major to include a few business courses in his curriculum, and for all students to enroll in a small-business or independent enterpriser course. The latter suggestion may furnish information that need never be put to actual use in later life, but how can the student know this? Also, the broader outlook obtained should make for a more intelligent choice between salaried employment or independent enterprise, as well as furnish a basis for a better appreciation of our complex economic system.

A basic decision as to the field of one's activity will be helpful in making the best preparation possible for self-employment. For some the decision will be an initial one which is based on already existing talents, interests, or training. Others will make this decision as they gain knowledge and experience in the field of business. Consideration should be given to the major fields of retailing, wholesaling, manufacturing, and the service industries; to choice of function, such as accounting, advertising, personnel, or purchasing; as well as to the commodity or service to be handled, such as groceries or wearing apparel, personal or repair service. Individuals are likely to be better suited by temperament and other personal traits to one of these alternatives than to the others.[8]

Acquiring Trade Experience

In addition to taking business courses every student should endeavor to obtain some employment experience in the field selected for a career or one closely related to it. It is difficult, if not impossible, to provide conditions on the college campus that are truly representative of full-time postgraduate employment. What an employer expects in return for his investment in wages and how to get along with coworkers and customers are subjects difficult to teach in the classroom. Vacation work and part-time employment, especially in connection with a cooperative or in-service training program sponsored by the school, may serve two purposes: (1) provide work for pay in the environment representative of a chosen career; and (2) provide an opportunity to work with and for others on an income-earning basis. The first of these may result in disillusionment in the selected career, since many vocational choices are made on scanty knowledge of the field. But how much better it is to discover this while still in training and while an opportunity to change goals and prepare for another occupation still is open. Since a man's future happiness often depends on his occupational fitness, this recommendation deserves emphasis.

An example of an enterprising young man who gave himself the opportunity to study and work in his field of initial interest is Denny Swails of Iowa City, Iowa, who started working after school in a drive-in restaurant as soon as he turned sixteen. He began by doing a variety of jobs from clean-up to food preparation. In his senior year of high school he enrolled in the high school distributive education program. For this class he prepared a 160-page book on the drive-in business, based on his first-hand observations and information received in replies to over 150 letters sent to manufacturers of drive-in equipment. The report won him second place in a state-wide DE contest. About this time the restaurant for which he worked suffered serious fire damage. In the course of rebuilding he suggested and designed several new features for the interior, including an infrared oven for keeping the food hot between the kitchen and the pickup window. He also devised a faster method for handling orders.[9] Dennis now owns his own drive-in.

Students often ask about the amount and type of experience that will best prepare them for operating their own enterprises. Some believe it is better to learn the best methods developed by big business; others feel they can learn all the functions of management and get broader experience by employment in a small concern. The beliefs are more widespread than well founded that experience needs to be obtained in a firm similar to the one a person plans to operate, and that it must be first-hand experience.

[8] See Appendix A for a list of reading references of value to those who wish to organize and operate particular types of small business.

[9] *Iowa City Press-Citizen*, May 30, 1966, p. 6.

Balancing experience.   Experience should be balanced and should include managerial responsibilities. Balance refers principally to the acquiring of experience in all of the major functions, such as selling, buying, production, personnel, finance, and accounting. Balance is also provided by knowledge of how concerns of appreciably different size operate in the same field. The man with several years' vacation and part-time experience in all divisions of a small store should consider seeking his additional experience in one or two functions that the large companies are known to have developed efficiently, such as merchandising and accounting in chain stores. Conversely, the former chain or department store employee should obtain experience in a smaller independent concern to get the overall viewpoint of managerial duties and to learn what the owner-manager has to do for himself that is normally done by headquarters for the manager of a chain store or for a buyer in a department store.

It is sometimes difficult to obtain exactly the type of experience desired. Certainly it is well to know the type of experience needed, to realize when you have learned as much as possible in one job, and when to move on to another. If at this time your employer is unable to transfer you he may make it possible for you to learn something about the other functions in various ways. Sometimes you may need to change jobs to round out your experience.

In-service training.   If an in-service training course is offered by your school there is an excellent opportunity to obtain desirable experience and to multiply its benefits. In such a program the trainee is recognized by his employer as such, rather than as just another college student working part time. Job experience is usually rotated or diversified and the trainee has access to management for questions and consultation. Often in larger concerns he is invited to sit in on junior executive meetings. The fact that the student's grade depends upon his work analysis report, ratings by his supervisor, and participation in seminar discussions add greatly to the benefits obtained. Many students who have worked part time for several years in the same firm learn much more about the business during their one semester as a trainee. With a group of students all in different training stations meeting to exchange experiences and to discuss problems during their seminars, each one has his own perspective vastly enlarged. Questions raised during a seminar stimulate each trainee to seek an answer from his employer.

Learning to Be a Manager

Actual managerial experience is not so easy to secure within the few years which ambitious prospective enterprisers allow for preownership employment. When actual managerial experience is not obtainable on the job, other methods of learning to be a manager may be effective.

The employee, for example, can observe and study the management of the firm for which he works. Such analysis involves critical observation of the management, determination of just which management activities are performed and why and of the reasons they are done in a certain way, appraisal of their effectiveness and possible improvements, checking on the soundness of ideas for improvement, and learning to visualize how he would carry out each managerial responsibility. These steps call for keen observation, creative imagination, discreet questions, and discussing ideas or suggestions with the manager and coworkers. If questions are tactful and well timed, an inquiring mind is certain to be approved by progressive management. In fact it is one of the key criteria in the newer methods of selecting future big business executives. Even though it often happens that an employee's ideas for improvement may be impractical because they neglect something he does not know about, making suggestions may be the best way to learn of factors not readily apparent, and imagination is still considered by management to be indicative of promising executive ability.

The management of men, or personnel management, is discussed in detail later in this book. In essence, it consists of getting others to want to do what you want them to do, and to do it efficiently. Unless a student operates his own business on the side, or has a part-time job involving the management of others, most of his efforts in this area will be for nonfinancial goals. Club affiliations and other extracurricular activities afford opportunities to develop and test leadership ability. Even classroom activities, oral reports, class discussion, committee or panel memberships, and the like afford similar opportunities. Many students are very proficient in managing their instructors — learning the latters' pet ideas, idiosyncrasies, and motivations and using this knowledge effectively.

An almost infinite number of capsule or pilot-plant projects are available to any student who cares to make an honest test of his managerial ability. He can play his hobby for a potential profit, become a free-lance agent for some large concern, or act as a resident buyer for out-of-town (usually rural or small-town) consumers. The idea is to set up an actual business venture — accurate in every detail except size, like the scale models of navy ships and airplanes — then manage the venture profitably. Dollar profits may be small but they must be earned profits.

If an individual first learns to manage his own life well, this in itself is preparation for business management. Among the qualities he should develop and practice are self-reliance, good use of time, and wise money management. All are as important to successful business management as to well-organized living.

In summary, the following points merit emphasis: (1) good management is basically the same in a drug store, automobile factory, or family enterprise: (2) one *can* and should learn from the experience of others; since (3) it is humanly impossible for one person to acquire all the knowledge and skill needed for entrepreneurship from personal experience alone.

PREOWNERSHIP EXPERIENCE "ON LOCATION"

Many prospective enterprisers may choose between starting a new concern, buying a going concern, or buying into an established one, and a few may have a fourth alternative, that of entering or taking over a going family business. Chapter 5 deals with buying a going concern, especially from strangers. Chapter 6 considers starting an entirely new enterprise. Our interest now is with the remaining alternatives, where preownership experience is more directly involved.

Much may be said for, and a little against, buying a controlling interest from one's employer. By working in the business you plan later to own, the major dangers of buying a going concern from strangers are avoided. You have an opportunity to study strong and weak points of the firm that could easily be missed by an outsider. You can learn all the details of operation, study methods or policies that you might be able to improve under your own management, and get much better acquainted with the personnel, customers, and suppliers than would be possible otherwise. You may be able to take over managerial responsibilities gradually, profit by the experience and knowledge of the retiring management, and transfer to yourself most of the goodwill associated with the personality of the former owners.

The experience of eighteen-year-old James Dove of Ashland, Ohio, is a case in point. He bought a food store in Ashland immediately following his graduation from high school. This neighborhood grocery and meat market has been located in the same building for fifty years. It is modern in every respect. Young Mr. Dove worked in the store after school during his last two years of high school. His purchase of a going concern would seem to have respected most of the accepted standards recommended for such transactions. Mr. Dove has experience in the trade, he knows the area and its people, and he is familiar with the condition of the store's inventory and fixtures. With a fifty-year record behind it, a good building in good condition, with no zoning problems, good merchandise sources, and established banking relationships, the odds are in favor of his success. He is in a position to inherit much of the goodwill earned by the present owners.[10]

It is probably this latter advantage, goodwill by association, that makes this method preferred by those planning to enter professional practice for themselves. A recent graduate in medicine, dentistry, law, or accounting usually finds that the endorsement of the well-established, reputable practitioner with whom he becomes associated is accepted by the clientele, and he has an opportunity to prove his own ability much sooner than if he were to attempt to practice alone. Even in nonprofessional fields the method has similar advantages, though to a lesser degree. A unique feature about many small businesses is that their goodwill is directly related to the personality of the owner, rather than to the brands or company reputations of large corporations.

Before taking over the owner-management of a family enterprise there may be a valid need to appraise the soundness of the enterprise and to decide whether it would be worth taking over in preference to other alternatives; but such cases differ little, if at all, from the continuous need for management to appraise its position and future prospects. More important is proving the managerial ability of the heir. So many case histories are known in which a founder built a successful enterprise whose profitable operations were enjoyed without effort by his son, only to have the grandson ruin the business by his incompetence, that the expression "three generations from shirt sleeves to shirt sleeves" has gained widespread acceptance. Employees, and sometimes other family members, tend to resent and suspect the boss's son who steps into a top management position right out of school. Thus we have both a potential lack of managerial competence and a need to prove one's ability to others when a family enterprise is acquired.

The heir to a family business might avoid or at least minimize the dangers just mentioned in several ways. Most common is for him to work in the firm during vacations and part time during the school year. If his work is coordinated with business courses it can be extremely valuable experience. Principles and methods discussed in class can be considered closely as to their application to the company. One difficulty in the case of many college courses taught in terms of big business is

[10] *Cleveland Plain Dealer*, July 25, 1965, p. 7B.

to appreciate applications to the small independent concern. The very effort of seeking to find ways to utilize those that are appropriate can greatly enhance the value of the coursework and indicate possible ways the family concern might be improved. This is not to say that the company's methods and policies should be changed as each new topic is developed in class. Rather it is an exploratory exercise to determine what would be necessary to make any indicated changes and the probable effects such moves would have. The process resembles class discussion of a case problem.

A second approach is for the son to learn the business through part-time work while still in college if possible, but as soon as feasible on a full-time basis as an understudy to the management. He is upgraded in stages as he develops proficiency. This plan may be successful even when the son does not start to work in the company until after graduation, but is usually better if pregraduation experience in the firm is obtained. While he is still the boss's son, and considered by other employees to be a favored person, he does have an opportunity to make friends and demonstrate his ability. It is far better than coming in as a total stranger to the organization and starting in a top management position.

A third plan is for the son to prove his ability in an outside organization before becoming associated with the family enterprise. Although more time-consuming than the other plans, it does reduce the danger of an incompetent person becoming the owner-manager purely by inheritance, and tends to reduce employee feeling of favoritism. It also has an equally important advantage, that of bringing in an outside viewpoint. The dangers inherent in inbreeding are reduced. Just as many large companies often employ executives from other concerns to keep a flow of new blood and outside ideas coming in, so it is with this method. Probably the more serious limitations upon a college graduate going directly into the family enterprise center around this danger of inbreeding.

In the final analysis a decision should be based on circumstances in the particular case. No two family enterprises will be identical in all factors, such as attitudes of other family members, potential rivalry for control of the business, ambitions and attitudes of employees, qualifications of the prospective owner-manager at the time of graduation, or needs of the business. The basic guide in all cases is adequate planning and preparation far enough in advance to make it really effective.

SUMMARY AND CONCLUSIONS

Whether to be self-employed or a dependent employee is a major decision for many individuals. It warrants careful consideration.

Free entry into business is an essential feature of the American way of life. Opportunities for reward in proportion to effort and contributions have always made independent business ownership attractive to energetic individuals. However, the requirements needed for success as an independent enterpriser are rarer than some people believe, and the authors carry no banner promoting self-employment for everyone. The purpose of this book may as well be to warn away the unqualified as to encourage those who might succeed as entrepreneurs. The authors, as instructors and consultants, take some pride in having influenced individuals in both directions.

As part of the process of planning his future, the reader should compare the advantages and disadvantages of both employment and business ownership with his own traits in mind. If he decides he is the type to operate his own business, then he should survey the opportunities, risks, and requirements. Next, he should begin his pre-business-ownership planning and preparation. Finally, before starting out on his own, he should study the modern principles and practices discussed in the balance of this text.

Appendix A has been prepared for those who decide to go into business for themselves and who desire information on the starting and managing of specific types of business. Also of value to the prospective entrepreneur should be the authors' checklist for organizing and operating a small business in Appendix B.

REVIEW QUESTIONS

1.   What are the advantages of working for someone else? The disadvantages? Discuss.

2.   Compare the financial security of big business employment with that of self-employment.

3.   How may an executive in a large company be affected by changes in top management? Explain.

4.   What are the advantages of going into business for oneself? The disadvantages? Discuss.

5.   Under what circumstances might it be advantageous or preferable to operate a part-time business?

6.   What are some of the commonly cited reasons for going into business for oneself? Discuss.

7.   Why are more and more young people today choosing self-employment as a means of earning a living?

8.   Why are more and more members of minority groups looking upon self-employment as a means of earning a living?

9.   What qualities do entrepreneurs have in common as indicated by the Western Reserve study?

10.   Discuss the personality characteristics of successful small businessmen as reported in Dr. Pickle's study. How do they differ from those reported in the Western Reserve study?

11.   Rate yourself as a prospective entrepreneur (*a*) using the scale in Figure 4-1, pages 68-70; and (*b*) taking the self-test, based on the Western Reserve study, on page 71.

12.   What is the first step in preparing and planning for business ownership? Why is this so important?

13.   How may one go about preparing oneself for small business ownership?

14.   Discuss the desirability of big business or small business employment for preownership experience. Which do you prefer for yourself? Why?

15.   Explain how business analysis can be used as a substitute for, or supplement to, actual managerial experience in preparation for business ownership.

16. Briefly summarize the discussion of preownership managerial experience in this chapter.
17. Compare buying a concern from strangers with buying into the concern you are working for.
18. Discuss the problems and other relevant considerations in taking over a family enterprise.

DISCUSSION QUESTIONS

1. Suggest how large corporations should deal with inventions and other innovations made by their employees.
2. Why do not all business schools offer in-service training courses? Should they do so? Explain.
3. Which is more important in preparation for business ownership — proficiency in time management or in money management? Justify your answer.
4. How can it be said that financial rewards are greater in self-employment than in salaried employment?
5. Someone has said that when a person goes into business for himself, he quits working for a boss who runs a business and hires people and starts working for his customers. If this is true, he is simply changing bosses — the customer now becomes his boss, his employer. Is that a fair statement? Discuss.

SUPPLEMENTARY READINGS

Donneley, Robert G. "The Family Business." *Harvard Business Review* 42 (July-Aug. 1964): 93-105. Examines the strengths and weaknesses of a family business. Discusses the morality as well as the effectiveness of family management of businesses.

The Men at the Top: A Study of Small-Company Presidents. Staff Recommendations of the Research Institute of America, New York. A study of the origins, motivations, and patterns of behavior of over 1,000 successful entrepreneurs — the broadest study ever undertaken of the men who shape the destiny of small business.

Pickle, Hal B. *Personality and Success: An Evaluation of Personal Characteristics of Successful Small Business Managers.* Small Business Research Series no. 4. Washington, D.C.: G.P.O., Small Business Administration, 1964. A study of those personality traits of a successful business manager which have contributed measurably to the success of an enterprise.

PART TWO
Getting Started

- BUYING A GOING CONCERN

- JUSTIFYING A NEW BUSINESS

- ACQUIRING A FRANCHISE

- SELECTING THE LOCATION

- PROVIDING PHYSICAL FACILITIES

- FINANCING AND ORGANIZING THE BUSINESS

5

Buying a going concern

For the prospective small business owner who possesses the necessary personal qualities, managerial ability, and capital, and who is not inheriting a family enterprise, there are two ways to get started: he can buy out an existing establishment or he can start from scratch with a new firm. In either case a franchise arrangement may be an important consideration. This chapter will discuss the many factors to be considered in buying a going concern; determination of the economic justification for a new firm in the selected area will be considered in Chapter 6; and franchising opportunities will be examined in Chapter 7.

Because the mortality rate of new businesses is high, the opportunity to buy a firm already in operation appears attractive. It seems to be a way to avoid many of the beginner's hazards. The existing firm is apparently a proven success, the typical serious errors have either been avoided or are already corrected, the "bugs" are out of it and it is apparently running along nicely. It is like a ship after its "shakedown cruise," or a new automobile after the usual small adjustments have been made.

Or is it, in fact, more like a *used* car? Most owners do not sell their cars until they feel they need considerable mechanical attention.

Even if the beginner does not plan to buy a going concern, the methods of evaluating one will be useful to him as criteria for appraising the success and, therefore, the salability of any firm, perhaps his own at a later date.

The Need for Evaluation

In most instances the business under consideration will already be on the market, but in some cases the prospective purchaser, seeing an establishment operating in a certain location, makes an offer. In either case the value of the business must be determined by buyer and seller alike before an agreement can be reached. Both parties are anxious to secure full value in the exchange.

83

General Considerations

A going business can be evaluated with reasonable accuracy. First one needs a checklist of points to be considered; then one must be able to differentiate between the good and the bad, and recognize advantages and disadvantages. A great failing of amateur buyers, as with amateurs in any market, is that they often fail to observe certain vital factors which are present. Successful analysis of the value of any business requires the following qualifications on the part of the analyst: (1) enough experience in the trade to recognize the evidence for or against the business; (2) enough knowledge to adequately evaluate information provided by records or from other sources as to the level of past performance and probable future developments; and (3) a sufficiently objective approach to the matter to avoid excess enthusiasm which might blind him to the facts.

It is not the purpose of the authors to be pessimistic in this matter but only to recommend caution and encourage consideration of all available information. At a minimum the following questions should be asked about the business:

1. How long has it existed? Who founded it? How many owners has it had? Why have others sold out?
2. What is the profit record? Is profit increasing or decreasing? What are the true reasons for the increase or the decrease?
3. What is the condition of the inventory? Are the goods fresh and new, or obsolete, soiled, and deteriorated?
4. Is the equipment in good condition? Who owns it? Are their liens against any of it? How does it compare with that of the competitors?
5. How long does the lease run? Is it a satisfactory lease? What are its conditions? Can it be renewed?
6. Are there dependable sources of supply? Are any franchises or other special arrangements expiring soon?
7. What about competition, present and future? Are new competitors or substitute materials or methods visible on the horizon?
8. How about the area surrounding it? Are there new shopping centers or any buildings to be torn down? Are traffic routes or parking regulations likely to change?
9. Does the present owner have family, religious, social, or political connections that have been important to its success?
10. Why does he want to sell? Where will he go? What is he going to do? Is his wife's health as bad as he says it is? What do people think of him and his business?
11. Is the personnel situation satisfactory? Are key people efficient and willing to remain?
12. How does this business, in its present condition, compare with one you could start and develop yourself within a reasonable time?

All of these questions can and must be answered. Seldom are all of them answered properly before the buyer takes the plunge. It seems that some very brave people are afraid to ask the right people the right questions. Talk to the people who have been dealing with the business. Talk to those *you* would be dealing with in the future. See the local banker, the suppliers, the neighbors, the former owners, the customers, the employees, and even the competitors.

PROFITS

Profitability

A study of the authentic records of the business will quickly reveal whether or not it has consistently rewarded the owner for his efforts. The prospective purchaser must weigh the question of whether or not this income would be satisfactory to him and his family and, if not, whether it could be increased. He will want, therefore, to study the records of operating expenses, comparing their percentages with those of efficiently run enterprises, in order to detect opportunities for reduction or extension. Among bankers, suppliers, and lawyers, most of whom deal frequently with problems of business failure, there is a common acceptance of the principle that most failing businesses do so for lack of intelligent management. Those who are accustomed to studying the records of bankruptcies and other discontinuances can as quickly spot the discrepancies causing the failures as a physician diagnoses the common human ailments that cause most illnesses and deaths.

The seller's books alone should not be taken as proof of sales or profits stated therein. Insist upon seeing the record of bank deposits for at least five years or for the length of time the business has been operated by the present owner, whichever is shorter. If possible, obtain the deposit records of previous owners in case the present one has been in business only a short time. Ask to see the owner's copy of his income tax return, which any honest seller should be willing to show. Inspect all bills paid to suppliers and reconcile purchases with sales and markup claimed. Do the same for sales tax receipts. Be sure fixtures and equipment are fully paid for and be aware of the debts you would assume. Make certain all back taxes have been paid. It is better not to include any delinquent customer accounts in the purchase price unless they are heavily discounted.

Profit Trend of the Business

A study of the records of any business will indicate whether sales volume is on the upgrade or downgrade. It it is going up, it is worthwhile to know which departments or items account for the increased volume, and whether or not it is profitable volume. If it is going down, a similar determination of areas of lost volume should be made. Many businesses have failed after selling great quantities of goods at such low margins as to make net profits impossible. Some of these have allowed their competitive lines to crowd out their profit lines.

If the volume is decreasing, the question may arise as to whether it is due to failure to keep up with competition, inability to adjust to changing times, or simply lack of energetic sales promotion. A familiarity with the trade plus a few pertinent questions put to bankers, suppliers, and others will usually bring out the facts.

The Expense Ratios

For every size and type of business there are generally recognized ratios of expenses to sales that are accepted as proper throughout the trade. Some of these are collected and consolidated by trade organizations, such as the National Retail Hardware Association or the National Association of Retail Grocers. Others are developed by interested manufacturers for retailers, such as Eli Lilly and Company has done for the druggists, and City Products Corp. for independent variety stores. Figures for manufacturing concerns have been collected by Dun & Bradstreet, Robert Morris and Associates, and others. Operating ratios have also been calculated by Westinghouse (radio repairs and appliances), the American Foundry Institute, and the National Association of Dyers and Cleaners. Dun & Bradstreet operating ratios for retail concerns are the standard for this field. Useful figures are also available in books and government bulletins that may be secured in most public and school libraries.

A study of the figures of any concern offered for sale, compared with standard ratios for the trade, will quickly bring out any discrepancies. Learn the gross margin and the net profit in percentages and dollars. In the course of explanation of these by the seller, the intelligent buyer will quickly become aware of operating problems that may be important factors in helping him make up his mind to buy, or for determining the worth of the business. Some conditions are due simply to poor management. An excessive operating cost may be caused by carelessness, and a less than normal expenditure may indicate the neglect of a particularly vital activity that would bring results if properly financed. Frequently if the same amount of money is intelligently spent on one activity, instead of being misspent on another, desirable results in volume and profit promptly appear. The following is a simple illustration of how operating ratios are used in appraising a business.

A grocery store offered for sale has had average annual net sales of $70,000 for the past three years with no appreciable increase or decrease. Analysis of the company's records discloses the following operating ratios expressed as a percentage of net sales, for the preceding three years.

	19 –	19 –	19 –
Total expenses	15.8%	16.2%	16.5%
Wages other than owner's	4.0	4.5	4.9
Rent	3.5	3.5	3.5
Advertising	0.5	0.3	0.1

Dun & Bradstreet standard operating ratios for this kind and size of store for the years covered were as follows:

Total expenses	15.9%
Wages other than owner's	4.1
Rent	2.6
Advertising	0.6

Certain differences significant to the prospective purchaser may be noted from these ratios. Obviously the rent is too high. Possibly a talk with the landlord would result in a new lease that would bring this expense into line. The payroll has increased steadily. Why? Investigation would possibly disclose a situation that could be corrected by the new owner, such as carelessness in employing more help than needed, or laxness on the part of certain employees. Further analysis shows that both total expenses and payroll were close to the standard ratios the first year; total expenses increased each year by approximately the same amount as payroll. If the new owner could bring payroll into line, total expenses would be satisfactory. However, if conditions are such that dollar payroll could not be reduced enough to adjust the ratio, there is still another possibility. Notice that total sales remained constant over the three-year period while advertising expense declined from 0.5 percent to 0.1 percent. By increasing this item it is quite likely that total sales could be increased enough to bring both payroll and total expense ratios into line.

Even the casual reader will notice the frequency with which "if" was used in the preceding illustration. Operating ratios are standards or guides. Their effective use depends upon the ability of the new owner to change conditions that have caused any ratios to be appreciably different from the standard.

TANGIBLE ASSETS

The Inventory

A wise buyer's stock of goods is made up of timely, fresh, well-balanced selections of materials or merchandise, which in the well-managed store will consist of those items the public wants, provided in the proper sizes, designs, and colors and priced to fit the local buying power and purchasing habits. In a well-run factory there will be a representative collection of raw materials and supplies that will be used up within a reasonable period of production. Sometimes quantities of metals, lumber, oils, compounds, or other ingredients will be found on hand that are no longer used or for which there is no reasonable expectation of future use. "Close buying" is as essential to profit in one line as in another.

In merchandising there is an old saying that "goods well bought are half sold." Goods well bought are those for which there is a proven demand, or which the seller buys to fill the needs of customers whose requirements and tastes he can anticipate. Determine the monthly sales volume, monthly purchases, the value of the average inventory, and thus the stock turnover. This information will not only have a bearing on the profits which may be expected, but also help in evaluating how well the inventory is meeting the needs of the customers.

Every bankruptcy sale brings bad buying to light. A crossroads store in a recently electrified community was found to have six gross of chimneys for kerosene lamps. Another had four dozen pairs of specially constructed, expensive miner's gloves to meet the needs of six local men who were infrequently employed in a mine twelve miles away. Another store had drawer after drawer full of yellowing stiff collars, and numerous boxes of one-piece men's underwear long after their popularity had waned. Not only had they been poorly bought, but they had not been "cleared" in time to prevent a substantial loss.

The purchaser of a going business is not particularly concerned with the errors of his predecessor, except as an object lesson. His concern is that he does not become the loser on an aggregation of "dead" stock that the seller has listed as worth its original value – the loss is rightly the original buyer's, and the new buyer must beware that the loss is not passed on to him. "Age" an inventory before appraising it.

The Equipment and Fixtures

Because of the rapid mercantile and industrial progress in recent years, it is important that the modern business be equipped with machines and fixtures that are efficient. A row of punch presses that made a substantial profit twenty years ago are no longer competitive with those that produce several times as many units in the same time, nor can those old machines even be made to produce at the greater speed. Office equipment must be investigated very closely, since obsolete calculating, addressing, or duplicating devices are almost worthless; to use them is generally inefficient, and parts and supplies may be unobtainable. This is particularly true of little-known makes.

Fixtures that dignified the store and pleased the customers a few years ago are now as out of date and uneconomical as carbide lamps for automobiles. A cash register designed for the bookkeeping requirements of fifteen years ago will usually not record the information now required for computing figures for taxation. Obsolescence is often characteristic of the business about to be sold, for in many cases the usefulness of these items, representing a substantial capital investment, has been outlived long ago, and their cost has long since been written off. The owner has delayed so long in replacing them that they have no trade-in value, and without this discount he finds the prices of new equipment to be exorbitant. Hence he decides to sell the business — any financial realization he makes on the fixtures and equipment is now clear profit, an extra bonus on his period of operation.

Ask to see the owner's insurance policies. Is his coverage in line with assets claimed?

Other Assets

Certain assets in addition to the more obvious physical goods and equipment have a real value to the purchaser. Among these are the following:

Lists.   Mailing lists, general lists of customers, lists of customers interested in certain products, and other lists have very definite value. Selective lists may often be sold or rented. A veterinarian's list of wealthy dog owners, for example, could bring a good rental fee from a store introducing a line of dog accessories; a custom tailor's list of customers would be worth money to a seller of made-to-order shirts.

Credit records.   These, if carefully kept, are of great value to the buyer of a business; without them he may lose heavily in granting credit or be forced to pay for credit reference information.

Sales records.   Carefully kept records that show normal seasonal demands are a valuable insurance against under- or overstocking.

Franchises.   These have a sale value even if they were granted without cost. Even informal franchises have value if the supplier will continue delivering to the new owner.

Contracts.   Favorable leases and other advantageous contracts have monetary value. In the winding up of many profitable businesses, the sale of leases has produced unexpected profits for the owner.

Incidentally, purchasers of businesses should have their attorneys make sure the foregoing assets are included in the sale. The authors know of at least one instance in which the sales agreement did not include the list of customers; the seller came around the next day and got his own price for the list from the helplessly stymied buyer.

INTANGIBLES

This Thing Called "Goodwill"

All of us know of business concerns that have existed for years without ever establishing sufficient goodwill to be regarded favorably by the average customer. These stores and shops and manufacturing plants do business, to be sure, but it is done *in spite of* their policies, their goods, their service, their handling of customers. Strong competition would have driven them out of business long ago. Their position in the public mind, from a preference standpoint, is at the bottom of the scale.

This public attitide cannot be changed quickly. Most observers will agree that it takes far less time to ruin a good name than it does to make a bad one good.

A successful business has goodwill as an asset. Ill will is a liability. Taking over a popular business may bring with it public acceptance that has been built up over a period of many years, and which is therefore valuable. Taking over an unpopular one may mean years of promotional effort to remove the taint of unsatisfactory customer relationships accumulated over as many years. Only then can goodwill be acquired.

Because many sellers of businesses seek to place a premium on goodwill that really is, in fact, ill will, care should be taken to determine whether or not the business in question is selling an asset or a liability. This may be done by questioning unbiased persons, including customers, bankers, and others who will have bases for an opinion. Statements obtained from such individuals may then be compared with the ledger entries to support conclusions regarding the status of the business in the public mind.

The Business World's Opinions

Occasionally businesses, like people, have dual personalities — one for home use, and one for work and the public. Some enterprises, too, have more than one pattern of behavior — one for customers, and another for employees and other business firms. The attitude of the average employee is important to business success; the attitudes of suppliers or contemporaries can make or break any business at critical times. A firm that has the reputation of underpaying employees, of overworking them, or of failing to promote the proper individuals is weakened in its operations. The business that has broken contracts, schemed to get advantages, or generally established itself as a hard bargainer with no sense of cooperation or loyalty is in an unfavorable condition for sale.

Resources and Franchises

Every manufacturer and wholesaler has among his accounts many whom he considers for one reason or another to be undesirable. If there are favors to be granted, some customers receive them automatically and others on request, while a third group receives as few "breaks" as possible. This last group represents the marginal customers, or those whom the supplier has decided are not worth the effort to keep. In fact, they may eventually be displaced in communities where other outlets promise more satisfactory volume. Occasionally a business owner, knowing that he is soon to lose this resource contact, desires to dispose of his business. This is most frequently true in the case of a franchise or a restricted representation for strong lines of goods that in the opinion of the suppliers has been abused. The buyer should, in any case, obtain satisfactory assurances, and new contracts if necessary, with the supplier if a franchise is involved.

Ask the owner about any franchises he has for preferred merchandise lines, then verify his statements by writing directly to the firms concerned. Find out if they will continue the franchise if you buy the business, and if they know of any competition about to begin in the district. Also consult the Chamber of Commerce and local bankers on the latter point.

ESTIMATES

Competition

Healthy competition is most desirable where there is an ample market. In manufacturing businesses the nearby presence of a competitor improves labor resources, and the two organizations working together can obtain concessions from railroads, utilities, and others that neither could get alone. Since their markets are not entirely local, the fact that they are near together is not a handicap. In the mercantile field the effect of competition, even in areas where the market is large, will vary according to lines of merchandise carried. In staple goods, such as notions, groceries, drugs, and small hardware, close proximity of large-store competition is often undesirable, since trade will be limited to the particular area and there may not be enough to go around. In regard to shopping goods, like furniture, appliances, and apparel, the fact that two stores are side by side is in favor of both, for people will go a great distance to buy shopping items and will go more readily if there are two or more stores in which to shop.

Service industries depend entirely upon the local market and share available business with competitors in proportion to the reputation, aggressiveness, and goodwill of each establishment. Ordinarily the advantages just mentioned resulting from locations near competitors do not apply to service industries; however, the presence of progressive retail stores in the vicinity is usually desirable.

The only dangerous competition in most cases is unscrupulous competition, and that type of business is usually short-lived as compared with longer-established, more ethical concerns. Occasionally, however, unethical practices can be carried on over a long enough period to make business impossible for the smaller, legitimate operator. The presence of any such competitors, or the likelihood of their presence, should be carefully determined and considered if the business is in a highly competitive trade. If a permit is required to start a business in the town, consult the government officials in charge for clues of new competition.

The Manpower Situation

Businesses generally are made up of four elements — materials, money, machines, and manpower. When a business is being purchased, manpower must be considered as of equal importance with profits and production, for it will usually be desirable to retain certain key people to keep the business on an even keel. New people who are both properly trained and steady workers can seldom be secured readily. The prospective buyer will want to know:

1. Are enough qualified people presently employed?
2. Will any of these people depart with the old owner?
3. Are there any key individuals among the workers who will for any reason be unwilling or unable to continue working indefinitely for the organization under new ownership and supervision?

WHY IS THE BUSINESS BEING SOLD?

When the owner of a business decides to dispose of it, the reasons he presents to the public may be somewhat different from those known to the business world, and both of these may be somewhat different from the actual facts. As a rule, there are numerous contributing factors in business sales as well as in business discontinuances and bankruptcies. However, the businessman who is about to lose his contract or franchise for a strong line of merchandise, or who knows of a new law or civic development that will affect him unfavorably, will not tell his prospective purchaser all that he knows. The city planners may give a prospective buyer information about proposed changes in streets or routing of transportation lines that might have a serious effect upon the business in the near future. The man whose business is threatened by intensive competition usually does not give the real reasons for selling. If he also "needs a rest," or if owing to his wife's illness she needs a change of climate, he may decide to emphasize these reasons to the total exclusion of the really decisive factors. If poor health is mentioned, determine whose health is poor and verify the claim by consulting the physician in charge.

The Seller's Personal Plans

Experienced business buyers often investigate the reputation of the seller, in addition to the public's attitude toward the business. Talking with customers may furnish information of both types.

Although there is no intent here to cause the prospective purchaser of a going concern to feel that all sellers of businesses are subject to questionable ethical and moral principles, *caveat emptor* has through the years been a reliable maxim for buyers of horses, used cars, and going businesses. There is just enough ignorance on the part of the average buyer and just enough avarice on the part of the typical seller to make buying a business somewhat hazardous. True, there are laws against fraud and misrepresentation, but such cases are usually very difficult to prove in court. Also, pride and the desire to avoid publicity frequently prevent the injured purchaser from taking any legal action.

A few years ago in a small midwestern city an enterprising young man bought what had always been a prosperous men's wear store. The seller took his check and left for Florida to retire. Six months later the new owner received notice to vacate, for the building was to be torn down by order of the state. At about the same time, a new clothing store opened across the street, financed and supervised by the former owner of the old store. Strangely enough, also at the same time, another unfortunate event took place. A second new store was opened one block away by the manufacturer of the line of clothing that the purchaser had hoped to distribute at a profit. Needless to say, the new owner suffered considerable loss.

This is not a typical case, but merely an example of what may happen. Most such calamities can be avoided by careful study of leases and franchise contracts, and by writing protective clauses into contracts of sale. Any hesitancy on the part of the seller to bind himself against undesirable later behavior or consequences may be regarded as indicative of some danger from that source. Be sure you receive an agreement in writing that he will not enter the same kind of business as a competitor for some reasonable number of years.

SETTING THE PRICE

Buying a business is a serious matter involving a substantial financial investment. This investment should bring personal gratification and occupational enjoyment as well as provide an adequate living. A business bought at the wrong price, or at the wrong time, or at the wrong place costs the purchaser and his family more than the dollars invested and lost. After a potential buyer has thoroughly investigated the business, weighs the wealth of information collected, and decides that his expectations have been suitably fulfilled, a price must be agreed upon.

What Is the True Value?

We frequently use three terms to indicate value:

1. *Book value* — What it cost or is worth to the present owner from an accounting viewpoint; the amount shown on the books as representing its value as a part of the firm's worth.
2. *Replacement value* — What it would cost to go into the current market and buy the same materials, merchandise, or machinery. Relative availability and desirability of newer items must be considered here.
3. *Liquidation value* — How much the seller could get for this business, or any part of it, if it were suddenly thrown on the market, to be bid on by sophisticated buyers.

The differences between these three approaches to the determination of value are obvious and sobering. Certainly, in terms of asset valuation, book value may not "hold up in the marketplace." Specialized equipment, obsolete inventory, or bad debts will rapidly depreciate book value, especially if actual earnings are down. Nor is replacement value a reliable figure because of opportunities to buy in the used-equipment market. In short, liquidation value is a realistic approach, for dismaying as it may be to the seller, it can serve as a base for original negotiation.

Past earnings of the business and earnings trends in the industry are excellent indicators of a business's worth. Cash flow is another measure of value. Cash flow may be described as net profits after taxes plus noncash charges such as depreciation, depletion, and amortization. Cash so defined is that which is available for debt reduction or expansion. The cash flow rate is an increasingly important indicator of the true value of a business, though its accurate determination may call for the services of a qualified accountant.[1]

Pricing the Assets

We have discussed some of the things a buyer should look for as he considers the assets of a going concern. When the price is being set the bargaining should begin only after the value of the following items has been determined:

1. The cost of the merchandise at wholesale, adjusted for slow-moving or obsolete items
2. Cost of the equipment, less depreciation
3. Prepaid expenses
4. Supplies
5. Accounts receivable, less bad debts
6. Market value of building
7. Goodwill

The buyer must be very realistic in determining what he can afford to pay for goodwill. Is the public's attitude toward the business an asset worth money, or is it a liability the owner ought to pay to be rid of? Few businesses that are for sale have much goodwill value. Those which have are more accustomed to turning down offers to buy.

The amount paid for goodwill will reflect itself in the excess of selling price over the objectively appraised value of goods, equipment, and supplies, after liabilities are deducted. Actually it will be the price, above cold appraisal of the balance of assets as against liabilities, paid by the new owner for the old owner's constructive efforts in developing the business to its present condition. The amount to be paid for goodwill will depend on:

1. how long it would take the new owner to set up a similar business and at what expense and risk;
2. the added amount of income possible through buying a going business as against starting an entirely new one;
3. the relative prices for goodwill asked for other businesses of similar type with similar advantages; and

[1] See: G. H. B. Gould and Dean C. Coddington, "How Do You Know What Your Business is Worth?" Management Aid no. 166 (Washington, D.C.: Small Business Administration, 1964).

4. the extent to which the old owner agrees by contract to remain out of the same business within a competitive area.

What is the value of goodwill on a statement of assets and liabilities? The prospective buyer had best regard it as valueless, as such, rather considering any premium he must pay above true "book value" as (1) compensation to the owner for his losses on beginner's mistakes the new buyer might otherwise make, or (2) payment for the privilege of carrying on an established and profitable business.

In either case the premium paid should be small enough that it can be made up from profits within a relatively short period. Excessive amounts paid for goodwill are most common where competition for the purchase of a business exists; and frequently, for various reasons, the "other prospective purchaser" can stand excessive beginning costs better than the enthusiastic but unanalytical novice. Goodwill, in the usual sense, can be lost overnight; but a proven opportunity may be worth paying for.

The following formula has been suggested by the Bank of America as one method of arriving at a price for a business:[2]

Step 1. Determine the tangible net worth of the business on the basis of its liquidation value. (The market value of all current and long-term assets less liabilities).

Step 2. Estimate how much the buyer could earn with an amount equal to the value of the tangible net worth if he invested it elsewhere. . . .

A reasonable figure depends on the stability and relative risks of the business and the investment picture generally. The rate [*of return*] should be similar to that which could be earned elsewhere with the same approximate risk.

Step 3. Add to this a salary normal for an owner-operator of the business. This combined figure provides a reasonable estimate of the income the buyer can earn elsewhere with the investment and effort involved in working in the business.

Step 4. Determine the average annual net earnings of the business (net profit before subtracting owner's salary) over the past few years.

This is before income taxes, to make it comparable with earnings from other sources or by individuals in different tax brackets. (The tax implications of alternate investments should be carefully considered.)

The trend of earnings is a key factor. Have they been rising steadily, falling steadily, remaining constant, or fluctuating widely? The earnings figure should be adjusted to reflect these trends.

Step 5. Subtract the total of earning power (2) and reasonable salary (3) from this average net earnings figure (4). This gives the extra earning power of the business.

Step 6. Use this extra, or excess, earning figure to estimate the value of the intangibles [or "goodwill"]. This is done by multiplying the extra earnings by what is termed the "years of profit" figure.

This "years of profit" multiplier pivots on these points. How unique are the intangibles offered by the firm? How long would it take to set up a similar business and bring it to this stage of development? What expenses and risks would be involved? What is the price of goodwill in similar firms? Will the seller be signing a noncompetitive agreement?

If the business is well-established, a factor of five or more might be used,

[2] "How to Buy or Sell a Business," *Small Business Reporter*, vol. 8, no. 11 (San Francisco: Bank of America National Trust and Savings Association, 1969), p. 11.

especially if the firm has a valuable name, patent or location. A multiplier of three might be reasonable for a moderately seasoned firm. A younger, but profitable, firm might merely have a one-year profit figure.

Step 7. Final price = Adjusted Tangible Net Worth + Value of Intangibles. (Extra earnings × "years of profit.")

The step-by-step application of this formula is illustrated below:

1. Adjusted value of tangible net worth $50,000
2. Earning power at 10% . . . . $ 5,000
3. Reasonable salary for the owner-manager . . 10,000
                                                   $15,000
4. Average annual net earnings before
       subtracting owner's salary 17,000
5. Extra earning power of the business
       (line 4 – lines 2 and 3) . . . . $ 2,000
6. Value of intangibles — using 3-year
       profit figure for moderately well-
       established firm (3 × line 5) 6,000
7. Final price (line 1 + line 6) $56,000

If, in the above example, the average annual net earnings of the business before subtracting the owner's salary (line 4) was only $14,000, the seller would receive no value for goodwill because his business, even though it may have existed for a considerable time, is not earning as much as the buyer could earn through outside investment and effort. In that case the buyer's price would be determined by capitalizing the average annual profit (net earnings after deducting all expenses, including the owner's salary) by the desired rate of return. The calculations are as follows:

$$\$14,000 - \$10,000 = \$4,000 = \text{profit}$$
$$\$4,000 \div 0.10 = \$40,000 = \text{buyer's price}$$

ADVICE TO THE NOVICE

Using a Broker

Unfortunately for the prospective buyer, something approaching a "business opportunities racket" has developed in many cities. Brokers may advertise and sell the same business time after time to a succession of newcomers, each of whom lasts only long enough to lose his accumulated savings. Naturally this does not mean that all businesses advertised for sale are necessarily white elephants.

Nearly every city has one or more business brokers. Most inspect and appraise a business establishment offered for sale before listing and advertising it, and some also assist a buyer in financing the purchase. Business brokers normally receive their commission from the seller, but a well-established, reputable broker can be helpful to a prospective buyer, assist in locating a suitable business offered for sale at a fair price, and aid in negotiating terms and similar matters.

Considering that it is not easy to find a profitable business with good future prospects on the market at a reasonable price, a good broker may be very helpful to both buyer and seller, but the basic advice contained in this chapter still should be followed — check and double-check, and take nothing for granted. It may be that the authors are being excessive in their admonitions. However, this kind of business transaction does, in fact, represent very dangerous ground for the novice.

Check and Double-Check

Recommended practice is to make several independent appraisals and then to compare each appraisal with others arrived at through different methods. "Check and double-check" is the formula to use.

An individual should make checks on customers to be sure they are not fakes and should be suspicious if customer traffic increases every time he appears at the store. He should also do some secret checking for at least one week, talking to any suspicious customers and following up on the information they give him.

There are many schemes used to defraud innocent buyers, such as falsification of inventory figures, of customers' and suppliers' accounts, and of sales and other records, to mention only a few. It is well to check with several of the owner's more important merchandise resources to see if all bills are being paid when due and to verify his statement of current balances due to vendors. The prospective businessman should familiarize himself with the bulk sales provisions of the Uniform Commercial Code to protect himself against future loss resulting from the protection this law gives to creditors.[3]

The National Better Business Bureau, often called into action because of unscrupulous purveyors of "business opportunities," such as "make money at home" schemes and "partner wanted" appeals, warns prospective business buyers as follows:

> 1. *Advance Fee.* If your business needs financing, don't fall for an unscrupulous promoter who offers to arrange a loan if you first pay his expenses. Front money operators may offer to incorporate your business and assist in selling stock. But, when advance fees have been paid to them or their associates, service usually stops or is found to be worthless.
>
> 2. *Business Brokers.* Some business brokers, in acting as agents for sellers of businesses, are irresponsible, unfair to prospective purchasers, avoid all liabilities, and are interested only in collecting a fee. Do not be rushed into a deal. Get all verbal understandings in writing from the seller. Put the deal in escrow with a third, reputable, disinterested party. Before you sign an agreement to purchase, have all papers checked by your attorney and all books and records showing earning capacity, past profits, inventory, equipment, obligations, etc., checked by an accountant.
>
> 3. *Buy-Back Contracts.* Buy-back contracts, like money-back guarantees, are no better than the guarantors. They are frequently worthless promises made by dishonest promoters.
>
> 4. *Job Investments.* Invariably large earnings or a better than average weekly salary

---

[3] See pp. 487-88 for a discussion of the bulk sale provisions of the Uniform Commercial Code.

are offered to those who will "invest" in the business of a promoter who misrepresents.

5. *Listing Fee.* This is a variation of the Advance Fee Scheme. The fake business broker gets you to pay a fee for listing your name with him for finding the type of business you wish to engage in. Listing fees are sometimes disguised as expenses for advertising or circularizing prospects.

6. *New Promotions.* Decide whether you can afford to lose before you invest in any new enterprise. A large number of new enterprises fail.

7. *Partner Wanted.* Partner-wanted propositions are sometimes nothing but deceptive frauds to get your investment in a supposedly profitable business claiming the need of new funds. In a partnership each partner is responsible for all the debts of the firm. *Know* your partner.

8. *Patents and Inventions.* Investments in new inventions, patents, or patent litigation ventures are usually risky speculations and sometimes frauds.

9. *Territorial Rights.* Should a high pressure promoter lure you with the right to sell his product in exclusive territory, reserve your decision until you possess the facts. Some promoters misrepresent their products to get quantity orders and often sell several people the same territorial rights.[4]

Although there are many opportunities to mislead or defraud an inexperienced business buyer, a man who really knows the field places more weight on his ability to analyze the market, judge the competitive situation, uncover adverse future developments, and estimate the profits he could make from the business than upon the present owner's reasons for selling. These "reasons" are too hard to verify.

SUMMARY AND CONCLUSIONS

There are, in this country, at least 10 million business enterprises. Twenty percent of these do 80 percent of the nation's business. Some are profitable, others are losing money. Some owners wouldn't part with their livelihoods "for love nor money," while others would be happy to get rid of theirs as quickly as possible at a maximum gain or, possibly, at a minimum loss.

None of us wants to buy a "dead horse"; and we must face the fact that there are far more sick, dying, or dead businesses for sale than there are thriving profitable ones. We must make a careful appraisal of actual and potential *volume, profit,* and *growth.* These are the factors which determine the real worth of the business, *now,* to us.

The more important factors to consider in appraising a business may be grouped under four main headings according to objectives and process of evaluation. These are: (1) profits, (2) tangible assets, (3) intangibles, and (4) estimates. With sufficient care, both the profit aspects and the tangible assets can be appraised objectively and quite accurately. Intangibles include attitudes of the public and the trade as well as goodwill. They may be more difficult to appraise accurately, yet they are real and often are of great importance in determining the real value of a going business. Estimates deal either with probable future developments or with comparisons of

[4] *Facts You Should Know About Schemes*, rev. ed. (New York: National Better Business Bureau, 1964).

alternatives: whether to buy, or to build a business "from scratch." Preparing a list of "pros and cons" helps clarify the distinctions.

Arguments for buying an established business	Arguments for starting an entirely new business
Proven location	Can select own lines
Resources known	Can plan own layout
Equipment available	Can hire own employees
Stock already selected	Can select own clientele
Established clientele	No precedents to follow
Competition known	Newest equipment

Some firms have prospered equally well under a series of owners; many have not. The successful business is often the result of one individual's hard work over a long period of time. He has operated it in harmony with his own philosophy, with his own business goals, with his own ideas and methods. Hence the business and he are often inseparable, for its personality is his personality. This is a common characteristic of the smaller firm, which is often a one-man operation. This should be remembered when consideration is given to purchasing a going business.

Buying a going business is risky at best. One may not secure all the benefits anticipated, even if they are honestly presented by the seller, but a person will inherit all ill will and other handicaps the business has acquired. Do not be rushed into a decision to purchase on inadequate information, for there are so many difficulties in securing legal satisfaction in case of deception. *Once the business is purchased, it is yours "for better or worse."*

Dealing or not dealing with a broker is less important than verification of all aspects of the transaction, using your own lawyer or accountant as needed. Remember that in a small business even genuine goodwill may attach to the owner-manager rather than to the business or its location. Be certain *you* can earn the goodwill and retain it if you must pay for it.

REVIEW QUESTIONS

1. How can a person "get started" in establishing his own business?
2. What are some arguments for buying an established business rather than starting "from scratch"?
3. In buying an established business, what are some of the questions you should ask about it? From whom might you seek information about the business?
4. Identify and discuss some of the more important factors to consider in appraising a business.
5. Which is more important in appraising a business — profitability or return on investment? Why?
6. Should one ever consider purchasing a presently unsuccessful business (i.e., one with relatively low profits, or none at all)? Explain.
7. What factors warrant special attention in appraising (*a*) merchandise inventory? (*b*) fixtures and equipment? and (*c*) accounts receivable? Explain.

8. How can the amount of insurance carried by the current owner be used as a guide by a prospective business buyer?

9. Why should the buyer be careful in assuming that goodwill is an asset to the new owner?

10. What should a prospective buyer know about the seller's merchandise sources? How is this information obtained?

11. Does competition help or hurt a business? Explain.

12. What information should the prospective buyer have on the firm's manpower situation?

13. Discuss the three ways in which "value" is defined in the text. What is the most realistic approach to "true value"? Why?

14. What items should have their value determined prior to sales negotiations? Discuss.

15. What determines the price paid for goodwill?

16. How can a buyer determine the "rate of return" to use in evaluating the worth of a business?

17. Discuss the advantages of dealing through a business broker. What precautions should one take when dealing with a business broker?

18. What is meant by a "bulk sale"? Explain how the bulk sale provisions of the Uniform Commercial Code can help the buyer of a business to protect himself.

DISCUSSION QUESTIONS

1. A business broker in Pat's city advises him to invest his $8,000 in a business for sale and to borrow the $2,000 balance from his bank. The broker says he would make the loan himself but has too many such requests. Pat figures he could launch a similar business for $11,000. What should he do, and why?

2. Affable Clifford Stubbs of Iowa City, Iowa, sold his home and used his life savings to purchase a thriving neighborhood food market located in a rented building on the triangular point of a busy intersection. The store had operated in this location for more than 40 years. The store is well managed and popular. Business has been excellent, with customers coming from all over town to buy his prime cuts of meat. One year after he purchased the market all parking on the streets bordering his store has been made unlawful. Now Mr. Stubbs is selling out his current stock and has put his fixtures and equipment up for sale at an 80 percent loss to himself.[5] How might this financial disaster have been avoided? What alternatives other than closing his store might have been considered?

SUPPLEMENTARY READINGS

Bunn, Verne A. *Buying and Selling a Small Business*. Washington, D.C.: Small Business Administration, 1969. Discusses some of the principal facts to be ascertained about a small business before any buy-sell decision is made.

[5] *Iowa City Press-Citizen*, September 10, 1966. p. 1.

Suggests some approaches that may be helpful in negotiating a buy-sell transaction.

Schreiber, Irving, ed. *How to Buy and Sell a Business Taxwisely*. New York: Macmillan Co., 1968. A reference book for the businessman and tax accountant on the tax implications and consequences of the purchases and sales of businesses.

Robinson, Roland I. "The Market for Small Businesses." In *Financing the Dynamic Small Firm*, pp. 94–104. Belmont, Calif.: Wadsworth Publishing Co., 1966. Deals with the market for small businesses sold as a unit. Views the problem from the point of view of both the seller and the buyer.

6

Justifying
a new business

Many small businesses are successfully started "from scratch." A prospective entrepreneur may have a brand new idea he hopes to introduce and market successfully, or he may believe he can provide certain goods or services better than is presently being done. This chapter will consider how to determine if a proposed business venture is sound, whether or not it is a genuine business opportunity. A genuine business opportunity may be defined as a need for the proposed goods or service in sufficient volume at a high enough price and a low enough cost to allow a businessman to operate at a profit. Once an idea is justified as a genuine business opportunity, a sound basis for establishing a general policy for the proposed enterprise is provided; that is, the aim or the purpose of the business can be adequately defined. Justification shows the entrepreneur how best to meet the needs of those people he proposes to serve and whether he is likely to do so at a profit.

The approach used to justify starting a new business depends on the intent of the prospective entrepreneur. He may wish (1) to appraise the need for another business similar to those already established, or (2) to test an idea for a new type of business. In the first instance the prospective small business owner can analyze historical data and project industry trends, and in some cases, perhaps, may be in a position to study the records and operations of similar enterprises already in operation. These methods are precluded when a completely new type of business is being contemplated, and the risk is obviously greater.

Evaluation of opportunity or justification for a new business may be provided by consumer surveys, market analysis, and other types of study and research. Often a genuine business opportunity is uncovered as a result of making a location study. Some businesses can be justified in one location but not in another. Though this chapter needs to consider location as a factor in business opportunity, a more detailed discussion of selecting business locations will be found in Chapters 8 and 9.

101

SOURCES OF INFORMATION

Whatever kind of a business is being contemplated, whatever the prospective businessman's intentions, he should have facts on which to base his decisions. He may seek these facts himself or he may engage a consulting firm or a market research specialist to collect the information necessary to help him make a wise choice.

Various statistical techniques can be used in determining whether or not a good business opportunity exists in a given community. From census data the investigator can calculate the number of businesses of each kind per given unit — say 10,000 — of population, either for a particular state or for the entire country. The situation in any town can then be compared to the average. If the town falls above or below average for a certain type of business, it will be a guide as to whether there is room for another. Some trade associations also furnish data on the number of persons in a trading area required to support a business of a given type.

Another approach is to utilize an index of sales potential, such as the per capita consumption for a particular line of goods — or perhaps an index of consumer purchasing power. There is probably no better source of information regarding markets than *Sales Management* magazine's "Buying Power Index," published annually. This publication contains a wealth of information helpful in setting sales quotas, planning distribution, locating warehouses, and studying sales potential. It includes information on population and income for every state by counties and cities, including per capita and per household incomes. Retail sales estimates are also made for every state by county and city. This information is combined and weighted to produce a "buying power index" to be used in predicting sales in a particular locality.

Once all available information is assembled from these and other sources, such as Chambers of Commerce and industrial development commissions, the entrepreneur should undertake personal investigation. This often provides the decisive information he needs.

ROOM FOR ANOTHER SIMILAR BUSINESS?

There are two situations in which another business similar to those already present may be justified: (1) where an expanding market can support additional enterprises of the same type; and (2) where the market is not being adequately served because of the inefficient management of existing firms.

Assume that a community of 150,000 persons has 14 stores of the type a young man is interested in starting; census data show an average of one store for 9,000 population. Experts calculate that this type of business requires an average of 10,500 in the trading area. Apparently there is such a slim margin that another store would be quite a risk. This is where additional guides are needed. If an index of sales potential shows the town to be well above average, this may be sufficient justification. More important for most lines of small business is the personal investigation. Assume for the foregoing example that the investigation reveals an increase in population from 120,000 to 150,000 during the past few years; no new stores in this line have been opened, and those already in existence are rushed and apparently very prosperous. The conclusion is obvious: the young man should select a location carefully and get his enterprise started.

The second situation justifying another business of the same type – poor management of existing concerns – requires first-hand familiarity with the local situation. Some symptoms will be evident if it exists: high prices, extensive out-of-town consumer buying, poorly kept stores, shoddy merchandise, frequent out-of-stock conditions, incompetent clerks, slow service and poor quality of workmanship in service establishments, high business turnover, lack of customer loyalty, prevalence of consumer gripes, and exaggerated advertising. Where these conditions abound, there is a "natural" for a progressive, alert newcomer. In a situation like this there is no need for the prospective enterpriser to be concerned about the population required to support another business of this type in the trading area – there may already be twice as many outlets as the national average, yet one good store is needed. Consumer surveys, if available, or if one has the resources to conduct his own, are often useful to reassure the new enterpriser that his disapproval of the management of existing stores is shared by the local population and evidenced by its buying habits.

Consumer Surveys

Often independent surveys of consumer buying are made by colleges and universities and Chambers of Commerce. Some of these surveys indicate the preference for certain stores and reasons for patronage and for shifting trade from one establishment to another.

From such a consumer survey an analysis should be made of the reasons certain businesses acquire patronage. If the prospective businessman plans to draw trade by making certain goods available, he should determine the potential demand for his product and study his competition. Perhaps he plans to offer unusual value in terms of price, buying at low prices and operating at low cost. First he must know there is demand for this kind of an operation. Offering repair or maintenance service may be another drawing point, but he must know whether there is a need for such special services and whether he will have a sufficient volume of business to support them.

Trade-area surveys provide information on which communities consumers prefer to shop. The amount of out-of-town consumer buying and the reasons people travel to shop should be studied. Capturing this out-of-town trade might be the justification of a business. The extent that customers shop away from home is a rough measure of the alertness of home-town merchants to customer wants. Customer beliefs and preferences regarding prices, merchandise assortments and quality, services, credit terms, advertising, the newness of merchandise, and modern store facilities are usually disclosed as major reasons for out-of-town shopping. Although the tendency is for trade to gravitate toward the larger cities, this is not always true, especially among nearby towns that differ in size by not much over 100 percent. Numerous studies indicate that some communities attract a sizable amount of trade from other towns having nearly double their population, mainly as a result of more wide-awake and aggressive management.

In some small towns the quality of management of local businesses may be obviously low and out-of-town shopping extensive. This does not *always* indicate a genuine business opportunity for a newcomer. Whether such an opportunity exists depends upon the ability of the proposed venture to attract customers from the surrounding territory, the attitudes of local businessmen, and the size of town relative to accessible larger cities. If under efficient management the business contemplated could be profitable entirely from resident trade a genuine business opportunity is apparent. When, however, customers must be attracted from out of town, whether from rural areas or nearby towns, studies show that the quality of management of the leading retail and service establishments is more important than what one small enterpriser can do alone. Unless other businessmen will cooperate in a self-improvement program to make the town a more attractive shopping center, the new business is likely to be short-lived. If, on the other hand, they will cooperate under the leadership of the newcomer, an excellent opportunity may exist for the enterpriser to reverse a trend of declining business. Several small towns have been revived in this manner.

It is also necessary to evaluate the effects of traffic congestion and the lack of customer parking facilities. Established firms may be reluctant to move out of the congested business districts so long as their concerns are profitable. A new firm that provides adequate customer parking and locates not too far from the central district may easily obtain a generous share of the business quickly and even provide the nucleus for a secondary business district.

INTRODUCING A UNIQUE IDEA

From a virtually infinite number of sources individuals can secure ideas for a new business. Some of these ideas may be practical from a technical standpoint but impractical either in terms of use value or cost-price relationships. Many ideas are based on known facts and may seem practical until put to the test of justification: Does the idea promise a sufficient volume of business at a high enough price and low enough cost to yield a profit?

A large proportion of our currently important goods and services were unknown or considered impractical a generation ago, and many fortunes have been made by exercising creative imagination. There are two aspects to the problem of starting a new business by introducing a unique product or service. One is to consider the practicality of the idea, the other is how to capitalize on it. Both contribute to the important but expensive pioneering function of independent enterprise.

Contrary to popular belief, the practicality of an idea often depends more on its market acceptability than on technical aspects of production. The latter can almost always be solved if demand or potential demand is strong enough. Thus ideas that meet a widespread basic need or solve some recognized consumer problem are almost certain to succeed even though some may require more technical research than could be provided by the average prospective enterpriser. Ideas for basic innovations occur most often to the alert observer with a creative mind. He need not at the time be seeking a businesss opportunity but is alert enough to recognize an unsatisfied basic need and some possibility for meeting it. It is unfortunate that the beginner in business is inclined to choose the business *he likes,* and the goods or production methods or standards of service *he likes,* and the location *he likes* without enough objective thinking in terms of what the *customer likes and wants and is willing to buy.*

Procedures for the discovery and development of new product or service ideas are described in several excellent books on the subject. In summary, the following steps are recommended:

1. Record and file examples encountered where a widespread need is not currently provided for, or where annoying experiences or hazards are encountered; for example, when objects slip out of hands, containers topple over and spill contents, bottles drizzle or drip, people often slip and fall, certain foods are easily spoiled, certain household or business duties become chores, needed objects are too heavy to move or difficult to store, and so on.

2. Mull over the problem at odd times and record *every* idea that comes to mind for a possible solution, for later testing and development.

3. Keep alert to observe developments in other fields or ideas encountered anywhere that might furnish a solution and record them. When James Ritty, for example, observed the mechanism for recording the revolutions of a ship's propeller, he recognized that the idea could be adapted to the recording of sales transactions in a business, a problem he had long been seeking to solve, and thus laid the foundation for the modern cash register.

4. Relax occasionally and let your subconscious mind make suggestions. Experiment with possible solutions, test their practicability, seek advice, and stay with the search until a solution is found that meets the test of a genuine business opportunity.

Following is a recent illustration of the discovery and development of a new product:

[James Billingsley, a Prairie City, Iowa, auto dealer, invented a snow removal blade, called the Jiffy Auto Blade, which can be attached to the rear of any car in three minutes.] The polyethylene plastic blade is attached with two seamless tubing connecting rods over the rear axle of the car and one pin in the center of a trailer hitch. [The direction angle of the unit is changed by means of adjusting pins on the back side of the blade. In a test last winter in the driveway of Mr. Billingsley's home, the blade removed snow as deep as 11 inches.]

[Patent rights to the blade are pending and have been assigned to a small Prairie City manufacturer — Dowden, Inc. The firm has started production on the complete snow removal unit, which will be sold through dealers and other distributors in the snow belt of the United States.[1]]

Usually, however, it will be easier to justify the need for a new project based on a combination of two existing types of business or an adaptation of some kind now operating than for one based on a radically new idea. If average business judgment is used in selecting types of business to combine, or adaptations to be offered are decided upon only after an analysis of customer needs, the chances for success are good. Of course, the test of volume, costs, and price must still be met in every case. This situation may be summarized for the prospective businessman under the following five headings:

[1] *Des Moines Register,* August 22, 1971, p. 4-F (abridged).

1. He can offer a new service to the community;
2. He can offer a new line of goods to the community;
3. He can offer a new service with an established line of goods;
4. He can offer a new line of goods with established services;
5. He can offer a new line of goods and new kinds of service.

In any case a market analysis must be made and the proposed business evaluated in terms of the consumers' buying motives.

Buying Motives

The study and understanding of buying motives may well be considered as vital before the establishment of a business. Certainly if the people in the community in which the concern is to be established have no particular motivation for buying certain goods, or if those motives or their relative strengths are unknown, sales and advertising efforts will be wasted in almost all cases.

People want many things, and nearly everyone wants the same things, although in varying degrees, to satisfy his personal needs. The presence of many individuals with similar preferences in the same community makes it a good or a poor market for specific goods and services, depending on what a firm has to offer.

Buying motives, as generally listed, include the following satisfactions that people seek, thus determining their needs, which usually can be met with business offerings of goods or services:

Comfort — the desire for physical or mental ease and well-being

Convenience — the desire for a minimum of effort, for saving of time and energy

Security — the desire to know that the future is provided for with their welfare assured

Prestige — recognition of the individual as personally outstanding or a member of a desirable group

Health — the desire to feel and look physically fit

Economy — the desire to secure full value for each penny spent, to save money

Groups and communities differ. Certainly a traditionally low-paid group would respond to any offering stressing *economy;* they might forego the *convenience* and *comfort* of certain services to achieve this *economy.* Others will buy exotic and similarly unusual goods to secure *prestige*; which may be more important to them than *economy.* These preferences will differ among people of different incomes and ages and sexes. If the good or the service contemplated offers *health* or *security* with *economy* as well, then the prospective operator will find ample business volume in communities containing many older people living on limited incomes.

There are many other reasons why people buy things, including the desire to gain and hold the affections of others, the desire to belong to the crowd, the desire for recreation and amusement, and so on. Those that have been listed above, however, serve to illustrate the influence of consumer buying motives in the justification of a business within any community or market.

Market Analysis

Market analysis is not a practice limited to large organizations. The businessman contemplating the establishment of a small concern also has a job of market analysis to do in determining: (1) what a given community wants so that he can offer the right thing, or (2) which community wants the thing or service he is capable of offering.

Such analysis is customary in large businesses, where it prevents many misplaced stores, shops, and plants. The thousands of dollars spent for this purpose are considered good investments. The lack of such a precautionary step is an important reason for many small business failures.

The absence in small business of adequate consumer and market studies is doubtless due to the lack of funds and time for adequate programs of research, and to the small operator's impatience and stubbornness that are natural corollaries of his economic independence.

Market analysis is not necessarily complex. It is essentially logical. There are many variations of a basic pattern or procedure, but in general a scientific approach is taken involving steps such as the following:

1. state the problem or question clearly;
2. get the facts; insist on adequate information;
3. organize and study the facts;
4. develop possible actions; review pros and cons for each alternative;
5. select the alternative that seems best, and start using it;
6. observe progress alertly and adjust as necessary.

The approach used by the manufacturer of a set product who seeks a market will be different from that of the producer who wishes to find out what the public wants in design and performance and then makes his product accordingly. The procedure, however, will be similar.

Let us consider the problems of an established manufacturer seeking a product to produce and market profitably. The kind of analysis useful to him also would be applicable to a man justifying a new business. Let us assume that this manufacturer has available various types of woodworking machinery with which he could, given designs and plans, make any one of many wooden items – even items with which he is not now familiar. He has previously turned out toys, but demand for them is slackening; he fears he may have to stop making them altogether. He wonders how best to use his machinery and manpower. He will not want to change the equipment or the people involved, but he can choose his materials and his product. The problem, thus, is to choose a product to manufacture under the conditions described.

Getting the facts. He goes about getting information with a series of questions such as:

1. Is there any product I have previously made for which there is now a demand?
2. What requests have I had recently for goods that I could make?

3. What items now made of other materials might be made either better or cheaper of wood?

4. What items are my competitors making and selling?

5. For what items that I can make are stores and wholesalers being asked?

6. Is there any other material that can be handled like wood which I might use to make new items?

7. What are the actual facts as to why my old product is not selling as it did?

To get the facts to answer these questions, he consults: (1) his own records, (2) retail buyers, (3) wholesale buyers, (4) trade journals, (5) trade associations, and (6) users of various products.

Organizing the facts. After the various facts are organized, and irrelevant and uninteresting findings have been eliminated, he notes the following results from his study:

1. He has had requests for:
   a. Other kinds of toys
   b. Improvements in toys he has made
   c. Toys of other materials
   d. Miscellaneous kitchen items.

2. The toys he has been making are too bulky and heavy.

3. The sides of many of the toys he has made have split.

4. A new kind of wallboard is replacing wood in kitchen equipment.

5. One manufacturer is making toys of a kind of cardboard that is lighter than wood, but is not sturdy enough.

6. Retail and wholesale buyers could sell his wooden toys if they were lighter and sturdier.

7. He has many friends and a good reputation in the toy field.

8. His status-of-sale and discount arrangements are not as good as those of his competitors.

Reviewing the possibilities. After studying the findings of his records and correspondence and the results of interviews and questionnaires, he finds that the following possibilities present themselves:

1. He can start making kitchenware instead of toys;

2. He can make kitchenware to supplement his toy business;

3. He can make a new kind of toy, of wallboard;

4. He can make the same toys, with material currently popular or recently developed;

5. He can sell his goods on terms to meet competition.

Reviewing each possibility he builds his business plans accordingly. He feels that since he knows the toy business, has an established reputation in it, and knows the people to whom he sells, he had better not try the kitchenware. He adjusts his terms to meet competition and starts out on his new program. Now, as always, his trouble is that toys are seasonal. Soon, however, he finds that he can make and sell a beach toy of wallboard and tin that will give him a summer business. He also discovers an export possibility through the U.S. Department of Commerce.

Trying out the plans.   After six months he has settled down to routine business, with a year-round program that keeps his plant busy. One final adjustment is to contract for two years' full production of his major item, the entire output to be sold to a large mail-order chain. This transaction will give him broad distribution, does not cost him much to sell, and assures steady production and income for a long period. Contact with the buyer for this mail-order chain came about in the course of his inquiries about his product and prospects.

DISCOVERING BUSINESS OPPORTUNITIES

A great variety of opportunities exist for new businesses. The particular opportunity which has appeal to an individual entrepreneur will depend on his abilities, motivations, and goals. He may wish to:

1. "get in early," to capitalize on trends such as "do-it-yourself" and the self-service shops;
2. put a hobby to productive use, such as woodworking or other handcraft;
3. "cash in" on special abilities or training, like a store buyer who opens his own resident buying office;
4. put new discoveries to use, like the product sold as "Silly Putty";
5. meet needs resulting from population shifts, changing age composition of the population, or changes in economic conditions;
6. put new materials or waste products to profitable use; or
7. meet needs neglected by big business, possibly for minority groups or those requiring individualized products.

Even though the entrepreneur has made a tentative selection of the type of business to enter, a survey approach may prove valuable either as a test of his present idea or in suggesting more promising alternatives. To discover an opportunity for starting a new business, the following procedure is suggested: (1) set the course, (2) study the trends, (3) evaluate markets, and (4) think creatively.

Setting the Course

Start with what you are prepared or equipped to offer. What can you do with your preparation and equipment? Who wants the products or services you could offer? In what form? Where? When? How? At what price and volume?

Studying the Trends

Note community and industrial trends. Study communities in different stages of development, such as larger cities and smaller towns. What businesses exist in the cities that the town will soon need? Compare classified sections of the telephone directories, or other business directories. Make personal observations. Communities in different sections of the country may be compared.

A study of the community might reveal particular enterprises that are needed.

Perhaps there is no sporting goods store in the town and the population is sufficient to support one. Or a particular service may be needed. Find out why people go out of the community to have certain services performed. A study of existing businesses in the community might suggest a new business that would dovetail with them – perhaps a small manufacturing industry making products local businesses have to import.

Population movements.   One of the most significant trends affecting modern business is that of population moving to the suburbs. The result is that new and active shopping centers have been growing up on the outskirts of the big towns. Even smaller cities are finding it desirable to plan for a more decentralized growth, with new neighborhoods being developed as entities served to a considerable degree by their own community shopping and service centers. It may be important for a prospective businessman to watch developments of large-scale housing projects. These will create new business opportunities, but will also cancel some of the present ones. Another trend to watch is the changing age composition of the population – over 16 million senior citizens (sixty-five years of age and older) with money to spend, and the increasing market domination by teenagers.

Industrial opportunities.   A study of industries in the community may lead to other ideas for a small business. The use of waste products or by-products of other industries offers many opportunities in the manufacturing field. Examples of products using waste materials are Celotex, made from sugarcane stalks, and pressed wood, made from sawdust. In a lumbering area, opportunities may exist to use bark or other parts of trees considered waste. In a citrus fruit area, the peelings of fruit might be made into a profitable product. Certain plastics can be made from waste or by-products.

Prospective entrepreneurs might also consider the business implications of the recent interest of environmentalists and others in the recycling of waste products. The U.S. Bureau of Mines, for example, has recently established a pilot plant in Edmonston, Maryland, to determine the economic feasibility of mining "urban ore" – so-called because it consists of tin cans, old bottles, and other trash that is customarily buried in town "dumps." Almost anything that can be made with virgin materials can be made with reclaimed materials. "Based on the content of metals," the director of this project states, urban waste "must be classed as a high-grade ore," and is the country's only growing natural resource at a time when other resources are being consumed to the point of extinction.[2]

The use of local products or raw materials in industry is becoming increasingly important. In an agricultural region find out who is processing the commodities that local farmers grow. If this processing is not done locally, find out why. In a predominantly forested region there might be opportunities in the chemical treatment of wood, in charcoal and wood distillates, in pulp mills and paper mills, in toys, in handicrafts, or in Christmas greens. Plywood fabrication is another industry upon which there has been much emphasis because of prefabricated housing and new uses of such wood in product manufacturing.

In an agricultural area there may be a need for custom-built farm equipment, for a parts and service agency for farm machinery, or for apiarists', dairymen's, and

---

[2] David Mahsman in the *Washington Post,* as reprinted in the *Des Moines Register,* August 15, 1971, pp. 1-G+ et passim.

poultrymen's supplies, or for rental and operation of farm machinery. In an industrial region opportunities may exist in the operation of small shops for custom welding, in custom-built shop equipment, in research laboratories for industrial use, in machine tool service and repair, or in materials, parts, or containers for the local industries.

New outlets for manufacturers or wholesalers may be needed in a particular area. It might be well to contact the maker of a new product, with a good future, having few outlets at the present. Wholesalers are a good source of information regarding needed outlets in their trading area.

Evaluating the Markets

Analyze each market: children, newlyweds, home seekers, businessmen, professional men, single women, homeowners, bachelors, students, working women, older people. The presence of these and many similar groups in every community constitutes markets within the market. Consider how occupation or other characteristics of the group may give rise to the need for special goods and services.[3]

If there are many working girls in a community they might patronize establishments offering a personal-shopping, meal-planning, housekeeping, or similar service. Jobs related to family or personal living perhaps will also provide opportunities in the service field. Examples are reminder services for appointments, birthdays, and anniversaries and labor-saving services, such as paying the family's monthly bills and yard or house maintenance. Services to professional men might include cooperative buying of supplies, office layout counsel, specialized employment service, secretarial or accounting service, or the servicing, renting, and repairing of office equipment. Daycare centers and diaper rental or laundering are services that can be made attractive to mothers of small children.

It might be a good idea for the small businessman to get in touch with retailers, wholesalers, manufacturers, and institutional establishments to determine the products they need to import. He could find out why these products are not manufactured locally. After a definite need in the community for a particular type of business has been established, the population trend and major type of industry in the community should then be considered. Preference would be given to a growing town that has stable industries.

Determine also the dislikes, complaints, and problems of businessmen and other groups (such as housewives and professional women), with reference to goods and services available to them in the community. If consumer buying-habit surveys are available, these may suggest consumer complaints to be investigated further. Another fruitful source of ideas are publications that list ideas for new or improved products.

Thinking Creatively

Study the existing products, merchandise assortments, services, and other business offerings for possible improvements or combinations that would make for

---

[3] In addition to those cited below, see Chapter 3, pp. 42–46, for more recent examples of new businesses which have been started to satisfy the demands of segmented markets.

greater utility or greater customer convenience and comfort. Opportunities may exist even though people are apparently satisfied with the products and services they are using and may have given little or no thought to their possible improvement.

Observe people's habits of living — leisure-time activities, hobbies, amusements, recreation, modes of transportation, methods for care of the home and business premises, group activities, and the like — with an eye to possible business opportunities. Is a catering service or boxlunch or packaged picnic outfit supply needed? Naturally, these are only illustrative suggestions.

Why not put idle equipment to use? Occasionally owners of partially used, high-cost equipment will help set up an individual in a separate business. Or leased departments or concessions may be obtained in retail stores or markets.

Hobbies have often led to the establishment of small businesses. A photography shop might be needed in a community, or a small machine shop specializing in job-order work for local farmers, businessmen, and homeowners might be profitable. In a tourist region opportunities may exist to retail local handcrafts.

Otto F. Reiss offers a number of suggestions for developing new ideas. He says, "Why not ask yourself why a thing is the way it is today — why not change it by making it larger or smaller or by changing its shape?"[4] He suggests taking a cue from the past and adding a new twist to a product or service.

Capitalize on some trend by getting in on the ground floor. Demand is dynamic, always changing. Certain periods of our economic history have seen the rise of entirely new industries — several of major importance, such as the automobile, radio and television, electronics, and aerospace industries. Many more have been of lesser importance, sometimes fairly short-lived, but have provided opportunities for small business to expand while enjoying the higher profits of the early years.

To carry out one or more of the foregoing suggestions may necessitate keeping an idea file, involving the clipping of news items on new developments, visiting and talking with people, note taking, and perhaps a little "snooping." It may take time and may often lead to several false starts before the big idea is discovered. But it should be fun and good training, and will provide a waiting period while the prospective entrepreneur accumulates adequate funds and makes connections of future value.

CHOOSING A NAME FOR THE NEW BUSINESS

In most cases when a going concern is purchased the name of the firm is retained by the new owner, particularly if the business has been successful and has merited the goodwill of its customers. When an entirely new business enterprise is launched however, and if it is not a part of a national franchising organization, the entrepreneur must choose a name for it.

The name of the firm is important; in a new business, it is more important than the name of its owner or owners. Here are some simple rules to follow in choosing a name for your business:

[4] Otto F. Reiss, *How to Develop Profitable Ideas* (Englewood Cliffs, N.J.: Prentice-Hall, 1945). See also Alex F. Osborn, *Applied Imagination: Principles and Procedures of Creative Thinking* (New York: Charles Scribner's Sons, 1953).

1. Make it short, simple, easy to remember. "Schlevinsky's Hardware," for example, is as difficult to remember as it is to pronounce.
2. Let it tell the customer what you offer him. "Jones and Co." means nothing except that Mr. Jones is in a business of some kind. "Alexander, Richardson and Weston Co." sounds like a law office — but what do they sell? The firm name should indicate its goods or services and its particular goals or features.
3. Avoid family names or first names unless you are already well known. You may be proud of your name, but it doesn't say anything about your business to the customer! It is also easier to sell a business with a nonfamily name when the time comes you want to dispose of it.
4. Avoid worn-out words and phrases in the firm's name, such as "Quality" and "Discount Store."
5. Be sure you aren't using a name someone else is already using. In some cases the name of the firm should be filed with the county clerk. (See p. 495, Chapter 24, for a brief discussion of registration requirements.)

SUMMARY AND CONCLUSIONS

The objective of a businessman should be to give the customer what he wants at a profit to himself. The customer, in turn, must consider that in accepting a product or service in exchange for money he is participating in an activity which is as profitable to him as it is to the businessman.

Wherever there are people there are unfilled needs. The challenge to the person who wishes to start a new business is to determine what these needs are and how they may best be satisfied. He must justify his proposed venture before he begins if he is to have a fair chance of success. Justification must be based on facts. These facts may be acquired through market research, consumer surveys, study of existing businesses, consideration of local and general social and economic conditions, and intelligent observation. These facts must then be organized and evaluated.

The particular approach to be used by the prospective entrepreneur, and the facts he needs, will depend on whether he is seeking to market a preconceived idea, whether he wishes to locate a specific kind of business in the best possible area, or whether he seeks the best business opportunity in a particular place.

Suggestions and advice given in this chapter for the development of radically new enterprises should appeal to those gifted with imagination or a love for pioneering. This is the area where great opportunities may exist for making a fortune while performing a valuable service to society.

REVIEW QUESTIONS

1. How does the text define a "genuine business opportunity"?
2. Discuss the various types of business opportunities and how they arise. Which carry the greatest risks to the prospective enterpriser? Do these opportunities exist for large firms as well as small firms? What are the unique business opportunities, if any, of the smaller firm?
3. How is the justification of a new business related to its location? To its business policies?

4. How can you determine whether another similar business would be justified in a given location? State your assumed conditions.

5. What information is available in *Sales Management*'s "Buying Power Index"? How may it be used?

6. Discuss inefficient management of existing concerns as a justification for another business of a similar kind.

7. Differentiate between consumer surveys and trading-area surveys.

8. If you know that many people in a town of interest to you do a considerable amount of out-of-town shopping, how would you use this information to uncover a genuine business opportunity?

9. How is marketing likely to be the factor determining the practicality of a radically new idea? Discuss.

10. What steps are involved in the discovery and development of ideas for new products or services?

11. Discuss the James Billingsley case (p. 105) and cite other recent illustrations of the discovery and development of new products or services of which you are aware.

12. What are some frequently named buying motives? Of what relevance are they in justifying a business?

13. What can a small businessman determine from a market analysis?

14. What are the basic steps involved in making a market study? Discuss and illustrate each step.

15. How is the particular business opportunity which has appeal to an individual enterpriser related to his abilities, motivations, and goals?

16. How would you go about discovering an opportunity to start a new business?

17. Give some simple rules to follow in choosing a name for the new business, and illustrate the application of each rule.

DISCUSSION QUESTIONS

1. Distinguish between justifying and appraising a business. In what ways may these activities be similar? Show how some of the guides and methods useful in appraising a business for possible purchase would be useful in justifying a proposed new business.

2. What sources of information would you consult in determining the economic feasibility of starting a new service station in your community? A job-order machine shop? A diaper rental and laundering service?

SUPPLEMENTARY READINGS

Hilton, Peter. *New Product Introduction for Small Business Owners*. Small Business Management series no. 17, 2nd ed. Washington, D.C.: Small Business Administration, 1961. Provides basic information about placing a new or improved product on the market.

Rotch, William. "Starting a Business." In *Management of Small Enterprises: Cases and Readings,* Small Business Management Research Report prepared for the Small Business Administration, pp. 3-58. Charlottesville: University of Virginia, 1963. Cases examine potential businesses to decide whether and how each business should be started.

7

Acquiring a franchise

A full time income with only part time effort. Modest investment acquires exclusive franchise territory yielding unlimited earnings potential. No prior experience necessary. We provide you with the intensive training and supervision to guarantee instant success.[1]

Even the most casual observer of business today is likely to be somewhat familiar with the concept of franchising. He is likely to be solicited through the mail and in the classified sections of his local newspaper. He has heard fabulous success stories and, perhaps, some that were not so successful. And he cannot help but be aware of the myriad of fast-food service drive-ins lining the nation's highways and the arterial streets of our urban areas; "Franchise Row" – or the "Franchise Strip" – is a common sight in many of our larger cities and towns. The franchising of small businesses today is "big business."

Franchising offers genuine business opportunities to many prospective entrepreneurs, but the inference that a franchise is a gold mine and that the typical franchisee can become an instant millionaire, or at least earn an income several times higher than that which he is presently earning, is indeed misleading. Also, while most franchising offers are sound business proposals, there are some that are not. It is the purpose of this chapter to point out the weaknesses and the pitfalls of franchising as well as its strengths and its inherent advantages to the prospective franchisee, so that he may better judge each franchise offer on its individual merits.

FRANCHISING DEFINED

Franchising is a system for selectively distributing goods or services through outlets owned by the franchisee. Basically, a *franchise* is a patent or trademark license, entitling the holder to market particular products or services under a brand name or trademark according to prearranged terms and conditions.

The brand identification is an important aspect of this form of distribution. It

---

[1] Prepared by the Federal Trade Commission to warn prospective investors that not all franchising ads offer legitimate business opportunities. "Advice for Persons Who Are Considering an Investment in a Franchise Business," *Consumer Bulletin No. 4,* (Washington, D.C.: G.P.O., 1970), p. 1. See also: Harold Brown, *Franchising: A Trap for the Trusting* (Boston: Little, Brown & Co., 1969).

consists of standardization throughout the system. The various outlets in the system are similar as to class of trade, merchandise carried or services rendered, and other factors that have a bearing upon joint merchandising and management through common policies. Also, all of the outlets in a franchise system are identified as members of the system. They operate under a common name and/or insignia, and the establishments often have a distinctive appearance common to all members of the system. This standardization is ensured and controlled by the terms of the franchise contract.

Essentially, therefore, a franchise system is a "voluntary" chain, that is, a chain of individually owned businesses. Franchising, in fact, has been the salvation of many independent wholesale and retail merchants in the face of increasing competition from corporate chains and discount operations. By joining a jobber-sponsored voluntary chain, for example, an independent retailer can get all the benefits that are available to a corporate chain store: central buying as well as assistance in merchandising, promotion, and management.

The franchising or licensing technique is more often utilized today, however, when a company comes up with an idea for a product or service and finds that it does not have adequate resources to market its own new idea. By licensing prospective entrepreneurs to perform the marketing function for him, the franchisor is enabled to achieve rapid expansion at relatively low cost, a substantial part of the investment being contributed by the franchise holder.

Another advantage of franchising to the franchisor is that the owner of his own business (the franchisee) is likely to be more diligent and strive harder for success than the hired manager of a company-owned outlet. Pet Milk officials, for example, declare that franchising combines "the initiative and incentive that can come only from an owner operating his own business and the supervision, coordination, and management help that only a national business can provide."[2]

Since franchising is a form of selective distribution, the typical franchise agreement prohibits the franchisee from setting up competing outlets within the franchise area. The franchisee is also often precluded from operating a similar business within a specified time and radius after termination of the agreement. Though some franchise agreements do not contain such a clause, the franchisor has a corresponding obligation to ensure that any one geographical area is not oversaturated with competing franchised outlets; some contracts, of course, may grant exclusive territorial rights.

Since the franchisor utilizes only a limited number of outlets for the distribution of his product or service, he naturally expects and demands results from his franchisees. For this reason, a franchise is usually valid only for a specified period of time, after which the franchisee's performance is evaluated for possible renewal of his contract. Similarly, a franchisee is often precluded from selling his franchise without the approval of the franchisor. Some franchise agreements also contain sales quotas.

There's nothing new about franchising, of course. The automobile, gasoline, and soft drink firms have been doing it for years; for them it is "old hat." The automobile industry, for example, started to franchise dealers in the early 1900s, "and for

[2] Robert Rosenburg, *Profits from Franchising* (New York: McGraw-Hill Book Co., 1969), p. 154.

many of the same reasons that caused a later generation of businessmen to select it over other available means of distribution: lack of ready capital to establish large numbers of retail outlets in a short period of time, and lack of trained administrative personnel to operate these same outlets and provide the needed, personalized ongoing service required."[3] Henry Ford was the first to utilize the franchise system and was closely followed by his competitors.

In the 1920s and 1930s, independent wholesalers of groceries, hardware, automobile accessories, and other products adopted the franchising concept and began to build vast networks of voluntary chains.

Though there is nothing new about the franchising concept, there is a new scope to this method of distribution. In recent years, franchising has spread to businesses as disparate as art galleries, nursing homes, automobile transmission repair shops, muffler shops, gift stores, travel agencies, supper clubs, rental services, part-time secretarial help, computer dating services, diet services, modeling schools, dental technician schools, management consulting, and data-processing services. The most rapid growth has been in quick-service food drive-ins dispensing such culinary delights as hamburgers, beefburgers, fried chicken, pizzas, doughnuts, and hot dogs.

GROWTH OF THE FRANCHISING CONCEPT

Franchising today is used to distribute almost any conceivable product or service. Its growth has been primarily dependent upon two factors: the desire and need of business to establish many outlets with minimum capital, and the desire of individuals to be independent businessmen.

The first big spurt in franchising came right after World War II. A tremendous backlog of demand had been built up for peacetime goods and services, and the postwar expansion of many companies (particularly the newer ones) was restricted by lack of capital. Returning war veterans with a desire to own their own businesses, with bonuses in their pockets, and the availability of G.I. loans guaranteed by the Veterans Administration provided an obvious source of much-needed capital. Thus there were mutual benefits to be obtained, and the franchise system began to boom.[4]

The growth of the franchising concept in recent years is nothing short of phenomenal. Of the franchising companies in business today, 90 percent were not in existence prior to 1954.[5] In 1969-1970, annual sales reached an estimated $90 billion through the joint efforts of over 1,000 franchisors and 600,000 franchisees.[6] Franchise sales today account for approximately 10 percent of the nation's gross national product and over 25 percent of total retail sales.[7]

---

[3] Ibid., pp. 9–10.

[4] See Harry Kursh, *The Franchise Boom* (Englewood Cliffs, N.J.: Prentice-Hall, 1969).

[5] *Franchising,* Small Business Reporter, vol. 9, no. 9 (San Francisco: Bank of America, 1970), p. 1.

[6] U.S. Senate, Select Committee on Small Business, *Impact of Franchising on Small Business* (Washington, D.C.: G.P.O., 1970).

[7] Rosenburg, *Profits,* p. 3.

FRANCHISING SYSTEMS

Franchising systems may best be classified by the kind of organizations which sponsors them: (1) manufacturers; (2) wholesalers; (3) corporate chains; and (4) companies in the "franchising business."

Manufacturer-Sponsored Systems

As noted previously, automobile manufacturers and petroleum refiners were among the first to franchise entire retail outlets. Manufacturers of farm implements and earth-moving equipment also license dealers who sell only the products of their sponsor. Such dealers sell their products under specified conditions with respect to pricing, inventory levels, advertising, and sales quotas. They may or may not own the physical facilities of the business; in the petroleum industry, for instance, service stations are often leased by the operator. No fee is paid for the license — the manufacturer merely requiring the franchisees to buy his products. Dealers take full title to the goods they sell.

In some cases, however, the franchisee may actually manufacture the goods he sells, the franchisor supplying the patterns, molds, and manufacturing specifications on a royalty basis. Such a practice is common in the distribution of burial vaults and other concrete products, where weight and the transportation cost factor make it economically more feasible to manufacture the product in the local markets.

Not all products lend themselves to this form of distribution by manufacturers. A product must possess at least one of the following characteristics before it can be marketed through franchised dealers:

1. The product price and/or amount needed in inventory at the retail level requires the dealer to make a large investment.

2. Consumer buying habits indicate they are willing to put forth more than a usual amount of effort in purchasing the item. That is, comparison of brand, price, quality, and other features is recognized as the likely buying process for the consumer.

3. A product requires installation in the home, an inventory of parts at the local level, and dealer responsibility for maintenance of product guarantee provisions.

4. A manufacturer introduces a new product and finds many dealers adverse to carrying the product. By restricting outlets the manufacturer can offer substantial advertising and sales support not otherwise possible.

5. The basis for the purchases is heavily determined by the consumers' confidence in the retailer.[8]

Some manufacturers, of course, distribute their products to selected retailers who sell a wide line of other products; this practice is common among manufacturers of such products as electrical appliances, television sets, furniture, shoes, paint, and tires. Many of the tire companies, for example, have secured distribution rights for well-advertised products, such as General Electric and Kelvinator refrigerators, to be sold through their dealer stores.

---

[8] Edwin H. Lewis and Robert S. Hancock, *The Franchise System of Distribution* (Washington, D.C.: Small Business Administration, 1963), p. 7.

Mr. H. L. Hayward, manager of the Dealer Department at the Goodyear Tire and Rubber Company, describes his company's authorized dealer plan as follows (the Goodyear plan is typical of similar agreements made by other tire manufacturers):

> Goodyear is a dealer company and our distribution has always been primarily through dealers. We have approximately 9,500 direct franchised dealers in the U.S.A.
>
> The essential . . . qualifications of Goodyear retailers are primarily that the dealer have or be capable of developing the proper reputation in the community, the necessary management and merchandising ability, and sufficient finances, to warrant his being extended the proper line of credit. We make no charge to our dealers for the Goodyear franchise.
>
> The buying advantages offered consist of . . . supplying our dealers with products we manufacture bearing our own name, and with certain other lines of nationally advertised merchandise which we do not manufacture but which we offer to our dealers . . . to round out their selling opportunities and to give them a complete business franchise.
>
> Many merchandising and management aids are available to our dealers — these include the personal advice and counsel of our field representatives, special representatives on certain products (such as truck tires [and] farm tires . . .), district credit managers and district sales managers.
>
> In addition to the personal advice and counsel by the qualified people just mentioned, our dealers get the benefit of comprehensive employee training programs, both in meeting form (consisting of movies, sound slide films, charts and quizzes) and of printed booklets, folders, etc.
>
> The obligations . . . assumed by our dealers consist primarily of taking full advantage of the sales and profit possibilities of our complete business franchise, backed up by the merchandising helps available, and of seeing that the people to whom they sell Goodyear products are given the right kind of service.
>
> It is expected that our dealers will buy from Goodyear those lines of merchandise we [offer] which the dealers want to handle. We have no objection to a dealer handling lines of merchandise which we do not carry, and these, of course, he may buy from any source he desires.[9]

In contrast to voluntaries in other lines, the nature of tire products leads to a dual system of dealer outlets — the retail store and the service station.

Though originally organized as a buying cooperative, Rexall drugstores today comprise the largest drug voluntary chain in America. The original association built their own manufacturing plant and in 1920 adopted the franchising technique as a means of expansion. All Rexall drugstores are independently owned stores which operate under an agreement with the Rexall Company. They feature Rexall products and agree to participate in specified national sales promotions. Rexall provides national advertising, and various other merchandising aids as requested. Affiliated Rexall stores may carry as full a line of other brands of merchandise as they wish.

The network of Midas Muffler Shops is another example of a well-known manufacturer-sponsored franchise system.

Franchising arrangements between manufacturers and wholesalers are similar to those between manufacturers and retailers. Here also, the franchisor derives his income solely from the sales of his product to the franchisees. Franchising at this

---

[9] H. L. Hayward, personal communication, June 29, 1971.

level of distribution occurs principally in the soft drink industry. The wholesaler purchases syrup from the manufacturer, adds water and carbon dioxide, and bottles or cans the completed product for sale to retailers in his exclusive territory. Beer also is commonly distributed by franchised wholesalers; however, they perform no bottling or canning operations.

Wholesaler-Sponsored Systems

Wholesaler- or jobber-sponsored voluntary chains usually carry the wholesaler's own or "private" brand merchandise, have a common name and appearance of the store front, and offer advertising and other merchandising aids that vary with each organization. The retail stores are individually owned but agree in joining the "voluntary" to assume certain obligations such as to feature the company's merchandise, to cooperate in advertising, and to maintain acceptable standards of appearance for the store front and interior. Most organizations specify the minimum amount of merchandise that must be purchased through the sponsoring wholesaler. The affiliated stores usually do not need to purchase their right to participate, since wholesalers are merely seeking good new outlets for their products.

The following discussion of a selected number of wholesaler-sponsored voluntary plans for independent merchants describes some of the outstanding features of the various types of programs.

Groceries. Clover Farm Stores, organized in 1926 with headquarters in Cleveland, Ohio, is a wholesaler-sponsored voluntary group of retailer-owned stores. The Clover Farm field representatives help wholesalers and retailers with their individual problems – finances, selling, operating efficiency, and so on. Headquarters publishes a monthly magazine, the *Clover Farm Bee*, which contains articles, editorials, and advertisements. It also publishes the *Four-Leaf Clover* for advertising to the home; this newspaper, although edited by the main office, is printed and distributed without cost by the various divisions. The retailer receives the *Clovergram*, a mimeographed publication containing information about store operations, promotion, merchandising, and clerk training. In addition to this, Clover Farm headquarters sends posters, price cards and pennants, and other advertising material to the various divisions.

Other well-known retail food voluntary chains include A. G. (Associated Grocers), St. Louis, Missouri, with 865 members in Illinois, Missouri, and Kansas; Super Valu Stores, Minneapolis, Minnesota, serving the north central states area; Red and White Stores; and I.G.A. (Independent Grocers Alliance), with headquarters in Chicago and over 3,700 retail members and 69 independently owned supply depots. Organizations such as these are alliances of independently owned retail stores. They have membership contracts and usually collect dues; they feature their own private brands, but also carry national brands; and they furnish merchandising and management assistance in varying amounts to franchise members. Advertising and promotional aids, as well as some help on layout, accounting, and sales clerk training, are furnished in most cases, but the use of supervisors varies among the different firms.

Variety and general merchandise.   The Ben Franklin Division of City Products Corporation entered the variety field in 1927. There are over 2,100 locally owned Ben Franklin stores, featuring variety and general merchandise, operating in cities and towns all over America. In 1970 these stores had returns on sales of 8 to 15 percent, and on investment of 20 to 35 percent.

Before recommending that a prospect invest in a particular store, the Ben Franklin Division makes a careful study of facts pertaining to his background, experience, likes, and dislikes. Every effort is made to see that each prospect is a perfect "fit" for the store he takes over. Special attention is given to a prospective owner's suitability for the task, to the type of community most appropriate for him, to his ability to meet capital requirements for stores of the size under consideration, and to similar factors. Various locations are carefully evaluated; population, trade area, shopping habits, spendable income, traffic counts, and building requirements are studied before establishing a store. Ben Franklin lease-location men are responsible for sound lease protection to provide each owner with security and the certainty of having an adequate building at a fair rental. The Ben Franklin Division matches, man for man, function for function, the organization and supervision found in the corporate chains.

Experts in merchandising, advertising, display, and sales promotion devote their entire time to servicing this program and to keeping retailers abreast of the best that competition can offer. Professional guidance for individual store owners is as necessary as having a dependable merchandise source. Zone managers make periodic calls on each owner in order to give him every assistance possible on problems of merchandising, financial control, personnel, displays, and other management duties. The total charge for this printed and personal service amounts to about 0.75 percent of the store's annual volume.

Upon entering the Ben Franklin program, the owner agrees to purchase merchandise of the type and quality offered by the company's buying division, and to put into practice all the guidance and retail know-how provided by the program.

The buying division makes available practically all of the well-known nationally advertised brands. In addition, it has a packaging and brands department for the purpose of providing Ben Franklin store owners with exclusive brands that can be obtained only in their stores. Since these brands cannot be purchased from local competitors, it is to the owner's advantage to create a demand for them.

The Ben Franklin Division has regional offices in Chicago, Baltimore, Minneapolis, Dallas, Kansas City, Memphis, Los Angeles, and Stow (Ohio), and national headquarters in Des Plaines (Chicago) Illinois.[10]

Hardware.   True-Value and V. & S. hardware stores are dealer-owned hardware stores which hold membership in Cotter and Company, warehouse distributors. Cotter and Company, founded in 1947, is a mutual wholesale organization which is entirely owned by the retail dealers who patronize it. Dealers purchase an equal amount of voting stock and have an equal voice in controlling broad policy. In 1971 there were more than 2,200 such individually owned stores committed as a group to buy nationally known merchandise. Most Cotter Company stores are located east of the Rockies, though rapid expansion is taking place to the west.

---

[10] Comments regarding the Ben Franklin Division are from a letter to the authors, dated July 6, 1971, from Mr. John M. Gaunt, attorney, City Products Corporation.

Semiannual trade shows are held for the members, and ordering is done from a comprehensive, frequently updated catalogue. Though merchandise may be ordered from other suppliers, the dealer's interests are best served by ordering from his own company. Cotter and Company provides a full range of merchandising aids to stores requesting them. The entire net profits of the company are returned to the dealer-members in the form of patronage dividends averaging over 8 percent annually.

Another well-known hardware voluntary chain is the group of Ace Hardware stores, located in the Midwest.

Auto accessories.   Another example of voluntary chain stores sponsored by a wholesaler is Western Auto Associates, selling automotive supplies, sporting goods, household appliances, toys, and hardware. There are over 4,000 of these stores which are independently owned and operated businesses, but which have working agreements with Western Auto Supply Company of Kansas City, Missouri. Western Auto provides a two-week training course for the prospective store owner; helps to find a location in a market of the entrepreneur's choice; and assists in lease negotiation, floorplan design, and stock selection. It assists in promotional events, provides counsel on financial management, and advises in other areas of the business as requested. Financial assistance is offered through financing a portion of initial investment and in extending credit, including the carrying of accounts receivable.

Agency Stores

Some of the larger corporate chains have sponsored retailer-owned affiliates (or "agency stores") that bear a relationship to them that is similar to that of the voluntary chain store to its sponsor. Thus a corporate chain may supply both company-owned and retailer-owned stores from the same warehouses. The company-owned and retailer-owned stores will usually be similar in appearance. Two examples of chain-store-sponsored voluntaries are the Gamble-Skogmo Stores (general merchandise) and the Walgreen Agency (drugs). These voluntaries are more likely to be located in small towns, with the company-owned stores operating in shopping centers or larger cities. Some of the larger tire manufacturers also have both corporate chain and agency stores. It is only when the tire company desires an outlet in a town where there is no suitable opportunity for an independent store that the company-owned stores are operated. Corporate chains which operate both company-owned and voluntary chains are concerned primarily with maintaining outlets for their own brands of products.

Drug stores.   Walgreen Drugs, which also operates a corporate chain, inaugurated the Walgreen Agency Plan in 1931. It is a complete merchandising plan for independent druggists. A Walgreen agency may be established in registered drugstores, if they fulfill the requirements of the plan and conform to certain standards. All the merchandising facilities of the company are available to the agents – construction and layout plans, advertising, display, and merchandising aids. Other services may also be obtained on an advisory basis.

Agents operate under a franchise for the exclusive sale of Walgreen merchandise within their trade area. A wide variety of sundry items are also sold. A minimum purchase requirement is stipulated, based on sales. The usual term of an Agency Agreement is ten years. Agencies are invited by the company to join in certain sales promotion and merchandising events throughout the year. The Walgreen Agency Plan does not disturb the regular jobber-retailer relationship insofar as national brands are concerned, but Walgreen merchandise is stocked in addition as an exclusive.

General merchandise stores.   In the general merchandise field Gamble-Skogmo, Inc., of Minneapolis has 3,900 retail outlets of which over 3,100 are franchised dealers in its various divisions. Its company-owned merchandising chains are augmented by a parallel wholesaling organization serving franchised dealers.

In 1972 there were 208 company-owned and 1,406 franchised Gamble Stores. For the most part, they market hardlines such as automobile accessories, tires and batteries, hardware, appliances, housewares, radio and television sets, lawn and garden equipment, and sporting goods, in stores ranging in size from approximately 5,000 to 15,000 square feet, at downtown locations in cities and towns of fewer than 50,000 people throughout the central and northern states.

Franchised Gamble Stores are locally owned and operated, and benefit from the operating, promotional, and merchandising concepts developed for them by the company. A complete plan of merchandising and management aids has been developed and is provided by field men in each region. No charge is made to franchised dealers for these services. More than 125 franchised Gamble units now carry softlines, and 435 carry furniture and home furnishings and similar merchandise in addition to the hardlines, and it is probable that this trend will continue.

Skogmo Stores, of which 199 are franchised (as of 1972), are primarily softlines outlets. Similar in size to the Gamble franchised stores, they are aggressive marketers of men's, women's, and children's clothing and related items in smaller communities, often serving a wide rural shopping area. As in the case of the Gamble franchised stores, the company provides strong merchandising and merchandise support for its franchised Skogmo dealers, and other services such as accounting, insurance, time payment, display, and advertising as well.

Franchising Companies

In the franchising systems discussed on the preceding pages, no fee is usually charged for the franchise or license per se — or, if there is an initial charge, the fee is nominal. The franchisor, in most cases, earns his profit solely from the sale of his products to the franchisees. Also, it is the *established* manufacturer or wholesaler, who is already in the market, who takes the initiative in forming the chain.

In recent years, however, many new coporations have been established which specialize in the *sale of franchises* as a means of gaining entry into the market. Their programs are built around a management and merchandising "service." Franchisees gain the right to sell a nationally advertised product or service under a well-known brand name, and have continuing access to all the merchandising and management knowledge the franchisor possesses. The profit to the sponsoring organization lies as much in the payment for services rendered to the retailer as in the volume of products sold. For these services, the franchising organization usually receives an initial fee plus a percentage of the gross.

In some cases all that is required of the franchisee is that he buy all ingredients, supplies, and equipment from the parent company. Chicken Delight, for example, derives its income from sales of original equipment, food service containers, paper goods, and the like; in this regard, it functions much the same as the wholesaler-sponsored voluntary chains described earlier.

Other examples of this new type of franchising technique include McDonald's hamburgers, Col. Sanders' Kentucky Fried Chicken, Dairy Queen soft ice cream, Holiday Inn motels, AAMCO transmissions, Hertz auto rental, and Manpower part-time secretarial and clerical help, to mention just a few of the more readily recognized franchise "names." The *Directory of Franchising Organizations*, published annually by Pilot Industries, Inc. (347 Madison Avenue, New York City), lists similar "management packages" for the distribution of almost any kind of product or consumer service.[11]

This is the fastest growing type of franchising system – the system described in detail by Harry Kursh in his book, *The Franchise Boom*.[12] In fact, most of the members of the International Franchise Association represent companies in the "franchising business," that is, companies whose primary source of income is the sale of franchises.

One of the most successful franchising operations of this kind is McDonald's chain of hamburger drive-ins. Since it is also fairly typical of most other systems that have sprung up in the 1950s and 1960s, it is described here.

Started in 1954, McDonald's has grown from a single hamburger stand in San Bernardino, California, to over 1,500 franchises. Only Kentucky Fried Chicken, Inc., has more franchised outlets – more than 3,000. In 1970 the national average gross sales for a single McDonald's outlet was over $430,000, individual owners pocketing anywhere from $60,000 to $80,000 before taxes, according to company officials. There is no fixed charge for a McDonald's franchise, the parent company receiving its income solely by assessing the outlet owner 11.5 percent of his gross sales. In return, the franchisee receives thorough business and restaurant training at the parent company's famous Hamburger University in Elk Grove, Illinois; continuing business training and consultation; and a national advertising program that has established McDonald's as one of the leading advertisers in the United States. The financial requirement for all fees, deposits, and equipment (at 1971 prices) is approximately $70,000 cash prior to opening the business, plus an ability to finance an additional $50,000.

Thorough standardization is required for the success of this type of franchise chain. Usually, the outlets in the franchise system look the same and distribute an identical product or service. For example, a hamburger that is purchased at a McDonald's drive-in in Iowa City will taste the same (supposedly) and come packaged the same as one purchased in New York City. Similarly, the room that is

[11] See p. 118 for a brief discussion of the ever-widening scope of this method of distribution.

[12] Op. cit.

rented at a Holiday Inn in Cleveland will look much the same as one rented in Chicago.

Standardization is even more important in operating procedures – the franchisor's proven "formula for success." Thus the key element in most franchising systems is the copyrighted operations manual, in which every conceivable detail of business practice is spelled out. In a food-service operation, for example, the manual will include such items as recipes, portions, menus, and food storage and handling instructions. Inventory and financial record-keeping procedures are also spelled out, as are personnel policies and practices. Even the days of the week and hours of the day the business must be open are specified. Adherence to these and other standards in the system is controlled by company field representatives or "franchise coordinators," as well as by the terms of the business franchise.

Although no two franchise contracts are identical, the following list includes those elements common to most:

1. The franchise fee
2. The required investment
3. Royalties
4. The operations manual (including inventory and recordkeeping requirements)
5. Promotional activities
6. Management assistance
7. Termination of franchise (including contract term and condition of cancellation)
8. Sale of franchise license
9. The area of protection for the franchise

The dramatic success enjoyed by many specialized franchising companies has prompted some of the older, established firms to develop similar programs. The Howard Johnson restaurant chain is a case in point. Originally, it was a small local corporate chain in western Massachusetts, started in the mid-1930s; it was not until the early post-World War II years that the company began to franchise individually owned establishments under the Howard Johnson name. In recent years, the company has diversified by entering the motel franchising business as well.

Most of the older firms, however, entered the franchising business by way of corporate mergers. In some such cases – such as Ralston-Purina and Jack-in-the-Box, and B. F. Goodrich and Rayco – the merger objective was vertical integration. But more frequently the objective has been to diversify the product base, and thereby offset seasonal factors inherent in single industries. Among the conglomerate corporate franchising mergers are the following:

Consolidated Foods — Abbey Rents
                          Chicken Delight
General Foods — Burger Chef
Great Western Sugar Co. — Shakey's

International Industries	— International House of Pancakes
	United Rent-Alls
	House of Nine
	Orange Julius
	Sawyer Business Schools
Marriott Inns	— Hot Shoppes
	Big Boy Properties
Pet Milk	— Stuckey's
Pillsbury	— Burger King
RCA	— Hertz (joint ownership with American Express)
	Arnold Palmer Corp.
United Fruit	— A & W Root Beer
	Baskin-Robbins

The success of the franchising method of distribution has also been underscored in recent years by the attempts of many of the leading franchisors, including Kentucky Fried Chicken and Howard Johnson, to repurchase a number of their franchises — indicating that they have accumulated so much capital that they no longer need franchising for inexpensive expansion. Thus the individually owned outlets bear a relationship to the parent company that is similar to the status of "agency stores" described previously.

PROS AND CONS OF ACQUIRING A FRANCHISE

Claimed to be "America's answer to monopoly capitalism,"[13] franchising offers distinct advantages to the prospective owner of a small business. Acquiring a franchise eliminates most of the risks that bankrupt so many small businessmen during their first few years of operation. With a quality franchise the prospect is set up in a going business, one with a successful, nationally advertised or identifiable product or service. He usually also receives thorough training in a proven business technique; assistance and/or backing in locating, constructing, equipping, and financing his enterprise; the purchasing advantages of combined buying power; and expertise in merchandising and management practices and control. Since 90 percent of small business failures are attributed to lack of business know-how, the value of a good franchise is clearly evident.

Most franchisors, in fact, will go to great lengths to avoid having failed franchises on their hands. Franchise failures are bad, not only for profits but for the "image" of the franchisor as well; the latter's desire to see the franchisee succeed is based on mutual self-interest. Significant is the fact that fewer than 10 percent of all franchises fail. McDonald's, for one, boasts that not one of its franchised outlets has ever lost money. In dramatic contrast with this is the fact that one out of every two businessmen who start on their own fails within two years, and eight out of ten fail within five years.

[13] Rosenburg, *Profits*, p. 5.

A franchisee does not launch a *new* business in the strict sense of the word. He is really opening a new "outlet" of a well-established organization with a record of acceptance and success.

There are, however, some major drawbacks in operating a franchised business. Even though he may own his own business, the franchisee must necessarily sacrifice a certain degree of independence. The franchisor's constant monitoring and supervision of its franchises is unpalatable to many businessmen of independent temperament.

A number of restrictions are also imposed upon the franchisee. His freedom to expand into other lines is often limited, and he usually does not have the right to sell his business to the highest bidder or to leave it to a member of his family in his will without the concurrence of the franchisor. Such rights are usually preempted by the terms of the franchise contract.

Also, since franchisors generally reserve the option to buy back an outlet upon termination of the contract, the franchisee operates under the constant fear of nonrenewal. His franchise may fail to be renewed if he fails to meet the franchisor's sales quota or does not follow his rules. Also, some franchisors (as noted previously) have initiated policies of buying back franchises and operating them themselves, particularly the more successful ones. Thus the franchisee sacrifices a certain degree of security as well as independence.

And finally, it should be emphasized that not all franchising arrangements produce happy results. Some franchisees have suffered severe financial loss, and others have not achieved nearly the profit potential that the franchise promoters had led them to expect. The factors accounting for the lack of success of some franchises are discussed in the following section.

FRANCHISING ABUSES

One of the most apparent reasons for the unhappy results of some franchise operations is that in some localities there are more fast-food emporiums, motels, and other kinds of business than the market can absorb. As one cynic has asked, "Just how many hamburgers, pizzas, and fried chicken can the average person be expected to consume?" Thus the rapid growth of franchising has led to an oversaturated market in some industries, with the result that a number of franchisors have recently filed petitions for bankruptcy.

Uncontrolled competition in the franchising business is obviously an important cause of this condition, but it is also the result of overexpansion on the part of individual franchisors, some of whom may be more interested in the sale of franchise packaging or equipment than in the profits of their franchise holders.

Franchisors sometimes dictate that prospective franchisees make sizable deposits *before* seeing the contract. Subsequent refusal of the franchise offer results in forfeiture of the deposit.

Some promoters also fail to screen or train their franchisees carefully, to make sure that they are capable of operating a business. A few even encourage absentee ownership, suggesting the purchase of franchises as investments with hired managers running the store. The "training programs" promised by some franchisors often turn out to be nothing more than a sheaf of "canned" reading material. And in some cases prospective franchise buyers are not given sufficient information, financial and otherwise, on which to base a decision to buy or not to buy. Exaggeration of prospects is also commonplace among the "fringe" or "fly-by-night" operators who virtually have invaded the burgeoning franchising field.

Another undesirable practice relating to the sale of franchises is the use of a celebrity name to help sell the franchise when the prominent personality has little or nothing to do with the operation of the business. Even where the celebrity participates to a significant degree in the management of the business, as some do, the more important consideration for the prospective franchisee is the soundness of the basic franchise operation.

Also questionable are the termination and renewal provisions in most franchise agreements. The basic concept of franchising enables the parent company to grow rapidly. But at a certain point it is likely to "go public" because of its increased access to capital. Historically, with additional capital, franchisors have frequently tended to acquire their own outlets. McDonald's, for example, is 15 percent company owned.[14] The problem with reacquiring franchises arises when the parent company seeks to buy at the lowest price. One reason for the close scrutiny or monitoring of outlet operations is that certain inconsequential actions, under the terms of the franchise agreement, may result in a forfeiture of the franchise. Franchises are of varying durations, and renewals are sometimes refused on the grounds of supposed poor performance. Though both of these practices represent extremes they are not uncommon. "Weeding out marginal franchisees" is the term that is used for the process of company repurchase of outlets at bargain prices.[15]

The legal status of a franchise has significant ramifications. Probably the most commonly cited reason for establishing these independent businesses is the desire to build equity in a business that can be passed on to one's children. In the case of company repurchase, however, the price is often designated in the contract, and usually it is stipulated that the repurchase price will not exceed the original franchisee fee or investment. Such provisions effectively preclude the franchisee from being compensated for the goodwill or increased equity which he may have contributed to the business. Franchising promotions, nevertheless, frequently emphasize equity potentials.[16]

Even more interesting is the fact that, because of their vague legal status, franchises technically have not been included as parts of estates. Since most contracts specify that one is allowed to sell one's franchise only to a party approved by the franchisor, there is no assurance that franchises can, in fact, be passed on to heirs.[17]

Several other practices of some franchising organizations are even more

[14] Charles G. Burck, "Franchising's Troubled Dream World," *Fortune,* March 1970, p. 121.

[15] Harold Brown, *Franchising: A Trap for the Trusting* (Boston: Little, Brown & Co., 1969), p. 23.

[16] Robert Metz, *How to Select a Business of Your Own* (New York: Hawthorne Books, 1969), p. 43.

[17] "Caveat Emptor, Keyword of the Franchising Boom," *Publishers' Weekly,* August 18, 1969, p. 51.

questionable from a business or legal point of view. For example, a questionable accounting practice of some promoters is the inclusion of the entire franchise fee in their first-year statements of earnings, thereby making their businesses look a lot better than they are. In some cases this practice has been followed even before the franchised outlets have been opened for business; such "paper franchises" are misleading both to prospective franchisees and prospective investors in the stock of the parent company. One of the first stock market bubbles that subsequently burst was the Minnie Pearl's Chicken System. Those who invested in this fast-food franchising system saw their stock drop sharply from $45 to $3 a share.[18] As one wag put it, the company was guilty of "counting its fried chickens before they were hatched."

Equally questionable is the "multilevel distributorship" or "pyramid sales" technique. Like a chain letter, franchises are sold to franchisees who may, in turn, receive commissions for selling franchises to others. The promoter's sales of franchises is thus unlimited, potentially continuing endlessly until franchisees end up by trying to sell to each other.

A major grievance of some franchisees is that they are obligated by the tie-in provisions of the franchise contract to pay higher prices for supplies and equipment than they would pay elsewhere for goods of similar quality. One witness at the U.S. Senate committee hearings on franchising practices, for example, testified that a well-known franchisor of pizza charges its franchisees $21.50 for a spice blend that it can package for $3.[19] In addition to the markups on its own supplies and equipment, a franchisor may also receive kickbacks from "approved" suppliers. Also, since it is common practice for advertising media to pay 15 percent of the fees they collect to the agency responsible for the advertisements, franchisors frequently incorporate their advertising departments as "independent" agencies and stipulate in contracts that all promotion be placed with this agency.[20]

In a class action on behalf of Chicken Delight franchise holders, a U.S. District Court jury in San Francisco has recently ruled that such tie-in agreements violate the Sherman Anti-Trust Act and are thus illegal. Attorneys for the franchisees maintained that there is a built-in conflict of interest between franchisee and franchisor. The decision has been appealed, but "until a final ruling is obtained [it is likely that] the agreements between more than 1,000 franchisors and many thousands of businessmen are going to be [similarly] challenged."[21]

Up to the present time there has been little franchising legislation as such. The first such legislation at the federal level was enacted in 1956 after much opposition had been expressed by automobile dealers to the short-term cancellation provisions found in many of their franchise agreements. Such provisions, it was argued, enabled automobile manufacturers to overload dealers' inventories, or to set unrealistic sales quotas, under threat of contract cancellation or nonrenewal.[22] The

---

[18] *Des Moines Register,* April 5, 1970, pp. 1 et passim; see also Burck, "Dream World," p. 116.

[19] U.S. Senate Select Committee on Small Business, *Impact.*

[20] Brown, *Franchising,* p. 17.

[21] John Cuniff, AP business analyst, in the (Iowa City) *Press-Citizen,* April 15, 1970, p. 6C.

[22] See Charles M. Hewitt, "The Furor Over Dealer Franchises," *Business Horizons,* 1 (Winter 1958), pp. 80–87.

Good Faith Act, signed into law on August 8, 1956, gives the franchised automobile dealer the right to sue for damages in a federal court if he can prove that the manufacturer failed to exercise "good faith" in carrying out the franchise or in terminating it.[23] The duty to act in "good faith" is defined in the act as "the duty of each party to any franchise . . . to act in a fair and equitable manner towards . . . [the] other so as to guarantee the one party freedom from coercion, intimidation, or threats [thereof] . . . ." All automobile manufacturers and some oil suppliers have extended the duration of their franchises since the passage of this law.[24] Though originally aimed at franchising abuses in the automobile industry, its provisions are equally applicable to franchising agreements in other industries.

More recently, a subcommittee of the U.S. Senate Select Committee on Small Business has been taking a long, hard look at other franchising abuses, and is currently preparing legislation aimed at protecting both the franchisee and the stock investor. According to Senator Harrison A. Williams, chairman of this subcommittee, the proposed bill will include provisions for the following:

1. disclosure by the franchisor of his financial standing, all the terms of the franchise operation, potential profits, and other information needed by the prospective franchisee in making a wise decision;
2. federal help for members of minority racial groups who want to acquire franchises;
3. curbs on indiscriminate use of celebrities' names in franchise operations where the celebrity actually has little or nothing to do with the business.[25]

A number of states have also enacted legislation to curb franchising abuses. The franchise investment laws of California, Massachusetts, and New York contain essentially the same provisions, as follows:

1. registration of franchisors and franchise salesmen, and sales agencies;
2. registration of a franchisor's sales presentation, the latter regarded as being similar to a stock prospectus (California has ruled that a franchise is a security and is therefore subject to "Blue Sky" laws);
3. investigative and injunctive powers to declare unfair methods of competition granted to the attorney general;
4. holding of franchise fees in escrow accounts to guarantee franchise performance and to keep them out of earnings statements that would overstate profits.[26]

Other restrictions on franchising operations are contained within the provisions of the Federal Trade Commission Act. The Federal Trade Commission has recently cited the following guidelines for fair practices in franchising:

1. If the best locations have been assigned to insiders that fact should be disclosed;
2. The amount of assistance to be provided in managing and operating the franchise must not be overstated;

[23] 70 U.S. Code (1956), sec. 1222.
[24] Hewitt, "Furor," p. 87.
[25] Cuniff, op. cit.
[26] "A Chain of Laws for Franchising," *Business Week,* April 4, 1970, p. 26.

3. The advertising and promotion that is to be financed from royalties must be described accurately;

4. Prospective earnings must not be exaggerated;

5. Franchisors must reveal any significant unfavorable news, litigation, or claims pending;

6. Franchisees who can buy comparable goods or service on the open market at better prices than from designated suppliers have grounds for complaints.[27]

Franchisees do not rely solely on legislation to protect themselves from franchising abuses, or on litigation to remedy these abuses. In the past few years an increasing number of them in particular companies or industries have organized themselves into bargaining units for the collective renegotiation of contract terms and airing of grievances. The recently formed National Association of Franchised Businessmen is a bargaining and lobbying organization representing franchise holders in all industries across the country.

The bulk of the franchising companies, however, are ethical businesses who are equally concerned about undesirable franchising practices. To police the industry, a number of leading franchisors recently formed the International Franchise Association. As part of its program it has prepared a code of ethics wherein each member company subscribes to the following principles:

1. The advertising practices of members shall be governed by the Association's Ethical Advertising Code, the provisions of which are:

   a. All advertisements shall comply, in letter and spirit, with all applicable rules, regulations, directives, guides and laws, promulgated by any governmental body or agency having jurisdiction with respect thereto.

   b. An advertisement containing or making reference, directly or indirectly, to performance records, figures or data respecting income or earnings of franchises, shall be factual, and, if necessary to avoid deception, accurately qualified as to geographical area and time periods covered.

   c. An advertisement containing information or making reference to the cost of a franchise or its investment requirements shall be as detailed as necessary to avoid being misleading in any way and shall be definite and specific with respect to whether the stated amount(s) is a partial or the full cost of the franchise, the items paid for by the stated amount(s), financing requirements and other related costs or investment charges.

2. No member shall sell, offer for sale, or distribute any product or render any service, or promote the sale or distribution thereof, under any representation or condition (including the use of the name of a "celebrity") which has the tendency, capacity, or effect of misleading or deceiving purchasers or prospective purchasers.

3. No member shall imitate the trademark, trade name, corporate name, slogan, or other mark of identification of another franchisor in any manner or form that would have the tendency or capacity to mislead or deceive.

[27] Sidney A. Diamond, "Federal Trade Commissioners Warn of Abuses in Franchising," *Advertising Age,* July 21, 1969. pp. 86–89. See also the FTC's Consumer Bulletin no. 4, "Advice for Persons Who Are Considering an Investment in a Franchise Business" (Washington, D.C.: G.P.O. 1970).

4. The so-called pyramidal distribution system is inimicable to the interests of the consumer, the distributor, and the franchise concept, and no member shall engage in this method of doing business.

5. Full and accurate written disclosure of all information material to the franchise relationship shall be given to prospective franchisees within a reasonable time prior to the execution of any binding document.

6. The franchise agreement shall set forth clearly the respective obligations and responsibilities of the parties and all other terms of the relationship, and be free of ambiguity.

7. The franchise agreement and all matters basic and material to the arrangement and relationship thereby created shall be in writing and executed copies thereof given to the franchisee.

8. A franchisor shall select and accept only those franchisees who, upon reasonable investigation, possess the basic skills, education, personal qualities, and adequate capital to succeed. There shall be no discrimination based on race, color, religion, national origin or sex.

9. A franchisor shall exercise reasonable surveillance over the activities of his franchisees to the end that the contractual obligations of both parties are observed and the public interest safeguarded.

10. Fairness shall characterize all dealings between a franchisor and its franchisees. A franchisor shall give notice to its franchisee of any contractual breach and grant reasonable time to remedy default.

11. A franchisor shall make every effort to resolve complaints, grievances and disputes with its franchisees with good faith and good will through fair and reasonable direct communication and negotiation. Failing this, recourse should be made, if possible, to arbitration, with litigation pursued only as a last resort.[28]

MINORITY FRANCHISEES

Various sources have suggested that members of minority racial groups are unable to establish their own businesses almost solely because they are unable to obtain financing and proper training and advice. Both these obstacles are surmounted by the franchise method of establishing a business and by provisions of the Economic Opportunity Act of 1964.

As part of the federal government's effort to create viable business opportunities for minority businessmen, the SBA and OMBE jointly sponsor the "25 X 2" franchise program. The purpose of this program is to encourage franchisors to seek out and support prospective minority franchisees. For those with the potential to successfully operate a franchised (or other) business, but whose credit rating is such that they cannot qualify for a commercial bank loan, low-cost SBA "economic opportunity" loans are available up to $50,000. Additional financing, if needed, is often provided or underwritten by the participating franchisors. Among the active participants in this program, on a national scale, are McDonald's Corporation and Kentucky Fried Chicken, Inc.

[28] Reprinted through the courtesy of the International Franchise Association, 1025 Connecticut Avenue N.W., Washington, D.C.

Another active participant is the Shell Oil Company, which has recently inaugurated a five-year program to increase the number and quality of black-owned gasoline service stations in the Washington, D.C., area. Along with start-up loans and station-modernization programs, the company furnishes each dealer with five weeks of full-time training before he launches his business.

Experience with these programs indicates that minority businessmen are earning incomes comparable to their white counterparts. Records also show that the failure rate for minority franchisees is about the same as it is for white franchise holders.

SUMMARY AND CONCLUSIONS

There are several reasons why franchising has grown so rapidly in recent years. The most important of these are that it provides opportunities for the establishment of new small businesses as well as a method of financing corporate growth that otherwise would be much slower. While the franchising concept has great merits, it also has weaknesses which have led to unscrupulous exploitation.

For prospective entrepreneurs contemplating the acquisition of a business franchise, the authors offer the following advice:

1. View the franchise offer in the light of the material presented in this chapter, as well as the material (on "justifying" a new business) presented in the preceding chapter.
2. Personally contact several of the company's franchise holders and find out how they like the deal.
3. Call your local Better Business Bureau or Chamber of Commerce and ask for a business responsibility report on the franchise promoter.
4. Have your lawyer go over all provisions of the franchise contract.
5. Make sure that all areas of uncertainty are resolved before making a decision and signing the contract.

In any case, regardless of whether the new business is a franchised operation or not, some state laws and municipal ordinances require the licensing of certain types of businesses activity or otherwise restrict the number of firms in these industries. (Business licensing requirements are discussed on pages 502-3.) Before his business is launched, the entrepreneur should check with government authorities to see if his proposed venture is subject to these requirements.

REVIEW QUESTIONS

1. What is franchising?
2. What are the benefits of franchising to the franchisor? To the franchisee?
3. How do you account for the rapid growth of franchising in recent years?
4. How do the authors classify the various franchising systems? Give several examples of each.
5. What kinds of products are commonly marketed through manufacturers' dealerships?

6. What kinds of products and services can be marketed through "franchising companies"?
7. What is the key ingredient in franchising systems of the type in question 6? Explain.
8. What are some of the other "services" provided by franchising companies to its franchisees?
9. What are some recent developments which suggest or underscore the success of the franchising method of distribution?
10. Give some examples of corporate franchising mergers. What are the objectives of such mergers?
11. What are some of the disadvantages of acquiring a franchise?
12. What are some of the questionable practices of some franchisors? How can you explain the increasing number of franchising abuses in recent years? How can these abuses be corrected or remedied?
13. What legislation for franchising control has been passed, or is under consideration, at the federal level? Discuss the provisions of this legislation.
14. Describe the provisions of similar legislation at the state level to curb franchising abuses.
15. What guidelines have been adopted by the Federal Trade Commission for fair practices in franchising?
16. Discuss the federal government's role in encouraging the acquisition of business franchises by members of minority racial groups.
17. What advice would you offer the prospective purchaser of a business franchise?

DISCUSSION QUESTIONS

1. If you were starting a business where voluntary chains were in existence, would you prefer to affiliate with one or to "go it alone"? Why?
2. From the viewpoint of member independent merchants in the same field, would you expect a corporate chain or a manufacturing wholesaler to be the more useful sponsor of a voluntary chain? Explain.
3. What do you think of the opportunities for a qualified person to start a small business as a member of a voluntary chain? Discuss.

SUPPLEMENTARY READINGS

Rosenburg, Robert M., and Madelon Bedel. *Profits from Franchising.* New York: McGraw-Hill Book Co., 1969. Discusses whether franchise ownership is right for you, and if so, what areas are best for your skills and aptitudes; where to get financing, including typical arrangements with franchising companies as well as banks and government agencies; how a formal control system works in an actual franchise system in maintaining standards and transmitting financial data; and how to evaluate franchise agreements.

U.S. Senate, Select Committee on Small Business. *Impact of Franchising on Small Business*. Washington, D.C.: G.P.O., 1970. Report on hearings before the Subcommittee on Urban and Rural Economic Development, where an in-depth examination was made of the franchising concept. The committee's conclusions and recommendations, with support data, are given.

8

Selecting
the merchandising
or service location

Choosing the right location for one's business can be a major factor in its success or failure. A good location may allow a mediocre business to survive, but a bad location may spell failure for the finest of businesses. There are certain basic things to consider regardless of the kind of business being contemplated. These considerations, however, must be weighted according to the needs of the particular enterprise and the entrepreneur's intentions and goals.

There are two major aspects of locating a business: (1) deciding on the particular community, and (2) choosing a site within that community.

Selecting the region and town is relatively more important in terms of economic factors for the small factory or wholesale concern than for most retail and service establishments. Conversely, choosing the district and site within a particular town is usually of more importance to the retail store or shop. However, the beginning wholesaler usually plans for a modest market within his community with economical access to his customers, and so is influenced by some factors similar to those that govern the selection of a retail or service location. Since choosing a location for a factory involves several additional considerations, it will be discussed in the following chapter.

In selecting a town for a retail, wholesale, or service establishment the following factors must be evaluated: the local economic base; population and income trends; customer demographic data; competition; living conditions; and the attitudes or plans of those in a position to influence the future of a given area. The small businessman should be sufficiently familiar with the specific requirements for his business to rate each of these factors in terms of his needs.

In determining the best site for a retail establishment the retailer thinks in terms of the place which will be most accessible to the customers who need the kind and quality of goods he intends to sell. While some wholesalers may also need to consider accessibility, they are more likely to regard as important their delivery costs or the cost of the space they occupy. Service establishments, to a greater or lesser degree, have characteristics of retailing, wholesaling, or manufacturing, and

137

their operators must evaluate accessibility, space costs, and other pertinent facts in terms of the functions they will perform.

Rent and its complement, advertising, are a large part of operating cost, and it is important that these dollars be spent wisely to produce maximum profits. Since location tends toward greater permanency than many other aspects of business, and since a lease is usually involved, a business must anticipate the future correctly and continuously adapt to the changing conditions affecting its site. Ownership of the site aggravates this problem.

SELECTING THE TOWN

Towns and cities vary greatly in their desirability as locations for different kinds and sizes of businesses. Ordinarily the small businessman will be faced with either of two basic types of problems: (1) comparing the merits of a number of possible towns or cities within which to locate his particular kind of business, or (2) deciding whether or not a given town is a good place in which to enter one of a few closely related kinds of business. Similar procedures will be followed in either case.

Personal Factors

In selecting the location for a small business, personal factors are of far greater importance than they are for the large concern. Pragmatically, they may limit the individual's range of choice to his immediate environment, either because of his lack of knowledge of more distant locations, or because he does not have the necessary time or funds to investigate a wider area. Of even greater importance are the highly personal factors that lead to deliberate choice. Some of these are:

1. A desire to locate among family and friends
2. The desire to locate away from relatives or to be where one is unknown
3. A personal preference for one region or part of the country
4. A need to locate in a particular climate because of health
5. An opportunity to take advantage of established trade connections in a particular territory
6. A preference for a small town, a suburban location, or a big city
7. The need to personally supervise other business interests or investments held in the area

Although it is often considered risky to go into business in a particular town solely because one is well known there, sound business reasons often favor such a decision. Credit is easier to obtain where the entrepreneur has already established a good reputation. Also, friends and acquaintances can give good word-of-mouth publicity. However, the beginner should not count too heavily on receiving their patronage *merely* because of friendship. The native's intimate knowledge of the people of the community, their buying habits, their likes and dislikes and other characteristics, and his knowledge of the community's economy and its industrial base may be an advantage that a total stranger would acquire with difficulty.

The Town as a Place to Live and Do Business

In choosing a town the entrepreneur should consider whether it would be a pleasant place in which to live. Those factors which contribute to a pleasant environment for him and his family also have an important effect on the ease of doing business. He should consider the general appearance of the town. Are the homes neat and attractive, and are lawns and streets well maintained? Next, he should determine if adequate facilities are available, such as banking, transportation and highways, professional services, and suitable utilities. The quality and kind of public and private institutions such as schools, churches, amusement centers, and hospitals which a community supports indicate a great deal about the concerns of the people of the community and also greatly affect the kind of life one can lead in a particular place. This also serves as a barometer to predict the direction in which a town is moving.

Sometimes unfilled economic needs in a given community, or the business opportunities it provides, will seem more important than esthetic considerations or the convenience of doing business. However, in general, a progressive city will also provide the best business opportunities.

Economic Characteristics

The kind of work pursued by the majority of the local population is an important factor in selecting a community in which to locate. A suburban area made up largely of professional leaders and business executives contrasts notably with a densely populated district located on the "wrong side of the tracks."

Retailers will want to locate where customer income is regular and assured. Both the amounts of money paid to workers in different occupations, and the regularity and frequency of payments, differ. Some communities serving farmers must expect to grant long-term credit; others do a week-to-week credit business, because their customers are paid weekly. The cash business volume of many communities fluctuates according to the pay days of establishments in which sizable groups of citizens are employed.

The town's industrial base also affects the amount and kind of goods the customers will want. As measured by the value of farm products sold and "value added" by manufacture and the extractive industries, the wealth produced in or near the community has important consequences in terms of local employment, income, and population growth.

Hopefully, the new businessman will be able to locate in a community which is not entirely dependent upon one firm or industry. Enterprises located in a one-company or one-industry town are subject to the same seasonal and economic fluctuations of that firm or industry.

A prospective businessman can learn a great deal about a town by looking, listening, and studying available census data and other business statistics. Some danger signals are:

1. The necessity for high school and college graduates to leave town to find suitable employment
2. The inability of other residents to find jobs locally

3. Declining retail sales and industrial production
4. An apathetic attitude on the part of local businessmen, educational administrators, and other residents

Favorable signs include:

1. Opening of chain or department store branches
2. Branch plants of large industrial firms locating in the community
3. A progressive chamber of commerce and other civic organizations
4. Good schools and public services
5. Well-maintained business and residential premises
6. Good transportation facilities to other parts of the country
7. Construction activity accompanied by an absence of vacant buildings and unoccupied homes or houses for sale

The purchasing power of a community is reflected in:

1. The number of people employed and the trend in employment
2. Total payrolls and the average wage or family income
3. The amount and trend of bank deposits
4. Per capita retail sales
5. The proportion of home ownership, and home values

Preference should be given to a growing town. A rare opportunity would be needed to compensate for a static population or one that shows a long-term declining trend. It is always possible that with enlightened civic leadership and other favorable conditions such as the rerouting of a major highway, a static or declining town may stage a rebirth, but it should not be counted on.

Labor-management relationships in the community are also important to the small businessman, both as a shopkeeper and an employer. Strikes may result in violent fluctuations of retail volume in the cash store, or in the overextension of credit. If the town is a "union town" the employer should find out if industries and businesses operate as "closed shops," since this will affect his hiring practices.

The Potential Customers

Wise business decisions can only be made if, as a first step, the market which the entrepreneur wishes to serve has been carefully defined. Sociologists roughly divide people into "social classes." Social class is determined by evaluating income, occupation, and education. It has been shown that people tend to have predictable tastes and modes of behavior which are determined to a great extent by the class to which they belong. These differences are reflected in buying habits. The entrepreneur must decide what class and type of customer he wishes to serve. When this is known the community can be evaluated in terms of (1) purchasing power of the potential customers, (2) their residence (whether rented or owned, houses or apartments), (3) their place and kind of work, (4) their means of transportation,

(5) their age, (6) their family status, and (7) their leisure activities. Conversely, once the retailer is established in a location he must always be aware of these same customer characteristics, because as communities change and customers change, the businessman must be prepared to either change his location or change the definition of the market which he wishes to serve. Failure to follow one of these courses can mean reduced profits or business failure.

For a better understanding of consumer buying habits, statistics showing the breakdown of family expenditures are available for the United States as a whole and are classified by type of community, location, occupation, size of family, and size of money income. These data may be obtained from the Bureau of Labor Statistics of the U.S. Department of Labor, and the Agricultural Research Service of the U.S. Department of Agriculture.

Competition

Whether competition is good or bad for a business depends to a great extent on the kind of business one is contemplating and on one's competence. Some establishments thrive on it while others are destroyed by it. Many lines of business do well if located in a market or shopping center with the right type of competitors. Retail stores that handle shopping goods or general merchandise sold to customers who live in a large trading area surrounding the town generally do better when they are located in proximity to one another for the convenience of the shopper. Small wholesalers or manufacturers who are not dependent on the local market, such as dry goods wholesalers and furniture makers, also find that healthy competition attracts buyers and suppliers' representatives from out of town. In contrast to this, the small grocery wholesaler intent on serving the local market would view the presence of many alert competitors as undesirable.

The other aspect of competition is the small businessman's ability and ambition. Where an inexperienced and less ambitious individual might rate strong competition undesirable, an experienced, well-qualified, ambitious person might welcome such a situation as assurance of a healthy condition likely to make for greater permanence and stability. He would count on being able to get his fair share of the business.

The prospective small businessman should note the presence of chain stores, which frequently present strong price competition since they can operate on narrow profit margins. He should also consider whether competing stores are attractive and if they draw as customers the people who live in the community.

Competition between communities is defined in terms of trade areas. The size of a trading area, for a community or for a store, depends largely on competition from neighboring towns or trading areas. Competition will express itself in lower prices or better quality, wider assortments or more services. In general, as towns increase in size their trading areas increase at a much greater rate than the town's population.

Size of Town or Trading Area

The size of the town, or the extent of the trade area which a business district serves, determines to a great extent the opportunities which exist for the small businessman in a particular place. A *trade area* may be defined as that territory within which the people live who trade or shop in a specific community. In general, it may be said that the larger the community the farther the people will come to trade there. However, the size and proximity of neighboring towns, as well as the merchandise or service provided by each community, affect the operation of this rule.

The size or extent of a community's trade area can be estimated in a number of ways, as follows:

1. Taking license numbers from parked cars and then locating the owners' addresses from the tag registration office
2. Checking newspaper circulation which usually covers a trading area
3. Sending questionnaires to people to find out where they buy
4. Securing addresses of customers from established stores in the territory, or by interviewing customers as they leave the store
5. Asking local bankers from what territory they draw depositors
6. Applying "Reilly's law of retail gravitation"

The last is a mathematical formula which is used to determine the breaking point between competing trade centers, that is, the point between towns where a consumer will purchase equal dollar amounts of goods and services in each town. The theory behind the formula assumes that the size of a town's trade area for shopping goods depends on two factors: (1) the population of competing towns, and (2) the distance to each of these towns. For illustrative purposes, the formula is applied as follows to determine the point between Town A and Town B beyond which the majority of people will make the majority of their retail purchases in Town A rather than in Town B:

$$\text{Breaking point in miles from Town B} = \frac{\text{Distance between Town A and Town B}}{1 + \sqrt{\dfrac{\text{Population of Town A}}{\text{Population of Town B}}}}$$

$$= \frac{19}{1 + \sqrt{\dfrac{15,247}{32,430}}} = \frac{19}{1 + \sqrt{0.470}}$$

$$= \frac{19}{1.688} = 11.3$$

From the formula it can be seen that the size of a community's shopping goods trade area varies directly with the community's population and with the distance to competing communities.

There is a close relationship between the number of customers served by a trading area and the types of business that the trading area can support. The number of persons required to support a representative independent store varies greatly according to how specialized or widespread is its merchandise appeal; highly specialized stores, such as toys or sporting goods, may require 100 times as large a population to draw from as those having an almost universal market, as groceries or food service. Table 8-1 shows the population required on the average, in the country as a whole, to support 16 different kinds of retailing in the late 1960s. Similar ratios can be calculated for particular geographic areas (locations) and for other kinds of business.

Table 8-1

Population Required for Selected Kinds of Retailing

Restaurant or lunchroom	840	Jewelry store	8,400
Grocery store	910	Radio and television store . . .	8,720
Gasoline service station	920	Florist	8,860
Cocktail lounge or beer parlor . . .	1,790	Household appliance store . . .	9,560
Drugstore	3,700	Retail bakery	10,150
Furniture store	5,980	Sporting goods store	12,400
Women's read-to-wear	6,240	Department store	34,580
Hardware store	7,320	Cigar store	35,770

Source: *1967 U.S. Census of Business: Retail Trade*; and 1967 estimate of population, U.S. Bureau of the Census.

Any state or city may deviate considerably from the average for the entire country; it may be difficult except for census years to secure data for a particular town; and even when data are available they indicate merely the status quo. Despite these limitations this approach is useful to the beginner, especially if ratios for the kind of business being considered are determined for the entire country, his state or region, and his particular town. For large cities ratios may also be estimated for the particular retail district under study. In using ratios such as these it should be remembered that different kinds of stores vary considerably in drawing power or trading area; ladies' fashion apparel may attract customers from several miles away, whereas a drugstore or grocery may be limited to its immediate neighborhood. The composition of different communities may also cause deviations from the average; where most families are large and have many children, food expenditures as well as those for children's wear are likely to be well above average, just as in a district containing an unusually high proportion of sportsmen sales in this line may be substantially above average.

Small Towns — a Special Opportunity

The sales image of a small-town business is created by having better service, high quality, friendliness, and interest in the community. This creates a strong favorable image because of the personal involvement of the small-town businessman. However, weak images are created by a limited variety of merchandise and generally higher prices.

In any case, there are certain businesses that are "naturals" for the small town. In each of the following types of establishments, for example, 40 percent or more of the nation's total business is done in towns under 5,000 population:

Type of Business	Proportion of National Sales
General stores	90%
Feed and seed stores	60
Farm implement, tractor, hardware dealers . .	55
Hybrid seed corn	50
Filling stations	45
Hardware stores	40

Source: 1967 U.S. Census of Business: Retail Trade.

Variety stores, lunch counters and stands, drugstores, and liquor stores appear to do equally well in both small and large communities. On the other hand, large department stores, delicatessens, optical shops, and specialty stores for the sale of office and school supplies, cameras, furs, books, and cigars are likely to be missing from the small-town Main Street. Most of this merchandise is found in the smaller town but in different kinds of stores.

Although payroll is normally the largest item of expense in retail stores, many small-scale retailers, at least at the start, actually hire few, if any, employees. This makes rent their major operating cost. Data assembled by Dun & Bradstreet, by sizes of town and store sales volume groups, show that in most major lines of business occupancy expense is relatively lower in small towns than in larger towns.

Still another factor favoring small-town locations is that most of the larger chain organizations have a minimum size limit for towns in which they will locate. For the independent merchant in towns below this size standard, this means that he will not be forced to meet direct local chain store competition. He can study chain methods and other examples of modern big city retailing in larger communities and bring them to the small town. Chains do not open their own stores in towns below a minimum size because of the volume needed to support the higher total expenses of a company-owned store. Thus the progressive independent is given reasonable assurance of a protected position. This does not mean that chain store competition is bad and should be avoided in all cases. It is rather a matter of each type of store, independent or chain, capitalizing on its respective inherent advantages. Where an independent has direct chain competition, he is more likely to succeed if he plans his operations to dovetail those of the chain, rather than attempting to meet the chain on its strongest grounds. Where no chain competition is present, the field is wide open for the independent.

It also seems likely that in the future the rate of rural-to-urban migration will be slowed down. Many of the almost insurmountable problems of welfare, transportation, pollution, and crime can be traced to the overcrowding of people and the excessive concentration of industry. The increasing concern with the "crisis of the cities" has resulted in a strong rural development movement, in which business enterprises are encouraged to be launched or relocated in economically underdeveloped areas of the country to provide jobs for the young people of these communities. Federal legislation is currently pending which would provide tax incentives for the creation of new business enterprises in rural and small-town America. The National Federation of Independent Business has been an important lobbyist for such legislation.

SELECTING THE SITE

After the prospective small businessman has decided upon the community in which he wishes to locate and understands some of the special requirements of his business, he is ready to select a site. There are some rules of thumb which will be helpful for him to keep in mind, whether his goal is to establish a retail, wholesale, or service business.

Retail and service establishments have many of the same location requirements. Site selection for a service establishment is affected by the same considerations affecting retailers to the degree it engages in retail trade. Wholesalers have special requirements that need to be considered separately; however, even wholesalers are influenced by many of the factors affecting other merchandisers. To lessen repetition we shall first consider some basic factors to be evaluated in site determination in any of these businesses, and then discuss special needs later in the chapter.

Business Districts

Every community has a downtown or central business district and some neighborhood shopping areas. A large city may also have one or more large outlying shopping centers. In addition, there are highway and interceptor locations to consider. Each type of business district is discussed below in some detail. But first, a few concepts warrant explanation.

Locations and stores may be generative or suscipient. A generative location is one to which the consumer is directly attracted from his place of residence; to shop there is the principal purpose of the consumer in leaving his residence. Such a location is selected expressly to be easily accessible to the greatest proportion of persons away from home for the primary purpose of shopping.

A suscipient location is one to which the consumer is impulsively or coincidentally attracted while away from his place of residence for any primary purpose other than shopping. It takes or receives rather than generates business.

Downtown Locations

Downtown locations may be on the main street or on side streets. Until recently every city had its "100 percent block" or hard-core area where the heaviest concentration of shopper traffic was present – including branches of the national variety chains. This traffic was generated by the extensive advertising and pulling power of the leading department stores. The decline in the relative importance of downtown in many cities has caused many variety chains and some department stores to abandon these former 100 percent districts. The department stores that remain, however, are still the chief generators of pedestrian shopper traffic.

In the central business district are located a large collection of stores carrying shopping and specialty goods. In addition to the department and variety stores are departmentalized speciality stores, such as furniture, wearing apparel, shoes, and jewelry. There are also a number of convenience goods retailers such as drugstores and cigar stores.

In large cities the central shopping district may be a composite of several districts, usually adjacent to one another, and each noted for a particular price range or kind of goods, such as the general department and specialty store district, women's department and specialty store district, women's apparel district, men's clothing district, and others. Each central business district will have one or more streets parallel to the main street and several at right angles to it. The latter are the secondary retail areas. Most of the centrally located, smaller retail stores and some service establishments will be found here. Wholesalers are often grouped together on the fringe, accessible to highways or railroads.

Leading out from the central district will be "string" streets connecting this district with various sources of customer traffic. Some of these streets are main traffic arteries. Specialized districts with stores and shops catering to automobile traffic grow up along these traffic lanes, frequently for many blocks outward from the central business district.

Downtown has become increasingly important as a center for administrative, financial, and professional services, while declining in relative importance for most lines of retailing and services. It still has the major hotels and convention facilities, libraries and other cultural attractions, bus terminals, financial institutions, and office buildings. Many new office buildings and close-in apartments have been erected downtown in recent years. So long as present conditions continue in most large cities, downtown stores will cater increasingly to three major classes of customers:

1. The downtown working people, who have characteristic buying habits and practices
2. The "cliff dwellers" (apartment house occupants), who tend toward higher style and less casual wear
3. The regional shoppers or occasional visitors[1]

Stores and service establishments located in the large downtown office and apartment buildings are typically small-scale independents. Many that locate on the street level, either on side streets or the main street, are also small independents. The best locations tend to intercept pedestrian traffic from large buildings, attracted to the department store districts; the same kind and size of store located between the large building and the department stores will do much better than if

[1] Richard L. Nelson, *The Selection of Retail Locations* (New York: F. W. Dodge Corporation, 1958), p. 326.

located at an equal distance from the building but in a direction *away* from the department stores.

Downtown has enjoyed over a century of retail supremacy. In many cities it still has the largest assortment of offerings in merchandise and in professional services, as well as being the hub of financial, administrative, and cultural establishments. Although plagued with traffic congestion, parking problems, high occupancy expense and taxation, antiquated buildings, and slum areas, it is not dead yet. It may stage a comeback, slow and expensive, but ultimate. For department stores with suburban branches, the parent store downtown is often important — although Wanamaker's in New York and other leading firms have closed their downtown stores.

Federally and locally supported urban renewal programs are bringing new hope and new opportunity to many big-city shopping areas. Sometimes this has meant the razing of existing buildings and redevelopment with new buildings, malls, and courts. Other communities have emphasized redevelopment and rehabilitation by private investors and have added parking ramps and malls.

Shoppers must be able to find adequate parking facilities. If the ramps are occupied by the cars of people who work in the central business district, or by those seeking only entertainment, they are not available to shoppers. The shopper who has free parking available in shopping centers close to home may choose to shop there instead. Established stores in many cities have been reluctant to reimburse customers for their parking expense.

In very large cities, such as New York and Chicago, access to downtown has been over 90 percent by public transportation for many decades. In almost all other large cities, however, public transit is woefully inadequate. It *may* be revived through generous public subsidy. Until there is some evidence of a real improvement in public transportation, the prospective small businessman would be well advised to "think twice" before selecting a downtown location.

Shopping Districts

Large cities are divided into districts and then neighborhoods. The districts are often centered around a school or hospital, and have physical boundaries such as a river, railroad tracks, or arterial highways. Each of these sections is likely to develop its own well-balanced business district. This includes a combination of shopping and specialty goods as found in the central business district, but the stores are not as large and the variety of specialty goods is more limited. There will be a larger proportion of convenience goods stores, including groceries.

The districts are in turn subdivided into neighborhoods, each with its own shopping facilities but with a smaller assortment of stores. The emphasis here is on service establishments and convenience goods.

A district or neighborhood of a city in many ways assumes the characteristics of a town of comparable size. The number, type, and size of stores in a particular group, whether in a city district or in a town, reflects the size of the trade area which it serves. Thus the cluster of stores found in a city neighborhood which might be defined as having a population of 100,000 would be comparable to that found in a town of the same size. As pointed out previously in the discussion of trade areas, the size and composition of the grouping also depends on the proximity and size of other shopping areas. Superior and aggressive merchandising methods extend the size of the trade area, allowing it to support more stores which will show bigger profits.

Shopping Centers

Shopping centers may be classified by (1) character of merchandise featured, (2) degree of integration, (3) layout and facilities, (4) size, (5) extent of control, and (6) sponsorship. These are not mutually exclusive classifications. Each deals with one aspect. Thus a supermarket may open a fairly large convenience goods center with inflexible control excluding other supermarkets.

Type of merchandise featured. There are convenience goods centers and shopping goods centers. Convenience goods tend to be standardized items of relatively low unit price. Shopping goods are less standardized, if at all, and tend toward higher unit prices; examples include most wearing apparel and department store types of merchandise.

Degree of integration. Earlier shopping centers were mere clusters of stores and service establishments each independently owned and operated. These are the familiar strip centers that often lack even a name for the center. Parking, if provided at all, consists of space in front of each store and barely out of the main flow of automobile traffic. Not all of the land is necessarily owned by one person, although sometimes it is.

Layout and facilities. The newer strip centers provide off-street parking. Stores and parking run parallel to the traffic artery and sometimes on both sides of it. Some are L-shaped around a corner location. In these centers the first group of stores to appear is usually on land owned by one person or a small group. Later other developments often take place adjacent to the first center but on property owned by different people. Such centers share a common parking space, often have a name for the entire center, but do less group promoting than the controlled centers. Often tenant selection is neither planned nor controlled.

Although there are many other shapes and layout arrangements that shopping centers have taken, the trend in the larger ones is toward the mall type. The mall may be simply an area reserved for pedestrian shoppers with all stores having access and visibility along its sides; many provide amenities such as greenery, flowers, protection from the elements, and even year-round air-conditioning. Parking is outside the stores that surround the mall, on two, three, or four sides. Mall centers usually have two department stores with numerous independent and chain units between them on both sides of the mall.

Size. Shopping centers may be of the neighborhood, community, or regional type. Neighborhood centers usually specialize in convenience goods. Community centers have from 20 to 40 stores with ample assortments of shopping and convenience goods and services to serve the entire community or the part of town in which they are located. Regional centers are the largest, with 40 to over 100 stores. They expect to draw shoppers from well beyond the city limits.

Community and regional centers are planned, usually controlled, and operated as an integrated going concern. Tenants have leases that stipulate a minimum monthly rental plus a certain percentage of sales, often also above a stated minimum. Many tenants like this arrangement. The center management strives to have minimum guarantees sufficient to cover fixed financing and, usually, maintenance expense. The center advertises and promotes as a unit even though individual stores may also do their own advertising.

Sponsorship and control.   It is the control aspect of many shopping centers that is most controversial. Control refers to tenant selection and certain provisions in the leaseholds. The degree of control varies from one type of shopping-center sponsor to another. Most large planned centers have been sponsored by industrial real estate promoters. Many have been promoted by department stores, and a few by supermarkets, discount houses, and corporate chains.

Many controlled centers sponsored by real estate promoters and department stores exclude discount houses and sometimes supermarkets. The latter have reacted by sponsoring their own centers. Often such centers give the sponsor an "exclusive" for his type of business. Since both supermarkets and discount houses are generative of shopper traffic, they tend to attract smaller stores, both independent and chain, that capitalize on the presence of these shoppers. The character of shoppers may differ, however. Those attracted by the supermarket are usually interested in convenience goods; those drawn by the discount house usually behave more like department store bargain hunters. Although there may be exceptions, centers sponsored by department stores, supermarkets, and discount houses are less likely to feel the impact of the financier's demands in tenant selection than those sponsored by real estate promoters. Their established financial rating and contacts are probable explanations.

Real estate promoters who sponsor large shopping centers require generous financing, available chiefly from insurance companies and similar institutional lenders. These financiers insist upon well-established, financially strong "big name" tenants. This usually means national corporate chains and the dominant local department store. With the power to make or break a developing center still in the planning stage, these two types of retailers are often able to dictate their own terms by demanding very low rent, exclusive representation for their types of retailing, and restrictions on the type of merchandise that other tenant stores may carry.

Because of the financial risks involved, shopping-center sponsors or promoters are generally reluctant to accept small tenants. However, a small firm can now have its lease "guaranteed" by the Small Business Administration. The firm pays three months' rent in advance, plus a premium calculated as a percentage of the total rent to be paid during the term of the lease. These funds are held in escrow and are returned to the firm, with interest, when the lease expires.

Two major difficulties arise for controlled shopping centers: excessive competition from other centers, and interceptor highway enterprises.

One danger of too close control is the stimulation of competing centers that may exceed the local market potential; that competing centers may be launched by supermarkets and discount houses has already been mentioned. Normal free enterprise competition could also lead to the launching of more shopping centers than warranted by demand. In either case, operation of competitive forces will determine the outcome, but with results weighted against the center and those tenants that sought a monopoly through their attempts to obtain exclusives. Probably more serious for most shopping centers, and of special interest to small businessmen, is the expansion in the number of highway retail and service establishments.

Highway Locations

Car ownership and the use of cars has expanded tremendously in recent years, providing a new pattern of living and shopping. Many workers drive 50 miles each way daily in car pools. Women are doing more taxiing of family members and more shopping by car. Earlier distinctions between urban and rural people are blurred, and highway business extends beyond city limits.

Although independents pioneered highway retailing, chains and department stores have joined the movement. "Solo" locations are common, especially for department stores, furniture and floor coverings retailers, supermarkets, and discount houses.

Highway stores are free of architectural and merchandising restrictions, price restraints, and coercion for group efforts found in integrated shopping centers. They can often capitalize on traffic drawn by the shopping centers, either as interceptors or spillover recipients.

Also, "scrabbled merchandising" is typical of many highway locations. Restaurants, for example, carry a wide range of nonfoods; discount houses carry foods; supermarkets carry more nonfoods than usual.

The expansion of drive-in businesses of all kinds is also noteworthy. On arterial highways and string streets mere off-street parking may be sufficient for the typical retail store and service establishment, but newer types of business enterprise are based strictly on drive-in service where patrons do not need to leave their cars. These include drive-in theaters, banks, dairy products stands and snack bars, and batteries of vending machines accessible from the driver's seat, as well as conveyor systems for dispensing foods and refreshments. A "motormat" restaurant in Los Angeles is representative of the latter type of development. A wheellike layout has twenty parking stalls, each served by an electrically controlled food carriage. The motorist writes his order, puts it in the carriage with sufficient money to pay the bill, presses a button, and the carriage moves off to the kitchen. There an attendant fills the order, makes change on the bill, and sends the carriage back to the car.

For many independent enterprisers the multibillion-dollar recreation market offers numerous opportunities for highway drive-ins, motels, and many types of business located in or en route to recreational areas. The market in transient regions has expanded greatly in recent years, and appears likely to continue expanding with increases in the amount of leisure time available to workers and their families.

Basic Factors in Site Selection

In selecting a business district within a community, or on its fringes, several factors warrant attention. The more important ones are the rent-paying capacity of the business, the nature of the merchandise to be carried or services rendered, clientele desired, and anticipated volume.

Rent.   Usually the rent-paying capacity of a business will be a major factor in site selection. Certain businesses such as drugstores, men's and women's apparel stores, restaurants, beauty and barber shops, and department stores can afford to locate in a high-rent area. Others such as furniture and furnishings, and hardware and food stores, must stay in the low-rent areas.

The following table lists important characteristics of stores suitable to each district:

High-Rent District	*Low-Rent District*
1. High value of merchandise in proportion to bulk	1. Low value of merchandise in proportion to bulk
2. Window display highly important	2. Large amount of floor space for interior display
3. High rate of turnover	3. Low rate of turnover
4. Appeal to transient trade	4. Established clientele

In general, convenience goods stores locate wherever a sufficient number of potential customers have quick and easy access to the store. Usually they are large-volume units able to justify the high rents demanded for such sites. This may be on streets of heavy transient traffic, in outlying shopping centers, in well-populated neighborhoods, in industrial or other business areas, as well as in the downtown shopping center. Small food stores, notions and variety stores, small drugstores, and similar enterprises often do better outside the larger shopping centers and closer to the homes of their customers.

Shopping goods require a location in one of the shopping districts. This may be the central area or one of the suburban or outlying shopping districts or centers.

Class of trade.   The class of trade desired influences the choice of business district. In most cities, for example, certain districts are more "exclusive" than others in terms of income level or occupational status. Population patterns are also important, business subdistricts often catering to special groups such as business executives and office workers, transients (hotel guests), students, and various racial or ethnic groups.

Volume.   The anticipated volume of the store to be operated likewise has a direct bearing on the selection of the retail district. Usually only large-volume stores, one for each line of merchandise, can locate in the central shopping district. The small-volume stores may find it preferable to locate in a central or secondary district in a smaller town rather than in one of the poorer districts of a large city.

Specialization by type of merchandise carried tends to be greater in the central district. The individual who desires to locate in such a district must be able to justify the higher overhead of the location. He should have the advantage of merchandising experience, ample capital, and command of buying sources to a higher degree than the neighborhood storekeeper, for not only must he compete with other stores selling the same or similar goods, he also must vie for the consumer's dollar with all other kinds of stores.

Naturally the number and variety of retail districts varies with the size of the town. In small towns there may be only one shopping district, with a few grocery stores scattered around in neighborhood locations.

THE RETAIL LOCATION

Once the store's policies are formulated and the region selected, the next job is to appraise the present and future prospects of each town under consideration. Wholesalers and manufacturers can often help, as can agencies of the federal, state, or local governments, Chambers of Commerce, local banks, building and loan associations, and real estate agencies. The activities of the larger chain stores in establishing or closing branches in the town can serve as an indirect but usually reliable indicator. A personal investigation should be made of the town to compare it with others as well as to select the area and possible sites within it. In general, high-priced merchandise requires a trading area of above-average income, a more refined or exclusive shopping district, and the presence of suitable environment or "atmosphere."

Probably in no other type of business, however, is the building *site* as important a factor in determinine the success of a business as it is in retailing. Some studies have found poor location to be among the chief causes of retail failures. The following factors are usually of maximum importance in retail site selection: (1) accessibility of the site to prospective customers; (2) proximity to competitors and other types of retail stores; (3) rent and terms of the lease; (4) restrictive ordinances; and (5) history of the site.

Accessibility of the Store

Since the typical store depends for profits upon a sufficient number of customers coming into it, customer accessibility is an all-important consideration. For the small retailer accessibility is mainly a question of the ease with which his customers can reach the store. A site with the heaviest volume of pedestrian traffic would be ideal except that the rent might be beyond his means. Accessibility to pedestrian traffic for other sites will be influenced by distance from the traffic generators, terrain, dangerous street crossings or other hazards, or similar factors. The nature of the entrance may be important if it is even slightly above sidewalk level, or if the store has an off-the-street location, such as an upper floor.

To an increasing extent accessibility should also be considered in terms of automobile travel and parking facilities.

The accessibility of a site is sometimes related to the sequence of shopping. For example, food stores located on the right-hand side of an artery leading away from a major shopping district are more accessible because grocery customers usually shop on the way home, whereas a laundry or dry cleaner located on the right-hand side going into town is more accessible because customers prefer to unload the wash or cleaning before continuing to town.

Proximity to offices of professional men is desirable, especially in outlying shopping centers. People having appointments with doctors, dentists, optometrists, and so on quite often will become shoppers if stores are conveniently accessible.

Traffic analysis.   From careful analysis of experience in numerous outlets, chain store managers have determined the approximate sales value of each pedestrian passing a given location. Pedestrian traffic is thus used by chain stores as a direct guide to the evaluation of any site. The small independent retailer can imitate chain store methods in comparing and appraising various possible locations. Two factors are especially important: total pedestrian traffic during business hours, and the percentage of it that is likely to enter the store.

In making traffic counts, the checker should select a few half-hour periods, especially during the normally busy hours of the day. Only possible customers for the particular kind of business should be counted, with men and women recorded separately. Children may also be put in a separate category if they are likely customers. Even two 15-minute counts daily will enable the analyst to estimate the total eight-hour traffic fairly accurately.

To estimate the probable number of pedestrians who would enter a given kind of store, sample counts may be made of the percentage of them that enters stores of the same kind in each district. The results may be checked against similar surveys made by others.

The mode of transportation used by customers is an important consideration. When most customers come to the store in their own cars, a site several blocks from the shopping center that has ample parking space is often more accessible than a downtown store. Corner locations with entrances on each street have similar advantages for pedestrian traffic.

The rent-advertising relationship.   Some merchants utilize shopping traffic where they find it; others try to attract shoppers to their stores by means of newspaper, TV, or radio advertising. Rent and advertising expenses are often so closely related in the retail business that their relationships should be clearly understood. (We refer here to expenses incurred for advertising in media *outside* the store. This qualification is necessary here because a store's window displays are commonly regarded as its most valuable advertising medium.)

Rent is payment for the opportunity to make a profit by selling merchandise. The highest rents are paid for locations having the greatest volume of profitable shopper traffic. Competition for these locations tends to keep the rent up to the maximum that can be paid for their most effective use by the most efficient businessmen. A profitable business may be operated in these so-called 100 percent locations without expenditure for external advertising.

For years variety chains have followed the policy of selecting sites in the line of customer shopping traffic built up and maintained by the larger department stores.

Some specialty stores — such as those selling apparel, furniture, or food products — also locate near the large department stores. But in contrast to variety stores, they often find it pays to advertise: first, because they carry shopping goods that are suitable to advertising; second, because their central location makes possible effective use of the low-cost-per-reader mass media like newspapers; and third, because they can often "ride the tail" of department store advertising. Shoppers coming to the center anyway will often respond to these advertisements, though they might not make a special trip in response solely to the smaller store's advertisement.

Other specialty stores locate several blocks from the major shopping district, and pay lower rent for these locations but require higher advertising expenditures. Although the returns per dollar of advertising expenditure alone may be less for these fringe stores, the combined effect of low rent and moderate advertising may be very profitable. Thus it is the rent-advertising combination that is the largest item of expense in retail stores except for wages and salaries.

Proximity to Other Businesses

A retail store, like an individual, should keep the right company. It is well known that certain kinds of stores do well when located close to each other. Customers who patronize stores of one type in such a group are the best prospects for others in the same "affinity" class. Studies of these natural clusterings of stores have disclosed the following:

1. Men's and women's apparel and variety stores are commonly located near department stores;
2. Restaurants, barber shops, and candy, tobacco, and jewelry stores are often found near theaters;
3. Florists are usually grouped with shoe stores and women's clothing stores;
4. Drugstores may be found in any of the above groupings;
5. Paint, home furnishings, and furniture stores are generally in proximity.

Customers are people with habit patterns and buying needs that are often associated with other activities, as the foregoing illustrates. The same type of analysis may disclose other natural business groupings. For example, in recent years launderettes have been established in thousands of towns. What does the woman who brings in her clothes do during the fifteen or twenty minutes while the washer does the work? She shops in nearby stores to fill frequently recurring needs for items such as groceries, variety goods, and possibly magazines or similar articles.

In contrast to complementary or related store groupings, certain kinds of stores do better if not located close together. For the exclusive sale of convenience goods, unless the customer traffic is unusually heavy, stores of the same kind do not locate close to competitors. An apparent exception to this generalization arises where an alert independent in the drug, variety, or similar line finds advantageous a location adjacent to a chain store in the same line. The "spillover" traffic attracted to the chain may provide sufficient business for the independent. By making his merchandise offerings fit in with those of the chain he may secure additional volume. This means that some of the chain's customers who normally buy standardized popular styles or colors will be attracted by similar goods in novel designs, unusual colors, or other variations. Good examples of this are party novelties, popular-price gift items, unusual but low-price toys, and seasonal greeting cards.

The small independent's natural tendency is to want to avoid competing stores. The foregoing discussion should demonstrate that often locations close to the right kind of competitors are sometimes desirable.

There are certain neighbors that usually are undesirable for nearly any kind of retailer. Proximity to places that are normally avoided by shoppers — funeral parlors, hospitals, garages, saloons, and industries having disagreeable noises, odors, dust, or smoke — is unfavorable. Some environmental conditions may be temporary, such as broken sidewalks, vacant lots or stores, and construction in progress, but during the time they exist shopping traffic will shun the vicinity.

Rent and Terms of the Lease

Most retailers rent rather than construct the store building. Of major importance to the small retailer is that the building be suitable to his type of business, or that it could be made so, preferably at the landlord's expense. (Requirements of the store building will be discussed in Chapter 10.)

Two types of lease agreements are used in retailing — the flat rate and the percentage lease. Under the flat-rate plan, an annual rental of a definite amount payable monthly in advance is stipulated in the lease. For each line of retailing this amount should be consistent with the standard operating ratios in the field, modified according to the size of store, size of town, and the combined rent-advertising ratios discussed earlier. The percentage lease usually guarantees the landlord a minimum monthly rental, with additional payments at some percentage of sales agreed upon by both parties. For either type of lease, however, the objective is to stay in line with the standard rent ratio or to compensate for any deviation by more or less advertising, superior managerial ability, or similar considerations. Consequently, the standard ratio for the particular line of business should be known, and the rental demanded for any site under consideration should be appraised in terms of the site's potential volume of sales and the volume necessary to achieve this ratio.

Leases may be secured for periods ranging from one to ten years or more. Usually it is desirable for the beginning retailer to get a one- or two-year lease with an option on renewal for five to ten years at an agreed rental. This is not always possible, but he should bargain for the best terms at the time the lease is under discussion.

The lease usually provides for many other important points, such as any remodeling to be done, who is to pay for it, liabilities and duties assumed by each party, and permission or authority for the tenant to erect certain external signs, engage in additional lines of business, or make alterations to the premises in the future if needed. If the landlord owns adjacent property, it is sometimes possible to incorporate in the lease provisions governing the kinds of business for which these sites will be rented. A lease is an important legal document, and the small businessman should always seek competent legal counsel before entering into a formal lease agreement.

Restrictive Ordinances

Sometimes unusual restrictive ordinances may be encountered that would make an otherwise ideal site less desirable than another, such as limitations on the hours of the day when trucks are permitted to load or unload. Zoning and similar regulations are of importance when an individual attempts to open a store in an area restricted against his kind of business.

Site History

At least the *recent* history of each site under consideration should be known by the prospective retailer before he makes a final selection. Although most Americans no longer believe in haunted houses, experienced merchants know that hoodoo locations do exist. These are sites that have been occupied by a succession of retail failures. Naturally there are logical reasons why the site has not been a successful one at certain times in the past, but there are also the dangers that prospective customers have formed a habit of avoiding the location, or that the next prospective renter will overestimate his ability to succeed where his predecessors have failed.

LOCATION OF SERVICE ESTABLISHMENTS

The kind of service business to be established will probably have more bearing on the requirements for a good location than in other major fields. A personal service, professional or semiprofessional, where clients call at the place of business should be as accessible as possible. This may mean an office location in the financial district or a shop location in one of the better retail districts. If the customer does not visit the business, then the site may be selected in terms primarily of rent, space requirements, and owner's convenience.

An interesting characteristic of most service businesses is that a reputation for extra high quality of workmanship will attract customers in spite of a poor location to a far greater extent than is true of other kinds of business. However, since this is an exception, and since it comes about only after the reputation is earned, the beginner especially should seek the best location in which to build such a reputation.

Some kinds of service businesses require a factory type of location where the actual work is performed, and a retail site for customer contact in addition. For example, a laundry or dry cleaning firm may do a large amount of cash-and-carry business.

Policies relating to the market or type of clientele desired will influence the choice of town and area within a town whenever: (1) a special type of customer constitutes the market, such as office workers or factory workers; (2) the service is one for which there is widespread demand; or (3) existing competition deviates appreciably from normal.

Both in selecting the town and the district within a large city, care should be exercised to learn the facts. Assumptions that appear to be logical are not always borne out by reality. For example, although a heavy concentration of car ownership means a good market for automobile service establishments, clean cities are better markets for dry cleaning establishments than dirty ones.

Drive-ins are important in many service fields where the customer brings the article to the shop. These include many types of repair shops and laundry and cleaning establishments. A location close to the central business area on an arterial street and on the side nearer the better residential districts is considered best. Delivery services are becoming increasingly costly; the present trend is toward service at the shop rather than in the home, and customers are willing to do the transporting in most cases. For these reasons service business not yet launched on the drive-in principle should consider this possibility whenever it is appropriate. Even some personal services like beauty parlors and barber shops are finding advantages in this type of location. As mentioned earlier in this chapter, drive-ins have expanded to nearly every field. They are best suited to services where (1) the customer prefers to remain in his own car — as drive-in theaters, restaurants, and banks; and (2) where parking facilities may be dominant in determining customer patronage, as for fairly standardized services such as cleaning and self-service laundries.

Some services have special location requirements. Readers who are interested in the location requirements of a particular type of business are directed to the references in Appendix A.

THE SMALL WHOLESALER'S LOCATION

In the long-established lines — groceries, hardware, drugs, dry goods, and general merchandise — the country for some time has been pretty well provided with wholesale establishments that many years ago passed the "small" stage. Most of these firms have continued to operate in the small towns where they were originally established 30, 40, or more years ago. Annual sales volume of many of these houses, even in towns of the 10,000 population class, runs close to the $1 million mark. In some of the newer fields, such as wholesaling of electrical goods, radios, certain appliances, and various specialties, small-town markets have not been so profusely supplied from local wholesale houses. In both new and old fields, however, there has been an influx of newcomers operating as small businessmen.

Selecting the Town

Usually the small wholesaler depends more on the local market; that is, retailers within his town or within a trading area radius of less than ten miles. This means that the income in the community is of major importance in selecting a location. In this respect the small wholesaler emphasizes the same location factor as do his retailer customers, except that a wholesaler is also interested in the incomes in adjacent towns.

There are a few situations where a wholesaler's selection of the region or town is influenced by important factors other than the income of the town's immediate trading area. Four, in particular, deserve mention: (1) If a wholesaler, even though he starts on a small scale, has definite ambitions to expand rapidly and aspires to sectional or national distribution, it would be wise for him to locate in one of the key distributing centers for his line of goods. (2) With the recent expansion of franchise and cooperative buying plans a beginning wholesaler may wish to consider affiliation with one of them in the near future; such an ambition may influence his choice of location. (3) A small wholesaler may wish to handle a specialized line where the customers are small manufacturers and manufacturing retailers located in a few well-defined market centers. At one time, for example, southern California had many special or custom-built automobile body factories served by a few such wholesalers. (4) The middleman — a functional wholesaler, the resident buying office, or the purchasing agent — may need to be located in the major markets, such as New York for women's wear or Chicago for furniture.

The small wholesaler is primarily interested in a town with stability of income, diversified industry in the trading area, prosperous retail stores, and lack of competition. The last includes competition from other wholesalers in nearby towns. In special cases an individual may also lay some stress on availability of local financing, local taxes, and the attitudes of established businessmen.

Personal factors play a major role in the selection of the region and often the town in which many small wholesalers locate. A large majority of small wholesale houses develop in one of two ways: (1) An established retailer may experiment with quantity buying and start selling at "wholesale" to other retailers; thus the town is automatically selected by virtue of the retailer's original location. (2) A salesman for a wholesale house may team up with an experienced wholesale bookkeeper or office man and start a company in a promising territory that he has had under observation for several years.

Well-informed persons estimate that as high as 90 percent of all small wholesale houses are started in either of the two ways just discussed. Those resulting from a retailer's expansion into the wholesale field are said to be less likely to continue successfully than are firms started initially as wholesale houses by men experienced in wholesaling. A salesman calling upon retailers in many different towns has a much better basis than any one of his customers for selecting a particular town in which to locate a small wholesale business.

Selecting the District within a Town

The average age of wholesale establishments is greater than that of establishments in other fields. Most cities have wholesale districts. Usually these were in operation long before the automobile and truck appeared. Naturally they were located adjacent to water or rail transportation and frequently to both. Chicago and other cities served by these types of transportation are specific examples. In smaller inland towns the established wholesale district is adjacent to the railroad freight facilities.

In recent years there have been two significant developments leading to new wholesale locations within the town: highway transportation, and the rise of cash-and-carry wholesalers, especially in the grocery field.

In many situations the small wholesaler must still decide between locating in the established wholesale district or elsewhere in the town. Usually the advantages of locating outside of the wholesale district are far more compelling. The principal exception occurs when the need to pick up "shorts" from other wholesalers happens frequently, as it does sometimes in the drug business.

Within the wholesale district space is limited, plants are multistory because of high ground rents, warehousing costs — which usually constitute a major item of expense — are high, and traffic congestion is prevalent. Largely because of these conditions it is improbable that the small operator will be able to secure the efficient street-level type of plant he needs. Although rent is a relatively minor expense for service wholesalers (as compared to "cash-and-carry" wholesalers) in most fields, warehouse labor is a big item. Particularly for the small wholesaler who is not in a position to use labor-saving material-handling equipment, a wholesale district location would seem to have most of the disadvantages and almost none of the advantages of other locations.

Selecting the Wholesale Site

Since small wholesalers serve principally the local market, their location should be selected with this fact as a primary consideration. However, there are many aspects to be considered. The rise of truck transportation and the increased speed of all forms of transportation are important. For example, many small wholesale grocers located in small towns use their own trucks to deliver to customers as well as to bring in warehouse stocks. In nearly every city of 100,000 population or more there are public warehouses where commission men and brokers maintain stocks of goods. A small wholesaler located 200 miles from such a city sends his truck up to 75 or 100 miles to make customer deliveries, and the driver then continues on to the city distributing point where he picks up small lots of assorted goods from the warehouse stocks of commission men and brokers. Obviously this practice frees the small wholesaler (who could not ordinarily buy in carload lots anyway) from any dependence upon locations close to railroad facilities.

The preceding example assumes truck delivery by the wholesaler to his retail customers, location in a relatively small town, and distribution to a trading area that includes out-of-town customers. There are other situations to be considered, however, that bear heavily upon the intratown site. A primary consideration is the amount of "store" business, that is, the extent to which retail buyers visit the warehouse as compared to sale and delivery at the retailers' stores. "Store" business is of two types. The older form, still used in variety and general merchandise lines, is where the wholesaler maintains a showroom with displays from which visiting buyers make their selections. The goods may be taken by the buyer or delivered later by the wholesaler, the former practice being common with out-of-town buyers. For this type of business a site near other wholesalers with moderate parking facilities is desirable in order to obtain "shopping-center advantages."

The second example of "store" business is the cash-and-carry type of warehouse. There are many more small wholesalers operating this type of "store" business than the other. Often one or two persons can operate a cash-and-carry plant doing several hundred thousand dollars annual volume of business. Usually most of the patronage comes from retailers within the town, and a site of maximum convenience to these retailers that also has adequate parking and truck loading facilities is needed. This means higher rent expense. However, the total operating expense is likely to be less.

Recently small wholesalers, and a few large concerns that have built new plants, have chosen sites near the edge of town. The chief advantages are lower rent and ample space, the latter making possible the construction of the most efficient type of ground-floor warehouse with transportation access on all sides. More rapid transportation and good highways, less traffic congestion, and new types of construction that provide better light and ventilation all have contributed to this trend. Probably many of these operators also have had in mind the use of some air travel to markets and air transportation to the warehouse.

Small wholesalers who make truck deliveries, or whose salesmen travel, have a different problem of site selection from that of those doing "store" business. Here the relative amount of city business compared to out-of-town business is a major factor. The objective is to locate near the center of the desired trading area so as to keep the total distance traveled by salesmen and trucks at a minimum. A difference of one mile between two possible sites would be a large factor in such a case. Traffic congestion and highway facilities are important. Rent is usually a minor item of total expense, the major ones being salesmen's expenses, warehouse expense, and delivery costs in that order. To illustrate this situation, assume there are two small wholesalers, one having 90 percent of his business within the town, the other only 50 percent. The former would locate in town, close to the retailers served, and at the best site available in terms of rent, traffic conditions, space, and type of building required. The other would determine the direction in which the out-of-town half of his business is concentrated, and then would logically pick a site at the appropriate edge of town or about midway between his two groups of customers.

The increase in large shopping centers affects wholesale locations in a number of ways: (1) A wholesaler located to serve several centers may well be in a suburban area of relatively low land value; this in turn makes possible the construction of a modern one-story, economically operated warehouse with ample parking and loading facilities. (2) In some lines, notably drugs, retailers often want frequent emergency deliveries. (3) In some other lines, notably dry goods and variety items, retailers often express a desire to be able to visit the warehouse showrooms conveniently.

SUMMARY AND CONCLUSIONS

There are two aspects to consider in locating a merchandising or service establishment. The first is choosing a particular community, and the second is selecting a site within that community. These choices are of necessity interrelated and often dependent one upon the other. A business cannot be located in a community if there is no suitable site available in that community. Sometimes suitable sites are available in several communities, and then the various advantages of each community are considered.

The requirements for a retailing, wholesaling, or service establishment are determined by the type of goods or service to be sold and the market which is sought. This market must be clearly defined.

The choice of a town may be influenced by personal factors, the economic characteristics of the town, the size of the trade area, or by competition.

The site within the town — whether downtown, neighborhood, shopping center, or highway location — will be determined by the type of goods to be sold, the class of customers desired, and the anticipated volume. The entrepreneur must consider accessibility and convenience for his customers in relation to the rent he will pay, the amount he will advertise, the prices he will charge, and the nature of his business.

REVIEW QUESTIONS

1. What are the two major aspects of locating a business? Discuss the importance of each with particular reference to wholesale concerns, retail stores, and service establishments.

2. Under what circumstances might a prospective entrepreneur give greater weight to personal than to economic factors in selecting a retail location?

3. What are some of the major social and economic factors that should be evaluated in selecting a community in which to locate a merchandising or service establishment?

4. How can the purchasing power of a community be estimated?

5. How can the size or extent of a community's trading area be estimated?

6. What is the relationship between the number of customers served by a trading area and the types of business that the trading area can support? Explain why stores specializing in merchandise like cigars and sporting goods need a much larger population than grocery stores or drugstores. How can the prospective entrepreneur determine if a given community can "support" an additional business of his type? What are some of the limitations of this procedure?

7. What are some of the advantages of locating a merchandising or service establishment in a small town? The disadvantages?

8. How do you account for the decentralization of shopping areas? Do you expect this trend to continue? Why or why not?

9. What types of downtown businesses seem to be less affected by the trend toward outlying shopping centers? To what major groups of customers do downtown stores and service establishments cater?

10. For the merchandising or service business, what are some of the basic factors to consider in choosing the business district in which to locate?

11. What are some kinds of business which have relatively high rent-paying ability? What kinds of business have limited rent-paying ability? What conditions account for these differences?

12. What factors usually are considered of utmost importance in selecting the building site for a retailing business?

13. What is meant by the "accessibility" of the store or shop? Discuss.
14. What is meant by "traffic analysis"? What is its value in determining the suitability of a retailing site?
15. What is a "100 percent" location? Do all retailers strive to obtain such a location? Why or why not?
16. What are "retail affinities"? Give several illustrations.
17. List the kinds of businesses that could effectively use a drive-in type of location.
18. Contrast the differences in the location requirements of retailers and small wholesalers with regard to (*a*) the choice of a community in which to locate the business, and (*b*) the selection of a building site within that community.

DISCUSSION QUESTIONS

1. How would you expect location to be related to factors like the following: layout; credit and delivery policies; financing; supplier relations; customer relations and sales promotion; government regulations and taxation; and personnel? Discuss.
2. For a retail grocery store doing exclusively telephone-order and delivery business (no customers admitted to the store), describe the ideal location.
3. Mrs. Jones, a widow with two preschool children, has a small doughnut shop one block from the college campus, from which she earns a modest living. A larger store downtown, one block off Main, near a conventional restaurant, is available for 50 percent more rent. Additional equipment would be required and some modernizing needed for the vacant store. Mrs. Jones's funds are limited, but she dislikes the late night hours required at her present site. What do you think she should do and why?
4. Discuss each of the following statements:
     a. "Most people will go out of their way for 'good' service; therefore, store location is not too important."
     b. "An area with high unemployment and irregular income is not a good location for any type of store."
     c. "It is ordinarily desirable to locate as far from your competitors as possible."
5. Frank Gilbert operates a short-order restaurant (open 6:00 a.m. to 10:00 p.m.) on Elm Street where he has been for 10 years. His sales have averaged $65,000 per year. His largest volume is in the morning (early) and at lunchtime (drawn from route men — bread, milk, etc. — and nearby business establishments). He feels that his volume could be increased significantly if the seating capacity of the restaurant could be expanded. This is impossible in the present building; however, three blocks to the west of his present location there is a space available which would make the expansion possible. This new store is within 300 feet of a high school. Parking is also available on a similar basis to his current location. What should be considered before deciding upon such a move?

SUPPLEMENTARY READINGS

Davidson, Thomas L. *Some Effects of the Growth of Planned and Controlled Shopping Centers on Small Retailers.* Small Business Management Research Report prepared for the Small Business Administration. Storrs: University of Connecticut, 1961. This study of 81 shopping centers disclosed that the financial requirements of the lender calls for AAA tenants in 70 percent of the available space and, in effect, excludes many small businesses without this top credit rating. The survey offers suggestions for resolving the problem of gaining entry for more small businessmen in shopping centers.

Journal of Small Business Management 10 (Jan. 1972). This issue is devoted exclusively to problems of business location. Among the articles of particular interest to small retailers are the following: "Identifying the Key Factors in Retail Store Location" (pp. 17 ff.); "Obtaining Competitive Locations for Small Retailers in Shopping Centers" (pp. 21 ff.); "Improved Pedestrian Traffic Counts for Better Retail Site Location" (pp. 27 ff.); and "The Interstate Highway Market: An Overview of Relevant Criteria in Site Selection" (pp. 32 ff.). The article, "Deciding on Location for a Small Business" (pp. 1 ff.) is of general interest.

Thompson, Donald L. *Analysis of Retailing Potential in Metropolitan Areas.* Small Business Management Research Report prepared for the Small Business Administration. Berkeley: University of California, 1963. A report on trading-area analysis to help the small retailer choose the right community for his store location. Two approaches are used: one based on economic factors, and the other on consumer shopping habits.

Zimmer, Basil G. *Rebuilding Cities: The Effects of Displacement and Relocation of Small Business.* Small Business Management Research Report prepared for the Small Business Administration. Providence, R.I.: Brown University, 1964. Describes what happens to small business when small enterprises are forced to move because of urban renewal or highway construction, based on the experiences of 300 displaced firms. Also describes the suburbanization movement and its effect on small business.

9

Selecting
the industrial location

Regional economic analysis indicates that there is a close relationship between the center of population and the center of manufacturing. Wherever there are factories, there are people — employees and their families. To satisfy the wants of these people there must be wholesale establishments, retail stores, and service enterprises. Then there may be other businesses which complement the larger industrial concerns, such as the producers of packaging materials or the manufacturers of component parts and other supplies. To satisfy further the requirements of these businesses and the local population, transportation and communications facilities and other public utilities are necessary. Thus, in the complex of any metropolitan area, we find the core of business to be that of production. For the people whose employment and income is largely dependent upon the area's manufacturing activity, schools and churches must be provided, as well as a host of governmental services. In addition manufacturing activity broadens the tax base, bringing increased tax revenue to the community.

Probably, therefore, no type of business has been more aggressively sought, highly praised, generously aided by various levels of government, given more credit for our high standard of living, and yet subjected to as many restrictions when it tries to locate than has manufacturing. Industrial growth, as observed, makes possible and necessary the expansion of trade, services, research, the professions, recreation, and similar activities where independent enterprise flourishes. It also provides work for the continuous surplus of farm labor, and is the catalyst necessary to boost the economy of depressed areas.

LONG-RUN IMPORTANCE OF PLANT LOCATION

The location of any business is a risky *long-run* commitment. It is manifestly impossible to move the business to a new location once the physical facilities have been constructed, and it will be too costly to sell or junk these facilities until some time in the future. It is for this reason that small manufacturers, particularly, are encouraged to rent rather than buy or build the first building they occupy – as most merchandising and service establishments do.

In some cases, however, the small manufacturer has no choice but to buy his plant. As noted, once the plant is located in a particular place the heavy fixed capital investment is virtually immobile. The prospective manufacturer is therefore interested more in *future* conditions than in some immediate but temporary advantage. One city, for example, may have below-average taxes, but if its streets need repair, if the water and sewerage systems and the fire and police departments and school system are substandard, the tax advantage would certainly be temporary. To bring local conditions and public services up to an acceptable level might well result in a tax cost which is above average.

Another reason for initially renting factory space, whenever this can be done, is that it is usually harder when a manufacturing firm ceases operations to get another company to take over than it is to transfer ownership of a retail or service establishment. A factory's plant and equipment are specialized. When conditions make it unprofitable for one company to produce in a given plant it is unlikely that new owners could make the same product profitably. Conditions making it difficult or impossible to operate a given factory profitably are likely to be beyond the individual company's control. When the market for a product evaporates, or shifts to other products, a manufacturer is powerless unless he can shift with the market – or hedges against this by diversifying his product line.

Nor are industrial plants easily adapted to other uses. They are sometimes difficult to dispose of, as abandoned plants seen in various parts of the country bear silent witness.

SMALL PLANT LOCATION

Industry, despite its relative immobility, follows market shifts and changes in technology and economic conditions. It is particularly drawn to those areas in which labor and/or transportation costs are lowest and where the prospects for future growth are highest.

Because of high freight rates, for example, industry in general tends to seek its market. Thus as new population centers have sprung up (principally in the West and Southeast), the mass-production firms have established branch plants each of which is located in the center of its own regional market.

Naturally, the small manufacturer – whether oriented to the manufacture of producers' goods or of consumers' goods – in the long run is affected by the same conditions that promote or retard the growth of larger firms. Larger manufacturers have more experienced men at their disposal and a wider range of choice in selecting their locations. Their decisions may well serve as a guide for the small manufacturer.

Before attempting to analyze his particular business as to location requirements, the small manufacturer should be familiar with (1) the major factors to be considered in selecting a plant location, and (2) the available sources of information and assistance.

BASIC LOCATION FACTORS

Industrial plant location is a twofold problem. In which section of the country should the manufacturing enterprise be established? Should it be located in a community in a traditional industrial area such as New England or the Middle Atlantic region, or should it be located in a community in one of the relatively less industrialized areas, such as the South, West, or Southwest? In addition to selecting the *general geographic area* in which to locate the plant, as manifested in the choice of a community, the businessman is faced with the problem of selecting a *plant site* within or near the community. Different factors, or approaches to the problem, must be considered in making each of these plant location decisions.

Selecting the Area or Community

Regardless of the kind of manufacturing enterprise, the small businessman will consider each of the following basic factors in determining the region, state, or community in which he will operate his plant:

1. Nearness to market(s), including market trends
2. Nearness to suppliers
3. Labor supply and cost
4. Power supply and cost
5. State and local regulations and taxes
6. Transportation services and costs

By locating closer to its customers the small manufacturing firm can provide them with quicker service. Conversely, by locating closer to its sources of supply the small plant will receive quicker deliveries of raw materials and component parts. In addition, in each case, there is a lowering of freight cost. The manufacturer pays the cost of transporting the materials and other supplies it buys ("freight in") as well as the cost of transporting the finished goods it sells ("freight out"). Most freight rates are closely correlated with the value of the commodity that is shipped. Because of the "value added by manufacture," these rates are considerably higher for completely processed products (finished goods) than for raw materials and parts; that is, they can "bear" a higher tariff. For this reason, *most* manufacturers find it more economical to locate closer to their market than to their sources of supply. Industry in general, as previously noted, tends to seek its market.

The ideal situation, of course, is where the areas in which the plant's customers and suppliers are located overlap or coincide. Usually, however, they don't.

Freight rates vary with the mode of transportation as well as the value of the product. Of interest to most small manufacturers is the observation that for relatively short hauls (up to about 500 miles), truck transportation is more economical than rail transportation.

Another important factor in plant location, and particularly in smaller firms where there has been little or no development in automated processing, is labor supply and cost. Area wage rates vary considerably, and often this is the factor which tips the scale in favor of one community over another. The seasonal factor is an important consideration in both the supply and cost of labor, and the small businessman should acquaint himself with the activity and characteristics of prospective neighboring industries.

Though their requirements may vary considerably, all manufacturing enterprises need power to operate production machines. Therefore, the supply and cost of power is another common factor affecting plant location. However, with the recent development of electric power "grids" in many of the relatively less populated parts of the country, this has become less important.

State and local industrial regulations and taxes should also be considered in choosing the community in which to establish a manufacturing plant. A favorable attitude toward industry is increasingly being stressed by industrialists seeking plant locations, particularly since they usually have a choice of several communities which are more or less equally desirable from other points of view. The local attitude toward industry is reflected, in part at least, by the industrial regulations and taxes it imposes. Tax costs may also vary widely.

The above factors in plant location are *general* factors which should be considered in locating *any* type of manufacturing enterprise. In addition to these are other factors which may be of some importance in *particular* industries or situations. Water, for example, is necessary in the operation of a paper mill, where it is used in production processes and in transportation as well as a source of power. Before the advent of air conditioning, climate was important in certain types of processing, such as textiles, tobacco, and candy manufacture. It is still an important consideration in the location of airplane plants, where year round testing of the aircraft is a desired objective. Certain locations may have advertising value for firms in certain industries, such as Grand Rapids for furniture or California for pottery. Local tax concessions and other inducements, such as a free site, might also have a bearing in the plant location decision in individual cases. Personal factors often influence the decision, particularly among small plant owners.

It is obvious that a community may rate high on some factors, and low on others. Also, many of the factors interact and cannot be considered in isolation. Ignoring personal and other intangible considerations, the decision rule is this: *select that location at which the combined cost of production and distribution is at a minimum.*[1]

Selecting the Plant Site

After the community is selected, the next step is to select the site on which to construct the plant. This site may be within the corporate limits of the community, or it may be a suburban location. Among the factors considered in making this decision are the following:

1. Land (and assessment) values
2. Property taxes
3. Room for expansion and for employee parking
4. Contour of the ground, or shape of the plot

[1] An analytical technique for determining this is presented in a later section of this chapter.

5. Disposal of waste

6. Utilities and public improvements, such as water, sewer, gas, and electric connections; paving, gutters, and sidewalks; and street lighting

7. Building restrictions or codes (zoning)

8. Trackage and shipping facilities, or highway access

The above factors in selecting a plant site are self-explanatory and merit no detailed discussion. In connection with this aspect of plant location, we wish to cite particularly the present trend toward *suburban* locations. The suburbs of a large city provide practically all the advantages of the city with relatively few of its disadvantages. For example, in-town traffic congestion, lack of parking space, the scarcity and high cost of land, and high taxes have caused many manufacturing firms to "bypass" large-city locations. On the other hand, the suburban plant is close to suppliers and service industries.

It is obvious from the discussion on the preceding pages that a tremendous amount of information needs to be obtained and correlated if the small manufacturer is to select the most advantageous location for his plant. The National Industrial Conference Board has prepared a summary of the sources from which various types of information may be obtained. It is reproduced in Table 9-1.

AGENCIES ASSISTING IN PLANT LOCATION

Nearly all states, and many cities, in both industrial and nonindustrial areas, have established agencies to assist industries seeking new locations as well as communities seeking new industries. These may be government agencies, such as the Department of Commerce of New York State; state and local Chambers of Commerce or other businessmen's associations; or special agencies established for this purpose, such as the various industrial commissions and planning boards. In recent years there has been a pronounced trend for the less industrialized areas of the country, both states and communities, to establish agencies and seek aggressively to promote industrialization of their localities.

There are three typical situations where such agencies aid industry in finding desirable locations: local concerns seeking to expand, out-of-state companies looking for sites for branch plants, and local individuals wishing to start new factories. Types of agencies to be considered may be grouped into five classes: (1) state and local governments, (2) federal government, (3) community financial organizations, (4) commercial services, and (5) public utilities.

State and Local Government Agencies

Most states have a Planning and Resources Board, State Planning Commission, Department of Commerce and Industry, Industrial Development Commission, or similar agency. State agencies vary in the scope and nature of their activities, but in general they serve as liaison between local communities in the state and persons seeking information, whether for travel, plant location purposes, or other reasons.

Table 9-1   Summary of Information Sources for Plant Location

Community

General infor- Bankers
mation about Chamber of Commerce
attitude, ser- Customers in locality
vices, type of Industrial associations
community, Industrial real-estate firms
etc. Libraries
Manufacturers
Merchants
Municipal officials
Newspapers
Railroads
Real estate brokers
State, local development
agencies
Utilities

Construction Costs

Architects
Contractors
Manufacturers
Trade paper indexes

Electricity

Availability Chamber of Commerce
and rates Edison Electric Institute
State, local development
agencies
U.S. Department of
Commerce
Utilities

Gas

Availability American Gas Association
and rates Chamber of Commerce
State, local development
agencies
Utility

Housing

Availability Civic officials
Newspapers
Real estate brokers
State, local development
agencies

Industries in Area

Customers
"Editor and Publisher
Market Guide"
Industrial associations
Municipal publications
State, local development
agencies

Area Labor Situation

Availability Chamber of Commerce
and skills Industrial associations
Manufacturers
Municipal authorities
State, local development
agencies
State employment service
office

Bonus and Manufacturers
fringe benefit Unions
practices

Union con- Manufacturers
tracts Unions

Wage levels "Help wanted" ads
Manufacturers

Markets

Present cus- Sales records
tomers' loca-
tion, volume,
type of prod-
uct

Growth poten- Company forecasts, sales-
tial of individ- men, customers
ual markets Studies by:
(present custo- Advertising agencies
mers, possibil- Chamber of Commerce
ity of opening State, local develop-
new markets) ment agencies

Transportation Carriers serving area
costs to cus-
tomers

Table 9-1   (cont.)

Effects of new plant on marketing areas of existing plants	Sales records	**Taxes** (cont.)	
			State, local development agencies
			Tax assessors
			Tax attorneys
Site			
Availability	Railroad development department	**Transportation**	
	Real estate brokers	*Freight rates, schedules, services*	Carriers serving area
Flood history	City and Army engineers		
	U.S. Geodetic Survey maps	*Railroad sidings*	Carriers serving area
Options	Real estate brokers		
Price	Real estate brokers	**Water Supply**	
Title	Legal assistance	*Availability*	City engineers
Zoning	Municipal authorities		Fire insurance carriers
	Real estate brokers		State, local development agencies
			U.S. Department of Interior
Taxes			Utility
Local and state	Industrialists		
	Municipal officials	*Rates*	Utility

Source: "Highlights for Executives," *Techniques of Plant Location,* Studies in Business Policy No. 61 (New York: National Industrial Conference Board, 1953), p. 2.

Usually material descriptive of the state is published and sent on request. Many maintain files of industrial prospects for use by local communities, and refer certain types of inquiries to appropriate city agencies. Although the aids rendered by state and city agencies vary widely, this source is usually a good starting point in seeking information about a particular part of the country.

A liaison office, such as the agencies under discussion, needs information about communities within the state that are seeking new industries as well as data on the requirements and preferences of industries seeking sites. Information of the former type consists of complete lists of all available buildings and industrial sites, and data on basic industrial location factors. Most state and community agencies make surveys to discover available buildings and sites and relevant information about each, such as area, rental, type of building, and equipment.

It is the larger manufacturer seeking to locate branch plants, however, who is most likely to utilize the services of these state and local agencies. Relatively few requests for information or assistance are received from the prospective small manufacturer. Agency executives cite at least three reasons for this: (1) individuals seeking to enter manufacturing on a small scale are not well informed about the services available through state and local industrial development agencies; (2) many such factories are started in the home community, where the need for location advice is not felt; and (3) sometimes the principal need is for financial assistance.

A recent survey by the authors of the types of public aid available to the industrialist trying to locate a plant indicated that: (1) 43 states allow municipalities to issue bonds, either full faith or revenue, for erection of new or expanded plants; (2) 36 states have development credit corporations employing private capital; (3) 17 states allow temporary local property tax exemptions; (4) 24 states have tax-supported industrial development commissions or agencies that help bring plants to the community, and (5) 21 states either make direct loans or guarantee private loans for the construction of new plants.

Federal Government Agencies

Agencies of the federal government include the Economic Development Administration of the U.S. Department of Commerce, and the Small Business Administration. In addition, relevant data are published by the Census Bureau, Office of Business Economics of the Department of Commerce, Bureau of Labor Statistics, and other federal agencies. In most cases the prospective owner of a small manufacturing plant should seek advice from an appropriate office of the Department of Commerce or Small Business Administration.

Community Financial Organizations

Community financial organizations are of three main types: (1) private venture-capital companies, (2) industrial funds or foundations, and (3) credit pools. The first is concerned with new firms that show promise for the development of radically new products or processes, and would not be of help in locating or financing existing enterprises. Community industrial foundations have engaged in the purchase, development, and sale or lease of industrial sites and buildings. The foundations have also made loans to or purchased the securities of firms in the area and have when necessary offered management and technical information. Somewhat similar to the community industrial fund has been the growth of development credit corporations. During recent years they have been established in all but 14 of the states. Frequently, after a thorough investigation by a development credit corporation, financial institutions which are not members of the organization either assume the entire loan or agree to participate. Although referred to here as financial organizations, the primary purpose of the industrial funds, development credit corporations and credit pools is to encourage industries to locate in the state or community.

Especially in the little-industrialized towns, however, there has been some tendency to use the funds of these organizations to assist only established out-of-state industries in setting up branch plants. In other situations funds are available to buy sites, construct buildings, or do other things needed by a new industry that is suited to the community, especially when it will complement already established industries, regardless of whether the organizers are local individuals or out-of-state concerns.

The prevailing attitude toward local financial assistance was aptly expressed in a letter to the authors by an official of a state Chamber of Commerce as follows:

In matters of financial assistance to a prospective industry we insist that all arrangements be based on sound business policy. We do not encourage any plan which involves "something for nothing." We always insist that the current interest rate be paid by the prospect for private funds invested by local citizens in constructing a plant. Local citizens are advised by us to do all possible to keep costs down and many services are rendered by them without cost during the construction period. Good co-operation and a friendly welcome is far more valuable to all concerned than free land and free rent.

Commercial Services

The major commercial services to consider in selecting a plant are real estate brokers and developers of industrial properties, industrial or management consultants, and those specializing in plant locations, such as the Fantus Factory Locating Service. Certain architectural engineering or factory construction firms could also be included in this group, as many aid in securing locations as well as provide construction services. For most beginners a reliable broker experienced in factory locations would probably be the logical choice.

Public Utilities

Two major types of public utilities have been active in assisting with factory locations: railroads and power or fuel companies. In both groups assistance is naturally restricted to the areas served by the companies offering aid.

ANALYSIS OF INDIVIDUAL REQUIREMENTS

When the small manufacturer has become familiar with the basic location factors and available sources of information and assistance, his next step should be to analyze his particular business as to location requirements. His choice of region or community will be limited to those suitable to the nature of his concern. Otherwise he will weigh the relative importance of each basic factor and select the community most advantageous from the standpoint of personal preferences and future prospects. The personal aspect is the one outstanding difference between plant location for the average small factory as contrasted with the large concern. For industries in the "footloose" category, it may be the only consideration for the small businessman as far as his choice of a particular region or community is concerned.

In most cases of small plant location where personal factors are not of great importance there will be some choice as to size of the city and character of the area. The small manufacturer may choose between industrial or agricultural regions, mature or expanding regions, and central city or suburban locations. Since we have eliminated personal factors, preference should be given to the newer, expanding areas, and suburban rather than central locations. If other factors are the same, the small manufacturer should weigh carefully certain advantages of locating in agricultural rather than industrial regions.

Of interest to the small businessman are two important aspects favoring rural locations. The first relates to cost. Not only is labor more loyal, dependable, and of lower unit cost (in spite of the manufacturer paying well above prevailing local wage rates), but other costs, with the possible exception of transportation costs, are also lower. Since his product is in price competition with other products, whether of the same type or not, lower total unit costs are especially important. This is particularly true during the "small" stage, when volume of output is not large and a greater margin per unit is required for satisfactory total profits.

The second aspect relates to the possible effects of future industrial development of the community. If the product manufactured can be sold locally, the industrialization and growing demand occurring in some agricultural communities is an advantage. If the market is widely but thinly distributed over the country, however, a rapid industrial expansion of the community in which the factory is located may become an economic disadvantage by increasing total production costs per unit.

Selection of a site for the small factory within a city will be governed by the same factors that apply to larger industries: comparative cost of rent or construction, accessibility of inter- and intracity transportation, parking facilities and accessibility for workers, zoning regulations, and similar considerations. Only to the extent that the small concern may require less land, a small work force, and other factors on a smaller scale will the import of these be significantly different.

An illustration.   The Acorn Company is planning to construct a new plant to meet the increased demand for its products. The company is considering building the plant in either community A or community B, located in different states.

Due to differential wage rates in the two communities in the building trades, construction costs would be approximately 10 percent higher in community B than in community A. It is estimated that it would cost about $500,000 to build the plant in community A. The plant would have an estimated useful life of 40 years.

Site costs would also be higher in community B. The desired site in community B would cost $20,000. The cost of a desirable site of equal size in community A would be $15,000.

Local property taxes in the two areas are approximately equal, but on the basis of the company's average annual profit in the past the company's state income tax liability is estimated at $10,000 per year in community B, or approximately $5,000 lower than the estimated state income tax in community A.

A particular advantage in locating in community B would be an annual estimated savings of $50,000 in shipping the company's goods to its numerous retail outlets. The total outgoing freight charges from community A are estimated at $90,000. On the other hand, since community A is located nearer the company's sources of raw material supply, annual incoming freight charges at this location are estimated at only $10,000 per year, or $20,000 less than similar costs at community B.

Labor costs would vary somewhat, the estimated $110,000 annual labor cost in community B being 10 percent higher than in community A. Indirect labor typically accounts for about 20 percent of the total labor cost in the Acorn Company.

Supervisory costs are also 10 percent higher in community B, where they are expected to total $11,000 annually.

The costs cited above are the only ones which vary by location; administrative and other operating costs will be the same regardless of location. On the basis of this information, and assuming an annual interest rate of 6 percent, where should the Acorn Company locate its new plant?

The following tabulation is a comparison of all annual operating costs affected by location, and indicates that the combined costs of production and distribution would be lower if the plant were located in community B:

Average Annual Operating Expenses Affected by Location

	Community A	Community B
Depreciation on building	$ 12,500	$ 13,750
Interest on *average* investment in building	15,000	16,500
Interest on investment in land	900	1,200
State income tax	15,000	10,000
Outgoing freight	90,000	40,000
Incoming freight	10,000	30,000
Direct labor	80,000	88,000
Indirect labor	20,000	22,000
Supervisory costs	10,000	11,000
	$253,400	$232,450

The cost calculations in the tabulation are self-explanatory, except perhaps for the handling of the interest costs on investment. Here, we wish to point out that depreciation is a form of "capital recovery" to the plant owner, since it is included in the price that the manufacturer receives for his product. Therefore, the manufacturer's investment in the asset becomes progressively smaller over the period of depreciation. Where the *straight-line* method of depreciation is used (as is commonly the case in calculating the depreciation on buildings), the average investment is always *one-half* the original investment. Since land does not depreciate, that is, does not waste away physically, the manufacturer's investment in this asset remains the *same* for each year he holds the asset.

The difference of $20,950 in annual operating expense in favor of one community over another is sufficiently large that in most plant location decisions it would probably outweigh personal and other intangible considerations. Where the cost differential is small the latter factors loom more important, particularly among small, independent plant owners.

SUMMARY AND CONCLUSIONS

A factory location usually represents a relatively immobile heavy fixed investment. Consequently, selection of the region and community should be made with a long-range viewpoint. Even substantial inducements offered by local development groups should be appraised against the likelihood of their permanence and the future growth probabilities of the community.

Locating a small plant differs from locating retail and service establishments chiefly in the much greater importance of the region and town rather than the site within a community. Personal considerations are, however, as important in factory as in other small business location decisions.

The prospective small manufacturer should familiarize himself with the numerous agencies available for assistance in selecting a location, should study carefully the basic location factors and how each of these may vary in importance for different cases, and should then analyze his own needs and weigh the relative importance of each factor before making a final decision.

REVIEW QUESTIONS

1. Why are long-range considerations more important in the location of factories than in the location of merchandising or service establishments?
2. What major factors do industrialists nearly always consider in selecting a town in which to locate? Why is each so important?
3. What additional factors may be of some importance in some industries? Give some examples.
4. What is the decision rule for selecting the best location for a plant?
5. What factors influence the selection of a factory site?
6. How do you account for the current trend toward suburban locations for industrial plants?
7. What kinds of information are needed for an analysis of alternate communities and plant sites?
8. Classify the groups of agencies available for assistance to a manufacturer seeking a location for his plant. Give examples of each.
9. Why are large companies seeking to locate branch plants more active in securing assistance from agencies offering help than are most beginners?
10. Why do industrial foundations and credit pools render aid in locating business enterprises?

DISCUSSION QUESTIONS

1. Should an industry long established in one town be permitted to migrate to another region mainly to secure lower labor costs? Discuss.
2. Bill has perfected an economical converter for a car to permit use of 12-volt accessories on a 6-volt battery or generator, and vice versa. He expects five years of active sales, during which time he plans to develop other auto accessories. He is considering locating his plant either near his home in Oklahoma City or near Detroit. Which factors should he weigh most heavily? Which location would be better, and why?

SUPPLEMENTARY READINGS

Journal of Small Business Management 10 (Jan. 1972). This issue is devoted
   exclusively to problems of business location. Among the articles of particular
   interest to small industrial plants are the following: "The Small Manufacturer's Guide to Plant Location Services" (pp. 5 ff.) and "Space for Small
   Industrial Business in Older Central Cities" (pp. 11 ff.).

Kinnard, William N., Jr., and Zenon S. Malinowski. *Highways as a Factor in Small
   Manufacturing Plant Location Decisions.* Small Business Management Research Report prepared for the Small Business Administration. Storrs:
   University of Connecticut, 1962. The purpose of this study was to determine
   the influence and significance of existing highway systems on location
   decisions by small manufacturers. Reasons for site selection, taking into
   consideration highway access, are analyzed.

Malinowski, Zenon S., and William N. Kinnard, Jr. *The Place of Small Business in
   Planned Industrial Districts.* Small Business Management Research Report
   prepared for the Small Business Administration. Storrs: University of
   Connecticut, 1963. A survey of 271 industrial parks with particular emphasis
   on the availability of such sites to small manufacturers. Discusses formation
   and control, operation, rental costs, and characteristics of occupants.

Thompson, James H. *Methods of Plant Site Selection Available to Small
   Manufacturing Firms.* Small Business Management Research Report prepared
   for the Small Business Administration. Morgantown: West Virginia University, 1961. An analysis of the various techniques commonly applied to site
   selection. Covers the experiences of small firms of many different types.

10

Providing
physical facilities

A good building effectively used is as valuable to an operating plant as are good home facilities for a household. As with any other asset in business, such as money, personnel, equipment, or materials, the building housing the operation can be poorly selected or poorly utilized. The degree to which it is properly selected and used is often a major factor in determining the amount of return on the entrepreneur's expenditure of time, effort, and money.

ADAPTING THE BUILDING

The building should lend itself to activities that are of greatest importance in the particular business enterprise. Four major considerations are: (1) function; (2) construction; (3) appearance; and (4) lighting, color, and air-conditioning.

Function

So far as function is concerned, the building should be evaluated from the point of view of (1) suitability for its intended use, (2) accessibility, (3) internal transportation or traffic, and (4) layout.

A building is good or bad in direct proportion to its suitability to the activities that must be performed. Excellent housing for one business may be next to impossible for use by some other business. Simple protection from the elements and from burglary may be sufficient for many lines of retailing, whereas heavy construction and solid concrete floors might be required for certain manufacturing or service industries.

Accessibility requirements vary by kind of business. In retailing, customer accessibility is of greatest importance, but adequate facilities for receiving merchandise and making deliveries should be provided. In manufacturing, easy receipt of raw materials and shipment of finished product are dominant considerations. Service industries usually require accessibility for customers or clients and often also require easy access for delivery equipment. Accessibility to a retail store building is hampered by steps, a narrow entrance, or any type of obstruction, such as a post. Steps represent an accident hazard as well as an obstacle to customer traffic. A nonskid ramp may be the best solution if no way can be found to eliminate differences in elevation.

Receipt of goods may be difficult if there is no door to an alley or if goods must be unloaded from a heavy-traffic lane without an offset for trucks. Delivery through the main customer entrance is most undesirable. Where merchandise traffic is heavy, unloading platforms at truck level are useful; gravity chutes may be used if the receiving room is below ground level. Recently, portable roller chutes have come into use.

Closely related to external accessibility is the question of internal transportation and traffic facilities provided by the building. Movement of materials is particularly important in manufacturing. Retail stores naturally wish customer traffic to be unhindered by columns, different floor levels, irregularly shaped buildings, and similar conditions. Movement of merchandise within the store may be important for items like furniture, heavy appliances, or especially bulky containers. In service and manufacturing establishments the nature of the process largely determines the importance as well as the type of internal transportation facilities. A beauty parlor and a job type of machine shop obviously have very different requirements.

The flow of materials or the movement of customers or employees is directly related to layout; both must be considered together. The basic purpose behind physical plant layout is to integrate men, materials, and equipment so as to move material as easily as possible over the shortest distance or to attract customers to the merchandise or service offered for sale. Either of these objectives can be accomplished by providing a natural sequence of operations, in a safe manner and in a pleasant atmosphere. The achievement of these objectives should result in a lower cost of operation.

Good layout often depends upon the nature of the building. At one extreme is the industry that almost requires a specially constructed building; at the other is the type of business for which any strategically located building is suitable. An example of the former might be a machine shop; of the latter, the typical small retail store. Building layout will be developed in greater detail later in this chapter.

Construction

Our primary concern here is for the safety of customers and employees. Condition of the roof, foundation, supporting columns, and floors should be investigated, especially in the case of older buildings.

Architecture or building design should also receive attention when a building is appraised. Modern design is more functional and less ornate than traditional architecture. It permits remodeling to secure a greater amount of glass for light and ventilation, or the removal of supporting columns that obstruct internal movement or visibility. Load-bearing walls used in older buildings make certain types of remodeling difficult and constitute a hazard in case of fire. Modern design also develops a favorable corporate image among prospects and customers. However, wonders have been accomplished in modernizing many old buildings. It is not so much the age of a building as the feasibility of remodeling it that is important.

Naturally the tenant will want the landlord to bear the cost of modernization or other structural changes required to make the building suitable, and very often this can be arranged.

Improvements in construction materials are constantly being made, particularly in floor coverings. Terrazzo, asphaltic tile, inlaid linoleum, hardwood or composition blocks, and special waterproof, rubber-base, and antiskid paints are examples of fairly recent developments. Floors should be selected with their intended use in mind. Reinforced concrete floors reduce vibration and are ideal for heavy warehouses; resilient materials increase employee and customer comfort; nonslippery surfaces reduce accident hazards; some materials are resistant to special chemicals or unusual wear; and others are attractive and particularly suitable for lighting requirements. Areas visited by customers may have sales promoting features, guide lines, trademarks, or "atmosphere" inlaid in the floor.

Will the building permit expansion or alterations that may be needed later? Is it flexible enough to be adapted to other possible uses? Potential growth and changes in the proposed business during the term of the lease and possibly for the next five to ten years should be considered. Will the occupant want to add new departments? Where can they be housed? If one is starting a service business and may contemplate adding retail sales later, is the building, as well as its location, suitable? Is the area or space such that he can use it economically? What about subleasing part of the building now in order to have it available later for expansion? Is extra space that can be used effectively during dull seasons available for recurring peaks of selling, storage, or processing? These are some of the many questions that should be investigated before a final decision is made, and many of them should be provided for in the lease.

Appearance

The external appearance of the building is important in many ways. In the capacity of an advertising medium it should represent the character of the business, identifying it and at the same time distinguishing it from others. Some attempts to make the building represent the character of the business take extreme forms such as the massive columns and thick marble walls, floors, and fixtures of many bank buildings. A building of this kind may become a white elephant if the bank moves to different quarters and the building cannot be converted to other uses. However, modern architecture can achieve the desired impression of safety, stability, permanence, and dignity by less expensive means. Even the store front may present the character of a business, the luxurious front of the exclusive shop being contrasted to the practical, economical appearance of the popular-price store.

The building, including the front, may distinguish a particular business merely by being different, yet fashionable, or by attempting to visualize the nature of the business or its name. The Brown Derby in Hollywood is an example. For the small businessman entering a line of business in which such novel treatment of the appearance of the building is neither too costly nor too permanent, it may be an effective way of capturing and holding the interest of potential customers. If successful, the design may be patented and serve as the basis for granting franchises, as was the case with Clarence Saunder's unusual Piggly Wiggly store fronts, or it may be used if one decides to open additional stores of a similar nature. Often this idea of the theme of the business is carried out for the interior. A luggage shop in Little Rock, Arkansas, for example, was constructed in the form of a Pullman car. Unless watched carefully, however, these attempts to visualize the nature of the business may result in a single-purpose structure which can be adapted to other uses only at great cost.

Lighting, Color, and Air-Conditioning

Other aspects of building modernization include lighting, color, and air-conditioning. Modern lighting is both functional and decorative. Artificial light must be not only of sufficient intensity, but it must be uniform and properly diffused. Light which is properly diffused is light which causes no glare, either directly or through reflection. If light is uniform throughout the store or work area, there will be no marked shadows or sharp contrasts.[1]

Another requirement of good lighting is the "quality" of the light. Different types of lamps have different lighting qualities. Mercury-vapor light, for example, contains no red rays which cause glare. The absence of red glare, together with the bluish cast of the light, also results in a clearer definition of surface – a prime consideration in many factory operations. However, this type of light distorts colors. Where accurate color determination is important (as in purchasing a new suit at a men's store), tungsten-filament lamps are recommended. Because they generate less heat, fluorescent lamps are becoming more popular. Local public utilities can give the small businessman good advice on proper lighting.

Color-conditioning implies that the effects upon people produced by the colors of walls, ceilings, floors, fixtures, and even merchandise may be controlled to secure desired effects. In general the trend is toward lighter (pastel) colors, because they usually are more pleasing as well as more economical in light-reflecting ability. Warmth can be simulated, if desired, by the use of warm colors of the red and yellow varieties. Apparent size can be increased through the use of receding colors like white or decreased by use of advancing colors. Although blue ranks higher in abstract color preference, each color should be used to accomplish the particular result desired.

Air-conditioning has become a virtual necessity in retail stores located in warm climates and has increased worker efficiency in many plants. It is now expanding to include odor-conditioning. Not only are temperature and humidity being controlled, but often pleasant or even sales-stimulating odors are provided.

THE STORE BUILDING – SPECIAL REQUIREMENTS

Most of what has been said about the appearance and interior of buildings probably applies to retailing to a greater extent than to other kinds of business. A retail store should be attractive and inviting to customers. Colors of walls, background, and fixtures should be selected to set particular kinds of merchandise off to greatest advantage. In this regard, lighting should be used as a silent salesman.

---

[1] There should be some contrast or shadow, however, for the perception of third dimension. Entirely shadowless objects appear flat.

The store front, especially the windows and entrance, should be designed with care to be in keeping with the type of merchandise sold and the style of retail architecture prevalent in the community. Although the general trend is toward the all-glass front, this is not suitable in all cases. Paint, furniture, food, and wearing-apparel stores may use this type of front to advantage, but jewelry stores and others dealing in small items may find the traditional window more desirable. Valuable help may be secured from trade associations and from equipment manufacturers and store-front engineering firms.

THE FACTORY BUILDING – SPECIAL REQUIREMENTS

In the case of buildings for small factories and for the processing type of service establishments, requirements center around the nature of work processes and the types of machinery and equipment to be used. Adequate provisions for the economical installation of necessary piping, ventilating equipment, foundations for heavy machines, and similar requirements will vary according to the nature of the business. The trend is toward the rectangular rather than the U- or L-shaped building and toward single-story structures if ground values permit. Other building requirements are related to layout or to the arrangement of machinery and other equipment, and are discussed below.

Although little has been written about the small factory, many companies have constructed decentralized branch plants throughout the country. Most of these would be considered small businesses if they were independently owned and operated. A personal inspection of these buildings in any area should provide a wealth of ideas on modern small factory building design.

THE SERVICE BUILDING – SPECIAL REQUIREMENTS

Service businesses are so diverse in nature that building requirements vary greatly. Certain consulting and other personal services may require nothing more than facilities for a telephone, desk, chair, and filing equipment. Personal services like beauty shops require an attractive, comfortable interior arrangement and provisions for adequate electric power and plumbing, as well as rest rooms for patrons and display space for the promotion of merchandise and services for sale.

The principal factor in determining service building requirements is whether the service is predominantly of the merchandising or the processing type. Many service establishments sell enough merchandise to make provisions for adequate display, stockkeeping, and selling space important considerations. Examples of such service include shops that repair electrical appliances, radios, refrigerators, watches, and similar articles. Often shops such as these will need a building wired for heavy-duty electrical equipment.

Another group of service businesses with special plant requirements is composed of those working with heavy, bulky materials or products. Examples include automobile, truck, and tractor repair shops and storage places, and sheet metal and heavy machine shops. In general a single-story building without basement is preferable for such establishments. Large open spaces free of supporting columns and heavy, level, nonsagging concrete floors are also important. The latter may be essential for accurate welding and other operations commonly performed in sheet metal shops. The industrial, rather than commercial, type of building has many advantages for such shops. Exposed steel ceiling beams may be used for the suspension of hoisting and monorail overhead crane equipment. Steel columns may serve similarly for jib cranes and strong walls for supporting storage racks. Wide aisles and entrances are needed to accommodate delivery trucks as well as vehicles to be repaired. Frequently special facilities for ventilation may be necessary. Safety codes governing ventilation, exits, fire walls, floor loads, and similar conditions may introduce unusual building requirements.

Gasoline service stations will have some of the special requirements already discussed and in addition will need facilities for petroleum storage tanks, a hydraulic car lift or grease pit, and an appropriate exterior appearance to attract motorists. Floors and service areas should be easily cleaned and resistant to grease, oil, gasoline, and other chemicals. Other types of service businesses that require work areas resistant to certain chemicals and fumes are battery repair shops, photoengraving plants, and electroplating firms.

ARRANGING THE LAYOUT

Layout deals with the arrangement of machines, fixtures, and other equipment, *according to a plan*. A distinction must be made between "making" a layout and "planning" a layout. Too often machines are moved without a plan. Because of this it is important that qualified industrial engineers and retail executives supervise major layout revisions. Retailers can often turn to their equipment manufacturer or supplier, their wholesaler, or their franchiser for assistance. In most of the retail and many of the service fields, trade associations have developed model layouts best suited to the needs of the particular business. Consulting firms also supply helpful advice concerning layouts for all kinds of businesses.

The best layout is the one which makes the most effective use of space for the particular business. The principal factor here is not area or volume, but *location*. The same area or volume in one part of a store, for example, may be worth many times more than an equal area or volume in another part of the same store.

Layout starts with an analysis of the activities involved in operating the business, the objectives sought, and the facilities for achieving them. In manufacturing and in many service businesses the primary objective is to facilitate productive operations. In the retail store it is to direct the flow of customer traffic for maximum sales.

Certain factors must always be considered in arrangement and layout. They are:

1. *Logical and optimum psychological arrangement of equipment and merchandise with reference to production flow for manufacturing and to customer buying habits for merchandising.* Having machinery in proper sequence and conveniently located expedites the flow of material and saves factory workers much lost motion. Also, having merchandise in the right place at the right time increases sales per customer and reduces steps for salespeople.

2. *Maximum use of light, ventilation, and heat, to take full advantage of natural conditions resulting from the building construction.* Effective use of windows, doors, vents, and skylights will save eyes, improve work and health, and reduce the costs of lighting, heating and air-conditioning. Customers will also appreciate the fact that arrangements made with these factors in mind facilitate their personal comfort and their selection of proper merchandise.

3. *Maximum efficiency in the use of equipment.* Improper location of equipment may cause workers to do entirely by hand work that should be done by existing equipment. If the machine for putting "the finishing touch" on the final processing or packaging of goods requires extra steps, for example, employees may tend to do this work manually or to avoid it entirely.

4. *Location of materials or merchandise in such a way as to be readily available to workers or customers.* By thus reducing steps for workers and reminding customers of their needs, an orderly arrangement saves workers' time in locating materials and permits customers to study and handle the merchandise.

5. *Maximum facilities for a clear view of the establishment by management, worker, or customer.* Thus management can readily observe all activities of customers and employees, workers can observe customers' presence and movements, and customers can readily see all the store's offerings and the location of particular groups of merchandise.

The same principles of layout apply to various types of businesses, since the following factors are always present:

1. *People* — workers, customers, management
2. *Equipment* — machinery or fixtures
3. *Goods* — materials, merchandise, or supplies
4. *The building and its features* — windows, doors, stairs, and so forth

To summarize, layout for any kind of business — merchandising, manufacturing, or service — involves the arrangement of equipment, machines, and other elements to secure maximum efficiency in use. The relative importance of meeting the needs of customers, workers, and management varies according to the type of business, but must be considered in planning the layout.

Store Layout

The retailer has three objectives for his layout: customer satisfaction (through convenience, service, and attractive appearance); maximum sales (by proper selection of fixtures and arrangement of merchandise); and economy of operation. Influencing this layout are a number of factors.

Stores vary in the relative amount of business secured from telephone orders and from customers who visit the store. Telephone orders demand the same efficiency required by a manufacturer in his layout, usually the process type of layout.[2] Where most of the sales are made on the premises, a selling rather than an efficiency type of layout is suggested. The amount of self-service compared to clerk service also influences store layout.

[2] See the discussion of manufacturing layout, pp. 188-95.

Space locations within a store can be used more effectively in some ways than in others. It is usually poor business to try to increase the volume of a slow-selling department by giving it one of the better locations when this requires shifting another department better able to take full advantage of the good location.

The diagram in Figure 10-1 shows an approximate distribution of the total rent or value of space in a small store according to location on the main floor when the store has only one entrance. When a one-floor store has entrances on two or more sides, such as the front and rear or front and one side, the relative amount of traffic through each door is the important consideration. In such cases the diagram can be used to indicate the relative value of space inward from each entrance reflecting the differences in traffic volume.

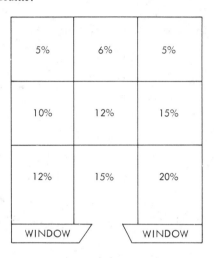

Figure 10-1.   Plot of Sales Floor Values

It is the space nearest the traffic flow, and which therefore offers the greatest exposure to customers, which has the greatest sales potential. Thus the value of space in a retail store decreases as one moves from the front of the store to the rear. Some authorities use a straight-line approach, or the "4-3-2-1 rule," in measuring this decline in space value. This approach is illustrated and explained in Figure 10-2.

It is observed that a roughly straight-line approach was used in estimating the floor space values in Figure 10-1. It was also assumed in Figure 10-1 that the space toward the right, as one enters the store, is more valuable than the space at the left. The rationale for this is explained by Professor Aspinwall as follows:

> Customers moving in and out of your front door behave just about as do people on the street. Those who know what they want try to go directly to that item. People with no specific items in mind move from place to place as their interest is caught by goods on display. These two types of traffic are known as *destination* traffic and *shopping* traffic.
>
> Destination customers tend to move in a logical, thought-out sequence. Shopping customers, taking a largely random approach, almost always *turn to the right* after they enter your front door. Destination traffic generally will not drift to the right, because of

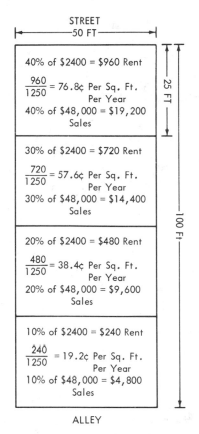

STREET

|←———50 FT———→|

40% of $2400 = $960 Rent

$\frac{960}{1250}$ = 76.8¢ Per Sq. Ft. Per Year

40% of $48,000 = $19,200 Sales

25 FT

30% of $2400 = $720 Rent

$\frac{720}{1250}$ = 57.6¢ Per Sq. Ft. Per Year

30% of $48,000 = $14,400 Sales

100 Ft

20% of $2400 = $480 Rent

$\frac{480}{1250}$ = 38.4¢ Per Sq. Ft. Per Year

20% of $48,000 = $9,600 Sales

10% of $2400 = $240 Rent

$\frac{240}{1250}$ = 19.2¢ Per Sq. Ft. Per Year

10% of $48,000 = $4,800 Sales

ALLEY

The rent contracted by lease is $2400. per year. Therefore 5000 square feet divided into $2400 = 48¢ per year. This is the average rent per square foot per year for the whole store.

Under the 4-3-2-1 rule, 40% of the total rent is assigned to the front 1/4 of the space; 30% of the total rent is assigned to the second 1/4 of the space; 20% of the total rent is assigned to the third 1/4 of the space, and 10% is assigned to the rear 1/4 of the space.

Typical rent or occupancy cost for a drug store is 5% of sales; so that $2400 = 5% of sales, and 1% = $480, and 100% = $48,000 total sales.

Figure 10-2.   The "4-3-2-1 Rule" in Estimating Sales Floor Values

the slower and unpredictable movements of the shoppers. Instead, these customers *usually turn left* upon entering a store. As a result, shopping traffic tends to circulate through a store in a counter-clockwise direction, while destination traffic moves clockwise. Recognition of this movement provides a key to the layout of goods not only near the door but also within the entire selling space.

Goods with low gross margins and high replacement rates should be located . . . to the left of the entrance. This location will afford destination customers immediate access to the staples they buy frequently. It will help them complete their purchases quickly. In contrast, the high gross margin items with low replacement rates should be arranged on the right. When this is done, these goods are seen by the bulk of the shopping traffic; as a result, sales of these items tend to increase.[3]

Whether the owner plans to make his own final layout or to call on the assistance of a management consultant or other "outside staff" source, he should make a tentative layout of his own as carefully as possible. First, he should make a

[3] Leo V. Aspinwall, "Are Your Merchandise Lines Paying Their Rent?" *Small Marketers Aids Annual No. 3* (Washington, D.C.: Small Business Administration, 1961), pp. 8–9.

drawing of the floor space to scale and divide it into areas as indicated in Figure 10-1, noting the percentage value of each area in relation to sales potentials. Then he should list the space needs, and evaluate each in terms of several factors, such as the performance of essential nonselling functions, the ability to capitalize fully on heavy customer traffic through impulse sales, the ability to draw customers to remote sections of the store, and miscellaneous factors such as employee conveniences and nearness to other activities.

A preliminary step is to separate selling from nonselling activities. Nonselling work is in turn divided into essential store activities like officework, receiving and storing goods, display construction, and "customer bait" like telephones, package checking, and postal substations. Facilitating activities may be assigned the least desirable locations from a traffic viewpoint. Customer service departments will be strategically located to lure customers past tempting displays of impulse goods.

Selection and arrangement of fixtures and merchandise within any store building will be determined in part by the merchandise sold, the customers it seeks to serve, and the service it offers. As to fixtures, an exclusive shop selling but one kind of merchandise — apparel, furniture, or leather goods, for example — should possess an atmosphere of dignity, comfort, modernity, and perhaps even luxury. Stores selling primarily to men will need to present a rugged, masculine, "he-man," and businesslike atmosphere; those serving women will have "the feminine touch" characterized by carefully harmonized colors, decorative figures, and diffused lighting.

Another factor in arranging merchandise is to separate "impulse" goods from "demand" goods, that is, goods which are bought on sight without previous deliberation as opposed to those which customers have in mind when they go to a particular store. The druggist, for example, keeps patent medicines, hospital supplies, and his prescription department in the rear of the store. To get to these, the customer must pass many displays of impulse goods. The wise shoe store operator has his staple shoes in the rear; as the customer goes to them, he passes attractive hosiery, house slippers, and sundries such as shoestrings and shoepolish.

A question faced by many retailers is this: should the merchandise be arranged by price, by size, by line, or on some other basis? In the case of men's suits, arrangement by size seems to be the best plan, because the customer is not so likely to be attracted to a suit not available in his size, and the mixture of price lines more readily permits trading up by showing and selling better lines. Placing the same colors together might make a more expensive suit look drab in comparison with a cheaper suit of a brighter shade. Also, if a merchant has a large stock of one style in different colors and sizes, he should not put them all on display, for this makes the garment look "common" and the customer may feel that he would meet himself everywhere he went. The avoidance of large one-style displays is a rule that applies generally to all types of apparel. The problem of arranging merchandise may also arise in home furnishings, electrical appliances, paints, or shoes. Since shoes, for example, are stored in boxes, ease for the salesman in locating them is of major importance. In this connection it may be noted that, contrary to the common practice of keeping shoe stocks by lot number for convenience in reordering, one store found that keeping them by size saved salesmen many of the steps they had previously wasted in going from one lot number group to another looking for the size wanted.

There is an increasing trend toward an "open" arrangement of merchandise. The success of the Woolworth Company and other variety stores has been attributed to the use of open display. The modern department store, having discovered the value of spaciousness, puts it to use in wide aisles and low display cases. Most store owners agree with the findings of one study that indicated that open display in a drugstore doubled face powder sales, tripled soap sales, and increased candy sales over five times.

Some stores have found that having the wrapping desk in the rear draws people back, as they tend to follow the merchandise and the salesman as he moves in that direction. The value of this location, however, may be offset by the loss of the salesman's time in making the trip back that far for each sale.

Wrapping and cashiering facilities are often mislocated. They are usually together for employee convenience. As noted, they may be at the rear of the store to draw trade past other goods. Frequently, however, they comprise a rather bulky unit consisting of a large counter and a cash register. Many stores have found that facilities for the handling of cash sales may be arranged at strategic points in the store. Under this arrangement only larger items or those sold on credit and requiring credit approval will require wrapping and the use of the larger facilities, which may be placed in space at the rear that is less expensive from the traffic viewpoint.

Guiding traffic is helpful, and many devices are useful in managing this. Some stores, not fully relying on the "keep to the right" habit or perhaps wishing to counteract it, place obstacles in the way of customers in some paths and make wider entrances to others. A pile of boxes on display or a sizable showcase is an effective barrier to control traffic. People's tendency to act by habit and to follow the line of least resistance can be capitalized on by the alert merchant.

The manufacturers of store fixtures, recognizing the changing nature of merchandise and the desire of merchants to experiment, have for several years produced fixture units of such uniformity, mobility, and ready interchangeability that they permit various combinations. Although they are separate units, when properly placed they join together so readily as to appear to be one unit built to store specifications.

Layout in Wholesaling

Layout of the wholesale establishment is based on the primary function of the business: order filling. Optimum use should be made of the force of gravity, mechanical conveyors, and materials-handling equipment, since about 60 percent of the cost of operation is likely to be payroll. Often forward stocks (say six to ten days' supply) or a frequently purchased item can be arranged along a conveyor or order assembly line. Major functions like receiving, "dead" storage, order assembly, breaking packages, packing and shipping, and officework should be physically separated. An exception might be combining the receiving, packing, and shipping functions in the smaller plant. In general, the wholesale layout will resemble more closely that of a factory, and many good ideas can be adapted from factory layouts.

Most wholesale-warehouse activities lend themselves to a production-line type of operation (or "order-pick" line pattern), as illustrated in Figure 10-3. Unlike a

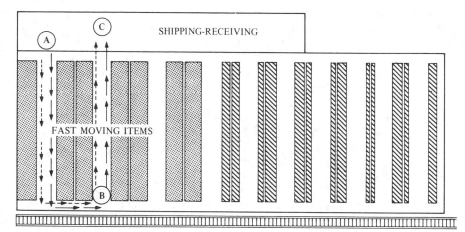

Figure 10-3. A Wholesale Warehouse Layout

manufacturer, who turns out goods that are identical, however, the wholesaler turns out orders of goods that are seldom alike. The wholesaler's problem is to arrange an order-picking route and routine that will enable him to handle the unpredictable assortments without special adjustment for any of them. Therefore, both the routing and the routine should be flexible enough to meet any reasonable contingency.

An important objective in any type of work-center layout is to reduce the amount of employee "travel." A wholesale-warehouse employee ordinarily walks several miles each day in the routine of order filling. As illustrated in Figure 10-3, this "mileage" can be effectively lowered by (1) laying out picking aisles so that they are perpendicular to the shipping dock, and (2) storing the fast-moving (large-volume) items on pallet racks nearest the shipping dock. The aisle space between the pallet racks and shelf stock should be four to six feet, depending upon the type of merchandise.

Order filling can also be speeded up by splitting orders into "trip routes." For example, in the illustration the order picker travels up one side of one aisle (A), loading only one side of the trailer. Then, he travels down the opposite side of the next aisle (B), loading the other side of the trailer, and finishing his trip right back at the shipping dock (C) — no dead travel time. Meanwhile, other men follow similar picking routes, filling other splits of the order.

When preparing warehouse layouts, wholesalers should also determine the feasibility of using mechanical materials-handling equipment and other labor-saving devices. Pallets and gravity chutes frequently offer a means of simplifying materials handling under certain conditions.

Factory Layout

In general, manufacturing processes may be classified into three basic types: intermittent, continuous, and repetitive manufacture. In intermittent manufacture, products are made only to customers' specifications. Since the product is nonstandard it cannot be produced for stock; thus it cannot be manufactured "continuously." A plant engaged in this type of manufacture is called a "job shop."

In continuous manufacture, on the other hand, one or only a few standard products are manufactured continuously to the company's own specifications in anticipation of sales. If two or more products are manufactured, they are manufactured simultaneously on separate production lines. Such a shop is commonly called a "mass-production shop."

The repetitive type of manufacture falls between the intermittent and continuous types. In this type of manufacture, a large and diverse line of standard products are manufactured, each product being processed from time to time in lots of economic size. No single product is produced in sufficient volume to justify its manufacture on a continuous basis, yet since it is a standard product the processing of additional quantities or lots can be "repeated" from time to time without change in departmental or machine routing or in operation method and allowed operation time. This type of shop is known as a "miscellaneous shop."

Obviously, the type of manufacture determines not only the kind of production equipment that is used, but also the manner in which this equipment is "laid out." In the intermittent and repetitive types of manufacture, for example, a *functional* (or process) layout of production equipment is required. In this type of layout, there is a separate department for each process; that is, each type of operation is performed in a single department on all types of product. Hence, production equipment is of the *general-purpose* type. This type of layout is typical of most small manufacturing plants and is illustrated in Figure 10-4.

The continuous type of manufacture, on the other hand, requires that the production equipment be laid out on a *line* (or product) basis. In this type of layout, there is a separate department for each product; that is, all operations on a single product are performed in one department, the equipment being arranged in a "line" according to the most economical sequence of operations. Hence, production equipment is of the *special-purpose* type. The best-known example of this type of layout is automobile assembly.

The most important advantage of the functional type of layout is its *flexibility.* Different products or customers' orders can be processed on the same (general-purpose) machines. Similarly, changes in the "product mix" (the elimination of unprofitable products and the introduction of new ones) can be made without changes in the layout. Also, since the machines are functionally independent, a breakdown in one machine does not delay operations on the other machines. Thus the flexibility of this type of layout results in a greater utilization of both machines and labor.

Another advantage is a lower capital investment in production equipment, since general-purpose machines are standard (stock) items which can be made at high volume and sold at a lower cost than special-purpose equipment.

However, since general-purpose machines are less efficient than special-purpose machines, unit operation costs are higher. Also, because the manufacturing requirements of the various products or job orders often conflict, there is a considerable amount of backtracking of work in process; for this same reason a flexible system of shop transportation is necessary (a sporadic movement of work in process by lift trucks, rather than the continuous movement of material by conveyor), resulting in lengthy delays between operations and long manufacturing-

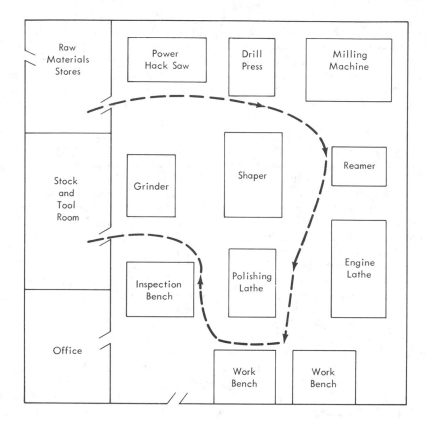

Figure 10-4.   A Functional Layout of Equipment in a Metalworking Shop, Showing Flow of Material in the Original Method of Processing Wringer
Drive Shafts

cycle times. The longer processing time, in turn, requires more storage space for
work in process in addition to larger inventories. It is also difficult to estimate costs
and completion times on many jobs, and detailed daily planning and scheduling of
work is necessary to avoid costly congestion at certain work centers.

The functional layout is strong where the line layout is weak, and weak where
the line layout is strong. The advantages and disadvantages of the latter type of
layout may thus be inferred from the above discussion. The disadvantages of the
line type of layout (principally high fixed costs and lack of flexibility) can be
overcome if the volume of production is high and reasonably stable. However, this
type of layout is not feasible for most small manufacturing firms. As we have
indicated many times in this text, it is the small firm's flexibility which gives it
certain advantages over the larger firms.

Considering the foregoing variations in layout, we can summarize some of the
principles of plant layout as follows:

1. Materials and semifinished products should follow the shortest and quickest possible
   route from entrance to exit.

2. A minimum of physical handling, with as many operations being performed at each "stop" as possible, is essential.

3. Through layout, management must seek to eliminate "bottlenecks" in the production process caused by the slowing down of any one process at a strategic location. (Though this depends in part on the adequacy and care of machinery, the location of the machinery is a vital factor.)

4. The misuse of space must be recognized as being of equal importance to wasted use of machinery and manpower.

5. Complete elimination of "backtracking," overlapping of work, and unnecessary inspection should be achieved through constant awareness of possibilities for new sequences and combinations of steps in processing or fabrication.

Although management consultants may be needed to solve the more complicated problems of factory layout, there is much the owner-operator of a small manufacturing plant can do for himself. First he should construct a *process chart* for each part or product he manufactures. A process chart shows the sequence of everything that happens to the material while it is being processed. Such a chart is illustrated in Figure 10-5, which portrays graphically the original method of processing drive shafts for a wringer-type washing machine. The manufacturing process illustrated is of the "repetitive" type previously described.

For purposes of analysis and possible simplification the details of the manufacturing process are conveniently classified, each detail being represented on the process chart as either (1) an operation, (2) a transportation, (3) a storage, or (4) an inspection. Storages of material are further classified as "temporary" or "permanent", and inspections, as "quality" or "quantity."

To assist the analyst in interpreting at a glance the detailed information about a manufacturing process, the various manufacturing activities are symbolized as well as verbalized on the process chart. A large circle is used to represent an "operation." An operation occurs whenever the material is changed in its physical or chemical characteristics, or is assembled to, or disassembled from, other material. "Operations" are the only reasons for the performance of the other steps in the manufacturing process. A small circle represents a "transportation," or a change in the location of the material from one work center to another. Changes in the location of material from one work station to another may result from either manual or mechanical handling, hence an "H" is placed in the circle for a transport by hand, a "C" for movements by means of a conveyor, "E" for elevator, "T" for truck, etc. A double triangle represents a "temporary storage," or the waiting (or idle) period between operations. Temporary storage refers only to material "in process" (as contrasted with the permanent storage of material "in stores" or "in stock"). When material in process is in temporary storage it is simply lying in wait in the work center until an operation or inspection is performed upon it or until it is transported to the work station next in sequence for further processing. Since material on a conveyor is either being moved or "operated" on (or inspected) at all times, temporary storage occurs only in the intermittent or repetitive type of manufacturing process, in which the functional layout or arrangement of equipment is most appropriate. A "permanent storage," on the other hand, represented by a large (single) triangle, occurs whenever the material is not "in process." In the case of raw materials and finished goods the material must remain in the storeroom or stockroom until the proper written authorization is received to

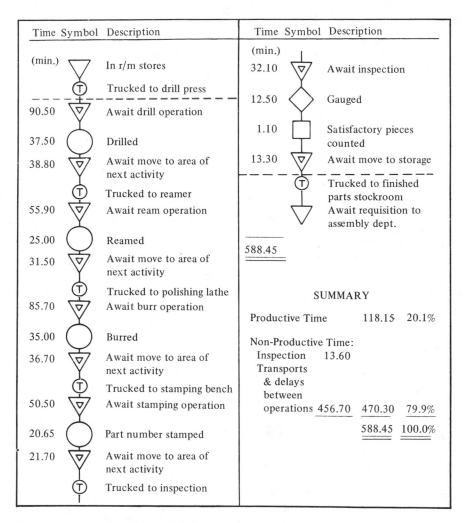

Time	Symbol	Description	Time	Symbol	Description
(min.)	▽	In r/m stores	(min.)		
	Ⓣ	Trucked to drill press	32.10	▽	Await inspection
90.50	▽	Await drill operation	12.50	◇	Gauged
37.50	○	Drilled	1.10	□	Satisfactory pieces counted
38.80	▽	Await move to area of next activity	13.30	▽	Await move to storage
	Ⓣ	Trucked to reamer		Ⓣ	Trucked to finished parts stockroom
55.90	▽	Await ream operation		▽	Await requisition to assembly dept.
25.00	○	Reamed			
31.50	▽	Await move to area of next activity	588.45		
	Ⓣ	Trucked to polishing lathe			SUMMARY
85.70	▽	Await burr operation			
35.00	○	Burred			
36.70	▽	Await move to area of next activity			
	Ⓣ	Trucked to stamping bench			
50.50	▽	Await stamping operation			
20.65	○	Part number stamped			
21.70	▽	Await move to area of next activity			
	Ⓣ	Trucked to inspection			

SUMMARY

Productive Time		118.15	20.1%
Non-Productive Time:			
Inspection	13.60		
Transports & delays between operations	456.70	470.30	79.9%
		588.45	100.0%

Figure 10-5. Chart Illustrating Original Method of Processing an Order of 50 Wringer Drive Shafts

release it to the bench or machine area for processing or to the shipping department for delivery to the customer. A diamond-shaped figure is used, appropriately, to represent a "quality inspection," or the measurement of the qualities of the material in terms of established standards with respect to shape, dimension, finish, color, composition, hardness, strength, and other characteristics. A "quantity inspection," such as the counting or weighing of material, is represented on the process chart by a square.

Each transportation, operation, storage, and inspection of material — from the time it leaves the raw materials or parts storeroom until the finished product is placed in stock — should be listed on the process chart in the exact sequence of its occurrence in the manufacturing process. The construction of such a chart (see Figure 10-5) is the first step in the systematic analysis and improvement of work routing and plant layout.

Of the activities listed on a process chart, those which will be examined most closely by the analyst are the nonproductive materials-handling activities, particularly material transports and "temporary storages." The latter activities increase the total manufacturing time, thereby lengthening delivery schedules and decreasing the turnover of work in process and finished goods inventories. Large inventories result in increased materials-handling costs, such as greater depreciation and obsolescence and higher insurance and interest charges on the working capital tied up in excessive inventories. Thus materials handling adds to the cost of the product without adding to its value. In addition to longer delivery schedules and higher materials-handling costs, excessive inventories increase the need for floor space and often result in plant congestion. Hence it is the purpose of the analyst to devise a simplified work routing or plant layout requiring the least amount of materials handling.[4]

In achieving this objective, however, a knowledge of both the operation sequence and the standard operation time is necessary. The operation sequence, for example, suggests the most economical arrangement of machines and work benches. Arrangement of production equipment in accordance with the sequence of operations results in the shortest flow of work with no backtracking of material and, hence, the least amount of materials handling.[5]

Similarly, data on standard operation times are of importance to the analyst in reducing temporary storage time (and, therefore, the amount of space required for material "float") between progressive operations which are not properly coordinated or "balanced" on a time basis. Greater production balance may be obtained by simplifying the more time-consuming or "bottleneck" operations, particularly where the differences in unit times are reasonably small. Where there is great disparity in the standard operation times per unit, production balance may be obtained by varying the amount of equipment and applied labor, or by combining two or more of the shorter operations.

The process chart technique of analysis is as applicable to the miscellaneous or job-order shop as it is to the mass-production factory. If the problem is one of devising the best possible layout for the manufacture of a miscellaneous line of standard products, the analyst should construct a process chart for the item that is produced in the greatest volume or at the highest cost. If the layout is for a job-production shop, then the product that is considered to be most representative of the diverse classes of work should be analyzed. The net result of confining the analysis to a single representative or repetitive product is the development of the most efficient layout for the work *as a whole*, since it is obvious that straight-line

---

[4] Excessive materials handling and shop transportation caused by inefficient work routing or by poor factory layout often results in wastes which may balance or even exceed increases in production resulting from more efficient job performance. Except in the conveyorized mass-production plants, materials handling may consume as much as 80 percent of the total manufacturing-cycle time; thus productive labor is applied to material only about 20 percent of the time that it is in process.

[5] Pure line layout of equipment, however, is often impractical because of the existence of physical or technological factors which limit the location of work stations.

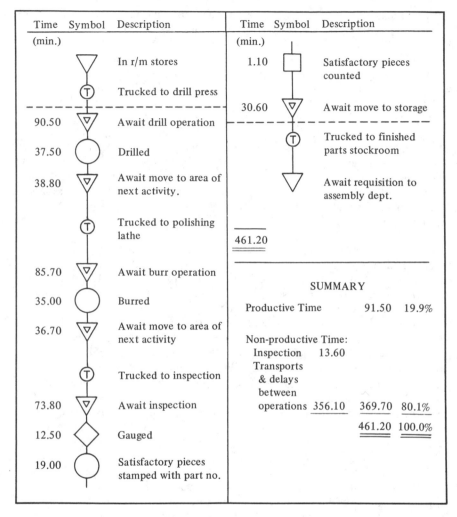

Time (min.)	Symbol	Description	Time (min.)	Symbol	Description
	▽	In r/m stores	1.10	☐	Satisfactory pieces counted
	Ⓣ	Trucked to drill press			
90.50	▽	Await drill operation	30.60	▽	Await move to storage
37.50	○	Drilled		Ⓣ	Trucked to finished parts stockroom
38.80	▽	Await move to area of next activity.		▽	Await requisition to assembly dept.
	Ⓣ	Trucked to polishing lathe	461.20		
85.70	▽	Await burr operation			
35.00	○	Burred			
36.70	▽	Await move to area of next activity			
	Ⓣ	Trucked to inspection			
73.80	▽	Await inspection			
12.50	◇	Gauged			
19.00	○	Satisfactory pieces stamped with part no.			

SUMMARY

Productive Time	91.50	19.9%
Non-productive Time:		
Inspection 13.60		
Transports & delays between operations 356.10	369.70	80.1%
	461.20	100.0%

Figure 10-6. Chart Illustrating Improved Method of Processing an Order of 50 Wringer Drive Shafts

flow cannot be provided for all products because of conflicting manufacturing requirements.

Material flow can be visualized by delineating on a scaled layout drawing (such as the one in Figure 10-4) the path or route taken by the material as it is moved from one production area to another. Such a *flow diagram* is a valuable supplement to the process chart.

Another supplementary aid in making the layout consists of attaching to the floorplan of the shop, templates or three-dimensional models of machinery and other equipment. The floorplan, of course, should show the location of walls, partitions, windows, doors, columns, service areas (such as washrooms, locker rooms, tool rooms, offices, storerooms, and stockrooms), elevator shafts, and other structural features which limit the arrangement of machinery and other equipment.

In listing on a process chart the detailed sequence of activities or steps in the present manufacturing process, and showing on a flow diagram the movement (flow) of the material from one work station to another, the analyst collected the body of facts with which to work. He is now ready to analyze these facts. Each step in the present process is scrutinized and questioned, with particular reference to the possibilities for its elimination or to its combination with other process activities. Possible improvements resulting from the relocation of equipment, and the cost and convenience of doing so, are also considered. After the manufacturing process has been improved, a process chart is constructed as a means of describing and recording the improved process and as a means of comparing it with the old process. A flow diagram is also drawn to show the improved work flow and layout of equipment.

The improved method of processing wringer drive shafts is illustrated in Figure 10-6. When compared with the original method (see Figure 10-5), it is noted that there is a 22 percent reduction in the overall time that the material is in process – from 588 minutes (for a lot of 50 drive shafts) to 461 minutes. It is further observed that most of this decrease is accounted for by the decrease in the number and length of the delays between operations. One way in which this improvement was brought about was by combining the stamping and inspection activities; this resulted in better production "balance" and in the elimination of two lengthy "temporary storages." Also, by enlarging slightly the diameter of the drill in the first operation it was possible to eliminate the reaming operation; this, in turn, eliminated two other delays between operations.

Layout for the Service Establishment

The appropriate layout and building design for a service establishment depends upon whether the enterprise is of the merchandising or the processing type. The former includes motels, restaurants, and most personal service establishments. Customer convenience, pleasing appearance, and similar considerations are of relatively great importance in the "merchandising" type of service business.

The processing type of service business has, on the other hand, much in common with a factory. Here various operations, such as cleaning, repairing, or altering, are performed on articles owned by the customers. In many cases the customer never sees the work being done and may not even come to the plant at all. Factors governing productive efficiency are of relatively great importance in such cases with regard to both building and layout. The principles governing factory layout, as discussed in the preceding section, will apply to service establishments of this type.

In the well-established service fields, trade associations and trade periodicals can be very helpful in solving problems relating to layout, equipment selection, and building construction. Many equipment manufacturers have an engineering or service division to assist in this work. There are also several independent firms and freelance specialists whose services may be obtained for a fee on a basis comparable to that of the consulting engineers used by manufacturers.

SUMMARY AND CONCLUSIONS

The building should be expanded or modernized as business conditions warrant such moves, and layout is most important in meeting this challenge. Layout involves the concept of "flow" – flow of people through a store or flow of materials through a factory. Since business is not static and both building and layout requirements change, an alert businessman must give continuous attention to building design and layout.

For the small businessman valuable information is available in the trade press, from his trade association, and from other agencies mentioned in the chapter. However, he can often make worthwhile improvements by analyzing his needs and studying operations as they are being performed to locate waste motion, uneconomical use of labor, and other weaknesses. By making a process or flow chart and flow diagram, further improvements may be made. Often suggestions made by employees or customers will lead to valuable changes in layout, equipment, or construction. Planning layout is a fascinating undertaking that usually more than repays the effort and study given to it.

REVIEW QUESTIONS

1. What major factors should be considered in evaluating a building to house the business operation? How should the building be evaluated in terms of each of these factors?
2. What factors must always be considered in laying out or arranging the equipment in the building, regardless of the type of business?
3. What are the layout objectives for a retail store? For a wholesale house? For a manufacturing plant? For a service establishment?
4. What factors influence the layout of a retail store? Of a wholesale house? Of a manufacturing plant? Of a service establishment?
5. What are the three basic types of manufacturing processes? What type of layout would be applicable in each case? What type of processing equipment? Materials-handling equipment?
6. Summarize the advantages and disadvantages of (*a*) the functional type of plant layout, and (*b*) the line type of layout.
7. Summarize the principles of plant layout discussed in the text.
8. What is a material process chart? What activities does it describe? Define each type of activity. How are these activities symbolized? What is the significance of each type of activity so described?
9. Distinguish between a process chart and a flow diagram.
10. Describe the various ways in which a manufacturing process may be improved. Are these approaches equally applicable to layout problems in other types of business? Explain.

DISCUSSION QUESTIONS

1. Select some particular kind of business and tell how the best layout affects requirements of the ideal building.

2. Tom wants to modernize his 30-foot-front, 100-foot-deep food store and convert it to self-service. He has ample funds for any justifiable alterations. Describe what he should do and give your reasons.

SUPPLEMENTARY READINGS

Immer, John R. *Profitable Small Plant Layout.* 2nd ed. Small Business Management Series no. 21. Washington, D.C.: Small Business Administration, 1964. Describes how to improve a poor layout when present space is sufficient, or how to start from scratch to plan an entirely new process layout. Discusses the various factors to be considered in each case.

Pintel, Gerald, and Jay Diamond. *Retailing,* pp. 48–57. Englewood Cliffs, N.J.: Prentice-Hall, 1971. Discusses the selection of merchandise displays and lighting fixtures, and the location of selling, service, and administrative areas in the retail store.

11

Financing and organizing the business

The short- and long-term capital needs of a business should be determined as accurately as possible before the business "gets off the ground." The capital structure of a business, in turn, is intimately related to its legal structure or form of organization (proprietorship, partnership, or corporation). Whether either should be considered this early in a book such as this, or deferred until after all other aspects of small business organization and operation have been explored, is a moot question. Certainly the beginner should have generally studied such things as where he wishes to locate, his prospective layout, his policies on credit, his projected sales, his personnel budget, and so forth before he can arrive at any meaningful proposal for financing. Banks and other financial institutions often require a fairly detailed business proposal before advancing funds, and certainly the small businessman should postpone final decision regarding both financing and organizing until he has appraised every operating function of his proposed enterprise.

That old, inspirational cliché, the "challenge of success," seldom is encountered more immediately than when prospective small businessmen must come to grips with financial problems, both before starting in business and after having embarked on entrepreneurship. Money, either in hand or in the form of credit, is the key to profitable enterprise, but it is extremely mercurial and will not tolerate careless manipulation nor imprudence in handling. This is as true today as it was in grandfather's time. There are other conditions that affect small business: the winds and tides of inflation and recession, rising material costs, and shrinking or diffident markets. Even the tax factor has not been greatly altered, except in degree. Then there is competition, which is always with us. But the method by which the beginner manages his investment capital and credit is perhaps a more vital factor in his business success or failure.

Capital and Profits

Capital, as we are using the term, means command over purchasing power — the total of owned and borrowed funds, plus credit accepted. Thus, for a business that requires beginning capital of $15,000, the owner with only $8,000 in cash or other usable assets may secure a bank loan of $4,000 and obtain goods worth $3,000 on credit from suppliers, equipment dealers, and others. Often it is not necessary to borrow the full amount at once, but a line of credit equal to the maximum amount required should be established. Bankers, prospective creditors, and other sources of financial assistance usually agree that the owner's equity should be about two-thirds of the total capital required, but this is an arbitrary and somewhat conservative rule.

Capital must be regarded as a business tool requiring skill in its use. Pressure on the beginner's usually limited funds is so great that he is likely not to reserve enough working capital, and he seldom makes adequate provision for the one serious mistake most new businessmen are likely to make during their first year of operations. By "one serious mistake" we refer to no *particular* error, but to the fact that one is usually made, and of a costly nature, and should be anticipated. No such mistake may occur, but as it is expressed in the insurance field, "It is better to have it and not need it, than to need it and not have it." The contingency may be provided for by a previous agreement with some understanding lender or by keeping suitable assets unencumbered for possible use as collateral if and when needed. Whichever method is used, it is important to stay with the original purpose and keep the source of extra capital available strictly for emergency use for at least one year. It is common for some beginners to lack cash reserves to meet unexpected expenses during the first year. Others do not anticipate all their expenses and find that their capital is gone before they have adequately set up their businesses. Still others go out of business partly because they are unable to take advantage of cash, quantity, and other discounts.

All money invested in a business, whether in fixtures, equipment, stock, or in operating expenses, is expected to yield a "profit" to the investor. Because of the risks incurred in going into business for one's self, this capital should yield a higher rate of return than could be obtained from investment in government or corporate securities having a guaranteed rate of interest. But this requires careful management by the entrepreneur.

Capital and Its Uses

There are two basic kinds of capital, depending upon the uses to which the capital is put and upon the liquidity requirements of the firm's assets. Assets that will be retained for a long time, such as land and buildings, machinery, furniture and fixtures, and other equipment, are classed as *fixed capital. Working capital*, on the other hand, includes the firm's cash reserves and all assets that can be readily converted into cash, such as inventories and accounts receivable. Working, or circulating, capital is used to buy materials or merchandise and to pay off current obligations such as rent and wages.

The relative requirements of fixed and working capital will vary. The retail store's ratio of working capital to total assets, for example, will differ from that of the service business, and that of a factory will be still different.

In determining capital needs the small businessman must allow for a reasonable period of time to elapse, usually from three to six months, before income from the business will cover regular monthly expenses, and he must include in his estimated needs a minimum salary or drawing account sufficient to provide for his living expenses. He should prepare a budget even before the final decision to start the business is made, and great care should be exercised to include all expenses and needs for capital, including taxes and other less obvious requirements.

Financial management.   Extensive experience shows that difficulties in financing often arise from a few common causes, such as lack of knowledge of available sources of funds, inability to present a convincing case to possible investors, and failure to plan and prepare in advance for likely needs. Long before his programmed date for hanging up an Open For Business sign, the prospective enterpriser should become acquainted with a banker or two and with other influential people in his community who are potential sources of funds and sound advice. It would be helpful to have an established consumer credit rating. Before starting a career as a business operator, the prospective entrepreneur will find it wise, perhaps essential, to create records of his financial responsibility as a part of his business history. This may be done in several ways – by maintaining a solvent checking account, for example, or by negotiating a few small loans when larger-than-casual expenditures are being considered. Even the record of small but regular deposits in a savings account may help when the need for financing arises.

For the established concern, careful financial planning is a continuing necessity. A current shortage of funds is often the result of the unwise use of funds in the past. In particular the firm should: (1) avoid an excessive investment in fixed assets, (2) maintain receivables and net working capital in proper proportion to sales, and (3) avoid excessive inventories. There is no financial difficulty of any firm, regardless of size, which cannot be traced to the violation of one or more of these three basic principles of financial management.[1]

WORKING WITH THE MERCANTILE CREDIT AGENCY

Young businessmen and prospective entrepreneurs often ask how they can obtain a favorable credit rating with an agency whose business is to provide such ratings as a service to business clients. In answer to this inquiry addressed to Dun & Bradstreet, the following comments were received:

> This is a little difficult to answer because a favorable rating implies that there must be an unfavorable rating. We do not have "unfavorable" ratings. There is no symbol in our *Reference Book* that indicates that an account should not be sold or that credit should not be granted. The story of the business is in the report, and if the situation is such that it is difficult to describe the case through the use of a rating, the *Reference Book* says, . . . "Better read the report on this." . . . This may seem technical, but it is fairly basic in understanding what the small-business man will expect when he comes in to obtain a "favorable" rating.
>
> So far as our own company is concerned, the best way to get off to a favorable start is to come voluntarily into the nearest Dun & Bradstreet office (of which there are 150) and explain the story of the new business before the enterprise is launched. It is easy at that time to work out all the details of the report.
>
> The Dun & Bradstreet reporter will be glad to show the new businessman the report on his business so that the merchant will be fully aware of what is in our files and what

---

[1] Financial management of the established small business is discussed in Chapter 23.

will be used to answer inquiries from subscribers. The only things that we do *not* show him are any opinions or trade experiences that we have received from others in confidence, for to do so would be violating the confidence of those who have given us information.

Now after talking things out, it is possible that there may be certain weaknesses in the new setup. The weaknesses may consist of inexperience, lack of capital, or perhaps a location that is not too good. But through frank and open discussion, we are also able to show what are the *strengths*. In the end, therefore, we are able to present a fair and impartial report which shows both sides of the story. This information is then reflected in the symbol, which is the rating.

So I would put it this way. When a man is going into business, he might just as well put his best foot forward. If he will provide figures showing his financial information, describe his plans, and generally discuss his affairs with us in the same way that he would talk over these things with a principal supplier, we feel that we can, in turn, give him the most favorable send-off.

I think it might be of value to the readers of your book to know that we will provide operating statistics . . . to the man who intends to enter business. These figures will give him an idea of what sales, expenses, and profits may be expected, based on the experience of others in the same business. We are glad to give whatever information we have gathered so that the new businessman can get off to a successful start. This is generally free of charge.

A typical situation in the reporting of a new business is this. Our reporter first makes a direct call on the businessman and asks questions regarding the amount of experience, the source and amount of capital, the legal ownership, and what the new businessman plans to do. Then the reporter will ask for financial statements, particularly a balance sheet and operating figures. If the business has not opened, the reporter will ask what sales volume is anticipated, and will try to talk out with the man how much of his capital will be going into fixtures, and how much merchandise he needs to buy.

After interviewing the businessman directly the reporter then supplements his call with an investigation in outside sources. It is quite likely, for example, that he will call on the bank to ask questions regarding the name in which the account has been opened. And if loans are granted by the bank, he will inquire into the circumstances. He will also gather information from suppliers as to the previous payment record of the owner, and may check public records to see if any items such as chattel mortgages have been recorded.

Now with this information the reporter writes a report. He weighs the varying factors and comes up with a judgment — which is a rating. He considers the experience and background of the owners, the financial condition and payment record. In all, there are seven major factors which go into making a composite appraisal.

All through this process the reporter is able to reduce error by recognizing inconsistencies in the information which he is receiving. Examples: A fine looking balance sheet does not tie in with slow payments to suppliers. A young may who says he is starting in with $25,000 from savings *may* have this capital, but it is unusual that a young man will have accumulated this much money. The chances are that there is a gift involved or an advance of capital from perhaps a friend or from relatives.

The second kind of checking comes from the opinion of outside authorities, that is, people who have known the businessman. All these checks and balances, coupled with the fact that nearly all businessmen are honest, allow the reporter to end up with a reasonably small margin of error. There may be error in an individual case, but across the board, taking 10,000 ratings, the degree of accuracy is quite high in the opinion of many people. I think this will be confirmed by the experience of credit men who use the Dun & Bradstreet Reference Books regularly. Financing agencies, and insurance companies whose loss ratios depend in many instances upon the use of our ratings, will, I think, also indicate that in the mass, the error is small.[2]

In summary, the following factors are used in arriving at the Dun & Bradstreet credit appraisal:

1. Proper organization of the business according to law, and a clear identification of ownership
2. Length of time in business
3. History of management — successful or unsuccessful
4. Balance of management experience
5. Financial condition
6. Trend — going ahead or going back
7. Promptness in paying bills

When all of these factors are strong, the rating is "high." When a little less strong but still quite satisfactory, the rating is "good." Where there is a deficiency, the rating is "fair," and when deficiencies have persisted the credit potential is regarded as "limited."

The above comments from the Dun & Bradstreet credit reporting agency might well be supplemented by the following admonition: Unless a business, small or large, enjoys a charmed life, it will sooner or later suffer occasional reverses. There will be times when the enterpriser must walk a financial tightrope. In such instances the first persons to hear about the emergency should be the enterpriser's creditors and he should be the one to tell them. The business woods are full of "rumor birds" capable of irreparable damage to the business. The only way to silence them is by dispassionately telling the unvarnished truth in the proper places. This would seem to be elementary wisdom, yet humans are stubbornly reluctant to admit they have erred in judgment or have been nipped in a vise not of their own contriving. Too many enterprisers wait until the roof is sagging before they make an effort to shore up the structure. It is then often too late.

CAPITAL REQUIREMENTS FOR
THE SMALL MERCHANDISING BUSINESS

In the following discussion of capital needs it will be assumed that the building is rented rather than purchased. Not only is this true for most beginning small businesses, but it is recommended practice in the vast majority of cases.

It is also recommended that the rental agreement include provision for the landlord to remodel when needed, because the small operator's need for working capital is so great that none of it can be spared for improvements if the landlord can be made to provide them. It is better to pay a small amount more per month for rent, if necessary, to obtain this kind of lease.

[2]From previous correspondence with Dun & Bradstreet, confirmed by Mr. Frederick T. Staats on June 21, 1971.

"The smaller the capital, the greater the risk" might well be the axiom of small business. Certainly it applies to small-scale retailing or wholesaling. The man who begins on a small personal investment with limited backing is working against many obstacles, such as the following:

1. Because he will be unable to afford many employees, he must run the store alone. His duties will include all store work, everything from sweeping the floor to keeping the store's records. This means long hours, little opportunity to leave the store, and calamity if he becomes ill.

2. Because he will be operating against stiff competition, customer credit may be a problem that requires careful handling. The added capital required for a credit business may deprive him of funds needed to pay for new goods or for goods already bought on credit.

3. The small store owner cannot afford to invest much in fixtures, for this money is taken out of essential working capital. Five hundred dollars spent for an unnecessary showcase represents money that could otherwise be invested and reinvested in merchandise for resale (from whence profits are derived).

4. The average beginner will be so short of capital during the first few months or even the first year or two that he will need very lenient terms from his creditors, especially suppliers. These represent a part of his provisions for working capital, because for all practical purposes he is borrowing this money from them.

In determining the capital requirements for a small merchandising business, one of three procedures might be followed: (1) the "desired income" approach, (2) the "rental rate" approach, or (3) the "cash available" approach.

The "Desired Income" Approach

A useful approach to determining capital needs is in terms of the amount of capital required to produce a given amount of annual personal income.

Assume, for example, that the entrepreneur has some personal funds, a good background of experience working for someone else, and the desire to avoid much experimental and groundbreaking work before his business can become established and profitable. In the case of a store, he might go about determining his financial needs by answering the following questions.

Basic premises:

Questions	Answers
1. How much income do I wish to be making when the business is established?	1. Assume . . . . $ 30,000
2. At the percentage rate of net profit common in this business, what volume must I "do"?	2. @ 8 percent . . . . 375,000 $\left(\dfrac{\$30{,}000}{.08} \right)$
3. At the common rate of turnover in this business, what stock must I carry?	3. @ 4 times . . . . 93,750 $\left(\dfrac{\$375{,}000}{4} \right)$

Capital requirements:

Questions	Answers
1. At the common rate of margin, what will this opening stock of merchandise cost me?	1. @ 30 percent . . . . $ 65,625 ($93,750 × .70)
2. How much will I require as a maximum in store fixtures and equipment?	2. (Estimate) 35,000
3. How much should I set aside for pre-opening expenses such as advertising and miscellaneous essential but unanticipated expenses?	3. (Estimate) 10,000
4. For what contingencies should I set aside added funds? How much?	4. Peak merchandise needs . . . 7,500 Cash funds, reserve for personal and business emergencies 8,500
5. Allowances for expenses for one turnover period.	5. (Estimate) 10,000 $136,625

The last item listed above refers to rent, wages, and other current expenses for at least one turnover period — in this case, three months. Enough cash should be on hand or readily available to pay these unavoidable operating expenses, leaving a maximum of working capital for stock adjustment and replacement. In this case these items might call for the following amounts over a three-month period:

Rent	$3,000
Wages	4,500
Advertising	1,500
Miscellaneous expenses	1,000
	$10,000

Thus a total of almost $137,000 would be required.

This example assumes that a particular kind of store is under consideration. The standard operating ratios used are those typical of hardware stores.

The "Rental Rate" Approach

Another approach to determining capital needs proceeds on the assumption that only a limited number of appropriate sites will be available to the beginner who would like to open a particular kind of store. Each site has a fixed annual rental. Since this is the only known fact, the first step is to calculate the necessary annual sales, using the standard operating rent ratio for the line of business selected. If further investigation shows this volume to be a reasonable possibility and offers a satisfactory prospective income, the determination of capital needs is carried out in a manner similar to that described in the previous example.

Assume that there is consideration being given to operating a women's ready-to-wear shop in a town of 50,000 population. The only suitable location rents for $400 a month for two years with a renewal option. Occupancy ratios[3] for this kind of business are close to 6 percent, or about 5 percent for rent alone. Capitalizing $400 at 5 percent gives $8,000 — the monthly sales needed to justify this rent — or required annual sales of $96,000. Average operating expenses for this proposed business are assumed to be 29 percent, or $2,320 per month ($8,000 X .29). With a stock turnover of four times a year average inventory would be $17,040 (or $96,000/4 X .71). From these data initial capital may be calculated as in our preceding illustration.

This method enables a person to determine the required sales to justify a given dollar rental and, from the sales figure and standard operating and merchandising ratios, to calculate initial capital and specific operating expenses. When the initial capital required has been determined, it should be checked against other ratios, such as capital turnover, ratio of sales to investment or dollar sales per dollar invested, ratio of sales to inventory, sales to working capital, and similar standard ratios applicable to the proposed business.

A retail store's greatest investment is usually in its merchandise. The stock of a retail store or wholesale house will frequently represent a considerably greater investment than its fixtures and sometimes more than its building space. Complete lines of many kinds of goods call for a substantial investment. However, daily cash receipts from customers permit circulating capital to flow back into the business constantly with no long delays. Granting credit delays this flow to the extent of the credit terms, requiring further funds for investment in goods sold but not paid for. In a retail store, wages and other overhead items do not represent as large an investment as that in most manufacturing trades.

Capital requirements vary widely according to the kind of merchandise handled, price zone or income group of customers, managerial ability and trade connections of the merchant, location of the store, economic conditions and the general price level, time required to establish the business on a self-supporting basis, attitude of the enterpriser toward risk taking, and many other factors. Within one line of merchandise the initial capital required for the elaborate fixtures, expensive location, liberal customer services, and other requirements needed to attract the fastidious upper-class trade may easily result in initial capital requirements far in excess of those considered satisfactory for less exacting lower-income customers. Economic conditions and price levels existing at different times within the past few decades have caused initial retail capital requirements under otherwise similar conditions to vary by over 200 percent from the lowest to the highest.

In view of conditions such as these, it is obviously impossible to present an example of initial capital requirement in dollars that would be accurate as a standard for any individual situation. However, the procedure for determining capital needs, the operating expense and merchandise ratios used in the computations, the acceptable distribution of initial investment, and similar factors remain fairly constant for each line of business regardless of variations in conditions such as those just mentioned.

[3] The ratio of rent and store maintenance costs to sales.

The "Cash Available" Approach

A third approach to determining the initial capital requirements of a business is to start with an amount of capital assumed to be available; the objective is to determine probable income resulting from its efficient use in terms of standard operating ratios and practices.

In the following example the most reliable guides available and the advice of competent authorities in the field have been utilized. The results have been carefully checked with the latest reliable survey reports. A conservative attitude toward the distribution of initial equity capital has also been taken; this results in slightly larger inventory investment (current assets) than surveys show to be representative of recently established stores in this line. Also, somewhat larger reserves are suggested than might be necessary in individual cases. A general merchandise store operating under approximately average conditions has been selected because of the widespread interest in this kind of store and the availability of recent data regarding this line of business.

Assume that, possessing experience, trade connections, and a good reputation, an entrepreneur can raise $30,000 to invest in a business, and that a suitable building is available at an annual rental of $3,600 with a satisfactory lease and renewal option. After consulting his prospective wholesaler, equipment manufacturers, the local banker, and business friends, as well as published data in the field, he arrives at the following estimates.

The bulk of the investment would go into inventory. His major wholesaler suggests a balanced inventory that could be purchased for $18,000, with a reserve of $2,400 for reorders and stock adjustments once the store is in operation. With a merchandise turnover of three times a year annual sales are estimated at $90,000, since the average inventory would be $30,000 at retail, assuming a gross margin ratio of 32 percent: $\left(\dfrac{\$18,000\ +\ \$2,400}{.68}\right)$. Merchandise could be reordered and received on an average of twice a month, and regular 30-day credit terms would be available. Thus the desired average inventory could be maintained from current sales and trade credit. The size of this would be consistent with the accepted standard of 65 percent of the total investment in inventory. The monthly rent of $300 is 4 percent of the estimated monthly sales of $7,500, a rent ratio which is standard for stores of this type.

Fixtures and equipment may be purchased for $7,200, payable one-fourth down and the balance in 18 monthly installments of $300 with carrying charges included in the initial price. This investment is also consistent with the recommended practice of spending from 20 to 30 percent of initial capital on fixed assets. Total operating expenses (rent, salaries, etc.) at the standard ratio of 25 percent would be $1,875 a month. Thus the gross margin of $2,400 (or $7,500 × .32) would cover monthly operating expenses and the monthly payment for equipment, leaving a balance of $225. From this balance should come a reserve for taxes of $60, leaving a surplus for reinvestment in the business of $165 a month during the first 18 months and $465 per month after that.

Distribution of initial investment under this projected program may be summarized as follows:

Beginning inventory at cost (open to buy: $2,400)	$18,000
Down payment on fixtures and equipment	1,800
License, insurance, and opening expenses (estimate)	900
Operating expenses, one month	1,875
Reserves:	
Merchandise reorders $2,400	
Expenses, two months 3,750	
Cash 1,275	7,425
Total initial investment	$30,000

Thus we have approached the financing of a small retail store from three points of view: (1) the desire for a given income, (2) the need to support a given rental, and (3) the availability of a given amount of capital.

Although the analytical procedures presented are recommended in the vast majority of cases, another viewpoint that deserves mention permits starting a business with less capital than the minimum usually considered necessary for success. There are always a few businessmen, including some successful ones, who believe the essentials of starting out are the idea, the desire, and the opportunity, with the fact of having less capital than the estimated minimum acting as a secondary consideration. They admit the going will be hard, but claim the experience will be worth the effort and the limited funds available will be used much more carefully than if the business were more adequately financed. They further observe that if one keeps waiting for a safe margin of finances, his opportunities may be lost or other conditions may later prevent him from starting out on his own. There is much evidence in their favor. They cite many examples of successful businesses that were grossly undercapitalized at the start. Certainly not all successful firms have met the theoretical requirements.

The authors hold no brief for or against this viewpoint. Certainly overcapitalization is not to be recommended. Also, it is probably better in rare cases to be opportunistic and, if it is "now or never," to take the plunge. But at least one should do so with his eyes wide open and be willing to accept the greater risks and harder work required.

Use of Operating Ratios

Ratios show the relationship between two items and are commonly used in business management to measure financial conditions or financial changes. In estimating the capital requirements of a new business, *operating* ratios are particularly useful. "Operating" ratios show the relationships of projected or actual expenses and income items in the firm's profit-and-loss (or operating) statement; for example, the rent and profit ratios cited in the examples above.

Although standard operating ratios have been developed for most kinds of business, they are probably used most extensively in retailing. They are useful not only to the beginner in determining his initial capital requirements, but as guides in operating the business once it is established. The small businessman should familiarize himself with the standard operating ratios in his particular business.[4]

CAPITAL REQUIREMENTS FOR THE SMALL FACTORY

The approach to financing a small factory, which differs somewhat from the approach to financing a store, must be based on potential earning power, for unlike the retail store it seldom has reclaimable assets in the form of merchandise. For this reason the enterpriser's funds and those he may borrow are subject to a greater hazard. Money paid out for labor, overhead, and partly processed materials cannot be recovered readily in case of default or other difficulty. In this connection three things are generally true of a manufacturing business:

1. Real worth — that is, market value or desirability from an investment viewpoint — will depend almost entirely on its earnings, actual or potential. Obviously it cannot depend on its assets or collateral, for used machines, expended labor, and half-processed materials have little market value. Many raw materials have little value because of transportation costs and limited markets.

2. First capital, therefore, will necessarily come from those who have created the business and who may expect to participate in its earnings. The general public is hesitant about investing in an unknown quantity. Only after the project has proved successful will they seek to "get in on a good thing."

3. The length of time required for processing will be a large factor in determining working capital requirements. This fact is of greatest importance when the business is first started, growing less vital as sales become frequent and cash income becomes regular and dependable.

The man who would set up a manufacturing establishment might use the following "income desired" procedure in determining his financial needs:

Questions	Answers
1. How much income must I have to make this venture worth while?	1. Assume . . . . $ 24,000
2. At the percentage rate of net profit possible in this business, what volume must I "do"?	2. @ 8 percent $300,000
3. How many pieces or units must I produce to net $24,000?	3. If the piece sells @ $1.50, @ 12¢ (8 percent) net profit per piece; 200,000 units
4. How many machines will it take to produce 200,000 units in the course of a year?	4. Assume: 4 machines @ $10,000 . . . $ 40,000 2 " @ 5,000 . . . 10,000 4 " @ 3,000 . . . 12,000 2 " @ 2,000 . . . 4,000

[4] See Table 23-1 for sources of standard operating ratios for various kinds of small business.

Questions	Answers	
5. How much of a supply of materials will be required, assuming turnover of four?	5. Enough for 50,000 units — with supplies (est.)	15,000
6. How much will wages be for one complete turn of 50,000 units?	6. Three months for eight men (est.)	30,000
7. How much rental for three months?	7. (Estimated)	7,500
8. How much for sales expenses?	8. (Estimated)	6,000
9. How much for office expense?	9. (Estimated)	2,500
10. How much should be set aside for unexpected incidentals?	10. (Estimated)	5,000
11. How much for personal expenses?	11. (Estimated)	5,000
		$137,000

The difference between the expenditures for this manufacturing business and those of the hardware store previously described is that the manufacturer invests in equipment which is subject to depreciation over a period of several years, whereas the store's major investment is in goods to be sold within three months. The total financial requirements of the two are similar, yet a potential creditor might clearly prefer one over the other.

In a manufacturing industry an important consideration is whether to buy rather than rent the plant and/or equipment. Decisions made here will obviously have an important bearing on the plant's long-term financing.

In establishing a small manufacturing business one can either pay cash for the initial stock of materials, parts, and supplies or seek to establish credit immediately. Credit obtained for these items will greatly reduce the initial working capital needed.

A small manufacturer should also consider whether it would be cheaper to manufacture his own components, considering cost of equipment, space, capital tied up, and so forth, or to buy all parts and merely assemble them. A well-established plant may be able to sell him parts for assembly at a lower cost than he can produce them. Purchase of components may reduce fixed and working capital requirements.

The tax structure has influenced business financing in many ways. Prior to 1954 it was often better to lease than to own land, buildings, fixtures, equipment, or other fixed assets because depreciation rules were rigid whereas rentals are valid deductions as business expense.

Since 1954, however, the Internal Revenue Service has eased the burden of capital financing through a loosening of depreciation rules:

a. The Internal Revenue Service is now more likely to take the word of the businessman as to the economic life of his asset. However, the life expectancy selected by the taxpayer must be within a range specified for specific classes of assets.

b. An additional 20 percent depreciation can be taken in the first year, on assets costing up to $10,000 (or $20,000 for a husband and wife filing a joint return), provided the asset has a useful life of six or more years.

c. The "double declining balance" method of depreciation is now allowed, increasing the amount of depreciation taken in the early years.

d. The investment credit is no longer tied to depreciation computations.

In December 1971 Congress further encouraged business capital expansion by extending the 7 percent investment credit in the federal income tax structure to *used* (as well as new) machinery and equipment purchases. This legislation should be of considerable help to the small entrepreneur, who often buys used equipment. The investment credit on used equipment that can be claimed in any one year, however, is limited to equipment costing no more than $50,000. Any amount of new equipment is eligible, but the maximum amount of the credit is limited to the first $25,000 of tax liability plus half of any above that.

Though recent changes in the tax laws have made the purchase of equipment — whether new or used — more attractive, the *leasing* of equipment has certain advantages not related to taxation. Not only are funds released for working capital purposes, but the lessee is exempt from maintenance costs which he would otherwise incur. The possibilities of leasing, as opposed to outright buying, must not be overlooked.

Its use by businessmen has so increased in recent years that it is now estimated that half of all plants, stores, and offices in the United States lease some of the equipment used in their operation. In addition to the advantages just cited, new models of equipment are usually more readily available to the user, and under short-term contracts the leased item is removed and no longer an expense when its use is no longer required.

CAPITAL REQUIREMENTS FOR THE SERVICE ESTABLISHMENT

The problems of financing the service business will depend on which characteristics predominate — those of the merchandising or those of the manufacturing business. To the extent that it carries goods for resale it will call for funds with which to buy them; to the extent that it sells the labor or machine work it will require capital for equipment and wages in much the same manner as a factory.

These considerations may be observed: (1) The fact that most service businesses are operated on a cash basis reduces their capital requirements. (2) Because the average service business renders its service in a comparatively short period of time, no great amount of capital may be required for investment in labor and overhead between the time the job is brought in and the time it is called for. (3) A service business, because it may depend on machine operation, may justify larger expenditures in equipment to save expensive manpower. A machine that will save one man's work may cost considerably less than what that man's wages would be over a relatively short period of time.

The usual type of service business shares features of both store and factory.

SOURCES OF FUNDS

The small businessman has a number of sources he can tap for funds. The sources from which he obtains funds will depend to a large extent on the manner in which he intends to use the funds.

The business is generally faced with three types of financial need — the need for initial capital, for working capital once the firm is in operation, and capital for expansion. Initial capital includes that necessary to get the business started and enough to keep it going until returns from operations provide sufficient funds to meet normal recurring expenses. That is, initial capital includes the beginning operating or working capital. As the volume of business increases, as it ordinarily does during the early months of operation, the amount of working capital needed tends to increase until the normal level of operations is reached. Whether this additional capital is provided for initially, or is obtained from profits or from other sources after the business has been operating, depends upon the conditions in each enterprise.

As to source, two types of capital are recognized — equity and borrowed. Equity capital is that invested in the business with no legal obligation to return the principal, or to pay interest upon it, to another party. It is ownership capital, although in the small family-sponsored enterprise the ownership aspect is often relinquished or donated by the contributor (frequently a parent or close relative of the proprietor) to the beginning entrepreneur. Borrowed capital implies the obligation to return the principal together with some interest or other compensation for the use of the funds. It is often called debt capital. In the small business this distinction between equity and borrowed capital is often blurred. Investigators have found that loans made to beginning businessmen by relatives or close friends sometimes resemble investment in the enterprise. No definite time for repayment is set; interest charges are deferred until some indefinite future date when the business can afford such payments. In most cases, however, funds borrowed to supplement initial owner-equity capital, even when obtained from relatives and friends, are secured with the intention that both principal and interest will eventually be repaid.

The tendency in recent years toward debt (rather than equity) financing is the result of the changed tax structure. To the small businessman who can obtain capital on reasonable terms within approved ratios to his own equity, this situation may have advantages. He can deduct interest paid as a valid business expense, enlarge the funds under his control, retain control over his enterprise, and take advantage of conditions causing more people to be willing to lend rather than to invest savings.

The average "going" small business in need of working capital, funds for expansion, or for some special purpose should analyze its own resources carefully before seeking outside financing. Inventories, for example, are a frequent source of idle funds. Usually from 20 to over 50 percent of the merchandise and materials on hand in the average small business is in excess of needs, and often some of the surplus items are currently being reordered. When surplus stocks have been identified, dispose of them as quickly and economically as possible — and make sure they are not still being reordered.

When credit is extended by a small business in need of funds, it is very likely that too much capital has been tied up in slow or doubtful accounts. A vigorous campaign to collect all past-due accounts and the adoption of careful credit control for future operations is necessary in such cases. It might be advisable to explore the possibilities of shifting to a cash basis.

A small business may have idle assets in the form of fixtures, equipment, materials, and other "odds and ends" that could be sold without affecting business operations adversely. Excess space may be rented or subleased, or the firm's telephone or display facilities may be leased to secure extra income, if this does not encroach on regular business activities.

Since the usual tendency for beginners is to buy many assets, such as trucks, office machines, and other equipment, extra capital may often be secured by selling such articles and shifting to a policy of renting or leasing equipment. This practice is becoming increasingly common and practical. Many rental or leasing firms are available, covering widely varied items. As noted elsewhere, tax advantages might accrue since rental is considered as an expense.

On a continuing basis some of the larger sources of capital from within the average small business are likely to be available through more effective expense control. Three aspects are of special importance: (1) owner withdrawals should be consistent with the needs of the business and can often be cut drastically when capital is needed; (2) certain operations performed in traditional ways may be shifted to less expensive methods, as personal service to self-service; and especially (3) closer control over payroll, rent, publicity, and other major expenses may be possible. This does not necessarily mean reduction of the dollar expenditures but, rather, securing maximum profitable returns from every expenditure. These procedures also greatly strengthen the firm's borrowing position if outside financing is still needed.

Other than the capital which may be freed or conserved through more adroit management of a "going" concern, additional funds may be obtained from the following sources:

1. The owner and his associates, including his family and friends, who may or may not become partners or shareholders in the venture
2. Partners and shareholders of a corporation
3. Representatives of banks or other established lending institutions whose business includes making loans to business organizations
4. The Small Business Administration financial assistance program
5. SBA-licensed small business investment companies
6. Members of the trade, including suppliers of materials, such as manufacturers and wholesalers; and, in some instances, customers who prepay their contracts
7. Other businesses, local capitalists, securities markets, community pools or groups, sales finance companies, and miscellaneous other sources

Borrowing from Friends and Relatives

Traditionally, beginning businessmen have gone to relatives and friends for financial assistance. Although this approach is considered poor business practice and is often based on erroneous assumptions, it may be necessary in many cases.

Yet business and family or social relationships should not be mixed if the most desirable results are to be obtained.

Securing funds from friends and relatives builds a highly personal financial relationship that conflicts with both independence and business. The businessman whose backing requires him to weigh personal considerations constantly is in a weak position when he makes decisions for the business itself. Furthermore, these financial associates frequently feel impelled to assert their proprietary interests by offering advice or even by insisting that certain business actions be taken, and their recommendations may not be in harmony with the wishes and objectives of the proprietor.

A *business* loan should be a *business* transaction, not a favor. One's friends and relatives may be more easily convinced of the possibilities involved, but they are seldom in a position to pass sound business judgment. The evaluation given the proposed enterprise by a business organization will be based on expert knowledge and experience, and will be constructive and therefore valuable to the beginner. In the lending institution's efforts to place its trust wisely the new operator will find assistance in properly planning and soundly establishing his enterprise.

Sometimes forming a partnership or even a closed corporation is one way of securing financial aid from close acquaintances. A partnership is the association of two or more individuals who pool their capital and talents for the purpose of operating a business. All partners may invest money only, but one or more usually becomes active in running the business.

Financing through Lending Institutions

Commercial banks are a primary source for debt rather than equity capital. Some banks have consumer loan departments and many more make small loans to consumers in a manner similar to business loans. Actually, a great many small loans made to individuals as personal loans are used for small business financing. Some banks have established small business loan departments and others delegate the financing of small enterprises to particular officers.

An undetermined, but probably substantial, amount of "semiterm" loans made by banks on a 60- to 90-day basis are subject to virtually continuous renewal under favorable circumstances. As a business proves to be successful both the amount and duration of such loans tend to increase.

Although short-term loans for less than a year predominate, many banks make long-term loans ranging from one to ten years with an average maturity of about five years. About four-fifths of the latter term loans are "collateral loans," that is, they are secured by assets having a value well in excess of the amount of the loan.

Term loans which are unsecured are called "character loans." Although they tend to be for shorter periods and smaller amounts than collateral loans, so much depends upon the individual borrower that exceptions to this generalization are easy to find. A person with proved managerial ability, an excellent reputation, and a good business proposition may receive a character loan for several thousand dollars on a long-term favorable-interest basis in the same bank where another, less well known individual is obliged to put up collateral worth $500 to secure a short-term loan of $200 at the bank's maximum rate of interest.

Banks also make special types of loans, one of which is the installment loan, ranging in amount from $100 to $3,000 or more. Most installment loans are repayable monthly, with a maturity of one year or less. Another variety consists of loans secured by accounts receivable, which may be on a notification or nonnotification basis. On the former the bank notifies the borrower's accounts and undertakes to collect from them. On the latter the borrower's customers may never know their accounts were assigned unless they fail to make payment as agreed. In such a case the bank is likely to notify the delinquent debtor and to assist in making collection.

A third variety of loan is one secured by negotiable receipts for warehouse or field warehouse stocks. These are common for manufacturers and for some dealers in furniture and heavy equipment. A fourth type is the equipment loan, which may be obtained on more favorable terms from the local bank than from the equipment manufacturer or supplier. And, finally, mortgage loans are sometimes made on the basis of either chattel mortgages or personal or business property or real estate mortgages, which may in turn be real estate owned by the business unit or by the individual enterpriser apart from his business.

The loan contract.   The loan contract is drawn up by the bank. It includes all provisions which the banker feels are necessary to ensure payment.

The loan contract sets forth the basic conditions of the loan and may include the following:

1. Length of loan period and schedule for repaying in installments
2. Interest and other charges
3. Provision that the entire balance of the loan be made due and payable immediately if any default is made in repayment
4. Any warranties that may be necessary
5. Requirements to maintain working capital at the proper level
6. Restrictions on other borrowing during the life of the loan
7. Description of assets, if any, pledged to secure the loan, and the terms under which they are pledged
8. Restrictions on the payment of salaries and dividends or distribution of earnings during the life of the loan[5]

Bankers' bases for lending.   The following standards are considered important by bankers when making loans to small businessmen:

1. The character of the applicant: he should be an excellent moral risk
2. The managerial ability of the applicant
3. The productive nature of the loan, as evidenced by the past record for an established business or the banker's appraisal of profit prospects for a new venture
4. The collateral offered to insure repayment in case the expected profits do not materialize or to protect the lender whenever the borrower's reputation has not been well-established

In making decisions regarding loan applications, the banker needs reliable facts.

[5]Paul G. Hastings, "Term Loans in Small Business Financing," *Small Marketers Aids Annual* no. 2 (Washington, D.C.: Small Business Administration, 1960), p. 61.

Usually the balance sheet and profit-and-loss statement will be requested for a going concern or, in the case of a new venture, a prospectus stating estimated sales, expenses, and anticipated profits. The use to which funds obtained will be put is a major consideration.

Since collateral is so often required to obtain bank loans, the small businessman should understand the nature of assets considered to be good collateral. These are usually "quick assets," or property that can be converted readily into its money value. Other things that the enterpriser often pays good money for may be poor collateral for bank loans. Among these would be items such as the following:

1. Specially made machines, equipment, fixtures, or built-in construction not salable to others in the same or similar trades — examples: canning, wrapping, labeling, or processing machines; store or restaurant fixtures built to fit particular spaces; wall decorations and floor designs.

2. Stationery, signs, wrapping paper, souvenirs, or other items carrying the name of the concern for which they were purchased and therefore salable to others at only a fraction of their cost, if at all.

3. Style merchandise or other goods likely to become outmoded; supplies of materials used in a declining industry or to meet a passing need — examples: cast-iron items that are being replaced by aluminum; kerosene lamps and equipment; makeshift or temporary substitutes.

4. Partly finished products, such as mechanical parts and materials intended for particular assemblies, and even completed assemblies for which a market has ceased to exist — examples: metal parts made to specifications for one buyer.

There are generally accepted guides in each line of business as to the proper ratio of long- and short-term loans to owner equity and other standards. The beginner may secure advice on the standard ratios for his business from his banker, accountant, or trade association. So far as the proper cost of borrowed capital is concerned, however, there appear to be no well-established guides; the cost of capital varies widely from one firm to another even in the same line of business.

Minority-owned banks.   Minority-owned businesses rely heavily on minority-owned banks as a major source of capital, particularly since both the banks and the business enterprises are located where there is a concentration of minority population to support them. However, of approximately 14,000 commercial banks in the United States, with total deposits exceeding $500 billion, only 48 are minority-owned-and-operated and their deposits (as of July 1972) total less than $900 million. To increase bank funds available for minority business development, the Office of Minority Business Enterprise of the U.S. Department of Commerce — with the endorsement of the National Bankers Association — is encouraging large corporations, educational institutions, religious organizations, foundations, labor unions, and state and local governments to establish deposit relationships with minority-owned banks. Since the inception of this program in October 1970, deposit balances in these banks have increased more than $400 million. These additional funds will significantly increase the impact these banks will have on minority business enterprise.

Borrowing from the SBA

Under section 7(a) of the Small Business Act of 1953, as amended, SBA is empowered

> to make loans to enable small-business concerns to finance plant construction, conversion, or expansion, including the acquisition of land, . . . equipment, facilities, machinery, supplies, or materials; or to supply such concerns with working capital to be used in the manufacture of articles, equipment, supplies, or materials for war, defense, or civilian production or as may be necessary to insure a well-balanced national economy.

However, under the act the Small Business Administration can make no loans that can otherwise be obtained on reasonable terms. Further, SBA's share of such loans cannot exceed $350,000 in any one case. At times, SBA places lower limits on its share of loans in order to conserve its funds.

SBA also guarantees eligible bank loans to small firms up to 90 percent or $350,000 of the loan, whichever is less, provided the bank's interest rate is not more than 8 percent. It may also participate with a bank in making a loan, up to $350,000 as the SBA's share, provided that the interest on the bank's share of the loan does not exceed 8 percent. Interest on SBA's portion of an immediate-participation loan and its interest obligation under a loan guarantee is limited to $5\frac{1}{2}$ percent.[6]

SBA loans for purposes of construction or expansion, or for the purchase of machinery and equipment, may be made for as long as 15 years. Those made for working capital purposes are usually limited to 6 years.

In addition to business loans, the SBA makes certain types of "disaster" loans for as long as 30 years, and for as much as $500,000. Under one type of lending program the SBA helps a small business restore or replace property damaged by a flood, hurricane, earthquake, or other natural disaster. Under a second type of lending program this business would also be helped to overcome economic injury suffered by it as a result of such a disaster. SBA loans of the latter type are for the purposes of stocking normal inventories and paying financial obligations which the small businessman would have been able to meet had he not lost revenue because of the disaster. To receive either type of loan the firm must be located in an area officially declared as a "disaster area" by the president or the secretary of agriculture. The damage or injury must also have been "substantial." Both "physical disaster" and "economic injury" loans may be made by SBA entirely on its own, or in participation with a bank or other lending institution.

Another type of "economic injury" loan is designed to assist the small firm that is forced to relocate because of federally aided urban renewal and highway construction programs. Loans of this type may also be made by SBA directly or jointly.

The maximum rate of interest on an SBA loan or on its share of a joint loan is 3 percent in the case of "natural" disasters, and usually between 4 and $5\frac{1}{2}$ percent in the case of economic "disaster" suffered by displaced businesses. No specific figure is set as the maximum rate of interest on the bank's share of a participation loan, but it must be within "reasonable" limits.

[6]Interest on "direct" SBA loans is also limited to $5\frac{1}{2}$ percent.

Since 1964 the SBA has been making "economic opportunity" loans, in addition to regular business loans and disaster loans. The purpose of these loans is to help low-income people with the potential to successfully operate a business, but who cannot qualify for SBA's regular business loans. Such persons can borrow up to $50,000 for up to 15 years. The interest rate is the same as for regular business loans ($5\frac{1}{2}$ percent). However, in considering "economic opportunity" (EO) loans, SBA relaxes traditional credit standards and places greater emphasis on the character and ability of the individual. In late 1972 the benefits of the SBA economic opportunity loan program were extended to honorably-discharged veterans of the Vietnam War.

As noted in Chapter 2, individual small firms are often at a competitive disadvantage with large firms in obtaining raw materials, supplies, equipment, or the benefits of research and development. To help them overcome this handicap, SBA will provide financial assistance to any local group corporation formed and capitalized by two or more small business firms for the purpose of making *joint* purchases or establishing *common* research and development facilities. The maximum amount of an SBA *pool loan* is $250,000 for each firm in the group. For example, if four small firms were to incorporate they would become eligible for a loan of $1 million in federal funds. If a bank participates, the loan amount may exceed this limit by the amount the bank provides. Pool loans are repaid over a period of 10 years, except when construction of facilities is involved. In the latter case, the loan may be amortized over a 20-year period. The interest rate on SBA's share of the loan is 5 percent per year.

The SBA also helps small business concerns *indirectly* in the acquisition of land, construction, conversion or expansion of buildings, and the purchase of machinery and equipment through loans to state and local development companies. These development companies are formed for the express purpose of promoting and assisting the growth and development of small businesses in the state or local area by supplying them with needed long-term loans and equity capital.

In August 1971 a new program was launched to provide SBA-guaranteed revolving lines of credit to small building contractors. The line of credit is available at any bank which has entered into an agreement with SBA to participate in the program. The amount of the line of credit cannot exceed a reasonable estimate of the contractor's current cash requirements needed to finance the work that he has the capacity to perform and which he can reasonably be expected to generate under firm contracts. Guarantees are limited to $350,000, or 90 percent of the line of credit, whichever is less. The line of credit will be in force for one year, but 60 days before it is due to expire it will be reviewed for possible extension for another year. This program will remove a major handicap to small building contractors, since they often have difficulty in obtaining government and other contracts because of inadequate financing for the early part of the work. It will also encourage large building contractors to subcontract a larger share of their work to small firms.

Another way in which the Small Business Administration assists in the financing of small business is through the licensing and regulation of small business investment companies, or SBICs as they are commonly called; these are discussed in the following section.

Small Business Investment Companies

The licensing and regulation of privately owned small business investment companies by the Small Business Administration was made possible by the Small Business Investment Act of 1958. The purpose of the act was to meet the needs of small business for long-term debt funds and equity capital which the Congress felt were not being adequately met by other lending institutions. Section 102 of the act reads as follows:

> It is declared to be the policy of the Congress and the purpose of this Act to improve and stimulate the national economy in general and the small business segment thereof in particular by establishing a program to stimulate and supplement the flow of private equity capital and long-term loan funds which small business concerns need for the sound financing of their business operations and for their growth, expansion and modernization, and which are not available in adequate supply: *Provided,* however, that this policy shall be carried out in such manner as to insure the maximum participation of private financing sources. . . .

In addition to the making of long-term loans, an SBIC may finance a small firm by purchasing its capital stock or debt securities, or by purchasing debentures which are convertible into stock of the business. However, it is limited by law to a maximum investment in any single firm to 20 percent of the SBICs combined capital and surplus. If a small firm needs more money than one SBIC is permitted to provide, several SBICs may join in the financing. Loans and debt securities must have a maturity of not less than 5 years. Loans may have terms for as long as 15 years, and there is no maximum maturity provision on debt securities, except as may be imposed as a policy of the individual SBIC.

A small business investment company may issue its long-term subordinated debentures to SBA in an amount equal to twice its private capital, but not more than $7.5 million. Under certain circumstances in which an SBIC is specializing in venture-capital financing, the maximum loan available from SBA is $10 million. Such loans may be subordinated with up to 15-year terms. No SBIC will be licensed by SBA, however, unless it has a combined private capital and surplus of at least $150,000.

Minority Enterprise Small Business Investment Companies.   In November 1969 the SBA, in cooperation with the Department of Commerce, instituted a Minority Enterprise Small Business Investment Company (MESBIC) program to provide financial, management, and technical assistance to new and expanding black, Puerto Rican, American Indian, and other minority-owned businesses. MESBICs represent a specialized application of the SBIC principle. One may be formed with a minimum investment of $150,000, which is matched on a 2-for-1 basis by the Small Business Administration.

Trade Financing — the Use of Credit

Trade financing is essentially a method of buying materials, merchandise, or equipment on credit. Equipment manufacturers and dealers know that the average small businessman is not financially able to pay cash for expensive installations and may have difficulty in securing local bank loans for this purpose. All major companies have financing plans to stimulate the sale of their equipment. Usually a down payment of from 20 to 30 percent is required, the remainder to be paid in monthly installments over a period of one to two years or more.

Credit from suppliers for the purchase of materials, merchandise, and supplies is the most common and most widely used type of financing in the small enterprise. It often provides a major part of the small businessman's working capital needs, especially in the retail fields.

Miscellaneous Sources of Funds

It is sometimes possible for an enterpriser to find other businesses that would profit by financing his venture. This may happen, for example, when a manufacturer is seeking a dealer outlet in a certain town, or when the established industries in a community feel the need for a new enterprise, such as a specialized repair shop or other type of facilitating industry. Many small businesses have been started in one of these ways.

People with property interests may be induced to aid beginning enterprisers, and often to construct buildings for them and to help secure initial financing of equipment and fixtures. Real estate agents, especially developers, and shopping-center promoters have occasionally aided in financing small businessmen who buy or lease through their agencies.

Many large distributors have financed small manufacturers to produce items for private-label merchandising. Other sources of credit available to the small businessman include commercial credit companies that make loans on manufacturers' or wholesalers' accounts receivable, sales finance companies that specialize in buying dealers' installment account paper at a discount, and others. Although in theory "G.I." loans (secured by the Veterans Administration) may be made through approved private lending institutions or by an individual, maximum limits on loan size and interest rates have made them for all practical purposes a thing of the past.

Within the past few years some state governments have inaugurated programs to support minority enterprise. Illinois, for example, recently established the Illinois State Equity Council to provide long-term and equity capital for minority businessmen.

The U.S. Department of the Interior also contributes to the development of minority enterprise through its Bureau of Indian Affairs. In July 1970 the bureau initiated the Indian Business Development Fund to assist Indians with the financing necessary to start or expand small businesses. The fund provides grants to serve as cash equity for those Indians having less than sufficient equity to qualify them for small business loans from either public or private sources. Most Indians have found it difficult to take advantage of even the 90 percent loan guarantee program of the Small Business Administration, because most private lending institutions have required a 100 percent guarantee for Indian loans.

Another source of funds is the Economic Development Administration of the U.S. Department of Commerce. To promote economic redevelopment in areas of substantial unemployment or low median family incomes, small firms located in these areas may receive long-term loans (up to 25 years) from the EDA at 4 percent interest.

The Economic Development Administration also participates with the Ford Foundation and other private groups in the funding of a new national program to assist minority contractors in the construction industry — the Minority Contractors Assistance Project (MCAP). Lack of capital and inability to meet bonding requirements are major reasons why minority contractors have had difficulty in competing for construction jobs. Usually they have been limited to small projects not requiring large seed capital. MCAP was launched in 1971 to help overcome this difficulty by providing interim construction financing and bonding assistance to minority contractors.

SELECTING THE FORM OF ORGANIZATION

In deciding what form of organization to adopt, several aspects should be considered. Since each has both advantages and limitations, a good plan is to weigh these in the light of one's needs and objectives. At least the following aspects deserve consideration:

1. A need for additional funds may sometimes be met better by forming a partnership or corporation than by borrowing or using mercantile credit. However, this means sharing profits as well as risks and losses.

2. A need for certain managerial abilities or experience may be met by taking in one or more partners possessing the requisite qualities. An alternate method of securing these benefits without sharing ownership is to affiliate with a voluntary chain or franchising organization. In either case the additional abilities are secured at the expense of sharing authority and placing some restrictions upon one's "independence."

3. The choice of organization form to use may be influenced by the desire to achieve such objectives as limiting liability, distributing the risks involved, and taking advantage of the tax structure in operation at the time and place where the business is to be started. Federal and state income tax laws may make one form of organization superior to others for the small businessman; profits from a corporation, for example, may be taxed doubly, once as corporate profits and again as invididual income, whereas the proprietorship or partnership may be exempt from this double taxation. Sometimes one form or organization is given advantages by particular laws or regulations, such as those limiting the power of a corporation to engage in certain activities open to the proprietorship or partnership.

As the best form of organization to use, the final decision will probably be a compromise based upon weighing the relative importance of certain needs against the limitations of each form of organization. The person in business must be familiar with these pros and cons for his own welfare and protection in order to take full advantage of his rights and at the same time avoid undesirable consequences due to his ignorance of his exact status. For these reasons it may be desirable to review these three types of organization.

The Single Proprietorship

The simplest way to go into business is to rent space, buy goods and equipment, and start working. Except where federal, state, or local licenses or permits are required, this is all that is necessary for the single proprietorship. This form of organization has numerous advantages:

1. Organization entails no formality.
2. Ownership has perfect freedom of operation. When business decisions are made or when actions are taken, it is not necessary to get the consent of anyone else in the organization.
3. All profits are the property of the owner and need not be shared with anyone else.
4. Earnings may be retained in the business for its improvement and expansion.
5. Business losses are deductible from personal income when federal income tax is determined.
6. As compared with the partnership:
   a. Liability is limited to the owner's errors or obligations.
   b. There is no danger of loss resulting from the death or withdrawal of a partner.
7. As compared with the corporation:
   a. No double tax when profits are distributed.
   b. No capital stock tax.
   c. No corporate reports or inspections.
   d. No restrictions on the nature of business
   e. No penalty for retaining earnings in the business.

There are, however, certain disadvantages in the one-owner type of organization:

1. The many abilities required for successful business operation (selling, bookkeeping, production methods, administration, and so forth) are seldom all possessed by one person.
2. Limited personal assets do not encourage lenders and cannot always provide the required capital to meet unusual needs.
3. In case of business failure the owner's personal assets, including his home, automobile, and other properties, are subject to claim by creditors.

The Partnership

Certain conditions accrue when a partnership is formed, some favorable and some definitely undesirable. Arguments in favor of the partnership include the following:

1. "Two heads are better than one." Two viewpoints, although they clash, may result in a desirable compromise.
2. Personal abilities are complemented. The salesman and the bookkeeper, with different personalities and abilities, may succeed together when neither could alone.

3. Added capital is made available by combining the assets of two or more partners and less borrowing is necessary.

4. Business losses are deductible from the personal income of each partner for income tax purposes.

5. As compared with the corporation:
   a. There are no state incorporation fees, no capital stock tax, and no double tax on dividends.
   b. Income may be divided through "family partnership" or on bases other than investment, such as talents or time spent in the business.
   c. Partners' "salary" is not subject to payroll taxes.
   d. No penalty results from retaining earnings in the business.

Among the disadvantages of the partnership are:

1. Each partner is liable for all debts incurred by the business.

2. Each partner is responsible for the action of all other partners that creates an obligation for the business.

3. The partnership is automatically dissolved by the death or voluntary withdrawal of a partner (except in the case of limited partners).[7]

4. Profits must be shared among the partners.

The Corporation

The corporation is a legal form of organization made possible by state laws that govern the provisions under which its charter, or authorization to operate as a business entity, is granted. Since the corporation is a creation of the law, it is impersonal and exists without reference to the particular individuals who may share its ownership and direct its activities. Advantages may be summarized as follows:

1. Legal liability of owners or stockholders for suits for personal injury or other activities connected with operating the business is limited to the amount of funds invested in the business.

2. The corporation is long-lived, being able to continue in existence up to the time limit granted in its charter, whereas the proprietorship ceases with the death of the owner and a partnership with the death of any partner (except in the case of limited partners).[8]

3. Capital may be accumulated from many sources: sale of common or preferred stock, loans made by issuing bonds, exchange of assets, and reservation of profits from the business.

4. Ownership in a corporation is easily transferred merely by sale or exchange of stock and entry of the new ownership on the books of the corporation. Permission of other stockholders is not required except in rare cases of separate contractual agreements.

5. Management of the business may be concentrated even though ownership is widespread.

6. A large number of owners may obtain for the corporation a considerable amount of free publicity and goodwill.

[7]Under the laws of some states the partnership agreement may provide for the continuance of a partnership for a specified period after the death of a partner.

[8]See footnote 7.

A corporation has certain disadvantages, however:

1. Its activities are limited to those specifically granted in the charter. A firm incorporated to engage in the retail dry goods business could not legally handle groceries or engage in manufacturing unless a "catchall" clause granting almost unlimited scope has been included in the charter.
2. Its geographical area of operations is limited to the state granting its charter until permission is secured from each state in which it desires to operate. This means also that additional license fees must be paid and regulations observed.
3. If active management is employed in lieu of owner-management, the personal interest and incentive associated with ownership are lessened.
4. The corporation must make numerous reports for taxation and other purposes to each state in which it does business.
5. Federal and state regulation of corporations has been increasing for some time.
6. A corporation is subject to more taxes than is the proprietorship or partnership (unless it can and does elect to be taxed as though it were a partnership under subchapter S of the Internal Revenue Code, discussed below).
7. More paperwork for reports and records is necessary, and the amount increases greatly as the corporation grows in size.
8. In the small corporation the advantage of limited liability is often circumvented in the case of business debts by the custom of requiring major stockholders to guarantee or endorse notes due to banks and to major merchandise suppliers.

TAXES AND THE FORM OF ORGANIZATION

Since taxes, especially federal income taxes, have become a major business and personal expense, the form of organization may be the deciding factor between profit or loss to an enterpriser. In addition, the tax structure has become so complicated and subject to so many changes that it is difficult to make a wise choice of legal structure. In all but very simple cases expert legal or accounting advice should be obtained.

For *income tax* purposes three basic forms of organization are recognized. The two most common ones are the corporation and the partnership, the sole proprietorship being subsumed under the latter since both are treated as income to individuals. The third legal form is relatively new – the "tax-option" corporation, a small business corporation which can avoid paying income tax if its stockholders elect to report the corporate income on their individual income tax returns. The latter organization form was created by a 1958 amendment to the Internal Revenue Code. Congress's purpose was to remove tax considerations as a factor in the small businessman's choice of a legal form of organization for his enterprise.

In order to appreciate more fully the lawmakers' intent in permitting this tax option, it is desirable that we first review the tax considerations in choosing between a partnership and a "regular" corporate form. The authors wish also to point out that in the great majority of cases these will be the alternatives most seriously considered by the small businessman. In the first place, not all small business corporations are eligible to exercise this option; and secondly, of the eligible corporations, only a small percentage of them have done so.

Partnerships vs. "Regular" Corporations

One of the most important practical features for small companies is the extent to which the owners can obtain income in the form of salary or in some other manner which represents a deduction for corporate tax purposes.[9] If all corporate income could be paid out to stockholder operators in this fashion, corporation taxes would not be a factor for closely held companies in which the shareholders are active. The most immediate way to narrow the effect of the artificial tax discrimination against corporations is by compensating the owners from company income. If salaries, rentals, stock options, and pensions to the shareholders are validly deductible items for the corporation, the double tax resulting from dividend payments is reduced to that extent.

This is an obvious device to minimize corporation income tax, and it has been abused by taxpayers through the use of inflated and fictitious claims. The taxing authorities are alert to guard against this kind of tax evasion, and with the courts have worked out various standards of a general character as a guide in testing the validity of different forms of compensation. Under the general tests, deductions for officers' salaries and bonuses are allowable if the compensation is "reasonable" in amount and payment was for services rendered.

An additional way of getting money out of the corporation is for the owner to capitalize with debt equity as well as ownership equity. The effect is the same as drawing out a salary; the interest would be a taxable item to the owner, of course, but would be a deduction by the corporation. This is a scheme that is widely used in order to remove the double-taxation effect.

The ultimate feasibility of the corporate form for small, closely owned organizations depends on the measure to which the shareholders may benefit from corporate income in ways other than through dividend payments. Aside from salaries or other compensations from current income, the chief benefit to a shareholder arises from appreciation in the value of his stock, and its eventual sale either before or after his death. The appreciation in value depends in practically all cases upon the growth of the company. Growth and reasonably anticipated needs are the primary reasons for justifiable retention of corporate earnings in the business, in excess of the $100,000 allowable without question under the 1958 revisions, without the penalty surtax on corporations improperly accumulating surplus.

The most undesirable feature of the corporate form is the fact that dividends are not deductible in arriving at the company's net income, and the individual shareholder pays income tax on the dividends he receives in excess of $100. The effect of this disadvantage may be minimized, however, by judicious arrangement of the capital structure. If the interests of the owners are represented to as great an extent as is possible by bonds of the corporation rather than by stock, a substantial part of the corporate gross income may be paid out to the owners in the form of deductible interest. In computing credit based on invested capital, 75 percent of borrowed capital is recognized as part of the invested capital.

[9]The balance of material in this section, except as noted, is adapted from Chapter 8, "Tax Factors in the Choice of Form of Business Organization," in the book by Dan Throop Smith, *Tax Factors in Business Decisions* (Englewood Cliffs, N.J.: Prentice-Hall, 1968), with modifications reflecting the Tax Reform Act of 1969.

Upon the organization of a corporation, there is nothing to prevent the "owners" from setting up their capital investment partly in stock and partly in bonds. There is no set rule on just how "thin" the ratio of bonds to stock may be. The tax advantages may be summarized as follows:

Loans	*Capital Contributions*
1. Corporation gets interest deduction.	1. Corporation gets no deduction for dividends.
2. You pay full tax on interest received.	2. You pay tax on dividends received in excess of $100.00.
3. You pay no tax when the loan is re-paid.	3. Redemption of stock might be held a taxable dividend.
4. Should the corporation become insol-vent, you get a full or limited deduction.	4. Insolvent corporation leaves you with only a limited loss deduction.[10]

The mechanics and the immediate tax effects of creating a partnership are more simple than in the case of a corporation. The principal problems are: the validity of the partnership form for tax purposes; the selection of the type of partnership — whether it should be general or limited; the formulation of provisions for acquisition of a decedent's interest; and the anticipation of the effect of the partnership form upon the basis of assets.

In almost all states there are statutes allowing the creation of limited partnerships, usually requiring at least one general partner who has unlimited liability. The limited partnerships may have a number of corporate characteristics: the limited liability of some members, transferability of interests, or survival of the partnership entity on the death of members. Under the laws of some states a partnership may continue for a period after the death of a partner if the agreement so provides.

Under the federal tax law, the limited partnership may be treated as a partnership if it does not have more corporate than noncorporate characteristics.

	For a $10,000 Business			*For a $75,000 Business*		
	Prop.	*Part.*	*Corp.*	*Prop.*	*Part.*	*Corp.*
Net income before salaries .	$10,000	$10,000	$10,000	$75,000	$75,000	$75,000
Salaries to principals	10,000	{ 5,000 { 5,000	{ 4,000 { 4,000	75,000	{ 35,000 { 40,000	{ 30,000 { 30,000
Net income after salaries . .			2,000			15,000
Personal income taxes. . . .	1,596	{ 557 { 557	{ 367 { 367	34,655	{ 10,703 { 13,203	{ 8,411 { 8,411
Corporation taxes			440			3,300
Total taxes	1,596	1,114	1,174	34,655	23,906	20,122
Income after taxes.	8,404	8,886	8,826	40,345	51,094	54,878

[10] *Eight Keys to Bigger Tax Savings for Smaller Companies and Their Owners* (Englewood Cliffs, N.J.: Prentice-Hall, 1953), p. 17, with modifications reflecting the Tax Reform Act of 1969.

The preceding table illustrates the effects of corporate and individual income taxes. It is observed that the corporation may be advantageous for a larger small business, whereas a partnership may have tax advantages for a smaller enterprise. In the example the principals are unmarried, have no dependents, take a standard personal tax deduction, and receive income from no other sources.[11]

The "Tax-Option" Corporation

The "tax-option" corporation, also known popularly as a "subchapter S" corporation (after the subchapter of the Internal Revenue Code which created it) or a "Small Business Corporation" (as it is termed in the Code itself), is a corporation which pays no income tax, the corporate earnings being taxed as "partnership income" to the stockholders. Thus the most undesirable feature of the corporate form of organization – the double tax on dividends – is avoided.

In order to exercise this tax option, however, the corporation must have no more than ten stockholders, none of whom can be a corporation, and all of whom must give their consent. A second requirement is that no more than 20 percent of the corporate income can be derived from investments (dividends, interest, rent, capital gains, etc.). The law also stipulates that more than 20 percent of the corporate income must be derived from business operations within the United States.

The advantages to those eligible small business corporations which elect to exercise this tax option are summarized by Clarence F. McCarthy and other tax authorities as follows:

> Use of a Subchapter S corporation can provide the small business man with the benefits of the corporate form of business organization without burdening him with the double tax ordinarily associated with corporations. At the same time it gives the shareholder the tax benefit of any net operating losses of the business. . . .
>
> Another advantage of the Subchapter S corporation, which may be quite valuable in the proper circumstances, is the ability to time the taxation of Subchapter S income by the use of a fiscal year. If the Subchapter S corporation adopts a fiscal year ending shortly after the end of the shareholders' taxable year, the taxable income of the corporation can be put into the preceding year of the shareholders by payment of dividends before the end of the shareholders' year. On the other hand, if it is desirable to carry the income of the corporation over and have it taxed in the next taxable year of the shareholders, the Subchapter S corporation can defer the payment of the dividend until after the close of the shareholders' taxable year. If no dividend is paid, the corporation's income will be taxable as undistributed taxable income in the taxable year of a shareholder within which the taxable year of the corporation ends. This ability to time the year in which the corporation's income will be taxable to the shareholder can be of considerable value, particularly if a shareholder's outside income is subject to significant fluctuations from one year to the next.[12]

[11] Reprinted by permission from *Changing Times* (The Kiplinger Magazine), June 1951, pp. 15–16. Copyright 1951 by The Kiplinger Washington Editors, Inc. Figures revised to reflect current (1972) corporate and personal income tax rates.

[12] Clarence F. McCarthy, Billy M. Mann, and William H. Gregory, *The Federal Income Tax: Its Sources and Applications,* 2nd ed. (Englewood Cliffs, N.J.: Prentice-Hall, 1971), pp. 679–80.

"Every coin has two sides," so the saying goes. Approximately 80 percent of the eligible small business corporations have *not* elected to exercise their option of being taxed as partnerships. Professor Mauriello suggests that this may be because of the lower maximum tax rate on corporate income (48 percent, as opposed to a top incremental tax rate of 70 percent on personal income). Where the tax-option corporation is earning substantial profits, "the stockholders may be taxed at a rate appreciably higher than the maximum corporate rate."[13] Professor Raby, on the other hand, points out that the effective tax rate on accumulated (undistributed) earnings is higher for the tax-option corporation than it is for the regular corporation; he also points out that "most state income tax laws do not recognize the Small Business Corporation as differing from any other corporation, and they thus tax the Small Business Corporation on its income."[14]

SUMMARY AND CONCLUSIONS

Although there is no one best way to finance or to organize a business under all conditions, *great care should be exercised in determining capital needs, sources from which funds are to be secured, and the form of organization that best suits the particular circumstances.*

For the foreseeable future, the tax situation in relation to income brackets and objectives of the owners must be considered, and may be the dominant factor in selecting the best form of organization to use at a particular time. Legal and accounting counsel is often desirable in making the right decision.

Although financing is usually associated with securing funds external to an enterpriser's own resources, discussion in this chapter is intended to demonstrate that often internal sources of capital are overlooked and that this aspect of the question should receive major attention.

The form of organization is not only closely related to the problems of financing, but very often also affects the financial liability of participants and the transfer of equities. It also affects taxation, regulation, and various management practices. We must therefore conclude that the various considerations reviewed here tend to be inseparable.

REVIEW QUESTIONS

1. Define the following terms: capital; fixed capital; working capital; operating ratios; financial management.

2. What factors are taken into consideration by Dun & Bradstreet in arriving at a credit rating for a prospective business borrower?

[13] Joseph A. Mauriello, *The Irwin Federal Income Tax Course* (New York: Richard D. Irwin, 1971), pp. 577–80.

[14] William L. Raby, *The Income Tax and Business Decisions,* 2nd ed. (Englewood Cliffs, N.J.: Prentice-Hall, 1972), p. 81. In addition to Raby and the references cited in footnotes 12 and 13, see Smith, *Tax Factors*, pp. 136–38, for a discussion of the advantages and disadvantages of the tax-option corporation, and Robert S. Holzman, *Tax Basis for Managerial Decisions* (New York: Holt, Rinehart, 1965), pp. 154–66, for a discussion of the accumulated earnings tax.

3. Why is it usually more desirable for a beginning small businessman to rent rather than purchase his business premises and other physical facilities?

4. What are some of the obstacles encountered by a small wholesaler or retailer with limited capital?

5. Describe the different methods illustrated in the text for determining the capital requirements for a small merchandising business.

6. Discuss the thesis that it is a good idea to go into business for yourself when circumstances are right even though your finances are below those considered "desirable" or "necessary."

7. In what ways do the problems of financing a small factory differ from those of financing a small store?

8. In what ways do the problems of financing a small service establishment differ from those of financing a small store or factory?

9. Differentiate between "initial capital" and "working capital"; between "debt capital" and "equity capital." Why does the small businessman ordinarily prefer debt financing to equity financing?

10. Explain the statement in the text that "on a continuing basis some of the larger sources of capital are likely to be available from within the firm."

11. What are some of the "outside" sources of capital for the small firm?

12. Describe the various types of "collateral loans" mentioned in the text.

13. What criteria do bankers usually use in evaluating applicants for a business loan?

14. What are some of the restrictions and stipulations usually deemed necessary by a banker in drawing up a loan contract?

15. What kinds of loans can the Small Business Administration make to small business enterprises? What restrictions are imposed for each type of loan?

16. What are some of the indirect ways in which the Small Business Administration assists in the financing of small business?

17. What are small business investment companies? For what purpose was the Small Business Investment Act passed? What are MESBICs?

18. What are some of the factors which influence the entrepreneur's choice of a form of ownership organization to adopt?

19. List the advantages and disadvantages of each of the following types of organization: (*a*) proprietorship; (*b*) partnership; (*c*) corporation.

20. In what respects does a "tax-option" corporation differ from a "regular" corporation? What are its advantages? Its disadvantages?

DISCUSSION QUESTIONS

1. Indicate the circumstances under which you could justify a ratio for your prospective business well above the standard (in that type of business) for each of the following:
   a. Rent or occupancy expense for (i) a retail store; (ii) a factory; (iii) a service establishment.
   b. Total payroll, excluding withdrawals of owners
   c. Bad debt losses for (i) a retail store; (ii) a factory

2. Select some kind of small business and after consulting businessmen and other sources of information prepare a prospectus of the capital required to start the business.

SUPPLEMENTARY READINGS

Carson, Deane. *The Effects of Tight Money on Small Business Financing.* Small Business Management Research Report prepared for the Small Business Administration. Providence, R.I.: Brown University, 1963. Circumstantial evidence developed in this study points to discrimination against small business firms by commercial banks during periods of tight money. Recommends a program of financial education to small businessmen so that they will be better equipped to seek out the most suitable source of external funds.

Davies, Robert N., and Kelwyn H. Lawrence. *Choosing a Form of Business Organization.* Small Business Management Research Report prepared for the Small Business Administration. Durham, N.C.: Duke University, 1963. Discusses advantages and disadvantages of the various forms of business organization. Cites the many complex tax and managerial control considerations that govern the proper choice.

Robinson, Roland I. "The Financial Aspects of Starting a Small Business." In *Financing the Dynamic Small Firm*, chapter 2. Belmont, Calif.: Wadsworth Publishing Co., 1966. Discusses the financial problems of starting a brand new business. Tax considerations bearing on the choice of a legal form of organization are also discussed.

PART THREE
Operating the Business

- POLICIES — THE BUSINESS PERSONALITY

- MANAGEMENT AND LEADERSHIP

- UTILIZING "OUTSIDE STAFF" SERVICES

- INSURANCE AND RISK MANAGEMENT

- PERSONNEL AND EMPLOYEE RELATIONS

- PROCUREMENT AND SUPPLIER RELATIONS

- PRICING FOR PROFIT

- ADVERTISING AND SALES PROMOTION

- CREDIT — A SALES TOOL

- INVENTORY CONTROL

- PRODUCTION CONTROL IN THE SMALL PLANT

- PROFIT PLANNING AND COST CONTROL

- REGULATIONS AND TAXES

- SIMPLIFIED RECORD SYSTEMS

12

Policies—
the business personality

A firm's policies reflect the management's attitudes, goals, and manner of doing things. One can "feel" the policies of a business the minute one deals with it, for policies set the firm's attitude toward costomers, employees, products, equipment, money, and so forth, and thus determine its atmosphere, its "personality," its way of doing business.

Whether it plans one or not, every business acquires a reputation of sorts — for low prices, exclusive merchandise, prompt customer service, rapid delivery, reliable quality, freshness of stock, always having something different, or for numerous other distinguishing attributes. Policies enable it to build the particular reputation desired.

"Policies are standing plans or guides to action. . . . They set the limits within which specific operating units or activities must function."[1] They direct the business and control its activities to keep them in line with established objectives. To be effective they should be based on adequate information. They also should be definite and stable, yet flexible enough to be adjusted to meet fundamental changes.

The elimination of inconsistencies by a well-regulated set of policies results in less lost effort and less working at cross purposes. Policies enable the small businessman to conserve his energies and resources by directing them consistently toward an established goal. This concentration increases his effectiveness and chances for success by lessening dissipation or dilution of effort. Experience can be utilized to the greatest extent, because policies show what not to do as well as what should be done to accomplish a particular purpose.

Many business policies are stated in writing, but some are not. Written policies are more definite and can be followed more easily, but unwritten policies in the small business may be equally effective. The most important requirement is that the policies be understood and followed by all members of the firm. Customers, competitors, and suppliers should be informed of all policies that affect their dealings with the company.

[1] John G. Hutchinson, *Organizations: Theory and Classical Concepts* (New York: Holt, Rinehart, 1967), p. 40.

233

It is also important that policies be strictly adhered to in practice. A policy is not like a rule to which exceptions can be made. Under no circumstances should even a single exception be made to a policy. If the policy is too strict, change it, but *never* make an exception so long as the policy is in force.

Policies are of three types — general, major, and minor. A general policy relates to the business as a whole and expresses the overall purpose and aims of the business. It defines what the business is to accomplish and is vital to its success. Illustrations of general policies that provided the basic idea for the business itself include Henry Ford's concern for "economical transportation," J. C. Penney's belief in "The Golden Rule," and F. W. Woolworth's initial concentration on the sale of "merchandise that can be sold profitably for ten cents." General policies should be the result of much forethought and planning, and may need to be changed somewhat with time.

Major policies also relate to the business as a whole, but they are subordinate to the company's general policy. They provide guiding principles for such important companywide activities or concerns as finance and expansion, personnel and labor relations, research and development, and public relations. Other major policies deal with answers to such questions as: Shall we simplify or diversify our product line? How should we distribute our products? What geographic markets or market segments shall we serve? Shall we enter foreign markets or not? Deciding upon these and other major matters of policy are probably just as vital to the success of a business as its general policy.

Minor (or departmental) policies are those affecting the operations of a particular department. They relate to such questions as: What advertising media shall we use? What kinds of credit, if any, shall we extend? Shall we provide clerk service or stress self-service? Shall we offer trading stamps? Shall we make trade-in allowances? Shall we "recommend" resale prices for our products? Shall we open the store on Sundays? Minor policies are determined by departmental executives, but they must be consistent with the overall policies of the firm.

Policies should capitalize on whatever advantages a business may have, including special skills and knowledge the owner or firm members possess. Limited resources, however, may at times require the rejection of an otherwise desirable policy. Financial resources, for instance, are usually a major limitation for small businesses. The abilities of available personnel must also be considered.

Most successful businessmen have the faculty of making prompt decisions. Since well-formulated policies guide these decisions, in one sense the decisions were all made well in advance, at the time of policy formation. In most cases the businessman tests each problem as it arises in the light of his policies and decides accordingly. This is one of the important advantages of having a good set of policies.

Occasionally the proprietor is required to make a hasty decision of far-reaching importance without having time to investigate all the ramifications of the question or to deliberate upon the possible effects of his decision. In such cases his established policies are the safest. No matter how attractive a proposition that violates his policies may seem, he should reject it without hesitation if he does not have time for an investigation at least as thorough as that involved in establishing the policies.

POLICIES FOR THE NEW BUSINESS

In the launching of an entirely new business, there is always an experimental or pioneering period during which initial policies will be on trial. Two dangers are to be guarded against. First, after every reasonable effort has been made to justify the need for the new business as recommended in Chapter 6, and after the real opportunity has been defined, great care should be taken to formulate policies most likely to enable the business to satisfy this need at a profit. All too often a small business is started not only with little serious attempt to justify its need, but also with only vague ideas as to how the assumed need can best be satisfied. It is better to formulate the policies one considers desirable, even though later experience proves the advisability of changing them, than to have no policies at all. Thus one will at least profit by directed experience. Changes can be made as required and the firm will be basing on experience a coordinated set of policies that will continue to develop as the business progresses.

Second, general policies should not be abandoned before they have had a fair chance to prove their worth. A beginner often fails to realize how long it may take people to become familiar with something new and to approve of it. As the sponsor of the idea, the proprietor is understandably enthusiastic about it. When potential customers fail to show their interest and appreciation, it is natural for him to become discouraged. Slow progress at first may make the enterprise seem hardly worth the effort. At this stage it is easy to be tempted to revise the policy. A change in general policy, the basic idea upon which the new business was founded, should not take place until the business has had a fair chance to succeed.

It is admittedly difficult to tell at just what point a general policy proves unsound and should be abandoned. However, the danger of becoming discouraged too soon is so great that every reasonable effort should be made to give a carefully determined policy sufficient time to prove itself. About the only guides that can be offered as to when policy abandonment is desirable are: (1) if experience shows actual errors of fact or judgment in formulating the original policy; (2) if unforeseen changes destroy the soundness of the policy; and (3) if the time required to establish the business on a paying basis is greater than the owner is able to stand financially.

This discussion relates primarily to the general policy of a new business. During the experimental period it is to be expected that some major and departmental policy changes will be made as the business finds its place and tests the desirability of minor variations in policy. For example, although a policy of accepting no special orders may have been decided upon at the start, an adjustment would be called for if it developed that only a few requests for special orders were received, that these came from some of the most profitable customers, and that the trouble and expense of handling special orders was less than had been expected.

In addition to a general policy, certain major policies deal with such fundamental matters that they must be considered for all lines of business. Of fundamental importance to the success of any firm in any line of business are major policies relating to products, finance, and personnel and organization.

Customer and Product Policies

"Whose needs do we hope to satisfy?" "What needs do they have?" "How can we best provide for these needs?" These are questions which must be answered by anyone planning a new business.

Decisions governing products to be made, merchandise to be handled, or services to be offered should be guided by what is variously referred to as the product, merchandise, or merchandising policy. Merchandising in a policy sense deals with designing, adapting, or selecting the goods or services to be offered by the business. Naturally the producer designs or adapts the goods, whereas the merchant selects goods to suit customer demands. Although closely related to general policy, which defines the field in which the business will engage, product policy goes beyond this by designating a particular area of operation as well as the methods to be followed. For example, a small factory that plans to make furniture must ask itself: What kind? For what customers? What principles will be followed as guides in designing and restyling? Will it cater to custom designs or work toward standard articles? Will it attempt to introduce or pioneer new concepts of style, such as improvements in functional design? When will designs formerly made be abandoned? What standards will be used in making these and other decisions affecting the goods to be offered?

Similar questions must be decided in the merchandising and service fields. In retailing and wholesaling, merchandise selection rather than product design is involved, although this difference is less significant than is commonly assumed. Actually some retailers have contracted with manufacturers who make products according to specifications or designs dictated by their customers' needs. Also, some small "manufacturers" merely submit their product designs to private label firms or subcontractors for actual production.

In the service industries competition, new developments, and market strategy are continually raising questions of adapting present services to customer needs, of adding new services, and of dropping old ones.

Two other policy guides may be suggested. Especially in the initial selection of products to make, merchandise to carry, or particular services to offer, a decision must be made as to whether to enter an already established though possibly crowded field, offering goods or services the same as those of competitors, or to differentiate the new firm's offerings in some way. The latter policy is usually better, if practical, as it gives the company a new market within the already established field, a strong claim for patronage, and a good talking point for its advertising. Many beginners merely copy the policies of firms already established, often without investigating how successful these have been.

There is one situation in which the adoption of policies similar to those of established firms may be justified. If careful investigations shows these policies to be the best for the conditions and if the newcomer has a good chance of competing successfully, these would be the logical policies to adopt. When existing firms are lax or careless in following stated policies or have other obvious weaknesses, the new entrant would have a good chance for success. Policies are often publicized in general terms with principles phrased for public approval rather than as guides that the business sincerely intends to follow. Many excellent business opportunities are found if investigation discloses this to be the case.

Finance and Expansion Policies

"Are we an aggressive, an adventurous, or a conservative firm?" "How do we feel about borrowing money from others?" "How large do we want to be ten years from now?" Answers to these questions set the pace for growth and development.

Policies regarding finance and expansion are so closely related for the small business that they may well be considered together. Two opposing attitudes are distinguishable: the conservative and the adventurous. For example, the financial policy should state the proportion of the concern's total capital the small businessman plans to own or what his equity will be at all times. Ownership equity in the assets of the firm should be more than half the total, and preferably larger.

Since inadequate, often "shoestring" ownership financing is a major cause of many small business failures, some authorities recommend that the portion of ownership equity be two-thirds or more. Thus if the capital requirements of a new or expanding business total $45,000, the entrepreneur should put at least $30,000 of his own money "on the line." This is a conservative policy, but the probabilities of success for the venture would be increased considerably.

On the other hand, the adventurous or heavy-risk-taking attitude is based on premises like the following: any business ownership is a risk; if the risk is worth taking at all, it should be exploited to the limit. That some limit exists is implied, but it is accepted only when necessary. Waiting for a conservative opportunity or condition is likely to defeat the very purpose of independent business ownership. By the time a person has accumulated adequate capital and experience and a good business opportunity occurs, he is too old and too saddled with family responsibilities to take advantage of it. A small business waiting to expand conservatively may sit by and see competitors become entrenched before conditions arise to permit its expansion by conservative standards.

Since numerous examples can be cited of success on a shoestring, of fortunes made from expansion against conservative advice, and of hundreds of thousands of individuals who waited too long to satisfy their business ownership ambitions, as well as of conservative small businesses that are still small, this adventurous policy must be recognized as having some merit. However, it is to some extent a matter of individual attitude and ability, and it varies so greatly with circumstances that probably the best approach is to use the more conservative principles as a starting point. After that, each individual may proceed at his own risk.

Policy needs to be established also with respect to outside financing. From what sources and under what terms will the businessman secure funds needed for initial capital, fluctuating amounts of working capital, and future expansion? Capital secured from the outside should be on terms that allow more-than-ample time for repayment out of reasonable expected earnings from the business.

A serious danger to most small businesses is the need to finance fixed capital from short-term loans. Even if renewal is promised orally, it may not come as expected when needed. One form of fixed capital is that invested in fixtures and equipment. Since both of these generally may be purchased on installment, the temptation to overspend is great. A better policy is to follow the recommendations of bankers, trade associations, management consultants, and other authorities as to the approximate amount of capital to invest in fixtures and equipment. In either case, adequate depreciation should be taken each year in order that a reserve may be accumulated for replacement of the assets when they become worn out or obsolete. The company policy should also provide for cash payment with borrowed funds, when need be, if the banker's interest charge on loans is less than the vendor's carrying charge on installment sales.

The monetary factor is the common denominator or thread connecting various activities of the business. Sales volume, for example, is related to production or merchandise needs by furnishing the dollar revenue with which to pay all expenses and costs of materials or merchandise sold. The financial budget is the device used by business to coordinate all its activities over a period of time. Policies should be formulated covering the scope of budgetary control, the steps in developing and administering the budget, and the extent to which a long-range budget — a five- or ten-year plan — will serve as a guide for future expansion.

Borrowing for expansion.   Although the conservative policy is to expand from earnings only, this is not always the most profitable. It "takes money to make money," but borrowed money works just as well as owned capital. There is always the possibility that many excellent opportunities will be lost if expansion is based solely on accumulated surplus. A decision to expand with borrowed capital, however, should be guided by the same adequate information and good judgment as required for initial entry into business. Two policies especially important during the early years of a business career are (1) to pay off all indebtedness in the shortest possible time, and (2) to leave as much of the profit in the business as possible. The latter policy requires that the owner's drawing account, or "salary," be minimal — somewhat less than what he could earn working for someone else.

Discounts on purchases.   Another aspect of financial policy is the firm's reputation concerning the payment of bills and the taking of discounts. At one extreme is a policy of paying cash for every purchase and seeking the largest allowable discounts. The average small business will usually take advantage of regular credit terms, however, because this is an important source of working capital. But too many are careless about taking advantage of cash discounts, and some tend to be slow in making payment even when bills are due at the net amount. A reputation for paying bills promptly is a valuable business asset. By always taking advantage of cash discounts the business can enhance its reputation even further. In addition, cash discounts alone amount to important savings in most cases. The typical terms "2 percent, 10 days, net 30" are equivalent to an annual interest rate of 36 percent when cash discounts are taken. For example, an invoice dated January 1, amounting to $100 with terms of 2 percent, 10 days, net 30, would carry a 2 percent discount of $2 if paid on the 10th. If it were paid 20 days later, on the 30th, the gross amount, $100, would be due. Assume it is necessary to borrow from the bank at 6 percent to discount the bill. Interest on $100 (actually only $98 would be needed) at 6 percent would be due for only $\frac{20}{365}$, or approximately one-eighteenth, of a year to secure $2 or 2 percent of the principal. The annual rate would be 18 times 2 percent or 36 percent. Thus by borrowing at 6 percent to discount the invoice the businessman actually makes 30 percent interest. A bill with terms of 5 percent, 10 days, net 30 would net him an 84 percent return on a bank loan at 6 percent; one with terms of 6 percent, 10 days, net 40 would give him a gain of approximately 72 percent on a 6 percent loan.[2]

The policy should be emphatic about paying bills promptly when due. If cash discounts are offered by vendors, the policy should provide for taking full advantage of every cash discount. If funds are inadequate for this purpose, procedures for increasing the cash flow should be formulated. These may include short-term bank loans, special sales, use of a revolving reserve fund set up by the business for such emergencies, and special efforts to collect accounts due the business.

Personnel and Organization Policies

"What shall our hiring standards be?" "How much authority and responsibility shall each individual have?" "What criteria will govern salary increases and promotions?" Such decisions as these affect the attitudes of the employees toward the company and the customers.

Personnel and organization policies in the small business can hardly be considered separately. An organization policy should cover the way in which responsibility and authority are distributed to different members of the firm. Decision must be made as to the extent to which the proprietor will delegate authority of various sorts to others and what authority he will retain for himself.

An axiom of good organization is that responsibility and authority must always be equal. No person should ever be held responsible for a job unless he has the authority to do it, nor should anyone be given authority in a business unless he is held responsible for the results. Unless a policy is absolutely clear and definite on this point, it will lead to confusion and low morale.

A common weakness in many small businesses is failure to delegate sufficient responsibility and authority to leave the owner free to devote himself to the more important management functions. It is this condition that often discourages good men from staying with a small business. A correct balance between delegating sufficient authority of the right type to relieve the owner of certain responsibilities, on the one hand, and maintaining sufficient control over the business, on the other hand, is the goal of good organization in the small business. In most cases the owner will want to reserve final authority over all major expenditures, the employment of persons for important positions, and final settlement of especially difficult customer or vendor complaints. Naturally final approval of all policies above the minor or departmental level will be the prerogative of the owner. The burden of final decision in all important matters relating to labor and public relations will also be the proprietor's.

Because the human element is a factor common to all businesses regardless of type, application of the basic principles of human relations is necessary in any business. Two standards of paramount importance in any personnel policy are: (1) fair treatment; and (2) the recognition of each employee as an individual, not as a mere cog in the machine. Fair treatment is not easy to define, but its absence is

---

[2] The examples assume continuous discounting of invoices throughout the year. Other qualifications have been omitted to keep the illustrations simple.

quickly detected by employees. Promotions or pay raises for reasons other than merit and seniority, for example, soon become known and increase the difficulty of securing and retaining loyal, dependable, and efficient employees. Morale in any organization is directly related to the formal or informal personnel policies of the management. By provisions for employee merit rating, worker-management cooperation in job rating, and other matters of mutual concern, a procedure for the airing and settling of workers' grievances, an employee suggestion system, and other employee-related programs, personnel policies serve as a constant reminder to supervisors of the importance that the entrepreneur places on the human relations aspects of their work.

Some other important aspects of the employment relationship, of course, are matters of law – such as minimum wages, maximum hours, minimum working age, safety precautions, workmen's compensation, Social Security insurance, and collective bargaining. For some employers civil rights laws inject a new dimension into hiring practices and policies. The stipulations of these laws vary from time to time, but absolutely must be considered in the formulation of personnel policies.

The policies discussed above – relating to customer and employee relations, finance and expansion, products and services, and internal organization structure – are sufficiently basic to all kinds of business to have warranted general consideration. Our attention is now directed to the consideration of policies which are unique to or of marked importance in particular types of small business enterprise.

POLICIES FOR MERCHANTS

The most important policies of the retailer are those relating to prices and customer service. Also important are their buying policies and the attitudes they maintain toward customers.

Attitudes toward Customers

Successful retailers do not leave the treatment that customers receive to the whims of employees. Rather, they are careful to establish and enforce a policy specifying the attitude that is to be maintained toward customers. This may cover the type of greeting customers are to receive, procedures for handling troublesome customers and embarrassing or ticklish situations, employee conduct while in the presence of customers, and meeting unusual customer requests.

An important policy for any store concerns the class of trade desired. It is usually difficult for a store to cater successfully to more than one income group. Sometimes catering to particular age or occupational groups is desirable. Clientele policy should be consistent with the store's location, the class of merchandise carried, and related policies such as sales promotion and customer services.

In general, three types of stores are recognized on the basis of the aggressiveness of their sales effort: promotional, semipromotional, and nonpromotional. Promotional stores rely heavily on advertising and special sales, whereas nonpromotional stores rely upon their regular customers and use a limited amount of advertising and very few, if any, special sales. The average store falls somewhere in-between (semipromotional).

Successful stores usually try to cultivate some outstanding point of superiority over competitors by consistently following a policy emphasizing this particular point. It may be the completeness of its assortments, fashion leadership, fashionable merchandise at popular prices, lower-than-average prices, unusual customer services, or one of a limitless number of other "hallmarks." Price policies and customer service policies are of particular importance in a retailing establishment.

Customer Services

Policies must be selected with reference to credit extension, delivery, returns and allowances, telephone and mail orders, layaways, check cashing, special orders, and a variety of other customer services. Certain factors will influence the selection of the best policy in each case. The services demanded or expected of the retailer will be determined by such factors as customers' shopping habits, class of trade, competition, location, and the nature of the merchandise (necessitating delivery of furniture and heavy appliances, for instance). Offsetting these are what the retailer is willing and able to furnish. Credit may be customary in the area and expected by customers, but the merchant's financial resources might prevent him from offering this service.

Setting the Prices

Another policy of special importance to the retailer is his price policy. Two price policies often confused are the one-price and the single-price. The latter, which is of limited application, relates to stores that handle merchandise at only one retail price, such as $5 shoes or $6 hats. The one-price policy means that goods are plainly marked and are sold only at the one price marked, regardless of who the customer is. It implies no bargaining over the price, but does not preclude policies giving special discounts to institutions or other large buyers. A one-price policy is representative of most retail stores in this country. However, a small retailer selling higher-priced merchandise having a short selling season, like fashion goods, is often tempted to deviate from this policy. Since markdowns must be taken on some of his merchandise, price shading can be easily rationalized as reducing necessary markdowns. Such a procedure will soon be discovered and the retailer will then find it difficult to adhere strictly to the one-price policy.

Other aspects of the price policy relate to (1) the markup taken, (2) the number of different prices for each line of goods, and (3) the general level of prices, or the price zone. Low markup and large volume or rapid turnover at low prices go together. The nature of the merchandise and the clientele desired are the principal factors governing the markup policy. It is usually necessary to average markups within a department instead of trying to set a fixed markup on all items. For "shopping goods" and some other lines in which numerous grades exist, price lining (that is, maintaining only a few best-selling prices in each line) is usually desirable. A policy of concentration on about three prices within a zone or range of prices suited to the store's class of trade is recommended. Selection of the zone is determined by the income of the class of trade desired; obviously men's shoes at prices of from $10 to $15 would not appeal to customers in the top income group.

Buying Policies

An important decision for many retailers is whether to affiliate with some buying and merchandising group or to buy independently. If a retailer decides to affiliate with a cooperative buying group, his policies should be formulated to capitalize on all the advantages that such a group offers. Concentration of buying and full cooperation with the group is usually desirable, if the affiliation is one worth forming.

If buying is to be done independently, policies should be formulated to cultivate vendor goodwill. Prompt payment of bills and courteous treatment of salesmen are particularly important. The buying policy should also cover such matters as the selection of suppliers and the number of brands of each item to carry in stock.

POLICIES FOR THE SMALL FACTORY

A manufacturer's production policy should define the extent to which he will make or purchase various parts and fabricated materials. At one extreme is the use of private-label firms to do the actual manufacturing. This policy has many advantages for the beginner with limited resources, even though he may plan at some future date to do the manufacturing himself. Private-label firms have machinery and know-how not available to the beginner. They can furnish advice on design and production methods that would be almost impossible for the small manufacturer to obtain independently. The real disadvantage in using these firms is that the beginner is not gaining experience as a manufacturer, but is merely a sales and distributing organization posing as a factory.

Sources from which raw materials and parts will be secured, and under what conditions, must also be covered in the purchasing policy. The basic principle of concentration should be considered here, even to the extent of buying all parts at first and concentrating on their assembly into the company's finished product.

Product identification should be considered early in the life history of the business. At first the company name may suffice, but a suitable brand name should be sought and adopted early enough to be exploited in the firm's advertising, packaging, and other sales promotion.

Production standards regarding quality of materials, workmanship, inspection, and packaging will be governed largely by the policies governing the class of customers desired and the prices of the company's products. Policies must be consistent with the class of trade desired.

Distribution, selling, and advertising policies must also be consistent with each other. Present and future costs of marketing the company's product, however, as well as market strategy, will be influential in making these policies.

Manufacturers of consumers' goods sold through retail stores find that all practical steps taken to help the dealer resell the product are well worth the effort. At first the small producer may be limited in what he can do. Attractive packaging and appearance of the product, even though it adds nothing to its utility, is the first step. Later, advertising and dealer aids such as signs and display racks may be used. The manufacturer should keep the dealer's problem of reselling the product in mind at all times.

Manufacturers of industrial or business goods, using manufacturers' agents or selling agents, have found that their success in this relationship is dependent on good communications between principal and agents. Although the contacts, talents, and aggressiveness of these agents are important, the manufacturer himself has the responsibility for keeping them informed about new products, price changes, and changes in policy. In fact, the small factory owner must regard them as their "sales force," truly members of their marketing organization, even though their services are shared with other manufacturers. From another viewpoint it may be recognized that with numerous principals to represent, the agent or other middleman will give most attention to those principals who encourage him most and those products with which he is most familiar.

POLICIES IN THE SERVICE BUSINESS

Policies in the service-type enterprise should stress the basic nature of the business — service — and emphasize those particular aspects of the service that are most desired by customers, and which the company is best equipped to furnish. Before service policy is adopted, at least three groups of factors should be investigated: (1) the market or potential demand for the type of service contemplated, (2) the availability of adequately trained personnel competent to render this kind of service, and (3) the owner's financial resources. Naturally the nature of existing competition should always be studied.

Since customers are less qualified to judge services than they are to evaluate physical goods, the policies of the service business should also stress the company's reputation. To achieve this reputation, product and inspection standards to maintain the desired level of quality should be provided for in the policies and rigidly adhered to in practice; in addition, the quality of the service should be publicized continuously.

In many types of service business, policies to guide the relative emphasis on the sale of service as compared to the sale of related merchandise are also desirable, at least until the shop is well established. Otherwise there is the danger that a division of resources and effort between these two activities may result in doing a poor job of both.

SUMMARY AND CONCLUSIONS

Policies are basic to every business, whether put in writing or formulated only in the mind of the owner. The general policy and usually certain provisions of the major policies should be formulated before a new business is actually started, although many modifications may be required later to keep the policies flexible enough to meet changing conditions. Policies constitute a form of management control that should be followed without exception. Change the policy, if necessary, but never make an exception or the policy is automatically destroyed. *All basic, long-run phases of the business's activity should be guided and controlled by policies.*

Modern business operated in a complex and continuously changing environment. Change is the only constant factor. Daily the businessman is faced with new conditions and questions requiring decision and action. Some stabilizing force must be present to guide all the activities of the business in one direction or it will flutter around aimlessly like a leaf in an autumn breeze. This stabilizing force is policy, without which a business is like a mariner without a compass or an automobile tourist without a road map.

REVIEW QUESTIONS

1. What are policies? What purposes do they serve? Under what circumstances, if any, should exceptions be made to a firm's policies?
2. Differentiate between major and minor policies and the firm's general policy. How are they related?
3. What are some of the limiting factors in policy formulation?
4. Should policies ever be changed? Why or why not?
5. Differentiate between the policies of a new business and those of a well-established business.
6. How do the product policies of manufacturers and merchandising establishments vary?
7. What are some of the important aspects of the firm's financial and expansion policies?
8. What are some of the important aspects of a firm's personnel and organization policies?
9. Cite examples of policies which are unique or of particular importance to each of the following types of business: (*a*) merchandising, (*b*) manufacturing, (*c*) service business.

DISCUSSION QUESTIONS

1. If you owned a shoe store in a small town of 12,000, selling men's, women's, and children's shoes, what service policies would you establish? What price policies? Explain.
2. Interview several small businessmen in the same kind of business to learn all you can about the policies of each. Analyze and report your findings and conclusions.

SUPPLEMENTARY READINGS

Buchele, Robert B. *Business Policy in Growing Firms,* chapters 1-8. San Francisco: Chandler Publishing Co., 1967. The first eight chapters of this book provide insights into the policy-formulation processes of the small firm. Case histories are used liberally in illustration.

Rotch, William. "Developing a Business." In *Management of Small Enterprises: Cases and Readings,* pp. 61-142. Small Business Management Research Report. Charlottesville: University of Virginia, 1963. The focus of this group of cases is the examination of policies for small businesses which have just been started or which have been in existence for only a brief period of time.

13

Management and leadership

The same money, materials, machinery, and men will, when managed differently, yield entirely different results. One man's store, shop, or factory shows a profit and a promising growth, while another man's business struggles for existence.

Successful business management may be described as the profitable use of those factors that are necessary to the conduct of the business. Effective utilization of assets is necessary and evident in any successful effort. In athletics, for example, one coach will have a string of team victories while another, using the same players, may suffer only losses. In engineering or construction great differences can result from the use of the same steel, bricks, and mortar by different men. The same canvas and paints may become an artistic masterpiece or only trash, depending on the hand that holds the brush.

Management is sometimes called a skill, sometimes an art; but it is increasingly a science. A skill or art may be more easily developed in some men than in others; but the science of management can be learned by most people for it is, to a great extent, the ability to make rational decisions based on fact and free of emotional bias. Decisions represent judgment, and sound judgment can only be based on solid facts.

BASIC MANAGEMENT FUNCTIONS

Management is the effective utilization of the elements of production: labor, materials, capital, and equipment. To use them effectively involves the basic functions of management, which may be listed as planning, organizing, staffing, supervising, directing, controlling, coordinating, innovating, and representing. This list summarizes the responsibility of a manager and sets forth these responsibilities in a logical sequence which must be followed.

Planning

Before a businessman begins to plan he must have defined his purposes. What contributions does he expect his business to make? What benefits does he hope to

245

derive from it? These questions and similar ones may have been answered in the process of appraising a going concern or justifying a new business. If not, they must be answered now. The need for determining a company's policies has been discussed in Chapter 12. This includes setting general rules of behavior and deciding how the company will regard its customers, its products, its employees, and itself. Policies serve as the guidelines for attaining goals.

Planning involves determining both long-term and short-term objectives, and deciding what methods will be used to achieve them. Goals include establishing the total volume desired: with which products, to what customers, by what methods. It also requires preparing a schedule which anticipates when various goals will be met. The manager must be able to forecast the social and economic environment in which he will operate and how he will use the available resources to attain his goals under various conditions.

Lack of long-range planning accounts for the untimely death of many businesses which made spectacular starts. Failure to insure a reliable source of raw materials or parts, failure to consider how to maintain an adequate volume of repeat sales to justify high initial promotional costs, or failure to outline a course of action should there be a loss of customers when changes in traffic or competition take place are typical omissions that occur frequently. A simplified application of Benjamin Franklin's ledger, in which was recorded all factors to consider before making an important decision, is helpful. The essence of this procedure is to list every possible factor that may have a bearing on the enterprise or project (providing the broadest possible base of available information), to study and evaluate this information, and then base decisions or plans on the results. One of the most fundamental principles of this procedure is to secure the widest possible diversity of viewpoints, and then to use this compilation of opinions and suggestions.

Short-run planning includes forecasting demand, determining production or sales goals, and then preparing budgets and production schedules accordingly. Some of these aspects of short-run planning are discussed in Chapters 21, 22, and 23. Short-run planning is the first step in establishing "control" (see p. 249). Once goals are established, management must impress employees with the nature of these goals and how they can be fulfilled. The need for good and continuous communication is obvious. Only through awareness of goals can workers cooperate in maintaining standards of production and in meeting sales quotas, or assist in controlling costs.

Organization

Even the smallest business needs good organization. Basically, organization involves two steps: a division, by analysis, of the particular business into the functions or activities that must be performed, and assignment of each to certain individuals. It is one of the most powerful tools of management. Organizing ability is universally accepted as a characteristic of the successful manager.

A simple approach to organization is to write down what the business must accomplish to be successful, and from this to subdivide or list *all* the activities that *must* be performed. These should then be grouped in *related* activities such as selling, producing, and recording. For a new business, effort should be made to secure individuals well qualified to perform each of these functions. For an established business, the job is to assign functions and subfunctions to members of the firm according to their respective abilities, capacities, and interests, being careful not to overload the better-qualified individuals.

In assigning duties to individuals, there are certain principles that extensive experience has proved to be of vital importance. Authority and responsibility should always be assigned equally. If you make an individual responsible for a certain job, give him the authority necessary to do it. Also, as was stated elsewhere, do not permit any individual to exercise authority — that is, to give orders or make commitments *for the business* — unless that person is held accountable for results. One's relatives should never be excepted from this rule.

Division of authority and responsibility in the small business is especially important in the case of a partnership, since the acts of either partner with respect to outsiders are usually legally binding. Also, employees recognize each partner as an owner and will take orders from him. If no agreement has been reached between the partners as to their division of authority, conflicting orders often result.

However, a principle useful in securing employee loyalty and cooperation is to give each member of the firm *some* authority and responsibility. This helps to build men as well as business. In the small business the tendency is for the owner to retain all authority, thus truly making it the one-man enterprise. The successful manager constantly considers his responsibilities in terms of those which he can delegate, and with respect to the effect of his actions on his own work, on that of his assistants, and on the rest of the organization.

In practice, organization must be the answer to the particular problems of a particular business. This means that the conditions existing in the business should be more important determinants of the kind of organization than arrangements illustrated on a generalized organization chart. Even big business has started placing less emphasis on formal organization as depicted in charts and is paying greater attention to the informal organization that seems to develop, largely as a result of employees selecting their own authority and responsibility according to preferences and abilities. Very often it is the informal organization that actually functions most effectively.

Staffing

Staffing is finding the right person for the right job and is the next logical step after organization. In organizing, the manager establishes positions and decides which duties and responsibilities belong to each. Staffing may become a part of organizing if an established concern already has employees to fill the positions available. Nevertheless, staffing is a separate and essential function of management which requires continual attention as new employees are needed to replace those who leave the organization and is required to serve a growing or changing organization. How to hire the best possible employee for each job, and how to keep him an efficient and loyal worker, is discussed in Chapter 15.

Supervision

Supervision has at least three aspects that are important even in the small business. First, to supervise implies observation, to see that duties are being performed or that work is being done correctly. This means that jobs or responsibilities have been assigned to individuals and that the supervisor knows the correct way of doing the work. For example, the manager observes a salesgirl demonstrating an article to the customer. Was the demonstration correct? To answer intelligently he must know the most effective or approved ways of demonstrating this particular article. This example suggests another aspect of supervision. Assume that the girl used a method of demonstration totally new to the manager. If so, it was either good or bad. If bad, the manager would take the first opportunity to discuss it with the girl and show her the correct or more effective ways to demonstrate this merchandise. This is the second aspect of supervision, the training or remedial phase. In the absence of supervision, the girl's sales record would eventually show that something was wrong, but it would not disclose the reason for lost sales.

If the new demonstration had been especially effective, the manager would have complimented the girl and adopted her method for future use, also telling all the other salespersons about it. This illustrates the third aspect of good supervision — "upgrading" of work by making all improvements general practice.

In all but the one-man enterprise some responsibility for supervision should be delegated. The modern trend is to use more supervisors and to treat them as members of management, encourage them to operate their divisions with initiative and ingenuity, and to experiment with promising new methods. Top management should go to the supervisor and discuss operating problems with him in his familiar environment instead of calling him to the manager's office.

Supervisors deal chiefly with men, materials, methods, and machinery or equipment used by the men whom they supervise. It is men who are the most complicated, unpredictable, and difficult to handle. Personalities, emotions, and conditions outside the business affect most workers and make many intangible elements important in achieving effective supervision. Family problems loom large with many workers. Others are upset by the details of their jobs. A good supervisor understands the place of these personal factors in his workers' lives and is alert to the symptoms which indicate trouble is brewing. He strives for the confidence and cooperation of his people and succeeds as a supervisor in almost direct ratio to earning this confidence and cooperation.

A supervisor must instruct, explain, train, and sometimes demonstrate what his workers are to do. In some cases an explanation is helpful, especially for anything quite new. Close observation and follow-up are needed as soon as the worker is on his own. This is the crucial stage — the experienced supervisor knows it but the beginner does not know it unless he is adequately warned. Communicating instructions and ideas correctly takes time and skill. Five fundamentals are important: (1) emphasize the use and job applications of information given; (2) stir the learner to activity, get him to take part; (3) give the employee time to digest what he learns; (4) help him to see what is especially important; (5) help him to understand the meaning of what he is learning.[1] When the worker has demonstrated his ability and willingness to do the job as requested, the supervisor need only make periodic checks to see that no deviations are occurring.

[1] *Getting Work Done with Fewer People: Suggestions to Supervisors,* Training Manual no. 8 (Washington, D.C.: U.S. Department of Health, Education, and Welfare, Division of Personnel Management, 1964), pp. 12–14.

When several workers are involved, some will work better together than others. The alert supervisor pairs off or groups his men on this basis. Individual abilities, attitudes, and ambitions also differ, and the good supervisor makes the most effective use of these differences both in assigning work and in spotting men for promotion or other recognition. All people like praise, recognition, and treatment as individuals. Praise and encouragement stimulate and inspire workers and constitute a part of the modern positive type of leadership. When criticism or correction must be given, real tact is needed, but it is better to "help the worker to help himself" in such cases early than to delay remedial action too long. This is, at times, one of the unpleasant but essential duties of a good supervisor.

Direction

Direction is the logical supplement and sequel to supervision. The duties and responsibilities which are designated to each employee are often stated in rather general terms. The worker may know how to perform his routine tasks independently and well; but in the day-to-day operation of a business, special problems often arise which are new and unusual and defy classification under any of the stated policies of the concern. These problems could not be anticipated during the training of the employee and he will be at a loss to handle them. Sometimes a major unexpected expense is involved, an accident may occur, or a delivery may not have been made as promised. A manager must be prepared to help his employees deal with such situations; or he himself should wrestle with the customer, client, machine, or material which presents the special problem.

Control

Control requires (1) setting standards or objectives for accomplishment; (2) maintaining current operating records for comparison with standards set; and (3) acting promptly when operations deviate too much from the goals established. Control systems deal with the measurable quantities like money, units of production, or sales. Managerial control requires an appraisal of the *reasons* why operating results are different from those planned, and intelligent decisions as to what action is needed. Example: Production control in a small factory plans a daily output of 30 units, based on anticipated sales department needs. Daily reports show actual production to be averaging only 25 units. Investigation discloses recurring delays because of repeated breakdowns of one machine. Review of sales estimates verifies the need for 30 units daily. Immediate action by management will prevent an increasing amount of back orders, broken promises, and lost sales. If possible, the defective machine should be repaired or replaced at once. Otherwise it would be better to slow down on sales immediately to keep it in bounds with productive capacity than to have disappointed customers and the other likely results of failure to coordinate sales and production.

Coordination

Coordination is an essential aspect of good organization. It is required because all members of an organization are interrelated and therefore what each one does in some way affects the others.

Perfect coordination is an ideal seldom, if ever, achieved. Management is always striving, however, through supervision, direction, and control, to secure the maximum coordination of all the activities of the business. Each important decision must be made in the light of its effects on all divisions of the business. Policies are important coordinating devices because they set common goals or objectives toward which various departments work. Budgets, schedules, and other types of control assist in securing coordination because they help management to plan and secure a balanced relationship between the operation of different divisions of the business. Coordination represents the culmination of effective management — nearly perfect balance between the elements of sales and production, of expansion and resources available, and of revenue and expenses plus profits.

Innovation

A manager may perform all the previously discussed basic management functions to perfection, but if he does not stop now and then and take the long view of his operation it will soon cease to be a dynamic, progressive business. He must evaluate his concern and consider how well it is fulfilling its original purposes. He must also look at the industry, the community, and the country. Is he keeping pace with a changing world? What are the things that could be done differently? What are the things that could be done better? Now is the time for creative thinking, and for innovation.

If a manager just keeps on doing what he has done in the past, his organization will become a static one. In fact, if the field in which he operates is a competitive one he will soon lose his place and not even hold his own. A good manager views his business as a challenge to his creativity. He should develop new ideas, combine old ideas into new ones, adapt ideas from other fields, and stimulate others in his organization to think creatively as well.

Good planning recognizes the ever-changing environment in which a concern operates, and it considers how to adjust an organization to these changing conditions. Innovation goes beyond this. It is a deliberate, creative process which consists of always looking for a better way to perform every function in the organization.

Probably every business also has some continuous problems where existing conditions never seem to be entirely satisfactory. A few of these are: building goodwill, making most effective use of personnel, physical facilities, and finances, and achieving the best rate of expansion.

Whatever the more important continuous problems may be, it is advisable to devote some time for deliberation and planning under conditions that are free of the pressures and interruptions characteristic of a normal business day. Good time management should permit much of the planning to be done during business hours. These planning periods should be respected by other employees as essential managerial activity.

Representation

The manager must also represent his business to many groups outside his organization. This may include his membership in the community service club or holding office in his trade association. He may need to meet with government officials or representatives of unions which may represent or wish to represent his employees. He must also be the spokesman for his business in dealing with financial institutions, other companies in the industry, suppliers, customers, and the general public. Sometimes only his presence is required; at other times community leadership is expected; and on yet other occasions great tact is required as he handles very delicate negotiations.

SPECIAL MANAGEMENT CONSIDERATIONS

Time Management

Time management is always important, but especially so to the small-scale beginning enterpriser. It has two major elements, (1) ranking the importance of duties, and (2) making effective use of timesavers. With all of its advantages, even being one's own boss has a maximum price in terms of time that can be devoted to it, and still permit the enterpriser to live. A major goal of time management is to keep this price for success reasonable. It may be less than forty hours per week in some cases and well over seventy in others, but it has a definite limit in all cases.

A major weakness of the ambitious beginner is to glorify his unusually long hours devoted to achieving success – a modern version of the martyr complex. Good *time* management in most such cases could reduce these long hours from 25 to 35 percent and produce better results.

Time is limited, fixed within absolute and reasonable limits. Managerial and other duties are virtually unlimited for the small-scale beginner. Choice is essential, and ranking is the only intelligent approach. "First things first" should be the guide, but like other maxims it is often difficult to accomplish mainly because of lack of planning. Which should come first, serving a customer when all other employees are busy and you, the manager, are doing essential paperwork that must be completed before tomorrow? The customer's arrival could not have been predicted a few minutes earlier, but your essential paperwork was known in advance for days or even months. You be the judge – it's your enterprise.

The first steps in time management are to: (1) rank the various jobs in order of importance; (2) divide them into at least two classes based on the manager's ability to control the time when they will be performed; (3) decide which ones can best be delegated to other members of the organization; (4) determine those where time can be saved in the long run by adopting suitable procedures; and (5) select or formulate suitable aids to time economy. Each of these needs some explanation.

Ranking involves valuation. First are those mandatory duties required by law: keeping adequate records for income tax, sales tax, Social Security, excise, and other tax reports; filing all tax reports and making payments according to times specified for each; and maintaining any other legally mandatory records, reports, permits, and payments. Next are provisions necessary for protection: appropriate insurance with its necessary records and payments made on time; adequate safety provisions for the premises and property; meeting contractual obligations for the payment of interest and principal on loans, rent, and other current operating expenses, and for merchandise and other purchases.

The foregoing are nearly all dated obligations, most of which can be taken care of at any convenient time up to the deadline. To avoid a last-minute rush and possible penalty for tardiness they should be cared for as time permits, well in advance of the deadline. This method also permits planning in advance so as to be adequately prepared, doing much of the work during slack periods, interrupting such work temporarily to take care of an emergency or immediate need — such as service to a customer when all other employees are busy — and doing a more thorough job on each activity by allowing ample time for it. A simple device to use is a tickler or reminder file or desk calendar. For every duty at least two dates are recorded, the deadline and the beginning or warning date, if ample time is to be allowed. Most businessmen take these steps, but do so mentally instead of recording the dates on a calendar or setting up a card file. The result is that frequently important duties are overlooked in the rush of day-to-day tasks. Even the tickler file will be of little value unless it is used constantly, consulted each day or often enough to insure its effective use.

A second group of managerial duties consists of all acts necessary to maintain continuous day-to-day operations. Most of these are routine, recurring regularly: opening and closing the shop; maintenance of the premises, merchandise or machinery, and having adequate personnel; operating the enterprise by serving customers or maintaining production; and conducting such activities as advertising and communication. They should be performed in a systematic and businesslike manner, but need not require the personal attention of the owner-manager except in the one-man enterprise. Most can and should be delegated to other members of the firm so as to economize the time and effort of top management. Adequate guides can be formulated, such as policies and regulations, and limits to authority clearly defined, so that only unusual or exceptional cases need be taken up personally with the manager. This is the very important *exception principle of management.* Failure to apply this principle is a major weakness of the management in many small concerns, and the chief reason the manager is so busy with day-to-day tasks that he lacks time for planning, deliberation, and attention to important duties that he alone can perform satisfactorily. The difficulty usually results from an unwillingness to delegate authority and uncertainty as to how it should be done.

In the one-man enterprise it is, of course, not possible to delegate duties, just as in the two- or three-person firm the owner-manager is likely to bear some responsibility for routine tasks. Time management is important, however, even for the lone operator. Routine duties are not all of equal importance, nor do they all have the same degree of urgency from a time standpoint. In a customer-service type of enterprise the shop must be open for business at regular or announced times even though some maintenance may have to be deferred. Also, in other respects serving the customer properly takes precedence over all other duties except extreme emergencies such as fire or serious misfortunes. But serving customers on the premises is usually irregular and difficult to predict. All time not required for customer service should be used most effectively for other duties in the order of their importance. These other duties include the dated ones discussed earlier, as well as daily tasks. A useful device is a daily memorandum, or "order of work," that lists the important jobs to be done, if possible, during each business day. This list is prepared in advance, away from the pressure and interruptions of business hours, and is partial protection against two dangers — failure to complete essential work on time, and dissipation of available customer-free time on odd jobs that appear continuously but are less important than those on the "do today" list.

Time management involves self-discipline. We all sometimes dissipate time on such things as idle conversation, newspaper reading, or just daydreaming. A businessman must keep up with important news events that might affect his business or family life, but many spend more time than necessary in the process. Conversation also is needed to spark fresh ideas, to make new friends, and to build goodwill, but a lot of time is often wasted on unimportant exchange of comments regarding the weather, storytelling, and the like. Of course, time-consuming habits such as these are often relaxing and enjoyable. The main point is that unless controlled they frequently use up the only time the enterpriser has to use for deliberation and planning. Experience shows that from one to two hours per day can often be obtained from these sources alone.

Records and Supplies

A business operator in some respects faces the same problems that a housewife faces in storing general supplies and in deciding what to keep and what to throw away. Adequate space and orderly storage for idle equipment, records, and supplies can greatly enhance the ease with which either a home or a business is run. Storage space can only remain adequate and orderly when the right decisions are made as to what should be retained and what should be destroyed. Retaining the useful is as important as disposing of the useless.

Records. Record keeping is essential to a well-operated business. Knowing what to keep and how to keep it is an important part of good management. The guide is "a place for everything, and everything in its place." Studies by the National Records Management Council show that, of the records of an average business, less than 10 percent must be kept permanently, 20 percent should be retained currently, 30 percent should be transferred to inactive status, and 35 percent should be destroyed.[2] Alphabetical, subject, and chronological bases for filing will serve most purposes at first until more specialized needs become apparent. Certain financial records used in reporting taxes must be retained as specified by law at the time. Purchase and sales records tend to go through three stages: active, reference, and dead. If the use to which they are put during each stage is considered in planning the filing system, time and space will be economized, particularly in the reference and dead stages.

Once invoices have been paid they may be useful for a few months to a year in analyzing past purchases by kinds of goods, vendors, price and terms, delivery dates and services, and providing information as to any significant differences between goods purchased from different suppliers. After they have served such purposes there should be some important reason why these records are retained, and the sensible alternative to dead storage should be disposing of them permanently. In

[2]*A Basic Plan for Record Retention and Destruction* (New York: Remington Rand, Management Controls Division, n.d.), p. 2.

most cases sales records should also be retained long enough for careful analysis to aid in future buying, sales promotion, and customer control as described in later chapters. After this period of reference use they should be disposed of. Records of physical inventories should receive similar treatment. After their active period of use for verifying the book inventory and preparing financial statements, they should be analyzed for management action to guide future buying, and then held in safe dead storage just long enough for emergency use in case of fire or other loss. Two extremes cause most beginners trouble: they either (1) discard records before analyzing them adequately during the reference stage; or (2) they store all records indefinitely without making effective use of them once they become inactive.

Whenever data from records must later be compiled for reports, such as income taxes and financial statements, setting up the record-keeping system to facilitate these uses not only saves considerable time later but gives more accurate results. A printed form lessens the danger of omitting essential information. Merely checking appropriate blanks replaces repetitious writing.

In connection with sales checks in retail stores several timesavers are being developed. Cash register receipts are suitable for cash-and-carry transactions where it is not necessary to identify by name each of several items purchased, and where trade-ins or other allowances are not involved. Modern registers are available that give the store a record of identification of each transaction by salesperson, department, and classification number. Additional data may be recorded manually on tally cards for a limited number of topics, such as special items, price lines, and the like. Duplicate unit-control labels may be accumulated where several variations (size, color, style) are involved for each item sold. These are all devices to save time and reduce errors likely to be made when writing out information at the time of each sale. They do not eliminate the need for some writing for send or charge transactions. A charge-authorization plate may serve as a stencil to print name and address and thus eliminate time-consuming writing. Such aids make record keeping easier and save time and space and contribute to reduced costs.

In service enterprises the trade association in the field, and sometimes the vendors, have developed procedures and forms that may be utilized to great advantage by the beginner. The resulting savings of time, effort, and expense which result from taking advantage of these aids, is worth the cost and effort of modifying procedures.

Equipment and supplies.   Storage of goods is somewhat different for each of the three broad classes: (1) merchandise, materials, or supplies currently used in the business, (2) equipment of various sorts temporarily not in productive use, and (3) miscellaneous used containers and odds and ends. Inventory or stores control is the subject of Chapter 21. Equipment not in current use is either of a reserve stock type, or is merely being held on the assumption that it may some time be useful. Fixtures kept in reserve should be easily accessible and require a minimum of time and effort to get at them when needed, and yet not occupy valuable space. Fixtures, often damaged or obsolete, become a problem in retail establishments and in some types of production. They are kept for spare parts or with the intention of repairing them, but it is often more economical in the long run to avoid such storage entirely. Miscellaneous used cartons, bits of paper, wood, and so on, are kept in case they may be useful in the near future; systematic storage of these may be made, provided that they are put in a safe place as they constitute a great fire and accident hazard.

Protection and Security

Consultation with a reliable insurance agent will disclose the types of insurance coverage needed. A major goal is protection against serious losses. A minimum of insurance should usually include fire, public liability, key-men, and burglary insurance. Other conditions, even though they may be covered by insurance, warrant special attention; they are accidents, theft, and — in retailing — shoplifting.

Most accidents are avoidable through training and constant vigilance. Serious accidents, whether to employees or outsiders, happen quickly. Conditions conducive to accidents should be recognized and remedied immediately.

Theft of cash, merchandise, or materials often involves trusted employees — even relatives. Spot checks of the cash register, or inventories at irregular times, may disclose "overages." Errors, especially in the records, is one cause. Another is an attempt by a dishonest employee to build up enough surplus cash or merchandise to warrant a theft. Unfortunately, every manager must be alert to suspicious activity on the part of any of his employees.

Shoplifting can easily wipe out any potential profit — particularly in retail stores using open displays. Shoplifters come from every economic and social class. Some shoplifters may be kleptomaniacs — those constitutionally unable to resist stealing; others may be either professionals or amateurs.

Professionals often work in pairs. One creates a commotion to distract employees while the other takes the merchandise and leaves. At least one employee in every selling area should remain on duty to supervise customers regardless of any disturbance and be prepared to take appropriate action if shoplifting is detected.

Amateurs usually work alone. They tend to lack finesse and may display signs of nervousness visible to experienced supervisors. Children comprise a large segment of amateur shoplifters.

Formerly, a shoplifter could not be accosted while still on the store premises. Several states now have passed laws that permit retail personnel to detain a suspect until a law officer can be obtained. These laws also lessen the danger of the retailer being sued in case of error. Despite these laws, the merchant should exert great care in handling suspected shoplifters.

Community Obligations

Though a small businessman usually expects to represent his business in certain community activities, sometimes he finds that the contribution of either time or money becomes a relatively heavy burden. He may also discover that friends and relatives put pressure on him for jobs or perhaps for prizes for a charity raffle. As a responsible businessman he wants to participate in civic development and belong to local service clubs. Often these activities demand and consume a large amount of his time. Also, because he is well known in the town, he may be called upon quite frequently for donations toward community development. While the larger organization with sales of $200,000 might contribute $20 to some "cause" and feel virtuous about it, the little fellow with $40,000 sales would probably feel ashamed to contribute a proportionate $4.

Although there is no single solution for such problems, there is a plan that, if followed tactfully, will assist in dealing with most such situations. First, the manager, in conference with specifically qualified individuals, should formulate policies covering each of these circumstances. Then (to cite one case in point) the owner may truthfully say to a job-seeking relative that on the advice of his suppliers and banker he has adopted a policy of not employing relatives. Similarly, to the friend soliciting contributions he may reply that on the advice of the Chamber of Commerce (or some other group) his firm has adopted a policy of making contributions in the same relative proportion to those of large concerns in the same field on a corresponding ratio of sales volume. It is much easier to handle these situations in this way than to have to depend upon direct, impulsive personal decisions.

LEADERSHIP IN MANAGEMENT

Modern management stresses leadership and the human element. Recognition of good work by the manager usually does more to encourage employees than incentives that are less personal. Criticisms of individual employees, when necessary, should be made privately, sympathetically, and constructively. Great care is taken by the real leader to treat all employees fairly and understandingly, as individual human beings. Employee suggestions are welcome; they are actively sought by alert managers, and the personal nature of the small concern can be used to advantage in getting employees to express themselves, to offer suggestions, and call attention to opportunities for improvement. In the more progressive organizations employees are consulted on management problems, and they are furnished with management information formerly of a confidential nature. Employee-management cooperation is one way for the small business to attract and hold personnel of excellent quality.

Achieving worker participation and distributing some responsibility among as many as possible usually enlists support and cooperation and leads to other objectives — to make workers conscious of the importance of costs, quality, safety, and preventive maintenance. Sometimes these goals may be achieved by a challenge to the workers, such as contests or awards which are significant as recognition symbols and need have no monetary value. But they are more readily attained by a constructive approach to personnel relations which gives workers a voice in making decisions that vitally affect them in their everyday work lives. Such an approach recognizes that in every individual there is a desire for self-expression, and that as a means of increasing worker efficiency the sense of participation is valuable in itself (regardless of whether the participants receive "awards").

The constructive approach to dealing with one's employees has always been deemed desirable, but it has become much more urgent or necessary in recent times. Employees who entered the work force prior to or during World War II were raised in an era in which discipline, both in the home and in school, was firmly established, and they were trained to accept the unquestioning authority of their parents, teachers, and employers. The present generation of employees, on the other hand, has been raised in an affluent society in which a permissive atmosphere prevails, and workers today have adopted a questioning, often arrogant attitude toward all forms of authority.

The small businessman in the 1970s must rely on his leadership qualities rather than his line authority to gain the loyalty, respect, and cooperation of his employees. He must recognize that holding the confidence of his employees is much more vital to the operating efficiency of the business than maintaining doctrinaire areas of authority. He must think less in terms of "management prerogatives" and more in terms of the benefits to be derived from the democratic self-expression of his employees. In the final analysis, just as political government functions with the consent of the governed, so also must management function with the consent of the managed.

Manager Reeducation

Change is a reality every business manager must face. The passing of each business day brings with it new pressures for possible changes in philosophy, product, program, processes, or procedures.

A craftsman depends most on his basic skills perfected through the years; many skilled laborers, such as carpenters, masons, or plumbers, find that their basic trade changes little from year to year. But business management, like many other professions, calls for constant reorientation. The businessman must recognize the changing economy, a new social structure, or the advent of competition; and he must be prepared to respond accordingly.

There are new techniques, new materials, new products, and new equipment being introduced and being used every day. A progressive businessman must actively seek information on change, both technical and social, and learn how to incorporate it into his plans or deal with it effectively. This may mean independent study or attending classes so he can learn what is necessary to continue to operate with the best possible methods, materials, and machines available.

Many organizations, government agencies, and schools provide opportunities for managers to expand their training and education. Trade associations, for example, often publish technical bulletins or sponsor management training classes, and local Chambers of Commerce also present useful programs. High schools, as well as college and university extension divisions, sometimes provide classes or promote conferences for particular industries or lines of business, such as retailing or metalworking; they also often provide classes in various business functions, such as accounting, marketing, or purchasing. The federal government sponsors courses and supplies material through the Small Business Administration and the Departments of Commerce, Labor, Agriculture, and Health, Education, and Welfare.

Many trade and professional associations hold annual management conferences for their members in cooperation with colleges and universities. In these meetings, speakers from the academic world are intermixed with speakers from industry who have achieved notable success in some activity. Meetings take the form of seminars, panel discussions, and workshops.

Management Succession

A common weakness in businesses of all sizes is their lack of a clearly outlined provision for a line of succession to key jobs in management. In larger concerns this may be due to lack of foresight, preoccupation with current problems, unwillingness to make the necessary investment, or the incumbent's fear of being replaced.

In the small firm it is due largely to the nature of the one-man operation. The manager sometimes refuses to delegate authority either for fear of subordinates' errors or for fear of losing control. This lack of provision for top management succession is apparent in many small concerns. Although most firms promote from within unless the special skills required are not possessed by any of the employees, few small businesses have any organized program for training potential managers.

SUMMARY AND CONCLUSIONS

Management consists of a series of decisions dealing with planning and operation of the entire enterprise and each of its components. Thus management begins before the enterprise is launched, and includes such preoperating decisions as selection of the kind of business, choice of a suitable location, provision of personnel and facilities, formulation of policies, and initial organization. It includes operation of functional divisions or departments, such as buying, producing, advertising, accounting, and inventory control. Many of these applications of management to special activities are fully discussed in Chapters 15 through 24.

It is top management's duty to see that a satisfactory return is obtained on the investment, that the business has an opportunity to continue as long as desired by its owners, that goodwill is maintained with employees and with the public. These are easier to list than to achieve.

A small enterprise pioneering some innovation, even when operated by a hired manager, may be concerned more with gaining customer acceptance and proving the future prospects for the innovation than with immediate profits or a continuity of the enterprise under its current ownership. Other small businesses are organized to secure only a modest immediate financial return, but many future nonfinancial benefits. These are unique features of some small concerns.

When the wide range of duties required of the manager of a small business is considered, the need for some outside aid is apparent, for he must coordinate every division and activity of the business; plan for the future while busy with pressing matters of the present; provide the right insurance; select, train, and supervise employees; conduct or direct research; and *manage* all activities of the business.

The opinion is widespread that success in small business requires long hours of hard work, and most enterprisers do put in long hours. Others equally successful, however, through adroit time management accomplish just as much and achieve the same results in more nearly normal working hours. In some cases, learning more rapid ways to perform essential tasks may be indicated. In other cases the time needed may involve sacrificing some social amenities, aimless scanning of the daily paper, or similar uneconomic, though pleasurable, activity. An employee has his time managed for him by company regulations, but the entrepreneur must do his own time management for success at a reasonable price.

Modern management must also stress leadership and the human element. This requires that employees be given some voice in decision making. If the results of group effort are as dependent on management as it most certainly appears to be in the operation of a business, then we can understand why athletic contests tend to become contests between the managers of the teams. A group of mediocre performers under strong leadership often will excel over a team of excellent individuals under a poor leader. Similarly, competition is between managements to a great extent. Products and services are indeed the weapons, and employees and facilities are important, but the contest is between the men at the top. Certainly the best team under the best coach will win.

REVIEW QUESTIONS

1. Explain why management is the most important factor governing the success of an enterprise.

2. Define briefly (in one or two sentences) each of the basic management functions discussed in the text.

3. How is planning related to good management? Illustrate.

4. Why is organization basic to good management?

5. Distinguish the formal from the informal organization in a business venture.

6. (*a*) Discuss briefly the important elements or aspects of good supervision. (*b*) How can the supervisor communicate instructions and ideas to his employees most effectively?

7. Distinguish between "direction" and "supervision."

8. At what point in management does control begin?

9. How does management coordinate the activities of a business enterprise?

10 Why is innovation an essential aspect of a progressive management?

11. Describe briefly each of the five steps in time management.

12. What is the "exception principle" in management? Explain how neglect of the exception principle of management results in many small enterprisers being too busy to do adequate planning and reviewing.

13. Why is a discussion of time management more appropriate in a small business text than in one for future big business executives?

14. Illustrate or explain how time management often requires self-discipline for a beginning enterpriser.

15. Why is record keeping important in the management of a small business enterprise?

16. What are the major weaknesses in the record-keeping systems of many small businessmen?

17. (*a*) What is meant by "leadership in management"? (*b*) Differentiate between the "boss" and the "leader." (*c*) Are employees today really any different than they were in past generations? Why or why not?

DISCUSSION QUESTIONS

1. Is efficient management of the small firm always concerned primarily with profit maximization? Discuss.

2. Select two independent enterprises where you will have an opportunity to observe the owner-managers for a reasonable period of time, choosing one that appears to be very well managed and the other poorly managed. Record, analyze, and report your observations.

SUPPLEMENTARY READINGS

Henderson, Philip E. *The Foreman in Small Industry.* 2nd ed. Small Business
    Management Series no. 14. Washington, D.C.: Small Business Administration,
    1962. Outlines the basic principles for developing well-qualified foremen.

Megginson, Leon. *Providing Management Talent for Small Business.* Small Busi-
    ness Management Research Report prepared for the Small Business Adminis-
    tration. Baton Rouge: Louisiana State University, 1961. This study shows
    some of the philosophies, principles, and techniques involved in selecting,
    developing, and motivating management in small business enterprises. Also
    discussed are the qualities necessary to fill the management position.

Raines, I. E. *Better Communications in Small Business.* 2nd ed. Small Business
    Management Series no. 7. Washington, D.C.: Small Business Administration,
    1962. Outlines a basis for developing the needed awareness and practical skill
    to help build better management by effective communications.

14

Utilizing "outside staff" services

Lack of managerial ability and the lack of sufficient time to perform all of the activities of management have been proven beyond any reasonable doubt to be the outstanding weaknesses in almost all small businesses which have failed. Adequate planning and preparation greatly lessens these weaknesses, but cannot for long remove them entirely as long as the enterprise remains small. Although the well-prepared manager has a big initial advantage over the typical beginner, conditions change so rapidly that unless he keeps abreast of developments even a good start is soon lost. Until a business becomes large enough to employ its own management specialists and staff experts it must make use of what is here termed an "outside staff," or eventually lose out in the competitive struggle.

Clarification of Terms and Concepts

Many specialists in big business have line rather than staff authority, but specialists in the same line functions who are not members of the firm may be utilized as "outside" staff. The sales manager of a large corporation, for example, is a *line executive*, a specialist in his function, but when sales consultants are employed they normally serve in a staff or advisory capacity. A small firm may have a man responsible for sales and still make effective use of many outside agencies to improve the performance of this function. The latter are specialists in a line function, but serve in a staff or professional advisory capacity only. Only in a dire emergency would the typical independent grant full, or line, authority to an outsider.[1] Our interest in this chapter is in the kinds of assistance available from outside a firm's own organization, where the decision to use or reject such aid rests with the management of the firm.

Scope of the Outside Staff

Outside staff assistance can be obtained by the small businessman in every area or function where similar assistance is furnished to executives of our largest corporations. Some types of assistance are more appropriate than others for the small enterprise, such as a simple but sound procedure for selecting employees

[1] Such as a creditors' committee to ward off bankruptcy.

rather than an extensive battery of scientific personnel tests that must be administered and interpreted by experts. Some are too expensive in one form, but available in other suitable but less expensive forms, such as a usually costly firm of management consultants as opposed to a part-time small business consultant. Some render individualized services (such as a detailed market analysis of a particular company's product and its competitive position), whereas others furnish basic data of a general nature with special applications to be made by the management of each firm (such as an analysis of basic statistics and trends affecting that class of product).

There are two types of business information provided by the outside staff: (1) technical, legal, and statistical information upon which management decisions may be based, such as industry sales figures and the various federal and state government census reports; and (2) "how to" or instructional information to assist the businessman in the efficient performance of various management functions such as plant layout, employee relations, and advertising layout. Most business information of interest to the small businessman is distributed by the following sources: trade associations; trade publications; colleges and universities; professional management consultants; specialized business-service organizations; equipment manufacturers; suppliers; and government agencies.

NONGOVERNMENTAL SOURCES OF BUSINESS INFORMATION

Several of the agencies discussed in this section provide many outside staff services, some of which overlap, but usually one type of agency will have advantages in a particular case.

Trade Associations

Almost every kind of business has a trade association. In contrast to Chambers of Commerce and other civic groups that cut across occupational or business boundaries, a trade association functions in a particular type of business or industry (such as hardware retailing, dry goods wholesaling, and bolt and nut manufacturing). They are typically membership organizations financed by dues that average a small fraction of 1 percent of the member's sales volume. In a few cases a requirement for membership is that the applicant must have been in business in the particular industry for a prescribed minimum period of time, usually one or two years.

Most of these restricted-membership organizations lend whatever aid they can to beginners, and a few have prepared kits to help newcomers get off to the right start. In addition, nearly all of them will accept subscriptions to their official journals and sell their other publications to nonmembers, though at prices higher than those charged to their own members.

Because trade associations are concerned with the needs and problems of member firms, their services are naturally designed more for the established than for the beginning enterprise. The prospective small businessman, however, can profit from the accumulated experience of older firms in the industry. Among the membership services typically supplied by trade associations are the following:

1. Promoting better accounting and record keeping methods

2. Sponsoring industrywide meetings and developing leadership within the industry

3. Operating a liaison service between federal agencies, the Congress, the industry, and its individual members; some trade associations also provide liaison service for their members with state and local governments

4. Providing publicity and public relations programs for the industry

5. Fostering industrywide technical research

6. Maintaining a labor relations service within the industry designed to prevent work stoppages and promote industrial harmony

7. Issuing special information bulletins to their members; these bulletins report on current affairs affecting the industry, on government orders and legislation, and other, similar matters

8. Gathering statistics for the industry

9. Publishing specialized data concerning their industries; many of these relate to such activities as promoting sales, educating the public to possible uses of the industry's products, or attracting qualified individuals into employment within the industry

10. Offering training courses to employees of member companies

11. Supplying other services to the industry such as credit-reporting services, savings on the purchase of insurance, and varied economic studies

12. Furnishing the industry with specialized technical advice that few small members, individually, would be able to afford[2]

Most trade associations have developed uniform accounting systems, standard record forms, and standard expense classifications. A major block to greater success for some small firms, however, is their failure to follow these simplified and standardized procedures. The National Shoe Retailers' Association, for example, encountered so much difficulty in getting small merchants to understand and use its uniform record-keeping systems and forms that it now advises members to consult with the local manager of the National Cash Register Company. This may be the result of special conditions in shoe retailing, but it also emphasizes a point basic to our book: Often the small independent needs help in applying the best practices to his own concern.

Compiling statistical data and other information for use by its members is another valuable service performed by trade associations. Uniform expense classification and accounting is essential to render such data useful for developing standard operating ratios, and for individual members effectively to compare their operations with others in the field. Annual surveys on the cost of doing business are conducted by the national association in the hardware, dry goods, men's clothing and furnishings, laundering, and other fields. Progressive small independents make effective use of their associations' cost and expense surveys to check on their own

[2] Reuel T. Elton, "How Trade Associations Help Small Business," Management Aids Annual no. 2 (Washington, D.C.: Small Business Administration, 1958), p. 116.

operations, to locate danger spots, and to take appropriate management action promptly that might otherwise have been delayed until conditions became really serious. Data on operating results of the industry are also valuable when managerial decisions involving a new enterprise, department, or other activity must be made.

In many fields of small business, industry cost studies and operating ratios are assembled by other agencies, such as producers, university research bureaus, accounting firms, Dun & Bradstreet, and the U.S. Department of Commerce, often with trade association cooperation. The trade association interprets such data, and reports to members pertinent conclusions and often the entire survey report. This type of activity — keeping in touch with all studies and developments of concern to members, and analyzing and reporting on them in terms understandable and applicable to members — is one of the major managerial aids to small independents.

Education and training is another important trade association service. This is provided through conventions, field contacts, and periodicals, and by correspondence and short courses — often in cooperation with a college or university. Increasingly, national associations have been publishing management "handbooks" or "manuals."

Many trade organizations also assist members through store or shop visitations, and all associations welcome member visits at headquarters to discuss individual problems. Trade association executives assist and advise on proposed layouts, and some even originate layouts from information furnished by members. Aid in modernization of building, fixtures, and methods is provided by leading associations, sometimes through their own staffs or from specialists approved by headquarters. The main method for receiving individual assistance is naturally by correspondence. Large, well-established associations answer many inquiries by mailing published materials, but endeavor to make the service as individualized as necessary.

On the local level, trade groups in the larger cities also render a large number of services to members. Many locals are affiliated with the national trade associations in their respective industries, and many of the services previously cited as being performed at the national level are also carried out through the local association. Among the national associations, there seems to be a trend toward state and local managerial training conferences. Conditions differ in various cities and among the states, so trade association services are often adapted to local needs.

In recent years interindustry competition has increased to such an extent that it is often more important than competition among concerns in the same industry. This is particularly true among industries producing consumer goods and services. Movies, for example, compete with television for a share of the consumer dollar. Similarly, food competes with drugs and hardware, clothing with automobiles and jewelry, and so on. Thus each industry, through the cooperative efforts of trade association members, endeavors to increase, or at least retain, its share of total consumer spending. Both types of competition — interindustry and intraindustry — complement each other. Healthy competition within an industry improves its competitive position ralative to other industries, but overemphasis or rivalry among firms in the same industry may not be to their combined self-interest. This means that competitors must subordinate their individual rivalries and pool their efforts at times to maintain their industry's proportionate share of the total consumer market.

Many trade association services to members require the pooling of technical information, statistics, and ideas for the benefit of the entire industry. To obtain maximum benefits from his trade association a member must give as well as take. The decay of industries in many foreign countries, in which individual firms so closely and jealously guarded their trade secrets, is mute testimony to the obsolescence of this independent approach or noncooperative attitude. In the United States the opposite point of view is evident by patent pooling and industrywide simplification and standardization programs, as well as by open membership trade association activities.

In addition to sharing information and furnishing statistical data requested by one's association, it is advisable for more small businessmen to attend their trade association conventions and participate actively in discussions. An independent owner-manager who takes a week away from his business to attend his trade association convention may share in and profit by the experience of 50 others having an average of ten years' experience or a total of 500 years of diversified experience in his line of business. In addition, he meets men who are superior in certain activities and can learn much from them through conversation. When meetings are not in session, he may want to visit stores or other types of business of interest in the convention city; sometimes they may be his own suppliers. Conventions are planned and conducted by experts to emphasize topics of current importance. Trade association officials understand the needs and problems of their members and are glad to talk about them. Many associations maintain model stores, complete libraries, and other facilities well worth study by visiting members. Time away from one's own business premises often leads to a "new look" approximating that of the outside viewpoint upon returning from a trip.

Trade Publications

For the independent enterpriser starting on a small scale, active participation or membership in his trade association may be difficult at first. However, familiarity with the trade publications in his field, both before launching his enterprise and continuously thereafter, is of the utmost importance.

Trade publications constitute one of the most economical sources for the small independent to use in keeping abreast of developments in his field. This category includes the official publications of trade and professional associations that are usually available to nonmembers by subscription. Both association publications and commercial trade and business periodicals are available in many libraries, and these sources may be useful. As a minimum, however, every small businessman should subscribe to at least one good trade journal in his field and to one good general news periodical or newspaper that carries significant reports on business developments and topics affecting the class of trade or industry with which he is concerned. Retailers should also subscribe to the popular magazines read by their customers, from which they may glean trends in consumers' tastes. Failure to do so results in a situation where customers are often better informed about new styles, new merchandise, or new materials than are many small merchants. In the fashion fields a number of periodicals issue retailers' editions that contain advance notices to the merchants of what their customers will soon be demanding.

Management Consultants

Recently an increasing number of small businessmen have come to realize the assistance they can obtain from management consultants, and more and more consultants are tailoring their services to the needs of small firms. This trend is likely to continue because it is the result of fundamental conditions. Management, as an activity, is becoming increasingly complex, specialized, scientific, and professionalized, and is distinct from the unique idea or motivation characteristic of a particular business. The operator of the firm is intensely concerned with promoting the firm's basic reason for existence or the unique idea that justifies continuing the enterprise. Thus, while the owner-manager of a small firm is thoroughly familiar with this aspect of the business, much more so than an outsider could be, he often lacks the expert organization and communications skills to manage successfully *any* business, including his own. It is this latter need that management consultants are equipped to meet. Many small businessmen fail to appreciate the place and value of outside consultants, but those who do utilize management counsel generally cite five reasons for doing so:

1. It provides an outside point of view.
2. It is based on wide experience.
3. It applies specialized knowledge to the problem at hand.
4. It emphasizes the scientific approach to problems.
5. It saves time.[3]

In individual cases there may, of course, be other more specific reasons in addition to these five for calling in consultants.

In many small concerns problems requiring the special abilities of a consultant are intermittent and of short duration. It would not pay such firms to have management specialists continuously on their payroll any more than it would pay an individual to employ a physician full-time when his services are needed only occasionally to help prevent or remedy an illness.

What most small firms need are: (1) specialized assistance when some serious difficulty is encountered, and (2) periodic checkups to detect hidden pitfalls that may be avoided if discovered in time.

There are over 15,000 management consultants or consulting firms in the United States. Although some limit their services to a special phase of management, such as plant layout, plant location, or communications, most of them are able to service all the needs of the average business, and specialize mainly in the sense of acquiring greater experience with firms of a certain type and size. Part of this results from the

---

[3] Robert E. Williams, "How Management Consultants Help Small Businesses," rev. ed., Management Aids Annual no. 1 (Washington, D.C.: Small Business Administration, 1958), p. 178. See also Donald R. G. Cowan, *The Small Manufacturer and His Specialized Staff*, Small Business Management Series no. 13 (Washington, D.C.: Small Business Administration, 1954).

way consultants are often selected — by personal recommendations of satisfied clients.

Choosing the right consultant for the small enterprise should receive careful attention. In sizing up a particular consultant the Association of Consulting Management Engineers suggests that the prospective client obtain answers to the following questions:

1. How long has the consulting firm been in business?
2. What is the background of the principals (partners)?
3. What is the firm's financial status?
4. What companies has it served?
5. What do its clients say about the technical quality of its work?
6. How much of its business is "repeat" business?
7. How well does the firm get along with people — its own employees as well as outsiders?
8. How much time do principals spend on the job?
9. Has the firm had experience applicable to your problem?
10. Has the firm a recognized expert on your kind of problem?[4]

"You can get help in answering some of these questions," say officials of this professional consulting organization, "but others you will have to decide on the basis of your own judgment. There are a few rule-of-thumb measures that can be applied. They are not infallible; they are only indicators. But, as a rule, you should be suspicious of a consultant who deviates from the normally accepted pattern.

Be wary of the fellow who employs high-pressure salesmen and high-pressure advertising. Broadly speaking what is meant by "high pressure" is this: the fellow who *promises* benefits from his counsel, who urges you to sign up *now*, who hints at dire consequences if you fail to follow his advice, or who advertises a special *limited time* offer.

Stay away also from the man who offers cut-rate services or promises results before he has had a chance to make a thorough study of your business.

Avoid the fellow who offers to make a study and a report on your business for a fixed fee. . . .He cannot possibly know how much work would be involved before he even starts on the job.

Don't expect much from the person who offers consulting services contingent upon the purchase of certain machines or merchandise.

Be cautious of the man who asks for payment in advance.

Look out for the tricky financial arrangement. Insist that the consultant tell you in writing precisely what he proposes to do, about how long it will take, and about how much it will cost, as well as what he thinks he will accomplish by doing it.[5]

Once a consultant is employed, it is of the utmost importance to cooperate with him in every possible manner, both during and after his employment. His work consists of two major parts: (1) diagnosis of the trouble or weakness, and (2) recommendations for improvement. His recommendations are of no value unless

[4] Williams, "How Management Consultants Help," p. 183.
[5] Ibid.

followed. In some cases it may be necessary to have the consultant carry through his recommendations. This need occurs when a recommendation calls for some technical job beyond the ability of the concern's own management, such as the installation of more efficient methods, a quality control system, or a new layout.

Management consultants are relatively expensive but may represent an excellent investment. A small consulting firm, or an individual consultant, may charge $100 per day or more, but may be needed for only a short time to remedy some trouble that would otherwise result in loss of profits far in excess of the consultant's fee.

The small business consultant is usually a limited-service type of management consultant. He is often currently employed by an educational institution or large corporation and does consulting work on the side. Progressive colleges and universities encourage their faculties to engage in a reasonable amount of private practice in their teaching specialties. Many of these men have had exceptionally fine training and considerable practical experience. The nature of their academic positions requires them to keep abreast of the latest developments, and exposes them to continuous requests for information and advice. They are obliged to observe high standards of honesty, integrity, and professional ethics.

In many cases the typical independent enterpriser will find a small business consultant better suited to his needs, and probably less expensive than a full-time management consultant, but he should not expect cut-rate or bargain services, and certainly not the free advice that the specialists so often are asked to give.

Specialized Business-Service Organizations

In addition to trade associations, trade journals, and professional management consultants, the small business owner-manager may receive assistance from an increasingly large number of specialized business-service organizations. The latter differ from management consultants in two respects, primarily: (1) they limit their service to a particular function or group of functions, and (2) in particular cases they may render only routine services at the operating level.

Many recurring tasks in the small concern, for example, may be "farmed out" to companies specializing in the performance of the particular tasks. These include such activities as window cleaning, setting up displays, copywriting, correspondence, machinery and equipment repair, parcel delivery, sign painting, comparative shopping for retailers, and so on.

On a higher plane of service, well-known examples of "outside staff" assistance to small business include the services of such organizations as Dun & Bradstreet and the A. C. Nielsen Company. These firms render invaluable service in such areas as credit reporting, advertising, and market research. In addition to these are other firms specializing in plant location studies, the analysis of traffic problems, the design of control systems, or other matters of primary concern to management. Also available to the management of a small firm, on a subscription basis, are a number of business reporting "services," such as those of the Bureau of National Affairs, Research Institute of America, Commerce Clearing House, Merten's, and Prentice-Hall. The latter reporting services keep management abreast of developments in tax laws, pension plans, profit sharing, and labor legislation and arbitration. Of particular interest to the small retailer are the subscription services which specialize in reporting fashion trends, shelf prices in chain food stores and supermarkets, or other kinds of market information.

A recent development is the renting of electronic computers from banks and data-processing firms. This may be for the purpose of solving a complicated but infrequently occurring problem, such as a new location for the store or plant, or for a continuous function such as inventory control. These data-processing services are not to be confused with the "datacenters" established in various cities by IBM and other computer manufacturers; the staff services of such equipment manufacturers are discussed in the following section.

Equipment Manufacturers

Manufacturers of cash registers, weighing and measuring scales, electronic computers, production machines, handling devices, and other equipment often render many complimentary services to the users or prospective users of their products in an effort to build and maintain goodwill. Some have established special divisions for the purpose of aiding or informing small businessmen, such as the Marketing Services Department of the National Cash Register Company.

These manufacturers provide a variety of services. Assistance on store layout and modernization, for example, is available from companies producing floor coverings, display materials and equipment, and modern store fronts. A similar service is performed for small industrial plants by manufacturers of machine tools and handling equipment.

As noted previously, another type of service is that provided by the "datacenters" which have been established by computer manufacturers in several of the larger cities. In addition to the hourly rental of machines, datacenter customers can make full use of the computer manufacturer's educational facilities, experience, and library of programming aids.

Many equipment manufacturers also maintain a series of publications to aid the small businessman. These publications cover a wide range of management subjects, and are available free upon request.[6]

Large-Company Competitors

Another valuable, but sometimes overlooked source of information for the small businessman, is any innovation by the larger concerns, especially the leaders in his industry. This does not mean that the small enterpriser should mimic every move made by large companies or spend undue time watching their activities. In some cases, however, what the leaders in an industry do today may be almost universal practice tomorrow. Needless delay in making adjustments can be serious. Independent retailers in the hardware and drug fields waited so long to adopt open displays and self-service counters that they may never fully recover business lost to customers who prefer these methods. In other cases some changes by large-scale competitors may open up new opportunities to small-scale independents, who might provide supplementary goods and services. Many additional ways the independent can utilize observable activities of leaders in the field are explained in later chapters dealing with special phases of management.

[6] Most manufacturers endeavor to provide single complimentary copies of publications dealing with a specific subject. However, there is usually a charge for quantity orders.

Other Nongovernmental Sources of Business Information

Many local public utilities have specialists available for consultation on lighting, heating, and air-conditioning. Public utilities also make surveys and advise on power installations. The customer's banker can render valuable assistance on financial and credit matters. The sources from which a business secures its merchandise, materials, and supplies are particularly important sources of information and will be discussed in Chapter 17.

GOVERNMENTAL SOURCES OF BUSINESS INFORMATION

More than two dozen agencies of the federal government furnish information useful to the small businessman at little or no direct cost. The most important of these are the Department of Commerce and the Small Business Administration, and the services of each will be discussed in some detail. However, a few others are worthy of mention.

Federal Reserve banks publish reports on business and economic conditions in their respective districts, including continuing series such as sales and inventory indexes and stock-sales ratios. These reports are available in local banks and in many libraries, and by direct request from the Board of Governors in Washington or the district Federal Reserve bank.

The Federal Trade Commission has been assigned the task of conducting many studies concerned with concentration of economic power, monopolistic practices, unfair competition, effects on competition of various laws, and possible needs for new legislation. Publications of the Food and Drug Administration catalog actions against numerous firms for alleged violation of the Federal Food, Drug, and Cosmetics Act, with brief digests of each charge and actions taken. Like the regulatory functions of the Federal Trade Commission dealing with advertising, actions taken by the Federal Food and Drug Administration are of interest to small businessmen largely because they suggest what *not* to do. Publications of research projects by both agencies, however, as well as their annual reports often contain information and ideas of great value to the independent businessman.

The U.S. Department of Agriculture has a large number of periodic series and many special research publications dealing with agricultural products (both raw materials and foods ready for consumption), the status of farm families, agricultural cooperatives, farm prices, consumer preferences and buying habits for foods and textiles, home economics topics, and, fairly recently, certain phases of retail food marketing.

For special studies and statistical series relating to labor, the status of wage earners' families, employment, and similar data, the Bureau of Labor Statistics of the U.S. Department of Labor publishes material that is often helpful in appraising economic conditions and in keeping abreast of developments affecting labor. The *Monthly Labor Review* is available in many libraries or by direct subscription.

The U.S. Office of Education of the Department of Health, Education, and Welfare administers the Vocational Education Amendments of 1968 in cooperation with state departments of education. Federal vocational education funds have been used in various states to sponsor management seminars, shoplifting clinics, and truth-in-lending seminars for merchants, and other programs related to small business operation.

Compliance with tax laws can be overwhelming – especially to the new entrepreneur. The Internal Revenue Service publishes each year the *Tax Guide for Small Business*. IRS has also prepared a tax kit to assist the small businessman. Entitled *Mr. Businessman's Kit*, it supplies the entrepreneur with every type of tax form he will need, and contains many convenience features to help him file his tax returns properly. Both the tax guide and the tax kit are available through local IRS offices. The small businessman is also encouraged to visit his local IRS office for assistance.

The ambitious enterpriser should purchase from the Superintendent of Documents, or obtain from his local library, the latest edition of the *United States Government Organization Manual* for a fairly complete listing and description of the activities of every federal agency. Only in some such manner is he likely to become familiar with certain agencies that may be useful to him.

U.S. Department of Commerce

Prior to 1953, when the Small Business Administration was established, the U.S. Department of Commerce was the government agency most active in conducting projects of interest to independent enterprisers. It is still the businessman's department of the federal government. From time to time bibliographies or compilations of the publications of the USDC are released which may be consulted in many libraries.[7] The small businessman may keep abreast of current publications in certain areas by asking that his name be put on the desired mailing list. The biweekly *Selected United States Government Publications* issued by the Superintendent of Documents, Washington, D.C., also lists many recent USDC publications.

During the 1940s the USDC conducted hundreds of studies of various management and operating functions of concerns in the major fields of small business, publishing the results in over 500 "Small Business Aids." Though most of these "aids" are now out of print, they are available in many libraries. Many are still useful for the ideas they express, and all of them are sound in the principles and basic concepts they present.[8]

Among the current publications of the USDC of likely interest to small independents is the monthly *Survey of Current Business*. This periodical is the standard reference source for data on production and distribution activities of the nation's basic industries. It also contains data on the business population and its changes, the level and distribution of income, and about 2,500 statistical series covering nearly every measurable factor of significance to the national economy.

The Department of Commerce maintains 42 field offices and over 600 local "cooperative offices" for the purpose of providing ready access to the reports,

---

[7] See *United States Department of Commerce Publications: A Catalogue and Index*, Annual Supplements (Washington, D.C.: Superintendent of Documents).

[8] The Small Business Administration has continued the practice of publishing small business management and marketing "aids." The SBA has, in fact, revised and reissued many of the numbers in the old USDC series.

publications, and services of the Bureau of the Census, and also those of the Bureau of International Commerce, the Business and Defense Services Administration, the Economic Development Administration, and the Office of Business Economics. Information on certain activities of the National Bureau of Standards, Patent Office, and the Institute of Applied Technology is also available. Experienced personnel will assist in the solution of specific problems, explain the scope and meaning of regulations administered by the department, and provide practical assistance in the broad field of domestic and foreign commerce. Field offices act as official sales agents of the Superintendent of Documents and stock a wide range of official government publications relating to business. Each office maintains an extensive business reference library containing periodicals, directories, publications, and reports from official as well as private sources.

Through its Census Bureau, the USDC also compiles and publishes, on a periodic basis, data on a wide variety of the nation's social and economic characteristics. The Census Bureau reports of major interest to the businessman are the following:

1. *The Census of Population*, taken every ten years, presents information on age, race, sex, marital status, family status, ethnic origin, migration, education, income, occupation, employment, and other characteristics of the population. These data are universally available for states and counties, and much of the information is also broken down for cities and towns with populations of 2,500 or more. Of special significance to the businessman are the trends in the level and composition of employment and income, the changing occupational pattern and age composition of the population, and the population migration pattern. These data have important marketing implications. Changing wants may be anticipated and opportunities for new enterprises, products, and services disclosed by careful analysis of census data.

2. The *Census of Manufactures* is taken every four or five years, most recently in 1972. Included in this census are data on the number of manufacturing establishments, the number of production and other employees, "value added by manufacture," cost of materials, value of shipments, and recent capital expenditures for each of the nation's manufacturing industries. These data also are compiled for each of the states, and much of the information is available for counties as well. To fill the gap between census years, the Bureau of the Census conducts *Annual Surveys of Manufactures* to yield estimates for the more important industrial classifications.

3. The *Census of Business* is also taken every four or five years, the latest occurring in 1972. This census provides information on all types of retail and wholesale trade and on selected services. Included are data on the number of establishements, gross annual sales or receipts, the number of employees, annual payroll, and the number of active proprietors of unincorporated enterprises. These data are compiled for each state and county, and for all communities with a population of 2,500 or more. Their usefulness, however, is limited, though not seriously so, by the number of years which elapse between census surveys; unlike the *Census of Manufactures*, there are no interim estimates or reports.

Other recurring censuses conducted by the Bureau of the Census include the *Census of Agriculture*, the *Census of Mineral Industries*, the *Census of Governments*, and the *Census of Housing*.

In addition to the publication of the above census volumes, the Bureau of the Census cooperates with the Bureau of Retirement and Survivors Insurance (Department of Health, Education, and Welfare) in the publication of *County Business*

Patterns. This joint publication is issued quarterly, and contains data for each major industry on the number of reporting units, "covered" employment, and taxable payrolls under the Retirement, Survivors, and Disability Insurance Program (RSDI).

No really intelligent decisions which are contingent upon the state of the national, state, or local economies can be made by the management of any firm, large or small, without reliable data of the type furnished only in the above-mentioned volumes. The typical owner-manager of a small business enterprise may not fully appreciate the significance of the work done by the Bureau of the Census, because ordinarily he does not read the various statistical reports. But his trade association editors read and analyze and make important conclusions and recommendations on the basis of them, as do university bureaus of business research and other agencies with which he has contacts. So, indirectly, at least, the small businessman has a vital interest in a continuation or even an increase in the frequency and coverage of these reports.

Small Business Administration

The Small Business Administration, established in July 1953, is the first permanent peacetime agency of the federal government created solely to advise, assist, and protect *all* small business enterprises. Previous agencies set up to render financial and procurement assistance to small firms were limited to helping manufacturers engaged in defense or essential civilian production. Since the SBA took over its predecessor, the Small Defense Plants Administration, it was initially more familiar with rendering financial aid to manufacturers than to distributors, retailers, or service establishments, although the latter types of business enterprise are included within its scope of operations. The SBA has 15 regional offices and 83 branch field offices. The latter are located in the larger cities in all 50 states and in Puerto Rico, Guam, and the Virgin Islands.

Three major areas of assistance to the small businessman are provided by SBA: (1) financial assistance, (2) the procurement of government contracts, and (3) management and technical assistance.

SBA financial "assistance" includes the lending of money as well as the counseling of small firms on financial matters. However, its lending function is restricted by law and is of lesser importance. The Small Business Administration as a source of capital for the small firm is discussed in some detail in Chapter 11. Much more valuable, and more germane to our present discussion, is the assistance which SBA officials can render the small businessman in securing loans from private agencies – what he should do anyway, if he knew how. Through its counseling service, SBA already has aided thousands of financially harassed firms to find relief through regular channels of financing. This experience of SBA again supports the thesis of our text, namely, that the financial problems of most small businessmen are symptoms of more fundamental ailments: lack of managerial ability, and lack of information or know-how.

A second primary purpose of SBA is to assist small firms that want to obtain government prime contracts and related subcontracts. This area of service to small business (which, like the lending function, is not strictly an "outside staff" activity) was discussed in Chapter 2.

The third major area of SBA operations deals with providing managerial and technical assistance to small business. Staff specialists in the Small Business Administration's field offices assist with many types of management problems. Their services are available to established businessmen who have a specific problem or who want authoritative information on various aspects of management, and to persons who are considering starting their own businesses. One feature of this counseling service is a system of business reference libraries, which the SBA has established in its Washington office and in each of its regional offices. These libraries contain textbooks, government and private publications dealing with business management, business papers and other helpful publications, and are available for reference use by the small businessman.

The Small Business Administration cooperates with leading educational institutions and distributive education groups throughout the nation in sponsoring courses in administrative management, providing instruction in the basic functions of planning, organizing, staffing, directing, and controlling small business enterprises. These courses, generally taught by experienced educators and successful businessmen, are usually held in the evenings and run from six to eight weeks. One-day "Workshops for Prospective Business Owners" are also conducted.

The SBA also sponsors the Service Corps of Retired Executives. SCORE, as it is popularly called, is a group of more than 3,500 retired business executives who make their management skills and experiences available to small businesses on a voluntary, part-time basis. By pointing out weaknesses in his management policies and practices, and how they may be corrected, SCORE volunteers help the small businessman improve his chances for business success. Many of them also serve as lecturers or coordinators in the above-mentioned administrative management courses and workshops.

SCORE's counseling services are available on request; such requests should be addressed to the nearest SBA field office. No fees are charged during the first 90 days. However, the business is asked to pay the volunteer's out-of-pocket expenses during this period. After 90 days, if it is desired to retain the volunteer's services, mutually satisfactory compensation arrangements may be made.

Also sponsored by the SBA is the Active Corps of Executives. ACE was organized to supplement the talents of SCORE by merging the expertise of active businessmen with that of the SCORE volunteers. As with SCORE, the ACE program is designed to help the small businessman who can't afford a professional consultant.

Continuing the practice previously followed by the Department of Commerce, the SBA also publishes several series of management and technical publications of value to established or prospective operators of small business concerns. These are:

1. Management Aids for Small Manufacturers
2. Small Marketers Aids
3. Technical Aids for Small Manufacturers
4. Small Business Management Series
5. Starting and Managing Series
6. Small Business Research Series

In addition, the SBA publishes sources of information (*Small Business Bibliographies*) on specific kinds of business or business operations in serial form, as well as a number of nonseries publications.[9]

Many contributions to the advancement of small business enterprise were made as a result of the 1959-1961 SBA Management Research Grant Program. Under this program, 230 SBA-funded management research studies were completed by various universities and state development agencies. Only a limited number of copies of the research reports were printed, but they are available for reference in any of the SBA regional offices and at many reference libraries. Summaries of these studies were also prepared, however, and these are available in reasonable quantities from any of the SBA offices, free of charge.

State and Local Agencies

The Department of Commerce of New York State is an excellent example of a state agency that undertakes extensive outside staff services for small businessmen. Most state officials will direct inquiries concerning their resources, license and tax requirements, and similar matters to the appropriate departments for reply. Many states publish statistics on business based on the amount of sales and income taxes they collect. In their efforts to attract industries, several states are expanding services designed to facilitate this objective; these were discussed in the chapter on industrial plant location (Chapter 9).

On the local or municipal level governmental "outside staff" services have been limited to those connected with seeking new industries, and to answering inquiries regarding licenses, permits, and zoning regulations. Semipublic agencies, community development organizations, and industrial boards, however, may be found in some cities, and the possibility of their existence in any case should always be considered. It is consistent with the original plans and policies of the Small Business Administration that more local governmental and semipublic organizations should provide outside staff services designed to meet special local needs.

SUMMARY AND CONCLUSIONS

No matter how extensive the manager's personal experience may be, it is no longer possible to operate a small business successfully if it is insulated or detached from the information and assistance available from "outside staff." Conditions have become complex and change rapidly. As competition continues to increase both within each industry and on an interindustry basis, staff contacts outside each firm will become even more essential.

Services of a high quality related to any function of management and to any phase of operations of the small enterprise are available from the outside staff.

[9] Selected SBA publications related to various types of business operation or functions in a general way are classified in Appendix C in accordance with the chapter organization of this book; SBA publications related to organizing and operating specific types of business are included (with other reference sources) in Appendix A.

Many of these were discussed in this chapter. In particular, strong endorsement was suggested for trade association and trade press services, and for those of the U.S. Department of Commerce and the Small Business Administration. It was also suggested that management and small business consultants, or "business doctors," may save a business life just as a physician or surgeon may save a human life.

Aids and services furnished on a goodwill basis by companies with a product to sell may also be of great value in many situations. Their brief treatment in this chapter is due to the wide diversity of such outside staff services and to the rigid demands for brevity in a book such as this.

REVIEW QUESTIONS

1. (a) What is an "outside staff"? (b) Why must most small businessmen rely heavily upon such a staff? (c) What types of business information are provided by the outside staff? (d) What are the major sources of this information?

2. What are some of the membership services typically supplied by trade associations?

3. What are the advantages to be derived by the small businessman in subscribing to trade publications?

4. (a) When is it most appropriate for the small businessman to hire a management consultant? (b) What are some of the advantages to be derived by the small businessman in hiring management consultants?

5. Cite some examples of "outside staff" services performed by specialized business-service organizations.

6. (a) How do you account for the numerous and valuable free staff services provided by equipment manufacturers? (b) What are some of the services they provide?

7. Cite some other examples of nongovernmental sources of business information.

8. What kinds of information may be obtained by the small businessman from each of the following agencies of the federal government: Federal Reserve Board; Federal Trade Commission; Department of Agriculture; Bureau of Labor Statistics; Internal Revenue Service.

9. Describe the major small business services available from the U.S. Department of Commerce.

10. Describe the major small business services available from the Small Business Administration.

11. In what ways do state and local government agencies assist the small businessman?

DISCUSSION QUESTIONS

1. Cite examples of how a small businessman can use basic economic and statistical data published by government agencies in policy formation and long-range planning.

2. Two seniors in business considered buying a country club five miles from the campus but outside the city limits, to be operated as a dinner club. Where should they seek primarily nonfinancial assistance?

SUPPLEMENTARY READINGS

Pomeranz, Janet M., and Leonard W. Prestwich. *Meeting the Problems of Very Small Enterprises.* Small Business Management Research Report prepared for the Small Business Administration. Washington, D.C.: George Washington University, 1962. An analysis of the need for management counseling of very small business firms.

Stevens, J. Richard. *Methods and Channels for Effective Communication of Management Information to Small Business.* Small Business Management Research Report prepared for the Small Business Administration. Tallahassee: Florida State University, 1963. A study of the methods and channels used to communicate management information to small businessmen. Evaluates the success or failure of these various approaches and offers recommendations for more effective preparation and dissemination of such information.

15

Insurance
and risk management

As risk is a part of our personal life, so is it a part of our business. Some risks are *reducible,* such as the reducible risk of accident by driving carefully, or the reducible risk of theft by more vigilant security measures. Some risks can be *transferred,* such as the purchase of fire insurance on our home or store building. Few risks can be eliminated completely.

In any business it is possible to have the result of years of hard work lost by a single fire, theft, or accident. Precautionary measures and proper insurance coverage can help avoid this kind of trouble.

THE RULES OF RISK MANAGEMENT

Knowing *what kind* of insurance to carry, and *how much* to purchase, is an important aspect of good risk management. In making these determinations, the small businessman should consider (1) the size of the potential loss, (2) its probability, and (3) the resources that would be available to meet the loss if it should occur. These factors are incorporated in the following "rules of risk management" developed by Professors Robert L. Mehr and Bob A. Hedges:[1]

1. *Don't risk more than you can afford to lose.* No firm can possibly eliminate or transfer all of the risks which it faces; it obviously must assume some of the risks. The most important factor in determining whether a particular risk should be transferred (to an insurance company) or assumed (by the firm) is the maximum potential loss which might result from the risk; if the loss would be likely to force the firm into bankruptcy, or cause it serious financial impairment, then the risk should not be assumed.

2. *Don't risk a lot for a little.* There should be a reasonable relationship between the cost of transferring the risk (the cost of insurance) and the value that accrues to the insured firm. For example, the additional premiums required to eliminate or reduce "deductibles" in many types of insurance is quite high in relation to the

[1] *Risk Management in the Business Enterprise* (New York: Richard D. Irwin, 1963), pp. 16–19. See also Emmett J. Vaughan, "A Mini-Course in Risk Management, Part I," *Underwriters Review,* January 1971, pp. 9, 14.

added protection. This rule also reinforces the first rule: The firm that neglects to purchase insurance against severe losses is risking a lot (the possible loss) for a little (the premiums paid).

3. *Consider the odds.* Contrary to popular opinion, a high probability that a loss will occur does not indicate that the risk should be insured. In fact, the contrary is true: the greater the probability of occurrence, the less appropriate is the purchase of insurance for dealing with the risk. In the first place, losses that occur with relative frequency are *predictable* and are typically *small* losses that can be assumed by the business without too much financial difficulty; they are often budgeted as "normal" costs of doing business and thus are included in the prices paid by customers. Some common examples are shoplifting and bad-debt losses. Secondly, where the probability of loss is high a more effective method of managing or controlling the risk is to *reduce* it by adopting appropriate precautionary measures.

As a final note, the reader is reminded of the overriding importance of the first rule of risk management, as discussed above: do not risk more than you can afford to lose. Clearly, the probability of a fire, theft, or casualty loss is less important than the possible size of the loss should the casualty occur.

INSURANCE PLANNING

Insurance planning begins with a consideration of the insurable risks faced by the business enterprise. In general, the following business risks can be covered by insurance:

1. Loss or damage of property — including merchandise, supplies, fixtures, and building
2. Loss of income resulting from interruption of business because of damage to the firm's operating assets
3. Personal injury to customers, employees, and the general public
4. Loss to the business from the death or disability of key employees or the owner

The insurable risks of the small business will be discussed in detail in the following section of this chapter. In general, the following types of insurance are available:

1. Fire and general property insurance — covering fire losses, vandalism, hail, and wind damage
2. Plate-glass insurance — covering window breakage
3. Consequential loss insurance — covering loss of earnings or extra expenses in case of suspension of business due to fire or other catastrophe
4. Burglary insurance — covering forcible entry and theft of merchandise and cash
5. Fidelity bond — covering theft by an employee
6. Fraud insurance — covering counterfeit money, bad checks, and larceny
7. Public liability insurance — covering injury to the public, such as a customer or pedestrian falling on the property
8. Product liability insurance — covering injury to customers arising from the use of goods bought in the store
9. Workmen's compensation insurance — covering injury to employees at work

10. Life insurance — covering the life of the owner(s) or key employee(s)

11. Boiler insurance — covering damage to the building premises caused by boiler explosion

After listing his insurable risks and the types of insurance available to cover them, the small businessman must then consider how much of a loss he can afford to bear himself, the possible losses which he would prefer to transfer, and the insurance company's fee for assuming part of his risk. The cost of the various kinds of insurance must be matched against the possible loss and the ability of the small businessman to bear the cost.

It is not possible here to cite exact figures as to insurance costs because individual business insurance rates depend on so many factors — such as store location, type of business, property value, the building's construction, average inventory level, etc. The small businessman should seek cost estimates from at least two reliable insurance agents for his consideration before buying any coverage. The feasibility of "package" insurance policies at discounted rates should also be explored.

INSURABLE BUSINESS RISKS

As noted above, insurable business risks can be classified under the following headings: (1) loss or damage of one's own property; (2) business interruption and other types of "indirect" or "consequential" loss resulting from fire or other damage to the business premises; (3) bodily injury and property damage liability; and (4) the death or disability of "key" executives.

Loss or Damage of Property

The small businessman usually owns considerable property. For many, the building in which the business is housed represents the greatest investment. Even when the place of business is rented or leased, the small businessman's investment in furnishings and inventory is substantial. These investments should be protected against fire and other perils such as smoke, windstorm and hail, riot, civil commotion, explosion, and damage by aircraft or motor vehicles. The latter forms of risk insurance — or "extended coverage" — can be added to the basic fire insurance policy at little additional cost. Vandalism and malicious mischief coverages can also be added. If the business owns or operates a steam boiler, steam boiler insurance should also be added, for the explosion coverage of the "extended coverage" discussed above does not include explosion of a steam boiler.

By accepting a coinsurance clause in his policy, the small businessman can get a substantial reduction in premiums. Under such a clause, the building must be insured to at least 80 percent of its value.[2]

Under the provisions of a coinsurance clause, the businessman agrees to maintain insurance equal to some specified percentage of the value of the property (e.g., 80,

[2] There are two basic measures of insurable value: actual cash value and replacement cost value. Replacement cost means exactly what it says: the cost of replacing the structure with a similar structure of like kind and quality at present-day prices. Actual cash value is based on replacement cost and is generally considered to be replacement cost minus depreciation.

90, or 100 percent) in return for a lower rate. In this sense, coinsurance works like a quantity discount. If, at the time of a loss, the insured has failed to maintain the specified percentage, he cannot collect the full amount of his loss, even if the loss is small. Payment is made under the coinsurance provision on the basis of the following formula:

$$\frac{\text{Amount of insurance carried}}{\text{Amount the insured agreed to carry}} \times \text{Amount of loss} = \text{Amount paid}$$

Thus if the insured owns a building with an actual cash value (i.e., a depreciated value) of $100,000 and insured it with an 80 percent coinsurance provision, he must have coverage equal to 80 percent of the actual cash value at the time of the loss in order to collect the full depreciated value of the property at the time of the loss. Suppose that a $10,000 loss occurs immediately after the policy is taken out and that the value of the building is determined to be $100,000:

$$\frac{\text{Amount carried}}{\text{Amount required}} \times \text{Amount of loss} = \frac{\$80,000}{\$80,000} \times \$10,000 = \$10,000$$

Now suppose that the loss does not occur for three years, and that during the period the actual cash value of the property has increased to, say, $125,000. Loss payment would be made on the following basis:

$$\frac{\text{Amount carried}}{\text{Amount required}} \times \text{Amount of loss} = \frac{\$80,000}{\$100,000} \times \$10,000 = \$8,000$$
$$= \$8,000$$

This example illustrates an important point: the coinsurance requirement is applied at the time of the loss, and the amount of insurance that is required to comply is based on the value of the property at the time of the loss. Furthermore, the burden of maintaining the proper amount of insurance is placed on the insured himself.

It may be noted that the above illustration is concerned with the depreciated value of the property. If the insured had elected to insure on the basis of the full replacement cost (i.e., without a deduction for depreciation), the same formula would be used, except that the amount of insurance that the businessman agrees to carry would be based on the full replacement cost, without a deduction for depreciation. If a deficiency in the coinsurance percentage exists, he will be able to collect only for a part of the full replacement cost of the loss, suffering a deduction for depreciation. If the deficiency is great enough, he may even collect less than the depreciated value of the property damaged.

A word of warning to the small businessman is warranted here. Building costs — which determine replacement costs — have approximately doubled in the past two decades. Thus older business buildings are likely to be more underinsured than those of more recent vintage. But because of inflation many new buildings have also rapidly slipped below 80 percent coverage. The small businessman should check frequently to see that his place of business is not underinsured. The increase in its replacement cost can be estimated by means of an "appraisal kit" that his insurance company will supply on request. These kits provide multipliers applied to the original cost of the building, based on its age and the geographical area in which it is located.

The *contents* of the building should be insured against at least the same perils as the building. Retailers, particularly, may find it desirable to purchase a special glass-insurance policy that covers all risk to plate-glass windows, glass signs, glass doors, showcases, and countertops. In addition, there should be insurance coverages on various forms of dishonesty. Employers should acquire a fidelity bond on employees who have access to large sums of money. Protection against the dishonesty of customers and transgressors may also be desirable, such as theft, burglary, and robbery coverage.

Burglary insurance coverage covers losses only if there are visible marks of the burglar's forced entry. Robbery insurance, on the other hand, protects the insured against loss of property, money, or securities by force, trickery, or threat of violence on *or off* the business premises; thus it would cover hijacking, for example, and other losses not covered by burglary insurance. Perhaps the best policy to cover the dishonesty exposure is the comprehensive dishonesty, disappearance, and destruction policy; this comprehensive policy, written especially for the small businessman, provides economical protection against all the forms of dishonesty mentioned above, in addition to counterfeit currency and forgery.

Many small businesses have had difficulty in obtaining property insurance coverages at reasonable rates, particularly if they are located in deteriorated urban core or "high-risk" areas; in some sections – known as "red-circle" zones – property insurance is not available at any cost through normal channels. Small businessmen in these areas may get help through the FAIR plan or through the Federal Crime Insurance Program.

The FAIR plan.   FAIR is an acronym for Fair Access to Insurance Requirements. Under this plan, the insurance companies operating in a particular state enter into a pooling arrangement whereby they share risks in high-risk areas and agree to pay their proportionate share toward the full sum of an approved claim. FAIR plans have been introduced in 26 states, and in Puerto Rico and the District of Columbia. The plan works as follows:

A small businessman (or homeowner) unable to get property insurance in ordinary channels obtains an application from the FAIR plan headquarters or from an insurance agent, broker, or company. He fills out the form and returns it. An inspection of his property is made, and if the property meets minimum insurance requirements, a policy is issued upon payment of a premium.

Even if certain dangerous conditions do exist, the property may be declared eligible for coverage – but at an increased rate until these hazards are eliminated. If the property is found to be uninsurable because of excessive hazards, the inspector points out these deficiencies and the owner may have them repaired and request another inspection. The principal deficiencies generally are faulty wiring, faulty heating units, generally dilapidated conditions that make property subject to trespass by derelicts, or poor housekeeping – such as accumulations of rubbish.

Protection offered through FAIR plans includes fire and extended coverage, covering (as noted above) riots, civil disorders, and other perils.

In only one of the FAIR plan states, however, does the FAIR plan include protection against crime losses – one of the most important problems of small businesses located in deteriorated urban core areas! To fill this void, the Federal Crime Insurance Program was launched by the U.S. Department of Housing and Urban Development on August 1, 1971.

Federal Crime Insurance Program.   In some urban core areas, privately under-written crime insurance is totally unavailable, or available only at prohibitive premium rates. As long as crime and civil disorder continue to flourish in these areas the responsibility for providing insurance coverage against these hazards would seem to rest with the government. The private-insurance sector just does not have the resources to provide protection against hazards stemming from social revolution – at prices that homeowners and businessmen can afford to pay. That the federal government was ready and willing to assume this responsibility was evidenced by the recent enactment in Congress of an amendment to title XII of the National Housing Act. Under the provisions of this amendment, the Department of Housing and Urban Development (HUD) is directed to review the types of crime insurance available in each of the states either through the normal insurance market or through a state FAIR plan. Crime insurance as defined in the amendment means insurance against burglary and robbery, and includes broad-form business and personal theft insurance, but not automobile insurance.

In any state where such insurance is not provided at "affordable" rates by August 1, 1971, HUD is authorized to make it available through the facilities of the federal government. The conditions of such insurance, including the setting of rates and determination of insurability, are at the discretion of HUD and may vary from state to state or from locality to locality within a state. HUD is also empowered to utilize insurance companies as fiscal agents – to market the coverage and service the insured business (or homeowner), thus making available to this program the expertise and experience of the private carriers. By 1972 federal crime insurance was available in the urban core areas of nine states and the District of Columbia, and three insurance companies were writing policies under this program. All licensed insurance agents in each of these states are eligible to take applications for insurance.

It is interesting to note that one of the conditions required for this insurance is that the businessman install adequate safeguards and security measures.

Consequential Loss

Though losses resulting from property damage may be fully compensated, the small business may also suffer other losses of an indirect or "consequential" nature. A fire, for example, may be so damaging that business operations, if not halted completely, can be continued only by moving to a temporary location at considerable expense. Business-interruption insurance can be purchased to cover (1) the fixed costs that would continue if the business were forced to cease operations temporarily – such as taxes or lease payments, interest, depreciation, utilities, and salaries of key employees – as well as the estimated profits that would be lost during the period of the shutdown; and (2) the extra expenses incurred in moving into temporary quarters.

Legal Liability

As noted previously, the most basic principle in determining the kind and amount of insurance that a small businessman should carry is that the probability that a loss may occur is less important than the possible size of the loss. On the basis of this principle it would appear that legal liability is potentially the greatest risk that a small businessman (or anyone else, for that matter) faces. The maximum loss that can occur to the business property is obviously limited by the value of that property. But in the case of the liability exposure there is no fixed loss limit, and a judgment against the small businessman in a bodily injury on property damage suit may be far greater than the value of the property itself. The size of damage-suit awards has risen sharply in recent years, and today liability coverage up to $1 million is no longer considered high or unreasonable. Adequate liability insurance is, therefore, *essential* to the small businessman; without it, a single judgment against him might well "put his back to the wall" financially, or even put him out of business.

In general, there are four types of liability exposure: (1) employer's liability and workmen's compensation; (2) liability to nonemployees; (3) automobile liability; and (4) professional liability. Of primary concern to the typical small businessman are the first three.

Employer's liability and workmen's compensation.   Under common law as well as under workmen's compensation laws an employer is liable for injury to employees at work caused by his failure to (1) provide safe tools and working conditions, (2) hire competent fellow employees, or (3) warn employees of an existing danger. Employee coverage and the extent of the employer's liability varies from state to state. At the present time workmen's compensation is *required* in about half the states. Though it is not required in the other states, the employer will lose certain legal defenses without it.

General, or third-party liability.   "General" liability is liability for any kind of bodily injury to nonemployees except that caused by automobiles and professional malpractice. In some cases this liability may even extend to trespassers. Also, a small businessman may be legally liable for bodily injuries sustained by customers, pedestrians, deliverymen, trespassers, and other outsiders even in cases where he exercised "reasonable care."

Automobile liability.   Cars and trucks are a serious source of liability. Most business firms own one or more of them. Even if they don't, under the doctrine of agency they could be held vicariously liable for injuries and property damage caused by an employee who was operating his own or someone else's car in the course of his employment. Of course, the firm would have some coverage under the employee's own liability policy *if he had one,* but even if he had, the limits of the employee's liability might be grossly inadequate. If there are many employees it would be impractical to check their individual liability coverages. In businesses where it is customary or sometimes convenient for an employee to operate his own car while on company business — as in the case of many road and route salesmen — the employer is well advised to acquire nonownership automobile liability insurance.

Summary.   The "best" form of general liability insurance for the small business firm consists of a comprehensive general liability policy. This, combined with a comprehensive auto liability policy and a standard workmen's compensation policy, represents the practical ideal.

Death or Disability of "Key Men"

More so than in a larger business the death or disability of a "key man" in the organization (or his employment by another firm) can cause serious loss to the small enterprise. If one person in the organization makes a significant contribution to the success of the business, which is often the case in the small firm, his death may be tantamount to the death of the business itself. Disability can be even more serious if the disabled key man happens to be an employee rather than the owner-manager, for then the business would lose not only the services of the disabled employee but may be obligated to continue paying his salary. Risks of this kind can be minimized by acquiring life and disability insurance on the key man, payable to the company, in some amount that would permit the business to make the adjustment in the event his services are lost.

Special Multiperil Program

A recent innovation in the insurance industry is a "package policy" approach for commercial risks similar to homeowners' policies covering personal risks. This is the special multiperil policy, or SMP program. Under this policy the small businessman can purchase *one* insurance policy to cover all the risks which formerly required separate underwriting agreements. Of the business risks described in the preceding pages, the only ones that cannot be included in a "package policy" are workmen's compensation and company-owned automobiles.

By combining most of the businessman's usual coverages into one package, policy-writing and -handling costs are reduced and these savings are reflected in reduced premium rates. This "package discount" can save the small firm as much as 25 percent of its insurance cost. But more significantly, the package concept causes the small businessman to view his insurance problem as a *single* problem, rather than as many individual problems; thus he is more likely to avoid overlapping coverage and to tailor his insurance program to cover only the important risk exposures — those which would be too great for him to bear alone.[3]

LOSS REDUCTION OR PREVENTION

Risk management is a much broader concept than just insurance buying. If a businessman has a fire in his store or shop, insurance can replace his damaged

[3] For a more complete discussion of the insurable risks of businessmen and others, see Curtis M. Elliott and Emmett J. Vaughan, *Fundamentals of Risk Management* (New York: John Wiley & Sons, 1972).

property, reimburse him for business interruption expenses, and even restore his lost profits; but there are *hidden* losses that he can never recover. He can never recover the loss of customer goodwill, nor the value of skilled employees who have gone elsewhere to work, nor the loss of momentum and continuity in the business. An adequate insurance program is only a part, not the ultimate goal, of risk management.

It is also important for the small businessman to realize that after a fire, theft, or other kind of loss he must use all reasonable means to protect his property or run the risk of having his insurance coverage cancelled. Even if his insurance is not canceled, his premium rates may rise if he has not taken steps to reduce the risk or to prevent the recurrence of a casualty. Risk management involves risk *reduction* as well as risk *transference.*

The Fire Peril

The small businessman can use a wide variety of protective devices and can adopt innumerable precautionary measures to reduce his business risks. The peril of fire, for example, can be minimized by installing automatic sprinklers, or by providing an adequate supply of fire extinguishers and instructing employees how to use them. Brick, concrete, and other types of fire-resistant materials can also be used in construction, as well as fire walls and doors.

The Crime Peril

One of the most serious threats to business property today is the *crime* peril – burglary, robbery, and theft. This is readily apparent to most of us as we go about our daily lives: the sign at the service station that says only checks or credit cards will be accepted after dark; and the sign at the store counter that says we are being monitored on closed-circuit television. A study of crime against small businesses sponsored by the Senate Select Committee on Small Business estimated the total cost of such crime at $3 billion in 1968, more than 250 percent greater than comparable losses ten years earlier. Between 1968 and 1972, annual business crime losses rose to $3.5 billion. This figure represents the reported property loss resulting from crime *on the premises* only; it does not include losses in the distribution and transportation of goods. Law officials agree, moreover, that *reported* crime is only the top of the iceberg; businessmen often fail to report thefts.

Burglary and robbery.   Small stores are prime targets of the burglar and robber. Among the protective devices that the small businessman can use to reduce perils of this kind are silent central-station burglary alarm systems and pin-tumbler cylinder and "dead-bolt" locks. Bank deposits, of course, should be made daily during daylight hours; if an armored-car service is not utilized, a different route to the bank should be taken each day and deposits should be made at different times of the day. Periodically during the day, excess cash should be removed from the cash register and placed in the safe. The safe itself should be visible from the street (not hidden in the back of the store) and should be bolted to the building structure. Overnight indoor security lighting is also desirable, and perhaps outdoor lighting as well.

Employee infidelity. In addition to the crimes from outside the walls of the business, and perhaps more serious, are the crimes from *inside* – from the businessman's own employees. Except for fidelity bonds which might be taken out on employees who have access to large sums of money, this type of loss is generally uninsured and most of it isn't even discovered. It has been estimated that in some stores, inventory shrinkage resulting from employee pilferage and other dishonest acts of employees is greater than that caused by shoplifting. The businessman can prevent employee theft, or at least make it more difficult, by adopting effective accounting and inventory control procedures. Among the safeguards that he can employ are: (1) the use of outside auditors; (2) countersignature of all checks; (3) the *immediate* deposit of all incoming checks, as well as their duplication; (4) bank statement reconciliation by employees other than those who make the deposits; and (5) *joint* access to safe-deposit boxes. Professional shoppers can also be employed to check for violations of the store's cash register and refund procedures. But the most obvious and most important safeguard is careful screening and selection of personnel.

The businessman must also contend with dishonest customers as well as dishonest employees. He faces two kinds of perils from customers: (1) shoplifting, and (2) bad-check passers.

Shoplifting. According to statistics compiled by the National Retail Merchants Association, shoplifting has increased by more than 220 percent across the nation in the last decade. On the average, retail merchants are losing from $2\frac{1}{2}$ to 3 percent of their merchandise – which, incidentally, is just about the profit margin for some of the stores. Some of the goods are lost by employee theft, but most vanishes by shoplifting.

Most shoplifting losses are uninsured because (1) much of it is undiscovered, and (2) many store owners are reluctant to prosecute shoplifters. It is much easier for some retailers to pass along shoplifting losses to customers as part of their costs. This is a dubious policy, however, for it will not discourage shoplifting activity, and may even encourage it. Merchants should also be reminded that shoplifters often steal handbags and packages from customers as well.

Shoplifting losses can be reduced by unrelenting prosecution. Even an antishoplifting sign prominently displayed in the store will help, by reminding the would-be offender of the consequences of such a practice. Many states have passed shoplifting laws which make it easier to apprehend shoplifters, by allowing store employees to detain a customer who has been *observed* to conceal merchandise on his or her person; in these states, it is no longer necessary to apprehend the customer off the store premises with the goods in his possession. Shoplifting losses can likewise be minimized by hiring extra clerks, or perhaps off-duty policemen, during the peak hours. Wide aisles, clear vision, and alert employees are also helpful in defending against this common merchandising problem. Various protective devices may also be utilized, such as two-way and convex wall mirrors and closed-circuit television. Such devices as these, as well as the precautionary measures outlined above, make sure that "customers" do not always get what they want!

Bad check losses. Bad checks pose another problem for many small businessmen. Here, also, protective steps can be taken to minimize losses. Checks, for example, should not be accepted for amounts in excess of the amount of purchase. Nor should postdated, illegibly written, or two-party checks be accepted. Proper identification should be requested before accepting checks from strangers, preferably an automobile operator's license; if the license does not have the operator's photograph affixed to it in addition to his signature, then a second form of identification should be requested.[4]

SUMMARY AND CONCLUSIONS

Every business faces risks. In general, a small business firm faces many of the same risks that confront the individual, and most of them are insurable. These risks can be broadly classified as (1) property damage or theft, (2) third-party liability, and (3) death or disability.

Fire or other peril may destroy the building or its contents. In addition to the loss of the property itself are the "indirect" losses suffered (including reduced profits) when business operations are halted or temporarily suspended because of such a casualty. Dishonest employees, customers, and others may steal from the firm. The firm may also become liable to others for bodily injury or property damage. And premature death or disability of the owner, a partner, or a "key" employee may cause serious loss to the business.

Risk management for the small firm begins with a consideration of the extent of the need for protecting itself against these risks. In this connection, it is the magnitude of the potential loss rather than the probability of its occurrence which is more important. Every means should also be taken to reduce each of the risks facing the firm, whether or not the risk is insured.

REVIEW QUESTIONS

1. What are some of the insurable risks faced by the small business enterprise? What kinds of insurance are available to protect the business against these risks?

2. How can the small business owner determine the kind and amount of insurance he should carry?

3. What is meant by "extended coverage" in a fire insurance policy? What specific business risks or perils are included in this coverage?

4. What is the meaning of a coinsurance clause in a fire insurance policy? From the property owner's point of view, discuss the pros and cons of such a clause.

5. What is meant by "actual cash value"? By "replacement cost value"?

6. Differentiate between burglary and robbery insurance. What are some of the other crime perils faced by the small businessman?

---

[4] Readers interested in exploring further the subject of commercial crime and how the small businessman can best deal with it are referred to Management Aid no. 209, *Preventing Employee Pilferage* (1970), and the following Small Marketers Aids, published by the Small Business Administration (Washington, D.C.): no. 119, *Preventing Retail Theft* (1967, rev. 1971); no. 129, *Reducing Shoplifting Losses* (1967); no. 134, *Preventing Burglary and Robbery Loss* (1968); and no. 137, *Outwitting Bad-Check Passers* (1969).

7. What is a "red-circle" insurance zone? How does a state FAIR plan help small businessmen in these areas?

8. Describe the Federal Crime Insurance Program. How extensive is this program at the present time?

9. Describe the various types of liability to which the small business is exposed. What types of liability insurance are required by law in most states? Some states?

10. What is business-interruption insurance? For what losses may the small businessman be compensated under such a policy in the event of a major fire?

11. Describe the special multiperil policy, or SMP program. Can such a policy be written to cover all business risks of the firm? Explain. What are the advantages to the small businessman of this "package policy" approach?

12. Why is it important for the small businessman to reduce his business risks as much as possible?

13. Enumerate some of the precautionary measures described in the text for combating: (*a*) the fire peril; (*b*) burglary and robbery; (*c*) employee infidelity; (*d*) shoplifting; (*e*) bad-check losses. Can you suggest additional safeguards in each case?

DISCUSSION QUESTIONS

1. Other than insurance, what measures can you suggest for reducing the risk of business losses resulting from the death or disability of the small business owner or of a key employee? Resulting from third-party liability?

2. Should a small retailer carry the same kinds of insurance as a large retailer? Why or why not?

3. What is meant by the "legal principle of indemnity"? If a business firm has two fire insurance policies on a building valued at $90,000 – one for $60,000, the other for $40,000, and neither with a coinsurance clause – what would be the total amount of insurance that the firm would collect on its two policies in the event of a total loss? How much of this total claim would be paid by each insurance company?

4. What are some the noninsurable risks of operating a business enterprise?

SUPPLEMENTARY READINGS

Greene, Mark R. *Insurance and Risk Management for Small Business.* 2nd ed. Small Business Management Series no. 3. Washington, D.C.: Small Business Administration, 1970. Discusses the various kinds of insurance that are the most practical for the small businessman.

Journal of Small Business Management 9 (July 1971). The theme for this issue is "Commercial Crime and the Small-Businessman," containing eight articles covering most aspects of the crime exposure in the operation of a small business.

U.S. Congress, Senate Select Committee on Small Business. *Crime Against Small Business.* Senate Doc. no. 91-14 (1969). A study of the impact of crime on small business concerns and how such concerns may protect themselves.

16

Personnel
and employee relations

The reputation a small business acquires in the community is closely associated with its employee relations. Customers are quick to sense employees' attitudes toward their management. A contented, well-treated staff of workers will reflect loyalty and enthusiasm in their dealings with customers and with the public and can be a major asset to the small business. Thus good employee relations are essential to good public relations.

Every progressive business seeks some point of superiority over its competitors. In the small business the major competitive advantage may well be the closer personal contact, and therefore the more effective communication and teamwork, between the owner-manager and his employees.

Materials, equipment, machines, and other things used by business are available to all competitors at approximately equal prices. It is the firm's personnel that is unique and susceptible to the greatest individual management development. The result of good employee relations — a loyal, efficient group of workers — cannot be copied or purchased by competitors. Furthermore, the increased worker efficiency which usually accompanies good employee relations is of greater importance in the small business than in the large concern. Whereas the larger firm is better equipped, having specialized machinery and mechanical aids, and is able to develop its own specialized staff, the small business must rely more heavily on its personnel alone.

The human element in the small business is complicated by the close personal acquaintance that normally exists between the owner and his employees. It often happens that many of the employees are relatives or lifelong friends of the owner. The result may be an unwillingness to follow approved personnel practices as developed in larger organizations, either because the owner feels that they are too impersonal for his small group of intimately known workers or because he lacks understanding of modern personnel practices and their adaption to the needs of the small firm. Offsetting these obstacles in the small firm is the owner's greater knowledge of each of his employees and the feeling of mutual friendship that so often exists. These are *real advantages*. Actually one of the main reasons for the development of most so-called modern personnel practices has been the need of the larger organizations to make up for this lack of personal contact and understanding between management and employees. Yet the importance of separating business from personal and family relations should be a major incentive for using modern personnel methods in the very small company.

The personnel methods discussed in the remaining pages of this chapter are "standard practice" in large concerns but may appear to some readers as unnecessary in the small firm. But people are human beings, whether employed by large or small firms.

If the small fellow limits his choice of methods to those used by other small operators he will probably repeat their mistakes and make very little progress. If one small shop appears to have good employee relations without using any organized personnel procedures, the reason probably lies in the personality of the owner — something very difficult for other businessmen to duplicate. Another small business may have very little labor turnover because its employees seem to be contented and satisfied with their positions. Closer analysis might disclose that the employer is lax in his supervision and requirements of worker efficiency. Employees realize this and are satisfied to enjoy the easy going. A favorable lease may have made it possible for another firm to show a modest profit in spite of relatively inefficient employees. Similar cases could be given to illustrate various ways in which a small business can exist without actually cultivating worker support, but they would prove only that inefficiency of operation is fairly common among many small concerns that have not as yet felt serious competition, or that many small businessmen are content with mediocre results. Good employee relations in such cases could convert these "average" concerns into more profitable, growing companies — to the mutual benefit of employer and employee alike.

Authorities on business leadership agree that a significant factor in a business owner's success is his ability to accept and use the ideas of his employees. A major obstacle is often that of incorporating them into his operational scheme of things as if they were his own, giving the employee full credit if they succeed and assuming the blame if they fail. Such courage begets contribution and cooperation of a high order, and fosters a true group spirit of aggressiveness that can readily distinguish the small firm.

A logical starting point in any personnel program is job analysis. It is from the factual data secured in job analysis that job descriptions and job specifications are prepared. A *job description* is a list of job duties — a description of what the job incumbent does — and indicates the types of objects handled (such as machines, tools, equipment, materials, or merchandise); working conditions (if these vary widely from job to job); and how the job is related to other jobs in the organization. A *job specification,* on the other hand, indicates the skill, effort, aptitudes, experience, knowledge or education, and other personal requirements needed to perform the job successfully. The selection, placement, training, promotion or transfer, and remuneration of employees should be based largely upon job descriptions and job specifications.

In the company with relatively few employees each "job" will naturally involve more duties than would be expected of one individual in the large concern. In making a job analysis it is well to take all employees into one's confidence and explain the purpose of the study. Each individual is then asked to make a complete list of all his duties or responsibilities; kinds of work performed; machines, equipment, tools, or merchandise handled; relations with other individuals in the organization; and difficulties and problems commonly encountered. Often this listing will be made in cooperation with a supervisor or department head.

At this stage certain lost motion, inconsistencies, overlapping, or unsafe practices may be revealed. Thus it may be advisable to undertake some methods studies for the purpose of job improvement before actually preparing the job descriptions and specifications. Simply stated, methods study involves an earnest, intelligent effort to find the best way of doing the job. Depending upon the nature of the work, it may stress saving time, reducing risk, saving physical effort, or determining the personal factors involved in selling or creative activity. Although large companies, where subdivision of labor is already highly developed, find it necessary to employ methods study "experts," the average small businessman can often make improvements resulting in a 50 percent (or larger) increase in efficiency by simple observation and analysis. Most work can usually be done faster, better, and cheaper. Each time a method of doing a particular job is improved it should be made standard practice, and cooperation in using the new way should be secured from all employees concerned.

RECRUITMENT AND SELECTION

The small business is usually limited geographically in recruiting employees and is sometimes further handicapped by the fact that the best local talent may prefer employment in big business. By paying wages comparable to those offered by large employers and by stressing promotional opportunities or a better chance to learn the business, however, the small employer can largely offset this handicap. Aggressive solicitation and selling of the company by the small businessman can further lessen some of these limitations and help to secure an adequate supply of the right type of job applicants. He should strive to create a public image of his plant or store as a "good place to work."

Another point of special importance to the small business is to seek out and select candidates rather than wait for applications. Perhaps the best source of manpower is the friends and relatives of present (satisfied) employees. Clergymen, teachers, and the company's customers and suppliers can also be solicited for their help in locating prospective employees who possess desirable skills or personality traits. In any case, when applications for employment are received, standard employment procedures should be followed, though perhaps more informally in the small business than in the large one.

Screening Potential Employees

Several procedures may be followed in screening job applicants. The most basic of these is the application-for-employment form. Its first use is in eliminating the obviously unqualified applicants. It also serves as a guide in interviewing other job candidates. In some cases, applicants who "survive" the interviewing process may be given a test or battery of tests.

The application blank. An application blank is a record of statements (presumably of facts) made at the time of seeking employment. It should include

APPLICATION FOR EMPLOYMENT

Date _____

Print
Name _____

Address _____

City-State _____ Phone No. _____

In case of in-   Name _____
jury notify:

Address _____

Marital   No. of Dependent   Other De-
Status _____ Children _____   pendents _____

Physical Defects (explain) _____
_____

Position
Desired _____

Earnings
Expected _____

Date
Available _____

Soc. Sec. No. [___ | ___ | ___ | ___]

Height _____   Weight _____

                        Birth
Sex _____   Date _____

Citizen of U. S.: Yes _____   No _____

Have You Ever Been Dis-
charged from a Position _____

EDUCATION

School	Name and Location	Dates From	To	Years Completed	Dipl./Degree Yes	No	Major Course (Subject/Degree)
Grade							
High School							
College							
Graduate School							
Business or Trade							
Other							

Extracurricular School
Activities _____
_____

Current Hobbies _____

ARMED SERVICES RECORD: Have you served in the U. S. Armed Forces? Yes _____ No _____

                                                                    Final
Dates: From _____ To _____ Branch _____ Rank _____

Type of Discharge _____ Current Draft Status _____

PERSONAL REFERENCES

Name	Address	Occupation

EXPERIENCE (in chronological order)

Present Employer		Address		Kind of Business	
Starting Date	Starting	Salaries Present	Reason for Leaving		
Job Title	Supervisor's Name		May we Contact?		

Description of Work _____
_____
_____

Figure 16-1a. Application for Employment

all information that will aid in deciding whether or not to employ the applicant, as well as certain facts that may later be useful if he is employed.

The application blank should be tailored to fit the needs of the particular company. At a minimum, however, it should contain basic hiring data such as age,

Figure 16-1b.   Application for Employment (cont.)

EXPERIENCE (continued in chronological order)				
Next to last Employer	Address		Kind of Business	
Starting Date	Leaving Date	Salaries Starting | Leaving	Reason for Leaving	
Job Title	Supervisor's Name			May We Contact?
Description of Work _____				

Employer	Address		Kind of Business	
Starting Date	Leaving Date	Salaries Starting | Leaving	Reason for Leaving	
Job Title	Supervisor's Name			May We Contact?
Description of Work _____				

Employer	Address		Kind of Business	
Starting Date	Leaving Date	Salaries Starting | Leaving	Reason for Leaving	
Job Title	Supervisor's Name			May We Contact?
Description of Work _____				

Employer	Address		Kind of Business	
Starting Date	Leaving Date	Salaries Starting | Leaving	Reason for Leaving	
Job Title	Supervisor's Name			May We Contact?
Description of Work _____				

ADDITIONAL EXPERIENCE AND INFORMATION (licenses, special machines, etc.)_____

_____

_____

_____

_____

_____

INTERVIEWER'S COMMENTS _____

_____

Date of Interview_____   Interviewed By _____

Source: Ernest L. Loen, *Personnel Management Guides for Small Business*, Small Business Management Series no. 26 (Washington, D.C.: Small Business Administration, 1961).

sex, marital status, military service status, education, previous employment, and Social Security number. It should *not* contain "discriminatory" information such as race, creed, color, or national origin. (Except for jobs for which this is a requirement, it probably also should not ask for information on union membership.) The only physical data necessary for preliminary selection is the height and weight of the applicant, and his physical defects if any. Character references (including the occupation as well as the name and address of each reference) should also be given, as well as the name and title of the applicant's immediate supervisor on each of his past jobs.

In addition to its uses in employee selection, the application blank provides an initial record of employment if questions of fact later arise, and serves as part of a permanent record in which added experience and training should find a place. Other helpful information may be noted on the typical application blank illustrated in Figure 16-1.

The employment interview.   As a selection procedure the interview is necessary to judge the applicant's appearance, poise, speech, and other characteristics. Also, since the objective is to hire an individual who satisfies the requirements of a particular position, the completed application blank should be studied prior to the interview, and the job descriptions and specifications likely to be needed should be at hand.

The interviewer should make a few reminder notes of important points to look for or ask the applicant about. He should have handy an interviewer's rating scale upon which he will enter evaluations of all the traits listed, which may be a few or many. This device is like a grocery shopping list, useful to insure complete coverage of essential items, to serve as a reminder, to guard against diversions, and to assist in directing and distributing effort.

The interview should be conducted in a suitable place, such as the office or a quiet part of the building. The applicant should first be put at ease. Often asking general questions designed to start the applicant talking and to "break the ice" is sufficient. Informality consistent with the dignity or importance of the interview is the goal usually sought. The trend in larger companies is to use two or three interviewers. Even the smaller employer may well have an applicant interviewed by different members of the organization. In addition to seeking information from him, the interviewer should furnish all important information regarding the company, the job, employment conditions, pay, company policies, and similar data, as well as answer questions the applicant may ask. If employed, the newcomer should be given specific instructions and encouragement. If rejected, he should leave with a feeling of goodwill toward the company.

The use of tests.   Three general types of tests or examinations are often used during the selection process: psychological tests, performance tests, and the physical examination. There are numerous varieties of psychological tests, some designed to measure intelligence or the ability to learn and others to rate aptitudes, interests, attitudes, and particular personality traits. Opinions differ regarding their value to the small firm. Where used, however, they should not be administered or interpreted without expert guidance. Such guidance is available from many educational institutions, personnel institutes, and practicing psychologists.

Performance or achievement tests should be used, even in the small business, if the nature of the work for which an individual is applying permits. These need not be elaborate; often a mere tryout preliminary to actual employment is sufficient. The physical examination should be used much more generally than it is, especially when the job requires strength, good vision, hearing, ability to stand continuously, stamina, or other qualities above the average and wherever the health and safety of the public or fellow workers are involved.

Checking References

The wise employer does not take an application at its face value. References given should be investigated, either in person, by letter, or over the phone. The telephone check has gained in favor. Naturally the applicant will select persons who he thinks will give him the best recommendations. Usually relatives, church officials, and politicians should be eliminated from further consideration, for the very nature of their positions precludes securing useful information from them regarding the applicant.

The logical references for an applicant to give are readily apparent to any employer: his present or former employer, banker, business associates, school officials (in the case of recent graduates), and possibly a few business acquaintances. An applicant who gives references other than these may be attempting to conceal certain "unfortunate" episodes in his past experience or he may have thoroughly justifiable reasons for doing so. In doubtful cases the prospective employer should exercise judgment supported by understanding.

Supervisors and employers are often wrong in their evaluation of an employee, and an unfortunate set of circumstances – personality conflicts, accidents, and so forth – may distort their opinions. In such cases the job applicant may justly prefer to give as references unbiased coworkers or others rather than his present or former ":boss." Organizations of all types and sizes have "internal politics." Often publicity given to this condition in a particular organization or a knowledge of its existence by various individuals will give the clue needed as to which recommendations should be given greatest weight by the prospective employer.

On the other hand, an employer may overlook an ex-employee's weaknesses so as not to jeopardize the latter's chances of finding other employment. Thus the small businessman should be as circumspect in judging the work references as he is in evaluating the personal references of job applicants.

Credit bureau reports.   Rather than rely solely upon the statements of a job applicant and his former employers, some firms adopt the simple expedient of obtaining an "employment character" report on him from the local credit bureau. An example of such a report is given in Figure 16-2. Unlike the ordinary credit report, it provides the educational background and employment history of the prospective employee, and presumptive information concerning his character as obtained from public records.

However, under the terms of the Fair Credit Reporting Act passed in 1971, if an employer orders such a report from his local credit bureau he must notify the job

NAME AND ADDRESS OF CREDIT BUREAU MAKING REPORT

S P E C I M E N

PERSONNEL REPORT

Credit Bureau of Anytown
1234 Main Street
Anytown, Anystate   77036

DATE RECEIVED	DATE MAILED
8/3/72	8/6/72

CONFIDENTIAL *Factbilt* ® **REPORT**   FOR   XYZ Corporation

IN FILE SINCE: 6/65

This information is furnished in response to an inquiry for evaluating credit risks. It has been obtained from reliable sources, the accuracy of which is not guaranteed. The inquirer agrees to indemnify the reporting bureau for any damage arising from misuse of this information, and this report is furnished in reliance upon that indemnity. It must be held in strict confidence, and must not be revealed to the subject reported upon. If adverse action is taken based on this report, the subject reported on must be so advised and the reporting agency identified.

REPORT ON (SURNAME):	MR., MRS., MISS:	GIVEN NAME:	SOCIAL SECURITY NUMBER:	SPOUSE'S NAME:
DOE	Mr	Albert Frank	562-24-2716	Evelyn

ADDRESS:	CITY:	STATE:	ZIP CODE:	FROM:	TO:
8888 Oak Circle	Anytown	Anystate	77000	6/67	8/72

FORMER ADDRESS:	CITY:	STATE:	ZIP CODE:	FROM:	TO:
2036 Irving Drive	Thattown	Anystate	78000	10/65	6/67

DATE OF BIRTH: (IF NEAR 21, CONFIRM)	MARITAL STATUS:	NUMBER OF DEPENDENTS INCLUDING SPOUSE
10/25/32	married	4

☐ OWNS RESIDENCE   ☐ RENTING   ☒ BUYING   ☐ BOARDING   ☐ LIVING WITH PARENTS   ☐ LIVING IN MOBILE HOME

EMPLOYMENT HISTORY

PRESENT EMPLOYER AND KIND OF BUSINESS:	POSITION HELD:	SINCE:	MONTHLY INCOME:
ABC Equipment Sales	Sales Manager	3/70	$ 1000

ESTIMATED INCOME FROM OTHER SOURCES

EXPLAIN: Wife employed part-time as receptionist: average $300 mo.

MOST RECENT FORMER EMPLOYER AND KIND OF BUSINESS:	POSITION HELD:	FROM:	TO:	MONTHLY INCOME:
DEF Corporation	Asst Manager	1/68	3/70	$ 900

ADDRESS OF MOST RECENT FORMER EMPLOYER:	REASON FOR LEAVING:	WOULD THEY RE-HIRE?
6006 Main Drive Thattown	Opportunity with ABC Co.	☒ YES ☐ NO

PREVIOUS FORMER EMPLOYER AND KIND OF BUSINESS:	POSITION HELD:	FROM:	TO:	MONTHLY INCOME:
GHI Sales & Service	Route Salesman	1965	1/68	$ 800

ADDRESS OF PREVIOUS FORMER EMPLOYER:	REASON FOR LEAVING:	WOULD THEY RE-HIRE?
2 Interstate Street	moved to Anytown from Thattown	☒ YES ☐ NO

EDUCATION:

		NO. OF YEARS COMPLETED	WHEN GRADUATED	GRADE AVERAGE	COLLEGE MAJORS AND DEGREES EARNED
HIGH SCHOOL	Washington High, Thattown, Anystate	12	1950		
COLLEGE	State University at East Bend	4	1954	3.2	BS in Business Admin.

PUBLIC RECORD:

RELATING TO ANNULMENT OR DIVORCE. SHOW DISPOSITION OF CASE.	none
RELATING TO CRIMINAL CONVICTION. SHOW DISPOSITION OF ANY CASE.	none
RELATING TO CIVIL SUITS, JUDGMENTS OR BANKRUPTCY. SHOW DISPOSITION	none
RELATING TO PROPERTY OWNERSHIP.	Property Deed filed Apr. 1967 Recorder Office for purchase of lot at 8888 Oak Circle

CREDIT HISTORY AND REMARKS WHERE SPACE IS INSUFFICIENT ABOVE:

KIND OF BUSINESS	DATE ACCOUNT OPENED	DATE OF LAST SALE	HIGHEST CREDIT	AMOUNT OWING	AMOUNT PAST DUE	TERMS OF SALE AND USUAL MANNER OF PAYMENT
B 601	1965	1967	$20,000	$16,500	00	I-1
B 500	1970	12/70	3,500	1,500	00	I-$79-1
D 608	8/65	9/69	342	00	00	0-1
H 302	4/68	1/72	1,342	450	00	I-$45-1

FORM 17   Member Associated Credit Bureaus, Inc.   PRINTED IN U.S.A. 6/70

Figure 16-2.   Personnel Employment, Credit, and Character Form

applicant in writing within three days after ordering the report (1) that the report was requested, (2) that it might contain information about his character, personal characteristics, and mode of living, and (3) that he has a right to request additional information concerning the nature and scope of the investigation; the employer is then obligated to comply with this request, in writing, within a period of five days. These notifications are required whether the person is employed or not. However, they are not required if the person has not specifically applied for the job and the employer is simply screening an individual to whom he might offer the job.

Where a person has applied for a job and is turned down, the employer must notify him in the same way he would notify a rejected credit applicant.[1]

PLACEMENT

Many small employers could use their wage dollar more efficiently than at present by capitalizing fully on the special abilities of each employee when assigning duties. The man who would never wear an expensive pair of dress shoes when doing his gardening is often the same man who would use a $180-a-week pharmacist or mechanical specialist to sell chewing gum or shoestrings. Since the time of either is worth $4.50 per hour, or $7\frac{1}{2}$ cents per minute, and selling costs are at least 5 percent of sales, an employee would have to sell 15 ten-cent packages of gum each minute for the store to get full value from his wages.

This example indicates that low-priced items should be sold by inexpensive help or by self-service and that the higher-paid salesmen should devote their time to "big-ticket" items exclusively. A store can carry both high- and low-priced items and have low-salaried people to sell one class of merchandise and qualified specialists to sell the other. Employee differentiation may be studied in the modern chain drugstore, although not all small retailers can carry the application of this principle to the same degree.

The production shop's problems along similar lines are obvious. A competent mechanic's time should not be misspent with menial tasks, nor should the apprentice or handyman be entrusted with exacting technical work. Misspent payroll funds come directly out of profits. Profit is jeopardized whenever the wrong employee is assigned to the wrong task at the wrong wage rate. Furthermore, the job may not be properly performed, and the employee is likely to become discontented as well.

The one- or two-man business may not find this plan of labor specialization advisable. It may be that it must sell all price lines and that contacts in selling small items serve as "leads" for the sales of large ones.

The first few days in a new position are usually the hardest. A newcomer should be introduced to his fellow workers, shown the location of employee facilities, informed of any regulations, and encouraged to ask for additional information as it may be needed. A good plan is to assign an older, more experienced worker to act as sponsor until the introductory period is over. The "boss" himself should follow up on the new employee by occasional visits with him until he feels at home in the organization. Consideration and reasonable attention at this time are a good investment in employee relations.

TRAINING

Some preliminary training in standardized work methods is an important part of the new employee's introduction to the job. This may require a few hours, a few

[1] Obligations of the small businessman toward rejected job and credit applicants are discussed in detail in Chapter 20.

days or even a few weeks or months, varying with the nature of the work and the previous training or experience of the worker. The need for *improvement training,* which should be offered as required, is fairly continuous in most cases. Improvement training may be *remedial* or *developmental* in nature.

Remedial training seeks to correct errors or mistakes made by individual workers regardless of how long they may have been employed. It is usually based on error reports of individuals, on reports by the immediate supervisor, or on periodic reports of the operations of each department, on the amount of spoiled work, lost sales, breakdowns, schedule delays, accidents, and similar indicators of a department's inefficiency or ineffectiveness. Either group or individual training methods may be used in remedial training.

Developmental training assumes that every job can be done better, that there is always something more an employee can learn about his job, and in many cases that certain workers wish to prepare for advancement to better positions. Continuous on-the-job training is recognized as an integral part of the responsibility of every supervisor and executive. Unfortunately it is a responsibility often neglected.

Regardless of the type of on-the-job training program — or whether the trainee is a new employee, or an old employee assigned to a new job — the following basic steps in the teaching process should be followed by those who have been charged with instructional responsibilities:

First Step:	*Preparing the Learner*
	Put him at ease.
	Gain his interest and confidence.
	Find out what he already knows.
	Show task's importance, appeal to pride.
	Show task's relationship to entire job.
Second Step:	*Presenting the Task, by Steps*
	Tell, show, and explain patiently.
	Be sure each step is understood.
	Stress key points, one at a time.
	Mention "tricks of the trade," knacks.
	Welcome the learner's questions.
Third Step:	*The Learner's Tryout*
	Have him perform the job himself.
	Be ready to help avoid mistakes.
	Keep him at ease, criticize diplomatically.
	Have him explain steps as he goes.
Fourth Step:	*Test and Follow-up*
	Put him on his own, doing the job.
	Check his performance after some practice.
	Have him reexplain key points, knacks, and so forth.
	Cause him to feel free to ask for further help.
	Taper attention to him down to normal supervision.

Many direct benefits result from a good remedial or developmental training program. It reduces labor turnover, improves the quality of work performed, reduces accidents, facilitates the discovery of promotion-worthy employees, and tends to lower the unit costs of labor.

There is no longer any need for the small business to neglect employee training because executives lack time or lack experience as teachers. Federal- and state-sponsored vocational training of various types, and covering a wide range of jobs, is available at little or no cost in nearly every community.

Adult training is available under the Manpower Development and Training Act which is administered by the U.S. Department of Labor and the U.S. Office of Education. Much on-the-job training is done in this program. In addition, nearly every state has a vocational division associated with the state department of public instruction. The divisions have specialists in the following areas: trade and industrial education, distributive education, office education, home economics, and agriculture. In most states, local school systems employ coordinators who represent the various state services previously mentioned. The coordinators are expert teachers. In addition, most are required to have at least two years of occupational experience in addition to college training.

There are two types of programs conducted by the coordinators which can be of direct, immediate benefit to small businessmen. One of the programs is a cooperative program for high school seniors in which the students spend part of the school day working in a business. The students are also enrolled in regular classroom work that is directly related to the business in which they are working. The work experience phase includes a cooperative effort on the part of the businessmen and coordinator to organize the experiences of the student so that real training occurs on the job as well as in the classroom.

In addition to the cooperative programs for high school students, most coordinators are willing to organize adult courses on request from local business people. Generally, one-half of the cost of instruction will be paid by the state and federal government for such classes. The subject areas are unlimited as long as the course is valid preparation for an occupation requiring less than a college degree. In addition, many state universities and colleges employ specialists in their extension divisions to supply instructors for adult training organized by local coordinators.

Training may be given to either adults who are currently employed in the occupational area or to those who wish to enter a field and whose aptitudes and abilities indicate that they can profit from this training.

These programs are a unique example of government agencies at all levels — local, state, and federal — cooperating with private businesses to strengthen the businesses participating and in addition, helping people advance themselves. Besides vocational education and Manpower Development and Training, there are training programs available under the Economic Opportunity Act and the National Defense Education Act.

In addition to government-sponsored vocational training and the on-the-job training of individual employees, weekly or monthly group meetings of the employees are often desirable. Such meetings provide a sounding board for employees' opinions on the firm's problems and practices, and provide the owner-manager with an excellent means of conveying information to his employees. Each meeting should have a definite purpose, one major objective. It might be to acquaint employees with trends and current developments in the industry or the company, or with a new product or the price of equipment. A contest or event planned by the firm might be the theme of another meeting. It is far better to make each meeting interesting and reasonably brief and to accomplish one single objective — something worthwhile for workers and management alike — than to have more ambitious objectives and risk a flop.

Group meetings may be for the purpose of providing instruction as well as information. Group instruction is particularly useful for special types of training — such as sales promotion and methods improvement. The owner-manager, or a qualified foreman or key employee, may lead a group training session. However, experts from outside the company — professors from the local university, representatives from the trade association or from the company's suppliers and distributors, and others — should also be invited to speak on certain subjects in which the workers need instruction.

In many cases motion pictures and film strips can be used to advantage in group training. They may be obtained from many suppliers, government agencies, educational institutions, and film-renting agencies. Many trade associations compile lists of available training films for use by their members.

Other training aids are also available, such as the various technical aids published by manufacturers and governmental agencies such as the Small Business Administration, training articles on specific topics published frequently in trade journals, and "courses" sold by commercial training organizations. Whenever visual aids — films, charts, and so forth — or any of the prepared courses or aids are used, it is of the utmost importance that the person who is to conduct the meeting become thoroughly familiar with them in advance. Every film should be previewed. Even complete courses prepared in lecture form should be mastered by the leader before each meeting.

TRANSFERS AND PROMOTIONS

Neither employees nor jobs are static. Jobs are continually changing, both in content and in the company's need to fill them. Employees also change, many becoming qualified for better jobs, while others become discontented or disillusioned on their present jobs. Adjustments to these changes are made principally by transferring or promoting workers to different jobs.

Transfers are changes in the occupation of workers not properly considered as promotions. The need for transfers arises from one of four conditions: (1) elimination of a job; (2) request for change by an employee; (3) belief by management that a worker has been misplaced; and (4) fluctuations in the need for certain kinds of jobs.

When a job is eliminated through no fault of the worker, every reasonable effort should be made to place him elsewhere in the organization. If this is impossible, the employer should help him secure a satisfactory position with some other company.

For various reasons employees sometimes ask to be shifted to another job. If the reasons given for the request are plausible, it should be granted if possible. In other cases management may take the initiative when it appears that a particular worker would be better suited to a different job. Usually a satisfactory transfer can be made in such cases if the reasons are discussed with the employee, but sometimes this is not possible. A surprisingly large number of workers resent any change in their job or duties, even when it involves a promotion, increases their income, or is otherwise to their own benefit. In some cases certain locations for a desk or even a work place in the shop acquire "prestige" for employees, and those favored by such locations show resentment when moved.

A promotion involves assignment to a job of greater difficulty, requiring greater skill or a larger measure of responsibility, and consequently is a better-paying job. In making promotions, merit and seniority are important factors. Only in cases where employees are approximately equal, however, should seniority be controlling. Since merit is of primary importance, there should be some provision for the systematic evaluation of employee performance on their present jobs. Operating reports should be supplemented by periodic ratings by supervisors and others in a position to make impartial evaluations of qualities like attitude, initiative, personality, self-development, and preparation for promotion. Often promotions may be preceded by one or more trial periods in the new position.

REMUNERATION

As job analysis provides the factual data needed for the intelligent selection, placement, training, transfer, and promotion of employees, so it also forms the basis for determining the relative worth or value of each job in the enterprise. The process of determining relative job worth is called "job evaluation." The most basic determinants of what the hourly wage rate of a job should be, relative to other jobs, are the duties that must be performed, the conditions under which they are performed, and the qualifications required to perform them. Jobs are evaluated with reference to one another and to their importance to the company in terms of skill, effort, responsibility, and similar factors. To the extent that equitable wage rates are established by this procedure, job evaluation minimizes a common source of employee grievance — namely, the belief of a worker that he is underpaid relative to other workers.

The wage that an individual worker receives, however, is dependent only in part upon the requirements of the job. It is also a function of his performance on the job. Thus it is common practice in wage administration to establish a *rate range* for each job by means of job evaluation, and to determine an individual employee's wage rate *within* that range on the basis of his seniority and/or merit. Merit rating (or the rating of the man on the job rather than the job itself), as noted in the preceding section, is also used in deciding whether or not to promote an employee to a higher-paying job when he has reached the top of the wage scale on his present job.

Wages also vary with the method of wage payment. The small firm is likely to find the simpler systems of payment better suited to its needs. These are straight salary or time payment, straight commission or piece rates, and simple bonus plans, such as regular salary plus a definite reward or bonus for achievement beyond a standard or quota agreed upon in advance.

Incentive systems based on time studies or other measured output may be used effectively in the small business if restricted to jobs where such plans are appropriate and if kept simple. Benefits to be derived from such systems must be compared with the added expense entailed and with employee attitude toward the method. An incentive wage plan should give the worker more pay for the same amount of time worked, give management a lower labor cost (or a predetermined unit cost for purposes of pricing and budgeting), be understandable and acceptable to the worker, and be economical for management to administer.

The negative attitude of some workers toward incentive plans is sometimes difficult for the inexperienced manager to understand. Not all employees are ambitious. Many prefer their present income to prospects for a higher income if this involves changing established habits. The majority of workers are suspicious and fearful of new plans to increase output even though they will share in the larger returns.

Probably more employees in small firms are interested in the stability and regularity of their incomes than in opportunities to enter higher income brackets. The following cases — one in the soft-drink industry, and the other in the rug-cleaning business — illustrate two different ways in which employment income can be stabilized in seasonal industries by good management.

Bottling soft drinks is a business affected by pronounced seasonal fluctuations. During the spring and summer the demand for soft-drink salesmen is strong and remuneration high. When business declines and earnings are low in the fall, many salesmen in this industry seek positions with other companies, expecting their old jobs to be available again the following spring. One company developed a plan that has enabled it to retain its salesmen throughout the year.

Analysis of the problem convinced management that salesmen became accustomed to the high standard of living made possible by the seasonally high incomes received during the warm months. When their incomes declined under the former method of paying salary plus commission based on current sales, many men became dissatisfied and quit. A new plan provides for a stabilized drawing account that is paid weekly and is the same throughout the year regardless of seasonal fluctuations in sales. Under this plan each of the company's salesmen draws a fixed sum of $125 per week throughout the year. This actually serves as a "salary," although it is charged against the salesmen's accumulated earnings account, and does not vary even if the salesman's actual earnings average less than $125 per week over a yearly period. If his earnings total more than the amount of his drawing account, he is paid a year-end bonus.

During the boom season for bottled soft drinks, some of the men earned more than $200 per week under the old plan; but during three or four of the cold months sales went down considerably and the men's earnings fell as low as $60 per week. The company's salesmen, who now draw $125 a week right through the slow winter months, feel no particular inclination to seek other jobs, since their salaries do not slump with the season. The plan adopted by this company might solve similar wage problems for other small firms.

In a different field of small business, rug cleaning, a problem of coping with seasonal fluctuations was solved by diversifying services offered and adding the selling of merchandise. During the seven dull months of the year one company promoted personalized cleaning and renovating services in private homes and institutions. The fact that such services brought company representatives inside these homes and institutions provided an opportunity for them to suggest the sale of remnants or other materials observation showed to be needed. Results were gratifying. After the adoption of the new plan, sales of merchandise represented 30 percent of total receipts and the combined sales of merchandise and service have permitted retaining key personnel throughout the year.

Profit sharing.   In recent years various types of wage *supplements* have come into vogue. The most common type of wage supplement is profit sharing. Profit sharing, which has been gaining ground among small businesses, has many advantages, in theory at least. In many respects it is better suited to the small than to the large enterprise. For it to be successful, there must be a feeling of mutual trust and confidence between management and employees. The company's books must be open to inspection by those included in the profit sharing, although not indiscriminately. A basis previously agreed upon for sharing the profits must be established and followed, and a satisfactory wage and salary scale must be maintained. Under no circumstances should profit sharing be used as a deferred wage-payment plan.

There are certain basic questions regarding profit sharing, especially for employees, that should be considered before adopting such a plan. Profit, which is a residual after all costs and expenses of the business have been paid, fluctuates widely, often as a result of causes external to the business, such as competition and general economic conditions. Even under favorable conditions only a few employees are likely to be in a position actually to increase or decrease the company's profits. For these reasons, profit sharing is not a form of incentive wage, except in a limited sense for the few persons in a position to affect profits materially. Profit is the reward to owner-managers for both risking their own capital and exercising good managerial ability. The owners bear losses when they occur; profit sharing does not contemplate loss sharing by those who participate in the profits when there are any. And finally, it is discouraging to employees who anticipate sharing in the profits and who may even have done extra work to help the company make a profit to discover at the end of the year that there are no profits to share.

MORALE BUILDING

Nonfinancial incentives have a place along with incentive payment plans in stimulating and rewarding employees. Recognition by management of good work or of valuable suggestions by employees is an important example. Soliciting worker participation in management is another that has been receiving increasing consideration.

An axiom in all human relations is that most major troubles result from neglected minor grievances. In the small business this is more serious than it appears. Employee grievances have serious effects on the community's attitude toward the employer concerned. Because of the very personal nature of most employer-employee contacts, many workers will be reluctant to talk about their "gripes."

Big business has organized systems to secure and use employee complaints for better employee relations. The small businessman who relies solely upon his "close personal contacts" in this area is courting unnecessary risks. He has three main avenues to use in arriving at the best solution to this problem. First, he can make an objective study of all conditions in his business likely to be irritating to employees. Second, he can use the exit-interview technique – that is, find out from each employee who quits just what his complaints about the company were. And third, he can institute a continuous plan of employee suggestions with frequent conferences and requests for ways in which the firm can improve employee relations. The small businessman has the big advantage of being able to establish a close bond of confidence and trust with his employees if he will take the initiative in doing so.

The attitudes of employees are particularly important in the small organization, whether the business be a retail or wholesale establishment, a manufacturing firm, or a service business. Employees who must be relied upon to produce a given amount in a given period, or to face customers and thus to represent the firm in human relations situations, must not only be thoroughly familiar with the firm's policies, philosophies, goals, and methods of operation, but must share the opinion of the owner-manager as to their desirability and justification. The fact that in the small concern each individual carries a larger share of responsibility makes these attitudes all the more important. In all phases of personnel administration, from selection through training and into normal supervision, the attitudes of the individual must be noted, evaluated, and cultivated constantly. Because of his importance to the organization, the dedicated nonconformist and the consistent malcontent — persons who may lower the quantity or quality of output, or damage relationships with clients or customers — cannot be tolerated and must be discharged from his responsibilities if his attitudes cannot be changed. Most modern personnel administration experts agree that the way an employee thinks about his job makes or breaks him as a contributor to the company's welfare.

Many things have been written concerning the need for employee loyalty to his employer. Perhaps the best known statement in this connection is by Elbert Hubbard, which reads as follows:

> If you work for a man, in heaven's name work for him. If he pays wages that supply your bread and butter, work for him, speak well of him, think well of him, stand by him, and stand by the institution he represents. . . . If I worked for a man I would work for him; I would not work for him a part of his time, but all of his time; I would give undivided service or none. . . . An ounce of loyalty is worth a pound of cleverness. If you must vilify, condemn and eternally disparage your employer, then resign your position; and when you are outside, damn him to your heart's content. But . . . so long as you are part of an institution, do not condemn it. Not that you will injure the institution, . . . but when you disparage the concern of which you are a part, you disparage yourself.[2]

One personnel consultant has these comments and suggestions:

> No simple ground rules for improving employee morale can be offered. Every situation is unique. No two individuals are exactly alike, nor are two companies identical. Nevertheless, from psychological research on morale and attitudes in business, certain practical suggestions may be made:
>
> 1. Tell and show your employees that you are interested in them and would be glad to have their ideas on how conditions might be improved.
>
> 2. Treat your employees as individuals; never deal with them as impersonal variables in a working unit.

[2] Elbert Hubbard, *Loyalty in Business* (East Aurora, N.Y.: The Roycrofters, 1921), pp. 79–80.

3. Improve your general understanding of human behavior.

4. Accept the fact that others may not see things as you do.

5. Respect differences of opinion.

6. Insofar as possible, give explanations for management actions.

7. Provide information and guidance on matters affecting employees' security.

8. Make reasonable efforts to keep jobs interesting.

9. Encourage promotion from within.

10. Express appreciation publicly for jobs well done.

11. Offer criticism privately in the form of constructive suggestions for improvement.

12. Train supervisors to think about the people involved insofar as practicable, rather than just the work.

13. Keep your people up-to-date on all business matters affecting them, and quell rumors with correct information.

14. Be fair.[3]

EMPLOYMENT RECORDS

Employment records are an important tool. An efficient but easy-to-manage record system makes use of an individual employee envelope measuring $9'' \times 11\frac{1}{2}''$ with the name of the employee on the tab and his employment application and birth and citizenship certificates inside. Personnel report forms are used by supervisors in reporting such things as outstanding work performance, breach of discipline, progress of employee on the job, tardiness, absence, change in work attitude, or any other important phase of the employee's work activity. This information is written on the personnel report form, dated, signed by the supervisor, and given to the individual in charge of personnel, who files it in the employee's envelope. This procedure accomplishes two objectives: it keeps the personnel authority informed about the employee, and with a minimum of record keeping and red tape forms a permanent file of the employee for use in promotions, counseling, and discipline, and in union negotiations of grievances.

PERSONNEL IN MERCHANDISING

Few lines of business compare with retailing in the wide fluctuations of need for personnel on an annual, monthly, daily, and hourly basis. The "standby" capacity demanded of retail personnel is enormous. This is both a challenge and an opportunity. Because customers want prompt service when they appear in the store, the merchant must always be prepared to handle unexpected busy periods. Fortunately, most fluctuations are regular and can be anticipated. On a daily and hourly basis, part-time employees can often be used to meet peak demands at certain hours of the day and on Saturday, usually the busiest day of the week. This arrangement gives the merchant an opportunity to try out or develop prospective

[3] Martin M. Bruce, "Managing for Better Morale," Small Marketers Aids Annual no. 4 (Washington, D.C.: Small Business Administration, 1962), pp. 59–60.

full-time employees, but it also increases the need for training. An excellent source of afternoon and Saturday workers is the local distributive-education program operated in connection with the high school. The local superintendent of schools can furnish information on this program.

In addition to general sources of training material, the retailer in most lines will find excellent help in publications by the School of Retailing of the University of Pittsburgh and the School of Retailing, New York University. *Controlling Merchandise,* published by the National Cash Register Company, Dayton, Ohio, is valuable for employee and management alike. Many trade associations also provide training for retail employees.

Many retailers pay a commission on sales in addition to a base salary. Some stores pay bonuses or "P.M.'s" (premium money) to encourage the sale of certain items such as slow-moving goods or higher-priced merchandise. Retail employees often receive, as a substantial fringe benefit, discounts ranging from 10 to 30 percent on merchandise purchased in the store in which they work.

PERSONNEL IN THE SMALL FACTORY

Large manufacturers have long recognized the importance of good personnel practices. At one time personnel management was widely considered as a preventive of unionization. More and more unions have taken part in working for better personnel management. Unions have been spreading their influence increasingly and have already entered many small factories. Some small manufacturers see in the introduction of a personnel program a means of forestalling the unionization of their plants. In the authors' opinion, this is the wrong approach; unions can be worked *with* to advantage.

Management has developed methods, tools, machinery, and skills to process and utilize materials efficiently. Little, and often nothing, is done to secure the maximum productive efficiency from the plant's manpower. This should be the aim of a personnel program. Excessive labor turnover makes it difficult to achieve.

Labor turnover costs are not as intangible as many suppose. First, there is the direct cost involved in training new employees. Also to be considered are the costs in the period during which a new employee is on the payroll but not producing at full capacity. This cost varies with the length of the training period. There are also costs from an increase in spoiled or wasted material, lowering of employee morale, and increased overhead. From this standpoint alone it is well to develop a personnel policy and program designed to attract the most desirable employees and to keep them with the company.

In a small shop there is a limit to specialization. It may be impossible to have even one man whose sole responsibility pertains to personnel management. Hiring and training may be the responsibility of one member of the organization, whereas sickness benefits, employment records, and savings associations may be handled by the auditor or an accountant; or, as is frequently the case, each department foreman may do his own hiring and personnel record keeping. Yet it is important for employees to know who heads the personnel function. They must know who is responsible for their job relations and to whom they can take their problems.

Supervisors in the small shop must be called upon to give much of the preliminary on-the-job training. Training the new employee should begin with an explanation by the supervisor of company products, policies, regulations and an explanation of the importance, in their manufacturing setup, of the first job the employee is to learn. Key workers in each department should then take over the actual job instruction of the employee. Worker-instructors should be carefully selected, not only for craftsmanship, but also for their loyalty and ability to explain and show how the job is done.

A safe shop is good business. Accidents are costly to management in lost time, in the weakening of employee morale, and in direct cash outlay. There are in general two causes of accidents — personal and impersonal. Personal causes account for accidents due to improper attitude, lack of knowledge or skill, physical handicaps, and poor health. Impersonal causes include hazardous work-handling arrangements or procedures, defective mechanical equipment, unsafe clothing, crowded aisles, improper lighting and ventilation, and inadequate guarding. It is good practice for the owner-manager of a small plant to delegate responsibility for safety education to one person in the organization who would also report both unsafe working conditions and careless workers.

Small manufacturers who have their own sales organization often slight the sales function because of their greater interest in production. The selection and training of salesmen is, therefore, of special importance. Since a high volume of sales and production is of industrywide concern, industrial groups and trade associations often cooperate in collective sales-training programs.

PERSONNEL IN THE SERVICE BUSINESS

Good personnel is important in all service fields, but the special needs and problems vary for each of three main groups. In one group the service rendered is highly personal and the caliber of employees may be the deciding factor between success and failure. Most professional services, such as medical and dental care, and many semiprofessional services are in this group.

The beauty shop affords an excellent illustration of the type of personnel problems faced by establishments in this group. Most states and communities have legal requirements governing employee's qualifications and sanitary working conditions for beauty shops and similar personal service establishments. These are minimum standards, and the shop owner endeavors to exceed them whenever possible. Usually operators must be licensed. Equipment and physical facilities must pass inspections. The owner, however, is more concerned with maintaining both personnel and plant standards well above legal requirements than with merely satisfying them.

Although *skill* is the greatest single ability required of a beauty shop operator, personality, voice, manners, and appearance are also very important. The ability to sell both the services and merchandise offered by the shop is a valuable asset for most employees.

Personal service establishments vary both in the degree of specialized service offered and in the extent to which individualized handling of each patron is encouraged. Beauty shop employees must be selected according to the shop policy of general or specialist service. Work should be assigned to each operator to take full advantage of special skills possessed. Most owners find it good practice to strive throughout the shop for standard procedures and methods, in which new employees should be instructed.

A second group of service businesses, considered from a personnel viewpoint, is composed of gasoline service stations, many repair shops, restaurants, and similar enterprises. This group shares to some extent the customer concern with the type of employees already noted for personal service establishments like beauty shops, but not to quite the same degree.

In general, service stations, repair shops, and restaurants – unlike beauty shops – have not played up the superior skill of particular employees. Rather, they tend to strive for reputations based on the quality of product or service rendered by the business. Surveys have shown frequently that factors relating to employees have been among the chief reasons why service stations have lost customers. Important reasons given include indifference, haughtiness, ignorance of products, overinsistence in sales efforts, and attempted substitution. Likewise, unless a restaurant has an outstanding reputation for superior-quality food, customers tend to be very sensitive to the appearance, personality, and general attitude of the hostess and food service employees. Establishments in this group would well put more emphasis on training employees in good customer relations than they sometimes do.

As a class both service station and restaurant employees are likely to have frequent contacts with tourists and other strangers to the community. Employees usually need special training to be able to answer questions asked by tourists even though many of these inquiries relate to the employee's home community. In addition to receiving special training, employees in such positions may need simple aids like local maps, mileage charts, and folders describing and illustrating nearby places of interest.

In the restaurant business it is sometimes required that all applicants for employment pass a physical examination that gives special attention to the possibility that the applicant may be a carrier of tuberculosis, typhoid fever, or other contagious diseases. Local regulations, such as the requirement that each food handler possess a health certificate, should be complied with.

Establishments such as commercial laundries and dry cleaning plants have personnel problems of a quite different nature than those described above, and these make up our third classification. Frequently the plant is located in a congested industrial district, which makes it difficult to attract and retain desirable employees. Working conditions are not likely to be pleasant, and wages are relatively low. There are fewer opportunities than in manufacturing to learn important industrial skills. Because of the greater difficulty of building and maintaining employee morale, personnel management is especially challenging. Particular concern should be paid to fair dealing, recognition of good work, friendly relations with employees, suggestions systems, and employee facilities.

SUMMARY AND CONCLUSIONS

Although every business operates through its personnel, probably less has been done to utilize this valuable resource effectively than has been done for the other factors of production. Since payroll is usually a major and often the largest item of expense in any business, the opportunities for financial improvement through better personnel relations are great. In addition, a firm's personnel is one thing competitors cannot copy or duplicate. Materials, merchandise, advertising and display ideas, and even product designs are generally available to all businessmen on approximately equal terms, but this is not true of a good group of employees. Only the workers' time can be purchased or hired; their attitudes, loyalty, cooperation, and productivity must be earned. This is the aim of good personnel work. *The many advantages small business has over big business in handling employee relations should be developed to their fullest extent.*

Small business also has some special problems in securing and maintaining competent personnel. Fortunately the more important ones can be solved if they are recognized and given proper attention. Often apparent handicaps, like limited opportunities for promotion, can be turned into advantages by stressing the greater range of training and experience to be secured by employment in the small company. This has a strong appeal to men who later hope to enter business for themselves.

Many techniques of personnel management common in larger concerns can be used to advantage in the small business. A worker is a human being whether employed by a large or small concern. Carefully selected and well trained, he becomes an investment of value. Methods for training workers or supervisors, or for enlisting employee cooperation are available for use by the small businessman. In addition, material on personnel in both book and periodical (trade journal) form is extensive. Finally, the public vocational education programs in operation throughout the country can furnish practical and related training even to the smallest concern without cost to the owner-manager.

REVIEW QUESTIONS

1. Compare the opportunities for management in large and small companies to maintain good employee relations.

2. What is meant by "job analysis"? In what ways is it useful in small business operation?

3. How can a small businessman obtain well-trained employees who might otherwise seek employment in a large concern?

4. What procedures may be followed in screening job applicants? Describe each briefly.

5. How can a businessman evaluate the responses on an employment application blank?

6. Differentiate between remedial and developmental training.

7. What are the essential steps in an on-the-job training program?

8. Discuss the federal- and state-sponsored vocational training programs most helpful to small businessmen.

9. Differentiate between promotions and job transfers. Why are job transfers often necessary?

10. Define "job evaluation." What determines the relative worth of jobs?

11. On what does an individual worker's wage depend? What is the purpose of a *rate range* for each job?

12.   What are "wage incentives"? Under what conditions might they be used in a small company? What benefits are to be derived from them?

13.   How can wages be stabilized or regularized in seasonal industries? Discuss the relative merits of each method suggested.

14.   Is profit sharing better suited to the large company or the small company? Why? What are the pros and cons of profit sharing?

15.   Are nonfinancial incentives relatively more important in the large company or in the small company? Explain.

16.   What are some of the ways in which the small businessman can build and maintain morale among his employees?

17.   What can a small businessman do to develop and keep employee loyalty?

18.   What information should be kept as a permanent part of each employee's record?

19.   Compare personnel requirements and the problems associated with the maintenance of good employee relations in the main types of business enterprise – merchandising, manufacturing, and the service trades.

DISCUSSION QUESTIONS

1.   Do you think employment tests or examinations are worthwhile to the small concern? Why or why not?

2.   What kinds of controls result from job evaluation, formal wage structures, time or production standards, and incentive-wage systems?

SUPPLEMENTARY READINGS

Loen, Ernest L. *Personnel Management Guides for Small Business.* Small Business Management Series no. 26. Washington, D.C.: Small Business Administration, 1961. Discusses hiring practices in the small company, employee training, wage and salary systems, and management-union relations.

Ufford, D. W. *An Employee Suggestion System for the Small Plant.* 3rd ed. Small Business Management Series no. 1. Washington, D.C.: Small Business Administration, 1964. Provides basic principles for the establishment of a suggestion system which benefits both the employees and the owner-manager of a small business.

17

Procurement
and supplier relations

Goods or supplies are necessary to the conduct of any business. The retailer and the wholesaler must have merchandise to sell, the manufacturer requires materials to fashion into finished products, and the service establishment needs supplies to function. The source from which a business secures merchandise, materials, or supplies may be called a "resource," "supplier," or "vendor."

The aim of successful buying is to obtain the best goods for the intended use. Favorable relationships with suppliers helps in achieving this goal. It also facilitates other aspects of buying. Although buying is a function that must be performed in all businesses, maintaining favorable relationships with sources of supply is one characteristic of successful buying that is particularly important in the small enterprise.

SOURCES OF SUPPLY FOR THE SMALL BUSINESS

Before the small businessman can effectively formulate his buying policies or undertake the actual purchase of goods needed to operate his business he must be familiar with the different types of suppliers available to him, the advantages and limitations associated with each type, and the conditions under which it is better to concentrate most of his buying with one or a few suppliers as compared to making purchases from many sources.

Types of Suppliers

Three groups of suppliers are usually recognized, and most small businesses will find that they must make some of their purchases with representatives of each group: producers, merchant middlemen, and functional middlemen.

Producers.   Manufacturers, miners, farmers, or processors of natural products all may be classed as producers. These business units may be of any size, ranging from very small to very large. Naturally, advantages claimed for concentrated purchasing

312

would not apply with respect to purchasing from many of the smaller producers. Another consideration is that many businesses, especially the larger manufacturers, have their own methods of distribution and may not be available for direct dealings with the small enterprise. Their products may be purchased, but only through middlemen or representatives used by the particular manufacturer.

Merchant middlemen.   Merchant middlemen constitute the chief source of supply for most small firms. These are marketing institutions that buy and take title to goods, for resale. Familiar examples are wholesalers or jobbers, supply houses, and merchant truckers. In many "hard lines," especially where the goods carried are used both by industry and retail-service businesses, "supply houses" are comparable to wholesalers. In the laundry and dry cleaning fields, suppliers are regarded as being in the "allied trades."

Wholesalers, especially in the general merchandise area, are classified as service or limited function wholesalers. A cash-and-carry wholesaler is one example of a limited function middleman.

Some service wholesalers also operate cash-and-carry departments. Since small businessmen often patronize local wholesalers, the possible savings through purchasing by the cash-and-carry method can be significant. The reason for the cash-and-carry policy is to reduce prices to retailers by lowering some of the wholesaler's operating expenses. It also enables the buyer to inspect his purchases, keep his payments up to date, and eliminates the clerical work necessary for buying on a charge basis. However, cash-and-carry takes the buyer away from his business where he may be needed, requires more working capital than many small businessmen have, and usually provides a more limited assortment of merchandise than that carried by the service wholesaler.

The service wholesaler, who is more likely to carry a broad line of goods, provides the opportunity to purchase from a single source products made by hundreds of producers; assurance at all times of a supply of new items made available locally through the wholesaler's constant scouting of all markets; quick delivery of goods as needed; opportunity to buy on credit; service and advice rendered through salesmen who visit the store; and assurance of the wholesaler's interest in the retailer's success because this is the only basis upon which the wholesaler can continue in business.

In merchandising, the small independent retailer has learned from experience that a reliable wholesaler is one of his best assets. The amount of confidence most retailers have in their wholesalers would surprise anyone not familiar with the field. This trust and confidence has been earned by the ever-increasing interest wholesalers have exhibited in the welfare and success of their retail customers.

Merchant middlemen differ in their degree of product specialization, such as general wholesalers versus drug houses, as well as in the range of services offered. The majority of merchant middlemen do not have any well-organized plan of voluntary cooperation for buyers, although many will work more closely with customers who concentrate their purchases than with those who do not.

Merchant truckers are wholesalers who operate in many lines of goods, such as raw and processed foods, bottled drinks (route men), and some hard lines. Some are erratic sources of supply, but often they have "good buys," whereas others carry regular lines and follow fairly definite schedules of calling on buyers.

Functional middlemen.   Small businessmen may also have occasion to purchase from functional middlemen. These are suppliers who do not take title to the goods for which they perform certain marketing functions such as selling, buying, or transporting. Familiar examples are brokers, selling or buying agents, manufacturers' representatives, resident buyers, purchasing agents, and freight forwarders. A broker serves either a buyer by seeking out sellers, or a seller by locating buyers. He brings buyer and seller together, and often has a wealth of market information available for both parties.

Small enterprisers will ordinarily use brokers when: (1) brokers are traditional in the field, such as in the textile industry and many of the food-processing industries; (2) the goods of a particular producer are available only through brokers (or other sales agents and manufacturers' representatives); and (3) on certain occasions when they are trying to locate a seller of goods not readily available in the established channels of trade. Resident buyers or purchasing agents are used by retailers and smaller wholesalers.

Apart from providing market information, most functional middlemen are not in a position to offer merchandising plans, although in some fields they are highly respected as technical advisors regarding uses of the product with which they deal.

One or Several Suppliers?

Retailers or service businesses holding dealerships or franchises usually are under obligation to concentrate purchases with the franchising organization. Only one supplier is used by manufacturers where a monopoly of supply exists or where the nearest supplier is traditionally the least expensive source of materials. Other businesses should decide whether to concentrate their buying with one or a few suppliers or to "play the market."

A small business which is free to choose its suppliers will give preference to those who:

1. can provide goods of the required quality, type, or model;
2. have goods available at desired prices and terms and in quantities needed;
3. are reliable — that is, where goods are continuously available;
4. provide reasonable and customary protection of the buyer's interests, such as quality guarantees, right to make legitimate returns, and limited agency or similar franchise rights;
5. supply good service, not only in making deliveries, but also in handling transactions and making adjustments;
6. make appropriate provisions for managerial or merchandising aids and technical assistance when needed; and
7. employ suppliers' representatives of the type with whom the businessman can work and cooperate successfully.

Whether to diversify or concentrate purchases will involve additional considerations, many of which are special applications of the foregoing standards. In any instance where the owner is a shrewd buyer who enjoys trading and procurement activities, when he wants various suppliers competing for his business, and believes that he is in a position to take advantage of any variations in lines, prices, or services different suppliers may offer, diversification would be the logical policy to follow. Another advantage is that this policy enables the business to match popular lines carried by competitors, with the exception of exclusively franchised or otherwise restricted lines. Finally, it protects the small business in case any one supplier should cease business, change its lines, or change its business policies.

To the small businessman advantages of concentrating purchases may be stated briefly as follows: By carrying the same lines continuously, his customers are not shifted from brand to brand, nor his employees from materials of one kind to another. As a good customer of one resource he may receive special favors or cumulative quantity discounts, valuable advice and assistance in merchandising the goods, tips on market changes, and special considerations during times of difficulty.

Those are the advantages on each side. There are, however, disadvantages not directly implied in either of the lists. Dangers encountered in diversification include stocking too many lines, perhaps attended by difficulty in maintaining complete stocks in any one, and inability to capitalize fully on the advertising program of any one brand of merchandise or on technical advice regarding the use of certain materials or supplies.

The businessman with a close working relationship with a single supplier must acknowledge certain drawbacks to such an arrangement: inability to take advantage of unusual offers in other lines; some loss if the supplier changes policy or becomes poorly managed; and the risk that the merchandising advice, assistance, and guidance offered may become irritating or of no use. The latter weakness is particularly likely to be present in some franchising systems. During periods of scarcity, some suppliers, unfortunately, use their available supplies to get new accounts instead of serving their regular customers adequately.

FUNDAMENTALS OF BUYING FOR THE SMALL BUSINESS

The art of careful buying involves six basic processes: (1) determining needs; (2) locating suitable sources of supply; (3) negotiating terms; (4) maintaining favorable relations with suppliers; (5) receiving, checking, and marking; and (6) follow-up after purchase.

Determining Needs

Too much buying in the small business is based on hunches instead of adequate information. Often it is spasmodic rather than planned. The buyer should know the type, quality, brand, and size of supplies or goods needed, and the quantities required. For the merchant this involves a study of the needs of his particular customers. Even for the same class of trade, demand may be quite different in two locations even though they are not far apart. The alert merchant will keep abreast of fashion changes — anticipating them whenever possible, perhaps by reading the same magazines and seeing the same shows as do his customers. Wholesalers and trade journals are valuable aids to the small merchant in anticipating customer demand.

For the small manufacturer and service operator the intended use for materials, parts, and supplies is the important factor. The small enterpriser should watch for opportunities to use new, improved, or even less expensive materials that will do the job equally well. Trade journals, suppliers' representatives, and manufacturers' catalogs or descriptive printed matter will help him in this task. Also, his own production workers often offer valuable suggestions if they are consulted.

In determining the correct quantities to buy, and when to buy them, the close relationship between purchasing and inventory or stores control becomes apparent.[1] Estimated needs minus quantity on hand (from inventory control records) gives quantity to buy. In merchandising, the usual guides followed are: basic stock list and past sales records for staples, the model stock for shopping goods or other lines involving an assortment like size or color, and sample tests before placing complete orders for novelties.

In manufacturing, estimated sales or planned production of each article is the starting point. Then a list of materials and parts is used to determine the quantities needed for each unit. By multiplying planned production in units by the quantity of each material or part required per unit, the various quantities to purchase during the planning phase are calculated. Transportation charges (if any), quantity discounts, and the manufacturer's standard packing sizes are among the factors to be considered before deciding the specific number of each item to order at one time.

Locating Suppliers

Once needs or requirements have been determined, the next step is to locate suitable sources of supply. Resources available to the small businessman usually are more limited than those for the big company. Often the small businessman is restricted to the particular market representatives or channels of trade used by the producers from whom he wants to buy. Sometimes he is limited to the immediate area in which his own business is located. Regardless of these limitations, he will nearly always have some choice between competing suppliers.

In selecting a supplier, he will consider which one carries the quality and variety of goods best suited to his needs as previously determined. Other important factors will be price for the quality desired, time required for delivery, transportation costs, services rendered by the supplier (including willingness to sell in the quantities desired), and market strategy. An example of market strategy might be buying in a different locale from one's competitors in order to provide a unique assortment of goods. One Iowa City dress shop, for example, features California fashions and includes fashion reports from its resident buyer in California in its advertising. Too much attention is often paid to price. Goods should also be bought with an eye to quality, past performance, and customer needs. The aim should be to obtain the lowest price, the most favorable terms, and the most adequate service, all consistent with satisfactory quality.

Both in selecting a supplier and in choosing particular items, the buyer should be as well informed as possible regarding important properties of the goods. In merchandising, the following points are considered important: materials, construction, reasons for different qualities, comparative values, intended uses, and care required. These are the factors of greatest concern to intelligent consumer buyers.

[1] For a complete discussion of inventory control, see Chapter 21.

When style or fashion is characteristic of the merchandise, its stylishness may be of even greater importance than other elements. It is not necessary for the merchant to be an expert on all kinds of materials, nor for him to attempt tests. Reliable suppliers provide this information through their salesmen, on labels, in descriptive advertising, or by other means.

Small manufacturers and service operators will be concerned with the way different materials and supplies act in their production processes. Again, suppliers' representatives will give valuable information if requested to do so.

Negotiating Terms

In negotiating prices and terms, the small buyer will do well to steer a middle course. If he really is an expert on the goods purchased, he needs no advice, but the average man should try to be a careful buyer, to keep as well informed as possible on current prices, and to insist on fair treatment. Any attempt to pose as a know-it-all, however, or a reputation for trying to beat down prices is likely to invite trouble. Nearly always the salesman is better informed on qualities and prices than is the small purchaser, and some salesmen enjoy "putting it over" on the "smart" buyer. The exact quality needed for the purpose, at a fair price, should be the standard to follow.

Terms available to the small buyer are of two principal types, cash discounts and "datings," or the length of time before the net amount of the invoice is due. Often the trade will have its customary terms, or they will be fixed for the smaller business. When opportunity for bargaining does exist, however, too many small businessmen are more interested in datings — that is, the length of credit extended — than they are in the cash discount. Unless a business is in dire financial straits, the cash discount is usually more important than the period of credit extension.

Maintaining Favorable Relations with Suppliers

Merely to buy goods is easy. To maintain favorable relations with vendors seems, at times, to be especially difficult for the small businessman. But it is always worth the effort. The smaller the business, the greater the importance of cultivating friendly relations with suppliers. In contrast to the big buyer, the small operator has far less to offer vendors in the way of profits. But he can be considerate of salesmen, prompt in paying his bills, and fair in all his dealings with suppliers.

Receiving, Checking, and Marking

Receiving, checking, and marking goods purchased are routine activities in most cases, and they may be performed carelessly unless provisions are made for their proper handling. In the small business this involves recognizing the importance of careful checking on quantity, condition, and transportation charges. Quality should be inspected in most cases. An alert small buyer has a good opportunity to build a desirable reputation, and to cement favorable future relations with his suppliers, by the way he handles these activities. Overages as well as shortages should be reported promptly to the seller. Damage claims should be made, insofar as possible, to the party responsible — either the vendor or the transportation company. In either case they should be made promptly and supported by adequate proof. Care in observing little details like these will help considerably in setting the small operator apart from the vendor's other customers, and stamping him as a "big businessman on the way up."

The way goods are marked upon receipt varies by type of business, the firm's policy, and other factors. Merchants should always mark on each item or container the date it is received. Whether size, cost, selling price, vendor's identification, or other data are marked on the individual items will depend on the needs of the business. Small manufacturers and service operators may need to do little or no marking, except where identification of the grade and source of materials is significant in operations control.

Follow-Up after Purchase

Follow-up relates to the history of the goods once they have been received. In merchandising, it includes data on how the article sold, rate of turnover, markdowns, customer complaints, returns, adjustments, and allowances. It is an always up-to-date picture of the item from the time it entered the store until it was finally disposed of. The small wholesaler will watch this record closely in terms of reorders by his retail customers. In either case, retailer or wholesaler, one of these situations will develop: the article will be a "hot" item to be reordered at once; or it will be an average piece of merchandise; or it will be a "buyer's mistake."

In small manufacturing and service establishments follow-up is more difficult and more frequently neglected. Of course, if a particular purchase turns out to be a "dud," appropriate action is taken. However, in the small firm most purchases are moderately satisfactory and too little effort is exerted toward tracing the success of each. Small operators could well give more consideration to follow-up activities, particularly in the purchase of materials and supplies.

When any firm has reached the size at which purchase records beyond those required for legal and accounting purposes are needed, a "resources file" is indicated. In this file is kept a card for each supplier that carries a complete record of the success of all transactions with him. It also contains data on prices, unit packages, discounts, and other purchasing information. Such a file serves as a current history record, which is a valuable guide to reordering.

BUYING BY THE SMALL RETAILER

Buying for the retail store has been developed to a highly skilled occupation, utilizing many aids and scientific methods — but it is still an art based on individual ability. Buying is the foundation for success in retailing. Small-scale retailers, since they are, at best, handicapped because of limited experience and buying power, should capitalize on the experience of larger stores, use the outside staff, or affiliate with some reputable cooperative buying group.

Consumer demand for many goods varies from one community to another as well as from time to time for the same group of people. The successful retailer understands the dynamic nature of consumer wants and makes strenuous efforts to keep his merchandise offerings adjusted to current demand. To do so usually involves anticipating his customers' needs to that goods will be on hand when they are needed.

Determining Customer Wants

Three main methods are used to determine what merchandise customers are likely to want: (1) analysis of sales records; (2) consumer surveys; and (3) the study of trade information.

Sales records.   Chain stores that deal in staple merchandise, such as grocery and drug chains, have developed a simple system of maintaining adequate stocks of articles in steady demand. Headquarters first prepares a list of the items each store should carry. Once a week the store manager compares his actual stock on hand with original quantities for each item on the checklist. For example, if the stock on hand of one brand of soap is 10 bars and entry for the previous week shows 22 were on hand, one dozen were sold during the week if none were received. Thus, without recording sales daily, the manager knows the rate of sale of each item and orders goods to keep his stock in balance with sales. Small retailers can use this checklist system by securing basic stock lists from their suppliers.

A different system is needed to provide information about the sale of merchandise whose style changes rapidly. Retailers who handle such goods find it advisable to record each sale and to make frequent (sometimes daily) analyses of these sales records. Thus they know what styles are selling rapidly and should be reordered at once, as well as the styles for which demand is declining. For the latter a small price reduction made in time may help to sell the goods before customers have lost all interest in the merchandise.

Consumer surveys.   Small merchants will not ordinarily make formal consumer surveys but may accomplish approximately the same objective by observing and talking with customers in the store. Trade journal staffs sometimes conduct surveys of consumer buying habits and report their findings.

Trade information.   A retailer has available to him many sources of information about developments in his field. Examples are trade papers written for other dealers like himself, fashion magazines, special market services that undertake to keep retailers informed about new merchandise and trends, manufacturers, brokers, and other salesmen. Many of these sources of trade information may reveal a customer demand in other localities before the merchant's own customers have expressed themselves.

Trade papers are especially helpful for informing a merchant of new goods for which there is as yet no active consumer demand, but which are likely to become popular later on. Such information is presented both in the form of articles and as vendors' advertising. If he is to avoid costly mistakes in buying unwanted goods, each retailer must know his own customers well enough to judge what new merchandise will, and what will not, be acceptable to them.

For style goods, and other lines where balanced assortments are of great importance, the model stock is the usual buying guide. A model stock plan means carrying a predetermined assortment of merchandise that is in proper balance by types, sizes, and colors with the sales of the line of goods. If the model stock plan were perfect, it would include the exact quantities of the right sorts of goods in relation to the desired rate of sale. In other words, if the estimates of the model stock plan were entirely correct, the merchant would sell all the goods projected in the plan; and in doing so, he would achieve exactly the stock turnover rate for which he had planned.

Forecasting Future Demand

Changing consumer wants make past sales far from a perfect guide to what and how much a retailer should purchase. Changes in trading areas, such as increases or decreases in population, make it impossible to use past sales alone as a reflector of future demand. A change in business conditions also to some degree nullifies the past as a guide for the future. When prices are changing rapidly, past records in terms of units sold should be used, instead of dollar sales volume, to forecast future needs. Changes in demand with respect to fashion, color, and material likewise weaken past sales records as a barometer for future purchases. The retailer should use market trends and sales forecasts to modify his preliminary decisions based upon past sales records.

Several of the sources discussed as useful in determining customer demand will be helpful in forecasting market trends — especially trade journals and manufacturers. The latter are in a favorable position to aid dealers in this activity because producers must forecast such trends for themselves if they are to experience profitable operations. Also, like wholesalers, manufacturers are continually receiving orders and inquiries from many territories. This furnishes them with the data needed to note important trends.

During the next decade pronounced changes in the composition of the population will be significant. The percentage of those past sixty years of age, with ample purchasing power, will continue to increase, while it is expected that the relative number of teenagers will decrease. Other important factors will be the higher level of educational achievement, the increase in the number of working wives, and the changes in the cultural, social, and economic status of various minority groups.

Salesmen who call upon the retailer are usually well informed about trends, particularly changes affecting the line of goods carried. Suggestions given by traveling salesmen are often very helpful to the small merchant. Of course, he should be careful not to let himself be oversold on certain goods an unscrupulous salesman may want to dispose of. Salespersons in the store also can furnish information on current trends in customer preference for certain merchandise.

Some retailers have each salesperson record every customer request for merchandise that is not in stock. "Want slips" are frequently used for this purpose. Care should be exercised in using information recorded on want slips. First, it is important to be sure that requests come from regular customers rather than from transients or from shoppers employed by other stores or even by vendors. Next the retailer should be satisfied that there are enough calls for the merchandise not in stock to indicate a trend and to justify placing an order for such goods.

Competitors, especially the progressive large stores in the trading area, may be studied by the small retailer to determine market trends. The advertising and displays of such stores provide clues to the increasing or declining popularity of certain merchandise. In using this method, the merchant should select a store that is normally slightly in advance of his own on the merchandise acceptance curve. This means that the customers of the store selected for observation usually buy new types of merchandise before his own customers do.

Sources of Supply

The majority of the purchasing for most stores, both large and small, is done on the premises. Many small retailers stock their stores by dealing with area wholesalers or their wholesaler affiliate. Where goods have a high turnover, as in the grocery, hardware, and drug fields, salesmen may call upon each customer once a week. Others supplement local purchases by making wide use of wholesalers' or manufacturers' catalogs, which provide a wider choice of merchandise than is offered locally. Some manufacturers have sales representatives who call on merchants once or twice a year.

Merchandise marts   In the general merchandise fields even small retailers find it desirable to "go to market" occasionally. "Markets" are sometimes located in a single building or mart where the leading vendors have displays and representatives. The Merchandise Mart in Chicago contains seven miles of display corridors with the offerings of some of America's best-known manufacturers. Atlanta's Merchandise Mart has over 400 lines of furniture, home furnishings, juvenile and gift wares, and has built a new 22-story building to provide space for appliances, luggage, jewelry, and wearing apparel. The Trade Mart in Dallas has 160 showrooms for 1,000 lines of furniture and accessories. Other major markets are located in San Francisco, Los Angeles, and St. Louis.

Trade shows.   Trade shows also provide an opportunity to examine merchandise and place orders. They are held in the principal market centers at least once a year. However, they are also held by state trade associations at their annual conventions. There are usually several hundred merchandise display booths in an exhibition hall. These are rented for the duration of the convention by manufacturers, wholesalers, and manufacturers' agents. Often demonstrations are made as to how the merchandise may be used or sold. Retailers thus have an opportunity to examine new and unusual merchandise and familiarize themselves with new trends and developments in their field, often without traveling more than one or two hundred miles.

Cooperative Buying Groups

Some retailers have formed cooperative buying groups to reduce buying costs, obtain price concessions, and benefit from the market and merchandising knowledge of others.

The retailer cooperative is owned entirely by the retail merchants, operates entirely for their benefit, usually has its own warehouse, and sells exclusively to member stores. In some respects, such as in the use of patronage dividends, it resembles the consumer cooperative type of organization. The retailer usually pays dues to the organization.

Market Representatives

Both large and small retailers located at some distance from the main central markets find it highly desirable to maintain contact with a representative situated there from whom they secure a large part of their merchandise. In the "soft lines" — wearing apparel, dry goods, and department store merchandise — these representatives are referred to as "resident buying offices." In hardware and "hard lines," the term "purchasing agent" is frequently used. (The discussion in this section applies to purchasing agents as well as to resident buyers, although it deals primarily with the latter.[2])

Resident buyers of interest to the smaller merchants are of two principal types — the paid buying office, and the merchandise broker.

Paid buying offices. The paid or independent buying offices maintain continuous contacts with a selected group of retailers on an annual fee and contract basis. In addition to buying merchandise for subscribing stores, they furnish a wealth of market information and forecasts. Many stores large enough to afford a paid buying office seem to be more interested in this market information service than in actually buying much merchandise through the office. However, when buyers from these stores go to market they work closely with the merchandise experts in their resident buying office, which saves the buyer's time as well as keeping him in touch with the latest trends and best resources. The buying office is normally used as the store buyer's temporary headquarters when in the market.

Although there are several hundred resident buying offices in New York City, and many in other major markets, such as Chicago, St. Louis, Los Angeles, San Francisco, and Dallas, about 17 have long been in operation and are widely known throughout the country. In general, these offices serve only one client (subscribing retail store) in any community. The usual practice is to charge an annual fee of approximately 0.5 to 1 percent of the subscriber's net sales. In pricing their services to individual stores, a few of the offices consider, in addition, the relative amount of the merchandise experts' time needed by the store. Some offices have minimum fees, which have been as low as $900 to $1,200 per year. Even the smaller of these figures would indicate a store volume of $90,000 or more per year to keep this fee within the customary one percent standard.

The Association of Buying Offices recently stated its objectives as follows:

1. To keep our member stores informed through timely bulletins of the latest fashion and market trends, as well as opportune purchases and new items presented in the various markets

---

[2] Important differences between "hard" and "soft" lines are: a larger number of manufacturers, greater weight per unit of merchandise, and fairly stable styles for the former; and frequent style and price changes, light unit weight, many new producers, and a somewhat smaller number of manufacturers for the latter.

2. To hold meetings or clinics at the beginning of the season to acquaint members with the current developments in fashion

3. To assist our member stores in the screening of resources and values

4. To seek to combine the purchasing power of our members in order to secure better prices on merchandise and supplies

5. To organize private-brand programs for our members

6. To engage in program merchandising with vendors on behalf of our members

7. To act for and represent member stores in the world's markets in the interim period between buyers' trips

8. To follow up and speed deliveries on-outstanding orders

9. To assist our member stores in the planning of promotions and regular selling events in line with prevailing market trends

10. To foster good relationships between manufacturers and our member stores

11. To provide merchandise in adequate quantities and increasingly improved quality, as reasonably as possible to the ultimate consumer

12. To counsel and advise with the management of our member stores in planning their stock and merchandising operations

13. To consult with store managements on their organization problems, their personnel programs, and analyze store figures in many constructive ways

14. To offer through branch offices a specialized knowledge of regional markets

15. To assist our members in replacing personnel

16. To advise our members on electronic data processing developments in the retailing area[3]

Merchandise brokers.   Merchandise brokers bring buyer and seller together. No charge is made to retail clients for the broker's services, but the vendor pays a brokerage commission based on a percentage of sales. The advantages to a retailer who uses a merchandise broker are that it saves him time on market trips, and he has access to goods which might not be available to him if he tried to locate them himself. The broker assembles a large number of lines from which the buyer makes his selection, or he may take the buyer to various wholesalers and manufacturers. The broker also can make additional purchases when the buyer is unable to come to the market. Because the broker's first concern is to sell the merchandise of his clients, some merchandise lines, regardless of their merit, may not be recommended by the broker to his retail customers. A merchandise broker usually limits himself to one customer in a particular city, which makes it more likely that a retailer's merchandise will differ from that of his competitors. Merchandise brokers investigate the credit standing of retailers before accepting them as customers; thus manufacturers and wholesalers may take their orders with confidence. Some brokers place a "floor" on the size of a retailer's purchasing power before accepting him as a client. Although no contracts exist between the retailer and the broker — contracts being made only between the broker and the sources of supply — brokers send market bulletins and advice to retail customers and assist them in many ways when they come to market.

[3] Mr. William Burston, Executive Secretary, Association of Buying Offices, Inc., New York, personal communication, June 18, 1971.

BUYING BY THE SMALL WHOLESALER

As a class, wholesalers are supposed to have large businesses. Actually many small wholesalers find it difficult to purchase in carload lots or other quantities of sufficient size to secure the low prices and economical transportation needed to justify their status as wholesalers. This has often led to the use of pooled buying, ordering through resident buying offices, and transportation arranged by freight forwarders or shippers who consolidate several less than carload shipments into car lots to secure lower transportation rates. Actual examples of practices followed by small wholesalers known to the authors are described in the following paragraph.

Three brothers, each operating an independent, noncompeting wholesale grocery, pool their buying to secure a 5 percent discount permitted for purchasing in car lots. A feed and flour wholesaler pools his buying with a few large retail customers. A seed wholesaler buys on contract from growers, sends scouts out to locate sellers, and orders from catalogs. A produce dealer uses truck drivers to scout for "good buys"; a small packer sends his buyers to the local stockyards on sale days; a radio wholesaler waits for visits by salesmen but does some ordering by mail. One small hardware wholesaler does not stock heavy, bulky, expensive items but buys them only on customer orders. These few examples illustrate the diversity of buying methods likely to be found among small wholesalers in many average towns. Several of these practices are quite similar to those followed by retailers.

In at least one other respect many small wholesalers resemble retailers; by virtue of it, they are, in fact, both retailers and wholesalers. Throughout the country, but especially in the small towns in the less densely populated states, small businessmen in fields like groceries, meats, hardware, electrical supplies, and some others, function as both wholesale and retail distributors. In such cases the wholesale division is influenced greatly by the needs and policies of the retail division in matters such as brands carried, price lines, and quantities to order. Much less frequently the wholesale activities have set the pattern for the retail store.

Policy decisions regarding brands to carry, assortments, number and completeness of merchandise lines, when to add new items, and the extent of quantity buying, are much more acute for the small than for the larger wholesaler although similar for both. Limited financial resources and a smaller market are the chief reasons for this condition. Also, the relative importance of short-run considerations as compared to long-run factors is greater for the small wholesaler.

In gauging demand, the small retailer-wholesaler may have a slight advantage over his large counterpart. Consumer demand is immediately reflected through the retail store. However, the man who is exclusively a wholesaler would anticipate this demand and would have stocks on hand to fill orders of retail customers as they come in. In practice many wholesalers try to maintain continuous contact with consumer demand and trends by means of frequent visits of their representatives to retail stores. In addition to this first-hand observation, small wholesalers should use all available sources of demand forecasting, including the advice of their resident buying offices, reports on market trends, and tips received from manufacturers' representatives.

At least partly because of this need to forecast market trends further in advance than retailers, wholesalers are more tempted to engage in speculative buying. For the small operator this is especially dangerous. *One wrong guess and he may be wiped out.*

In selecting suppliers the small wholesaler finds that available ones vary by lines of goods, methods of distribution used by particular manufacturers, and location. The wholesaler's buying power may also have a bearing on the best sources of supply to use. Concentration is more common for staples, limited lines, and exclusive agencies. Orders are placed through selling agents. Diversification exists when there are a large number of small producers, such as in dry goods, and where style changes are frequent.

Another factor that may be of relatively greater concern to the small wholesaler is the distribution policies of competing manufacturers. Some producers sell directly to chain stores and other cut-price retailers, thus undermining the market for the wholesaler. Others protect their independent wholesale distributors.

Additional factors that enter into the choice of suppliers are transportation rates and the vendor's speed of delivery, ability to supply quantities desired, prices, and services rendered, as well as his financial standing, credit policies, reputation, and the types of protection the vendor may give to small wholesalers.

To a greater extent than do retailers, small wholesalers order from catalogs and price lists by phone or mail. In the hardware and grocery fields, and for some electrical goods and other similar lines, this is common practice. Soft-goods wholesalers, on the other hand, seem to prefer market visits or salesmen's calls.

Accepted business practices are particularly important in the wholesaling field. Confirming a small telephone order in writing, for example, may seem like a waste of time to the small wholesaler. Failure to do so would be acceptable in many retail fields, but for the wholesaler it is a serious mistake. All orders should be in writing, with proper duplicate copies as needed. Other well-established business practices, such as the use of purchase schedules, card indexing of vendors, prompt discounting of all invoices, dealing ethically with vendors, and observing trade customs, are expected to an even greater extent from small wholesalers than from retailers.

An alert wholesaler will seek out appropriate sources of supply, secure and file catalogs, and aim at being informed in advance even if actual buying is done at the warehouse. Several compilations are used, such as the *Thomas Register of American Manufacturers* (published annually), *McRae's Blue Book*, and specialized directories such as the *Thomas Wholesale Grocery and Kindred Trades Register*. These directories are in addition to the usual trade press articles and advertisements. At first the very small wholesaler may want to consult a directory or register in the purchasing department of some large nearby institution until he feels financially able to obtain his own.

BUYING BY THE SMALL FACTORY AND SERVICE BUSINESS

All manufacturing and most service establishments require materials and supplies to carry on their operations. Whereas the merchant buys for resale and frequently will purchase new items on his judgment that they can be sold at a profit, purchases for a factory or service establishment are made only in response to the expected needs of using departments. Assuming these needs to be reported or estimated accurately, purchasing aims at keeping the inventory of materials, parts, and supplies in proper balance with the needs of the company.

Too often, however, many small operators buy supplies as needed at retail, instead of arranging for their purchase at wholesale prices and planning needs well enough in advance to warrant such consideration. Often group buying is also possible. In several instances small noncompeting shops have successfully pooled their buying of many items.

Many shops, during the beginning years especially, do not confine their operations exclusively either to manufacturing or to rendering services. The small business doing processing or performing a service, frequently also sells some parts or merchandise. A manufacturer of metal products needs raw material and supplies like fuel and oil. Because he maintains a stock of various kinds of metals, or parts, he often sells some of these with or without processing. Plumbing contractors, repair shops, beauty parlors, and other small establishments often derive a sizable proportion of their total income from the resale of materials, parts, or merchandise used in their kind of business.

To some degree at least, these small businessmen have a dual purchasing problem — buying for use, and buying for resale. Purchasing for these small operators usually is not a specialized function requiring the full time of one man or department. It is ordinarily done by the owner or under his close personal supervision. Because the owner-manager is more likely to be interested chiefly in the processing side of the business, buying may easily be slighted or carelessly handled. Unless the owner is capable of doing the job properly himself, and is willing to do it, definite responsibility for purchasing should be vested in one person who is also given adequate authority and facilities to do the job correctly.

The important considerations in the purchasing function for nonmerchandising establishments are discussed below.

Purchasing for the Small Factory

Purchasing for the small factory aims to maintain inventories that are balanced in terms of production needs. If only one product is made and the rate of production is fairly constant, purchasing can be simplified to become nearly a routine operation. In other cases, when items needed can be obtained regularly as wanted within a predictable time limit, it may be sufficient merely to establish maximum and minimum stock limits and the economic ordering quantity. However, when deliveries are uncertain, purchasing "lead time" becomes an important consideration. So that he may receive his production materials on a proper scheduling basis it is necessary that the manufacturer know how far in advance he must place his orders with a given vendor.[4]

Purchasing for the Small Service Business

The importance of purchasing in different kinds of service establishments will vary with the following factors: (1) the percentage of total revenue obtained from the resale of merchandise; (2) the ratio of material and supply costs to labor costs; and (3) the range of qualities available from different suppliers.

Many service establishments secure almost half of their total revenue from the sale of merchandise. It is likely in such cases that materials, parts, and supplies used in conjunction with services performed will also make up an important part of the

[4] See Chapter 21   for a detailed discussion of inventory control in the small factory.

total "service" charge to customers. Examples include television, radio, and electrical repair shops, plumbing contractors, and some beauty parlors. In establishments of this type, purchasing is a function of major importance. In many personal service types of business, such as bookkeeping or advisory services, the cost of materials and supplies used bears such a small ratio to labor costs as to reduce the importance of the purchasing function to a minimum. Whenever the service is performed upon the person of the client or upon his property that is of high unit value, there may be significant quality variations in available materials and supplies that would lead to considerable differences in the quality of the resulting "service." An expensive garment cleaned with a cheap solvent that is inadequate for the task is one example. By contrast, some establishments, such as sheet metal shops, work with materials that are so close to a standard that improvising or substitution is impossible or, at the least, difficult.

SUMMARY AND CONCLUSIONS

Businessmen have a wide range from which to choose when purchasing materials, merchandise, and supplies. This often leads to overbuying, and to dissipation of the already-limited buying power of the small business. Although good arguments may be presented in favor of distributing orders among many suppliers, *it is usually better policy for the small business to concentrate and work closely with one major resource.*

Moreover, for the small business, buying is so often associated with valuable assistance from the supplier in many management activities that the importance of purchasing from him is further increased. Voluntary chains and cooperative buying associations enable the small independent to compensate for his smaller buying power through headquarters' aids. Relationships with suppliers for most businesses are fully as important as relationships with customers or employees.

REVIEW QUESTIONS

1. Differentiate between the different types of suppliers.
2. What factors should a small businessman consider in selecting his suppliers?
3. Discuss the arguments for and against a policy of utilizing a single source of supply.
4. Discuss each of the different aspects of the purchasing function.
5. What are some of the methods used in determining the needs of retail customers?
6. How can the retailer forecast future demand for his merchandise? Discuss fully.
7. What are some of the major sources of supply for the retailer?
8. What benefits can the retailer derive through cooperative buying? The wholesaler?
9. What is a resident buyer? Distinguish between paid buying offices and merchandise brokers. What are the advantages and disadvantages of each?

10.   Summarize the main points of difference or emphasis in the purchasing
       activities of retailers, wholesalers, manufacturers, and service establishments.

DISCUSSION QUESTIONS

1.   Which type of resident buying office would be better for a retailer just large
       enough to use either type? Discuss.
2.   Fred's independent supermarket competes with both corporate and voluntary
       chains on price and service. Recently, frequent out-of-stock conditions have
       become serious, although business conditions are normal. Fred knows that
       many customers have started buying those out-of-stock items from competi-
       tors. What should he do, and why?

SUPPLEMENTARY READING

Hedrick, Floyd D. *Purchasing Management in the Smaller Company.* New York:
       American Management Association, 1971. Discusses purchasing policies, value
       analysis, legal aspects of purchasing, the measurement of purchasing
       effectiveness, and other aspects of the purchasing function in smaller
       companies.

18

Pricing for profit

Once a businessman has acquired merchandise, materials, or supplies from one or more of the various sources of supply discussed in Chapter 17, he adds "value" to these goods. For example, the manufacturer processes materials; the service establishment uses supplies in the performance of a requested service; the wholesaler, having shopped a wide variety of markets, makes the goods he buys available under conditions where they can be examined and then purchased in smaller quantities; and the retailer assembles an assortment of goods in sizes and quality suitable to his particular customers, and presents them for sale along with information as to their care and use. Each of these businessmen hopes to make a profit on the function he performs. How much additional value has he added to the goods? How much will his customers be willing to pay? What price level will bring maximum profits? Will selling a small volume at a high price be more profitable than selling a large volume at a low price?[1]

Formulating price policies and setting the price is one of the most important aspects of management. Whether maximum profit may be acquired by higher or lower prices depends on a wide variety of conditions. The businessman must know his costs, understand buyer motivation, and evaluate the competition.

ECONOMICS OF PRICING

Price reflects the cost of goods (or services) sold, administrative and selling expenses and, hopefully, some profit. If the seller is a manufacturer, the cost of goods sold is represented by the costs of manufacture. If the seller is a wholesaler or a retailer, the cost of goods sold is the amount paid for the goods originally. The

[1] Price is only one way in which the businessman can expand his market. Other marketing factors (or "instruments," as they are commonly called by marketers) include advertising, personal selling or salesmanship, quality or distinctiveness of product, and packaging. By varying the "mix" of these marketing factors to meet different situations, sales can be expanded and the most profitable volume obtained. However, price is usually the most important of these factors.

retailer or wholesaler calls the difference between cost of goods sold and selling price "markup," or "gross margin." Gross margin, then, includes marketing or distribution costs, such as rent, wages, administration, and advertising, plus an allowance for profit.

Correct pricing policies depend upon many factors in addition to costs. Among these other considerations are (1) the nature of the product or service, (2) company policy, (3) competition, (4) business conditions, (5) market strategy, and (6) distribution methods.

The Nature of the Product

The quantity sold of either table salt or sable coats will be little affected by raising or lowering the price. The demand for these products is inelastic. However, the demand for color television sets or ice cream is very responsive to a change in price and can be stimulated by advertising. These latter products have a demand which is both elastic and expansible. Whether the article is of great or small monetary value does not, in itself, determine the nature of demand; rather, it is how much and for what reason the article is needed or desired. The nature of the product will determine the elasticity or the expansibility of demand. Elasticity of demand refers to the change in dollar value of sales that accompanies price changes. If a lower price alone increases total revenue, demand is elastic; if it decreases total revenue (even though the number of units sold increases), it is inelastic; if price changes do not change total revenue, the elasticity is unitary. Different products and services also vary in the amount advertising increases sales. This property is known as expansibility or advertisability. An article that sells only slightly better when well advertised has a low coefficient of expansibility; one that sells much better has a high coefficient. In most cases both price reductions and advertising will be used simultaneously, but in amounts proportionate to the product's relative elasticity and expansibility.

Company Policy

Company price policy will normally be influenced by factors like location, size or position in the field, customer services rendered, and the owner's preference for a particular market or reputation. Certain businessmen seek a particular class of trade and consequently follow a price policy intended to appeal to this group.

A businessman may set out to establish a reputation for having either the lowest or the highest prices in his field. In such cases the price level is the starting point; expenses, location, organization, and policies other than pricing must be adjusted to conform.

Competition

The prices at competitive stores will guide price policies within certain limits. A seller must recognize the nature of his competition. If the product offered by a competitor is similar to his, a competitive price must be set. The value of a product at the time of sale, however, includes – among other things – the service which accompanies it, the location of the selling establishment, and any unique features of the product which set it apart. Also, whether a seller must place a competitive price on his product depends on the policy of the store, the elasticity of demand, and many of the other factors here discussed. It should be remembered that, in a competitive situation, the demand for a product which is considered to be inelastic becomes elastic for the individual store. For example, although the demand for bread is inelastic, if one store lowers the price on bread it can increase its own bread sales greatly.

Business Conditions

Manufacturers' and retailers' prices fluctuate less readily than do wholesalers' prices. The latter are most responsive to changing economic conditions, since wholesalers deal in large quantities on a narrow margin and their markets are well organized. Manufacturers' prices fluctuate less frequently because of the general attempt to stabilize or maintain prices on differentiated products. A retailer does not respond readily to economic change since, at this level of distribution, (1) customary or convenient prices are common; (2) many of the goods are "price-lined"; (3) it is impractical to re-mark goods frequently; (4) it is not convenient to make changes in fractional amounts; and (5) the wider operating margins are usually adequate to absorb minor variations in the retailer's cost of goods over a short period of time. When fluctuations in retail price do occur, however, they are more violent.

A businessman must decide whether his prices will reflect the cost of goods he has on hand, or whether they will be based on replacement costs which may be either higher or lower. Within the limits set by the level of distribution in question, if general economic conditions are good and the economy is expanding, the seller may be inclined to increase his share of the wealth by raising prices. Often at such times labor and other costs are also increasing, and he will probably want to pass this added expense on to the buyer. During periods of economic stress sellers are likely to ignore margins, for their greatest concern at such times is to retain their share of the market and, hence, price cuts may be taken which reflect more than merely the decrease in costs.

Market Strategy

Market strategy may involve deciding whether to seek a large volume at a low markup, or a low volume at a high markup. It may also involve "leader" pricing; this is the pricing of some merchandise close to or below cost to attract to the premises customers who may make other purchases.[2] Another consideration in market strategy is whether the item being sold is a long-run or a short-run item. For example, high-fashion items (midi-skirts) or fads (hula hoops) have a limited market or may have sales appeal for a short period of time. The optimum selling price is one that will net the most dollars (after allowing for applicable selling costs) during the time the product is on the market. Sometimes, also, a new product is

---

[2] Some states have *unfair practice* laws intended to prevent selling at a price below the "cost of doing business," or *antiloss leader* laws requiring a price no less than "landed cost" plus 6 percent. (Landed cost is the manufacturer's list price less all relevant discounts and deductions, plus the amount of freight-in.) For a further discussion of these laws, see pp. 491-92.

introduced at a price which is higher than that justified by the cost of producing it, in order to establish it as a "prestige" product. For example, Corfam shoes were first introduced only in the highest price lines in order to establish Corfam in people's minds as a quality product.

Distribution Methods

It is important to understand how certain characteristics of marketing costs and the method of distribution used may influence appropriate pricing, especially for the manufacturer and in some cases the service business. Distribution or marketing costs, relative to production costs, are "sticky" and do not change quickly with small changes in price. Since marketing costs for most consumer goods make up almost half of the price paid by the final consumer, this rigidity tends to lessen the benefits received by the producer who reduces his prices when costs of production are lowered.

Unlike unit production costs, which invariably decrease with increases in production, distribution costs per unit may remain constant or even increase with increases in the level of sales. These results are demonstrated in two of the pricing examples cited in the following section. In the first example, marketing costs remained at $0.36 per unit when both factory and retail prices were reduced and the quantity sold increased. Sometimes, however, distribution takes place under conditions of increasing unit costs. This is especially true after a certain volume point is passed. It explains why department store expenses usually become a larger percentage of sales as volume increases, and also why selling costs to final consumers remain fairly constant even when production costs are decreased.

For example, a small manufacturer may sell his initial production at a profitable price to local customers with relatively little expense. If he seeks to expand his market, all distribution costs tend to rise until a volume is reached sufficient to justify mass-distribution methods and extensive advertising. This situation is also illustrated in the following section.

A third situation is that in which distribution occurs under conditions of decreasing unit costs. This occurs less often than might be expected. The best example of this is a staple product that can be sold and distributed to one or a few buyers in ever-increasing quantities.

EXAMPLES OF PRICING STRATEGY

By studying some hypothetical cases of pricing policy the reader may learn how some of the economic factors discussed above can be applied to specific situations.

Price Reduction with Inelastic Demand

Whether a business markets its goods directly or indirectly will determine the control it has over final price. Some manufacturers, for instance, must distribute their products through dealers while others can sell directly to the user of the product. In the following case of a manufacturer who markets his product indirectly (see Table 18-1), it is observed that price reduction alone increases volume very little and has little or no effect on the profits of either the manufacturer or the retailer, despite reduced manufacturing costs. This is because demand is inelastic and unit marketing cost is inflexible or "constant."

Table 18-1.   Effect of Price Reduction with Inelastic Demand

Number of Units	Factory Cost per Unit	Total Factory Cost	Unit Factory Price	Total Factory Sales	Factory Profit	Gross Margin Unit Marketing Cost	Unit Retail Profit	Unit Retail Price	Retail Volume	Retail Profit
10,000	$0.50	$5,000	$0.60	$6,000	$1,000	$0.36	$0.04	$1.00	$10,000	$400
10,500	0.45	4,725	0.55	5,775	1,050	0.36	0.04	0.95	9,975	420
10,600	0.45	4,770	0.55	5,830	1,060	0.36	0.04	0.95	10,070	424
10,000	0.45	4,500	0.60	6,000	1,500	0.36	0.04	1.00	10,000	400

In this example (as summarized in Table 18-1), it is assumed that a factory produces 10,000 units per month of an article sold through several dealers to consumers; manufacturing cost is $0.50 per unit, net profit $0.10, factory selling price $0.60, and retail price $1.00. At this price the retailer's profit is $0.04 per unit. Thus marketing cost is $0.36 per unit. A way is found to reduce production costs 10 percent, or $0.05. If factory price is lowered by this amount from $0.60 to $0.55, and dealers pass along the full amount of this reduction, retail selling price will be reduced by only 5 percent. If this increases retail sales in units by 5 percent, sales will now be 10,500 units, with a retail value of $9,975 and a factory value (at selling price) of $5,775. The manufacturer would thus be selling 10,500 units for $225 less than he formerly received for 10,000 units, and his net profit would be increased by only $50. The retailer would receive $25 less (in total sales) for 10,500 units than he formerly received for 10,000. Even an increase in retail sales of 6 percent to 10,600 units would mean sales at retail of $10,070, or only $70 more than when the price was $1.00. To the manufacturer this would be only $5,830 in sales, a decline of $170, and $1,060 profit, an increase of only $60. Had price not been reduced, profit to the manufacturer would have been increased by 50 percent, or from $1,000 to $1,500, with no change in sales volume.

Price Maintenance with Expansible Demand

In a second example of pricing strategy — the same situation as above, but with an expansible demand — prices are maintained but advertising is used to promote the sale of the product. Both the sales volume and the net profits are dramatically increased.

Assume that the $500 gained by lower manufacturing costs, plus an additional $500 — a total of $1,000 — is used for effective sales promotion. If an additional 10,000 units were sold, at a factory price of $0.60, advertising cost would be only $16\frac{2}{3}$ percent of the increased sales ($1,000/$6,000), or $8\frac{1}{3}$ percent of total sales ($1,000/$12,000). This would double profits to the manufacturer, over and above his advertising expense. It would probably increase dealers' profits sevenfold by reducing expense per unit. Possibly later the dealers would begin to lower prices, thereby further stimulating sales. Larger volume would very likely lead to still lower production costs, and the cycle of expansion typical of most manufactured consumer goods would be under way.[3]

The foregoing example may be presented in tabular form as shown in Table 18-2.

Table 18-2.   Effect of Advertising on Profits (Price Maintenance with Expansible Demand)

	Before Cost Reduction	After Cost Reduction and Expenditure of $1,000 for Advertising
Manufacturer:		
Units sold	10,000	20,000
Total sales (@ $0.60 per unit)	$ 6,000	$12,000
Cost of production:		
@ $0.50 per unit	5,000	
@ $0.45 per unit		9,000
Advertising expense		1,000
Net profit	$ 1,000	$ 2,000
Retailer:		
Units sold	10,000	20,000
Total sales (@ $1.00 per unit)	$10,000	$20,000
Cost of goods sold	6,000	12,000
Gross margin	$ 4,000	$ 8,000
Expenses (estimated):		
Fixed or overhead $2,500		$2,500
Variable or selling 1,100		2,100
Total	3,600	4,600
Net profit	$ 400	$ 3,400

Price Reduction with Elastic Demand

If distribution costs per unit are constant, a firm cannot benefit from a policy of lowering prices unless there is a fairly high degree of elasticity of demand. With constant or only slightly increasing costs, sales promotion should be used with greater vigor in proportion to the expansibility of demand. For example, imagine two products, A and B, each selling for $1.00 per unit and having a constant combined production and distribution cost of $0.90 per unit. Assume that 10,000

[3] See Samuel Berke, "Breakeven Point Studies for Small Marketers," Small Marketers Aids Annual no. 5 (Washington, D. C.: Small Business Administration, 1963), pp. 24–31.

units are being sold; A has a very slightly elastic demand and B is highly elastic. Experiments with different prices might yield results as indicated in Table 18-3.

Table 18-3.   Effect of Price Reduction with Elastic Demand

Price	A	B
$1.00 Number of units sold	10,000	10,000
Total sales	$10,000	$10,000
Total expenses	9,000	9,000
Net profit	$ 1,000	$ 1,000
$0.97 Number of units sold	11,000	20,000
Total sales	$10,670	$19,400
Total expenses	9,900	18,000
Net profit	$ 770	$ 1,400

Under the conditions assumed, it would be profitable to increase sales by lowering the price for product B but not for A. If A has a high expansibility the procedure indicated for it would be to use extensive advertising while keeping the price constant.

When both production and distribution take place on a decreasing cost basis, an ideal combination of conditions exists for the small business that plans on expanding rapidly. In the short run, when distribution operates on a decreasing cost basis, the small businessman may well lower his price and push sales promotion to the maximum limit of his capacity to produce. His attention in this case should be directed primarily toward reducing production costs and expanding facilities, and next toward devising plans to continue this most fortunate condition.

APPROACHES TO PRICING

The above examples may help the small businessman to understand some of the basic, or theoretical, considerations in pricing. In practice, several different methods are used in determining the prices of goods:

1. *Full-cost pricing.* When this method is used the price is set to cover labor, materials, overhead, and a predetermined percentage for profit. However, few businessmen adhere rigidly to such a policy for each product, but instead recognize variations in demand and competition and use full cost as a "floor" or reference point to which flexible markups are added.

2. *Gross-margin pricing.* This method, widely used by wholesalers and retailers, adds a set markup to wholesale cost. The markup is sometimes computed as a percentage of wholesale cost, but more often as a percentage of selling price. Most firms using this method do not apply the same markup to all items at all times.

3. *"Going-rate" prices.* Many manufacturers or wholesalers suggest prices and many retailers use these suggested prices. Other retailers simply follow the prices of similar firms.

4. *A reasoned approach.* Though all the previously named methods have merit and are applicable in certain situations, a set of rules may not be responsive to changing conditions. As one author has stated:

A well-reasoned approach to pricing is, in effect, a comparison of the impact of a decision on total sales receipts, or revenue, and on total costs. It involves the increase or decrease in revenues and costs, not just of the product under consideration, but of the business enterprise as a whole. If a proposed price change leads to a greater increase in total sales receipts than in total costs, it will increase profits and should be favored. Or if it leads to a greater reduction in costs than in revenue, the decision should also be favorable.

It is quite possible that an item or service sold at less than a full-cost price may nevertheless make a worthwhile contribution to total revenue (1) if the facilities used would otherwise be idle or less profitably employed, or (2) if the sale of the item at the lower price has a favorable effect on other phases of the business. . . . A price that appears satisfactory from the viewpoint of strict full-cost pricing will sometimes be seen as unprofitable when its overall effects are taken into consideration.[4]

PRICING BY RETAILERS

The prices placed on goods to be sold in a retail establishment will be affected by many of the same general considerations which are basic to all pricing decisions: company policy, the nature of the competition, the amount of freedom to price as one wishes, and the type of product and resulting demand considerations.

Company Policy

A store's pricing policies should respond to the general policies of the company. A store which wishes to provide extra services or handle unique and distinctive goods will likely charge higher prices. Another store which specializes in a "bargain basement" atmosphere will plan for a high volume with a low profit margin. Most stores fall somewhere between these extremes, using normal markups which reflect differences in the quality of the goods being sold.

Competition

A retailer needs to recognize that his competition comes not only from similar stores in his own community but from specialty and department stores in neighboring towns and from catalog sales. The price of goods depends not only on the quality or character of the goods themselves but also on their degree of availability and the services which accompany them. The retailer must evaluate his own and his competitors' prices in these terms. Customers are quick to decide whether or not they are getting their money's worth.

[4] W. Warren Haynes, "Pricing Decisions in Small Business," Management Research Summary no. 44 (Washington, D. C.: Small Business Administration, 1961), p. 2. For a further discussion of this approach to pricing, see section on "Incremental Costs and Marginal Income" in Chapter 23.

Pricing Freedom

Retail price on some merchandise is set by the manufacturer by means of national advertising, price agreements, or law. Such prices can be enforced by exclusive or selective distribution or by depending on fair trade laws. A retailer who charges less than a minimum price may find that the line of goods is no longer available to him. Because the fair trade laws of some states have been challenged in many courts,[5] some manufacturers still seek to control retail price by selling on consignment, cutting retailers' margins, or refusing to pay cooperative advertising allowances if prices are not maintained. When vendors suggest retail prices or quote prices in national advertising, small retailers usually conform to them unless the store policy is to cut prices.

Laws in existence also forbid a store to have two different prices on the same item at the same time. For example, when new supplies have arrived for which the store has had to pay more or less than previously, and if the store desires to change its prices accordingly, the prices on identical merchandise already on the shelves must be re-marked to match.

The Nature of the Product

The elasticity of the demand, how goods are shopped for, and their special characteristics are important factors in the determination of the correct price.

Staple convenience goods. For staple convenience goods, which are fairly well standardized items available in a large number of stores, either customary prices or the going market price is used. These are usually the lowest prices at which such merchandise can be handled profitably. A serious danger in cutting prices on such items is that all competitors will quickly reduce their prices and no permanent increase in volume or traffic will result.

Another pitfall is to price convenience items in amounts which make it inconvenient for customers to pay for them. For example, because of inflationary pressures it has become necessary for many retailers to increase the price of "five cent" candy bars and packages of gum. Those retailers who increased the price by only a penny or two found that their sales of these items had dropped. Market analysts concluded that customers do not like to dig out several coins for a small purchase — that they would just as soon pay a dime as six or seven cents.[6]

Shopping goods. Shopping goods are nonstandardized items that change frequently in both quality and style. Retailers usually "price-line" these goods, that is, they establish a small number of prices within each merchandise classification. Knowing the price at which goods will sell, the retailer can purchase his stock with these retail prices in mind.

[5] See pp. 492-93 for a discussion of resale price maintenance.

[6] *Time*, February 8, 1971, p. 79. Manufacturers have also taken note of this. The recent increase in the price of a package of Wrigley gum from five to ten cents, accompanied by the increase in the size of the package from five to seven sticks of gum, was anticipated in the *Time* article. A similar pricing decision was also made recently by the Squibb Beech-Nut Co., makers of "Life-Savers."

Fashion and novelty goods.   Although most fashion goods and seasonal items are subject to price-lining, they show the additional influence of the time factor in relation to pricing. Store policy will determine whether fashion merchandise is first offered at the very beginning of the season, or somewhat later after the risk element and retail prices have been reduced. Initial fashion offerings should be priced high enough to allow for the greater amounts of risk, as well as for the larger markdowns as the fashion cycle develops and price becomes competitive.

A store catering to the middle or upper middle class but not to the fashion leaders in a community would price merchandise relatively high early in the season, expecting to take markdowns as the fashion cycle progresses and before the more popular-priced stores enter into competition. Initial prices would be somewhat higher than those in volume or "promotional" stores, but substantially lower than prices in fashion leadership stores. Markdowns to be allowed for in the initial price would be normal for fashion (not high-fashion) goods and would be similar for different styles, because the fashion acceptance of all styles carried would be assured before this type of store begins promotions. By contrast, the high-fashion store will offer many styles that do not receive public acceptance. These may be difficult to sell at any price, often even well below cost. Consequently, the few accepted fashion lines must bear the loss of less successful lines. Also, predicting even what percentage of styles offered at the very beginning of the fashion cycle will become fashionable is far more difficult than estimating markdowns for the more conservative store.

Novelties or specialties usually carry a relatively high markup. Also, they may often be selected with price strategy in mind. Since novelties are likely to have a short selling season, prices may be high at first but often must be lowered as the novelty demand wears off. As with seasonal or fashion items, drastic markdowns may be needed to close out stocks as the demand drops toward zero. Careful daily watching of prices is important with goods of this type.

Groceries.   Though individual grocery items may be classed as "convenience" goods, *total* expenditures for groceries account for such a large proportion of the typical family's budget that many housewives constantly shop for the "best buys."

In recent years the professional consumer movement has caused some grocery stores (particularly supermarkets) to adopt *unit pricing* for packaged products. (In some areas – notably New York City – unit pricing is required by law.) Unit pricing is the practice of listing the price of a product in terms of some common measurement, such as an ounce or a yard. For example, by listing the price *per ounce* on each box of corn flakes, as well as the price per box, the customer can tell immediately whether it would actually cost her less to buy the larger "family" size rather than the regular-size package; there is no need for her to do mental arithmetic. Obviously, unit pricing is most helpful in comparing different-sized packages of an identical product, such as Brand X corn flakes; when comparing different brands of a similar product, differences in quality, packaging, and other factors must be considered in addition to the price per ounce.

Though unit pricing has thus far been adopted largely as a competitive practice among supermarkets, it is likely that competitive pressures may also force the small, independent grocery store to follow suit.

Setting the Price

Although the retailer has some of his prices set for him by competitors' prices, manufacturers' or wholesalers' recommendations, and the existence of accepted or expected prices, he must still determine prices for many or most of the items he sells. In general, a retailer's selling price must cover the cost of goods (or landed cost), selling and other operating expenses, and a margin for profit.

Markup.   The difference between the cost of goods sold and selling price, as previously noted, is called markup or gross margin. Markup may be calculated for each item of merchandise, or the term may denote the average markup on all goods.[7] It may be expressed in dollars and cents or as a percentage. When expressed as a percentage, the calculation may be based on either cost or the retail price. Most retailers, however, state markup as a percentage of retail price. For example, if goods cost $0.50 and sell for $1.00, most retailers will call this a markup of $0.50 or 50 percent; if the goods cost $1.02 and sell for $1.50, the markup is expressed as $0.48 or 32 percent.

The calculation of markup as a percentage of cost makes it difficult to analyze one's business over a period of time. It is the percentage of what the retailer sells his goods for (*gross profit*) that is more meaningful, for that tells him how much of his sales dollar can be used to pay bills, and how much he will have left over for income (*net profit*).

Knowing the cost of goods and the average amount of markup needed to operate profitably, the retailer may use the following formula to determine the price to charge for an item:

$$\text{Retail price} = \frac{\text{Cost}}{100 - \text{Markup on retail}} \times 100$$

For example, if a retailer received a gross of T-shirts having a total cost of $172.80, and he wishes to provide for a gross margin of 36 percent (estimated expenses of 26 percent plus target profit of 10 percent), he would calculate his desired income from the sale of this merchandise as follows:

$$\frac{\$172.80}{100 - 36} \times 100 = \$270.00$$

Dividing this figure ($270.00) by 144 (a gross) yields a unit price of $1.88. However, the retailer would probably mark the T-shirts to the level of his next highest established price line, such as $1.89, or perhaps $1.98 or $2.00. A special promotion or other situation might require a price of less than this, but in such a case the retailer should recognize that these goods are marked below his average markup and attempt to compensate for this somewhere else.

Some retailers, particularly those of an older generation, follow the practice of expressing markup as a percentage of the cost. In this case, the calculation of retail

[7] The term *maintained markup* is often used when a distinction needs to be made between *initial markup* (as defined in the following section) and the gross margin on *actual* net sales.

price may be made by first converting the desired markup from a percentage of retail price to a percentage of cost. A convenient way of doing this is to use a "markup table," such as that illustrated in Table 18-4. This conversion may also be made by using the following formula:

$$\text{Markup on cost} = \frac{\text{Markup on retail}}{100 - \text{Markup on retail}} \times 100$$

Table 18-4. Markup Table

Markup as Percentage of Selling Price	Markup as Percentage of Cost	Markup as Percentage of Selling Price	Markup as Percentage of Cost
5%	5.26%	28%	38.89%
6	6.38	29	40.85
7	7.53	30	42.86
8	8.70	31	44.93
9	9.89	32	47.06
10	11.11	33	49.25
11	12.36	34	51.52
12	13.64	35	53.85
13	14.94	36	56.25
14	16.28	37	58.73
15	17.65	38	61.29
16	19.05	39	63.93
17	20.48	40	66.67
18	21.95	41	69.49
19	23.46	42	72.41
20	25.00	43	75.44
21	26.58	44	78.57
22	28.21	45	81.82
23	29.87	46	85.19
24	31.58	47	88.68
25	33.33	48	92.31
26	35.14	49	96.08
27	36.99	50	100.00

The derived percentage, whether read from a markup table or calculated by applying the above formula, is then multiplied by the cost of the article. This "markup" is then added to the cost of goods to arrive at the correct selling price.

For example, if the retailer wishes to price the T-shirts by this method (and in the absence of a markup table), he would compute his markup on cost as follows:

$$\frac{36}{100 - 36} \times 100 = 56.25\%$$

$$.5625 \times \$172.80 = \$97.20$$

Adding this markup ($97.20) to the cost of the goods ($172.80 per gross) yields $270.00, or a unit price of $1.88 (or, $270/144).

Markon.   For many goods the initial price the retailer sets must be high enough to allow for "retail reductions" such as stock shortages, markdowns, and discounts to employees, in addition to the cost of goods, operating expenses, and a margin of profit. The difference between the cost of goods and the first price placed on the goods is called the "initial markup" or "markon." Some goods require a higher mark-on than do others because of the need for larger allowances for reduction. Examples of goods which require high initial markups are: (1) high-fashion goods, which have a limited or unpredictable market; (2) seasonal and novelty items, because they seldom can be economically held over to another year; (3) goods easily damaged or soiled, such as delicate lingerie or white gloves; and (4) easily pilfered goods, such as pens or perfume.

To arrive at the initial retail price, a markon or initial markup percentage is figured as a percentage of the initial retail price. However, the markdowns, shortages, employees' discounts, expenses, and profits are customarily figured as percentages of net sales. Adjusting for this shift in the basis of percentages, the formula for deriving a markon percentage is:

$$\text{Markon } (\%) = \frac{\text{Gross margin } (\%) \ + \ \text{Retail reductions } (\%)}{\text{Net sales } (\%) \ + \ \text{Retail reductions } (\%)}$$

For example, for a retailer with operating expenses of 30 percent, a desired profit of 4 percent, and anticipated reductions of 6 percent, the markon percentage would be computed as follows:

$$\frac{34\% \ + \ 6\%}{100\% \ + \ 6\%} = \frac{40\%}{106\%} = 37.7\%$$

Thus when reductions are expected, to obtain a gross margin of 34 percent an initial markup (markon) of approximately 38 percent is needed. Once the average markon percentage for this class of goods is determined, it is applied to the cost of the goods in the same manner as a markup percentage is used to arrive at a selling price.

Although the retailer is not ordinarily able to price each item to cover its landed cost, expenses, retail reductions, and a fair margin of profit exactly, he should always consider these factors and aim to average the results of a line or class of goods, or at least a department, to achieve this goal. In the case of nonstandard goods, the small retailer's intimate knowledge of his customers will often enable him to select different styles for two or more retail prices from a lot of goods that all cost the same, or he may find it possible and necessary to sell for the same price lots of goods having different landed costs. These are both cases of averaging to achieve the desired gross margin.[8]

[8] For a further discussion of the relationships between price, volume, and profit, and various price policy considerations, see Edward L. Anthony, "Pricing and Profits in Small Stores," Small Marketers Aids Annual no. 2 (Washington, D. C.: Small Business Administration, 1960), pp. 36–42.

PRICING BY WHOLESALERS

In general, wholesale as well as retail prices are based on the markup or gross margin necessary to handle each line of goods profitably. Competition tends to keep margins small on staples, but larger margins are needed on lines affected by fashion or other influences resulting in large markdowns. Since wholesalers' prices[9] are much more sensitive than retail or factory prices, they may change frequently in many fields.

Most of the same forces afffect the prices and profits of wholesalers as operate at other levels of distribution, but some of them affect wholesalers in a distinctive way. For the customers of wholesalers, price is usually the determining factor in the buying decision. Price competition is more direct and more intense for wholesalers than at other levels of distribution. A wholesaler has many rivals, including the manufacturer who sells direct, the functional middlemen, and other wholesalers in the same or broader lines. Wholesalers' markets are well organized and are most sensitive to supply and demand factors. Since dealers buy and sell in large quantities a slight change in the price they pay involves substantial dollar amounts. Wholesale prices fluctuate much more than do retail prices or manufacturers' prices because wholesalers operate on narrower margins and are less able to absorb increases in cost, even over a short period of time.

The wholesaler carries so many thousands of items that he is most likely to use a formula approach to pricing broad groups of items. Such an approach sets the price of an item at its actual total cost plus a fair amount for profit. This cost includes the landed cost, and the expenses of buying, warehousing, selling, and administration. Since the latter are indirect costs they must be averaged in determining the gross margin to be added to the landed cost.

The wholesaler has several options in determining the "cost of goods." Some wholesalers use the average landed cost of the inventory on hand of an item at a particular time. Others use the landed cost of each shipment, or "first in, first out" method; or the landed cost of the most recent purchase, or "last in, first out" method. Since even small wholesalers purchase in large lots and prices may fluctuate greatly before the wholesaler has sold all of any one shipment, the method used in determining the cost of goods is a matter of considerable importance.

The wholesaler must also know what his competition is charging and, when necessary, must meet prices of rival firms. Some manufacturers seek to control resale prices on their products at both the wholesale and retail levels, and sometimes such control must be accepted or the dealer will not be allowed to market the product.

Even small wholesalers are likely to follow the varying price policy – that is, quoting different prices on the same merchandise to different buyers depending upon bargaining ability, size of order, and similar factors which can be substantiated under the legal requirements. Even under the one-price policy, actual

---

[9] The difference between *wholesale prices* and *prices charged by wholesalers* should be clearly understood by the reader. "Wholesale price" is a broad term to indicate the prices charged in all wholesale transactions, including the sales made by manufacturers, raw goods producers, and farmers, as well as those made by wholesale establishments.

prices may vary according to the services extended, such as credit and delivery. Usually a uniform discount schedule can be used, or a price schedule prepared for each grouping of services. Under the varying price policy it is desirable for the wholesaler's salesmen to have maximum and minimum prices for each product, and some incentive to sell at or near the maximum price whenever justifiable.

PRICING BY THE SERVICE ESTABLISHMENT

The variety of businesses classified as service establishments is enormous and among them the methods of determining price will differ greatly, but there are some concepts which should be useful in the wise pricing of all services whatever their character. Every service performed should contribute to the profit of the firm and bear its share of the expenses. Every service establishment should have a bookkeeping system which accurately records operating expenses and the cost of all materials used in providing the service. The manager must understand the distinction between direct costs (labor and materials, etc.) and indirect costs (rent, utilities, etc.) and have some suitable way to allocate the indirect costs to the cost per unit of service.

Sometimes there are special conditions in some areas of service that place limits on this approach to pricing, such as guild pricing used by barber and beauty shops, prevailing price schedules used by competing firms, or limitations placed by franchise agreements. When prices are fixed, the manager's challenge is to control costs and increase operating efficiency for maximum profits.

In the broad class of services, including personal service establishments and common repair or reconditioning plants, there usually will be several establishments of each kind with currently accepted prices for the basic or more standardized services.[10] Pricing in these fields often starts from fairly stable prices for a few of the usual services provided by each kind of business. For example, in dry cleaning plants a lady's plain dress and a man's business suit are commonly used as standards. Appliance and other repair services may take the typical cleaning and tuning-up job for a popular model of car, refrigerator, or radio, as the case may be, for the basic price. In barber shops a haircut is the same price whether it is an easy or complicated job. From these basic service prices a price schedule can be set up for other important and fairly standard services. Special jobs are priced according to the amount of labor required. In all cases adequate allowance must be made for wide variations in the amount of materials and supplies needed.

When prices are not based on well-known community standards the "multiplier method" of pricing may be used to fairly allocate indirect costs. It is particularly useful when the amount of service varies from customer to customer, and if the labor cost is the most significant item and the hourly wages do not vary greatly among the productive laborers. The multiplier is determined by dividing annual labor costs into annual total sales. A new firm may need to use estimates of costs and sales during a "trial run" period; adjustments can be made when actual figures are available.

[10] In some states minimum prices that may legally be charged for many kinds of personal services are set by state boards.

Three figures are multiplied to determine the price to charge for a particular job: (1) the worker's hourly pay, (2) time on the job, and (3) the multiplier. For example, if a welding and metalworking shop had annual sales of $25,000 and total productive labor costs of $10,000, and the average worker were paid $3 per hour, the multiplier and the price to be charged for a job which took 4 hours would be figured as follows:

$$\frac{\$25,000}{\$10,000} = 2.5$$

$$\$3 \times 4 \times 2.5 = \$30$$

To this amount would be added the costs of material required for the particular job.[11]

Because the multiplier is based on operating figures it must be kept up to date and reflect actual conditions.

Many small repair shops in the automobile, radio, appliance, and similar fields find that customers like flat-rate pricing. It can be used on 80 to 90 percent of the jobs that come to the average shop. Company agencies will ordinarily use the list prices suggested by the manufacturers they represent. Others may use published lists, or subscribe to a price-reporting service like those used by plumbing and heating contractors.

When price lists are published an average wage rate is the basis for the flat rate recommended for each service. The flat rate is based on the "standard" time to do the job, times the average wage rate, times a multiplier. If the local wage rate is very different from that used in a published list, flat-rate prices must be recalculated by substituting the local wage rate in the formula, but using the same multiplier as used in calculating the given list prices. The assumption is that a particular service industry will have similar indirect-cost-to-sales ratios.

Sometimes a small operator in applying wage rates to an industry formula for setting prices will use hourly rates that are too low. For example, a list may give the standard time for a particular job as $4\frac{1}{2}$ hours, the multiplier as 2, and the average hourly rate as $3. Thus the standard flat rate price would be $27 plus cost of materials used. A small operator may figure his price as follows: $4\frac{1}{2} \times 2 \times \$2$ (his hourly rate in dollars) = a flat price of $18. If his labor at $2 per hour is fully as efficient as the average $3-per-hour worker, he will be in the clear. The standard time is usually based on efficient labor skilled in the particular kind of work being priced.

PRICING FOR THE SMALL FACTORY

In manufacturing in general the price of each product is closely related to its cost of production. When only one product is made, unit cost is easily calculated by

[11] See Alfred A. Cox and Rowe M. Meador, "Pricing Your Services for Profit," *Small Marketers Aids Annual* no. 8 (Washington, D. C.: Small Business Administration, 1966), pp. 46–47.

dividing processing costs plus total costs of materials and parts for a given period by the number of units of product made during the same period. Then, to determine a minimum sales price, distribution or selling costs per unit plus a fair margin of profit must be added to unit production costs. A higher price than this minimum may be charged if there is a lack of competition, a demand greater than the company is able at present to supply, or the desire to create a prestige reputation. In setting a price above the calculated minimum there is always the danger of inviting competition. Usually it is better for the small business to figure a fair profit in the minimum calculation and to price at that point.

When two or more products are manufactured, cost accounting becomes necessary to arrive at the approximately correct minimum price for each product. Expenses are divided into two groups, fixed or overhead, and variable or direct; the sum of these two is the total unit cost. As volume increases, fixed or overhead expenses remain approximately the same in total amount but decrease per unit. Variable or direct expenses increase in almost direct proportion to increased volume but remain fairly constant per unit of output. Consequently, the cost of production can be decreased, per unit, in proportion to the relative importance of overhead or fixed costs. When additional products of a different nature can absorb some of this overhead, the effect is similar to that of manufacturing one product in greater volume.[12] When certain variable costs, such as that of raw materials, are small or even decrease with increased volume, as they may in the utilization of waste or by-products, actual additional costs of production for the by-product may be relatively very low. Finally, when several products are made in the same factory, the determination of unit costs becomes somewhat arbitrary, and standards for pricing should be shifted from so-called cost of production to other factors like competition, nature of demand for the product, and company pricing policy.

In pricing to meet competition the first question to decide is what competition the firm plans to meet. If a company has successfully differentiated its product, the pressure to meet direct price competition is greatly reduced. If there are products that nearly meet the same need as the company's product and are popular in the marketing area, competitive prices are necessary.

Another factor especially important for the small manufacturer to consider is the way competitors are likely to react to his prices. If pricing is keenly competitive and price changes take place frequently, it may be risky for the small business to take the lead in offering lower prices. At one extreme is a policy of administered prices, by which the leaders set their prices and stay with them for considerable periods of time. At the other extreme is the policy of meeting all price reductions and keeping prices at the lowest possible point. Between these extremes will be found the policies followed by the majority of companies.

The manufacturer, like the retailer, must understand the nature of his product and its elasticity of demand. It is well to remember that price is only one way in which the manufacturer can expand his market and should be emphasized only when it is more effective than advertising, personal selling, packaging, and changes in the quality level of the product. Frequently experimentation with customer response to different possible prices may be necessary to determine the relative

[12] See authors' discussion of the break-even and incremental cost and marginal income approaches to pricing, product-line diversification, and similar problems in Chapter 23.

importance of the price factor. In this experimentation competitors' actions should be noticed and care taken to avoid starting a price war.

Very often some pricing must be done before actual production takes place. This involves the necessity of estimating costs fairly accurately, because the price set will influence volume of sales; this in turn will react upon unit cost of production. Thus it is desirable to determine for each product the break-even point, beyond which further price reductions should not be made under existing conditions. It means that point at which the extra revenue obtained from increased volume just equals additional production plus marketing costs.[13]

Another condition likely to be encountered by the small manufacturer is that involving differential pricing. It may be desirable when the company's products are sold through two different types of outlets. For example, a small factory may contract to sell approximately half of its output to one large distributing organization, such as a mail-order house, chain store, or department store. Since these large firms perform the wholesaling functions and selling to them usually involves a low selling cost per unit of product, a low price can be quoted on this part of the plant's output. Pricing the rest of the product will follow the principles already discussed, except that in calculating costs of production allowance must be made for the fact that a large share of indirect or overhead expenses has already been absorbed by the sale of the large order. It is considered a violation of the Robinson-Patman Act to price the product to the large buyer so low that it does not include a proportionate share of overhead costs. A second consideration in such cases will be the effect of this dual distribution on the price necessary to induce individual dealers to handle the product. For the small manufacturer this may not be serious because the large distributor will probably resell the product under its own private brand name. It is only when the product is offered by the large distributor in easily identifiable form and in direct competition with individual outlets that pricing to the latter becomes a serious problem.

Another consideration in pricing by the manufacturer relates to the use of list prices from which discounts are granted, as compared to quoting direct net prices each time a sale is under consideration. The use of list prices has at least three advantages: (1) it suggests the retail price to the dealer; (2) it is often useful to the dealer in selling to the final consumer; and (3) it permits more flexibility in making price changes and quoting different prices to different buyers. A closely related question is the extent to which individual salesmen are to be given authority to determine prices at which the company's product will be sold.

Small factories, located in market centers for their type of product, often find it desirable to use wholesale price lines. When the goods produced are sold through retail stores that use price lines, as is the case with many articles of popular women's wear, this method of pricing is used. If the manufacturer thus has his prices determined for him, within narrow limits, his problem is the profitable manufacture of goods to sell at these price lines.

SUMMARY AND CONCLUSIONS

Pricing is a very important aspect of management. Most people are in business to make a profit. Profit is the difference between expenses and the price at which

---
[13] See Chapter 23.

goods or services are sold. The businessman should seek that exquisite point at which, with a particular sales volume, he will make the most profit.

For a businessman to set the "right" price which will result in the greatest profit, he must know his costs and his prices must reflect these costs. The wise businessman also recognizes that the more efficiently he is able to operate his business, and the better his costs are controlled, the larger will be his profit margin. When he sets his price there are many considerations affecting his decisions besides the cost of his goods and his operating expenses. These are (1) the nature of the product, (2) the amount of competition, (3) company policy, (4) business conditions, (5) market strategy, and (6) distribution methods.

When these factors are carefully evaluated the manager must weigh the role to be played by price in relation to the other marketing instruments such as advertising, packaging, product quality or distinction, and personal selling.

In general, price is the most dangerous of the major marketing instruments for the small businessman to use aggressively. This should not discourage carefully directed experimentation in pricing, but there is a need for careful study and understanding before changing prices or price policies.[14]

Not all goods can be priced for profit, but the aggregate price charged on all goods should yield a profit. Also, in some cases the volume of sales of certain items may provide substantial dollar profits even when the percentage markup on these items is low.

REVIEW QUESTIONS

1.   What can a small businessman do, in addition to his pricing policies, to expand the market for the goods he sells? Of all these factors — including price — which is the most important? Why?

2.   (*a*) What factors must be considered in the pricing policies of the firm in addition to costs? Describe how each may affect the price charged. (*b*) How do these factors differ in their effect on pricing policies in each of the principal types of business enterprise — merchandising, manufacturing, service?

3.   Explain and illustrate how marketing costs affect a manufacturer's pricing policies.

4.   Explain, or define, each of the following and describe how it affects a firm's pricing: (*a*) elasticity of demand; (*b*) expansibility of demand; (*c*) price lining; (*d*) markdowns.

5.   Compare and differentiate the following methods of pricing goods: (*a*) full-cost pricing; (*b*) gross-margin pricing; (*c*) "going rate" prices; (*d*) the "reasoned" approach.

6.   In what ways is the retailer restricted in his pricing policies?

7.   How should staple convenience goods be priced by the retailer? Shopping goods? Fashion and novelty goods?

8.   What is "unit pricing"? Illustrate.

9.   Differentiate between "markup" and "markon." How is each calculated?

[14] To help combat the rising tide of inflation, temporary federal wage-price controls were established in August, 1971, which place a ceiling on the prices which may be charged for various products; to this extent price experimentation is restricted.

10. Which do the authors believe is the preferred method of expressing markup or gross margin — as a percentage of cost, or as a percentage of retail price? Why? How may one percentage be converted to the other? Illustrate.

11. Why is price competition more direct and more intense for wholesalers than at other levels of distribution?

12. When are "multipliers" useful in price setting in a service establishment? Why are they used?

DISCUSSION QUESTIONS

1. If you were starting an entirely new kind of business, explain how you would endeavor to determine the most profitable prices to charge.

2. Name as many products and services as you can think of in which consumers rely chiefly on price as a guide to quality. Suggest probable reasons in each case.

3. In Bill's store dresses are priced at: $9.95, $14.75, $16.95, $19.75, and $22.95. The dress department data are: expenses, 30 percent; profit, 6 percent; and retail reductions, 12 percent. Landed cost of two dozen dresses just received is $180. At what initial retail prices should they be offered? Explain.

SUPPLEMENTARY READING

Haynes, W. Warren. *Pricing Decisions in Small Business,* Small Business Management Research Report prepared for the Small Business Administration. Lexington: University of Kentucky, 1961. Discusses pricing theory and methods, including full-cost pricing, flexible markups, gross margin pricing, suggested and "going rate" pricing. Brief cases illustrate various pricing problems faced by small businesses.

19

Advertising and sales promotion

Advertising, display, and personal selling constitute the major activities of selling; they are, with public relations, the major tools and methods of sales promotion. Perhaps the best definition, then, of sales promotion is that which describes it as the *effective coordination of all marketing activities having to do with the performance of the selling function.* The effectiveness of the coordination of time, effort, and money to achieve the efficient use of the sales dollar is the measure of success in sales promotion. Sales promotion is of vital importance to the business; but it must not be overemphasized to the neglect of the other functions, and it must be long-range as well as short-range in its viewpoint and approach. Good sales promotion is carefully planned and directed toward specific goals. Adequate records of promotion costs and sales volume should be maintained.

Sales promotion may be direct or indirect. Direct methods include a wide range of special sales promotions, personal selling, merchandising aids by manufacturers, publicity, advertising, and display. Indirect sales promotional devices are represented by customer services, favorable customer relations, product styling, packaging, and good public relations. Indirect methods pave the way for the increased effectiveness of direct methods.

To be continuously successful, sales promotion must be based on customer satisfaction, good customer relations, and sound sales policies. Only when customer relations are the best will advertising and other direct sales promotional efforts be completely successful. Effective sales promotion thus seeks to build goodwill as well as immediate sales.

PUBLIC RELATIONS

Public relations are those attitudes toward the public which are expressed in business behavior. Since every business by its very nature deals with the public, every business has a public relations program, whether or not it knows it.

These generalities may be observed concerning public relations efforts and results:[1]

1. Every person who in any way has anything to do with attitudes toward or contacts with the public, is creating good or bad public relations.
2. Public relations results can be measured to a degree by objective inquiry among customers and others affected.
3. Good public relations, as such, cannot be bought, except to the extent that advertising is a successful method of communication.
4. Public relations are built continuously and systematically, in terms of a well-developed philosophy carried out in wise store policies.

A business may create goodwill or ill will in the community. How the general public regards an enterprise may depend on the courtesy of its truckdrivers on city streets, the support given to a charity campaign, or whether the refuse of the business is properly disposed of. These and similar matters may determine whether a resident of a community will ever become a customer of the business.

Customer Relations

Those people from among the public who are attracted, who decide to buy, and later to rebuy, are the very life of a business. The objective of a business must be to attract and maintain a supporting clientele of satisfied user-customers.

Although customer satisfaction is the basis for the continued success of all business, casual observation of a large number of companies will show that this fundamental is often neglected. A large part of goodwill, that intangible asset which may be worth several thousand dollars to some firms, is the result of maintaining favorable customer relations. In big business goodwill usually accrues to the company or brand name; in the small business personal attributes of the owner are of relatively greater importance. How to establish good customer relations should be planned as carefully as any other major objective of the business.

An initial step is to define the company's customers and to recognize their likes and dislikes. Policies tailored to the customer will be an important means of building and maintaining good customer relations. For example, if a small manufacturing concern sells primarily to individual retailers, it may offend its customers by attempts in the company's advertising to gain the business of chain stores.

Other ways to secure good customer relations include the following: training employees in proper customer attitudes, over the telephone or in correspondence; strictly observing the company's product or merchandise guarantees; servicing the product after purchase when required; care and courtesy in handling customer accounts; providing services desired by customers, such as parking facilities; prompt answering of all inquiries; and scrupulously observing delivery dates and other promises.

[1] Raymond W. Miller and Robert W. Miller, "Public Relations for Small Business Owners," Small Marketers Aids Annual no. 3 (Washington, D.C.: Small Business Administration, 1961), pp. 48–55.

It is sometimes difficult for the employee to realize that to the patron or customer, he, the employee, *is* the store, the company, the firm. In the customer's mind, and in reality, the employee is delegated by management to represent the firm. Thus his behavior, representing the company as the customer sees it, can be constructive or destructive of the goals of the business.

Modern management provides routines and channels through which information regarding customer relations is continuously obtained. Some of these will be impersonal, such as customer surveys and periodic analyses of returned goods and of customer complaints and correspondence. In addition, executives as well as salespeople and other employees have personal customer contacts which provide a means of judging customer attitudes.

It has been said that the success of the businessman is in direct proportion to his desire, determination, and motivation to serve his fellow man. This need for devotion to service and for concern for the welfare of others, when combined with a respect for detail, gives that "something extra" that makes the customer desire to do business with one businessman rather than another.

Perhaps the most familiar example of this is the gas station proprietor who offers maximum service, as compared with his competitor who offers minimum service. The one offering the maximum anticipates the wishes of his customers. The one offering the minimum, or shall we say, grudgingly giving the minimum, must be *asked* to make the necessary or the desirable checkups for the customer. The repairman who works the full hour for which he charges, the supplier who anticipates when his customer may need another delivery, or the agent who checks with his client periodically to see if there are changes in a situation which may require an adjustment in the program provided — these are the people who understand what is meant by good customer relations.

Why do we as customers continue to patronize a given plumber, insurance man, barber, or clothing salesman? It is because he knows what we like and what we need. He makes our buying easier and he gives us a feeling of confidence and of security. He has dignified us by setting us apart from the crowd. The keeping of sales records and service records, and their constant analysis and use as guides to the offering of further service to the individual customer, is the "secret weapon" of many successful small businesses in sales promotion. The satisfied customer of long standing is the most valuable possession any business can have.

SPECIAL ASPECTS OF SALES PROMOTION

Without increasing his expenses a small businessman can promote sales through free publicity, timely displays, and special sales.

An alert businessman will use publicity to impress his public with the fact that he is continually seeking ways to give them better service. Dry cleaners in towns all over the country who attend the national convention to learn about new methods have their home-town newspapers carry news items to this effect. An apparel store in a southwestern town of 13,000 is operated by a man and his wife who make several trips to market each year. News items in the daily paper always report these trips with comments regarding the fashion showings to be attended. When the store became affiliated with a Los Angeles buying office a few years ago and the wife attended showings of California designers, the local newspaper publicized this step forward. Later, when their display director received high honors in a southwestern display convention in Dallas, Texas, the award was given ample free publicity to impress the "home folks" with the progressiveness of the store personnel. When the owner-manager of a small retail-wholesale jewelry business in the same town took several weeks away from his business to attend a school for advanced training in watchmaking and repair work, the paper carried an account of this and employees in the store commented on it to customers. Many local broadcasting stations have home-town news periods on which the activities of small businessmen and their employees are reported. A company picnic for employees, the promotion of John J. Jones, Jr., from salesman to buyer for the store, a new machine for testing radio and television sets installed in the local repair shop – these and similar items should be reported by the small businessman to his local paper or radio station. But they must be items of real news value even though the reason for giving them publicity is to keep the name of the business before the public in a favorable light.

An interesting example of the power of publicity may be seen in the case of a woman who had been making artificial flowers in her home two miles out of town on a main U.S. highway. A news release written about her by a reporter for the local newspaper was picked up by the Associated Press and reprinted in hundreds of newspapers throughout the country. Letters and orders began pouring in, and within a few weeks it was necessary to buy land across the road to construct a new "factory," to secure a business manager, and to start training employees to do the actual production. Form letters were printed to answer the avalanche of inquiries and orders, the process of taking out domestic and foreign patents on the production process was begun, and a brand name was adopted. All this was accomplished without the expenditure of one penny for advertising

Special Events

The distinguishing feature of successful promotions is their timeliness, either when planned in advance for certain days or seasons or when capitalizing on some unexpected development. Merchants have available to them calendars of suggested promotional events, usually prepared several months in advance by the trade association in the field, which give all important dates likely to be useful in staging promotions. Most of these are published in trade journals and in dealer material released by wholesalers.[2]

Sometimes the nature of the business provides opportunity for timely promotions of seasonal merchandise. Feed dealers, for example, time their promotions with the planting, cultivation, or marketing of customers' (farmers') products; auto accessory stores time their promotions to the weather and the vacation use of the family car.

Games and contests of local interest afford opportunities for timely tie-ins, often through displays in the small business. A scoreboard displayed in the store may

---

[2] *Annual Time Table of Retail Opportunities* (New York: Bureau of Advertising, American Newspaper Publishers Association) suggests ad timing and practices for advertising. (Published annually and available from member newspapers.)

keep customers informed on the progress of a local team. Some merchants place a radio in the store for customers to hear reports of important games that are broadcast.

Another group of promotional ideas, such as anniversary sales, relate to the company itself. The established business should keep records of each promotion and consult these records in planning future events. Contrary to popular belief, previously successful promotions of a seasonal or recurring nature are more likely to be effective when repeated than are entirely new ones. Each new promotion is an experiment that may or may not prove successful. Since the customers of one store do not change greatly from year to year, an event that has proved its appeal to the customers once is very likely to succeed several times more. Of course details may be changed, but the basic idea of the promotion will remain the same. This should not discourage careful experimentation, but it should be a warning against seeking change merely to be different.

The range of themes or ideas useful in building sales promotions is unlimited. Each issue of the trade journals contains suggestions and stimulating ideas from nearly every field of retailing. Often ideas developed by large city stores can be used to advantage by the small store, such as having customer juries select 100 perfect gifts for Christmas from the store's offerings. A useful approach to planning sales promotions is to follow a checklist to provide for all details and proper timing. Important points to be included are the following:

1. Opening and closing dates
2. Name of promotion and any explanations needed
3. Merchandise to be featured
4. Complete plans for advertising and window and interior displays, including coordination of media and use of all appropriate devices — signs, price cards, window streamers, banners, special layout, and display
5. Organization plans — including staff meetings, employee incentives, and provisions for extra help or special training

Trading Stamps

The trading stamp has become an increasingly important means of attracting trade in recent years. The idea is very old and its popularity has risen and fallen, over the past 50 years particularly. Basically, it is a payment of a "commission" to customers on their patronage through the issuance of stamps, usually one stamp for each ten cents of purchases. These stamps are saved by the customer and pasted in a book provided by the merchant. A completed book of several hundred stamps may be exchanged for cash, for gifts, or for merchandise. The stamps are usually sold to the merchant by specialized trading-stamp companies, who also redeem the stamps accumulated by customers.

The actual cost to the seller of stamps issued to customers is very low, even in those few cases where stamps are carefully saved and redeemed by great numbers of customers. Not all customers request or even accept the stamps, and in some instances do not bother to accumulate and bring in completed books. The popularity of stamps varies by areas and may be influenced by income level of the community or by the competitiveness of rival merchants and service businesses.

Arguments for and against trading stamps are plentiful. The purveyor who considers them as a means of cultivating and maintaining patronage may well ask himself these questions:

1. Would this promotional expense be in addition to an established program or would it replace a part of it?
2. Would the addition of this cost to each sales transaction call for increased prices?
3. What types of stores in the area are now using trading stamps and what customers do they attract?
4. Are there already great numbers of people in the area familiar with this "brand" of stamps, or would advertising the idea of stamps be an expensive undertaking in itself?

Trading stamps can be, and apparently are in most cases, a valuable device for attracting and maintaining patronage.[3] In general, it would seem that results depend on the local popularity of the stamps, the degree to which the prospective buyer chooses to make his purchases in those establishments which offer them primarily because they are offered there, and the degree to which they can be offered by the seller as a normal advertising expense without interfering with other promotional activities, with his prices, or with his profits.

ADVERTISING

Advertising includes those activities by which oral and visual messages are directed to the public for the purpose of informing and influencing them either to buy or act favorably toward the subject featured. Profit-minded businessmen use advertising because it is a quick and convincing way to increase sales. Although advertising is a tool which big business uses to great advantage, it can be a powerful force for the small businessman as well.

Since advertising is a message directed to a particular group of people, a basic principle to follow is to know your market. Careful selection of the logical prospects for a particular advertisement should be one of the first steps in planning. The message or theme and its form of presentation in copy, illustration, and layout, as well as the appropriate media to use, all depend primarily upon the particular group to be reached by each advertisement. A great deal of advertising would be much more effective if the businessman exerted effort to make certain the objective of his advertisement is sound.

Probably the greatest single waste in modern advertising results from the careless preparation of many advertisements and sales campaigns. Recognition of this fact has led an increasing number of businessmen to take steps toward testing and measuring the effectiveness of their advertising. Keeping adequate records of all advertisements and relevant conditions at the time each is released is important. Some retailers make a practice of asking each new customer how he happened to come to the shop. An analysis of these results as a basis for planning future advertising increases the number of successes and reduces errors.

[3] According to a 1969 nationwide public opinion survey of consumer attitudes toward trading stamps, conducted for the Sperry and Hutchinson Company by a leading market research organization, approximately 78 percent of U.S. families save such stamps.

Frequently it is possible for the small businessman to pretest advertisements before they are released on a large scale. This may be done by using a less expensive, more easily controlled medium like a display, handbills, or direct mail to test the effectiveness of various elements of the advertisement before completing it in final form for use in such media as newspapers. Another plan, sometimes called "elements research," is an adaptation of split-run testing as used by national advertisers. If the element to be tested is the headline, one-half of a sample mailing will receive the circular with one headline and the other half with another. On the next mailing the "heads" will be reversed. Results of each mailing will be carefully recorded, either by inquiries received or by calls in the store if a retailer is working the test. Comparison will show which headline is the more effective. Copy, illustration, or the theme to use may be tested in a similar manner.

Two types of advertising are recognized, according to primary purpose or objective, as *institutional* (selling the business) and *direct action* (selling the merchandise, product, or service the business has to offer). Both are necessary, although the small businessman will usually devote most of his limited advertising funds to the promotional or direct-action type. Selling the business and selling the goods are in many respects similar. Some businessmen will wish to promote many aspects of the business, while others will emphasize only one or a few. Some of the business attributes that advertising may sell are: services, integrity, brands carried, courtesy, business success, credit terms, prestige, location, size, price, quality, and fashion policies.

Some businesses seek to set themselves up in the public mind as possessing all virtues. As this is difficult to do, the wise business operator stresses one or two at a time. Likewise, in presenting merchandise it is easier to convince the prospective buyer that it has the one or two outstanding things he really wants than that it is the paragon of all virtues.

There are several basic factors a small businessman in particular should bear in mind about advertising:

1. Advertising is much more than simply laying out an effective advertisement or writing a clever sales talk.
2. The kind of advertising that is best for some types of business may not be right for others.
3. Money can be wasted in advertising by failing to have adequate information about potential customers, by poor advertising copy and layout, by unwise choice of advertising media, by spending too high a proportion of gross income, and in other ways.

Laying the Groundwork

The first step in advertising is to learn as much as possible about the market to which the advertisement will be directed. The businessman can begin by asking himself these questions:

1. Who are my potential customers?
2. How many are there?
3. Where are they located?

4. Where do they now buy the things or services I want to sell them?
5. Can I offer them anything they are not getting now? What?
6. How can I convince them they should do business with me?

A businessman should never cease to "survey" or study his customers. Neighborhoods and customers' habits change. If a customer drifts away, the businessman should try at once to find out why.

Consumers may not realize a need for certain products until "educated" by advertising. This is nearly always true of new products for which extensive pioneering advertising may be required. This explains in part why advertising expense may be higher during the first few years. However, if consumers do not want a product or service, advertising alone cannot *make* them buy.

Advertising has a cumulative effect. Response is slow at first but increases with time. Sporadic splurges rarely pay. It is much better to advertise regularly and continuously on a small scale than to use large advertisements infrequently.

How Much to Advertise?

Determining the right amount to spend for advertising is important because this expense is a major one. For the small business it is especially important that limited funds be used to the best possible advantage. Once the amount available for advertising is decided upon, a more intelligent campaign can be planned, involving the determination of items to promote, prospects to seek, media to use, and frequency of releases.

For a business in an established field, operating ratios are valuable guides in determining how much to spend. However, these are guides, not absolute standards. Many profitable stores and shops spend more than the standard for their fields. The correct amount of money to budget for advertising will depend upon the job to be done and the funds available.

Advertising Aids

Freelance specialists or independent small businessmen specializing in copywriting, layout, commercial art or illustration, photography, research, and display work are available in many cities. Their services may be secured for a fee as needed. This group forms an important segment of the outside staff for small businessmen, providing services similar to those of public accountants, bookkeeping firms, and others. For certain types of advertising, such as signs, handbills, and circulars and other direct-mail pieces, additional agencies stand ready to help the advertiser.

Valuable aids, prepared by manufacturers or commercial services, are "mats," which are heavy-paper impressions of complete advertisements or of advertising illustrations, headlines, or copy. From such mats the local printer can make the stereotypes (metal plates) used in printing the advertisements. Producers often help dealers who handle their products by furnishing them with mats to use in local advertising. These may be distributed direct to the retailer or through the wholesaler, trade association, or resident buying office. Usually they are available to the local merchant free of charge. Since they are prepared centrally for nationwide distribution, advertising specialists may be employed and information about the product and its selling features incorpoporated in the advertisement much more effectively than the local advertiser could do it. Mats are flexible, permitting the local advertiser to make such changes as he needs or desires. Even when little or none of the actual mat is used, valuable suggestions for advertising themes, copy, illustrations, and layout may be obtained from it. Trade journals often present suggested advertisements based on centrally prepared mats that may be obtained by the retailer on request.

Commercial mat services are available to the small advertiser either by direct subscription or through the advertising department of his local paper. Most lines of retailing and service businesses may find adequate the mats furnished at no extra cost by services subscribed to by the newspaper. These mat services are very comprehensive in covering the lines of business that do local newspaper advertising. Each month the subscribing paper receives a large book illustrating all the accompanying mats. This makes it very easy for the small advertiser to select material appropriate to his needs.

In addition to a score of mat services with broad business coverage, there are many more that serve particular lines of business, such as fashion apparel, furniture, foods, and some service fields. Subscription to one of these services by the small businessman may be a good investment when similar material is not available through his local paper, trade association, or other organization.

Advertising Media

Newspapers and radios are considered "mass" media. Though they are not always suited to the advertising needs of the small business, limited amounts of advertising in such media may be useful.

In appraising advertising media, or comparing them in effectiveness, the prospective advertiser should consider the following:

1. *Cost per contact* — How much is it actually costing to reach a prospective customer?
2. *Frequency* — How frequent are these contacts or message deliveries? In this business, is the single powerful advertisement preferable to a series of constant small reminders, or vice versa?
3. *Impact* — Does the medium in question offer full opportunities for appealing to the appropriate senses, such as sight and hearing in presenting design, color or sound?
4. *Selectivity* — To what degree can the message be restricted to those people who are known to be most logical prospects?

There are many contracting possibilities in media. The newspaper and radio offer broad geographical coverage of the general public, while direct mail is the most selective. The radio commercial may reach hundreds of thousands, only a few of whom are possible customers. An expensive direct-mail piece may reach only a limited number, yet the cost per contact may be the same. The extent to which the prospect can be readily identified beforehand will influence the choice of media. If unidentifiable, newspaper, radio, or TV advertising may cause him to reveal himself; if identifiable, the expensive direct-mail piece might be the best investment. These considerations are a few of the fundamental decisions concerning advertising media.

Newspapers.   Small stores located in medium-sized and small communities are most likely to find newspaper advertising valuable. Following are some of the things that can be done to make it profitable:

1. Buy space at the best rates. Often advertising will cost less if more space is purchased. For example, if the campaign calls for 45 inches of column space at a rate of $4 an inch, the cost will be $180. A study of the publication's rate card might reveal that 50 inches can be run at a rate of $3.50 an inch or a total cost of $175.
2. Do not scatter advertising. Skipping around from one publication to another seldom gets results. It destroys the effectiveness of consecutive advertising and, most important, loses the handling and consideration privileges afforded the consistent advertiser. This makes a great deal of difference when it is desirable to secure a favorable position for the advertisement.
3. Check circulation figures closely. The smaller the newspaper, the more chance of padded circulation. It is good business practice to demand certified statements as to how the total circulation figure is broken down. The *Standard Rate and Data Service,* which is published monthly in Chicago and found in many libraries, gives the total net paid circulation of a paper as well as the circulation by city zone and by retail trading zone.

The classified sections of most local newspapers present an opportunity for the businessman with a limited advertising budget. Because this form of advertising is not used by the large, integrated store operator, we may conclude that the "little fellow" has obtained his money's worth from it, for if the medium had failed to produce results, its use would have been discontinued.

Telephone-book classified sections.   Most telephone directories have a special section, commonly known as the "yellow pages," in which the local businessman may advertise his goods and services. Such advertisements are little different from those in newspapers except that they are more likely to be illustrated and to depart in other ways from a straight, agate-line appearance.

One insertion in a telephone book continues to function as an active advertisement until the next issue appears. The telephone book stays in the home or office, ready to serve as a source of information on where to buy anything. Every business that has a telephone receives without charge a one-line insertion in the classified section of the book. Any further advertising must be paid for.

Radio.   Radio advertising can and does sell goods for the small retail merchant. What many small businessmen do not know is that "spot" announcements cost as little as $3.50 each on some of the small local stations that reach a large proportion of the local market. These, now comprising the majority of the commercial stations in the United States, have a power of less than 1,000 watts and are therefore unable to reach beyond a limited geographical area. This limitation is an advantage to the small retailer, because when he buys time on such a station he has little waste circulation. The programs of the local station are directed to the market in his area. The best way to get the complete story of radio costs is to visit the radio broadcasting office, examine the station's rate card, and have a talk with an authorized representative of the station. In addition, the *Standard Rate and Data Service* will furnish the prospective radio advertiser with cost information.

The advertiser must give attention to the type of person he wishes to reach – including age, sex, and profession – before selecting the kind of program he wants and the time to put it on the air. Information of this type is provided by the A. C. Nielsen Company of Chicago. The *Nielsen Service Report* includes (1) the weekly audience of each station for each county or other economic area; (2) the composition of the weekly audience with respect to economic status, race, home ownership, and so on; (3) out-of-home listening; (4) homes reached per minute by large, network-affiliated radio stations; and (5) radio and TV ownership. The cost of the advertisement will be affected by the time of the day it is used, the power of the station, the population of the area covered by the station, the number of times it is used, and its length.

Unless the advertiser uses an agency, usually all he need do as far as writing the commercials is concerned is to tell the radio station time salesman that he would like to publicize a certain sale or a product that day or week. The station man gathers the details and writes the commercials without additional cost to the advertiser.

If the businessman wants an entire program, the radio station will suggest popular types that may be sponsored, or the advertiser may suggest a program himself. The national networks have "co-op" shows that are originated by the networks themselves but which are sponsored locally. Commercials are inserted by the local announcer when the network gives the cue.

Television. Television is the fastest-growing advertising medium. In its infancy (up to the mid-1950s), the cost of TV time to the potential small advertiser was prohibitive. However, the rapid growth of the television industry has caused the small enterpriser to focus new attention upon it. The mere fact that in 1972, 95 percent of all homes in the United States had one or more TV sets provides evidence of its effectiveness as an advertising medium.

Spot announcements or some type of cooperative sharing of program expenses are probably feasible. For example, a 10-second spot announcement on a Cedar Rapids TV station costs from $8 to $67, depending on the time of day. Other possibilities are (1) dual or cosponsorship, (2) alternate-week sponsorship, (3) participating sponsorship, or (4) regional sponsorship.

Television costs when prorated against the coverage of a potential market may be lower than many other media. For this reason, even the small advertiser cannot afford to overlook this powerful force.

Signs. Signs used to identify the place and kind of business represent one of the oldest advertising media. This type of advertising is well suited to reaching the buyer while he is traveling about the neighborhood on foot, by bus, or by automobile.

Some authorities consider the ideal outdoor advertising medium for the small retailer to be the hand-painted sign on a board located as near to his store as possible, preferably on the side of his building. Such a sign has the advantage of relative permanence, but it also has the disadvantages of fixed copy, since it is more difficult to change a hand-painted sign than a poster panel.

The outdoor poster is made in two sizes, the 24-sheet poster and the 3-sheet poster. The 24-sheet poster makes the familiar large signs that may be seen along any highway, mounted on a substantial steel or heavy wooden poster-panel structure 11 feet high and 25 feet long.

The 3-sheet poster can be effectively displayed on the side of a building. It is well suited to use by the small retailer. A space 4 feet, 10 inches by 8 feet, 7 inches is required for the whole display, including the frame. Such a poster makes a good point-of-purchase reminder or a colorful supplement to mail, newspaper, and handbill advertising. There are approximately 12,000 poster plants set up to handle such work in this country.

At one time or another nearly every member of the family uses the bus or subway and reads the advertising cards for lack of something more interesting to do. This is an effective advertising medium for the small, local business enterprise.

Storefront signs are often provided by manufacturers whose product or equipment is carried or used by the small establishment. Such signs naturally contain the name of the manufacturer as well as that of the local businessman. Many small retail and service establishments and most factories prefer to erect their own building sign which features the name of the firm or its business exclusively. It may feature package reproductions, neon lights, or other attention-getting displays.

Point-of-purchase signs may easily be used to excess, especially when the small businessman is too lenient in permitting every salesman to put up his own signs. The cluttered appearance of many small shops is testimony to this danger. Useful guides to follow are: make each sign justify its space in terms of sales volume or profit to the business; require that it harmonize with the "atmosphere" and overall appearance of the establishment; and reserve all spaces needed for the firm's own signs or other business uses.

Handbills.   Handbills can be a very effective and inexpensive form of advertising for small businessmen. They are especially useful for announcing the opening of a new neighborhood business, for periodic reminders of the merchandise or services offered, and for advertising special sales. Handbills should be planned carefully as to layout, message or appeal, headline, and appearance. A good printer can give advice on the quality of paper to use, overall appearance, size, cost, and similar factors, but should not be depended on for the sales message or copy of the advertisement. The printer, however, should be carefully selected since he can render many valuable services to the beginning advertiser.

Since the use of handbills is likely to be undertaken partly because of low cost, there is a real danger that efficient distribution may be neglected. It is advisable to select reliable distributors and pay adequately for the work. Either the owner or some other competent adult should supervise distribution. In many cities organized handbill distributors may be employed who will guarantee effective circulation.

Direct mail.   Direct mail can be defined as *the controlled distribution of a written message to a selected audience.* Compared with other media it allows more *flexibility* in promotional costs, and *selectivity* in choosing prospects. It provides a *personal* sales message.

Postal laws in this country provide special rates which allow businessmen to use this highly effective medium at a minimum cost.

The small businessman should make his direct mail advertising as personal, informal, and selective as possible. Careful study of charge account and delivery records, as well as the owner's personal knowledge of his customers, should make it possible to classify most of his clientele into groups based on their common buying interest. Direct-mail pieces can be thoughtfully worded in such a way as to have a strong appeal to each customer and create the impression of individualized attention.

Although as many as ten different forms of direct mail advertising are recognized, the most important for the average small businessman are envelope enclosures, mailing cards, and postcards. Envelope enclosures include the direct sales letter, self-addressed return card or envelope, and folders or booklets to supplement the letter.

A mailing card can be used to advantage for making an announcement in a dignified manner. It may be printed either with or without illustration on stock of good quality. Appropriate uses include announcing the addition of a new line of goods, the arrival of new models, or a change of business address. A mailing card of superior quality should be enclosed in an appropriate envelope and first-class postage should be used.

Many small-scale advertisers have made effective use of the postcard. It is an ideal direct-mail form for the retailer with a good prospect list and a limited budget. A good layout that combines well-selected type with a line-cut illustration presents a concise sales story and can carry on an excellent and economical sales campaign. A series of such messages mailed on a systematic follow-up basis is likely to produce a telling effect. In the presentation of the message, consumer benefits should be stressed in a friendly person-to-person manner. Each letter should contain all the essential information necessary to make the prospect want the offering. Descriptive folders or small booklets may be enclosed to supplement the letter.

Nearly two dozen shapes and sizes of enclosures are used in direct-mail work. Each variety has its advantages and special uses. For example, the "broadside" (a large sheet of paper, usually 25 by 38 inches) is very effective for creating a dramatic effect. The large size of broadsides makes it possible to use showmanship methods effectively. When the nature of the advertisement makes a reply by the prospect desirable, make it easy for the recipient to act by enclosing a return postcard or envelope. Whether to use a stamped, self-addressed card or envelope, or to take advantage of postal provisions permitting "postage guaranteed" returns, should be studied. The former is cheaper per letter, but the latter often costs less in the end, since usually not all the cards or envelopes are returned.

Direct mail is more expensive per message delivered than publication advertising, but when used properly it can be an inexpensive method of reaching selected groups. The mailing list is of the utmost importance. If it is necessary to economize, most authorities recommend using a less expensive mailing piece and the best possible mailing list. Each name on the list should represent a live prospect for the goods advertised. It is important to keep the mailing list current and to make every effort to have titles and first names correct.

Repetition will ultimately drive home the message. A single piece of direct-mail advertising may bring results, but it is a proved fact that regularly repeated mailings will do a better selling job.

SALES PROMOTION IN RETAILING

The small retailer's close personal contact with his customers provides many advantages in developing a well-coordinated program of sales promotion, based on customer satisfaction and good customer relations. The right merchandise and services consistent with the store's policies, backed up by qualified personnel, competent salesmanship, and a suitable physical plant, furnish the framework for effective sales promotion.

Salesmanship and Physical Factors

The retailer's challenge may be aptly summarized in the often quoted definition of good retail salesmanship: "Selling goods that won't come back to customers who will." Improving the quality of retail salesmanship seems to be a never-ending process. Surveys made by trade associations, schools of retailing, and others dealing with customer likes and dislikes and effective selling have consistently shown the importance of the salesperson and the quality of his sales training. The small retailer can secure help in sales training from representatives of his suppliers and from the distributive-education program if there is one in his community.

Everything about the physical plant and equipment — its appearance, "atmosphere," temperature, lighting, displays, and facilities for transportation between floors — contributes to customer comfort and convenience and will also influence the clientele's attitude toward the store.

Building Good Customer Relations

Alert retailers build favorable customer relations in many ways. Among other things, they

1. greet as many customers as possible by name;
2. have a personal word or two with customers, when possible;
3. greet customers immediately when they enter the store even though they must wait;
4. take the greatest care to assure the utmost courtesy in handling customers, even the difficult ones — all staff members avoid giving a flat "no" to a request for merchandise not in stock;
5. give special consideration to the tired shopper;
6. avoid the patronizing phrase, "We can let you have . . . ;" and say instead, "We will see that you get . . . .";
7. express genuine regret when unable to supply customers' requirements; and
8. consult customers regarding ways of improving service.

The care and courtesy exercised by nonselling employees will also affect the customer's attitude. If the merchandise is delivered in good condition at the promised or expected time by courteous, neat-appearing employees using attractive delivery equipment, goodwill is created. It is well that the representative, whether he be delivery man, credit officer, shipping clerk, installer, or repairman, remember that in the customer's thinking, and as of that contact, he *is* the company.

Although the small retailer is in close personal contact with his customers and thinks that he understands what they want, he may be wrong in this reasoning because (1) many customers do not express their wants or even dislikes, and (2) potential customers may be avoiding the store for causes unknown to the merchant. It is good business to study surveys of customers' wants as well as to analyze causes of complaints. Good customer relations are possible only with courteous, conscientious employees, and an application of good retailing practices from the stocking of the right goods at the right price in the right amounts, to properly wrapped and/or delivered goods which are correctly billed to the customer.

Moving Slow Items

Every store will at times have some slow-selling items that can be sold through proper promotions before they result in a loss. The merchant need not rely solely on price reductions to move such items. Showmanship and the creation of a "bargain atmosphere" may also offer advantages, if wisely done. The following suggestions are worthy of consideration:

1. Mass-display the product at the best traffic spot, even if it means separation from other brands of like classification.
2. Use hanging banners and pennants, strung from wall to wall, to promote "shelf-warmers."
3. Focus attention of customers on slow movers with different-colored price tags.
4. Focus colored spotlights on special mass displays.
5. Advertise that customers get a package of the featured item free if a clerk forgets to tell her about it. This makes both customers and employees conscious of the product.
6. Mass-display full cases offered at discounts of 5 percent or 10 percent on case lots.
7. Sell a "pig-in-a-poke" bag of slow movers for a nominal price.
8. Tell the truth in advertising or display material. Say, "I want to get rid of this stuff, so here's a bargain"; "We made a mistake and bought too much — take some away and we'll give you a bargain"; "The quality is good, but we no longer can get this brand — clean out what's left."
9. Advertise "certified bargains." Produce the original bills showing what you paid for goods now offered as bargains. Also show what you charged for them previously.
10. Gather all items that can be offered at a uniform price. Emphasize: "Look what 89¢ will buy." or "Look what 10¢ will buy."
11. Hold a penny sale: "One for 18¢ — two for 19¢."
12. Put slow movers beside fast movers. Contrast the two by sharply cutting prices of the merchandise you are trying to move.
13. Set up an automatic price system. Keep reducing prices by a fixed percentage every week until the merchandise is sold.

Promotion Gimmicks

For a period of three weeks a Phoenix, Arizona, carpet shop had laid a nylon carpet in front of the gas pumps of a nearby service station for cars and trucks to drive over, dripping oil and grease. The carpet was then removed, half of it cleaned, and put on display for customers to see. An ad heralded the laying and removal of the carpet. They proved that the carpet looked like new after being cleaned, and a good volume of this carpeting was sold following the promotion.

A Sioux City furniture store decorated its premises with balloons for one of the firm's most successful promotions. Inside each balloon was a discount slip guaranteeing the customer a discount on his purchase. After a customer made a purchase, he was allowed to select one balloon to puncture. Inside he would find a slip discounting his cost, ranging from 5 percent to one balloon with a 100 percent discount. They named the promotion the "Count Down" and customers were encouraged to be at the store for the "blast off." An eight-column newspaper advertisement promoted the event and guaranteed "no duds."

The key letter in a Cleveland department store's full-page ad was the "s" in "Foundation Departments." Designed to attract teenage shoppers, the ad applied to both the junior intimate apparel and the foundation departments. Announcing a drawing for a free ski weekend in the Laurentians, the ad also invited girls to drop in for a free figure analysis and booklets on grooming. Registration was open for a full week in both departments. The merchandise included girdles and bras from standard lines. These were not special teen sizes but regular merchandise isolated for special promotion aimed at teenage customers.

The closed-door "party" promotion held on the sales floor is becoming very popular. A limited group is invited to a "party" after normal store hours. Ice cream, cake, sandwiches, coffee, and the like are served while the group watches product demonstrations and learns about special features of merchandise.

To encourage self-service in the electric housewares section, one store uses elaborate "Tell-all" fact tags and large posters which graphically compare the various brands regarding features, cost, performance, and so on.

The stereo demonstration room, well insulated from the noise of the main floor, is proving helpful in moving higher-priced stereo equipment. Many retailers serve coffee or soft drinks in this room.

Few stores capitalize sufficiently on the news value of new merchandise. One store features "Just arrived" fashion merchandise in a main window. Another outlet has a special section set aside for new items.

For lunch-hour shoppers, one store stages fast-moving, 10-minute fashion shows every half-hour. The schedule permits attendance regardless of when the shopper's lunch hour begins, and still leaves time for shopping.

Retail Advertising

For the retailer, timeliness, advertising the right merchandise, selecting the best theme, and providing good window and interior displays are important.

Timing.   Timing the release of fashion advertising should be related to the store's position in the merchandise acceptance curve or fashion cycle. Fashion leaders in the community advertise heavily at the very beginning of the selling season; those catering to the middle class advertise just before the peak of the selling period; and stores in the "economy" group put out their ads just after the selling crest has been passed.

For staple merchandise and special sale events, advertising should be timed to fit in with paydays and shopping habits of customers for stores serving the lower- and average-income groups; those catering to the upper-income brackets will be more concerned with tax dates and special customer preferences.

Selecting the merchandise to advertise. Selecting the right merchandise to advertise is of great importance to the retailer because only about 15 to 20 percent of all goods carried are suitable for external advertising. Not only should goods selected produce enough sales of the advertised articles to cover the direct cost of advertising, but they should also attract to the store customers who will buy unadvertised merchandise. In other words, advertising should attract shopping traffic of regular customers rather than bargain hunters or specific item buyers exclusively.

Selecting items to advertise may be done in many ways. Preference should be given to goods representative of the store's character and with an established appeal. The store's record of past sales, advertising, want slips, customer complaints, and adjustments may be used for selecting the product to advertise. For new items customer response to display is considered the best guide. Opinions of buyers and salespeople are useful guides if time will not permit test displays before advertising.

Choosing a theme. To help in deciding upon the theme to be used in advertising, buyers should state the features about each article that caused them to buy it for the store. Current practice is to require each buyer at the time he purchases new merchandise to secure from the vendor the "sizzle" or selling story for each article. Salespeople should also be able to give valuable suggestions as to what features of the merchandise would be most attractive and interesting to customers. The question, "What advertisable features does the merchandise have?" should be asked before it is purchased by the store's buyers.

Naturally, certain merchandise suggests its own theme, such as fashion rightness, authenticity, or economy. Experience has shown, however, that such "obvious" points of appeal as durability, strength, economy, or assumed use of the article may differ widely from the *real* reasons why customers buy particular merchandise. Careful and continuous investigation is the safest course to follow.

Coordination of sales effort. Customers attracted by advertising can be encouraged to buy additional merchandise by attractive displays, informative signs, point-of-purchase advertising, and circulars, handouts, or lists of unadvertised items placed in convenient traffic locations throughout the store. Interior displays should be in character with the store and its merchandise. Appealing displays of impulse items adjacent to each listed item, as well as to merchandise displayed externally, will give real meaning to the expression, "It pays to advertise."

Window displays. Most authorities agree that windows are usually an indispensable advertising medium. Showing the merchandise in three dimensions, in all its true color and beauty, is a strong point in displays. Since they are at the point of sale, displays serve as reminder advertising in addition to stimulating impulse buying.

If any merchandise in the window fails to result in the volume of sales expected, it should be replaced at once — even in the middle of a busy selling day — by items that will produce the desired results. Not only is window display space the most valuable advertising space in the store, but goods on display help to make up the "face" of the store that impresses traffic.

Displays should be tied in with national advertising whenever possible. This may be accomplished in many ways, such as by timing displays to appear during national campaigns, and by including pages from the national media or placards stating, "As advertised in *Vogue*," and the like. Seasonal displays are usually effective, offer opportunities for originality and related item selling, and help to build the store's reputation for merchandising alertness. Important promotions in the community, such as National Cotton Week, Mardi Gras, Mother's Day, or Days of the Forty-Niners, can offer profitable advertising themes.

Interior displays.   Interior displays should always have price cards and usually informative signs. For impulse and convenience goods, mass displays are very effective, especially the jumbled type with nothing for the customer to knock down when selecting articles from the display. Grocers have found that the effectiveness of mass displays is noticeably increased by the addition of advertising placards calling attention to featured goods and giving the price. If the offering is a special-price feature and there is a time or quantity-per-customer limit, this information should also be given.

As a rule, the display cards and other dealer helps offered by manufacturers and distributors should be utilized, because they provide authentic sales information about the goods and provide space for pricing. Such dealer helps represent extensive and often expensive study to discover the appeal that will be most effective in presenting a product to the public, and they contain tested catch lines that are bound to help sell the goods.

Advertising of credit terms.   The advertising of credit terms is regulated by the 1969 Consumer Credit Protection Act. By the terms of this legislation, a retailer is prohibited from advertising that an installment plan or a specific down payment or amount of credit can be arranged unless the retailer *usually* arranges terms of that type. In addition, no advertisement may allude to a specific credit term, such as "No Money Down" or "36 Months to Pay," unless *all other* related terms are also spelled out — particularly the finance charge, expressed not merely in dollars and cents but as an annual percentage rate.[4]

SALES PROMOTION IN WHOLESALING

In a recent survey by the National Wholesale Druggists Association, it was found that good service and favorable relations with customers were more important factors in causing merchants to buy than were low prices and large discounts. Top-ranking reasons given by retailers for patronizing their major wholesaler were: quicker deliveries, "bought from him for years," fewer "shorts," more interest,

[4] See pp. 381-85 for a full discussion of the credit-term disclosure requirements of the Consumer Credit Protection Act (or "Truth-in-Lending" law, as it is popularly known).

"like his salesmen," "like his house employees." The same survey disclosed as one of the chief complaints that wholesale salesmen *lacked training in retail sales promotion and retail store management,* as well as an interest in retailing.

Wholesalers in other fields have discovered a similar need for assistance by their retail customers. In a study of business failures among confectionery stores, the National Confectioners Association found that a contributing factor to the firms' demise was the lack of sufficient advice and assistance from their wholesale salesmen. The merchants needed help on store management, especially with reference to advertising, display, buying, stock control, and sales promotions. Wholesalers who have been most successful in withstanding corporate chain competition are those which have inaugurated dealer-assistance programs. As one wholesale firm's president explained, "We have learned that our job is to help the retailer move the merchandise out the front door. Only then will there be a demand for us to bring more in through the back door."

Small wholesalers do relatively little advertising. For most lines of wholesaling, considering large and small firms together, the expense of personal selling is from 10 to 20 times as much as the amount spent for advertising.

If small wholesalers do "floor selling," buyers often come to inspect merchandise displayed in the sample rooms or on the selling floor. Since these buyers are mostly small retailers, the wholesaler can use appealing displays, both to increase immediate sales and to show the retailers how to present the merchandise effectively in their own stores.

Whether display rooms are operated or not, some small wholesalers do a limited amount of external advertising. Practically all of them use signs over the store front and on the side of the warehouse if possible. Most other advertising is directed to the trade rather than to consumers. Only when a wholesaler has an exclusive franchise line, or is trying to promote his own brand, does he use consumer advertising.

Catalogs, price lists, sales letters, and some dealer-aid material that is usually furnished by the manufacturer constitute the principal forms of advertising used. The objective is to pave the way for personal selling and to minimize the time spent on sales calls. Almost no direct merchandise advertising is undertaken by the wholesaler himself.

SALES PROMOTION IN MANUFACTURING ESTABLISHMENTS

Customer Relations

Small manufacturers may sell direct to final consumers, to merchandisers (retailers *or* wholesalers), or to both types of customers. In any case the following questions will guide the factory owner in establishing good customer relations:

1. Are letters and telephone calls answered promptly and courteously?
2. Is price or other information by telephone given by your employees without an air of impatience, and without causing long waits to annoy the person who calls?
3. Is it possible to obtain accurate information on deliveries to customers, shipping dates, or similar information from your employees?

4. Do your salesmen answer inquiries promptly and intelligently?

5. Are your truckdrivers and deliverymen courteous to customers?

6. Does it make your credit department angry, and do they show it, when a customer slips slightly behind in his payments?

7. Is it common talk among the trade you serve that you favor the bigger buyers and neglect the little fellows?

Handling Complaints

Experience shows that a systematic procedure in handling complaints is desirable. Good complaint handling by any company entails three steps: (1) making rapid and reasonable adjustments; (2) gathering facts about the complaints; and (3) using the facts to improve production and operational methods.

A single complaint may not be significant, but a concentration of complaints on a single subject is almost certainly so. Various methods are used to obtain customer information on the shortcomings of a firm's products or services, such as encouraging dealers and salesmen to pass on complaints to the manufacturer. Forms for easy forwarding of complaint information may be supplied to them and to customers.

Unless a company obtains, analyzes, and acts upon those facts about its products and service that a good complaint system turns up, a significant opportunity for good sales promotion is missed.

Informative Labels

The small manufacturer can make especially good use of informative labels, if they are appropriate to his products, in building both dealer and consumer goodwill as well as in supplying salesmen with selling facts. The larger concern may accomplish these objectives through extensive publicity and training programs not available to the small operator. The large firm may have a tremendous investment in past advertising featuring the brand name or particular selling points and thus not need to use informative labels, but the small manufacturer "on the way up" has no such advantage.

One feature of the informative label that recommends its use to the small manufacturer struggling to establish a favorable reputation for his product is that salespeople do not always tell the customer how to use and care for a product, and the customer sometimes forgets even when told. Extensive experience with the use of informative labels shows that they increase the proportion of customers who buy better-quality products. This helps the small producer with a superior quality product to overcome some of the effects of extensive advertising by large competitors.

Displays

In small factories merchandise may be displayed in the window, or the manufacturing process may be visible from the sidewalk through a glass store front. This is often possible in a candy shop, bake shop, or craft shop.

Sometimes a small factory located near a highway can make good use of highway displays. A small plant that makes artificial flowers displays orchids and gardenias in transparent individual packages ready for sale to customers. The plant itself is not visible from the highway but is close enough to service the highway displays. When the product made is attractive, has impulse appeal, and may be sold profitably direct to consumers, such a plan is particularly effective in promoting sales.

Advertising

The small factory will usually direct its advertising either to consumers or to dealers or business users (other manufacturers) of its product. Manufacturers of consumer goods selling only in the local market, whether through local dealers or direct, may use newspaper, radio, outdoor signs, and direct-mail advertising effectively.

Small factories selling through dealers or to other businesses will use principally direct mail and trade publications read by their prospects. When the area to be covered is regional or national in scope, trade journal advertising will probably be the best. Space rates are relatively low, and the circulation is selective. Small advertisements inserted frequently may be most effective. The purpose will be to solicit inquiries or secure leads to be followed up by direct mail, the distribution of samples, or by personal selling.

Direct mail is the suggested medium when prospects are relatively few in number and form a highly selective group, or when the advertising message requires a great deal of description and explanation. Lists for direct mail advertising should include present and former customers, as well as prospective customers.

The manufacturer, particularly, has a problem budgeting the amount to be spent for advertising. He has no standard ratios to serve as guides, as do retailers. Nevertheless, he must make some estimate as to how much of his selling job can be done by advertising as compared with the results he can expect through salesmen.

Although radio is used by small manufacturers less frequently than direct mail, "spot" announcements may be an effective way to get a new product off to a good start, to draw attention to other advertising media used, and to gain dealer acceptance and distribution for the product because it is being supported by consumer advertising. Advertising themes for the small manufacturer might be: (1) the product itself, if it is new or superior to competing products; (2) the package; (3) the price, if it is lower than competitors'; or (4) availability in terms of prompt deliveries and nearness to customers. Other themes may of course be used if certain unusual services are offered, if the product is better for certain special uses than those now on the market, or if other particular circumstances prevail.

SALES PROMOTION IN SERVICE BUSINESSES

Selling intangibles like services has long been recognized as more difficult than selling physical goods. Often it is difficult to convince customers of their need for the service and to prove to them that it has actually been performed. Many small automobile repair shops have a worn parts panel. Customers can actually see how bearings, breaker points, and other car parts look after considerable wear. It is then easier to "sell" prospects on the need for installing new parts, as well as on the importance of preventive maintenance. Radio and television repair shop operators often keep the replaced parts to show the owner why it was necessary to replace them, and as partial proof that new parts were actually installed.

Since services are performed upon the person or property of the customer, the qualifications of the operator are important to patrons. When life or health may be endangered, state laws usually restrict practice to those of proved competence. Signs displayed in the shop assure customers that all operators are certified to be competent. Even in fields where laws do not require such certification, many service operators employ this device for promoting sales. Examples that might be cited include AAA and other approval signs in hotels, motels, and restaurants, United Motor Service signs in auto repair shops, and Master Barber certificates. Many trade associations have established standards of operation which, when accepted and practiced, permit the individual business owner to display a distinguishing sign.

Another aspect of promoting the sale of services is the importance many customers attach to little "extras." Hotels often find that a flower for lady guests or a free newspaper for the men pays big dividends in greater spending and repeat business.

Salesmanship for the service establishment as well as for the retail store requires that the salespeople understand the working of the business. Even the stenographer who answers the telephone in a plumbing firm should be able to give the approximate time necessary to complete a repair job and should be instructed in the use of an appointment book.

Too many small service establishment operators are in doubt as to just how they can advertise effectively. A laundry owner might say, "A laundry is just a laundry; if the customers like the service, they will come back." This is true to a degree, but it shows a rather short-sighted outlook. He should ask, "How can new customers be won in the face of so much competition? Other laundries may have quality service too. How can the housewife be persuaded that it pays to send her family's textiles to the laundry rather than do them herself? How can a reputation for quality service be built? Why do people desire the particular service offered? Why do customers prefer to trade with one shop rather than another?" Similar questions can be asked by the operators of business establishments offering other types of service. The answers to these questions will help in planning an effective promotional campaign.

SUMMARY AND CONCLUSIONS

The broad field of sales promotion may be divided into three areas: (1) customer and public relations; (2) special sales promotional ideas; and (3) advertising.

Any effort to increase sales is more effective when relations between the business and its customers are favorable. Very often sales promotion or advertising ideas that have been successful in one business are failures in another because the "environment" is different; so advertising and sales promotion must be directed to a particular market and the methods used must be appropriate to the goods or service to be sold.

In most small businesses all personnel, including the owners, are very important in determining whether relations with customers will be favorable. Much of the effectiveness of advertising or other special promotions that may be undertaken can be destroyed by poor salesmanship or other undesirable employee performance. Consequently, our approach has been to emphasize conditions that influence the customers' attitude toward the store, including quality of salesmanship and the attitudes of all the employees.

The ideas a businessman will garner in sales promotion alone, from trade publications and membership in his trade association, will soon justify the expense, time, and effort required. To use advertising effectively requires understanding and skill. Trade associations and advertising agencies specialize in solving their members' and clients' advertising problems, and their help can often be profitably solicited.

With increased intensity of competition, marketers have sometimes resorted to methods of advertising and selling which, if not illegal, have been unethical and injurious to the public interest. Deceptive promotional methods not only harm individual buyers but undermine the public's faith in all business. In recent years particularly, the consumer movement is providing business – small as well as large – not only with a warning but with an opportunity to see itself as others see it.

Perhaps such warnings should not be points of emphasis in the closing lines of this chapter on advertising and sales promotion. Yet they are mentioned here because one of the major temptations of the beginner, particularly at times when business is "slow," is to forget the judicious plans and policies previously made, and in blatant advertising to make wild claims or promises in desperate appeals to the public for patronage. A good way to prevent such departures from responsibility is to be aware of their dangers and to remember that the great names in industry were built through consistent and unfaltering integrity in all dealings with the public, including those involved in advertising.

REVIEW QUESTIONS

1. What are the major tools and methods of sales promotion?

2. Differentiate between direct and indirect sales promotion.

3. What is meant by the "public relations" of the business? Differentiate between public relations and customer relations.

4. How can a small business achieve good customer relations? How can the small businessman gauge the attitudes of his customers toward the business?

5. Is personal selling or advertising more important to the small business? Discuss and give concrete examples.

6. What are some of the devices a small businessman can use to promote sales, other than advertising?

7. How can the small businessman test or measure the effectiveness of his advertising?

8. Explain how the small business can pretest advertising. Is pretesting worth the time and expense required? Discuss.

9.   Differentiate between institutional and promotional advertising. Cite some examples of institutional advertising.

10.   In what ways do some small businessmen "waste" money in advertising?

11.   How can a small businessman determine the amount he should spend on advertising?

12.   What are some of the advertising media that a small, local business can use? What factors should be considered by the small businessman in selecting advertising media?

13.   What advantage, if any, does the characteristic of privacy give direct-mail advertising? Discuss.

14.   If the budget for direct-mail advertising is limited, is it better to economize on the mailing list or on the mailing piece? Discuss.

15.   What are some of the important considerations in effective retail advertising?

16.   How should a retailer select the merchandise to be advertised? Discuss.

17.   In what ways does the Truth-in-Lending Law restrict advertising of credit terms?

18.   What are some of the ways in which small wholesalers can effectively promote the sale of their products?

19.   Why is the use of informative labels usually more advantageous to the smaller than to the larger manufacturer?

20.   Why is sales promotion more difficult in the service business than in the retail establishment?

DISCUSSION QUESTIONS

1.   If the standard expense for advertising in your chosen field were 4 percent, would you be justified in spending 6 percent during your first year in business? In spending 10 percent? 25 percent? Explain.

2.   If a retail store has to dispose quickly of a limited quantity of some item of outer wearing apparel representing good value, what medium or media would be best to use? Why?

3.   For some kind of small business of particular interest to you, name four or five unusual ideas that could be used for effective sales promotion.

4.   What advertising theme could be used for each of the following: A new record changer? A child's picture story book? A clock-radio? A launderette with adjoining beauty parlor? A home-study high school course?

5.   Ed advertised several slow-selling items over the radio and in the newspaper. Many people asked about these items, but none bought them. What errors are apparent here? What should Ed do, and why?

SUPPLEMENTARY READINGS

Cook, Harvey R. *Selecting Advertising Media – A Guide for Small Business.* Small Business Management Series no. 34. Washington, D.C.: Small Business Administration, 1969. Discusses the advantages and disadvantages of each medium of advertising and suggests ways to judge its probable usefulness by small business.

Miller, Robert W. *Profitable Community Relations for Small Business.* Small
Business Management Series no. 27. Washington, D.C.: Small Business
Administration, 1961. Discusses relations with the various business communities such as the economic community, the political community, and the
educational community.

Successful Sales Managing. Business Series no. 1. New York: Business Education
Division, Dun & Bradstreet, 1967. Discusses three vital areas of sales
management: (1) the development of a sales organization; (2) the recruiting,
selecting, and training of salesmen; and (3) the counseling and supervision of
sales personnel.

20

Credit—a sales tool

The use of credit in business has often been described as representing "man's faith in man." Since the beginning of time, provision for the postponement of payment by seller to buyer has characterized business transactions between responsible parties. Certainly, if in these times all business or domestic transactions were handled on a strictly cash (or C.O.D.) basis, the wheels of business would be slowed down appreciably.

Most businesses in determining their capital requirements include the need for funds representing goods sold but not paid for. The money represented in the cost of the goods may be regarded as being loaned to the buyer. Because the use of capital must be compensated for and because of the record keeping involved in the maintenance of credit accounts, the handling of credit relationships by the seller represents a business expense. As with any other tool or device or method whereby business is facilitated or expedited, the credit function must be carefully controlled if its use is to be a profitable one for the business.

The granting of credit when one business firm deals with another is traditional, as noted, and in most countries a substantial amount of credit business is also done at the retail level as a service to customers. In the United States, however, it has become a dominant characteristic of retail merchandising to the point that almost all retail businesses (even the variety stores, which a few years ago would never have thought of extending credit!) are now offering it as a means of attracting trade.

TYPES OF CREDIT

Credit may be identified as either *consumer credit* or *trade credit*. The former is extended to the final consumer for the purpose of facilitating the sale of consumption goods, which may be either merchandise or services. Trade credit, on the other hand, is credit which is extended by one business firm to another to facilitate the sale of commercial or production goods; it is often called commercial or mercantile credit.

Experience shows that, in the retail field, credit-granting firms are more profitable and do a larger volume of business than do strictly cash stores. This is true in spite of the fact that credit stores generally sell at slightly higher prices than do cash stores, and that some firms fail because of unwise credit extension.

Trade credit is that usually extended by a manufacturer to a wholesaler,

374

distributor, or retailer, or by a wholesaler to a retailer, or by a manufacturer or distributor to an industrial consumer. It may be less of a lending or financing device than a means of simplifying payment. A frequent buyer finds it quite convenient to postpone payment until a number of purchases and deliveries have been made, usually over a period of a month. In this way, when each party adds the figures on his copies of the invoices, including any returns, they should agree, and the obligation is settled by the buyer with one check.

For some business the financing aspect — that is, the lending factor — may be the uppermost consideration in the extension of credit. A retailer may not be able to pay until a part of the shipment is sold and paid for. A wholesaler may be unable to pay until his retailer clientele has paid him. A manufacturer is quite often unable to pay until the materials or parts purchased are assembled into the finished product, sold, and paid for. Thus we have a situation where creditor is dependent upon creditor and debtor upon debtor — a basic interdependence of business.

Credit may also be classified by the characteristics of the credit instruments used or the methods of payment. Many consumers, for example, purchase goods on open or ordinary charge accounts, the payments being due when the bill is sent to the customer. If the number of charge accounts is small, bills are usually mailed at the end of each month. Where the number of such accounts is large some retailers group them alphabetically and bill in cycles throughout the month, each customer receiving his statement on approximately the same date each month; this procedure is known as *cycle billing*. If the account is kept current there is no interest or service charge.

Most business firms (trade customers) also purchase their goods on open account. However, the trade customer's account is payable a specified number of days *after* his receipt of the statement (often 30 days, but sometimes varying with the length of the buyer's turnover period), and in seasonal industries billing may involve the use of "extended datings." Trade customers are also commonly offered the opportunity of a cash discount if the bill is paid in full shortly after its receipt (usually 10 days).[1]

Because of unusually large purchases, or perhaps the irregularity of their purchases, some consumers may find it difficult to pay their bills all at once. Hence, some may elect to buy some items on the *installment plan* (or some variation of it, such as the "budget" plan), or open a *"revolving credit"* account. These plans are common among consumer creditors, rarely among trade customers.[2]

Installment credit.   Installment selling provides a protection for the seller not available in open accounts. Procedures of credit application and investigation are similar. To protect the seller, two forms of legal devices are usual in extending installment credit: the conditional sales contract and the chattel mortgage.[3] The conditional sales contract states that the title remains with the seller until the full price agreed upon has been paid, even though the goods have been sold and delivered to the purchaser. In case of failure to make payments, it is easy from a

[1] Trade credit terms are discussed in detail on pp. 398–99.

[2] As noted in Chapter 11, however, some business firms *may* purchase capital equipment on installment.

[3] The Uniform Commercial Code, adopted in all states but Louisiana, requires these contracts to be referred to as "security agreements."

legal standpoint for the seller to repossess the goods. This device is more convenient from the seller's point of view. Under the chattel mortgage, title passes to the buyer at the time of sale, but he either transfers it back to the seller, on the condition that he will get it back when he has fulfilled all the provisions of the mortgage, or gives the mortgagee a first lien on the goods.

Installment credit should be used by the small retailer only for articles that have repossession value, and only after checking with the credit bureau to determine that the applicant is not already overloaded with debt payments. The National Cash Register Company suggests that the following principles be observed when selling on installment:

1. Merchandise should be priced sufficiently high to cover all costs, including the possible cost of repossession, reconditioning, and reselling.
2. Merchandise — not terms — should be sold. When terms are emphasized, the customer tends to think less of the merchandise and is more likely to return it.
3. Adequate down payments should be obtained to prevent the account from becoming bad. When a customer pays a sizable part of the price he feels that he is the owner and the merchandise will more than likely be paid for in full.
4. Terms should be made as short as possible, and within the customer's ability to pay.
5. Collections should be made regularly. Installment payments require more attention than regular accounts.

In the small business, installment credit is likely to be called for if fairly durable goods of high unit cost are sold. The "lay-away" sale, sometimes used for ready-to-wear, is a variation of installment credit. Some stores sell coupon books which are paid for in small weekly installments. The coupons are used as cash for purchases within the store. These methods may be a good way to secure regular payments from customers of limited income who want to buy on the same basis as credit patrons. State laws regulating these various credit plans may vary, and it is suggested that the interested reader consult local law. Carrying charges usually must be added to installment purchases because of the extra bookkeeping and other costs involved in carrying the account. The common practice is to charge from 6 to 18 percent interest on the unpaid balance. The customer pays for part or all of the added installment credit expense, whereas open-account costs[4] are levied against cash and charge customers alike.

Many retailers prefer to have installment payments made in person at the store. This enables the merchant to keep in touch with the customer and offers further opportunities to sell additional goods.

Revolving credit or option terms. A "revolving credit" plan has the conveniences of an open charge account plus the privileges of installment payment. Customers are assigned a fixed credit limit and must pay a specified percentage of the outstanding balance monthly. Interest is charged on the unpaid balance at the end of the month.

---

[4] *Open-account costs* are markups on costs to all customers to cover costs of extending credit, collecting outstanding debts, bookkeeping, and the like.

WHEN TO EXTEND CREDIT

In most kinds of business we find both cash and credit firms, with a sizable proportion of the concerns selling both for cash and on credit. The small businessman will consider his preferences and those of his customers, balance the cost and risk of credit extension against the extra business to be expected, and compare the capital needed for a credit business with his own resources before deciding which policy he will follow.

The businessman should weigh both the advantages and disadvantages of granting credit. Advantages are:

1. A more personal relationship can be maintained with credit customers, who feel a bond with the firm.
2. Credit customers are likely to be more regular than cash customers, who tend to go where bargains are greatest.
3. Credit customers are more interested in quality and service than in price.
4. Goodwill is built up and maintained more easily.
5. Goods can be exchanged and adjustments made with greater ease. If necessary, goods can also be sent out on approval.
6. A list of credit customers provides a permanent mailing list for special sales promotions.

Some disadvantages are:

1. Capital is tied up in merchandise bought by charge customers.
2. If the merchant has borrowed the extra money required when credit is granted, the interest must be added to the cost of goods sold.
3. Some losses from bad debts and customers with fraudulent intentions are bound to occur.
4. Some credit customers pay slowly because they overestimate their ability to pay in the future.
5. Credit customers are more likely to abuse the privileges of returning goods and having goods sent out on approval.
6. Credit increases operating and overhead costs by adding the expenses of investigation and of the bookkeeping entailed in keeping accounts, sending out statements, and collecting payments.

The relative importance of credit to a particular kind of business and to customers' basic needs are also necessary considerations. To illustrate, manufacturers selling to the trade may do over 80 percent of their volume on credit, but one firm selling almost entirely to a few large buyers could dispense with credit because it would not be needed. The type of credit called for will be influenced by the customer in each field as well as by the nature of the goods.

The decision to extend credit to a given customer begins when his first order is received and must be continuously evaluated from then on. On receipt of each order, the person granting credit must make a decision as to the probability that the merchandise will be paid for. This decision can be no better than the facts on which it is based.

Sources of information on which the individual credit decision may be based include:

1. A complete credit application form, properly filled out and checked, utilizing any references available
2. Local, state, or national "professional" credit bureaus
3. Trade association facilities insofar as they provide reliable credit information
4. Banks and the credit departments of other firms
5. Trade and general business bulletins and publications; newspaper articles on business changes and legal decisions
6. Records within the firm; salesmen's reports; information from other customers

Every customer will therefore have, as a part of his listing by the firm, a credit record and rating, which, being constantly subject to change, must be reevaluated with regularity. While considerations regarding individual customers will vary, many businesses require that the credit status of most buyers be checked quarterly and that a record of these "checks" be made. Obviously, some customers will require a recheck more frequently than others.

Many mercantile credit agencies and most retail credit bureaus have available a standard credit application form. Manufacturers and wholesalers may also have models for distributors and retailers. Information generally required of consumer credit applicants is shown in the sample form on page 387 (Figure 20-3). A credit application form for mercantile or trade use, on the other hand, should gather the following information:

1. Name of firm (or proprietor if unincorporated)
2. Street address and telephone number
3. Kind of business
4. Number of years in operation
5. Other firms who have granted this firm credit
6. Banking connections
7. Other financial references
8. Personal credit data on owners or management — previous connections, home ownership, and so on
9. Amounts of credit and terms desired

Space should be provided on the application form for noting the credit limits of "approved" applicants. In this regard it is important to emphasize that the quality of information used as a guide in deciding to extend credit or not to extend credit must be unassailable. Refusal of credit, or overzealousness in collections, can be as dangerous as it can be protective — alienating not only the customer but depressing the morale of salesmen or other sales representatives. It is also important to cite reasons for not extending credit to particular applicants.

To summarize, credit is a service provided by the business whereby the customer can buy more conveniently. It is a means of selling and often is employed as a device for sales promotion. For this reason it is most important that credit departments and sales departments, or persons representing those functions, understand their personal role in the business which each represents. The credit person must recognize the fact that his job is to see to it that selling is made easier because buying is made more convenient. The salesman must recognize equally well that the credit department's function is to protect the financial interests of the business. Thus they must work hand in hand in providing and exercising this important function of distribution.

CREDIT AS A SALES TOOL

Small businessmen who do a credit business are losing some of the advantages this method provides if they fail to capitalize on the information their credit records provide for additional sales promotion. This is particularly true of open-account customers. Stores call this "customer control analysis" and manufacturers and wholesalers refer to it as "sales analysis." In the small business it simply means watching each customer's account (1) to discover opportunities for suggesting the purchase of certain items considered appropriate in the light of previous purchases; (2) to gather material concerning sales by departments or by salesmen; and (3) to detect any decline in purchases that might suggest a drifting away from the firm. When such a trend is discovered in time, an alert merchant or manufacturer can often investigate the cause and take appropriate steps to prevent a permanent loss of regular customers.

Special services may be offered with a credit account so that customers will be more anxious to open one, to maintain their credit standing, and to make greater use of the account than they would if it is merely a means of deferring payment. Many stores, for example, cash personal checks and order special merchandise more willingly for charge than for cash customers. Manufacturers and other small businessmen who want to expand their credit business should investigate special services that could be used to make an account more attractive. Naturally, care should be exercised not to alienate cash customers.

Credit account records provide useful information on past purchases from which management may develop case histories for each customer, showing his purchasing power, buying habits, time of purchasing, special merchandise preferences, hobbies, and similar data. Similarly, as indicated, failure to purchase over a period may be noted and acted upon. This sales analysis information available from the records may be supplemented by that obtained directly from each credit customer at the time application is made for an account, through personal contacts and by means of a judicious use of questionnaires. Such information can be used for direct-mail advertising, special sales promotions, buying and the timing of merchandise showings, selecting small lots of special merchandise for particular groups of customers, and in many other ways.

Increased knowledge of the customer permits sounder management decisions. This knowledge should not, of course, be confined to credit customers. There are sound reasons, however, why the charge customers constitute a better group than do cash customers for providing information to assist in management decisions. First, charge customers as a class are usually steady repeat patrons of the company. Management action based on what this group wants is likely to be on firmer ground than that based mainly on other sources of information. Second, a fundamental principle of successful credit business is to keep the charge customer on the books. To do so requires continuous knowledge of the customer's needs, changing status, interests, and so forth. Successful management in any area of business involves forecasting and continuously adjusting to conditions, especially those relating to major groups of customers.

COLLECTIONS

For the small business which extends credit, the ability to collect accounts may spell the difference between the success or failure of the firm. Although credit business can be very profitable, too many slow accounts will probably cause the firm to suffer a loss and prevent making a profit because:

1. the older an account becomes, the harder it is to collect;
2. attempting to collect the money due takes time away from other duties;
3. former good customers avoid the firm because it is embarrassing to meet the one to whom they owe money; and
4. slow accounts tie up funds needed to operate other divisions of the business; as a result, the firm's own credit suffers and the firm is not able to take advantage of cash discounts.

Experience shows that unless the firm extending credit is continually alert to the danger of slow accounts, its owner may find himself in a hopeless situation before he realizes that something is wrong. Two basic methods are used to measure the trend toward slow accounts: (1) comparing charge sales to collections, and (2) comparing charge sales to the amount owed by customers. When a retailer's charge sales during a week amount to more than his collections on charge sales, it may mean either that his charge business is increasing or that his collections were poor. There should be a close relationship between collections and charge sales. The danger sign is when collections lag behind charges week after week.

Bad-debt losses, normally, are deductible from income before taxation. The full amount of the debt may be written off if it logically can be assumed uncollectible, or a part of it, if collection appears to be only partially possible. Naturally, debts written off but later collected are considered as income.

Once an account becomes past due, there is a twofold objective to accomplish: (1) getting the money, and (2) retaining the patronage and goodwill of the customer. Prompt follow-up after the due date is desirable, whether by letter, telephone, or personal call. Telephone conversation or personal contact permits ready adjustment of the caller's approach to the debtor's reaction. The collection letter calls for most careful preparation. It must be brief, worded tactfully and pleasantly, employ the positive approach (avoiding such words as "can't," "refuse," "unfavorable," "unsatisfactory"), and possess other qualities which will help collect the bill yet maintain the customer's goodwill.

The success of a mail collection program also lies in the care that is given to keeping letters and notices current. It is advisable, too, to change the wording of form letters frequently; this is especially necessary when mail studies indicate that a particular letter has lost its pulling power.

The Cost of Collections

The question often arises as to who must eventually "pay" for credit — for the use of funds involved, for collection procedures, for the risks involved, and for losses. Some authors in the field of credit feel that the credit department should support itself, and indeed this is true where credit extension is limited to that of the installment type. In the typical retail store the regular 30-day charge account still comprises a large percentage of the credit volume, although the percentage appears to be declining. The major portion of credit department work (and therefore, expense) is caused by those accounts not paid within the 30-day period.

These expenses must be reflected either in increased prices or in losses to the merchant; if it be in increased prices, the burden is on the "good paying" customer. It has been suggested that more firms should charge a penalty fee for past-due regular accounts as is done in mercantile credit. If this were done (assuming the customer had been advised to that effect at the time credit was requested), it should considerably reduce the overall cost of retail credit extension.

REGULATION OF CONSUMER CREDIT TERMS

A survey by the Federal Reserve Board early in July 1969 revealed that there was considerable confusion among consumers about the interest rates they paid on their credit purchases, particularly on "revolving" ("open-end" or optional) charge accounts. Since then the Truth-in-Lending law has gone into effect. The stated purpose of this law — known officially as the Consumer Credit Protection Act — is "to assure a meaningful disclosure of credit terms so that the consumer will be able to compare more readily the various credit terms available to him and to avoid the uninformed use of credit."

The key word in the above statement is *disclosure*. The Truth-in-Lending law is a *disclosure* law and does not set maximum interest rates.[5] It simply requires that the finance charge, expressed both in dollars and the annual percentage rate, be disclosed in writing before credit is extended to the consumer and in periodic statements on unpaid balances. The term *finance charge* is defined in the act to include not only interest but other fees involved in granting credit, such as carrying charges and the cost of appraisal or investigation reports. Costs that would be paid even if credit were not granted and the goods sold for cash, such as taxes and registration or title fees, are excluded. In effect, the finance charge is defined as the *cost of credit*.

To implement the Truth-in-Lending law (administered by the Federal Trade Commission), the Federal Reserve Board has issued "regulation Z," which states the detailed disclosure rules applying to the two common types of consumer credit: "open-end" or revolving charge accounts, and "closed-end" or installment contracts. Where revolving charge accounts are maintained by the creditor, the

---

[5] Regulation of interest rates, as such, is left to the states. At the present time 22 states have set maximum finance charge rates, varying in annual terms from 8 percent in Minnesota to as high as 18 percent (on some balances) in most of the others.

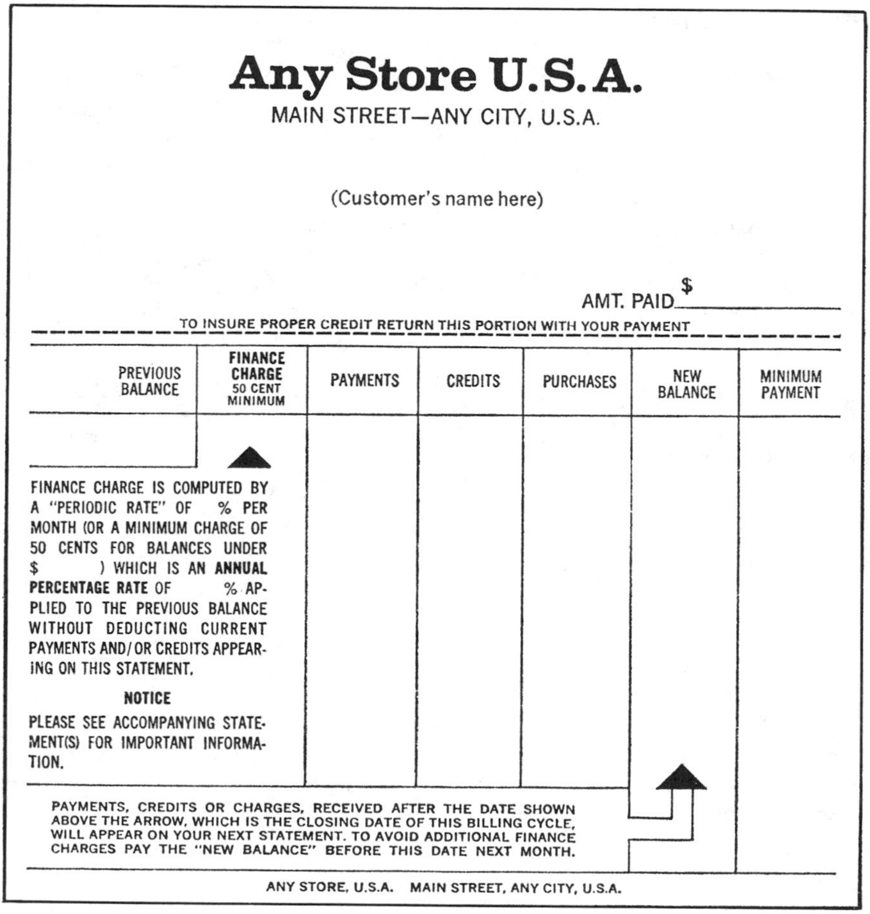

Any Store U.S.A.

MAIN STREET—ANY CITY, U.S.A.

(Customer's name here)

AMT. PAID $ _____

TO INSURE PROPER CREDIT RETURN THIS PORTION WITH YOUR PAYMENT

PREVIOUS BALANCE	FINANCE CHARGE 50 CENT MINIMUM	PAYMENTS	CREDITS	PURCHASES	NEW BALANCE	MINIMUM PAYMENT

FINANCE CHARGE IS COMPUTED BY A "PERIODIC RATE" OF   % PER MONTH (OR A MINIMUM CHARGE OF 50 CENTS FOR BALANCES UNDER $) WHICH IS AN **ANNUAL PERCENTAGE RATE** OF   % APPLIED TO THE PREVIOUS BALANCE WITHOUT DEDUCTING CURRENT PAYMENTS AND/OR CREDITS APPEARING ON THIS STATEMENT.

NOTICE

PLEASE SEE ACCOMPANYING STATEMENT(S) FOR IMPORTANT INFORMATION.

PAYMENTS, CREDITS OR CHARGES, RECEIVED AFTER THE DATE SHOWN ABOVE THE ARROW, WHICH IS THE CLOSING DATE OF THIS BILLING CYCLE, WILL APPEAR ON YOUR NEXT STATEMENT. TO AVOID ADDITIONAL FINANCE CHARGES PAY THE "NEW BALANCE" BEFORE THIS DATE NEXT MONTH.

ANY STORE, U.S.A.   MAIN STREET, ANY CITY, U.S.A.

Figure 20-1. Typical "Open End" Charge Account Statement

following information must be disclosed to the consumer *before* his account is opened:[6]

1. Conditions under which a finance charge may be made and the period within which, if payment is made, there is no finance charge
2. The method of determining the balance upon which a finance charge may be imposed
3. How the finance charge is calculated
4. The periodic rates used and the range of balances to which each rate applies, as well as the corresponding *annual percentage rate* calculated to the nearest quarter of a percent (0.25%)

[6] Board of Governors, Federal Reserve System, *What You Ought to Know about Federal Reserve Regulation Z – Truth in Lending* (Washington, D.C.: G.P.O., 1969). See also Benny L. Kass, "Understanding Truth in Lending," Small Marketers Aids no. 139 (Washington, D.C.: Small Business Administration, 1969).

Seller's Name: _____   Contract #_____

RETAIL INSTALLMENT CONTRACT AND SECURITY AGREEMENT

The undersigned (herein called Purchaser, whether one or more) purchases from _____(seller) and grants to _____ a security interest in, subject to the terms and conditions hereof, the following described property.

QUANTITY	DESCRIPTION	AMOUNT

Description of Trade-in:

Sales Tax

Total

Insurance Agreement

The purchase of insurance coverage is voluntary and not required for credit. ___(Type of Ins.)___ insurance coverage is available at a cost of $_____ for the term of credit.

I desire insurance coverage

Signed_____ Date_____

I do not desire insurance coverage

Signed_____ Date_____

PURCHASER'S NAME_____
PURCHASER'S ADDRESS_____
CITY_____STATE_____ZIP_____

1. CASH PRICE $_____
2. LESS: CASH DOWN PAYMENT $_____
3.   TRADE-IN   _____
4.   TOTAL DOWN PAYMENT _____$_____
5. UNPAID BALANCE OF CASH PRICE $_____
6. OTHER CHARGES:

   _____ $_____

   _____   _____

7. AMOUNT FINANCED $_____
8. **FINANCE CHARGE** $_____
9. TOTAL OF PAYMENTS $_____
10. DEFERRED PAYMENT PRICE (1+6+8) $_____
11. **ANNUAL PERCENTAGE RATE**   _____%

Purchaser hereby agrees to pay to_____ _____ at their offices shown above the "TOTAL OF PAYMENTS" shown above in _____ monthly installments of $_____(final payment to be $_____) the first installment being payable _____ 19_____, and all subsequent installments on the same day of each consecutive month until paid in full. The finance charge applies from ___(Date)___

Signed_____

Notice to Buyer: You are entitled to a copy of the contract you sign. You have the right to pay in advance the unpaid balance of this contract and obtain a partial refund of the finance charge based on the "Actuarial Method." [Any other method of computation may be so identified, for example, "Rule of 78's," "Sum of the Digits," etc.]

Figure 20-2. Typical Retail Installment Contract

5. How additional charges for new purchases are calculated
6. A description of any lien the creditor may acquire on the customer's property, such as the right to repossess a car, household appliance, or similar purchased commodity
7. The minimum periodic payment required

Periodic statements must also be mailed to the customer on all accounts with a balance of more than $1.00. Figure 20-1 is one of several formats prepared by the Federal Reserve Board which will permit a creditor to comply with the disclosure requirements of regulation Z. In general, periodic statements on "open-end" or revolving charge accounts – as noted in the illustration – must contain the following information:

1. The previous (or unpaid) balance at the beginning of the billing period
2. The amount and date of each purchase or credit extension, and an accompanying statement or brief description of each item bought (if not previously given to the customer)
3. Customer payments, and credits such as rebates, adjustments, and returns
4. The finance charge expressed in dollars and cents, as well as in terms of the annual percentage rate
5. The "periodic" rates used in calculating the finance charge, and the range of balances, if any, to which they apply[7]
6. The closing date of the billing cycle, and the unpaid balance as of that date (i.e., the "new" balance)

Similar disclosure requirements are imposed on "closed-end" or installment contracts. As noted in the typical retail installment contract in Figure 20-2, the following information must be disclosed to the customer:

1. The cash price (exclusive of trade-in allowance)
2. The down payment in cash, and trade-in allowance (if any)
3. The "unpaid balance of cash price" (cash price less trade-in allowance and cash down payment)
4. Charges not related to the extension of credit, such as taxes, registration or title fees
5. The total "amount financed" (sum of lines 3 and 4, above)
6. The finance charge expressed both in dollars and cents and as an annual percentage rate (lines 8 and 11 in the illustration, Figure 20-2)
7. The "deferred payment price" (cash price + finance charge + other charges as noted in line 4, above)
8. The date on which the finance charge will begin to take effect (if this is different from the date of sale)
9. The amounts and due dates of installment payments, and the "total of payments"
10. The amount that will be charged for default or delinquency of payment, and the method of calculating this charge
11. A description of the security (if any) held by the creditor
12. The penalty charge, if any, for prepayment of principal, and the method of computing this charge

Where the installment contract involves merchandise to be installed in the home, and where the retailer or contractor retains a lien on the home as part of the sales contract, the Truth-in-Lending law grants customers the "right of rescission," that is, the right to change one's mind and cancel the contract, if this right is exercised in writing within three business days following (1) the date of sale, or (2) the date

[7] In Figure 20-1, the finance charge is determined by a single periodic rate, with a minimum charge of 50 cents applicable to balances under a specified amount.

the required disclosures were made — whichever is later. The law also requires that two copies of a "Notice of the Right of Rescission" be given to the customer at the time he receives the credit-term disclosure information, or prior thereto.

Severe penalties are imposed on the creditor who inadvertently fails to disclose credit information or who willfully disregards the law, or who mistakenly overstates a finance charge which he does not rectify within 15 days after discovering the error.

CREDIT IN RETAILING

For many years the trend in retailing had been toward less and more closely controlled credit. The rise of strictly cash stores in many lines of retailing had demonstrated that credit was not the essential customer service it was earlier considered to be. Credit losses incurred in the Great Depression of the 1930s had encouraged cash business. The "cut-rate" store, the supermarket, the discount house, and almost all corporate retail chains were founded as cash institutions. Most voluntary chains encouraged member stores to sell only for cash. Now, however, the use of credit as a tool of sales promotion is general in locally owned stores as well as in many corporate chains.

Contributing to this change are such factors as the increased income of the average citizen, the general ineffectiveness of selling at the retail level, the development of novel credit plans by retailers, and the aggressive entry of banks into the credit-card business and the small-loan field. These and related factors have caused all retailers to seriously reconsider credit matters, and many have accepted and promoted the use of credit in self-defense.

Also, federal laws allowing certain personal and business expenses as income tax deductions have popularized the use of consumer credit for transportation, food, and lodging, because complete records of charges and payments are thus made available. There is no doubt that tax laws and regulations have encouraged the "charging" of many items by business and professional people.

Generally speaking, the following reasons explain and summarize why small merchants have employed credit in their efforts to attract, accommodate, and retain customers:

1. To secure additional business from present customers that can be handled at little or no extra expense

2. To attract new customers who need or want credit

3. To expand sales rapidly up to optimum capacity, and thus to reduce unit costs

4. To compete with large-scale retailers such as chain stores, mail-order houses, and "supers" who do not extend credit

5. To secure a financial return over and above merchandising profit in certain lines like durable consumers' goods that are purchased on installment contracts

6. To increase customer traffic by encouraging customers to pay their accounts in person at the store

7. To take advantage of the customer information available in credit applications and charge files

How much credit business is to be accepted or even encouraged will depend upon particular circumstances in each case. First, the local situation is important. While it is not always necessary to follow competitors' policies, if credit is extended by all other stores in the same line of business in the community, customers will probably expect it or an alternative benefit for paying cash.

Second, and of probably even greater importance, is the class of trade desired and what they expect in the way of credit. The fact that people in the upper-income bracket do not *need* credit is no assurance they will buy for cash. Rural customers may be in the habit of buying on credit, but when agricultural conditions are favorable they might prefer to pay cash. The retailer may find that even customers who think they want credit because of habit, convenience, pride, or financial need will discover the desirability of buying for cash when the right inducements are offered.

The final determinant will be the retailer's financial resources. Credit extension of any amount requires more capital and involves greater risks for the smaller retailer than most other activities. Total costs of open-account credit extension are likely to be from 3 to well over 5 percent of credit sales.

Using a Controlled Credit System

Properly controlled, credit can increase sales and bring the merchant steady, well-satisfied customers; handled in a slipshod manner, it can cause an overinvestment in accounts receivable, large bad-debt losses, and perhaps eventual failure of the business. A sound credit system is one in which (1) credit applicants are thoroughly investigated; (2) limits are placed on the amount of credit extended; (3) charge accounts are systematically monitored or "controlled"; and (4) delinquent accounts are followed up promptly.

The credit application and investigation. The first step in the credit investigation should be an interview with the applicant. During the interview the merchant's appearance, friendliness, and manner of obtaining information can help to gain the applicant's goodwill and confidence. Since an applicant usually will speak more freely when relaxed, the interview should be in complete privacy, if possible, and in a pleasant atmosphere. In order to have a record of the desired information, the merchant should have the customer fill out and sign a credit application, whether the customer takes the initiative in seeking credit or the store solicits the account.

The credit application should include the following information: (1) full name; (2) home address; (3) if less than two years at this address, previous place of residence; (4) business affiliation and address; (5) name of one or two personal references; (6) trade references (other accounts); and (7) his local bank. The International Consumer Credit Association, an organization composed of over 55,000 members engaged in consumer credit service, has adopted a standard form that the small businessman might find convenient to use (see Figure 20-3).

Three general methods are used in distributing credit applications. The most common plan is to have the applicant fill out the blank in the credit department, to which customers inquiring about credit are referred. In other stores salespeople give the application blanks to customers who are interested or appear to be good prospects. Some stores enclose the credit application with merchandise that is

GUARD YOUR CREDIT AS A SACRED TRUST

APPLICATION FOR CREDIT

International Consumer Credit Association

OFFICIAL RECOMMENDED APPLICATION

MR.
MRS.
MISS._____ WIFE'S NAME_____

HOME ADDRESS_____CITY_____STATE_____ HOW LONG_____ OWNS RENTS_____

PREVIOUS ADDRESS_____CITY_____STATE_____ HOW LONG_____

DATE OF BIRTH_____ NO. OF DEPENDENTS_____TEL. NO_____ SOCIAL SECURITY NO._____

EMPLOYED BY_____ ADDRESS_____

POSITION_____ HOW LONG_____ MONTHLY SALARY_____

FORMER POSITION_____ (if employed less than 1 yr.)

WIFE'S EMPLOYER_____ ADDRESS_____

POSITION_____ HOW LONG_____ MONTHLY SALARY_____ SOCIAL SECURITY NO._____

LANDLORD OR MORTGAGE HOLDER_____ADDRESS_____ MONTHLY RENTAL OR MORTGAGE PAYMENT $_____

NAME OF NEAREST RELATIVE AND RELATIONSHIP (OTHER THAN HUSBAND OR WIFE)
_____ADDRESS_____

BANKS_____ CHECK OR SAVINGS ACCOUNT NO _____ ☐ CHECKING ☐ SAVINGS

ADDRESS_____ ☐ LOANS

MAKE OF CAR_____YEAR_____ FULLY PAID: YES_____ NO_____ BALANCE DUE $_____

MAKING PAYMENT TO_____ ADDRESS_____

CREDIT REFERENCES

NAME OF FIRM	ADDRESS	TYPE OF ACCOUNT		ACCOUNT IS NOW	
		CHARGE	BUDGET	OPEN BAL.	PD. IN FULL

MEDICAL REFERENCES

HOSPITAL_____ADDRESS_____ BALANCE DUE $_____ PD._____

DOCTOR_____ADDRESS_____ BALANCE DUE $_____ PD._____

DOCTOR_____ADDRESS_____ BALANCE DUE $_____ PD._____

LIST ON REVERSE SIDE OF THIS APPLICATION ANY UNPAID BALANCES ON INSTALMENT ACCOUNTS AND MONTHLY PAYMENTS THEREON.

THE ABOVE INFORMATION IS FOR THE PURPOSE OF OBTAINING CREDIT AND IS WARRANTED TO BE TRUE. I AGREE TO PAY ALL BILLS UPON RECEIPT OF STATEMENT OR AS OTHERWISE EXPRESSLY AGREED.

I HEREBY AUTHORIZE THE PERSON OR FIRM TO WHOM THIS APPLICATION IS MADE, ANY CREDIT BUREAU OR OTHER INVESTIGATIVE AGENCY EMPLOYED BY SUCH PERSON, TO INVESTIGATE THE REFERENCES HEREIN LISTED OR STATEMENTS OR OTHER DATA OBTAINED FROM ME OR FROM ANY OTHER PERSON PERTAINING TO MY CREDIT AND FINANCIAL RESPONSIBILITY.

PLEASE READ BEFORE SIGNING APPLICATION.

DATE_____ SIGNATURE_____

CREDIT BUREAU

CREDIT LIMIT	APPROVED	IN FILE		DATE			
		FIRM	SINCE	HIGH CREDIT	TERMS	LAST PURCHASE	PAYS
$							

© INTERNATIONAL CONSUMER CREDIT ASSOCIATION, 1967
FORM NO. 1063B

Figure 20-3. Application for Credit

wrapped for certain customers. If the customer applies at the credit department in person — a procedure which in the small store may mean merely talking to the executive in charge of credit — a preliminary interview is usually held at this time.

Aided by information provided on the application blank and by credit references, a skilled interviewer can get some clues to the applicant's ability and willingness to pay his debts — the sole criterion for extending credit. The credit applicant's ability to pay his debts is obviously dependent upon his *capital* resources and his *capacity* to manage them well, whereas his willingness to pay is a matter of *character*. These factors — capital, capacity, and character — are commonly referred to as the "three C's" of credit.

The next step should be to obtain credit information on the applicant from the local credit bureau or, if there is none in the community, from other stores and businesses, the applicant's place of employment, and his bank and neighbors.

After completing his investigation, the merchant should evaluate the application. In this he should consider the applicant's character and credit record, his earning power and ability to pay, and his capital and property. Along with these factors the merchant must take into account the personal background of the applicant – his social standing, general reputation in the community, and business career.

Setting a credit limit.   The amount of credit granted to a customer should be based largely on his income and will vary, of course, with the type of store. A credit limit is usually set so that a customer will not buy beyond his capacity and by doing so jeopardize his credit record. To let him know that his account has been accepted, the store writes him a friendly letter telling how pleased they are to count him as a regular customer, and also restates the conditions under which credit is granted.

Establishing terms of payment.   As a safeguard against bad-debt losses, the merchant should have a definite understanding with the customer as to the credit terms. He may stipulate that payments are to be weekly, monthly, or on paydays. The time for which credit is extended on open accounts is frequently one month for salaried workers and weekly for wage earners, especially in food and other convenience goods stores. Usually payment by the 10th of the month for the previous month's account is customary on regular open accounts.

Monitoring or controlling the account.   From the day the account is opened, the merchant should watch it carefully to see that the customer upholds his part of the agreement. If credit is on a monthly basis, some merchants permit no further charges on an account if it is not paid by the end of the month in which payment is due. Others insist on giving personal approval to additional purchases on such accounts.

Credit control involves adequate records and prompt collections. For a small business, the best system of records has to be decided upon by the proprietor. The important provisions are an individual record for each customer, a filing system to keep the records straight, and a follow-up file to take care of delinquent accounts. The credit limit is often placed on each account record. It is important to observe the customers' habits – to know how much they owe and how they pay. Cultivate the best customers and if possible gradually drop the poor ones, remembering that they can frequently be converted into good cash customers.

Follow-up.   Prompt follow-up is likely to show delinquent accounts to be the result of (*a*) oversight on the part of the customer, (*b*) temporary financial difficulty, or (*c*) unwillingness to pay. In the first case, a reminder by the merchant will usually result in prompt payment. In the second case, if the retailer understands the customer's difficulty a mutually agreeable payment plan can be arranged. The third situation may be the result of customer dissatisfaction that could be settled agreeably if understood and acted upon promptly, or it may represent the typical "deadbeat" charge customer. When the dealer has determined the reason why each account is delinquent, the appropriate action to take is usually apparent. Aggressive collection procedures should be instituted if necessary, but should be delayed in favor of remedial action whenever possible.

Charge Plates and Credit Cards

Sometimes, instead of the customer applying for credit, the local credit bureau takes the initiative and issues charge plates or cards to a selected number of individuals who have already established good credit records. A group of stores may form an association with an agreement to extend credit to all customers to whom a charge plate is issued. Cooperating stores all accept this plate as evidence of credit approval.

The credit card, as developed originally by the oil companies, hotels, and others, has become a popular means of extending consumer credit, with advantages for both buyer and seller. The individual operator of a service station, for example, has the benefit of professional screening of applications at the headquarters of his resource, which also assumes liability for loss unless formal warning has been issued to the contrary. The consumer has the advantage of being able to charge at any of the affiliated establishments.

Credit-card service of this type is also available to other sellers of consumer goods or services. The American Express credit card, the Hilton "Carte Blanche," and the Diner's Club card, for example, are used by stores and restaurants of all kinds all over the world, and thus have been particularly helpful to travelers. For this service the card-issuing agency levies a charge on the subscribing business establishments amounting to approximately 6 percent of the amount of sale.

In recent years banks also have entered the consumer credit market. Originally introduced locally in New York City, bank credit cards are now available in most communities throughout the country. The three largest bank credit-card plans are "Master Charge" (issued by an association of banks called Interbank), "BankAmericard" (franchised by the Bank of America), and "Unicard" (issued by the Chase Manhattan Bank of New York in nine eastern states). In these plans the bank makes a credit investigation of an applicant for consumer credit, whether the application is made at the store or the bank. If approved, an embossed plate is issued that henceforth becomes identification and authorization when used for charge purposes in any cooperating store up to the floor limit. If a customer wants to charge more than the floor limit the merchant telephones the bank and secures the information needed immediately. Sales checks are furnished by the bank, and retailers record each charge transaction on these, insert the plate in a stamping machine, and usually secure the customer's signature if the purchase is made in person. Each day copies of the charge-sale checks are deposited with the bank, which then credits the merchant's account with the total amount less service charges. Service charges are usually 5 percent for open accounts and 6 percent for two- or three-payment budget accounts up to 90 days.

The bank does the recording and once a month sends a single statement to each customer accompanied by copies of all charge sales checks from all cooperating stores. The account is due and payable to the bank within ten days after billing. It is a nonrecourse plan, since the bank assumes full responsibility for approving credit applications and making collections.

Credit-card plans are variously viewed as an effort to aid small merchants to meet the credit promotion competition of large department stores, to separate financing from merchandising, and to furnish additional revenue for banks. The subscribing retailer (or service-business operator) gains the advantages of receiving immediate cash on an increased sales volume without the need to (1) investigate the customer's credit, (2) set up a credit bookkeeping system, (3) bill customers, (4) dun slow-paying accounts, (5) incur bad debts, (6) take time that could be more profitably devoted to merchandising, (7) tie up his own capital, or (8) incur possible ill will or loss of sales by refusing credit.

Credit Bureaus

Credit bureaus are service agencies organized to gather, compile, and distribute information concerning the resources, debts, and financial responsibility of individual consumers. They serve banks, department stores, small-loan companies, oil company credit-card and other national credit-card firms, local merchants, credit unions, and some professional people. Their master files contain complete credit histories consisting of facts obtained from the ledgers of the principal or representative credit granters of the community, as well as information from public records, the press, and employers.

Merchants, professional men, and hospitals are the chief supporters of credit bureaus. Since more than 2,200 retail credit bureaus belong to a national trade association, the Associated Credit Bureaus, a newcomer's credit record may be readily obtained by a local bureau, although the independent businessman would have a difficult time doing this for himself. Each member of the bureau agrees in his membership contract to supply ledger information concerning his customers, including those who are in arrears on their accounts. Thus the bureau secures and can furnish much more information about customers than any businessman could obtain on his own.

Figure 20-4 is an example of the report sent from one member of the Associated Credit Bureaus to a member bureau in another city. It shows the kind of data accumulated in the file of an individual credit user. A code has been developed for the most effective transfer of information. Businesses have been classified and given code letters such as A for automotive sales, D for department stores, and F for finance companies. The terms of sale are classed as either open accounts (O), revolving or option accounts (R), or installment accounts (I) – followed by the amount of the monthly payment ("I$100" and "I$150" in the illustration). The manner of payment is an explicit numerical statement of how prompt or how slow a customer is in paying his bills. This ranges from 0 to 9, with 0 representing a new but unused account, and 9 indicating a bad debt (or perhaps that the account has been assigned to a collection agency, or that the customer has disappeared). In Figure 20-4, Mr. Charles H. Brown has a finance company account which is classed as a bad debt. The remainder of his credit record is good.

Two methods, generally, are used to determine membership fees in credit bureaus: the meter plan and the flat rate. Under the meter plan, credit reports are purchased at so much per report. Many smaller bureaus use the flat-rate plan, by which each member is classified according to the approximate amount of service the business will use and is charged a flat monthly fee. In return for this fee, the member is entitled to as many telephone credit reports as he needs. The vast majority of credit reports are requested and given over the telephone. Precautions

S P E C I M E N

NAME AND ADDRESS OF CREDIT BUREAU MAKING REPORT

☐ SUMMARY REPORT ☐ SINGLE REFERENCE ☐ TRADE REPORT

☐ SHORT REPORT ☐ FULL REPORT ☐ PREV. RES. REPORT

Credit Bureau of Anytown
PO Box 600
Anytown, Anystate 77036

DATE RECEIVED	DATE MAILED	CBR REPORT NO.
10/16/72	10/17/72	

DATE TRADE CLEARED	DATE EMPLOY VERIFIED	INCOME VERIFIED
10/16/72	10/16/72	☒ YES ☐ NO

CONFIDENTIAL *Factbilt*® REPORT

FOR
EFG Sales Co., Inc

IN FILE SINCE: 10/60

This information is furnished in response to an inquiry for evaluating credit risks. It has been obtained from reliable sources, the accuracy of which is not guaranteed. The inquirer agrees to indemnify the reporting bureau for any damage arising from misuse of this information, and this report is furnished in reliance upon that indemnity. It must be held in strict confidence, and must not be revealed to the subject reported upon. If adverse action is taken based on this report, the subject reported on must be so advised and the reporting agency identified.

REPORT ON (SURNAME):	MR., MRS., MISS:	GIVEN NAME:	SOCIAL SECURITY NUMBER:	SPOUSE'S NAME:
BROWN	Mr	Charles H	111-22-3333	Henrietta

ADDRESS:	CITY:	STATE:	ZIP CODE:	SPOUSE'S SOCIAL SECURITY NO.:
1261 South Main	Thattown	Thatstate	87036	222-33-4444

COMPLETE TO HERE FOR TRADE REPORT AND SKIP TO CREDIT HISTORY

PRESENT EMPLOYER AND KIND OF BUSINESS:	POSITION HELD:	SINCE:	MONTHLY INCOME:
Original Designs Company	Designer	12/64	$ 1000

COMPLETE TO HERE FOR SHORT REPORT AND SUMMARY REPORT AND SKIP TO CREDIT HISTORY

DATE OF BIRTH:	NUMBER OF DEPENDENTS INCLUDING SPOUSE			
1/16/30	4	☐	☐	

FORMER ADDRESS:	CITY:	STATE:	FROM:	TO:
11810 Oak Drive	Anytown	Anystate	8/58	12/64

FORMER EMPLOYER AND KIND OF BUSINESS:	POSITION HELD:	FROM:	TO:	MONTHLY INCOME:
Clothing Fashions Company	Asst Designer	1950	12/64	$ 750

SPOUSE'S EMPLOYER AND KIND OF BUSINESS:	POSITION HELD:	SINCE:	MONTHLY INCOME:
City Abstract & Title Company	Stenographer	5/66	$ 375

CREDIT HISTORY *(Complete this section for all reports)*

KIND OF BUSINESS	DATE ACCOUNT OPENED	DATE OF LAST SALE	HIGHEST CREDIT	AMOUNT OWING	AMOUNT PAST DUE	TERMS OF SALE AND USUAL MANNER OF PAYMENT
H 403	11/66	8/72	260	156	00	R-1
A 451	10/67	3/71	2,980	2,680	00	I$100-0
C 388	9/65	6/72	68	00	00	R-1
D 155	1/66	1/70	181	80	00	0-1
O 663	1966	11/68	300	00	00	0-1
F 918	1964	1964	20,000	14,500	00	I$150-9

INDICATE IF FILE CONTAINS

☐ Items of Public Record   ☐ Any record of accounts placed for collection   ☐ Any reports received from other Credit Bureaus

IF ANY OF THE ABOVE ARE CHECKED, GIVE DETAILS

AFFILIATED WITH

Form 100 A   ▣ **Associated Credit Bureaus, Inc.**   Printed in U.S.A.

Figure 20-4. Inter-Bureau Report

are taken to insure identification of the inquiring credit granter and to give reports only to authorized persons.

The credit bureau does not give opinions. It is never a forecaster of the future. When information is called for, the prospect's credit record is given. The decision as to whether to extend credit is left to the credit granter. Only information applying to the subject's credit standing is given in such reports. The credit granter has an interest in the subject of a report when that subject is a user or prospective user of credit privileges, and credit information requested comes legally under the title of "privileged communications," and must be respected as such by all recipients. Information obtained from the credit bureau must be treated confidentially by the member and never disclosed to the subject of the report or to anyone outside the firm's credit department.

Some credit bureaus offer a valuable aid to members in the form of a "precollection service." This usually consists of a personal letter or other mailing piece appearing under the letterhead of the credit bureau and addressed to customers whose accounts are past due. The message may outline the purpose of the credit bureau and show how it benefits customer and store alike. The debtor is told that the past-due account is about to be, or already has been, placed on record in the credit bureau. The name of the creditor, the amount past due, and the due date are given. The customer is advised to pay the amount due immediately in order that the proper disposition of the account may be recorded in the credit bureau's files.

The Fair Credit Reporting Act.   Credit bureaus have a dossier on anyone who has ever purchased goods on credit — which includes almost everyone of adult age. A credit bureau's report on a consumer's credit application plays a major role in determining whether or not the retailer will grant credit to him. In recent years, however, there have been an increasing number of complaints against credit bureaus, centering around errors that have caused some consumers to lose their good credit rating. To protect consumers against the use of erroneous data in the files of credit bureaus, Congress in 1971 passed the Fair Credit Reporting Act.[8] Under this new law, if the consumer's application for credit (or for a job, loan, or an insurance policy) is rejected because of an unfavorable credit report, he must be told so by the retailer (or other businessman) who turned him down. He has the right to review the credit bureau's file on him, and to request a reinvestigation of any item which he questions. If the item is found to be inaccurate or can no longer be verified, it must be deleted from the file. In the event that the reinvestigation does not resolve the question — as, for example, when he has lost the receipt for a bill paid in cash, or when he is withholding payment for defective merchandise until the defect is corrected — he may have placed in the file a brief statement giving his side of the argument. The rejected credit applicant also has the right to be told the names of those who have received credit reports about him within the past 6 months (or who have received employment reports within the past 2 years), who then must be notified by the credit bureau of any corrections, additions, or deletions in the applicant's dossier. The credit bureau is not permitted to charge the rejected applicant for these services so long as the review of his credit file is requested within 30 days from the time he was denied the credit.

The new law also requires credit bureaus to delete from credit files adverse information that is more than 7 years old, except bankruptcy information, which may be reported for as long as 14 years. However, no age limits are placed on the

---

[8] The act is also designed to restrict the use of credit bureau dossiers for purposes beyond the exchange of routine business information; for example, their use in the investigation of taxpayers by the Internal Revenue Service, or of security risks by the Federal Bureau of Investigation. "Snooper reports" of this kind are beyond the scope of this book.

information in credit reports on those who apply for a loan or a life insurance policy of $50,000 or more or on those who apply for a job with an annual salary of $20,000 or more.

Retailers and other credit granters as well as credit-reporting agencies or bureaus also have certain obligations under the law. As noted above, a businessman who turns down a credit applicant because of a credit bureau report containing adverse information must give the consumer the name and address of the credit bureau supplying the report. But sometimes retailers contact credit references directly, so that a credit report from a credit bureau is not involved in their decision. In such a case, if a person is turned down for credit the retailer must inform him (at the time his credit application is rejected) that he has the right to request in writing within 60 days the nature of the information on which the credit decision was based. Although the law does not require the retailer to disclose the source of the information against the applicant, he must supply the consumer sufficient facts with which the accuracy of the information can be refuted or challenged.

Also, under certain circumstances a business may be regarded as a "consumer-reporting agency" under the law, and thus be subject to the same strict requirements as those imposed on credit bureaus. There is nothing in the law, for example, that would cause a retailer to hesitate to provide his own ledger experience about a consumer to the credit bureau of which he is a member so long as that information is accurate; this type of exchange is obviously basic to the operation of a cooperative credit-rating system and is not itself a "credit report." But suppose that the retailer granted credit to a customer despite a slightly unfavorable report on him by another retailer in town. Suppose, further, that the local finance company calls him to inquire about the customer and he relays the information given him by the second retailer. In this instance he would be regarded as a "credit-reporting agency" in the eyes of the law. Thus if the finance company rejects the customer's loan application and is thereby obliged to give the retailer's name and address to the rejected applicant, the retailer would be subject to the same requirements of the law as any other credit-reporting agency. Retailers and other businessmen would be well advised to leave credit reporting to the credit bureau and give out only *their own* factual ledger experience about consumers.

Another requirement of the Fair Credit Reporting Act with which the small businessman should be familiar is that any store which discounts consumer installment contracts through a bank or finance company must give the name and address of the third party to the indebted consumer. The bank or finance company, if it denies the loan, must then notify the consumer as required by the act.

The new law also restricts the use of credit reports, and credit bureaus are required to have those who request these reports certify in writing that they will be used for the expressed purpose. If a credit report is to be used for employment purposes, for example, *both* the credit bureau and the prospective employer have additional responsibilities under the act; these responsibilities were discussed in Chapter 16 (pp. 296-98).

Credit Management Associations

Whereas credit bureaus are credit-reporting agencies, credit management associations are dedicated to the personal and professional growth of credit administrators. One such group – the International Consumer Credit Association — is a nonprofit corporation which provides informational, educational, and other services for its members. Known for over 50 years as the National Retail Credit Association (prior to 1962), the ICCA is the only voluntary professional organization serving the entire field of consumer credit. Membership is open to any person actively engaged in any phase of consumer credit, including executives of banks; consumer and sales finance companies; credit unions; insurance firms; credit bureaus; educational institutions; and any business or profession which grants consumer credit.

A selected list of its services includes:

1. *Credit World,* a publication which presents a vast array of educational and informative material in easy-to-read and easy-to-understand form
2. Yearly industry conferences at the state, district, and national levels
3. Assistance in solving routine and special problems
4. A large selection of supplies, including credit and collection inserts and stickers, textbooks, credit application and age analysis forms, insignia, folders, booklets, posters, advertising materials, and many other items useful to the credit department
5. A monthly letter-writing service which provides subscribers with tailor-made credit and collection letters, as well as ideas for mail promotion.

Correspondence courses in various aspects of credit management are offered by the Society of Certified Consumer Credit Executives, a professional honorary society founded originally by the International Consumer Credit Association. Completion of specified courses leads to certification as a "Credit Counselor" (CC), "Associate Credit Executive" (ACE), or "Certified Consumer Credit Executive" (CCCE). Full membership in the society is limited to those who have been certified by the Board of Examiners, or who have earned the CCCE diploma. Correspondence courses are also offered by the extension divisions of certain universities. Ample material in book and pamphlet form is likewise available to the small businessman who cares to learn more about this subject.

Financing Credit Sales

Banks and finance companies help retailers finance their credit sales by purchasing retailers' installment contracts and unpaid open accounts. Whether or not these accounts or contracts are purchased at face value, or are discounted, depends on the lending institution, the nature of the contract, the customer, and local practice.

Conditional sales contracts may be direct- or indirect-collection contracts. Direct contracts are generally sold to the bank or finance company for the face value of the unpaid balance, plus the going rate of interest for such a transaction in that community at that time (perhaps 7 percent of the unpaid balance), plus additional collectable charges such as "credit life-and-disability insurance." The debtor signs a security agreement promising to pay the secured party (bank or loan company) a net amount each week or month until the unpaid balance and other charges are paid. Finance companies usually buy these contracts "without recourse" if the debtor is a reasonably good credit risk. Under such an agreement the retailer is free of further responsibility. Banks usually buy contracts "with recourse," so that if the debtor does not pay, the retailer is liable to the bank. However, often the bank charges a lower rate of interest than does the finance company.

Sometimes the retailer charges his customer as much as 10 percent interest, thus making an additional profit on the transaction. The justification for this is that if a buyer negotiates his own small loan he would be charged as much as this, or more, by a finance company. With an indirect collection contract, the debtor pays the retailer.

Finance companies are more likely than banks to purchase accounts receivable. Unpaid accounts are solicited and purchased (usually at a discount) from doctors, lumberyards, jewelers, fuel companies, and others. The finance company advances a certain percentage of the amount due on the account to the businessman, and holds another percentage in escrow as a "deferred payment reserve" that serves to increase the security of the advances made by the loan company. The loan company, then, through collection letters attempts to collect the account. Advances to the retailer by a bank range from 75 to 90 percent of the face amount of accounts receivable. The bank usually requires the retailer himself to be entirely responsible for payment of the accounts.

Although we have discussed elsewhere the use of banks in business financing, it should be recognized here again that (1) the credit grantor may find a bank loan necessary, as noted, to finance his "lending" at times; also (2) the customer may find the bank a more convenient or agreeable creditor than the establishment from which he is making the purchase; and (3) the seller and buyer may go to the bank together to solve the buyer's financing plan. Under the last arrangement, the seller may or may not find himself obligated in the buyer's borrowing agreement.

The "holder-in-due-course" doctrine.   Under existing federal and most state laws the bank, finance company, or other third party who purchases a dealer's installment contract is a "holder in due course" and is not responsible for any commitments the dealer might have made, such as the correction of a defect in the merchandise or perhaps an adjustment of some kind. If the dealer fails to make good on this commitment, the customer's only recourse is to sue the dealer; he has no recourse against the third party. On the other hand the third party, as the holder in due course, may sue the customer for collection of the debt. (If the third party purchased the contract "with recourse," as noted above, he may also sue the dealer.)

Consumer advocates, however, have criticized this doctrine and are seeking to have it abolished. By mid-1972 7 states required that all installment contracts include a notice that any third party buying the note is subject to any legitimate claims the consumer might have; nor can the consumer be forced to sign a contract clause which would waive his right to make such claims (the so-called waiver-of-defense clause). Approximately 20 other states have similarly restricted the holder-in-due-course doctrine in certain types of credit transactions, such as automobile sales, and comparable regulations are currently under consideration at the national level by the Federal Trade Commission.

CREDIT IN WHOLESALING

Wholesalers sell principally to small retailers, about 90 percent of whom need credit. The credit manager of the wholesale house is a valuable advisor for retailers who will consult with him. By granting or refusing retailers credit, he exerts a powerful influence on trade. If by extending credit he encourages an ill-advised business venture to start or a nearly defunct one to continue the hopeless struggle, the wholesaler does an injustice to all concerned – including competitors. The latter usually suffer when the failing business is forced to run closeout sales at a loss. Because of their strategic position in commerce, wholesalers are probably better able than any other type of businessman to give sound credit advice to retailers. The small wholesaler has the dual responsibility of protecting his own investment and encouraging promising small merchants while discouraging hopeless ones.

Credit Records as a Management Tool

Just as knowing more about credit customers can help retailers better meet the needs of customers and increase their own sales, a similar approach can be used by wholesalers. They can study their credit records, noting: the location of their customers, the type of business each operates, their distance from the wholesaler, the number of purchases they make, and the dollar volume of these purchases.

Recording this information on cards will make it possible to arrange the cards in a variety of ways to provide information such as the percentage of sales stemming from certain classifications of customers, the volume of sales per classification, the average size of sale, or the frequency of orders. The wholesaler may discover that it is not profitable to do business with a particular type of concern, or beyond a certain distance, or when orders are small or infrequent. Carefully planned and selective selling will eliminate unnecessary expense, secure more profitable sales, and increase net profits.

Mercantile Credit Ratings

The financial standing of many business firms is rated by credit-reporting agencies like Dun & Bradstreet. Since a favorable credit rating is highly desirable, businessmen strive to safeguard this precious asset. However, "ratings" are not always up to date, and many small-scale or newly established retailers do not have one. These facts limit the value of the mercantile credit-reporting agency's service in many cases, especially as far as the wholesaler is concerned. However, the agency may still be employed effectively in the case of doubtful credit prospects to secure special credit reports that are likely to be somewhat more reliable than the wholesaler's independent appraisal.

Credit Insurance

Unlike consumer credit, trade credit is insurable. Credit insurance is guaranty of accounts receivable as additional security for loans to business concerns. Briefly stated, credit insurance is a form of insurance to protect the merchant against loss arising from sales on credit to debtors who have one of the stipulated mercantile agency ratings. Credit insurance coverage is limited to manufacturers, jobbers, or wholesalers who sell to the trade. Experiments are under way for insuring retail credits.

The insurance policy provides protection against all known forms of debtor insolvency, and guarantees the payment of all past-due accounts filed with the insurance company within 90 days after due date in accordance with the provisions of the policy.

The insurance company does not attempt to replace the credit manager of a concern, but rather aims at widening the efficient credit work of businessmen and to educate them in the importance of building up well-equipped credit departments. The policyholder is required to bear a small percentage of the covered loss as coinsurance. The insurance is only against loss in excess of this normal loss, which is borne by the merchant himself. In practice, the merchant's expected loss is regarded as an expense of doing business.

CREDIT IN THE SMALL FACTORY

Credit management in the small factory has certain conditions in common with that in wholesaling. Both deal in mercantile credit, except when the small factory sells direct to consumers exclusively. Both use commercial ratings and other sources of information on the financial standing of business firms. However, the nature of their customers may introduce significant differences. For example, the small wholesaler is more likely to have a preponderance of retail store customers who either are not rated or whose ratings are less reliable than those of the small manufacturer's customers. Offsetting this is the wholesaler's more favorable position in becoming personally familiar with his customer's business.

Customers of the small factory will usually be other businessmen. Merchants or service establishments to which direct sales are made will be either established firms with ratings or small concerns in the vicinity of the factory. Other factories that make purchases are likely to be larger concerns. In any case it is well to be familiar with sources of information and the various services available in the field of mercantile or commercial credit.

Client Information

Dun & Bradstreet publishes reference books containing ratings of business concerns, issues special reports to members, supplies analytical reports, provides a continuous report service, offers a limited credit-checking service, prepares business analyses, may collect overdue accounts, will conduct special surveys, and publishes *Dun's Review and Modern Industry*. Except for a subscription to the last-named periodical, the services mentioned are rendered on a contract basis to members or subscribers of Dun & Bradstreet's services.

Information on new or prospective customers may be obtained from other creditors through direct exchange, either personally or by correspondence. Credit bureaus maintained by associations of credit men for the exchange of ledger experience and information are another source, and trade credit bureaus operated by trade associations are also useful. Information may be obtained from sales representatives who are familiar with the company under investigation, and salesmen of creditors, attorneys, and banks may be able to tell if the firm is a good risk. Other sources of information are corporation manuals, corporation financial services, and trade and financial publications. Before giving credit, of course, the manufacturer may wish to have a personal interview with the prospect and perhaps secure a financial statement directly from him.

Various special agencies provide credit services to business, many of them being of particular interest to smaller concerns that have no established credit department. Some are affiliated with trade associations. Many of these agencies are specialized as to industry, such as furniture, plumbing, textiles, shoes, paint, produce, and the like. Various state and local facilities also exist. They issue rating books regularly or from time to time, which are distributed to subscribers, and ordinarily provide a collection service as well, on a percentage fee basis. Some of these special agencies are the National Credit Office of New York City, the Manufacturers Clearing House, the Iron and Steel Board of Trade, the Credit Clearing House (a Dun & Bradstreet service), the Lyon Furniture Mercantile Agency, and the Shoe and Leather Mercantile Agency.

The rating books published by such agencies usually indicate, by symbol, the listee's general credit standing, current capital resources, and paying habits and method, supplemented by any pertinent special information. Such special items include evidence of continued unethical or troublesome practices, excessive returns of merchandise, chronic complaints without justification, disregarding of sales contract terms such as deduction of discounts not earned, or unreasonable requests for service. All such data are accumulated from field investigations conducted by the agency.

These agencies, as noted, provide a variety of services, from simple reporting of "slow-pay" firms, through listing of firms who have sold to a listee, to those who give credit data in extreme detail — some even providing insured recommendations. The strength of many lies in their specialization and the pertinent detail resulting, and the currency of their reports. The national or state trade association, to which the small businessman should belong, can refer him to a reputable credit agency. Local Chambers of Commerce often include a credit bureau as a part of their services.

If we consider the bank as a factor in commercial credit, as apart from financing the business establishment, the possibilities of the warehouse receipt or of field warehousing cannot be overlooked. A producer of seasonal goods, having produced for months but sold little, may require more funds, probably for more materials and further labor. He can store his manufactured goods in a public warehouse and receive a negotiable receipt approximating their value; the bank or his supplier will honor the receipt as collateral for further credit. Field warehousing, a service provided by licensed warehouse firms, permits similar arrangements under sealed, guarded storage on the premises of the maker or elsewhere; negotiable receipts are issued and employed as before.

Trade Credit Terms

If a prospect seems to be a good risk, credit is extended and an account opened for him. Terms must be decided upon at the beginning. Slow accounts are just as dangerous in a manufacturing or wholesaling concern as they are in a retail or service business. Not only do they tie up working capital, but if they are not collected over a period of time they will slow down production. In most trades, cash discounts are offered for payment within a certain length of time; otherwise the total amount must be paid. Such terms are stated "2/10, net 30," which means that a 2 percent discount is allowed if payment is made within 10 days and that in any event the total amount must be paid within 30 days. Some businesses buy in small quantities, and frequently. In such cases the manufacturer may extend M.O.M. or E.O.M. terms. Under M.O.M. (*middle of month*) terms, all purchases bought before the middle of the month are billed as of the 15th; if such a discount as that granted in the terms "2/10, net 30" is allowed, it can be taken through the 25th of the month. For example, an invoice dated March 3, terms 2/10, net 30 M.O.M., could be discounted at 2 percent if paid on or before March 25, the net amount of the invoice being due April 15. An invoice dated March 16, with the same terms, could be discounted up to April 25 or paid net May 15. E.O.M. (*end of month*) terms are very similar to M.O.M. except that all purchases are billed as of the end of the month instead of the middle, and discount periods as well as due dates are based on that date. Other terms often used are: R.O.G. (*receipt of goods*), which means that the discount period starts only after the goods have been received; *extra dating*, which indicates that the discount period is extended for so many days after the regular allowed term; and *season dating*, which is another form of *extra dating* but is for a much longer period of time, because buyers are reluctant to pay immediately for goods purchased as much as seven or eight months in advance of demand.

A misuse of credit insofar as cash discounts are concerned may occur when some firms remit the amount of the bill less the cash discount even though the discount period has passed and, in some cases, the net period as well. Permitting such a practice would certainly be unfair to the prompt-paying customer. Sometimes the remittance must be accepted, but no further credit should be extended. The amount of the discount may be added to the next bill, or the check may be returned with a note reminding the debtor that the discount was not to be taken and asking him please to remit the proper amount. Laxness in enforcing terms will only bring loss to the company.

Both wholesalers and manufacturers have occasion at times to sell on a C.O.D. (*collect on delivery*) basis. Goods sent C.O.D. are usually sent to credit risks that are known to be undesirable, or to simply unknown firms. Instead of sending merchandise C.O.D. and letting the shipping company collect for the merchandise, the manufacturer may wish to send a sight draft with a bill of lading attached. A bill of lading is evidence of title when the goods are shipped by a common carrier. When the merchandise arrives, the buyer is notified and he comes down to pay the amount of the draft and receive title to the goods. This applies only to a cash transaction.

Manufacturers and wholesalers often find it desirable to relate credit terms to the size of the order. This procedure has a dual purpose. By this limitation of credit to orders above a minimum quantity, customers are encouraged to place orders of sufficient size for economical handling; furthermore, encouraging the larger orders favors the better-established firms and thus tends to reduce the risk of granting credit.

CREDIT IN THE SERVICE BUSINESS

Because services are by their very nature intangible, nonreturnable, and "consumed" when rendered, credit extension is more risky and less common in this than in the other fields of small business. However, small service establishments with regular customers and frequent repeat sales, such as laundries and dry-cleaning establishments, often find credit extension a convenience that is attractive to many customers. This is especially true when it is accompanied by pickup and delivery service. Naturally, prices will have to be higher than if the business were run on a cash-and-carry basis.

Personal service establishments like beauty parlors and many types of repair services find that credit extension brings increased business. In all such cases, credit is primarily a customer convenience and is based on the willingness and ability of customers to pay. There can be no reliance on tangible goods as security, except in such special cases as when the law permits a hotel to retain the baggage of nonpaying guests.

Except for these differences, credit for the service business is similar to that for the retail store. Usually only open-account credit is appropriate, although major repairs on durable goods may be paid for on the installment plan. Account solicitation, sources of information, investigation of applicants, record keeping, and credit control are very similar in both fields.

Probably the typical service business has more to gain and less desirable business to lose by striving to reduce its credit business to a minimum than do firms in other fields. Since the quality of service rendered is of major importance, this will often be a more powerful means of attracting business than the credit extension.

SUMMARY AND CONCLUSIONS

Although credit carelessly handled can ruin any small business, carefully controlled credit has two major advantages. In many cases business gravitates to the credit-granting firm. *The mere availability of credit is sufficient to attract and hold many customers who would not trade with the firm if credit were not extended. Furthermore, information furnished by the credit customers' records can serve management.* Although credit is primarily a customer service, proper use of the information it provides can make it also a powerful tool of management.

Many surveys show the total cost of consumer credit extended by retail stores to be close to 3 percent of net sales, bad-debt losses accounting for about one-half of 1 percent. Credit-granting stores, however, tend to be more profitable than strictly cash stores.

Certain principles governing credit extension have been well established and should be observed. One is that the length of the credit period should not exceed the useful life of the merchandise. Another is that the longer an account is overdue the harder it is to collect.

Credit bureaus and other organizations provide useful information to small businessmen. Experience shows that using them greatly reduces losses resulting from credit extension.

The credit-card plans offered by banks, oil companies, and other organizations appear to be an ideal opportunity for independent enterprisers to secure the advantages of doing business on credit while avoiding many of the disadvantages. People may use these cards practically any place to purchase meals, lodging, gasoline, and other goods, and receive a single monthly statement that also serves as an expense and tax record. Certain types of small businesses should find this method of credit extension advantageous.

The purpose of credit extension is to help the customer to buy; but the purpose of business is to make a profit. Difficulties arise when the temptation to sell at all costs makes the seller forget there must be a "day of reckoning." A transaction is profitable only if the bill for goods or services is paid promptly. This lack of realism is one of the beginning businessman's greatest hazards. To say that profitable credit decisions often call for "nerves of steel" is no great exaggeration. Friends or relatives, former business associates, the big name, or the large order may constitute pressure for credit which is often hard to resist. Sound credit decisions must be based only on logical thinking and actions. If we criticize the banker's traditional "coldness" in lending situations, we must remember that friendly enthusiasm and blood ties have been an expensive luxury for many a businessman; better to be rational and objective and profitable in business than emotional and subjective and bankrupt. Those who have suffered believe that it is better to lose a friend quickly through refusal of credit to him, than slowly through the long trials surrounding his refusal to pay.

REVIEW QUESTIONS

1. What is "credit"? Why do most firms find it necessary to grant credit?
2. Differentiate between consumer credit and mercantile credit. Discuss fully the different types of credit arrangements commonly available to consumers and tradesmen.
3. What is "cycle billing"?
4. Differentiate between the conditional sales contract and the chattel mortgage.
5. When is installment credit likely to be appropriate? What principles should be observed in granting installment credit?
6. What are the advantages and disadvantages of granting credit?
7. What are the sources of information on which individual credit decisions are usually based? Discuss fully the "three C's" of credit.
8. How may credit be used as a "sales tool"? Discuss fully.
9. Why, in the authors' opinion, is it better to cultivate credit customers rather than cash customers?
10. What are the dangers of having too many "slow" accounts? How can the trend toward slow accounts be measured?
11. What is the purpose of the Truth-in-Lending law? How does the law define a "finance charge"? How are finance-charge rates regulated?
12. What is "regulation Z"? What are its major disclosure requirements?

13. What are the requirements of a sound credit system?

14. What are the advantages, to the seller of goods and services, of subscribing to a national or regional credit-card service?

15. What are credit bureaus, and what services do they perform for the local businessman? How do business firms themselves receive a "credit rating"?

16. What is the purpose of the Fair Credit Reporting Act? What are its major provisions?

17. Differentiate between credit bureaus and credit management associations.

18. How do banks and finance companies help retailers finance their credit sales?

19. Differentiate between direct and indirect conditional sales contracts. What is meant by the purchase of a conditional sales contract "without recourse"?

20. Describe the procedure by which banks and finance companies "purchase" accounts receivable.

21. Discuss fully the "holder-in-due-course" doctrine.

22. What sources of client information are available to the small manufacturer?

23. Describe some of the common credit terms granted by wholesalers and manufacturers.

24. Discuss warehouse receipts and field warehousing as instruments of commercial credit for the small manufacturer.

25. Why do manufacturers often find it desirable to relate credit terms to the size of the order?

26. Why is credit extension less common in the service trades than in other types of business enterprise? How does credit in the service business differ from that in the retail business?

DISCUSSION QUESTIONS

1. Since most surveys show that credit-granting stores are more profitable than stores selling only for cash, how do you explain the success of some cash-and-carry retailers?

2. Assume that you have purchased a going business in which liberal credit has been the policy for years and that you want to operate on a strictly cash policy. Explain how you would proceed.

3. Sam's small department store did 45 percent of its volume on open-account credit, 15 percent on installment, 5 percent on semi-credit plans, and 35 percent in cash. An increasing proportion of customers were younger families in their early twenties. Sam had complete records on all credit sales since 1962. Sales had increased rapidly from 1962 to 1967, then declined to mid-1972 when they were $2.3 million. Sam suspected that credit plans recently being promoted aggressively by several of his larger competitors were responsible for his failure to progress. What should he do and why? Consider at least three alternate approaches for him to use. Analyze and justify each.

SUPPLEMENTARY READING

Phelps, Clyde William. *Retail Credit Fundamentals*. 4th ed. St. Louis: International Consumer Credit Association, 1963. Instead of attempting to cover in superficial fashion all of the various subjects in which a consumer credit executive might be interested, this book — the official textbook of the International Consumer Credit Association — discusses in a thorough manner only those *basic* functions which every employee in the credit department of a large store, or every small businessman who extends credit to his customers, should know. In its practical approach it emphasizes not only the *what* and *how* of each functional credit-granting activity, but also the reasons *why*.

21

Inventory control

Every business requires some inventory of goods. In most lines this inventory of merchandise, materials, parts, or supplies represents a sizable investment of the owner's capital. In general, the merchant invests a larger proportion of his capital in inventories than does the small manufacturer, and the service businessman invests a smaller proportion than either.[1] Unless inventories are controlled they tend to get out of balance and result in loss to the business. It is the primary prupose of inventory control to maintain the balance that permits most profitable operations.

An inventory may be out of balance in either direction; that is, it may be too large or too small. If it is too large relative to the demand for it, the cost of carrying the inventory will be higher than it need be. Inventory carrying costs include such things as interest on the inventory investment, handling costs, depreciation and obsolescence, taxes and insurance, and storage or warehousing costs. Often these costs, per year, run as high as 25 percent or more of the inventory investment. Therefore, an important objective in inventory control is to reduce the average investment in inventory by increasing the turnover of the inventory. With each increase in the number of times the material "turns over" during the year, there will be a proportionate *decrease* in the annual cost of carrying the inventory. This is demonstrated in the following table, for a company with an annual sale of goods costing $120,000 and an annual inventory carrying cost amounting to 25 percent of the inventory investment:

Turns per Year	Annual Inventory Investment	Annual Inventory Carrying Cost
1	$120,000	$30,000
2	60,000	15,000
3	40,000	10,000
4	30,000	7,500
5	24,000	6,000

[1] It is not uncommon for a manufacturing concern to have 25 percent or more of its total invested capital tied up in inventories.

On the other hand, if the inventory is too small relative to the demand for it "stockouts" will occur, and these will add to the firm's operating costs. For example, rush orders or special orders not only require special handling, but they almost always involve uneconomic ordering quantities. If it is an item that is needed in the factory, it may also cause costly production delays. And if it is a consumer's item, then there will be dissatisfied customers and lost sales. Not only is the immediate sale lost, but an indeterminable amount of future business as well. Though stockout costs of the latter type are difficult to estimate, they are none-theless real. In any case, the businessman should estimate his stockout costs and strike a balance between these costs and the costs of carrying a larger inventory.

The faster the inventory turnover, the greater is the probability of running out of stock. For example, in the following table is listed the average *monthly* investment associated with the above inventory turnovers. This is done in recognition of the fact that the demand for almost any item is a seasonal demand – that is, it varies from month to month. This variation in demand, of course, can be determined from past sales records. Column 2 in the following table is based on the frequency with which the company experienced each of the monthly inventory demands during the past 10 years (120 months). Column 3 converts these figures into percentages or probabilities, and column 4 cumulates the probabilities. Thus with sales costing $120,000 per year, or $10,000 per month, and an inventory turnover of only 1, it is improbable that the company will ever run out of stock unless there is a shift in the demand pattern. At the other end of the spectrum (an inventory turnover of 5 times), there is only a 5 percent probability that the company will not run out of stock; similarly, there will be a 10 percent probability that the company will lose sales costing $500 (i.e., $2,500 – $2,000), a 70 percent probability of losing sales costing $1,333 (i.e., $3,333 – $2,000), and so on.

	(1)	(2)	(3)	(4)	(5)
Turns per Year	Average Monthly Demand = Average Monthly Inventory Investment	Frequency of Occurrence	Probability of Occurrence	Cumulative Probability	Annual Stockout Cost
5	$ 2,000	6	5%	5%	$4,210
4	2,500	12	10	15	2,416
3	3,333	84	70	85	750
2	5,000	12	10	95	250
1	10,000	6	5	100	0
		120			

Thus with each increase in the number of times the inventory turns over during the year, there will be a further *increase* in the annual cost of inventory stockouts. These increases are shown in column 5 (reading from bottom to top), and are based on the estimate that stockout costs amount to 50 percent of the original cost of each item. The stockout costs in column 5 were computed as follows:

$$5[(.05 \times \$0 \times .50) + (.10 \times \$500 \times .50) + (.70 \times \$1,333 \times .50)$$
$$+ (.10 \times \$3,000 \times .50) + (.05 \times \$8,000 \times .50)] = \$4,210$$
$$4[(.15 \times \$0 \times .50) + (.70 \times \$833 \times .50) + (.10 \times \$2,500 \times .50)$$
$$+ (.05 \times \$7,500 \times .50)] = \$2,416$$
$$3[(.85 \times \$0 \times .50) + (.10 \times \$1,667 \times .50)$$
$$+ (0.5 \times \$6,667 \times .50)] = \$750$$
$$2[(.95 \times \$0 \times .50) + (.05 \times \$5,000 \times .50)] = \$250$$
$$1[(1.00 \times \$0 \times .50)] - \$0$$

The factor 5, 4, 3, 2, or 1 represents the number of times each year the company runs the risk of running out of stock, which is equal to the inventory turnover (or the number of times each year the inventory is replenished).

To summarize, as the number of times the inventory "turns over," inventory carrying costs decrease and stockout costs increase. Thus the optimum inventory turnover occurs when these incremental costs when *combined* are at a minimum. From an examination of the following table, which summarizes these costs, it is observed that the optimum inventory turnover in the above case is 4 times per year.

Turns per Year	Annual Inventory Carrying Cost	Annual Stockout Cost	Total Annual Cost
1	$30,000	$ 0	$30,000
2	15,000	250	15,250
3	10,000	750	10,750
4	7,500	2,416	9,916
5	6,000	4,210	10,210

Inventory management may involve either *dollar* control or *unit* control. In the above example, the proper inventory level was determined in terms of the dollar value of the inventory. In many situations it is more convenient to establish average inventory levels in terms of the number of units of each kind of inventory. In either case, however, the general procedure is the same; the only difference is that carrying and stockout costs are expressed in terms of the cost per unit, rather than in terms of the cost per dollar of investment. For example, let us assume that the inventory in the above example represents the value (cost) of a single product sold or manufactured by the entrepreneur, and that this cost is $1.00 per unit. The annual cost of carrying this inventory, then, would be expressed as $0.25 per *unit*, and the stockout cost as $0.50 per *unit*. The optimum inventory turnover, of course, remains 4 times per year, and the average monthly inventory at this turnover rate would be 2,500 *units*.

Unit control is particularly important in the control of raw materials and parts used in manufacturing, and in those merchandising establishments which market a wide variety of products. But even in these cases, the entrepreneur may *also* be concerned with the total amount of capital he has invested in the inventory.

For example, the inventory may be well balanced in terms of the number of units of each item within a total amount, but be dangerously out of balance with regard to the dollar value invested. This is true especially (1) at the peak of a rising price trend, (2) just before a pronounced upward swing in prices, and (3) when shortages with controlled prices are imminent. Each of these three important but unusual situations requires management policy decision and lies beyond the normal scope of inventory control, although each may influence management's concern regarding present conditions of the firm's inventory.

Thus a major purpose in business is to have the right goods at the right place at the right time. This means having adequate merchandise on call and available to meet the demands of customers. Merchandise also represents an investment in funds, an investment which can be well or poorly controlled, well or poorly guarded and guided in use. In any measure of business efficiency the degree to which the wants of customers are satisfied readily, and the degree to which capital funds are used effectively must be given proper weight.

Some system must be used if inventory control is to be even moderately efficient. An early question in establishing a system is whether value or quantity is the factor controlled. In merchandising, especially, both dollar-control and unit-control systems are often used. Regardless of the system used, however, certain information must be fed into it. Effective inventory control requires accurate information from the using departments (sales in the case of merchandising, processing in the case of manufacturing or a service business) concerning the kind or quality of goods wanted, the quantities required of each, and the dates on which they are needed. Systems or methods used to secure the information essential for inventory control will usually operate through observation, physical checks, or a perpetual inventory record.[2]

Any form of inventory or stores control works with the following basic data: quantities needed, amounts on hand, additions to stock (purchases), subtractions (sales or issues), goods on order, and critical points at which action is needed. The last are usually expressed as "reorder points." Whenever the quantity on hand or available reaches a predetermined "reordering point," steps must be taken to replenish the inventory if it is to be kept in balance. The quantity to order at any one time is also predetermined, and is an important element in the operation of many inventory control systems.

Stores keeping, or the physical handling and storage of merchandise, materials, and parts, must also be performed efficiently. This requires adequate facilities to store each item in such a way that it will be protected and can be located quickly as needed. If some items are carried on consignment, stores keeping should provide for their special identification.

Finally, inventory taking, or the counting of articles on hand, must be carried out from time to time. When the physical-count or frequent-check system of inventory control is used for all items stocked, and each count is recorded on the inventory control card (or ledger), it may not be necessary to take additional inventories. However, if the perpetual inventory system is used, actual counts must be made from time to time to correct the book figures.

[2] "Perpetual" or "book" inventories vary with the type of business and are discussed in various parts of this chapter.

INVENTORY CONTROL IN MERCHANDISING

The small retailer's biggest investment is his inventory of merchandise carried. When this can be kept at the optimum amount, profits are increased. When inventories are well balanced at all times, the investment in merchandise is working most effectively. Among the major advantages of inventory or merchandise control in retailing is the fact that it enables the retailer to do the following: (1) balance stocks as to value, size, color, style, and price line, in proportion to sales; (2) "play the winners," as well as move slow sellers; and (3) secure the best rate of stock turnover for each item. Expenses and markdowns are reduced. The store's reputation for always having new, fresh merchandise in wanted sizes and colors is one of the major long-run benefits of good merchandise control.

Information provided by a good system of merchandise control that will improve both buying and selling activities includes the following:

1. Price preferences of customers
2. Items no longer popular
3. Right quantities to buy
4. Amount of a given item sold
5. Season or time a given item sells
6. Time to stop buying seasonable goods
7. Kind and style of goods customers want
8. Time to display and promote certain items
9. Slow movers
10. Particular items for which demand is falling off
11. Best buying sources
12. Best buying prices
13. Possibilities for new lines or kinds of goods
14. Whether stock is in proper balance[3]

A control system giving this information will eliminate guesswork and memory — both unreliable guides to inventory management.

Every store that has tried a stock control system for the first time has found that the greatest number of items in stock are rarely asked for or sold. Difficult as this is to believe, it has been found that from 20 to 25 percent of the items in a poorly controlled store produce from 75 to 80 percent of sales.

Efficient, profitable merchandise control need not be difficult, complex, or expensive. Many agencies, organizations, and associations can furnish good control systems to store owners in their respective fields. These system forms are economical, simple, and easy to operate. They are easy to install, can be brief or extended to fit the need, and can be handled in a few minutes each day.

[3] *Controlling Merchandise* (Dayton, Ohio: National Cash Register Company, 1958), p. 5.

Following is a tabular representation of an unguided buying policy. With an effective stock control system, A and C (as represented in the table) can be reduced:

```
If AB represents what you buy  . . . . . . . . . .  A        B
And BC is what customers want . . . . . . . . . . . . . . . .  B        C
Then B is what you sell . . . . . . . . . . . . . . . . . . . .  B
A are the "sleepers" . . . . . . . . . . . . . . . .  A
C represents the "outs" . . . . . . . . . . . . . . . . . . . . . . . . . .  C
```

Since inventory control tends to increase the rate of stock turnover, it may be well to illustrate how important this advantage may be to the small retailer. Figures and operating ratios used are representative of many small general merchandise stores. Consider a store with annual sales of $50,000, stock turnover 3 times a year, rent 5 percent of sales, and gross margin 40 percent. If a turnover of 4 times a year is standard in the field, the situation can be summarized as follows:

Present condition:

$50,000 ÷ 3 = $16,667 . . . . .Average inventory at retail

$16,667 × 60% = $10,000 . . . . Average inventory at cost

Goal or standard:

$50,000 ÷ 4 = $12,500 . . . . .Average inventory at retail

$12,500 × 60% = $7,500 . . . . Average inventory at cost

Excess inventory: $10,000 − $7,500 = $2,500

Interest on excess investment: $2,500 @ 6% = $ 150

Approximate rent for space used to store surplus inventory:

$50,000 × 5% ÷ 4 ($2,500 is ¼ of $10,000) = $ 625

The smaller inventory, turning more rapidly, might reduce markdowns, shrinkage,

and handling costs by 2% of sales (estimate):

$50,000 × 2% = $1,000

Total Probable Gain $1,775

Average net profit for stores of this class might be 3 percent; $50,000 × 3% = $1,500. Therefore, the total gain from increased turnover in this example is greater than the average net profit. The more rapid turnover might change a losing concern into one with average or better-than-average profits.

In the illustration it is assumed that the turnover of 4 times could be accomplished with no increased expense, that the space occupied by the 25 percent surplus stock accounted for 25 percent of the total rent, and that when this space was released it could be used effectively in selling the larger volume of merchandise. These would be reasonable assumptions in most cases. They are mentioned merely to caution the reader against overemphasizing the magic of increased turnover by failing to take related factors into consideration.

For most types of inventory control, as well as for other purposes, it is desirable to classify the goods carried into merchandise departments, i.e., to departmentalize the store. Similar and related items are grouped together, both in the store layout and in merchandise control records. Standard departmental classifications should be used as recommended by the trade association in the field.

Keeping Track of Inventories

Among the methods of securing the information needed for inventory control in a small retail store are the following: observation, physical check, and the perpetual inventory record. Observation may be sufficient in a very small store in which the variety of merchandise is not large, the rate of sale is fairly constant, and the owner keeps in very close daily contact with all goods. Usually, however, a physical check or count is necessary at intervals that vary according to the rate of sale and importance of the merchandise. It may be a simple or approximate check, as in the case of volume control of staple hardware items, or a careful and accurate one for higher-value shopping goods.

Perpetual inventory.   With a perpetual inventory record the merchant knows at all times the amounts of goods that should be on hand. Such a record is illustrated in Figure 21-1. The posting of sales to this stock record may be made from sales slips or from stub tickets or tags which are detached from the merchandise when it is sold. Separate running records are kept of individual sizes, colors, styles, etc. This method of merchandise control, however, is practical only for goods of high unit value and pronounced demand changes.

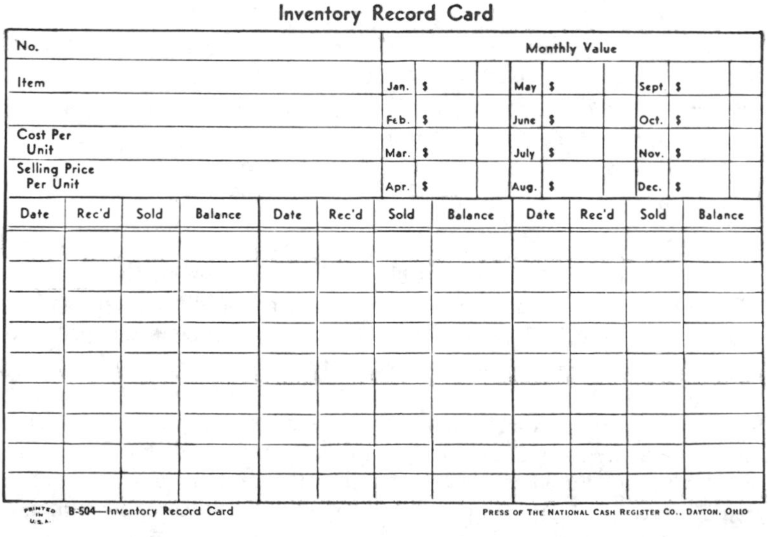

Inventory Record Card

| No. | | | | | | Monthly Value | | | | | | |

| Item | | | | | Jan. | $ | May | $ | Sept | $ | |

(form with columns: Date, Rec'd, Sold, Balance repeated; Cost Per Unit; Selling Price Per Unit; monthly value entries Jan.–Dec.)

B-504—Inventory Record Card   PRESS OF THE NATIONAL CASH REGISTER CO., DAYTON, OHIO

Figure 21-1.   Perpetual Inventory Record, as Commonly Used in Retailing

Physical count.   For most departments of an average small store periodic stocktaking is sufficient. The following tabulation, for example, illustrates how the retailer can order sizes, colors, or styles of merchandise in proper proportion without the expense of individual record handling:

| | Size or Style Number | | | | | |
	1	2	3	4	5	Total
On hand, June 1	18	26	21	16	15	96
Received during June		18	36	18		72
	18	44	57	34	15	168
On hand, July 1	6	21	24	9	3	63
Sold during June	12	23	33	25	12	105

The quantity sold is obtained by adding the number on hand at the beginning of the period and the number received, and deducting the number on hand at the end of the period. The amount needed to bring stock up to normal is estimated and the order made out. Assuming that no seasonal change in sales is anticipated, that a one-month supply is sufficient to order, and that 6 is the minimum packing for each size or style (or color), the order is estimated as follows:

| | Size or Style Number | | | | | |
	1	2	3	4	5	Total
Sold during June	12	23	33	25	12	105
On hand, July 1	6	21	24	9	3	63
Needed to replenish stock	6	2	9	16	9	42
Necessary to order, July 1	6	6	12	18	12	54

Though 12 units more than are required for the next period are being purchased, the stocks will be balanced again at the time of the next check and order.

Dating codes.   A dating code is a way of designating how long an item has been on the shelf. By means of the code, the older stock can be sold first (i.e., on a first-in, first-out basis), and thus the freshness of a packaged item can be kept from deteriorating to the point when it should be removed from the shelf. Formerly, dating codes were used that could be deciphered only by the retailer. For example, the code number "6206" might mean the item should be sold before December 20. The retailer determined this by adding the first and last digits to get the month, the middle two digits representing the day of the month.

Dating codes have long been used by many retailers to preserve the freshness of their stock, particularly in food stores. However, the consumer movement has lately focused attention on "open" or simple dating codes that can be interpreted by the purchaser as well as by the merchant; as, for example, "exp. Dec. 30." Though open-code dating is not required by law, it has nevertheless become a competitive practice of the corporate chain stores which more and more small retailers feel compelled to adopt.

Unit Control vs. Dollar Control

Stores having a very small volume of sales and limited amounts of merchandise may not need much of a merchandise control system. Continuous first-hand contact with stocks on hand may be sufficient. Even in larger stores where persons responsible for inventory control are in training for positions as buyers or managers, emphasis is often placed on daily personal familiarity with merchandise on hand and merchandise needed. However, in most cases the small retailer should take advantage of a suitable merchandise control system as an aid to his numerous managerial duties.

Before deciding what type of merchandise control system to use, at least the following factors should be considered: (1) what information is needed, (2) what uses will be made of it, (3) by whom it will be used, (4) how much detail is necessary, (5) what expense is justified to obtain this information, (6) the type of merchandise involved, and (7) what systems are used by other stores of a similar type. The last consideration may enable the merchant both to profit by the experience of other retailers in the same line of business in selecting the best system and also to compare his operating data with their results.

As noted previously, inventory management may involve either *dollar* control or *unit* control. In the former, standards are set, operations are reported, and corrective action is taken in terms of the dollar value of the inventory concerned. Thus planned sales for a department might be $10,000 for a six-month season; actual sales and purchases are reported in dollar value, usually at retail, and adjustments needed are made in terms of dollar value. This makes the buyer responsible for converting dollar amounts into specific items and quantities of goods. In unit control, the same steps are carried out in terms of number of items of each kind of merchandise or inventory. Dollar control is ordinarily used for all departments and kinds of merchandise; unit control is employed primarily when an assortment or variety is included under one class or line of goods. Unit control frequently involves some form of perpetual inventory to cover in physical quantity each important variation within the line of goods concerned. The type of unit control to use depends upon: regularity of the relative sales of each variety, unit value of the merchandise, length of the selling season, store policy, and possibly other factors.

When each variety within a line or class of goods sells at a fairly constant rate throughout the year, a basic stock system with periodic physical counts is sufficient.[4] A checklist may be used with clerical assistants to do the checking. In the case of seasonal goods or of others with a short selling period, such as skates, sports equipment, or rubbers, checking should be more frequent and greater attention should be given by the buyer to prevent loss from "outs" or end-of-season overstocks. When the unit value of each item is small, unit control can be operated in terms of reserve stock or full cartons rather than of individual items. This is sometimes called a "requisition system."

---

[4] A "basic stock" list is used for staple merchandise and should indicate not only the names of the items to be carried but also the minimum quantities to be maintained, reorder points, and the quantities to be reordered at any one time. In contrast, a "model stock" is most applicable to fashion merchandise and is a general breakdown of the line or class of goods in terms of such factors as size, color, style, price line, etc.

The most valuable area for unit control is in shopping goods and especially in fashion merchandise of fairly high unit value, such as wearing apparel, shoes, furniture, and many house furnishings and appliances. For such merchandise, unit control is obtained by keeping a daily running record of sales and stocks of each variety of each item within the line or class of goods. Two types of systems are in general use: merchandise tag and clerk tabulation. In the former each piece of merchandise has attached to it a tag of some sort, usually perforated and ordinarily with two duplicate parts. Each time an article is sold, one part of the tag is removed and either sent in to the office with the salescheck or deposited in a special container by the salesclerk. Small stores often have each salesclerk record or tabulate the specific size, style, color, and other characteristics of the merchandise as each item is sold. Sometimes this information is included on the salescheck instead of being kept as a separate record. Modern cash registers furnish stubs that are often used for unit control records. In all cases a unit control clerk, who may be the proprietor himself in a very small store, should summarize the data at least once a day so that a perpetual inventory in units of each variety may be kept.

To the small or beginning merchant, unit control seems like an unnecessary amount of trouble. However, it is the basis of modern merchandising. To be out of a particular size, style, color, price line, or other variety of a line or class of goods is the same as for a carpenter to have a saw but no hammer, a plumber to have pipe but no wrench, or a stenographer to be without a pencil. One lacks what it takes to do the job. Not only does the merchant lose the sale, but he helps his prospective customer acquire the habit of trading with competitors. There is probably no greater error in merchandising than to be out of wanted items, even occasionally! Naturally, however, this does not mean that a retailer should stock every item asked for by customers no matter how infrequently.

Our emphasis on unit rather than dollar control has been deliberate. The whole trend of merchandising for four decades has been toward greater unit control. Dollar control is necessary, especially for the huge organization with hundreds of merchandise departments and scores of buyers; but it is unit control that spells merchandising success or failure in the small store. If the unit control is right, dollar control will take care of itself — to the merchant's profit.

Staple vs. fashion goods.   The type of inventory control system most suitable depends upon the merchandise. Stability of demand and regularity of sale are major factors. For staple items, such as pins, needles, brooms, nails, toothpaste, bread, milk, chewing gum, and cigarettes — products which rarely change and have fairly regular sales — simple routine merchandise control systems are best. Certain items are staples for particular seasons, such as fireworks, Easter eggs, Santa Clauses, overshoes, skates, and water wings. Inventories of such items should be large at the beginning and as small as possible to secure maximum profitable sales during the closing days of the season. Whether to close out or carry over an inventory is a matter of store policy. In either case the inventory of seasonal merchandise should be at a minimum at the end of the selling period.

Staple items are fairly well standardized. In modern merchandising many staple goods consist of a series or assortment of individual items that are not substitutes for one another and that sell at different rates. Three types of variation are especially important: size, kind, and brand. Other characteristics that often operate are color, price, quality, or attributes peculiar to certain merchandise. There are few varieties or sizes of pins, but many of needles and still more of nails. With cigarettes, brand is important. In staple canned goods, brand, size, grade (quality), and price are major variables. Many items are staples with fashion-affected varieties, such as thread, bias tape, and most yard goods. White and black in popular sizes are likely to be staple, with other colors and patterns, as well as types of construction, affected by the current fashions.

Although it is not the function of merchandise control to predict demand or fashion changes, it is necessary to use different control systems when demand is erratic or subject to fashion influence. Buyers need information concerning (1) the quantity of merchandise on hand, and (2) reports or warnings in case the inventory changes from that planned. If proper information is furnished by the buyers, the inventory can easily be controlled, for a balance can be maintained or due notification sent to buyers. Appropriate action is their responsibility.

Assortments or variations within one line or kind of merchandise is one of the constant factors even for fashion goods. The proper inventory of staple goods in relation to sales is called a basic stock; that of fashion goods is called a model stock. Use of a good basic-stock list should keep a store supplied with items demanded well over 90 percent of the time; a model-stock list will help keep wanted items on hand about 80 percent of the time. In either case the inventory control must keep goods on hand for each size, pattern, color, style, price line, or other basic variable in proportion to its rate of sale. Unit control is often necessary for this purpose.

Inventory Valuation

Profits depend upon the maintenance of satisfactory relationships among sales, the *cost of goods sold,* and operating expenses; these are the three essential elements in a firm's profit and loss statement. Most retail stores (particularly the smaller ones) determine the "cost of goods sold" by recording the cost of all items purchased from suppliers, marking the unit cost in code upon each item in addition to its retail price, and taking a physical count of the items on hand on a cost basis at the close of an accounting period. The inventory at cost is then adjusted for depreciation or obsolescence of the stock to arrive at an inventory valuation at "cost or market, whichever is lower."

The "retail inventory method."   A widely used method of inventory valuation which does not require a physical count is the "retail method." This technique has been approved by the U.S. Treasury Department for income tax purposes.

The "retail method" is suitable for use by any store or department that has as its primary function the selling of merchandise without processing or alteration. In addition to providing a closing inventory at "cost or market, whichever is lower," it is a means of maintaining a perpetual merchandise inventory and of keeping records of markdowns, additional markups, and employee discounts. It also discloses stock shortages when the physical inventory is compared with the book inventory. However, our concern here is with its use for inventory valuation. The following table illustrates the steps in the procedure.

Table 21-1.   The Retail Method of Inventory Valuation

	Cost	*Retail*
Beginning inventory	$27,000	$ 45,000
Purchases	49,400	76,000
Add: Freight and express (cost column only)	460	
Add: Net markups (retail column only).		1,000
Goods available for sale (at cost and at retail)	$76,860	$122,000
Markup (retail minus cost) $45,140		
Markup of $45,140 divided by merchandise at retail of $122,000 = 37% markup		
Net sales $50,000		
Add: Markdowns, discounts to employees, and short- ages 3,000		
Goods sold or disposed of (at retail).		53,000
Retail value of goods on our shelves.		69,000
Cost percentage (100 % minus 37%).		0.63
Inventory at cost	43,470	
Cost of goods sold (cost of goods available for sale minus inventory at cost)	$33,390	
Net sales $50,000		
Deduct: Cost of goods 33,390		
Gross Margin $16,610		

The beginning inventory and all subsequent purchases are recorded at both cost and retail prices. Freight and express charges are added to the cost column, and net markups are added to the retail column. The resultant column totals are the cost and retail prices of goods available for sale during the period. The *cost* value of this merchandise is then deducted from the *retail* value to get the markup in dollars. Dividing the markup in dollars by the *retail* value of the merchandise available for sale, and multiplying by 100, will result in the markup as a percentage.

The next step is to add markdowns, discount to employees, and shortages, in dollars to net sales in dollars for the period. This sum, representing the retail price of the goods sold or otherwise disposed of, is then deducted from the total retail price of the goods available for sale to give the *retail* price of goods still on the shelves. The *cost* price of these goods is the objective. The retail price is multiplied by the cost complement of the markup percentage (100 minus percentage markup) to give the final figure for this ending inventory at cost.

Cost of goods sold is easily calculated by deducting the inventory at cost from the cost of goods available for sale. The explanation is that from the total cost of goods available for sale, the cost of goods still on the shelves has been deducted, the resulting figure being the cost of goods sold or disposed of.

It will be noticed that the markup percentage used (37 percent) was calculated without including markdowns, discounts, and (estimated) shortages, but these were added to sales as recorded to get the total value at retail of goods disposed of. Therefore, the calculated cost value of the closing inventory is less than actual cost, and this is proper because some of the goods were marked down. If, however, the price trend has been upward and additional markups (rather than markdowns) had been taken, these *would* be included in calculating the markup percentage, and the calculated cost would more closely approximate actual cost.

Physical inventories. Stores records must be correct in both quantities and values, and periodically it will be necessary to check the book inventory against the actual amount of stock on hand. In retailing the trend has been to take physical inventories more frequently than in the past, at least twice a year and sometimes monthly or even weekly. With proper planning and organization this is not too difficult in most stores, and experience proves it to be well worth the extra trouble. A "tickler" (reminder), file may be set up showing the dates to inventory each department.

Many small retailers regard a physical inventory as a necessary evil. Actually, it should be regarded as an opportunity to clean out old stocks and to reduce overstocks. A physical inventory should be taken carefully by important lines or classes of goods, and by age or length of time each article has been in stock. The inventory sheet in Figure 21-2 provides spaces for describing the merchandise (including the style or lot number), the quantity, the unit of measurement (yards, pieces, dozens, gross, etc.), and the retail price per unit. Where the cost method of inventory valuation is used the cost price is also indicated, as well as the adjustments for shrinkage in value of the merchandise.

Conclusions

The "retail method" is the only method of inventory valuation that the authors recommend for most stores in view of its many advantages. However, a beginning retailer might keep both retail and cost inventory records to advantage during the first few years. Under the "retail method" a perpetual inventory must be maintained at retail prices and careful records kept of all changes in the retail price. This gives a record of markdowns, discounts, and other changes and is a valuable management aid. It is independent of the unit type of control and has other limitations that should be understood by the proprietor. In particular, it must be used by departments or by merchandise classification, not on a storewide basis.

Dollar control in retailing may include the total store inventory, or any subdivisions as needed. Usually the following subdivisions for dollar control are useful: departmental, price line, and merchandise classification. Control should observe the rule of the golden mean — enough, but not too much.

Different merchandise control systems should be used as needed. The "retail method" is not suited to "manufacturing" departments like food service or alterations. Although some form of dollar control should be used for all merchandise, unit control may be needed to supplement dollar control, particularly in fashion lines.

INVENTORY

Sheet No.		Department			Date					19

| Called by | | Entered by | | | Extended by | | | | |

Description	V	Quantity	Unit	Price	V	Extensions			

Amount forward

Figure 21-2.   Inventory Sheet

STOCK CONTROL IN WHOLESALING

Wholesalers buy in large lots and carry heavy inventories. In the grocery field, for example, from 30 to 50 percent of the wholesaler's total assets represent investments in inventory. The trend toward widespread acceptance of the low-gross-margin-and-high-turnover principle, evident for many years in whole-saling, increases the need for accurate current information on inventories and good stock control. The aim of many wholesalers to supply to their independent retail customers all goods needed at prices competitive with those of chain stores and mail-order houses can be effectuated only with good stock control.

The key role played by the inventory control function in the flow of goods from the wholesaler to the retailer is shown in Figure 21-3.

Most trade associations in the wholesaling field conduct annual surveys of inventory control practices in member firms. In all such studies which have come to the authors' attention, it has been found that wholesalers with carefully planned unit stock control systems achieve a higher inventory turnover than those firms with no systematic stock control. Because of this higher inventory turnover, they also have a smaller percentage of capital in inventory and are able to operate on smaller gross margins. The practical measure of the effectiveness of stock control, however, is on the basis of earnings and profits, which invariably are larger and more stable in those wholesale establishments with unit-control systems.

The same basic methods of keeping track of inventories — observation, physical count, and perpetual inventory systems — are used in wholesaling as in retailing. The observation method is commonly used in small houses and by some larger firms. No record is made of the amounts on hand. Either the manager or the warehouseman is responsible for observing stock frequently. If the warehouseman notices that a pile of merchandise does not diminish in size, he notifies the manager and the latter decides what to do. Another duty of the warehouseman is to guard against out-of-stocks. When a stock gets low, he reports to the manager. Thus in small houses great dependence is placed upon the observation of warehousemen and the memory of buyers. The observation method, however, is often supplemented by the use of "short lists" or "outs," and "getting low" reports sent in to the office. "Short lists" are records of lines usually in stock but temporarily out, for which orders have been received that cannot be filled.

Periodic stock-count methods are used by many wholesalers. The periodic stock-count system is based on a regular count, fast-moving items being counted frequently and slow-moving items being counted less often. This means that some items may be counted daily and others only monthly. Like purchases and goods received, the counts are entered in a stock book, usually one for each department. Often "in and out" cards are used to record inventory counts as well as purchases, or a simple inventory card on which merely the date and amount of each count are recorded may be used.

Perpetual inventory control is receiving increasing attention from wholesalers. A committee of the National Electrical Wholesalers' Association in a report to the membership recently stressed many of the advantages of maintaining an adequate warehouse stock record system. Among the advantages cited were the following:

1. Convenience of having a continuous record in the office of items on hand and the quantity available for shipment
2. Ability to place replenishment orders without taking a physical inventory
3. Use of information contained on stock record cards to calculate rates of turnover and quantities to order for each item

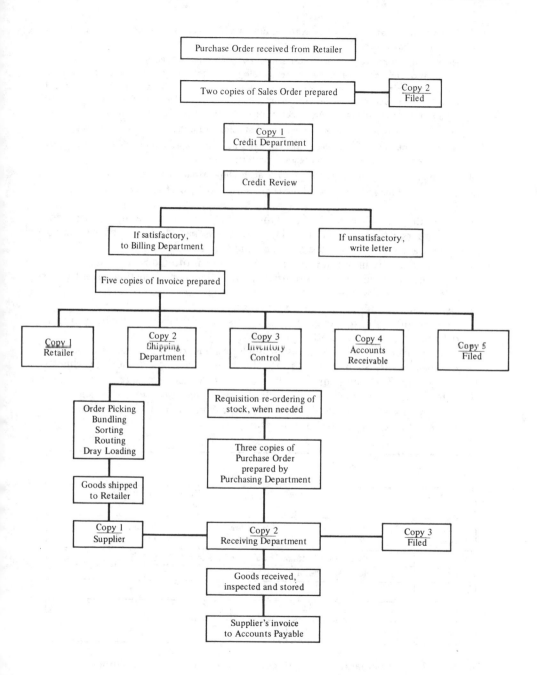

Figure 21-3.   Inventory Control and the Flow of Goods from Wholesaler to Retailer

4. Prompt filling of back orders when goods are received, by placing a "rider" listing customer back orders on the stock record

5. Reduction of costly errors in ordering, by including on each card such essential information as complete and accurate catalog numbers, description of the stock item, manufacturer's full name, standard package quantities, and terms of shipment if minimum list value or minimum weight factors are needed by the manufacturer to establish the most advantageous discount or most advantageous F.O.B. point

6. Use of the cards as a cross reference to indicate substitute items for "out of stocks"

7. Saving of the time of the sales manager, manufacturer's representatives, and salesmen by using the stock record cards to review inventory conditions

8. "Costing" of sales from data on the cards at the time of taking physical inventories

9. Disclosure of misappropriation of merchandise, especially of small stock items

Even in the small wholesale firm, the "office" where ordering is done and customer orders are received is usually physically separated from the warehouse where goods are stored. Thus the accuracy and frequency of reports on inventories on hand are especially important. In the warehouse it is often desirable to store part of a shipment in "dead storage" rather than with that part used for current order filling. This introduces the danger of overlooking part of a lot of goods when securing information for stock control reports.

In wholesaling, as in retailing, merchandise is usually classified into departments for stock control, layout, and other purposes.

Perpetual inventory systems, as used in wholesaling, rely on certain standards to control stock levels. Such standards include order points, which indicate when to buy; maximum and minimum stock standards, which are safeguards against out-of-stocks and overstocks; and standard-order quantities, which indicate how much to buy. These standards can be set up for each item in stock. See Figure 21-4 for a perpetual inventory record of this type.[5]

Unit of Issue:	Description:			
Location:	Unit Value		Time required to obtain:	
Maximum Stock:	Minimum Stock:	Reorder Point:	Ordering Quantity:	
Date:	Quantities in terms of units of issue:				Remarks
	On order	Rec'd	Del'd	Bal. on hand	

Figure 21-4. Perpetual Inventory Record, as Commonly Used in Wholesaling

The order point is based on the average time lapse that occurs between purchase and receipt of the merchandise and the maximum rate of sales during that interval,

[5] Cf. Figure 21-1, p. 410.

so that sufficient stock will be in the warehouse at the time of ordering to avoid out-of-stocks before the new goods are received. The minimum stock, which represents a margin of safety against out-of-stocks, is computed by subtracting the average sales during the time required to fill an order from the the the quantity established as the ordering point. The maximum quantity of stock is, of course, the maximum old stock expected to be on hand when a new shipment is received plus the standard order quantity. An example will clarify the concept of these standards:

Units

Minimum Stock

Order point (maximum amount likely to be sold during the time in which order is being filled as shown by the inventory control)	50
Less: Average amount sold during time in which order is being filled (as shown by the inventory control).	25
Minimum-stock standard	25

Maximum Stock

Order point.	50
Less: Minimum amount sold during time in which order is being filled (as shown by the inventory control).	10
Maximum amount likely to be on hand when new order is received.	40
Plus: Standard order	300
Maximum-stock standard	340

The order point and the minimum-stock standard are based on (1) the time required to fill an order, and (2) variations in sales during this period. These are relatively easy to determine. The maximum-stock standard depends largely, of course, upon the size of the standard order. Although a good inventory control system permits setting the order point at lower levels of warehouse stock without incurring the danger of out-of-stocks, the standard order size has a greater influence in determining the average inventory and thus has a greater influence on the expense of carrying inventory. The determination of standard order sizes is discussed in the following section.

INVENTORY CONTROL IN THE SMALL FACTORY

The frequency with which production would be slowed down or even stopped if some essential material or parts were not in stock led manufacturers years ago to recognize the importance of inventory control. Before stores control was introduced, an "out" condition of some important but inexpensive part was often accompanied by from one to ten years' supplies of other items.

In the small factory the variety of different materials and parts may not be large, and inventory control need not be complicated or expensive. But it is always important.

Some control is likely to be needed for raw materials, fabricated parts, and finished products, and perpetual inventory systems are commonly used. In controlling the inventory level of finished goods, a perpetual inventory system similar to that used in wholesaling is appropriate. (See Figure 21-4.) However, in controlling the inventory of raw materials used in fabrication, or the inventory of component parts used in assembly, it is often necessary that these materials be "reserved" to insure their "availability" when needed. A materials reserve system is required whenever a firm is engaged in either the intermittent or repetitive type of manufacturing process – the manufacturing processes most commonly found in small plants.[6]

For the purpose of illustrating the steps involved in this type of inventory control, let us assume that in the Acorn Company a production order (#47) has been issued for the manufacture of 100 air-conditioning grilles, requiring 100 steel plates of $42'' \times 36'' \times \frac{1}{4}''$ gauge. As these plates can be cut from $42'' \times 72''$ plates with no waste, the plant manager decides to use that size of stock. Filling out the top part of a *material reserve slip,* he requests the balance-of-stores ledger clerk[7] to "reserve" or earmark 50 plates for use on this production order. (See Figure 21-5.) This is done some time in advance of the date the first operation on this material is scheduled to start. On the bottom half of the material reserve slip the ledger clerk indicates whether the reserved material is in stores or on order or both; if all or part of the material requirements are on order, the clerk also indicates the expected delivery date. He then posts this transaction on the balance-of-stores ledger sheet, as illustrated in Figure 21-6.

As noted in Figure 21-6, the inventory of each kind of raw material is "controlled" on a balance-of-stores ledger sheet by means of four "balance" columns and four carefully determined quantitative standards.

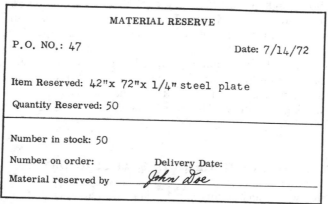

Figure 21-5.   Material Reserve Slip

---

[6] See section on "Factory Layout" in Chapter 10, pp. 188–95. In a mass-production plant, where material flow is "continuous," a reserve system is not appropriate.

[7] A balance-of-stores ledger is the same as a perpetual inventory record.

Description **Steel Plate 42"x 72"x ¼"** Min. Quantity **55** Ordering Point **440**

Code **PM-4** Max. Quantity **555** Amount to Order **500**

Unit of issue **Piece**

Date	Order No.	(1) Ordered			(2) Bal. On Hand	(3) Reserved			(4) Bal. Available
		Ordered	Received	Balance		Reserved	Issued	Balance	
1972 7/13					545				545
7/13	PO45					75		75	470
7/13	PO46					40		115	430
7/13	MPO8	500		500					930
7/14	PO47					50		165	880
7/14	PO48					150		315	730
7/17	PO45				470		75	240	
7/18	PO46				430		40	200	
7/18	PO49					75		275	655
7/19	PO47				380		50	225	
7/19	PO48				230		150	75	
7/20	PO49				155		75	00	
7/20	PO50				55		(100)		555
7/21	PO51					50		50	505
7/24	MPO8		500	00	555				

Figure 21-6. Balance-of-Stores Ledger Sheet (or Perpetual Inventory Record) for Control of Raw Materials and Finished Components

Balances "on order" (column 1) and "on hand" (column 2) are self-explanatory. The balance "on reserve" (column 3) denotes material which has been allocated to specific production orders but which has not yet been withdrawn from the storeroom. The balance "available" (column 4) denotes material which is unassigned and hence available for allocation to subsequent production orders. Material on order may be assigned (reserved) even though it has not yet been received from the vendor(s), and unreserved material on order is considered "available," because (theoretically) if the reorder point has been determined properly the quantity ordered will be in the storeroom before the present supply is exhausted. After each material transaction is entered on the ledger sheet, the balance on order (the quantity ordered minus the quantity received) plus the balance on hand should equal the balance on reserve (the quantity reserved minus the quantity issued) plus the balance available. Thus the ledger provides a continuous check on the accuracy of the entries made therein, in much the same way as does a double-entry bookkeeping system.

The two most important quantitative standards in the control of material inventories are (1) the ordering point, and (2) the amount to order. The ordering point is the predetermined level in the "balance available" column which "signals" the time at which the purchasing department[8] should be notified to order material in the specified amount, so as to reasonably insure that a sufficient amount of material will be on hand to meet all reserve obligations between the time the purchase order is placed and the time the material is received from the vendor. *If* the material was always ordered and received on time, and *if* it was always reserved and issued to shop at the same rate, the "minimum quantity" on hand when an incoming shipment is received would be zero. However, this theoretical minimum cannot be depended upon, and in practice a safety factor is applied in the determination of the ordering point. (A safety factor, or minimum inventory, of 55 units was established as a base in determining the ordering point shown in Figure 21-6.) The "amount to order" when the ordering point is reached should be that quantity at which the unit cost of procurement and maintenance is least. The theoretical "maximum quantity" on hand, of course, is the sum of the ordering quantity and the minimum quantity. Each of these quantitative standards, as well as the procedure for posting to a balance-of-stores ledger, are discussed in detail in the following sections.

Posting to the Balance-of-Stores Ledger

The following instructions on posting to a balance-of-stores ledger sheet will aid the reader in following the transactions recorded in Figure 21-6:

1. When materials are ordered, add to columns 1 and 4. The authority for entering this transaction is a purchase order.

[8] Or the person responsible for this function (who may be the owner-manager himself). In a large company, each of the various operating functions may be performed by several persons operating as specialists within "departments"; however, in a small plant it is likely that one person (in addition, perhaps, to other duties) may perform the purchasing function. Regardless of departmental organization and titles and degree of specialization, however, purchasing, receiving and the various other inventory control functions, as herein described, must be performed by someone.

2. When materials are received, subtract from column 1 and add to column 2. The authority for entering this transaction is a signed receiving department copy of the purchase order.

3. When materials are reserved, add to column 3 and subtract from column 4. The authority for entering this transaction is a material reserve clip. (See Figure 21-5.)

4. When materials are issued, after having previously been reserved, subtract from columns 2 and 3.

5. When materials which have not been reserved previously are issued, subtract from columns 2 and 4. The authority for entering transactions of the type indicated in this and the preceding instruction is either a raw material withdrawal slip or an accumulation notice.[9]

Each of the above types of material transactions is illustrated in the example, including the reservation and issuance of material on production order 47 (P.O. 47).

On July 13 the balance-of-stores ledger sheet for material coded PM-4 (steel plates of $42'' \times 72'' \times \frac{1}{4}''$ gauge) showed a balance on hand of 545 units. No material of this type was currently on order, nor had any been apportioned to apply on future shop orders; hence, the balance "available" on the morning of July 13 was also 545 units.

Later that day the ledger clerk "earmarked" (reserved) material to apply on production orders 45 and 46. The balance on reserve was therefore increased and the balance available for other orders was decreased by a total of 115 units. (See instruction 3.)

Since the above transactions decreased the balance available below the "ordering point" (440 units), the ledger clerk immediately initiated a purchase requisition for additional material in the specified amount (500 units). After receiving his copy of the materials purchase order (identified as M.P.O. 8), he records this transaction on the balance-of-stores ledger sheet, increasing the balances on order and available for future production. (See instruction 1.) A copy of the M.P.O. is also sent to the receiving department by the purchasing agent.

The material reserve slip for P.O. 47 (see Figure 21-5) was received by the ledger clerk on July 14. This provided the authority for making the appropriate entries on the balance-of-stores sheet, increasing the total amount of material on reserve and decreasing the total amount of material available for subsequent production orders by 50 units. Material was also allocated to P.O. 48 this same day. (See instruction 3.)

On July 17 the material required on P.O. 45 was issued, and on July 18 the material for P.O. 46 was likewise delivered to the shop. Since the material had been reserved for these orders 4–5 days previously, ledger entries were made reducing both the balance of stock on hand and the balance on reserve; the "available" column was not affected. (See instruction 4.)

Seventy-five units of material were apportioned to P.O. 49 on July 18, increasing the balance on reserve and decreasing the balance available by the same amount. (See instruction 3.)

[9] When the material to be withdrawn is raw material to be fabricated (as in Figure 21-6), the document conveying the storekeeper's authority to release the material is a "raw material withdrawal slip." If, however, the material to be withdrawn is a finished component, an "accumulation notice" is issued instead. The latter is a list of the component parts of an assembly, and specifies the number of units of each part which are to be delivered to the assembly floor.

The 275 units of material previously allocated to Production Orders 47, 48, and 49 were issued by the raw materials storeroom on July 19 and 20, and the appropriate entries were made by the ledger clerk in the customary manner. (See instruction 4.) These entries reduced the amount of material on reserve to zero and the balance of stock on hand to 155 units.

On July 20 an additional 100 units were issued to the shop on a rush order (P.O. 50). Since material had not been previously reserved to apply on the rush order, the balance on reserve remained unchanged, the ledger clerk merely reducing the balances on hand and available by 100 units. (See instruction 5.) However, a discrete entry is made in the "issued" column to indicate the actual number of units charged to the production order (as an aid to the cost department in costing the order), and the entry is placed in parentheses to indicate that this figure is to be ignored in determining the cumulative balances on reserve.

After the withdrawal of material for the above rush order, the balance on hand was reduced to the theoretical safe-minimum quantity (55 units). The quantity of "available" stock, however, is considerably larger, since it is anticipated that the 500 units on order will be received before additional material is released to the manufacturing floor. The balance-of-stores ledger clerk, therefore, was permitted by this careful systematized materials planning to reserve, on July 21, the amount of material required on P.O. 51, thus allowing further planning on this order to be done without delay.

On July 24, as anticipated, the receiving department received and inspected the shipment from the vendor on M.P.O. 8, and routed the material to the raw materials storeroom. The receiving clerk also signed his copy of the purchase order (M.P.O.), and forwarded it to the ledger clerk who was thus provided with the necessary authority to make the receiving entry on the balance-of-stores sheet. This receipt of new stock, of course, increased the balance of material on hand. (See instruction 2.)

After each transaction is entered on the ledger sheet as illustrated in Figure 21-6, the balances on order and on hand (columns 1 and 2) equal, in total, the balances on reserve and available (columns 3 and 4).

Determining the Most Economical Ordering Quantity

The most economical amount of material to purchase at one time, at a given price, is that quantity at which the total cost per unit of acquiring the material is at a *minimum;* this point occurs when the unit cost of preparing the purchase order for that quantity is *equal* to the unit cost of carrying the material in stores. That is, in determining the most economical quantity of material to order at one time, the costs of inventory *possession* must be balanced with the costs of inventory *acquisition.* These fundamental cost relationships are discussed below with reference to the material required on P.O. 47.

In the case of purchased materials, the acquisition costs are the incremental costs of preparing the purchase orders. These costs are determined by multiplying the "standard" cost of writing a single purchase order by the number of purchase orders which would be required each year at varying ordering quantities.[10] For

---

[10]The standard cost of preparing a purchase order is determined by dividing the total operating expenses of the purchasing department (or function) by the number of purchase orders written over a representative period of time.

example, let us assume that in the Acorn Company a total of 10,000 steel plates of
$42'' \times 72'' \times \frac{1}{4}''$ gauge are expected to be needed during the coming year, and
that the standard cost of preparing a purchase order is $15.00. Obviously, the
acquisition cost per unit of material (and hence the acquisition costs per year)
decreases when the amount of material ordered at one time increases. If only 100
units are ordered the unit acquisition cost is $0.15 (i.e., $15/100), and the total
acquisition cost per year is $1,500 (i.e., 10,000/100 × $15.00). For an order size of
200 units, both the unit acquisition cost and the annual acquisition cost would be
halved ($0.075 and $750, respectively). The acquisition costs per year on purchase
orders of other sizes are indicated in the following table, where

Q = Number of units ordered at one time

R = Annual requirements = 10,000 units

N = Number of orders written per year = R/Q

A = Acquisition (or order-writing) costs per order = $15.00

P = Possession costs, i.e., cost of holding one unit of inventory for one year = 20% of unit
purchase price = $1.20 (assuming a price of $6 per unit)

Table 21-2.   Tabular Method of Determining the Most Economical
Ordering Quantity

(1) Order Size (units): Q	(2) Number of Orders per Year: N = R/Q	(3) Acquisition Costs per Year: NA	(4) Possession Costs per Year: PQ/2	(5) Total Costs per Year: (3) + (4)
100	100.00	$1,500.00	$ 60.00	$1,560.00
200	50.00	750.00	120.00	870.00
300	33.33	500.00	180.00	680.00
400	25.00	375.00	240.00	615.00
500	20.00	300.00	300.00	600.00
600	16.67	250.00	360.00	610.00
700	14.29	214.35	420.00	634.35
800	12.50	187.50	480.00	667.50
900	11.11	166.65	540.00	706.65
1000	10.00	150.00	600.00	750.00
1100	9.09	136.35	660.00	796.35
1200	8.33	125.00	720.00	845.00
1300	7.69	115.35	780.00	895.35
1400	7.14	107.10	840.00	947.10

Certain incremental costs are associated with the possession, as well as the
acquisition, of materials. Inventory carrying (or possession) costs are comprised
mainly of taxes, depreciation and obsolescence, shrinkage, insurance, and interest
on the average inventory investment. Unlike unit acquisition costs, the cost of
holding one unit of material in inventory *increases* when the amount of material
ordered at one time increases. With larger order sizes and fewer purchase orders,
inventory turnover is lower and the average inventory level is higher. For example,

the cost of holding one 42″ × 72″ × $\frac{1}{4}$″ steel plate in inventory for one year in the Acorn Company, as noted above, is $1.20. If only 100 units are ordered at a time the unit possession cost is $0.006 (i.e., 1/100 × $1.20/2), and the total possession cost per year is $60.00 (i.e., 100/2 × $1.20).[11] For an order size of 200 units, both the unit possession cost and the annual possession cost would be doubled ($0.012 and $120.00, respectively). The possession costs per year on purchase orders of other sizes are indicated in column 4 in Table 21-2.

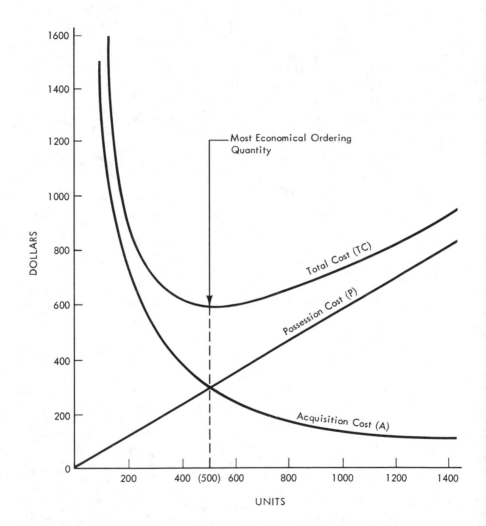

Figure 21-7. Graphic Representation of the Basic EOQ Formula

[11] If the entire 100 units were held in inventory for the entire period of $\frac{1}{200}$ year (inventory turnover period), the company's investment in each unit during this period would be the entire unit purchase cost, but since this material is used in production regularly throughout the period the *average* investment is only one-half this amount.

Figure 21-7 is a graphic representation of the above tabular data. From an examination of both the table and the chart it is observed that the most economical amount of material to order at one time, *at a price of $6.00 per unit,* is that quantity (500 units) at which the annual acquisition and possession costs are equal ($300.00 in each case) and at which these costs when combined are at a minimum ($600.00).

These fundamental cost relationships may be expressed more easily and conveniently by means of the following formula:

$$Q = \sqrt{\frac{2RA}{P}}$$

Thus,

$$Q = \sqrt{\frac{2 \times 10,000 \times 15}{1.20}} = \sqrt{\frac{300,000}{1.20}} = \sqrt{250,000} = 500$$

Quantity discounts.   The basic EOQ (economic ordering quantity) formula, as noted above, assumes that the purchase price per unit will be the same regardless of the number of units ordered. However, vendors often lower the unit price as the quantity ordered increases, because of the lowered unit costs of shipping and handling the order. When quantity discounts are offered, therefore, such savings reduce unit acquisition costs still further as the order size increases.

Suppose, for example, that the vendor offers the Acorn Company a price of $5.95 per unit if it orders 2,500 or more units at a time. Should the company take up this offer? The answer lies in a comparison of the total of all costs generated annually with orders of 500 and 2,500 units, respectively. For individual orders of 500 units at a unit price of $6.00, the annual costs are calculated as follows:

Purchase costs:	10,000 units × $6 =	$60,000
Ordering costs:	20 orders × $15 =	300
Inventory carrying costs:	250 units × $1.20 =	300
		$60,600

For individual orders of 2,500 units at a unit price of $5.95, the annual costs would be higher:

Purchase costs:	10,000 units × $5.95 =	$59,500
Ordering costs:	4 orders × $15 =	60
Inventory carrying costs:	1,250 units × $1.19 =	1,488
		$61,048

Therefore, the company should order the smaller quantity at the higher unit price.

Lot sizes in production.   The fundamental cost relationships noted above come into play in determining the size of production orders as well as purchase orders. In each case, the costs of acquiring the material must be balanced against the cost of possessing it or having it in stock. Where the inventory is to be replenished by means of *manufacture,* however, the acquisition costs include the cost of machine setups in addition to the cost of writing production orders.

The basic EOQ formula is again illustrated below, with reference to P.O. 47, which calls for the processing of 100 air-conditioning grilles. The cost parameters are as follows:

R = Annual requirements = 500 units

A = Acquisition costs per order = $50

P = Possession cost, or cost of carrying one unit of inventory for one year = $5

Thus,

$$\text{EOQ} = \sqrt{\frac{2 \times 500 \times 50}{5}} = \sqrt{\frac{50,000}{5}} = \sqrt{10,000} = 100 \text{ units}$$

Determining the Reorder Point

In addition to knowing *how much* material to order, it is important also to know *when* to order. If the material is ordered too soon, the inventory is increased unnecessarily; if ordered too late the present inventory might become exhausted, thus holding up production (in the case of purchased raw materials and finished components) or failing to satisfy customer demand (in the case of finished goods).

Two important factors in determining the ordering point are (1) the rate of consumption in units, and (2) the procurement time. In the Acorn Company, for example, the time it takes an order for steel plate to be delivered from the time it is requisitioned is two weeks; thus, with 10,000 units of material reserved and issued to the shop annually, the reorder point might (theoretically) be set at approximately 385 units (10,000 ÷ 26), which is the average biweekly rate of consumption. In such a case, the theoretical minimum inventory would be zero, for if the procurement time and annual consumption rate both remain unchanged, the balance of stock on hand will be depleted just as the new shipment of material is received.

Such preciseness, however, is seldom attainable. Sound management requires that a "safety" or "buffer" inventory be maintained for use whenever temporary exceptions to the normal or usual operating conditions occur. Furthermore, the demand for most materials is seasonal and fluctuates widely from month to month during the year. In the above illustration, the minimum safe inventory is estimated as being equal to the average production requirements for two weeks (55 units). This minimum quantity, or "buffer," is then added to the theoretical ordering point (385 units) to arrive at the actual reordering point (440 units), as used in Figure 21-6.

A-B-C Control

If the small factory carries stocks of different materials that vary widely in relative importance to production, in price, or in other significant ways, inventories should be classified and appropriate methods of control adopted for each classification. For example, relatively few materials often make up the bulk of the dollar investment in inventories. In one company it was found that 10 percent of the items in stock accounted for 75 percent of the inventory value, and that 70 percent of the items accounted for only 5 percent of the firm's inventory investment. For control purposes these are classified as "A" and "C" items, respectively. Between these extremes were the "B" items, which accounted for 20 percent of the total number of items and 20 percent of the total inventory value. Staples – the "C" items – may be controlled by using "bin minimums" or a simple "last container" arrangement, or perhaps by tying up the reorder point quantities in sacks or otherwise physically separating them from the remainder of the stock. Only the "A" and "B" items should be controlled under a stringent perpetual inventory and "reserve" system of the type described in the preceding pages; in addition, however, the high-value "A" items should come under the close personal supervision of the plant owner.

Bin Tags and Stores Control

All receipts and issues of each kind of material should be recorded on an inventory card placed in a bin or tacked on the wall near the place where the item is stored. By providing a running total of orders received and of removals, the bin tag shows, with reasonable accuracy, the stock on hand. If a perpetual inventory system is also maintained, each record provides a check on the other.

Several times a year both the bin card total and the perpetual inventory total should be checked against the actual count for all stock items. Occasional spot checks (a few scattered items at a time) in between regular inventory periods should be made to make sure that employees are noting removals on the card and that smaller items are not disappearing.

In addition to bin tags, effective stores control requires some systematic plan for storing each item so that it can always be located. Various systems are in use, including: (1) numerical storage – storing each item according to a parts number; (2) storage by type and, within each type, by size; and (3) index systems. The last are the most flexible and seem to be gaining increasing favor in spite of the extra paperwork required.

An index system operates by assigning location symbols to all storage space use. For example, "A10b" might designate aisle A, stack 10, shelf b. Usually similar materials are stored in the same section or area, but this is not essential. Card records show: (1) for each item, where it is stored, and (2) for each storage area, extent to which space is in use and available. Each item must be correctly described according to some standard nomenclature, and identification is facilitated by putting this identification mark on each item or container. Again symbols are often used. Whether to mark with pencil, rubber stamp, or tag depends upon the type of material and similar factors.

INVENTORY CONTROL IN THE SERVICE ESTABLISHMENT

Both in manufacturing and in service businesses – in contrast to merchandising – inventory control is entirely in terms of units and physical quantities. Naturally, the accounting records show the cost of materials and supplies purchased. In general, materials used in further production are of greatest importance.

Depending upon the nature of the service business, therefore, inventory control methods will be similar to those used in merchandising and manufacturing.

SUMMARY AND CONCLUSIONS

Properly handled, inventories of merchandise, materials, and supplies, which are one representation of the owner's capital, may be his major asset. The peculiar thing about many businesses, both large and small, is the extreme care with which cash is guarded and the lack of care exercised over "cash" in the form of inventories. A good rule for the small businessman is to regard his supplier as his banker as far as materials are concerned.

Good inventory control depends in part upon whether the businessman can rely on receiving shipments within an allotted time. Good vendor relationships, fair treatment of suppliers in matters of claims, and prompt payment of bills will help to make this possible. Even in the best of inventory control systems, emergencies will arise when unexpectedly depleted inventories must be replaced quickly. In such crucial times the value of good vendor relations is of the utmost importance.

REVIEW QUESTIONS

1. What is the objective of inventory control? What types of costs must be considered in determining optimum inventory turnover?

2. In separate columns list the ways good merchandise control in the retail store can aid (*a*) buying, and (*b*) selling.

3. What is a "perpetual" inventory? Does this type of inventory record preclude the necessity of taking periodic counts of the items on hand? Is a perpetual inventory record feasible for all kinds of stock? Why or why not?

4. What is open-code dating, and what purposes does it serve?

5. Why does the merchant emphasize the value of his inventory, whereas the manufacturer or service operator is concerned primarily with the number of units in his inventory? Explain the essential differences between dollar control and unit control of merchandise.

6. Differentiate between *model*-stock and *basic*-stock systems. What is the importance of making a distinction between these systems?

7. Explain the "retail method" of inventory valuation. Why is it widely used?

8. Why is merchandise control particularly important for the small wholesaler?

9. Explain the operation of a material reserve system.

10. Define "reorder point," "economic ordering quantity," and "maximum" and "minimum inventory limits." Of what value is each in controlling inventory?

11. What costs are associated with the acquisition of materials? What is the relationship between these costs and the standard order size?

12. What costs are associated with the possession of materials? What is the relationship between these costs and the standard order size?

13. Why is the total cost curve in Figure 21-7 U-shaped? What is an "incremental cost"?

14. How do quantity discounts affect the analysis of quantities to purchase, using the basic EOQ formula?

15. Explain the A-B-C inventory control policy.

DISCUSSION QUESTIONS

1. A hardware retailer wishes to establish minimum and maximum stocks for such items as screwdrivers, bolts, screws, and hammers. How should he go about it? Explain fully.

2. Summarize the main points of similarity and differentiate between the inventory control practices of merchandising and manufacturing establishments.

SUPPLEMENTARY READINGS

Harling, Edwin L. *Merchandise Control and Budgeting.* New York: National Retail Merchants Association, 1965. Stresses the importance of maintaining effective control over stock in retail operations.

Van DeMark, Robert I. *Wholesaler Inventory Control.* Dallas, Texas: Van DeMark, Inc., 1966. Suggests ways of providing adequate retailer service while keeping the inventory investment to a minimum. Samples of simple inventory control records for the small wholesaler are also included.

22

Production control in the small plant

The general pattern of production planning and control in a particular plant depends upon the kind of manufacturing process in which that firm is engaged. As noted in Chapter 14, three basic types of manufacturing may be discerned: intermittent, continuous, and repetitive manufacture.

The manufacturing process determines not only the type of equipment and machine layout but also the general pattern of production planning and control which is appropriate in a given case. There are two general patterns — the "flow" type and the "order" type. Since products processed continuously on specialized equipment laid out on a line basis permit the smooth flow of work from one production center to another, the *flow* type of production planning and control is common to the continuous (or mass-production) type of manufacture. As its name suggests, this type of production planning and control requires the maintenance of a predetermined rate of flow from each machine.

Order planning and control, on the other hand, involves the routing, scheduling, dispatching, and follow-up of a variety of orders for diversified production on common equipment. Hence, this type of production planning and control is common to the intermittent and repetitive types of manufacture.

The intermittent and repetitive types of manufacture, in turn, are most common in small plants. For this reason, order planning and control will be given major attention in this chapter.

For the purpose of illustrating the steps involved in this type of production planning and control, we will use production order #47 (discussed in the preceding chapter) as a point of reference. As previously noted, this production order calls for the fabrication of 100 air-conditioning grilles to be made from steel plates of $42'' \times 36'' \times \frac{1}{4}''$ gauge. The grille is one of six component parts of an air-conditioning register, and the 100 units on P. O. 47 will be needed on the assembly floor on August 2, 1972.

PRODUCTION ORDER PLANNING

Before the work specified on a production order can be processed in the shop, the balance-of-stores ledger should be checked and the "availability" of the needed raw material and component parts verified. The operation of a balance-of-stores and materials reserve system was described and illustrated in the preceding chapter. It will be recalled that 50 steel plates of $42'' \times 72'' \times \frac{1}{4}''$ gauge were "reserved" or earmarked for use on P. O. 47.

Master Routing and Scheduling

When products are fabricated to the customer's specifications, or when a standard stock item is manufactured for the first time,[1] a *master route sheet* must be prepared showing the following information:

1. Complete list of operations in sequence
2. Type of machine (or other equipment) on which each operation is to be performed, and/or the department in which each operation is to be performed
3. Material requirements for each operation (kind and quantity)
4. Tools, jigs, and fixtures required for each operation
5. Time allowance for each operation (time allowance per unit $\times$ the number of units on the production order + machine setup time)

This procedure may be made more clear, perhaps, by referring again to P. O. 47. The job is first broken down into its component operations – shearing, perforating, and rolling – and listed on the master route sheet in the sequence in which they are to be performed. (See Figure 22-1.) The work is then assigned to the appropriate machine group or department, and the setup and process times for each operation are estimated. Thus shearing – the first operation in sequence – is routed to the square shears (located in Department 10), and the production time is estimated at 5

Operation	Type of Machine to be Used	Department No.	Tools	Material	Set-Up and Process Time	Starting Date
1 Shearing	Square Shear	10		50-42" x 72" x ¼"	5 hrs	7/19/72
2 Perforating	Roller Press	20	Die 182		55 hrs	7/19/72
3 Rolling	Plate Roll	30			4 hrs	7/31/72

Figure 22-1.   Master Route and Schedule Sheet

[1] In the repetitive type of manufacture, master routing of the work in process on a production order need be done only *once*, for after a standard product has been placed in production for the first time the subsequent production runs or "repeat" orders will follow the same general routing. Accordingly, master route sheets for each standard product are placed in a master file, from which they are withdrawn for use whenever a production order is issued authorizing a new production run.

hours. The perforating operation is to be done on roller presses in Department 20 at an estimated time of 55 hours, and will require the use of a special die. The plate rolls (Department 30) are to be used in rolling the grilles, this operation requiring 4 hours.

The next step is to prepare a *master schedule sheet* for each part (or parts assembly). This is the same as the master route sheet, except that it also indicates the "starting" times (dates) for each operation. (See the last column in Figure 22-1.) The first step in this procedure is to estimate the total manufacturing cycle time. With reference to P. O. 47, the total setup and processing time is 64 hours. However, an allowance must also be made for "float" time, that is, the time *between* operations when the material is either being moved from one production center to another or is in "temporary storage" awaiting its turn at the machine. If this nonproductive time is estimated at 15 hours, the total in-process time would then be 79 hours, or approximately 10 working days, assuming single-shift operation. It will be recalled that the 100 units on P. O. 47 will be needed in a subassembly operation on August 2. Thus, the first operation on the order should be started no later than 10 working days before August 2. If it is assumed that the plant is on a 5-day week, with no work on Saturdays, Sundays, or legal holidays, then the starting date on this order would be Wednesday, July 19. Both the shearing and perforating operations are scheduled to start on this date. Rolling is scheduled to start on Monday, July 31. Thus the master schedule may be likened to a timetable, indicating *when* as well as *where* the operations on the part are to be performed.

In the master scheduling of an assembled product, each part must be scheduled with reference to the time it is needed for assembly to other parts. Hence, many of the component parts are in process simultaneously. The preliminary step in scheduling the production of an assembled product is to diagram the work to be done on the entire order. An air-conditioning register, for example, has 6 component parts. The total setup, processing, and float time for each of these parts, on an order for 100 units, is as follows:

Part 1: 6 working days
Part 2: 10 working days
Part 3: 15 working days
Part 4: 9 working days
Part 5: 16 working days
Part 6: 19 working days

Parts 1, 2, and 3 make up a subassembly used on the final assembly. The total cycle time for the subassembly is 3 days, and, for the final assembly 5 days. The manufacturing cycle time is 25 days, and at the present consumption (or demand) rate the inventory of air-conditioning registers would reach the minimum level on August 14.

In constructing the diagram, the final-assembly and subassembly operations and the parts on which the fabricating operations are to be performed are listed on a sheet of coordinate paper. A "workday" scale is drawn below a "calendar" scale at the top of the sheet. (See Figure 22-2.) The workday scale reads from right to left,

Date	July																August									
	10	11	12	13	14	17	18	19	20	21	24	25	26	27	28	31	1	2	3	4	7	8	9	10	11	14
Working days	25	24	23	22	21	20	19	18	17	16	15	14	13	12	11	10	9	8	7	6	5	4	3	2	1	0
Final assembly																					▬	▬	▬			
Sub-assembly																		▬	▬	▬						
Part 1												▬	▬	▬												
Part 2									▬	▬	▬	▬														
Part 3				▬	▬	▬	▬	▬																		
Part 4												▬	▬	▬	▬											
Part 5			▬	▬	▬	▬	▬	▬	▬	▬	▬	▬	▬	▬	▬	▬										
Part 6	▬	▬	▬	▬	▬																					

Figure 22-2.   Master Schedule Diagram for an Assembled Product

and is fixed to the calendar scale by assuming as a zero point the date (August 14) on which the order should be delivered to the finished-goods stockroom. Omitted from the calendar scale are Saturdays, Sundays, and legal holidays. The total setup, processing, and float time for each of the component parts is then marked off on both scales with reference to the time the completed part must be at the assembly station. The dates on which the *first* operation on each of the 6 parts in the above example should be started in process are readily ascertained upon examination of Figure 22-2. These dates are then recorded on the master route sheets for the various parts. With these starting dates as benchmarks, *subsequent* operations on each of the parts may be accurately scheduled.[2]

Detailed Routing and Scheduling

The master route and schedule sheet (Figure 22-1) indicates merely (1) the general *type* of machine or manual operation required on each part, and (2) the *dates* on which individual operations are to begin. The next step in production order planning is to make a more detailed routing and scheduling of the work. Involved here is (1) the routing of the work to a *particular* machine or work bench, and (2) the determination of the sequence in which the orders scheduled to "start" on a given day should be taken up for assignment to these production centers, that is, the approximate *time of day* the work should start on each order. With reference to the rolling operation on P. O. 47, for example, answers are sought to the following questions: (1) On which of the three plate rolls should the work be done, and (2) at what hour (approximately) should the operation begin? The same questions are asked with respect to each of the other operations required to complete this order.

[2] Figure 22-1 is the master route sheet for the air-conditioning grille, which is part #2 in the air-conditioning register assembly. From an examination of both Figure 22-1 and Figure 22-2 it is noted that the first operation on this part is scheduled to start on July 19.

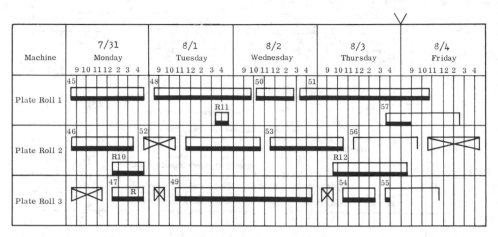

Figure 22-3. Gantt Schedule Chart

In routing and scheduling work to individual machines the production order planner often finds it helpful to utilize schedule and machine load charts of the Gantt type. The construction and use of these charts are explained below.

Schedule chart. The "Gantt schedule chart," as illustrated in Figure 22-3, is used for the purpose of assigning specific jobs or "orders." The chart is ruled vertically for hours and days, and each line on the chart is assigned to a particular machine or work bench. Thus in Figure 22-3, provision is made for the scheduling of work to each of three different plate rolls. Production orders are scheduled according to the "starting" dates on the master schedules unless the machines already are overloaded.

The time scheduled for starting the work on an order is indicated by an inverted L, open to the right (Γ), and the time for the order to be completed is indicated by an inverted L, open to the left (⌐). The total expected or allowed time for each order is indicated by connecting these (inverted L) symbols by a light straight line:

When an order is completed, no matter how long it required, it is indicated as complete by drawing a heavy line between the angles:

An incomplete heavy line indicates that the job is only partially completed.[3]

Jobs finished ahead of schedule may be indicated by overlapping lines – if the next job were scheduled on the chart at the same time that it was started in the

[3] These heavy lines indicate "accomplishment" or "progress" (in contrast with the light lines, which indicate "assignment"). The heavy lines are drawn to approximate lengths at the end of each working day, following reports of each worker's accomplishment for that day.

shop or if the schedule clerk knew positively that the operation was running consistently ahead of schedule, and how much ahead:

Since the left end of each line indicates the starting time, the amount of overlap indicates the time that the operation was finished ahead of schedule.

When jobs get behind schedule, additional time must be scheduled to allow the operator to come up to date. This is indicated by:

For example, an operator may be required to stop work on a regularly scheduled job to work on a repair job. Before additional orders are scheduled, additional time must be allowed for the interruption. If new orders are scheduled before the day's accomplishment has been reported, the length of the crossed blocks should equal the assigned length of the repair job. However, if the assigned work is done in less than the expected time and is completed before the next order is scheduled, the crossed block need be only long enough to cover the time the operation is actually behind schedule.

It is desirable to keep all regular production jobs on the same line if possible, with repair jobs (or other "interrupting" jobs) overlapping on the line below. The crossed blocks for extra allowed time usually should appear on the same line with the regular production jobs to show the continuity of time for the operation. These crossed blocks, therefore, will be added following the last order that has been scheduled. At the time the repair job is completed, the chart should appear as follows:

Here the short block represents the repair job, and the crossed block at the right indicates additional time which must be allowed for completion of the job which was interrupted. When both jobs are finished, the chart will appear as follows:

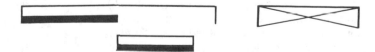

If the operator is behind schedule at the end of a working day, the chart will appear as:

where the vertical line at V indicates the time the chart is being read. If the operator was on schedule, the heavy line would extend to the vertical line. If the operator is ahead of schedule, the chart will appear as:

When an order is behind schedule the reason therefore should be indicated by a code letter. Customary code letters are as follows:

Letter	Cause of Idleness	Department or Person Responsible
G	Delay caused by unskilled or "green" operator	Foreman or Supervision
H	Lack of sufficient "help" or manpower	Personnel or Employment Department
I	Waiting for "instructions"	Production Planning and Control
S	"Slow" operator	Foreman or Supervision
M	Shortage of "material"	Purchasing, or Production Planning and Control
P	Now "power" available	Plant Engineer
R	Waiting for "repairs"	Maintenance
SU	Waiting for "setup"	Foreman or Production Planning
T	Waiting for "tools"	Tool Room or Production Planning

The identification or order number of each job is necessary to identify the orders with the various hours scheduled:

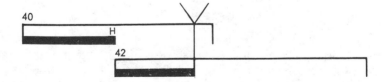

In this case, P.O. 40 is behind schedule because of lack of "help" and the operator had to "break off" this job to work on something else. P.O. 42 was substituted, and the operator is up to date on his allowed hours.

One of the Gantt schedule charts maintained at the Acorn Company is illustrated in Figure 22-3. A separate chart is kept for each group of machines or each production center. Figure 22-3 is the one maintained for the three plate rolls.

It will be noted that the work on P. O. 47 is assigned to plate roll 3 and that it is scheduled to begin at 1:00 p.m. on Monday, July 31. Since the estimated or standard time to complete this work is 4 hours (see last column, Figure 22-1), the order is scheduled for completion at 5:00 p.m. that same day. However, the operator had trouble with the machine and needed another 2 hours Tuesday morning to complete the job. The next order on this machine (P. O. 49), therefore, could not be scheduled to start before 10:00 a.m. When the rolling operation on P. O. 47 was completed at 10:00 a.m., the order was indicated as "complete" by a heavy line between the inverted-L angles. At the end of the working day on Thursday, August 3, the situation on each of the machines was as follows:

Plate roll 1: — 1 hour ahead of schedule

Plate roll 2: — on schedule

Plate roll 3: — 1 hour behind schedule (P. O. 55)

Load chart.   A load chart is a summary of all the schedule charts. It provides no detailed data on production orders; it shows only the work "to be done" in terms of man- or machine-hours. The chart is ruled vertically in terms of time units on a weekly basis, and a separate line is used for each *group* of machines (or workers). The first or top line represents the "average" load of the whole department or plant. (See Figure 22-4.) The scheduled loads for any given week are generally expressed as percentages of the available (or "capacity") loads; hence, the time units are expressed in tenths.

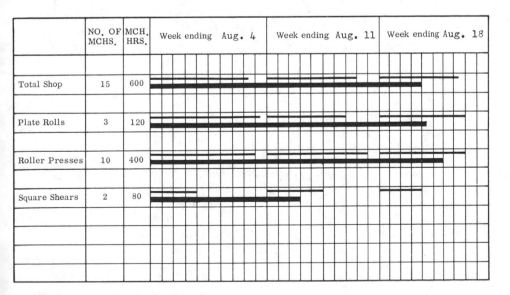

	NO. OF MCHS.	MCH. HRS.	Week ending Aug. 4	Week ending Aug. 11	Week ending Aug. 18
Total Shop	15	600			
Plate Rolls	3	120			
Roller Presses	10	400			
Square Shears	2	80			

Figure 22–4.   Gantt Load Chart

A light line drawn through the middle of the horizontal space indicates the amount of work assigned each week, and a heavy line drawn at the bottom of the space indicates the total work ahead (i.e., the *cumulative* load) of the group of machines over a period of several weeks.

Figure 22-4 is the load chart for the three groups of machines used by the Acorn Company in manufacturing air-conditioning grilles of the type specified on P. O. 47. The machines involved are 2 square shears, 10 roller presses, and 3 plate rolls. Since this plant operates on a 40-hour week the number of machine-hours available each week on each machine group are, respectively, 80, 400, and 120. The 15 machines of all types in the plant represent a combined weekly capacity of 600 machine-hours.

An examination of the schedule chart in Figure 22-3 reveals that 114 hours of work have been scheduled thus far for the 3 plate rolls during the week beginning July 31 (and ending August 4). This is 114/120, or 95 percent, of the available weekly load. Thus a light line is drawn across 95 percent of the space representative of this week. If it is assumed that as of August 8 a total of 84 hours of work has been assigned to this machine group for the week ending August 11, then a light line would be drawn across 70 percent of the appropriate space; similarly, if 96 hours have been assigned for the week ending August 18, a light line would span 80 percent of the space for that week. For the 3-week period, as of August 8 (when the last assignment was made), the cumulative load is 245 percent (95 plus 70 plus 80); thus a heavy line is drawn across the entire space representing the weeks ending August 4 and August 11, and across 45 percent of the space representing the week ending August 18. The same procedure is followed for the roller presses and square shears and for the plant summary.

Load charts (or schedule summaries, as they are sometimes called) are invaluable aids in production planning because they reveal overloads, bottlenecks, and other production inefficiencies quickly and effectively. Where such charts indicate problems of underload or overload, the following "remedies" might be applied:

Change of delivery dates

Decline (or try to get) specific types of orders

Improve congested processes

Operate equipment for longer period each calendar day

Get new equipment, or dispose of some

Route work to different equipment

Get more help, or shift it around where needed

Mechanical schedule and machine-load boards.   In recent years mechanical adaptations of Gantt schedule and load charts have appeared on the market, and the use of these is much less time-consuming than the original paper-type charts. One such device is known commercially as a "Productrol" board.

The Productrol board has two horizontal rows of small holes for each item being charted. These rows of holes correspond to the light and heavy lines used on the paper-type Gantt chart. In the top row are placed pegs, with strings or rubber bands attached, to indicate either the scheduled time for each order or the total scheduled machine load for each time period, depending upon whether the board is used for order scheduling or machine-loading purposes. When used for the former purpose, the pegs are numbered so that each order can be identified. Pegs, with strings or rubber bands attached, are also placed in the second row to indicate either the progress of each order ("accomplishment") or the cumulative machine load. A vertically placed string can be moved daily so that lagging production can be easily spotted.

Centralized vs. decentralized scheduling.   Up to this point it has been assumed that detailed routing and scheduling (i.e., the scheduling of work on individual machines) in the Acorn Company is a function of a centralized production planning department. In such a case the foreman of a production department is relieved of any scheduling (or machine-loading) responsibilities, and so is enabled to devote more time to problems of supervision. However, such a system is necessarily complex because the central planning department must be continually informed of each machine's activity. The flow of information of this kind to a centralized scheduling office involves a considerable amount of paperwork.

In most plants, particularly the larger ones, detailed routing and scheduling is decentralized. In such cases, the foremen either do their own scheduling or machine loading, or are provided specialized staff services by representatives of the planning department who are stationed in the various manufacturing departments.

Whether the detailed routing and scheduling function is performed centrally, or is decentralized, schedule and man- or machine-load paper charts or mechanical boards of the Gantt type (as described or illustrated above) may be effectively employed. However, where this function is decentralized (i.e., performed in the shop by the foreman or dispatcher), a dispatch rack or machine-loading board is often used in lieu of these devices.

Dispatch rack or machine-loading board.   A dispatch rack or machine-loading board has a section for each machine or workplace, under which there are three hooks or pockets to hold job tickets — one for the job in process, one for the next job ahead, and one for jobs temporarily assigned but not yet ready for work. By examining the job tickets which indicate the work ahead and in process on a particular machine, the foreman or dispatcher can determine whether or not new work should be assigned to it. As in the case of the schedule charts, the amount of work already scheduled to the machine and the due dates of the orders must be considered in making this decision.

After making detailed routings and schedules, the first phase of production-order planning and control — *plan the work* (planning) — is completed. The next and final phase of the total problem is to *work the plan* (production control).

PRODUCTION ORDER CONTROL

Production planning is futile unless a control *system* is set up so that the plans are followed. Production control systems, however, must be adapted to the needs of the individual plant — its size, personnel, physical facilities, type of manufacture and methods of processing, and internal organization structure. In this section a hypothetical production control routine, procedure, or "system" is described, but this is done merely to illustrate general *functions*. These functions must be performed regardless of "who" is responsible for performing them or "how" they are performed in a particular industrial organization.

Production control functions may be broadly classified as follows: (1) the dispatching of work in process; (2) the control of raw material and finished good inventories; and (3) the follow-up or expediting of work in process. In the coordinated performance of these functions by different individuals a certain amount of paperwork (sometimes called, facetiously, "red tape") is required. Production control "paper" evolves itself into two main classifications: *labor* "book" and *material* "book."

In the hypothetical situation described below, the labor book (which is incorporated as part of the dispatching routine) contains the following paper:

> Master route and schedule sheet (Figure 22-1)
> Move card
> Labor vouchers

As many labor vouchers are required as there are operations to be performed. The labor voucher for each operation is printed in triplicate.

The material book contains the following paper:

> Raw material withdrawal notice
> Raw material delivery slips
> Inspection tickets
> Finished stock delivery slip
> Identification tag

When material withdrawn from stores is material to be fabricated (raw material), the paper sequence as listed above in the material book is in effect. If, however, the material is a factory assembly, the raw material withdrawal notice is eliminated and in its place is used an "accumulation notice."[4] All other paper follows the sequence as previously listed. If the work is to be processed in more than one department, as many raw material delivery slips and inspection tickets are required as there are departments processing the work.

The labor books and material books are distributed as follows:

1. The labor books to the interested departments or dispatch stations (as discerned in the routing sheet)
2. The material books to the interested stockroom record clerks (as also discerned in the routing sheet)

The clerical time and cost of preparing the above "paper" for each part and parts assembly can be reduced considerably by making stenciled copies of the master route and schedule sheet, differentiating the use or purpose of each copy by color and/or preprinted headings. This technique of paperwork simplification is illustrated in Figure 22-5.

[4] An "accumulation notice" is a list of the component parts of an assembly, and specifies the number of units of each part which are to be delivered to the assembly floor.

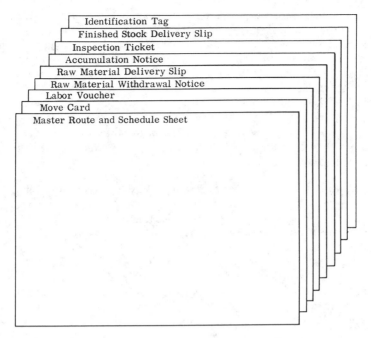

Figure 22-5. Master Form on Stencil for Duplication of Production Control "Paper"

Dispatching

The labor books are filed in the "dead load" file in the dispatch stations by P. O. number to await arrival of material. Upon arrival of material at the proper production center in the department, the move man detaches the raw material delivery slip and presents it to the dispatcher. The dispatcher then withdraws the labor book from the dead load file and places it in the "material-available" file by operation starting date. It is from this file that the dispatch board is loaded. At the beginning of each day shift, (1) if detailed routing and scheduling is decentralized, the dispatcher stacks the dispatch board from the material-available file to insure a full 8-, 16-, or 24-hour backlog of active work (the backlog depending on whether the plant is operating on one, two or three shifts); (2) if detailed routing and scheduling is centralized, the dispatcher stacks the dispatch board from the material-available file according to the operation schedule sheet, a copy of which has been previously forwarded to him.

Timekeeping. On dispatching a job (production order), the operator is given a name-stamped and clocked labor voucher for the particular operation. The original and duplicate labor vouchers for this operation, the labor vouchers for the subsequent operations (if any) in the department, and the move card are replaced on the dispatch board. In addition, the number of the machine at which the work is being performed is penciled on the master route and schedule sheet in the space preceding the operation number, so as to facilitate speedy identification should a set of labor vouchers be misplaced on the dispatch board. The master route and schedule sheet is then placed in the "live load" file by P. O. number.

When an operator has completed his operation, he returns his copy of the labor voucher. The time clerk then draws the original and duplicate labor vouchers from the dispatch board, collates them with the triplicate copy just returned by the operator, and clocks the vouchers. In all cases, before an operator can obtain the labor voucher for another job, he must return the labor voucher pertaining to the completed operation. After it is "clocked," this triplicate labor voucher is returned to the operator so that he may have a record of his production and incentive premium earnings. The duplicate copy of the labor voucher is sent to the payroll department, and the original to the cost department.[5]

Moving material in process.   An operation on a specific job now completed, the work must be moved to the next production center. The authority for this is a move card. At the dispatch station are two files for holding move cards; specifically, "jobs to be moved" and "jobs moved." The move man obtains move cards from the "jobs to be moved" file. Before moving the material (job), however, he sees that the material books are securely attached to the material and checks the quantity. Should there be any discrepancy between the physical count and the quantity as shown on the identification tag, the move man immediately notifies the dispatcher.

After moving a job, the move man verifies this by initialing the move card. The card is then returned to the dispatch station and placed in the "jobs moved" file.

At the time a card is placed in the "jobs to be moved" file, the dispatcher places the balance of the labor book in a suspension file awaiting movement of the material. After the move man moves the material to the next work center, the dispatcher withdraws the related labor book from the suspension file and reassociates it with the move card. If the material was moved to another production center in the *same* department, the dispatcher stacks the dispatch board for the performance of the next operation on this order in his department. If the material was moved to a production center in a *different* department for further processing, or to the finished parts stockroom, the dispatcher files the master route and schedule sheet in the "completed jobs" file. Before material is moved to the stockroom or to another production department, however, it must (or should) be inspected.

Inspection and its relation to the dispatching function.   The inspector inspects and counts material in process. To fix responsibility for defective work, this function is performed before material is moved from one department to another. If the work meets his approval, the inspector detaches the inspection ticket from the material book, initials it in the appropriate space, and forwards it to the dispatcher as notification that the job or the departmental operations are now complete and satisfactory. The dispatcher then places the master route and schedule sheet in the "completed jobs" file.

[5] Or the person or persons responsible for these functions (who may be the owner-manager himself). The number of copies of a labor voucher, or any other document used in the dispatching routine, is determined by the number of people who use the information it contains – which, in turn, is determined by the size and organizational structure of the firm. (See footnote 8, p. 424.)

```
┌─────────────────────────────────────────────────────────────────────────┐
│                           INSPECTION REPORT                               │
│                                                                           │
│  I. R. No. _____  P. O. No. _____  Date_____ │
├───────────────────────────────────────────────────────────────────────────
│  Part Name _____│
│                                                                           │
│  Department _____ Operation _____ │
│                                                                           │
│  Reason (s) for rejection of material: _____ │
│                                                                           │
│  _____ │
│                                                                           │
│  _____ │
│                                                                           │
│  Disposition:          □ Scrapped                                         │
│                                                                           │
│                        □ May be re-worked as follows: _____ │
│                                                                           │
│  _____ │
│                                                                           │
│  _____ │
│                                                                           │
│                        Signed: _____ │
│                                                (Inspector)                │
└───────────────────────────────────────────────────────────────────────────
```

Figure 22-6.   Inspection Report

If the material is rejected, an inspection report (or "I.R.") is issued. (See Figure 22-6.) The I.R. will indicate whether the material is to be "scrapped" or "reworked." Four copies usually are made out, one copy being distributed to each of the following persons or departments: inspection department, dispatcher, cost department (for costing the order), and the production planning department (for planning the additional work required).

Materials Supply

Upon receipt of the material book from the production planning department, the stockroom clerk files the book by starting date and thereunder by P. O. number. On the scheduled starting date, the material book is unfiled and attached to the material. If the material being delivered to the production center is raw material, the raw material withdrawal copy is removed from the material book and forwarded to the raw material stockroom. In the case of a factory assembly, the accumulation notice is removed from the material book and forwarded to the finished parts stockroom. One or the other of the above-mentioned papers are contained in the material book, never both.

The material is delivered from the (raw material or finished parts) stockroom to the production center of the first department in the routing. The move man removes the material delivery slip and gives it to the dispatcher. This is the dispatcher's notice that the material is on the floor, i.e., "in process." The dispatcher then pulls the labor book from the "dead load" file and places it in the material-available file in readiness for dispatching.

Raw material stockroom.   Upon receipt of the raw material withdrawal slip from the stockroom record clerk, the material is withdrawn from stock. The quantity used (feet, pounds, or units), date, P. O. number, and the balance of stock on hand are then recorded on the balance-of-stores ledger sheet. (See Figure 21-6, p. 423.) The material book is then securely attached to the material, and the raw material withdrawal copy is forwarded to the cost department.

Other duties of the raw material stockroom helpers are to receive and inspect incoming raw materials and to index stock bin locations. Receipts of incoming materials are entered on the balance-of-stores ledger sheet.

Finished parts stockroom.   The finished parts stockroom helpers receive finished material from the production departments, count and verify, index stock bin locations, initial finished stock delivery slips, and forward them to the production planning department. The material is then placed in stock according to the location index, and on the balance-of-stores ledger sheet are posted the date, P. O. number, quantity received, and the balance on hand. The identification tag remains in the stock bin until the last unit of that particular P. O. has been withdrawn, at which time the identification tag can be destroyed.

The finished parts stockroom helpers also make the accumulations for factory assembly purposes, and post the necessary data regarding these withdrawals to the balance-of-stores ledger sheet.

Follow-Up or Expediting

Dispatching is the function of *starting* work in process on schedule in accordance with the production plan. "Follow-up," on the other hand, is the function of recording the progress of work in the shop and taking remedial action in those cases where the work is not completed on schedule. In the latter event, the function becomes one of "expediting" or "stock chasing." Follow-up is a particularly important production control function in custom work, for job order customers make frequent inquiries concerning the progress of their orders and often request special services. It is, of course, also important in the "repetitive" processing of low-volume standard products.

At the end of the day the dispatcher withdraws the master route and schedule sheets from the "completed jobs" file and forwards them to the production planning and control department. There the follow-up man records the progress of the order. This is done most simply by circling the operation number on the department's copy of the master route and schedule sheet. Where schematic charts of the Gantt type are maintained, the progress of production orders is recorded in a routine manner by drawing the heavy "accomplishment" lines under the appropriate order assignments.[6]

[6] Where detailed routing and scheduling is decentralized, the follow-up function is performed by the dispatcher (or foreman) on Gantt schedule charts and/or master route and schedule sheets before copies of the latter are forwarded to the production planning and control department.

FLOW CONTROL

Where there is sufficient demand for the product special-purpose equipment can be set up for its "continuous" manufacture. In this type of manufacture the *flow* type of production planning and control is used; detailed order planning and control is not appropriate. Here, the planning function is the determination of the rate of flow of work in process from one production center to the next; the control function, obviously, is the initiation and maintenance of this predetermined rate of flow.

Production planning begins, as in all types of manufacturing, with an analysis of the product for determining (1) the most economical sequence of operations, and (2) the time allowance for each operation on each part or parts assembly. The next step is to install the production equipment in accordance with this master routing. Since the rate of flow from each production center should be as nearly equal as possible, the number of workmen and machines in each production center will vary, depending upon the capacity of each machine and the predetermined or standard times of the operations to be performed along the line. Thus once a production line has been set up for continuous manufacture, route and schedule sheets are no longer necessary. Routing is automatic because the layout of the equipment determines the direction of material flow throughout the plant. Likewise, scheduling is largely automatic because the rate of output is determined by the speed of the conveyor; so long as materials are supplied to the production line in the right amounts and at the right times, the volume of output can be calculated for any time period. Because of the steady "flow" or use of materials, balance-of-stores ledger sheets are not necessary; instead, a purchasing schedule is set up which is synchronized with the production schedule, thus minimizing the amount of storage space and working capital tied up in inventory.

The production control functions of dispatching and follow-up are also relatively simple. Once material is on the production line, the flow of material from one production center to the next is automatic. Dispatching in continuous manufacture, therefore, involves simply the "feeding" of material onto the production line in the amounts and times specified in the production program or master schedule. This is done by means of "track sheet" instructions which are transmitted to the appropriate line stations over a telautograph or other type of communications device.

The follow-up function involves simply a comparison of the actual rate of output with the *scheduled rate* of output over a period of time; this is in contrast with the follow-up function as performed in the intermittent and repetitive types of manufacture, wherein the progress of each order is checked. In intermittent and repetitive manufacturing, production order progress is checked on a schedule chart. (See Figure 22-3.) In the flow type of production planning and control, which is common to firms in continuous manufacture, a Gantt progress chart of the type illustrated in Figure 22-7 may be used. This chart shows the progress, on a weekly basis, of three products manufactured by a firm engaged in the continuous type of manufacture.

In Figure 22-7, for each product manufactured, the amount of work scheduled during a particular week, in terms of units of output, is indicated by a number

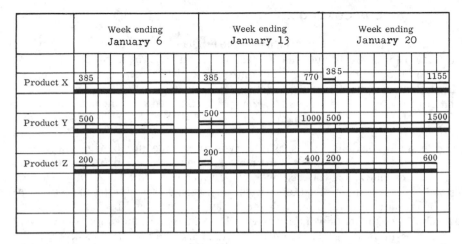

Figure 22-7. Gantt Progress Chart

placed in the upper left corner. A number in the upper right corner indicates the cumulative number of units which have been scheduled to date.

Horizontal light lines indicate the actual output or accomplishment in percentage of the standard amount scheduled for that week. For example, a light line drawn across half the space indicates that only one-half, or 50 percent, of the scheduled amount of work was completed during the week, and more than one light line through the space indicates that more work was done that week than was originally scheduled. Thus the scheduled 385 units of product X were completed during the week ending January 6; hence a horizontal light line was drawn across 100 percent of the space representative of that week. Due perhaps to a machine breakdown on the production line, only 347 units were completed during the following week; since this represents an "accomplishment" of only 90 percent, a light line was drawn across nine-tenths of the space. However, the output of this item was brought up to schedule by working overtime during the week ending January 20; the 423 units produced during this period is 110 percent of the standard weekly output, and this overproduction is indicated by drawing a second light line across 10 percent of the space.

The heavy lines in Figure 22-7 show the relation between the *cumulative* work completed and the *cumulative* work scheduled. The length of each cumulative line is plotted according to the scale of each individual column through which the line passes. Thus, for the three weeks ending January 20, the cumulative output of both products X and Y equaled the cumulative number of units scheduled to be completed by that time, but the cumulative output of product Z is lagging behind schedule by 20 units.

SUMMARY AND CONCLUSIONS

In conclusion, it is emphasized that while no two production planning and control systems are exactly alike, nevertheless the routine in one firm follows a

Table 22-1.   Production Control Patterns Common to Firms Engaged
in Intermittent, Repetitive, and Continuous Manufacturing

	Intermittent Manufacturing	Repetitive Manufacturing	Continuous Manufacturing
Type of Control		Order Control	Flow Control
Determination of quantity to manufacture	Requirements of the sales order	Economic lot size	Requirements of the production program
Routing of work in process	For each production order	Largely predetermined	Predetermined
Scheduling of work in process	For each production order		Production schedule prepared for entire manufacturing period—broken down into weekly and daily schedules
Dispatching	Release of labor and material "books" for each production order		Periodic release of manufacturing schedules
Follow-up	For each production order, compare with standards set for performance		Compare actual rate of output with scheduled rate of output

general *pattern* which is common to the system of other firms engaged in the same type of manufacturing. The similarities and differences between these patterns of production planning and control have been discussed and illustrated throughout this chapter and are summarized in Table 22-1.

REVIEW QUESTIONS

1.   What is "production control"? How does it aid in effecting economical production?

2.   How does production control in continuous manufacturing differ from production control in intermittent and repetitive manufacturing?

3.   Explain the use of a master route and schedule sheet.

4.   Differentiate between *master* routing and scheduling and *detailed* routing and scheduling.

5.   Differentiate between a schedule chart and a load chart.

6.   Differentiate between centralized and decentralized scheduling.

7.   Define and explain the use of "labor books" and "material books" in production order control.

8.   What is dispatching?

9. What part does a production order play in production control?

10 Differentiate between dispatching, follow-up, and expediting.

11. How does "flow" control differ from "order" control?

12. What is a Gantt progress chart. How is it used?

DISCUSSION QUESTIONS

1. What is the relationship of production planning and control to the following departments or activities of the firm?

    a. Sales
    b. Engineering
    c. Manufacturing
    d. Personnel
    e. Procurement
    f. Inventory control

2. How would you plan and control production in a three- or four-man metalworking job shop? Describe the kinds of information you would need and how you would obtain and coordinate that information. Describe your control system in detail.

SUPPLEMENTARY READINGS

Basso, Lee L. *Cost Handbook for the Small Manufacturer*. St. Louis: L. B. Associates, 1964. Discusses factors which the small manufacturer should consider in managing his production operations efficiently.

Gavett, J. William, and Allderige, John H. "Production Planning." In *Operations Analysis in Small Manufacturing Companies*, section 5. Small Business Management Research Report prepared for the Small Business Administration. Ithaca, N.Y.: Cornell University, 1963. Describes two types of production planning: the first relating to the flow of work through a job shop; and the second concerning the need for integrated decisions involving sales forecasting, production scheduling, and work force requirements for different models of a product.

23

Profit planning
and cost control

Profit is the motivating force in business. A business is "successful" only to the degree that it makes a profit; that is, to the degree that it continues to serve its customers so satisfactorily that they continue to support it as an enterprise. Profit may be described as that which is left over for the businessman after the goods are paid for and the bills are met. It is the businessman's "payoff."

PROFIT PLANNING

Profits, however, should not be left to chance; they should be *planned* for, not hoped for. In this section, two methods of determining profit goals or evaluating the profit potential of a small business are examined: (1) break-even analysis; and (2) marginal-income analysis. These techniques can be applied to certain types of problems in any line of business — merchandising, manufacturing, or the service trades.

Break-Even Analysis

Break-even analysis is the determination of the cost-volume-profit relationship. Cost and profit vary with the volume of sales. By separating that portion of total cost which varies in proportion to the volume of sales (variable cost) from that portion which exists regardless of the volume of sales (fixed cost), the relationship between cost, profit, and sales can be expressed graphically as shown in Figure 23-1 on what is known as a break-even chart.

The break-even chart is a square with a 45-degree sales income line drawn from the lower left to the upper right of the chart. The scale (in dollars) on which the total cost line is plotted is located on the vertical axis; the volume scale, which is identical to the cost scale, is located on the horizontal axis. The point at which the total cost line intersects the sales income line is called the "break-even" point. It is the point at which cost is equal to income, hence profit is equal to "zero." The area

453

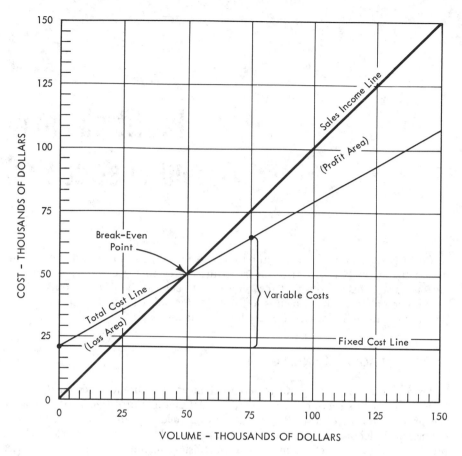

Figure 23-1. Break-Even Chart Illustrating Effect of Production Volume on Rate of Profit or Loss

between the total cost and sales income lines above the break-even point is the "profit area"; below the break-even point is the "loss area." The break-even chart in Figure 23-1 is based on the following data assumed for the Acorn Company:

Total sales income for the period		$75,000
Total cost at that sales volume:		
Fixed cost	$20,000	
Variable cost.	45,000	65,000
Profit.		$10,000

The total cost line in Figure 23-1 was drawn by first plotting two points: fixed cost of $20,000 at zero sales volume; and total cost of $65,000 at $75,000 sales volume. (The difference between these two figures, of course, is the variable cost at the indicated volume; in this case, $65,000 minus $20,000, or $45,000.) These points were then connected and the line extrapolated to the edge of the chart on the right. By inspection of the chart it can be seen that the break-even point is $50,000.

A break-even chart can be prepared from past cost records at various capacity levels. As noted above, a twofold classification of costs is used. *Fixed cost* is that part of total cost which does not change as volume changes. These are the costs which are necessary to maintain the essential skeleton of the business organization; hence, they are costs which are incurred even if the firm is temporarily shut down for lack of business (zero capacity). Examples of fixed cost are: rent, depreciation, salary of the owner-manager(s), property taxes, and interest on funded debt. *Variable cost* is that part of total cost which varies in direct proportion to volume, such as materials, direct wages, income taxes, and interest on floating debt.[1]

In relation to volume, there is in addition a "gray area" between the fixed and variable cost behavior patterns; that is, some costs increase with increases in volume but not in direct proportion. These are called *semivariable* costs. For example, when a firm first opens for business (or reopens its doors after a temporary shutdown) it must hire clerks and supervisors and incur other expenses which bear little relation to the initial volume of business; that is, they are "standby" costs which represent the difference in costs between shutdown and minimum operation.[2] For purposes of break-even analysis, however, these stand-by costs are considered "fixed." Therefore, break-even analysis is not applicable at production or sales volumes below the established minimum level of operation. But within the wide range of the smallest volume of business up to the practical or optimum capacity of the store or plant, break-even analysis is a most useful tool in evaluating the profit potential of the business.

The significance of the break-even chart for purposes of profit planning (see Figure 23-1) is that it clearly shows that above the break-even point the company is able to make increasingly greater profits. Thus above the level of sales at which the company "breaks even" its rate of profit increases faster than the rate of increase in sales. Conversely, the company suffers increasingly greater losses with decreases in sales. The break-even chart graphically illustrates to the small business owner-manager the importance of maintaining a high level of production and sales for the minimization of losses or the maximization of profits.

As a practical matter, of course, it is not necessary for the small businessman to draw a picture in order to determine his break-even sales point or the profit he could expect to make at a particular sales volume. For the break-even chart, after all, is merely a graphic representation of the profit equation:

$$P = S - (FC + VC) \tag{1}$$

where P = Profit (or loss)

    S = Sales income (or service-trade receipts)

    FC = Fixed cost (at minimum operating level, defined as "zero" capacity)

    VC = Variable cost

[1] Funded debt represents long-term funds borrowed for capital expenditure purposes; floating debt, in contrast, represents short-term funds borrowed to pay for materials, labor, and other needs which fluctuate with the volume of business.

[2] In a factory, similar standby costs are incurred between the one-shift capacity of the plant and minimum second-shift operation.

Since variable cost is that part of total cost which varies in proportion to the volume of sales, it is necessary to substitute the expression pS for the expression VC in the above equation. Thus:

$$P = S - (FC + pS) \tag{2}$$

where p = Variable cost per dollar of sales, expressed as a ratio

Applying equation (2) to the problem data on page 454, we first derive p as follows:

$$p = \tfrac{45}{75} = 0.6$$

Then, to compute the break-even point (where profit P is equal to 0):

$$P = S - FC - 0.6S$$
$$0 = S - 20 - 0.6S$$
$$20 = 0.4S$$
$$S = \$50 \text{ (thousand)}$$

Similarly, to compute the company's expected profit at $100,000 sales volume:

$$P = S - FC - 0.6S$$
$$= 100 - 20 - 0.6(100)$$
$$= 100 - 80$$
$$= \$20 \text{(thousand)}$$

Or the company's loss at $25,000 sales volume:

$$P = S - FC - 0.6S$$
$$= 25 - 20 - 0.6(25)$$
$$= 25 - 35$$
$$= -\$10 \text{(thousand)}$$

Each of the above calculated results can also be read from the chart in Figure 23-1.

At a sales volume of $75,000, the company's rate of profit on sales is $\tfrac{10}{75} = 13\tfrac{1}{3}$ percent. At a sales volume of $100,000, the rate of profit rises to 20 percent $(\tfrac{20}{100})$. Similar computations can be made in the "loss area." To repeat, as the break-even chart in Figure 23-1 graphically illustrates: *above the break-even point, increasingly greater profits are earned as sales volume increases; below the break-even level, increasingly greater losses are incurred as sales volume decreases.*

In addition to determining the effect on profit (or loss) of increases (or decreases) in production and sales, break-even analysis enables the small business owner-manager to determine changes in his break-even volume and rate of profit resulting from:

a. a change in cost (for example, a cost-reduction program, or a wage or tax increase); or

b. a change in price or product mix (under conditions of assumed product demand).[3]

All that is necessary is to "plug in" the assumed cost and income data and manipulate the above profit equation.

Another significant fact shown by the break-even chart is that the break-even point and the rate of profit or loss is directly affected by the *proportion of fixed to total cost.* For example, let us assume that in the Acorn Company a major change

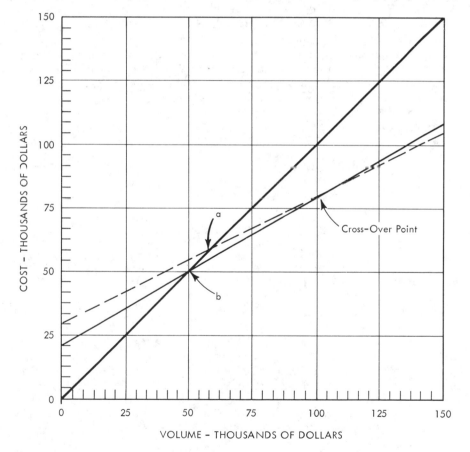

Figure 23–2.   Break-Even Chart Illustrating Effect of Fixed and Variable Cost Proportions on Rate of Profit or Loss

[3] For decision making in the area of pricing policy, another (and perhaps even simpler) approach is marginal-income analysis, discussed in the following section.

in equipment will add $10,000 to fixed costs (raising them to $30,000), but will reduce direct labor costs by an estimated $37\frac{1}{2}$ percent. At the current sales level of $75,000, at which direct labor costs are assumed to total $20,000, this would be a reduction in labor cost amounting to $7,500 (thus reducing variable costs to $37,500). The effect of this change in the company's cost structure is graphically illustrated in Figure 23-2 – the solid line depicting total cost "before" the change in equipment, and the broken line depicting total cost "after" the change in equipment.

It is observed that in the latter case the break-even point will be at a higher level of sales; $60,000 instead of $50,000. (The "before" and "after" break-even points are designated on the chart as b and a, respectively.) However, the rate of profit or loss at sales above or below the break-even point will also be higher.

At the current ($75,000) level of sales, total cost would be higher, and profit lower, if the change in equipment were made. But at what point in sales would the investment result in a larger profit? In other words, when would the investment begin to "pay off"? This also can be determined by inspection of the break-even chart in Figure 23-2. Profit is equal, of course, at the point where the two cost lines intersect. This "crossover point" occurs at a sales volume of $100,000. Beyond this volume, the rate of profit would be greater with the new labor-saving equipment than it would be without it.

The crossover point can also be calculated. Since profits are equal at this point, this is done by equating the "before" and "after" profit equations and solving for S, as follows:[4]

$$S - 20 - 0.6S = S - 30 - 0.5S$$
$$0.4S - 20 = 0.5S - 30$$
$$10 = 0.1S$$
$$S = \$100 \text{ (thousand)}$$

In making the investment decision, the small businessman would compare this volume with the company's short- and long-run sales forecasts.

Incremental Costs and Marginal Income

We shall now try a slightly different method of evaluating the profit potential of the business. The significance of this new approach can best be appreciated by first posing a problem, a not uncommon one among small manufacturers. Let us assume that the Acorn Company (whose cost structure was defined above) is operating at only half-capacity. It is primarily a job shop, more than half of its usual output consisting of products manufactured to customers' specifications. The company receives orders from two customers, as follows:

	Order A	Order B
Number of units to be delivered	250	200
Price customer is willing to pay for each unit	$5.00	$6.25
Estimated variable cost per unit	$3.00	$3.50
Estimated total cost per unit	$6.50	$8.00

[4] The new variable cost ratio, $p = 37{,}500/75{,}000 = 0.5$.

In order to meet the customers' delivery specifications, it would be necessary to start both orders in production immediately. However, though the plant is operating at only half-capacity, there is insufficient machine time available to process the orders simultaneously. Therefore, the owner-manager can accept only one of the orders. Of course, he need not accept either. What should he do? What would you advise him to do?

If your advice to him is to reject both orders, your decision would be typical of the decision which most small businessmen would make (and have made) in a similar situation. But it would be a wrong decision, as the following analysis attests:

	Order A	Order B
1. Price per unit	$5.00	$6.25
2. Volume in units	250	200
3. Variable cost per unit	$3.00	$3.50
4. *Added* income	$1,250	$1,250
(line 1 × line 2)		
5. *Added* variable cost	$750	$700
(line 2 × line 3)		
6. *Added* "profit-volume income"	$500	$550
(line 4 − line 5)		
7. Programmed cost (see p. 460)	0	0
8. *Added* "profit contribution"	$500	$550
(line 6 − line 7)		

As the figures indicate, the company's profit would be $50 higher if order B is accepted rather than order A — or, if the company is presently operating in the "loss area," its loss would be $50 less. And if neither order is accepted, the company would have foregone an opportunity to increase its profit (or decrease its loss) by as much as $550.

The important point for the reader of this book to bear in mind is that, for purposes of managerial decision making, it is the *incremental* cost associated with a particular plan or alternative course of action which is important, not the conventional cost-accounting concept of "average" or "total" cost. For example, if variable cost varies in amount with the volume of business but is always the same percentage of the business done (within a wide range of volume, as noted in our discussion of break-even analysis), while fixed cost is the same regardless of the volume of business, then the difference between 100 percent (as representing the business done) and the variable cost proportion may be called the "contribution to fixed cost and profit." In other words, if variable cost is 60 percent or $0.60 out of each dollar of business, there must be $0.40 out of each dollar of business applicable to fixed cost until it is offset, and thereafter, to profit. Thus in choosing between order A and order B, the small businessman should compare only the added income and costs associated with each order to determine the *net effect* on profit.[5] To use the accountants' concept of average cost, involving the allocation of fixed overhead cost, would be misleading.

[5] The terms incremental costs and marginal income are used interchangeably. Incremental costs are also often referred to as "out-of-pocket" or "differential" costs.

Incremental costs, however, may be fixed as well as variable in nature. Under the conditions as assumed for the Acorn Company (that is, under conditions of unused capacity), the building, machinery and supervisory staff already exist; the fixed costs associated with these factors remain the same *regardless of the course of action taken.* Hence, for purposes of management decision making they are *passive* costs and can be disregarded. However, if one of the orders required special tooling which could be used only on that job, the added cost is regarded as a fixed *programmed* cost which would be "charged" against the income produced by that order. On the other hand, if the plant was already working at full capacity, and the company decided to process both orders at overtime, the overtime labor cost of each order would be a programmed cost of a variable nature. For purposes of marginal-income analysis, therefore, we find it convenient to differentiate between fixed costs, variable costs, and programmed costs (which may be fixed or variable), and to consider as pertinent only the latter two classifications of cost.

This type of analysis has many practical applications in small business. Its usefulness can be further demonstrated by considering other management plans or "programs" under similar conditions, that is, when a plant has a large amount of excess capacity. One way in which production and sales volume might be increased is to lower the price. Let us assume, for example, that in addition to its job work, the Acorn Company manufactures widgets and a variety of other low-volume standard products. Last year, the company sold 20,000 widgets at $6.00 each. The *variable* cost per unit to produce them was $3.00. The owner-manager estimates that an additional 5,000 could be sold if the price were reduced to $5.60. If such a pricing policy were followed, what would be the added "profit contribution"? Using the same analytical framework as above, we find that the company's profit would be increased (or its loss decreased) by $5,000:

1. Price per unit	$5.60
2. Volume in units	25,000
3. Variable cost per unit (unchanged)	$3.00
4. *Added* income (line 1 × line 2 − $120,000 original volume)	$20,000
5. *Added* variable cost (line 2 × line 3 − $60,000 variable cost at original volume)	$15,000
6. *Added* "profit-volume income" (line 4 − line 5)	$5,000
7. Programmed cost	0
8. *Added* "profit contribution" (line 6 − line 7)	$5,000

Another way in which a small business might use its excess capacity is to add a new product to its line. Let us assume that, according to a market study, the Acorn Company could expect to sell an estimated 10,000 units of a new product during the coming year at a price of $5.00 per unit, with a special advertising and sales promotion effort costing $10,000. The new product can be produced on existing equipment, and direct labor and direct material costs would total an estimated

$3.00 per unit. If the company diversified its product line, what would be the added "profit contribution"? Proceeding as before, it is seen that there would be a $10,000 contribution to fixed cost and profit:

1. Price per unit	$5.00
2. Volume in units	10,000
3. Variable cost per unit	$3.00
4. *Added* income (line 1 × line 2)	$50,000
5. *Added* variable cost (line 2 × line 3)	$30,000
6. *Added* "profit-volume income" (line 4 − line 5)	$20,000
7. Programmed cost	$10,000
8. *Added* "profit contribution" (line 6 − line 7)	$10,000

Another familiar example of the incremental-cost or marginal-income approach to small business management decision making is the "make-or-buy" decision. If the company is currently purchasing an item, and it has excess machine capacity of a type used in its manufacture, the company may well consider manufacturing the item itself. On the traditional full-costing basis the company probably cannot manufacture the product as efficiently as the manufacturer from whom it had been buying the item, but so long as the company's out-of-pocket (or variable) cost is less than the purchase price it had been paying, the company's profit situation would be improved.

FINANCIAL STATEMENTS AND THEIR INTERPRETATION

Profit, of course, can be increased by way of a decrease in operating expenses as well as by an increased flow of income. In this section, we will look at the cost side of the profit coin. In addition to expense control, methods of determining or evaluating the adequacy of profits will also be discussed.

For the managerial analysis and control of both costs and profit, complete and accurate financial records are necessary. The two basic financial statements are the balance sheet and the profit-and-loss statement. The latter statement, as the name implies, is a summary of business transactions that have taken place during the year (or month) resulting in either a profit or a loss. It is like a motion picture of business operations during the period covered by the report; by careful analysis of the profit-and-loss statement, one can clearly see what has happened and determine why the business is now where it is. The balance sheet is the statement that shows exactly where the business stands; it can be thought of as a snapshot of the business as it stood on the last day of the accounting period. The balance sheet shows where the business is; the profit-and-loss statement shows how it got there. Used wisely, these two statements will give a good indication of what may be expected in the future.

The profit-and-loss statement summarizes the business transactions as follows:

Sales	$50,000
Deduct: Cost of goods sold	35,000
Gross margin	$15,000
Deduct: Expenses.	10,000
Net profit	$ 5,000

The financial records make readily available all these amounts except the cost of goods sold, which is easily computed from inventory records as follows:

Inventory, beginning of period	$20,000
Add: Purchases of goods during period.	45,000
Goods available for sale during period	$65,000
Deduct: Inventory on hand, end of period	30,000
Cost of goods sold	$35,000

From the balance sheet, the owner can see how much cash he has in his cash register and in the bank, how much inventory is on hand, how much the customers owe the firm, the value of his equipment, how much is owed to creditors, and the "net worth," the latter being the difference between what he owns and what he owes.[6] Here is a simple balance sheet:

Assets

Current assets:		
Cash on hand	$ 1,500	
Cash in bank	8,000	
Accounts receivable	6,500	
Merchandise inventory	9,000	$25,000
Fixed assets:		
Furniture and fixtures	$ 3,000	
Building	30,000	33,000
Total Assets		$58,000

Liabilities and Net Worth

Current liabilities:		
Accounts payable.	$ 3,750	
Notes payable	1,250	$ 5,000
Fixed liabilities:		
Mortgage payable		25,000
Net worth:		
Capital		28,000
Total Liabilities and Net Worth		$58,000

[6] *Current* assets include cash and assets that can be converted into cash within a short time (one year or less); similarly, *current* liabilities are debts that must be paid within a year. All other assets are regarded as *fixed*. *Net worth* is the equity of the owner or owners in the assets.

This is called a "balance sheet" because the total assets balance with, or are equal to, the total liabilities and net worth. It is closely related to the profit-and-loss statement, in that almost every entry made in the financial records affects both statements. An addition to cash in the balance sheet is usually an addition to an income account in the profit-and-loss statement. A deduction from cash in the balance sheet is usually charged to some expense account or to the cost of sales in the profit-and-loss statement. And when the two statements are drawn up at the close of the accounting period, the amount of net profit or net loss for the period as shown in the profit-and-loss statement is exactly the sum that is needed to effect a balance between the capital account plus liabilities and the total assets as shown on the balance sheet.

Ratio Analysis

Ratios show the relationship between two items and are commonly used in business management to measure financial conditions or financial changes. They are used in the analysis of financial statements because a businessman might be misled by a comparison of dollar figures. It is likely, for example, that increased sales volume would produce a greater dollar profit from one month to the next, although profit in relation to sales might be down by a rather large percentage.

Financial ratios can be used in the determination of policies for future operation of the business in two ways. First, the small business owner may find it helpful to compare his firm's ratios for the period under scrutiny with similar ratios for previous periods. Such a comparison would help him to pinpoint conditions in his business which merit attention. If profits are declining, he can quickly check the firm's financial ratios and ascertain possible reasons for the decline.

Secondly, the small business owner can compare the ratios for his business with the "standard" ratios in his industry. Standard ratios are averages of the results achieved by thousands of firms in the same line of business. Some fail and show very poor ratios. A few excel and provide ratios for the more ambitious to use as guides or bases for comparison. Such ratios are compiled and published annually by trade associations in many lines of business and by several universities, government agencies, and private enterprises. Among the best-known sources of industry ratio data are Dun & Bradstreet, New York (covering 72 lines of business activity), and Robert Morris Associates (the National Association of Bank Loan Officers and Credit Men), Philadelphia (covering 175 lines of business).

In interpreting the differences between the firm's ratios and the standard ratios, however, the small business owner should weigh the effects of seasonal fluctuations in both the firm and the industry as a whole. In addition, he should recognize and use standard ratios for firms of similar size and geographic location. Also, standard ratios are meaningful only if they are based on standard cost classifications and accounting systems.

There are three types of financial ratios: those which show the relationship of various items in the balance sheet (balance-sheet ratios); those which show the relationships of income to various expense items in the profit-and-loss statement (operating ratios); and those which show the relationship of a balance sheet item to one in the profit and loss statement ("mixed" ratios). Using the above financial statements, we will now proceed to calculate and interpret some of the more important ratios of each type.

Balance-sheet ratios.   The purpose of balance-sheet analysis is to assist the small business owner to make the most effective use of the resources at his disposal. Does he, for example, have enough cash on hand and in the bank? Are his current assets sufficiently large relative to current liabilities? Are his fixed assets too great in amount? Does he have enough capital invested in the business?

One of the most common balance-sheet ratios is the current ratio, which is the ratio between current assets and current liabilities. In other words, does the business have enough customers' accounts coming due to enable it, when they are added to its cash and to the income it will realize from sales during the next two weeks, to pay all the accounts that will fall due to creditors within the same period? Dividing total current assets by current liabilities will provide a current ratio that can be compared with the standard ratio or with former ratios of the business. In the above balance sheet, this ratio is $25,000/$5,000, or 5 times. A current ratio of not less than 2 to 1 is generally considered satisfactory. It is important to note, however, that the current ratio is affected by seasonal fluctuations. The high 5-to-1 ratio in the above case, for example, may reflect a "carryover" of inventory from one season to the next.

Because they may deteriorate or become obsolete, and be subject to write-offs or write-downs, some businessmen do not include inventories in computing the current ratio. Also, the conversion of merchandise inventory into cash takes more time than is true for other current assets. This more conservative ratio is called the "acid-test" ratio. In the above example, it is $16,000/$5,000, or 3.2 times.

Another common balance-sheet ratio is obtained by dividing the depreciated fixed assets (such as land and buildings, furniture, and fixtures, and machines and other equipment) by the tangible net worth.[7] Doing this for the data given above, we derive a ratio of $33,000/$28,000, or 1.2 times. In order to guard against purchasing too many fixed assets, the small businessman should try to keep this ratio not much more than 1 to 1. In other words, he should have enough capital invested in the business to pay for most, if not all, of his fixed assets. By this standard, the above ratio is too high. If fixed assets are high relative to net worth, earnings may not be sufficient to meet maturing installments on the long-term debt, and the small businessman may be compelled to seek new capital.

A business, of course, needs to borrow money in order to make money, but how much debt can it "safely" incur? In other words, what should be the ratio of total debt to net worth? Dividing, in our example, the sum of the firm's current and fixed liabilities ($30,000) by its tangible net worth ($28,000) yields a ratio of 107 percent. Many authorities feel that the equity of creditors in the assets of the business should be no greater than 75 percent of the owner's equity, and in some types of business perhaps even less.[8]

Mixed ratios.   Many important ratios relate data from one financial statement to data from the other. The four which the authors feel are the most useful for the

---

[7] *Tangible net worth* is the worth of the business minus intangible assets such as goodwill, trademarks, patents, franchises, etc. The latter are excluded from ratio calculations because of the difficulty of estimating their "worth" until they are actually sold.

[8] Richard Sanzo, *Ratio Analysis for Small Business,* 3rd ed., Small Business Management Series no. 20 (Washington, D.C.: Small Business Administration, 1970), p. 56.

small business owner are calculated as follows, using data from our sample statements:[9]

	Sample Computation
Net profit to average tangible net worth	$5,000/$28,000 = 17.9%
Net sales to working capital	$50,000/$20,000 = 2.5 times
Net sales to average inventory	$50,000/$9,000 = 5.6 times
Net sales to receivables	$50,000/$6,500 = 7.7 times

The small businessman can determine the amount his investment is earning for him by dividing his net profit (as shown on his profit-and-loss statement) by his average tangible net worth as shown on his balance sheets at the beginning and at the end of the period. If we assume that there was no change in his net worth during the period, the businessman in our example earned a healthy 17.9 percent on his investment in the business. This is a considerably higher rate of return than he could have earned by investing in corporate or government bonds, by purchasing time savings certificates, or by investing his capital in many other ways. The higher rate of return compensates the businessman for his risks and provides him with sufficient incentive. This, after all, is why he went into business.

A second important ratio of the "mixed" type measures the turnover of working capital. Working capital is the excess of current assets over current liabilities. It is working capital which allows the business owner to meet his weekly payroll, pay his monthly utility bills, and make regular payments on his suppliers' invoices. You will recall from our previous discussion of the current ratio that current assets "normally" should be no less than twice as large in amount as the current liabilities; this is equivalent to saying that working capital should be about equal to current liabilities. Thus the turnover of working capital, measured by dividing working capital at the end of the accounting period into the net sales during that period, is closely related to the current ratio. In evaluating the adequacy of a 2-to-1 current ratio in a given case, the businessman should give consideration to the number of times the working capital "turns over." With a fast turnover, a low current ratio might suffice. If the turnover is slow, then this should be compensated by a higher current ratio. Each ratio must be considered in relation to the other.

Inventory turnover is another important measurement for the small businessman to make. This is done by dividing the average inventory into the net sales over a given period. Ordinarily, the businessman should strive for as high an inventory turnover as possible without excessive "stockouts." With a fast turnover, inventory levels will be lower; hence, inventory carrying costs, and losses from depreciation and changes in style, will also be lower.

The net-sales-to-receivables ratio is also helpful in small business management. When a firm's sales are predominantly credit sales, the ratio may be used to estimate the average collection period. Net sales is first divided by 365 to derive the

[9] The following computations assume that there was no change in net worth or in the inventory investment during the period covered by the balance sheet; that is, both are assumed to be *average*. *Working* capital, as explained later in the text, is the excess of current assets over current liabilities.

daily credit sales. In our example, this would be $50,000/365, or $137. The daily credit sales is then divided into the total of the notes and accounts receivable to determine the average number of days the firm's working capital is tied up in credit sales. In our example, the average collection period is 47.4 days ($6,500/$137). This analysis will disclose important trends and danger signals very useful for successful credit management.

Operating ratios.   Operating ratios are used in expense control. Each item of expense in the profit-and-loss statement is expressed as a percentage of income as a common base. To keep the illustration simple, we will use the following condensed operating statement for our computations, although in practice the various types of expense would be listed and the percentage of net sales computed for each.

		Percentage
Sales	$50,000	100
Deduct: Cost of goods sold	35,000	70
Gross margin.	$15,000	30
Deduct: Expenses.	10,000	20
Net Profit	$ 5,000	10

   Ratio analysis provides the standards needed for effective expense control. The following approach to expense control seems to the authors to be a logical one: The owner of the business, in order to operate it once it is established, must have, as items or "tools" with which to work, a building, equipment, cash funds, materials or merchandise, and personnel. The effectveness with which he utilizes each of these, singly or in combination, determines his profit or loss and, therefore, his business success or failure. Over the years experience has shown that the importance of each of these is measurable in terms of what it produces, to be sure, but its value to the organization may also be measured in terms of the costs of its use. Thus effectiveness of use means profitableness of use. After a business has been in existence for a reasonable length of time, these costs, if the business is successful, tend to become rather fixed portions or percentages of the total expenses of the business, and in many industries desirable ratios (the percentages that these things have come to cost in representative successful firms) are well established. There is, therefore, a minimum percentage that each can cost and still provide proper service, and a maximum that each can cost before it reduces or prevents profit. While this is merely an explanation of "standard ratios," it seeks to emphasize the premium placed on the effective use of a firm's assets, and the need for expense records to check their effectiveness against these norms.

   Most ratio studies are concerned with operating expenses (rather than balance-sheet items), and the number of sources of published standard operating ratios runs into the hundreds. The expense items for which standard ratios are developed, of course, varies from one line of business to another, and within each industry there are differences among firms on the basis of size, geographic location, credit policies, type of ownership organization, and other factors. Expense control in retailing and wholesaling, and in factories and service establishments will be discussed in detail in the concluding sections of this chapter.

Budgeting

Closely related to ratio analysis in expense control is budgeting. An expense budget is a control device used by management to predetermine what each major class of expenses should be for the period of time covered, and to aid executives in conducting the business in line with these expenses as planned. It is a valuable management aid.

In modern business, control is always exercised in relation to some goal. There must be a desired objective, certain standards set or predetermined, current reports or records for comparison with these standards, and prompt executive action to keep in line with planned figures. These goals or standards may be time or output standards, or they may relate to production, inventory and employment levels, or other operating aspects of the business; but our attention here will be confined to business expenses. To repeat for emphasis, control requires: predetermined standards, current comparable reports, and prompt, intelligent executive action.

As applied to the expense budget, the objective may be to achieve a certain volume of business at minimum cost or to expand volume rapidly even though the cost of doing so will be high temporarily. In either case, standards will be set in terms of anticipated expenses appropriate to the objective planned; operating reports that show at frequent intervals what expenses have been actually incurred will permit comparison with planned figures. Appropriate action taken in time will prevent an unsatisfactory condition from continuing. In some cases it is possible to require authorization before certain expenses are incurred and thus to increase the degree of expense control exercised. One example is to require prior authorization before a department head can add an additional employee.

An expense budget is a "must" for every business. One author says: "Few, if any, techniques are more vital to the sound management of a manufacturing enterprise than budgeting. But many smaller companies unwisely neglect or ignore this simple, effective tool. Yet, smaller companies have a great need for it because of a pressing need for profitable utilization of working capital, and for the development of sound plans for meeting future competition and for expanding."[10] In launching a new enterprise, it is the basis for deciding whether the venture should be undertaken, or for satisfying the banker that the enterpriser has a good proposition for a loan. To the established business it means the difference between success and failure. It should be made in terms of an accepted expense classification for the particular business field and in line with available data from other successful firms. If a businessman aspires to higher goals, he should provide for improving on industry standards by reducing his expense percentages through better management.

Expense classification. If a firm is well established, the standard expense classification accepted for that particular line of business should be set up in the firm's accounting records. Usually, for the very small establishment, a simple breakdown of expenses into a few major divisions is suggested, with progressively detailed subdivisions recommended as the size or volume of the business increases. In so doing one will inherit the benefit of previous experience in the field. He will

[10] Howard Ellsworth Sommer, "Budgeting in the Small Plant," rev. ed., Management Aids Annual no. 1 (Washington, D.C.: Small Business Administration, 1958), p. 59.

also be able to use current operating ratios and expense data published by the trade association, Dun & Bradstreet, and other reporting agencies as a continuing guide to the success of his operations. If he selects his own expense accounts, definitions, or classifications, he will have no assurance that they are comparable to published data. For example, does the expense for advertising include only payment to newspapers and other media, or also payroll, "donations," and other such items? Are the same items included in the delivery, credit, or other expenses for customer services that other businessmen in the field include? Discrepancies in expense classifications such as the few suggested here will render comparison with average data for the field worthless.

For the small owner-operated business it is also important that *imputed* as well as actual costs be included in the standard expense accounts. Examples of actual expenses are payments made for utility services, labor, interest on loans, and, if the building is not owned by the proprietor, rent. Imputed expenses are those that would be charged for property or services of the proprietor if secured from someone else; they include interest on the proprietor's own capital invested in the business, rent for the premises he owns that are used for business purposes, and a fair salary for his own services as manager of the business.

With an accurate, complete record of the expense items which make up the totals in standard expense accounts, an operator can immediately tell whether one item that is too high can be cut down in future operations. Suppose one of the accounts is lower than standard. Ordinarily, he would experience a certain amount of satisfaction over this, but he should examine it anyway. Perhaps something is wrong. If this was his advertising account, he might have brought in a larger sales volume and a correspondingly higher profit if he had spent more for advertising. In studying expense control it is well to know how much can wisely be spent to increase sales volume and where adjustments, up or down, can be made to increase net profit in the long run.

Methods studies.   Methods studies are careful analyses of the way some activities are being performed, usually for the purpose of reducing the expense involved or making other improvements in the way the work is done. For repetitive operations that take a short time to perform, time studies may be used to assist the analyst in selecting more efficient methods. For most situations in the small business, however, critical observation and good judgment in making changes will usually be sufficient.

To repeat, expense control means *control*; if any item is too expensive, something should be done about it. This is the primary purpose of methods studies.

If a retailer cannot make a profit selling cereals with clerk service, he should put them on a self-service basis. If a product costs too much to manufacture, production expenses must be reduced or the business turned over to competitors. If a store is unable to operate a needed millinery department at a profit, it can lease it to one of the millinery syndicates.

To illustrate applications of the fundamentals of expense control further we shall now examine the major fields of small business. It must be remembered that within each major field there will be variations in application, different standard methods of expense classification, and similar adaptations to be made for each particular line of business.

EXPENSE CONTROL IN RETAILING

To the retailer certain items of expense are of major importance. They are labor, rent, advertising, and those items relating to inventory or investment in merchandise. In some lines customer services also account for large expenditures. Store policies regarding the class of customers desired and services to be rendered may affect expenses greatly.

A merchant can keep his payroll under control by employing the amount and kind of help needed. More use might be made of part-time employees such as former employees who resigned to get married, who would be willing to work occasionally when needed but who would not accept regular employment. Although the small retailer is not usually able to employ workers specially trained and skilled for each kind of task to be performed, he can try to secure more reliable and better qualified employees than those frequently hired. To do so will involve paying higher wages, but may actually reduce labor costs because of the greater productivity secured. Once qualified workers are employed, it is a good policy to assign duties to each worker to take full advantage of his special skills and abilities. Proper supervision and use of the techniques of good personnel management will help also to keep this largest item of retailing expense under control.

Store policy determines how rent, which is usually the second largest item of expense, can be controlled. Continuously adjusting policies to capitalize fully on all changes in the characteristics of the store's location will help to keep this expense in line.

Studying location trends in the region closely and planning future adjustments to them will provide for the long-run needs of the business. Sometimes a fundamental decision is involved, whether to remain at a particular site and adjust to changes in shopping traffic or to keep changing sites to follow the original class of customer.

Advertising is an example of an expense that might often be controlled more effectively by increasing rather than decreasing the amount spent. A merchant whose advertising expense ratio is below the standard for his type of store could probably increase his sales and profits by spending more money for advertising.

In some cases retailers can reduce fixed expenses by employing outside agencies to perform services where the volume of work is not sufficient to justify investment in equipment. For example, deliveries can be made through a mutual or consolidated delivery system. For infrequent small deliveries Western Union messengers may be used. Sometimes delivery trucks may be rented, maintenance and depreciation costs being borne by the firm from which the equipment is rented. The small businessman will find break-even analysis most appropriate in controlling fixed investment cost.

Some costs of a semifixed (or semivariable) nature, such as those incurred for bookkeeping and window-display services, can also be effectively lowered where the store is too small to hire its own specialists on a full-time basis.

The merchant's problem of expense control is unique because he carries a large number of articles of merchandise, many of his employees do several kinds of work, and he must continually defer to customer wishes or demands. In place of using cost accounting for particular products, as is done in manufacturing, the merchant "costs" entire lines or classes of goods. Since the functions performed by various retailers remain basically the same regardless of location, class of customers, kinds of merchandise handled, or other variables, and since many of the expenses incurred, such as those for labor, rent, and equipment, serve two or more functions, a dual system of expense classification control is often employed.

Expense Classification

Retail expenses, under the dual system, are classified as both "natural" and "functional." For example, the National Retail Merchants Association recommends for department and general merchandise stores 17 natural classes of expense as follows: payroll, property rentals, advertising, supplies, services purchased (other than professional), travel, communications, pensions, taxes, interest, insurance, depreciation, professional services, donations, bad debts, equipment rental, and unclassified. Then to each of five major retailing functions – administration, occupancy, buying, selling, and publicity – is distributed the proportion of the natural expenses it accounted for. These standard expense classifications are used by the Controllers' Congress and the National Retail Merchants Association in assembling and publishing operating data for department stores and general merchandise stores. Merchandising departments are also standardized and numbers are assigned to each so that a given number always refers to the same department in any store anywhere in the country. Such departmental operating data as inventory turnover, the stock-sales ratio, and total expenses, in the individual store, can then be compared accurately with national averages.

Similar standardized systems of cost accounting have been developed for many other types of retailing activity by various governmental and private agencies.

Operating Ratios

Comparison analysis and intelligent, timely action is the proved formula for expense control. Operating ratios help in this respect just as does the budget for the individual store. After comparing the firm's ratios with those of the trade, it is important, before taking steps to correct an out-of-line ratio, to find out why a ratio is different and to realize that the difference may be balanced by a difference in another ratio.

At the end of the year the retailer may find out whether he has made as much profit as he should have, or if he has operated efficiently, by comparing his business with others in his line of trade. If he finds that his expenses are too high, a comparison of his figures, item by item, with the expenses of profitable firms will enable him to ferret out those that are guilty of eating up the profits. Also, he may find that he is losing business by not spending enough in some places, and a supposed economy may be, in fact, increasing expenses in another area.

It is the total of all expenses that affects net profits; should one item be too high, some other must be decreased to keep profits at the average ratio. For example, a high cost-of-delivery ratio may be balanced by a low rent ratio. Also, increasing one expense item may cause a reduction in another that was formerly too high.

Standard operating ratios for various types of retail trade are available from trade associations and from a number of nontrade sources. The two principal booklets dealing with summary ratios in retailing are *Expenses in Retail Business*, published by the National Cash Register Company, and the *Barometer of Small Business*, published by the Accounting Corporation of America. These and other sources are listed alphabetically in Table 23-1 by line of business.[11]

Table 23-1.   Sources of Standard Operating Ratios, by Line of Trade

Line of Trade	Available Figures		
	National Cash Register Co.*	Account- ing Corp. of America†	Trade Sources
Appliance & radio-television dealers	√	√	
Automobile dealers, new.	√	√	"Average Operating Ratios for the Automobile Retailing Industry"; no charge; write to National Automobile Dealers Association, 2000 K St. N.W., Washington, D.C. 20006
Automobile dealers, used	√	√	
Auto parts dealers	√	√	
Bakeries	√	√	
Barber shops.	√		
Beauty shops	√	√	"Beauty Shop Facts and Figures"; no charge; write to Modern Beauty Shop, 59 E. Monroe St., Chicago, Ill. 60603
Bookstores.	√		"Operating Ratios for Booksellers"; no charge; write to American Booksellers Association, 175 Fifth Ave., New York, N.Y. 10010
Children's and infants' wear stores . .	√	√	
Cocktail lounges	√	√	
Confectionary stores	√	√	
Contractors, building.		√	
Contractors, specialty		√	
Delicatessens & other specialty food shops.	√	√	

[11]Other nontrade sources are Dun & Bradstreet and Robert Morris Associates, publishing standard operating ratios in wholesaling and manufacturing as well as in retailing.

Table 23-1.   (Continued)

	Available Figures		
Line of Trade	National Cash Register Co.*	Accounting Corp. of America†	Trade Sources
Department & specialty stores......	√		"Department Merchandising Operating Results of Department and Specialty Stores"; $15; write to National Retail Merchants Association, 100 W. 31st St., New York, N.Y. 10001
Drive-in restaurants..........	√		
Drugstores...............	√	√	"Annual Lilly Digest"; no charge; write to Eli Lilly and Company, Indianapolis Ind. 46225
Drugs, wholesale...........			"NWDA Operating Survey"; $2 for members, $5 for nonmembers; write to National Wholesale Druggists' Association, 220 E. 42nd St., New York, N.Y. 10017
Dry cleaners..............	√	√	"Cost Percentage Bulletin"; no charge; write to National Institute of Dry Cleaning, 909 Burlington Ave., Silver Spring, Md. 20910
Dry goods & general merchandise stores..............	√	√	
Farm equipment stores........		√	"Cost of Doing Business in The Farm Equipment Retailing Industry"; $2; write to National Retail Farm Equipment Association, 2340 Hampton Ave., St. Louis, Mo. 63139
Feed and seed stores.........		√	
Florists.................	√	√	
Furniture stores............	√	√	"Furniture Store Operating Experience Report"; no charge, but for members only; write to National Retail Furniture Association, 66 Lake Shore Dr., Chicago, Ill. 60611
Garages.................	√	√	
Garden supply stores.........	√		
Gift, novelty, and souvenir stores...	√	√	
Grocery stores.............	√	√	

Table 23-1.   (Continued)

Line of Trade	National Cash Register Co.*	Accounting Corp. of America†	Trade Sources
		Available Figures	
Hardware stores.	√	√	"Management Report"; no charge for members; $5 for nonmembers; write to National Retail Hardware Association, 964 N. Pennsylvania St., Indianapolis, Ind. 46204
Infants' wear stores.	√	√	
Jewelry stores	√	√	
Laundry plants	√	√	"Operating Cost Percentages"; no charge; write to American Institute of Laundering, Joliet, Ill. 60433
Laundries, self-service		√	
Liquor stores	√	√	
Lumber & building material dealers. .	√	√	
Machine shops		√	
Meat markets	√	√	
Men's specialty stores.		√	
Men's wear stores	√	√	"Annual Survey of Men's Wear Stores"; no charge; write to *Men's Wear Magazine,* 7 E. 12th St., New York, N.Y. 10003
Motels	√	√	"Motel Operating Averages"; $1; write to *Tourist Court Journal,* Temple, Texas 76501
Music stores	√	√	
Nursery and garden supply stores . . .	√		
Office supply and equipment dealers .	√		
Paint, glass, and wallpaper stores . . .	√	√	"PWAA Business Survey"; no charge; write to Retail Paint & Wallpaper Distributors of America, 8131 Delmar Blvd., St. Louis, Mo. 63130
Photographic studio & supply shops .	√	√	
Plumbing & heating equipment		√	
Prescription pharmacies	√		"Facts on the Operation of Prescription Pharmacies"; no charge; write to American College of Apothecaries, Hamilton Court, Philadelphia, Penna. 19104

Table 23-1.   (Continued)

| | | Available Figures | |
Line of Trade	National Cash Register Co. *	Account-ing Corp. of America †	Trade Sources
Printing shops		√	
Radio-TV dealers	√	√	
Repair services		√	
Restaurants	√	√	"Operating Results of Restaurants"; available on limited basis at no charge to firms in line if request is made on business stationery; write to Horwath & Horwath, 41 E. 42nd St., New York, N.Y. 10017
Service stations	√	√	
Shoe stores (family)	√	√	
Souvenir stores	√		
Sporting goods stores	√	√	"Cost of Doing Business Survey of the NSGA"; $1; write to National Sporting Goods Association, 23 E. Jackson Blvd., Chicago, Ill. 60604
Stationery stores	√		"Operating Results; Office Supply & Equipment Dealers"; no charge; write to National Stationery & Office Equipment Association, 740 Investment Building, Washington, D.C. 20005
Supermarkets		√	"The Super Market Industry Speaks"; no charge; write to Super Market Institute, 500 N. Dearborn St., Chicago, Ill. 60610
Taverns.	√	√	
Toy stores	√		"Toy Dealer Operating Profits"; no charge; write to Playthings, 71 W. 23rd St., New York, N.Y. 10010
Variety stores	√	√	
Women's accessory & specialty stores.	√	√	

Expense ratios per se do not indicate that a retailer may be failing to obtain an adequate return for some of the money he pays out. Even when the retailer's ratios compare favorably with the standard expense ratios, individual items may in reality be too high if he gets less for his outlay of money. For example, one retailer may deliver fewer packages than another who spends the same amount for this service. The remedy may be found in cost analysis based on the cost of doing a given piece of work, such as either cost per package, in the case of deliveries, or average cost per sale. This type of cost accounting requires that overhead costs be charged to lines of goods or to departments. How much of the rent bill for the store should be charged off to delivery expense, for example, might be figured out by estimating the percentage of total floor space occupied by the quarters devoted to preparing packages for delivery and loading them on trucks.

The ratio of net profit to sales should be interpreted in the light of sales volume and capital invested. A low ratio on the large volume may mean a good profit. Likewise, the same ratio is more satisfactory when volume is the same but investment less.

Even though the standard ratios are based on the figures of a group of similar stores, the ratios for a particular store may vary considerably from the standard ratios because of differences in operating conditions. Some of the reasons for variations from one store to another in particular ratios are discussed below:

Gross-margin ratio. A high gross-margin ratio may indicate either purchases at low prices, or sales at high prices, or both. A low gross-margin ratio, on the other hand, may indicate either inadequate markups, or high merchandise costs as a result of poor buying judgment and heavy inventory writedowns. Or, it may be the result of a deliberate merchandising policy (or campaign) of selling at low prices in order to obtain a large sales volume. To be profitable, such a policy must result in large sales volume and be accompanied by low operating costs.

Total operating-expense ratio. A higher-than-average total operating-expense ratio does not necessarily reflect any unfavorable conditions in the store. If it is accompanied by a high gross-margin ratio, and a satisfactory net profit ratio, it may reflect the character and policy of the store. For example, a better-than-average type of merchandise, or sales based on additional service to customers, may yield extra gross margin to cover the extra expense involved, and to provide a satisfactory net profit.

Nevertheless, a store with a total expense ratio much higher than that for similar stores is quite likely to be unprofitable. The typical unprofitable store has a high total expense ratio for its kind of business. This may be owing to small sales volume as compared with the profitable store, and not necessarily because it pays higher wage rates or higher rent rates. More frequently, however, a higher-than-average total operating expense ratio in an unprofitable store indicates low efficiency; that is, poor management in controlling expenses.

Net profit (or loss) ratio. The profit or loss ratio reflects the net results of the operation of the store. This ratio indicates the effectiveness of the management of the store and measures the efficiency of its operation. The net profit or loss ratio is influenced by many factors. A profitable store is usually the result of efficient management which, on the one hand, succeeds in maintaining a satisfactory dollar gross margin — from purchases at low cost and from sales at prices that are neither too high nor too low — and, on the other hand, succeeds in keeping all expenses under control.

Proprietor's wage ratio. Since many retailers do not make a distinction between money withdrawn for their wages and that which is a withdrawal of profits, a proprietor's wage ratio which varies from the average may have no significance. A higher-than-average ratio may indicate either that the store earns large profits, or that excessive wages are being paid to the owner. It is important that excessive portions of capital not be withdrawn, for this is limiting future growth.

A low owner's wage ratio, accompanied by small withdrawals of profits and a satisfactory net profit ratio, indicates that the retailer is building up his capital by leaving his profits in the business. On the other hand, a low wage ratio, accompanied by a low net profit ratio, indicates that the owner is getting a small total return from the operation of his store.

Employees' wage ratio. A relatively high employees' wage ratio is ordinarily an unfavorable sign. A high wage ratio may be the result of inefficient use of help, a poor store arrangement, the employment of too many clerks for the sales volume being obtained, or it may be the result of other factors. Like a high gross-margin ratio, however, a high wage ratio may be the result of a carefully thought-out management policy. It may indicate the retailer's policy of obtaining sales by providing more or better clerk service instead of spending more on rent, fixtures, or advertising. The degree of success of this policy can be determined by studying the sales volume, the gross-margin ratio, the rent and other expense ratios, and the net profit or loss ratio.

A low employee's wage ratio is usually evidence of efficient management, especially if it is accompanied by a low total operating-expense ratio and a satisfactory net-profit ratio. It may mean, however, that the store is not employing enough workers or not employing the right kind of clerks. An unsatisfactory sales volume may indicate that the latter is the case.

Rent (or occupancy) expense ratio. A high rent ratio may be the result of the store being larger than necessary to handle the present sales volume. On the other hand, a high rent ratio may mean that a favorable location has been obtained which makes it possible to obtain sales without high expenditures for advertising which might otherwise be necessary.

A low rent (or occupancy) expense ratio may mean that the retailer has been able to secure the store building at a low rental or purchase price. Or it may mean that the building is too small for the volume of business. A mutual comparison can be made with a rent-to-gross-margin ratio.

Advertising-expense ratio. An advertising-expense ratio that is in line with a standard ratio may not necessarily be favorable. The advertising may have been successful in increasing dollar sales volume, so that the added dollar advertising expense represents no greater percentage of sales than normal. But, if the added sales volume consists mainly of staples or low-margin goods, the advertising may not be profitable. To be profitable, advertising must result in added dollar gross margin more than sufficient to cover the added dollar advertising and other expenses. That is, the advertising should sell goods carrying high gross-margin rates as well as staples.

On the other hand, a low advertising-expense ratio, which is accompanied by small sales and net profits, may possibly mean that one of the causes of the unfavorable results is insufficient advertising.

Delivery-expense ratio. Unless the proportions of delivered sales to total sales are known, no worthwhile comparisons of delivery-expense ratios can be made. A store with two-thirds of its sales delivered will almost necessarily have a higher delivery-expense ratio than a store with only one-third delivered sales, and any difference between the ratios of two such stores will be of no significance. Only when a store has approximately the same proportion of delivered sales as that of the group with which it is being compared can significant comparisons be made. A high ratio will then indicate inefficiency in the delivery operation, and a low ratio the opposite.

Bad-debt-loss ratio. One of the factors to be considered in analyzing the bad-debt-loss ratio is the proportion of credit sales to total sales. Just as in the case of the delivery-expense ratio, a more worthwhile comparison can be made if the proportion of a store's credit sales is approximately the same as that of the group of stores with which it is being compared.

A low bad-debt ratio is usually evidence of a credit and collection policy that has been carefully planned and strictly enforced. Or it may be an indication that too much caution is being used in the development of credit sales. A high ratio usually indicates laxness in extending credit and in making collections.

Other expense ratios. Higher-than-standard ratios for any of the other expense items on the profit and loss statement usually indicate an opportunity for expense reduction. Heat, light, power and water, store supplies, and miscellaneous expenses, may be higher than average because of a deliberate merchandising policy of rendering extensive service, but more often they are high because of a lack of expense control. Depreciation of store equipment, being a noncash expense, may be high because of the methods of computing depreciation. A cash-shortage ratio that is too high is almost always the result of improper methods of safeguarding cash. Taxes and licenses may not be subject to the control of the retailer, but a high miscellaneous-expense ratio probably arises from carelessness in expense control.

Inventory turnover rate. A high inventory turnover rate is commonly considered to be favorable, but its importance may be exaggerated. In fact, a turnover rate that is too high may be just as unfavorable as one that is too low. A high rate sometimes means that the retailer has concentrated his attention on carrying small stocks of "fast movers." This practice may result in the loss of potential sales because of the increased risk of being "out of stock" and because of the lack of a sufficient variety of goods to satisfy customers. Also, the practice of buying fast-moving merchandise in small quantities may merely deprive the retailer of the wholesaler's lowest prices for quantity purchases, and increase the time he spends in ordering and receiving goods.

On the other hand, an inventory that turns over too slowly is probably loaded with slow items, that may not only tie up needed working capital, but also may lead to loss of sales because of the lack of fresh stocks of merchandise.[1,2]

EXPENSE CONTROL IN WHOLESALING

In wholesaling, materials handling is a major target for expense reduction. Clerical expense can also easily get out of line, since almost every transaction involves some paperwork. Other common areas of expense reduction are: simplification of stock; reduction in selling costs through closer cooperation with retailers; manufacturers' cooperation in packaging small units to eliminate the wholesaler's "broken package" room expenses; and selective distribution.

But cutting the cost of his service, the wholesaler can help his independent retailer customer meet the growing competition of chains, mail-order houses, manufacturer-controlled retail outlets, "supers," and new kinds of low-cost retailers in a market where price competition will be an important factor. Many wholesalers

[1,2] From the report of the Senate Special Committee to Study Problems of Small Business, 79th Congress, 1st sess., prepared by Charles H. Welch and Charles H. Sevin (Washington, D.C.: G.P.O., 1945).

are setting goals for expenses that will enable them to sell to independent retailers at prices low enough to permit the retailer to meet mail-order competition or at chain store prices adjusted for the difference in customer services. The more important wholesaler's expenses can be reduced only if retailers cooperate. This is especially true with reference to selling expense. Also, unless wholesalers can aid many of their retail customers in reducing expenses, the retail margin will offset most of the lower prices made possible by expense reduction.

Wholesalers share the advantages of manufacturers and process-type service businesses in being able to control expenses largely on an impersonal basis — as opposed to retailers, whose expenses arise mostly out of personal contact with customers. Wholesalers can profitably adapt many of the cost-reduction techniques developed in manufacturing.

In particular, the wholesaler should make distribution-cost studies on a unit basis. For example, experience shows that many retailers buy in such small quantities from any one wholesaler, and often demand so much service, that their accounts are found to be handled at a loss when all valid expenses are charged to the servicing of their accounts. If it takes a $20-a-day salesman one-half day twice a month to call on such an account and the wholesaler receives as a result monthly business amounting to only $150, it would be difficult in most cases to pay even the salesman's salary from the margin available. If in addition credit and other services are extended to the customer, an account of this type would clearly be unprofitable.

When a wholesaler has determined the minimum he can handle at a profit, expense control can be used more effectively in dealing with small-order buyers. Efforts are usually made to bring every order accepted up to the minimum, allowing for a few exceptions in the case of normally good customers whose annual volume would justify an occasional small order. Repeated small orders below the minimum may be refused. Usually the salesman can show the small buyer how he can plan his purchases to meet this standard. A few new customers who show promise of expanding may be carried at a loss temporarily. In general, however, it is better to refuse orders below the minimum and to reduce the expense of trying to serve "hopeless" customers.

EXPENSE CONTROL IN THE SMALL FACTORY

Although some of the best opportunities for small business in the field of manufacturing are in totally new or noncompetitive lines, expense control is nonetheless important in such cases for several reasons. No matter how new, different, or "noncompetitive" the product being made seems to be, it must compete on a price-usefulness basis with all other objects of consumer expenditures. Interindustry competition exists regardless of the size of business units involved. In pioneering the manufacture of a new product, the ultimate criterion of the commercial value of the item is the cost at which it can be made and sold. And finally, a new article that clicks with the market will soon be copied by competitors, making price competition based on production and selling cost inevitable.

During the first few years, while a new product is being perfected in design, expenses may be considered second to quality only if they are (1) in line with the owner's ability to pay, and (2) capable of future reduction to meet the inevitable competition that will quickly develop once the product gains market acceptance.

Fortunately for the small manufacturer, highly developed techniques for expense control have been perfected in this field. Cost accounting, methods studies, and almost every other tool of modern management were inaugurated in the field of production and later adapted to other fields.

Though industrywide operating ratios are available in a number of manufacturing industries, their usefulness as cost standards for the individual firm is somewhat limited because of the diversity of product mix, technology, and other factors from firm to firm, even among those of the same size. Consequently, most small firms will find it more feasible to develop their own standard costs.

One of the factory operating costs for which standards should be set is plant maintenance. Maintenance should be systematized, planned, scheduled, and controlled as carefully as production. The same principles of careful assignment of duties and responsibilities, good supervision, and budgetary control of expenses may be used to advantage. Providing maintenance workers with efficient tools and equipment is also good economy. Machine repairs should be so scheduled that it does not interfere with productive operations.

Many other expenses are significant to the small producer, such as packing and shipping costs and selling expense, and standards should be determined for these also. In general, there are six different types of expense which the average small manufacturer will find it profitable to control: (1) direct production costs, (2) indirect costs, (3) material and supply costs, (4) transportation costs, (5) costs of methods used for market promotion, and (6) miscellaneous costs.

Direct production costs are those which can be allocated to particular orders, products, or departments, such as direct labor and direct material costs. The control of material costs was discussed in Chapter 21, and is discussed in additional detail below. The control of labor costs involves the determination of a fair day's output for men and machines or the man-hour and machine-hour amounts required to produce each article. These become output standards with which actual production is compared to secure control. Before adopting such a standard, the operator of even a small factory should study ways of improving productivity. Perhaps subdividing the work and letting each worker become more skilled in performing a smaller number of tasks would increase total productivity. Or perhaps a better method of performing the work can be developed. A new layout might also increase manufacturing efficiency, as noted in Chapter 10.

Indirect costs include such overhead expenses as management and supervisory salaries, utility bills, rent, and similar costs. Though some of these costs are fixed and remain the same at all levels of production (such as rent), many others (such as maintenance, supervisory, and clerical costs) are semivariable and may be partially controlled. In small factories the number of employees engaged in paperwork, maintenance, and other activities involving indirect expense may be small relative to the number of direct production workers, and it is easy to be careless about efforts to control such costs. Managers of larger plants, however, are giving increasing attention to indirect costs, and have developed effective methods of reducing and controlling them. These guides should help the small plant operator do a better job of controlling indirect costs in his factory.

Control over material and supply costs involves much more than shrewd buying. It starts in the factory with a careful study of production needs and processes. One small manufacturer found that a slight change in design enabled him to use an unfinished molded metal part at less than half the price formerly paid for a similar part with finished surfaces. In another case, investigation and the advice of a local technician showed one plant operator how he could use a slightly more expensive lubricant for his machines and actually reduce total supply expenses 20 percent, because the new lubricant was especially made for the type of work involved. Since new materials and supplies constantly appear on the market, many designed for special purposes and others less expensive than ones traditionally used for the same purpose, the small operator always has opportunities for expense reduction in this area. However, few small operators are so well informed that they know the properties of the materials and supplies already on the market.

There are several ways in which transportation costs in the small manufacturing enterprise can be controlled. Careful study of alternate shipping routes, comparative freight rates, demurrage costs, damage claims, packing procedures and materials, and small-order shipments will usually disclose many opportunities for cost reduction. Careful stock control, for example, can avoid emergency ordering and expensive special freight costs. In some cases an alternate method of transportation, such as trucks instead of railroads or leased instead of company-owned trucks, may result in reduced costs.

Market promotion also offers many opportunities for expense control. At the start personal solicitation of orders may be necessary. Later the expense of personal selling may be lessened by using brokers or selling agents who operate on a very small margin, by selling through established middlemen like wholesalers or supply houses, or by using some of the many forms of advertising. Solicitation of *repeat* orders can often be done by mail or telephone.

This discussion of expenses in manufacturing concludes with the advice to use the regular methods of expense control previously discussed, such as ratio analysis, budgeting, and methods studies. In manufacturing, the opportunities for expense control are relatively greater than in other fields, because the producer is dealing mainly with materials and processes. He should learn all he can from the extensive writings on industrial management and adapt to his business every idea and technique possible.

SERVICE ESTABLISHMENT EXPENSES

Many service industries have standard accounting systems and expense classifications. For instance, in the laundry business the American Institute of Laundering has developed three systems for plants of each size group. For smaller plants the simplified system is used in which there are eight expense accounts: (1) productive labor; (2) productive supplies; (3) power plant costs; (4) building overhead; (5) laundry machinery overhead; (6) indirect overhead; (7) collection, delivery, and sales promotion costs; and (8) office and administrative costs. For expense control purposes, however, each of these is further subdivided. For example, among the categories under "labor" are "productive labor (laundering)" and "productive labor (dry cleaning)," and among those under "building overhead" are "rent of laundry building" and "repairs and maintenance." For each size group, operating ratios that may be used for comparison by individual plant operators are compiled each year.

Sources of information on standard accounting systems and operating ratios in other types of service industries are given in Table 23-1. Depending upon the nature of the service – whether of the merchandising or processing type, for example – service establishment expenses will be similar to those found in retailing or manufacturing.

DEMAND FORECASTING

An essential element in profit planning and cost control is the sales forecast. The demand forecast is particularly important in the budgeting of operating expenses, labor and material needs, and other costs which vary with volume.

There are many ways in which the small businessman can improve the accuracy of demand forecasting. By subscribing to the trade journals in his field and possibly in certain cases to those in his customers' fields, he can keep better informed of future conditions likely to affect the demand for his product. There are numerous forecasting services available, one or more of which should be helpful. It is possible to cooperate with business neighbors in subscribing to some of these services and thus reduce their cost to each. Attending meetings of trade associations, at which trends in the industry are frequently discussed by representatives of large companies that spend a great deal of money on their forecasting research, should pay the little fellow. Monthly reports of the Federal Reserve Banks for each district report major trends that can be used to forecast demand. Many state universities publish a monthly bulletin analyzing economic and business conditions within the state, often undertaking to forecast demand and supply conditions likely to have a bearing on the sales plans of local businessmen. The charge for these bulletins, when there is any, is seldom much more then the cost of printing and mailing. Every small operator should write to the college of business or bureau of business research of his state university to have his name placed on the mailing list for monthly bulletins and other useful publications. In many industrial fields, the U.S. Department of Commerce publishes monthly analyses and forecasts of conditions. This material, too, is either free or so inexpensive that no small businessman can afford to neglect using it.

SUMMARY AND CONCLUSIONS

Practically every other chapter in this book deals with the subject matter of this chapter – profit planning and cost control – in one way or another. In a sense this is the "keystone" chapter. Just as the keystone of an arch is put into place last and is said to lock or key the whole together, this chapter provides the material upon which all other chapters of the book depend. Without the knowledge of how to forecast and control profits, the small businessman can not be successful.

Profit is the motivating force in business. Though two firms may have the same production and sales income volume, one of the firms may be more or less profitable than the other because of (1) difference in cost "structure" (that is, the proportion of fixed and variable costs), and (2) differences in operating "efficiency." A firm's profit may be increased through more effective *profit planning* and/or more effective *cost control*. In either case, accurate and up-to-date financial statements and other accounting records are necessary.

In this chapter, two methods of determining profit goals or evaluating the profit potential of a small business were examined – break-even analysis, and marginal-income analysis. Cost control techniques which were discussed included budgeting and ratio analysis. These methods are not difficult to apply in a small business. The small-firm operator who learns them and applies them in the conduct of his business will be well repaid for his efforts by the greater profits that will ultimately result.

REVIEW QUESTIONS

1.　What is "profit"? What is profit "control"?

2.　Which costs vary directly with volume? Which costs do not vary with volume?

3.　How was the break-even chart in Figure 23-1 constructed? How would you use such a chart?

4.　What dangers exist in a heavy investment in fixed assets?

5.　What are "incremental" costs? What are some of the practical applications of incremental-cost analysis in small business?

6.　Why is it necessary that the small businessman understand accounting methods and procedures?

7.　What are financial ratios, and what purposes do they serve? What are the three types of financial ratios? Cite and discuss several examples of each type.

8.　What is a budget? How do budgets aid the small businessman in controlling the operation of his firm?

9.　Is it important to include both imputed and actual expenses to secure effective expense control? Discuss.

10.　Why should methods study be a part of expense control?

11.　What are the two major types of expense classification used in retailing? Give some examples of each.

12.　What are the three largest expenses in nearly every retail store? How can they be most effectively "controlled"?

13.　Outline some of the ways in which a wholesaler can reduce his operating costs. Do the same for a small manufacturer.

DISCUSSION QUESTIONS

1.　Considering the cost and income data assumed for the Acorn Company, as given in the text, what would be the effect on profit of a decrease in cost resulting from a methods-improvement program if *all* such savings were passed on to customers via lower price? Clearly state all assumptions.

2. What percentage increase in prices would be required to cover the cost of a 10 percent wage increase and still maintain the Acorn Company's current rate of profit?

3. Compare the operating ratios for the following retail fields and explain any similarities and differences: grocery, hardware, drug, jewelry, wearing apparel.

4. How would the topics discussed in this chapter be of use in appraising a business for possible purchase? In justifying a new business?

5. As the new owner of a store that has been declining in sales and profits for several years, Joe finds that the ratios for advertising are 20 percent and those for bad-debt losses 5 percent below the standard ratios for the field. What should he do, and why?

SUPPLEMENTARY READINGS

Bell, Robert W. *Business Budgeting for Small Department Stores.* Small Business Management Research Report prepared for the Small Business Administration. Fayetteville: University of Arkansas, 1963. Practical but simplified methods for budgeting by small department stores which provide a system for organizing and coordinating all store activities. Discusses three areas of budgeting: the merchandise plan; the expense budget; and the financial budget.

Cost Control in Business. Business Series no. 3. New York: Business Education Division, Dun & Bradstreet, 1967. Deals with cost control techniques of increasing profit. Stresses the importance of careful record keeping, budgeting, and cost analysis.

Sanzo, Richard. *Ratio Analysis for Small Business.* 3rd ed. Small Business Management Series no. 20. Washington, D.C.: Small Business Administration, 1970. Indicates how certain common business statistics can be compared so as to provide a basis for management control.

Zwick, Jack. *A Handbook of Small Business Finance.* 7th ed. Small Business Management Series no. 15. Washington, D.C.: Small Business Administration, 1965. Points out the major areas of financial management and describes various analytical techniques that can help the small businessman to understand the results of his past decisions and apply this understanding in making decisions for the future.

24

Regulations
and taxes

The business community, as with any other group that must work in harmony for the common good, has need for rules and regulations concerning the conduct of its members. Two classifications of such controls exist. One type consists of those developed and adopted voluntarily by the business people as codes of ethics or standards of conduct for and among themselves. The others are established and enforced by a legislative or other public authority and administered by properly authorized bureaus, commissions, and courts. These more generally concern business contacts with the public.

It is probably the latter that we usually think of first when speaking of laws affecting business. While codes of ethics and standards of practice as established in certain trades or industries have long been regarded as powerful forces within those groups, the increasing complexity of business operations combined with increasing tendencies toward protection of the individual citizen by governmental agencies has caused public laws to be of more interest and concern to businessmen.

Laws have various objectives as well as origins. Some are designed to prevent undesirable acts by prohibiting certain kinds of conduct. Others, such as tax laws, require particular acts and are mandatory for all concerned. A third group, permissive laws, permits individuals to enjoy certain privileges provided they meet stated requirements, such as permits to do business in particular fields or to engage in certain professional occupations.

The origin of laws — that is, the source of their authority — is significant because of our multipower type of legal authority. Ours is essentially a constitutional type of government. The federal government has been delegated in the Constitution the right to regulate commerce between the states (interstate commerce) and with foreign nations. Powers not delegated to the federal government are reserved to the states. Each state in its constitution is delegated, or presumes the right to exercise, certain powers that are generally of statewide interest, such as the regulation of intrastate commerce. Authority over purely local matters is usually left to the local governing agency, which may be the county, township, parish, city, or town.

Even though he may be engaged entirely in activities within the state, or solely within the city limits, the small businessman is interested in certain federal laws and taxes, as well as those of his own state and local governments, because they may affect his business and personal conduct.

484

There are many aspects of law that should be understood by the independent businessman, only a few of which can be given even brief mention here. Criminal law deals with acts (crimes) considered injurious to society for which a penalty such as imprisonment or a fine is imposed and for the enforcement of which society, through its duly authorized courts and law-enforcement officers, is responsible. Civil law, in contrast, is concerned with protecting the individual, especially his rights of private property, and allowing compensation for personal injury through lawsuit.

Almost all important modern laws are statutes — that is, acts passed by a federal or state lawmaking body — or constitutional provisions embodied in the original federal or state constitution and its amendments. Court decisions interpreting the various statutes and constitutional provisions provide guides to the meaning and application of every law. Trends in these interpretations tend to represent trends in public opinion with respect to the purpose or even the need for the law.

In recent years many important statutes have been enacted that incorporate a special board, commission, or other agency charged with the administration of the law. Examples of these administrative laws are the Clayton Act, which is administered by the Federal Trade Commission; the National Labor Relations Act, administered by the National Labor Relations Board; the Small Business Administration Act; and many state laws dealing with industrial relations, public health, and safety.

Finally, the common law, or old English guides and principles leading to justice and fair treatment, may govern in situations not covered by specific legal enactments.

As in other fields that have developed a similarly extensive body of knowledge, the independent businessman cannot hope to be an expert in law, nor can he afford to call on expert counsel for every decision. But he should endeavor to recognize those situations that call for legal counsel and be ready to secure and pay for such advice, for the investment will usually be more than repaid.

Furthermore, regulations and taxes have become so numerous and complicated that many people are of the opinion that they constitute one of the greatest hazards to the independent enterpriser. In contrast to most other areas of business, regulations and taxes are usually mandatory and carry severe penalties for even unintentional violations. Ignorance of the law is not accepted as an excuse, and even licensed attorneys are not always sure of certain provisions and their interpretations by the courts.

Certain general principles of law, important legal instruments, and particular laws that have special significance for the small businessman must be considered. An understanding of these principles, instruments, and laws should help the businessman to carry on his activities without either breaking the law or sacrificing the rights and benefits to which he is legally entitled. It should also help him to recognize when legal counsel is needed.

PRINCIPLES OF BUSINESS LAW: TYPES OF LEGAL TRANSACTIONS

The general principles of business law can best be presented, perhaps, by discussing the types of legal transactions in which the small businessman is likely to be involved. Such transactions are regulated by the Uniform Commercial Code

(UCC), adopted in all states but Louisiana (which still adheres to the Napoleonic code) and in the District of Columbia and the Virgin Islands. Most important are the laws relating to contracts, agency, sales, and negotiable instruments.

Contracts

Almost every business act is based on agreements or promises, most of which are contracts. Mutual confidence among the various parties involved in business activities is so basic to modern society that it is difficult to conceive of the continued existence of civilization in the absence of contractual relations. A contract is an agreement between two or more competent parties to do, or not to do, some lawful act for a stated consideration. Although a contract is an agreement, or meeting of minds, not all agreements are contracts. The essentials of a valid contract are:

1. *agreement* — an offer that must be accepted as offered;
2. *true consent* — not under duress;
3. *competent parties*;
4. *some lawful objective*; and
5. *consideration* — the value of which is not material.

It is important that if the person being offered the contract in any way manifests his acceptance, he may be legally required to accept the contract; it is the law that decides whether the contract exists, not the subjective intent. The offer may be made either orally or in writing. And there is of course an entire branch of law built around whether the contract is offered and accepted. The small businessman should consult his attorney in all matters dealing with contracts.

All persons are considered competent to enter into contracts except infants, insane persons, drunkards, corporations, and agents, fiduciaries, and other legal representatives. The specific laws relating to incompetency to enter contracts vary among the states, and one should carefully check the applicable local statutes.

Contracts must also have lawful objectives. Here it is important that they not be criminal, tortious (performing some private wrong), or opposed to public policy. Examples of such laws are usurious contracts, gambling and wagering contracts, and agreements that are injurious to the peace, health, good order, and morals of the people. Later discussion will detail how legislation tending to prevent restraint of trade, price fixing, and unfair business practices has made many previously valid contracts illegal.

The term *consideration*, in the law of contracts, does not mean that there must be an exchange of something having monetary value. Rather it indicates the doing of something or promising to do something that one is not otherwise legally obliged to do in return for the promise of another. Promises based upon a past consideration have only moral enforceability, and the promisor must be under legal contract to make his word legally binding. It is essential to have all important contracts in writing, and according to the law in many states certain contracts *must* be in writing. This is especially true of contracts not to be performed within one year and of those involving the sale of real estate. A written contract is usually desirable, even if not required by state law, whenever common sense indicates a possibility that certain provisions, or even the contract itself, may later be questioned or forgotten.

Agency

Agency implies a business relationship between two parties that involves a third party. An agent may be appointed to assume entire charge of his principal's business or to transact only certain types of business. It is best when dealing with an agent to insist upon proof of an agent's authority, or to have some evidence from the principal as to the delegated authority. The agent must "exercise good faith and the requisite degree of prudence, skill, and diligence," and is not allowed to act for himself or for another person with a conflicting interest. Persons usually deal with the agent as though they were dealing with the company or person (principal) he represents. Since agents are usually appointed by definite agreements or contracts, the law of contracts applies to agency.

The small businessman has many dealings with agents and may have occasion to appoint his own agents or to serve as agent for some principal. The purchase of insurance, many real estate transactions (whether for lease or purchase), and the procurement of equipment, materials, or merchandise often involves dealing through agents. A small manufacturer may prefer to sell through agents rather than through his own sales force. Even small-scale retailers may secure special or exclusive agency rights for certain prestige merchandise. A very important consideration whenever agency is involved is to ascertain and clearly define the authority delegated to the agent by his principal and the agent's duties or responsibilities.

Sales

The businessman is concerned with the sale of either real property or personal property. Property in this sense is the right that a person owns in something, whether land, material, or merchandise. Ownership may be transferred by gift or inheritance as well as by purchase and sale. Among the important provisions of the Uniform Commercial Code is the clear distinction between a sale and a contract to sell. Other points of law relating to sales covered in the code are the time title passes, identification of the goods, and the right or power of the seller to transfer title. Certain sales must be evidenced by a written bill of sale. If the goods are not delivered immediately, evidence of sale in writing is required when the amount involved is above some stated minimum.

There are so many variations of sales and payment plans that complete coverage would be impractical here. However, one question that arises frequently enough to deserve comment is the protection of the seller in case full payment is not made at or before time of delivery of the goods. For example, a retailer may buy merchandise on credit, sell the entire lot for cash to one or a few customers, and fail to pay the wholesaler or other suppliers. To protect the latter the Uniform Commercial Code requires advance notice (usually delivered in person or by registered mail) to each creditor before sale of the stock of goods; if advance notice is not given, the creditors can bring action against the goods even though they have passed into the hands of a third party. And even if notice has been given, the sale may nevertheless be voided if the intent of the transfer is to hinder, delay, or defraud creditors.

Businessmen contemplating doing any installment selling should ascertain the laws of their own state and of any states in which they have debtors with regard to permissible interest rates. Most states have statutes specifying the maximum rate of interest that can be exacted. All states have a legal rate of interest, to be used when an agreement says there is to be payment of interest but does not specify the rate. Penalties for charging illegal interest are very heavy, and it is important to know just what can be charged and under what sorts of agreements. The businessman must also make certain that he complies with the disclosure requirements of the Truth-in-Lending Law, discussed in Chapter 20.

A point that frequently causes confusion relates to the obligation of a business to sell goods or services to any person who may offer the full purchase price. A few broad classes of business enterprises, such as public utilities, common carriers, and hotels, are required to serve all persons alike who meet publicly announced requirements and are not obnoxious or otherwise objectionable to other patrons. The merchant is not in this class. He can refuse to sell to any person regardless of the latter's readiness to pay the full purchase price in cash. Manufacturers and other sellers not in the "public service" groups may also refuse to sell to any prospective purchaser at their discretion. Title II of the Civil Rights Act of 1964 prohibits discrimination or segregation in any "place of public accommodation" on the ground of race, color, religion, or national origin. Business establishments which are explicitly covered by this provision of the act are hotels and motels, eating establishments, gasoline stations, and places of entertainment.

Negotiable Instruments

Business transactions have been carried on to an increasing extent by means of negotiable instruments instead of money. Both serve as media of exchange; both facilitate trade and pass freely from person to person in business transactions. Money, or legal tender, is universally acceptable and is required by law to be accepted in this country as adequate settlement of financial claim. Although the same legal compulsion does not exist for negotiable instruments, custom, convenience, and confidence have all contributed to their widespread use. The common check or bank draft is a good illustration.

According to the Uniform Commercial Code, any instrument must satisfy the following requirements if it is to be negotiable:

1. It must be in writing and signed by the maker or drawer.
2. It must contain an unconditional promise or order to pay a sum certain in money.
3. It must be payable on demand or at a fixed rate or determinable future time.
4. It must be payable "to order" or "to bearer."

5. Where the instrument is addressed to a drawee, he must be named or otherwise indicated therein with reasonable certainty.

Negotiable instruments may be divided into two classes: (1) promissory notes; or (2) bills of exchange.

A *promissory note* is simply a written promise by one person to pay a sum of money to another person. It may or may not be secured by some form of collateral. A note secured by a mortgage on real or personal property is called a *mortgage note*. If given in exchange for merchandise, it is called a *conditional-sale note*; such a note stipulates that title to the merchandise remains with the seller until the note is paid. When the person who signs a note agrees that he will permit judgment to be taken against him without a trial if he fails to pay the note, it is called a *judgment note*. A *certificate of deposit* is a promissory note given by a bank, and a *bond* is simply a long-term promissory note. Other varieties could be cited, but these are the most common.

In contrast with a promissory note, a *bill of exchange* is an order by one person on a second person to pay a sum of money to a third person. If the order is drawn on a bank and if it is payable on demand, it is a *check*: If it is drawn by a bank on itself it is called a *cashier's check*, and if it is drawn by one bank on another bank it is known as a *bank draft*. A *traveler's check* is a special kind of cashier's check.

A check (such as those mentioned above) is a bill of exchange unconditionally payable on demand. The bank will ordinarily make payment unless (1) the person who made out the check lacks sufficient funds and has not made prior arrangements for an overdraft; (2) the drawer has stopped payment on the check; or (3) the bank has reason to believe the person presenting the check has no legal right to do so.

Another kind of bill of exchange that is of some importance to the small businessman is the *trade acceptance*. It differs from a check in two ways: (1) it is usually payable at some specified future date, and (2) payment on the note is conditional upon its "acceptance" by the person on whom it is drawn. It is sent by a seller to a purchaser with the understanding that if the latter approves the goods purchased, he will accept the draft. It is often used in selling goods on credit. The seller draws a draft on the buyer, often a retailer, for the exact amount of the invoice. This must be accepted before the goods are delivered to the buyer. Thus a promise to pay is created. The seller or drawer of the draft can often discount this trade acceptance at his bank and thus receive payment before the due date of the invoice while at the same time granting credit to his customers. Although drafts are sometimes accepted by a bank, by arrangement and for a fee, bankers' acceptances are far less common in domestic commerce than is the trade acceptance (such as the bank arranging to pay for the purchases in the above example).

Checks, trade acceptances, and other bills of exchange, as well as promissory notes, should be presented for payment when due or as soon as possible. Even though they may be legally valid claims for a reasonable time after maturity, practical considerations of security and custom dictate prompt presentation for payment. Special cases deserve special consideration and usually require competent legal counsel.

REGULATIONS PERTAINING TO COMPETITION,
TRADE PRACTICES, AND PUBLIC WELFARE

Laws concerning competition, trade practices, and public welfare are mostly restrictive or permissive. In general the aim is to encourage competition and stimulate progress by restricting anticompetitive and antisocial acts.

Competition

In most areas of business that are not natural monopolies, competition is considered to be desirable. However, unregulated business has repeatedly shown tendencies to seek monopoly powers in varying degrees. Our antitrust laws, both federal and state, have been enacted to protect business itself against those tendencies. The Sherman Anti-Trust Act of 1890 was passed by Congress after the states had tried unsuccessfully to check the growing monopolies of that time. Although not completely successful, it did make possible the dissolution of many monopolistic trusts in sugar, whisky, oil, and other industries.

A new approach was taken with the passage of the Clayton Act and the Federal Trade Commission Act in 1914. Emphasis was now placed on preventing the growth of monopolies by "cleaning up competition," or restricting practices that would lead to monopoly, such as price fixing and exclusive dealing and tie-in contracts.[1] In 1938 the Wheeler-Lea Act extended the coverage of the Clayton Act, especially with reference to misrepresentations in advertising. Administrative powers are vested in the Federal Trade Commission (FTC), which is charged with keeping competition both free and fair. Over the years the commission has built up a long list of unfair trade practices. Among these are the following: price cutting for the purpose of eliminating competition, misbranding, secret rebates, spying on competitors, boycotts, disparagement of competitor's goods, use of misleading names, false and misleading advertising, forced-line selling, bait advertising, bribing patronage, pirating employees, selling used items as new, merchandising by lot or chance, and offering "fake" buying advantages.

There are two FTC programs which are of particular interest to the small businessman. One is the Division of Trade Practice Conferences, which reduces to writing (after due notice and public hearing) rules which interpret the laws enforced by the commission as they apply to particular industries. The second is the Division of Discriminatory Practices, which investigates complaints of unfair practice and also will consult with small business owners regarding applicability to their own problems of laws administered by the FTC.

Although both the Sherman and Clayton Acts are federal laws and therefore apply only to interstate commerce, most states have enacted similar legislation to regulate intrastate commerce. In addition, the decisions of the FTC regarding unfair methods of competition have set the pattern both for state courts and for practices approved by the various trade associations. Final authority for approving trade practices, however, rests with the commission. Many of the trade prohibitions are prescribed only after extensive hearings and conferences between the commission

---

[1] A tie-in contract is one in which a buyer is obligated to buy products or services he does not want in order to obtain those he does want. An exclusive-dealing contract is one in which a seller obligates a buyer to refrain from the purchase of competitors' products.

and trade representatives. Although benefits to the small businessman resulting from the work of the FTC would be difficult to assess directly, there is no doubt that they have been substantial.

Price Regulation

In a truly competitive market, price acts as the regulator adjusting supply to demand. Attempts to manipulate prices in various ways have existed since the beginning of our price economy. In this country, there are four broad areas of regulation: price fixing, price discrimination, price cutting, and resale-price maintenance.

Price fixing. Price fixing, under court interpretations of the federal antitrust laws, includes agreements among competitors engaged in interstate commerce to stabilize prices or to hold competitive prices in a fixed relationship to each other. The term is not limited to the fixing of uniform prices. Also illegal are many "indirect" methods of price fixing, such as agreements to maintain uniform discounts, markup or methods of calculating markup, delivery charges, and many similar practices among competitors.

However, many states do not have antitrust laws, and in such states, so long as a small business is not engaged in interstate commerce, price fixing is not only legal but widely practiced. The setting of uniform prices or rates is particularly common among local service-trade establishments, such as barber and beauty shops, dry cleaning establishments, and automobile repair shops.

Price discrimination. In 1936 the Robinson-Patman amendment to the Clayton Act declared personal price discrimination to be illegal. Differences in the price of goods of like grade and quality to different buyers in competition are declared to be illegal unless justified by differences in costs of manufacture, selling, or handling. However, a seller is permitted to discriminate in price between buyers in order to meet the lower prices of competitors in regional markets.

The authors of the Robinson-Patman Act recognized that there are many ways in which a seller can discriminate in price other than varying the invoice price, and these also were declared to be illegal.

Specifically mentioned in the act are the following: (1) allowances for advertising and sales promotion that are in excess of a fair payment for services actually rendered by the buyer and that are not made on proportionately equal terms to all competing customers; and (2) brokerage fees collected from the seller when the "broker" was also acting with the buyer as principal.

The burden of proof that price (and service) differentials are economically justified rests with the seller, and the buyer who knowingly accepts such illegal price discrimination is made equally liable with the seller. The reason for making the buyer liable to prosecution for accepting a discriminatory price is the fact that many buyers for large chain stores and mail-order houses had formerly bargained for low prices that sometimes exceeded the economies resulting from their large orders.

Price cutting. Excessive price cutting when used solely for the purpose of eliminating competition has quite generally been considered to be an unfair method of competition used especially by large concerns to drive small competitors out of business. If permitted, it is normally followed by a high "monopoly price" once effective competition is driven from the market. The temporary benefits to consumers resulting from lower prices are lost during the subsequent period of high prices.

Most states have passed laws to prohibit below-cost selling that restrains the trade of competitors. These so-called anti-loss leader laws define cost as invoice cost plus a "fair share" of the expenses of doing business. Especially in merchandising, where a large variety of articles are handled, this is so indefinite and it is so impractical to determine the cost of individual items that these laws have been ineffective. A partial solution has been to interpret "cost of doing business" arbitrarily as some fixed markup over invoice cost – say, 6 percent.

Since anti-loss leader laws have proven to be unenforceable in practice, the necessary policing is usually done by each trade group rather than by state law-enforcement officers. However, the trade groups themselves have been lax in enforcement, and "loss leader" merchandising is common.

Resale-price maintenance.   Beginning with California in 1931, 45 states enacted "fair-trade" statutes that legalized resale-price maintenance contracts for trademarked articles or merchandise identifiable as to producer. These laws permitted vertical contracts between manufacturer and wholesaler or retailer stipulating either the price at which the identifiable article was to be sold or the minimum price below which it could not be sold. Contracts to set the resale price at the same level of distribution, between different manufacturers and different wholesalers or different retailers, were left unenforceable. A provision that a single contract between a manufacturer or his duly authorized wholesale agent and one retailer in a state became binding on all other dealers in the state (known as the nonsigner provision), was used up to 1951. By 1937 the majority of the states had passed resale-price maintenance laws, and the federal government made the practice generally legal in interstate commerce by passing the Miller-Tydings Act.

In the late 1940s, opposition began to mount against fair trade regulations. The courts were less friendly toward such legislation, and in May 1951 in the Schwegmann decision the United States Supreme Court decided that the nonsigner provision was not intended in the Miller-Tydings Act, thus releasing most retailers from the need to observe fair-trade prices. Pressure was immediately put on Congress, with the result that the Supreme Court decision was nullified by passage of the McGuire Act as an amendment to the Federal Trade Commission Act, making it an unfair practice for any retailer to cut an established resale price even though he was not a party to the fair-trade agreement. The commission was empowered and directed to enforce the act, an ironic situation in view of the commission's other duties and its opposition to fair trade laws.

Then, in state after state, courts began to rule against fair-trade laws, and when the large companies (such as General Electric and Sunbeam) which had attempted to enforce them stopped their efforts, fair trade was dead in 17 of the original states. The consumers had all along been opposed to "fair trade" and were willing to overlook its provisions. Also, retailers had refused to abide by its provisions, claiming the laws restricted their freedom to operate and resulted in artificially high prices. Finally, the manufacturers themselves became convinced that high fair-trade prices actually worked against their best interests because they often restricted volume production. The development of the discount house became possible with this new attitude toward "fair trade."

Retailing history in the United States has demonstrated that innovations will appear and expand in "soft spots" — where current retailing and marketing practices fail to meet widespread demands. Legislative efforts to block such American ingenuity have consistently failed since late in the last century; and current attempts to use fair-trade regulations as a crutch for incompetent management appear to bear out this long-time trend. Among the popular devices in recent use to bypass fair-trade regulations are: inflated trade-ins, non-fair-traded articles given free with each purchase at fair-trade prices, sales tickets made out at fair-trade prices accompanied by an unrecorded cash refund, and so on. No company or governmental agency can possibly detect and control all of these evasions; and even if they had virtually unlimited financial resources, the time factor alone would make enforcement impossible to achieve.

Our discussion in this section has been a deliberate attempt to warn the conscientious independent enterpriser against the long-run hazards of seeking security in legal devices in lieu of competent management. Efforts by businessmen to guarantee their profits by various laws and legal props have not been successful for any length of time. Especially in our dynamic, free-enterprise economy, efforts of this sort appear to be less desirable than rendering a genuine public service through efficient management conducted in the interest of consumers. The pros and cons of fair-trade regulation as a device for protecting small independents from large price-cutters are given in the footnote references[2] and in various bibliographies listed elsewhere. From a practical standpoint, however, the danger is real that in the long run any legal restrictive measures that place the interests of special groups above the public interest may react unfavorably to the very groups seeking protection.

Merchandise Regulation

So far as the product itself is concerned, the most important regulations are those relating to health, safety, labeling, trade names, patents and trademarks, and the interstate shipment of flammable or otherwise dangerous products.

Food, drugs, and cosmetics. Laws designed to protect the health of the consumer have been enacted by federal, state, and local governments. The Pure Food and Drug Act was passed by Congress in 1906, making it illegal to ship injurious, falsely labeled, or adulterated foods or drugs in interstate commerce. This law was revised in 1938 by the Food, Drug, and Cosmetic Act to include cosmetics (except soap) and certain curative devices or appliances. It also provided for testing before certain drugs that might cause sickness or death are put on the market. More complete disclosure of habit-forming ingredients as well as others that might be injurious to certain types of individuals is required. Like its predecessor, the 1938 law deals mostly with adulteration and misbranding, and with information that must be given

[2] See Stewart Munroe Lee, "Problems of Resale Price Maintenance," *Journal of Marketing* 23 (January 1959): 274–81; and Edward S. Herman, "Fair Trade: Origins, Purposes, and Competitive Effect," *George Washington Law Review* 27 (June 1959): 621–52.

on the label. The small businessman manufacturing or handling foods, drugs, therapeutic devices, or cosmetics should study and observe in detail the provisions of this law, even though he may not be engaged in interstate commerce. A 1953 amendment authorizes inspectors to enter any establishment where food, drugs, or cosmetic items are held and to inspect the establishment and materials and equipment therein.

A recent addition to the food and drug regulations concerns food additives. Under this legislation, manufacturers must certify to the Food and Drug Administration that the additives are harmless in the intended use. This is done by submitting certain required data, considerably detailed, in an application to the Department of Health, Education, and Welfare; the applicant is then advised by that body as to what he can use, in what amounts, labeling requirements, and so forth. There is also agitation for similar legislation for food coloratives and lipstick color components.

All states and most cities have legislation and regulations dealing with the processing and handling of food for the public. Many have laws governing drugs and similar merchandise. Pharmacy is recognized in every state as a profession which should be practiced only by qualified pharmacists, but the detailed regulations are not uniform in all states. Either the manufacture or the sale of certain other products – such as eyeglasses and similar optical goods, mattresses, and bedding – is frequently regulated by state law or local ordinances.

Product Safety.   The Food and Drug Administration also has the power, under the Child Protection and Toy Safety Act of 1969, to ban potentially harmful toys. A provision of this act requires retailers to refund the purchase price of a condemned toy. The store owner, in turn, can seek reimbursement from the manufacturer.

Since the publication of Ralph Nader's *Unsafe at Any Speed*, federal government attention has also been focused on automobile safety, and in recent years time limits have been imposed for the incorporation in new-car design of a variety of safety features prescribed by the National Highway Traffic Safety Administration.

Wool and fur products labeling.   According to the Federal Wool Product Labeling Act, all articles made of wool, except floor coverings, must be labeled as to the percentage of virgin wool and of reprocessed and reused wool content. If any fiber other than wool is present in excess of 5 percent, its percentage must also be given on the label. It is illegal for the retailer or other businessman dealing in such products to remove or deface the label containing this information.

In a similar manner, the Federal Fur Products Labeling Act outlaws the deceptive labeling of fur. Fur products must be guaranteed to consist of the type of fur indicated on the label. A retailer may replace a label provided he complies with all labeling requirements and maintains a complete record of the substitution for at least three years.

Both the wool and fur labeling acts are administered by the Federal Trade Commission. In connection with the fur act, the commission has issued a register of animal names, known as the *Fur Products Name Guide*, for use in properly describing furs and fur products.

Interstate shipment of flammable fabrics.   The Federal Trade Commission also administers the Flammable Fabrics Act. This statute prohibits the interstate marketing of wearing apparel or fabrics which are "so highly flammable as to be dangerous when worn." The act requires that five specimens of the fabric be tested in their original state, and in addition, in the absence of proof that a fire-retarding finish has been added, five specimens must be tested after dry cleaning or washing.

Company and brand names.   The company or firm name identifies the particular enterprise and may consist of all or part of the names of the owners or an assumed name. Sometimes a proprietor uses his first or last name only, or both, and partnerships frequently use the last names of each partner, as the Smith-Jones Company. A sole proprietor can ordinarily use his full name for his business without restrictions unless another firm in the same market and kind of business has this name well established and confusion would result if a newcomer were to use the same name. If an assumed or coined name is used, and usually when only the first or last name of a proprietor or partner is used, it is necessary to file with the county clerk the company name and full name of each owner. This is primarily to protect others who may deal with the concern and to have on record essential information as to who actually owns the business. For a corporation the name under which it will operate as well as the names of the incorporators are part of the application for a charter.

A brand name is used to identify a product or the line of products sponsored by one firm. It is a form of trademark. Often it is simply the company name; for example, Maytag washing machines or G.E. toasters. It may also be a name coined or appropriated for product-identification use by one firm; for example, a Dodge Dart or Ajax cleaning products. Though brand names are most often used by manufacturers, they are also frequently used by distributors; for example, Sears-Roebuck Coldspot refrigerators or A&P's Sultana canned goods.

Trademarks and patents.   A brand name, as noted above, is only one type of trademark. Sometimes a product, or the company itself, is more readily recognized by means of a symbol or emblem, rather than a name. Some of the more familiar trademarks of this type are Sinclair's dinosaur, MGM's lion, and Prudential's Rock of Gibraltar. Other symbols or emblems used as trademarks consist of unique arrangements of lines and/or colors, such as Chrysler's five-pointed star and Ford's blue oval. Package design may also be trademarked. Even the way the company name is written is a form of trademark. A point of major importance for the small businessman is to avoid any attempt to copy or imitate a company name or trademark already in use that might expose him to charges of unfair competition.

A trademark must have been used in interstate commerce before an application for registration can be filed with the Patent Office. Since July 1947, provisions of the federal Lanham Act replace those of the Trade-Mark Act of 1905. Under the Lanham Act, registration of trademarks on the Principal Register is essential to secure future protection. Also, a trademark need no longer be physically affixed to the merchandise; protection is thus given to well-advertised trademarks for such products as brands of gasoline and to "service marks" of service establishments. In addition to federal registration, many states have passed laws concerning the protection of trademarks used in intrastate commerce. A small firm would be well advised to employ a competent attorney in all trademark matters.

Securing a patent is also a highly complex proceeding and should be handled by an attorney trained in this specialized field. A patent gives an inventor the right to exclude all others from making, using, or selling his invention for a period of 17 years, and is granted only after there has been a determination of utility and a search to determine its novelty. No patent is granted upon a mere suggestion or idea; the invention must be described and illustrated in detail. The patent law affords no protection prior to the actual issue of a patent, although it is common practice to serve notice of application by stating that a patent has been applied for.

Consumer Credit

Significant consumer credit legislation has been passed in recent years. To protect consumers against the use of erroneous information in the files of credit bureaus, as well as the misuse of credit bureau reports, Congress in 1971 enacted the Fair Credit Reporting Act. Also passed by Congress, in 1969, was the Truth-in-Lending law to protect consumers against the uninformed use of credit. In addition, many states have established maximum rates which can be charged for the financing of consumer credit. These regulations, enforced by the Federal Trade Commission, are discussed in detail in Chapter 20.

Advertising

Federal regulation of advertising is administered by the Federal Trade Commission as part of its responsibility for the maintenance of fair competition. In general, false and misleading advertising is condemned. This includes the use of deceptive and misleading names and expressions like "Cylk" or "artificial silk." Many names formerly used to describe lower-quality furs in such a way as to suggest the expensive article have also been banned. The Wheeler-Lea amendment to the Federal Trade Commission Act gives the commission power to regulate advertising to meet the labeling requirements of the Food, Drug, and Cosmetic Act. It also gives the commission authority for the first time to prohibit advertising that is injurious to the *public* even though it may not directly affect competition, such as the ban on cigarette commercials on radio and television. The FTC also enforces the Truth-in-Lending regulations relating to the advertising of credit terms (discussed in Chapter 19). Many states also have laws regulating false and misleading advertising.

In 1953, the commission reversed its earlier position toward use of the word "free" in advertising and accepted its usage where the "conditions, obligations or other prerequisites to the receipt and retention of the 'free' articles" are clearly explained.

Labor Legislation

Federal and state labor legislation may be divided into five broad groups: (1) settlement of labor disputes; (2) fair employment practices; (3) regulations of wages, hours, and working conditions; (4) protective legislation for women and children; and (5) economic security legislation.

Settlement of labor disputes.   The National Labor Relations Act (Wagner Act) of 1935 was the first important law concerned with labor disputes and is administered by the National Labor Relations Board. It provides that employees shall have "the right to self-organization, to form, join, or assist labor organizations, to bargain collectively through representatives of their own choosing, and to engage in concerted activities, for the purpose of collective bargaining or other mutual aid or protection." According to the act, certain practices on the part of an employer are considered to be unfair, including the following: (1) interfering with, restraining, or coercing of employees in the exercise of their guaranteed rights: (2) dominating or interfering with the formation or administration of any labor organization; (3) encouraging or discouraging membership in any labor organization by discrimination in regard to hiring, tenure, or conditions of employment; (4) discharging or otherwise discriminating against an employee for filing charges or giving testimony under the act; and (5) refusing to bargain collectively with representatives of employees.

The Wagner Act was, unmistakably, one-sided legislation; it assumed that only the employer could "sin." By 1947 many unions had become such towers of strength that they often abused their powers from the public viewpoint. As a result the Taft-Hartley Act was passed whereby unions (as well as employers) could be held responsible for unfair labor practices; in particular, it outlawed the "closed shop," secondary boycotts, jurisdictional disputes, and "featherbedding."

However, due to Supreme Court interpretation and the complexity of the issues, a number of the congressional goals were not fully realized. Organized labor continued to grow in strength, and in 1959 the Landrum-Griffin Act was passed to protect the rights of individual members from the autocratic use of union power. In addition, the unfair labor practice provisions in the Taft-Hartley Act were strengthened.

Labor experts expect differences of opinion to arise between representatives of labor and management when negotiating a new contract. As a consequence, they are required to bargain in good faith in an attempt to reach an understanding. Furthermore, disputes will arise over the interpretation of an existing contract, and most agreements, to meet this contingency, provide for a grievance procedure culminating in arbitration.

One of the most important decisions in the field of labor law in the past 25 years concerns the question of agreements to arbitrate. Prior to 1957, state contract law controlled collective bargaining agreements, and neither an agreement to arbitrate nor an arbitrator's award were enforceable in court. In *Textile Workers Union* v. *Lincoln Mills*,[3] the Supreme Court decided that agreements to arbitrate could be enforced under the Taft-Hartley Act and that federal law, rather than state law, could control. And in subsequent decisions, the Supreme Court decided that courts could not, generally speaking, tamper with the decision of an arbitrator.[4] These decisions are extremely important because of the emphasis placed on arbitration rather than court maneuvering in labor disputes.

---

[3] 353 U.S. 448 (1957).

[4] See Irving Kovarsky, "The Enforcement of Agreements to Arbitrate," *Vanderbilt Law Review* 14 (Summer 1961): 1105–14.

Fair employment practices.   The most recent development in labor legislation has been the attack against racial discrimination practiced by employers and unions. Most states (none in the South) have enacted fair employment practice (FEP) laws, and Congress in 1964 passed the Civil Rights Act. In general, the state laws provide that complaints of discrimination be brought before an administrative agency which could, after investigation, attempt conciliation. If conciliation should fail, the administrative agency or commission would make a subsequent formal decision which could be enforced in a state court. Until the point of failure at the conciliation level all information is confidential; if a formal decision is made, it becomes a matter of public record.

The federal law differs in one important respect from the state laws. The federal commission can only conciliate the differences between the complainant and the employer (or union); that is, its members cannot make a binding decision. However, if the employer (or union) refuses to comply with the judgment of the commission, the commission can bring a suit in a federal district court, as though a decision had not been made before (per a 1972 amendment to the Act).[5]

The federal law pertains to firms and unions functioning in interstate commerce, but states with FEP legislation are entitled to priority of jurisdiction for 60 days. Other salient features of the federal law are:

1. Segregated locals and the complete exclusion of blacks from unions is forbidden. This changes the Taft-Hartley Act.
2. Professionally developed tests used for hiring and promotion are permitted. This provision has received much adverse comment because tests tend to discriminate against those people with a poor economic and educational background. Based on the 1971 Supreme Court decision in *Griggs* v. *Duke Power Co.*, an employer violates the federal law if the test used is not geared to the job description and if its reliability and validity is not checked.
3. A full-time agency, the Equal Employment Opportunity Commission (EEOC), was established to consider complaints[6] and conduct technical studies. Most of the state commissions are staffed by part-time members.
4. Unions and employers must provide apprentice-training opportunities for blacks. Rapid technological change tends to wipe out the unskilled and semiskilled jobs in which most blacks are employed.[7] The federal law is intended to help blacks move into the skilled job categories. The controversial Philadelphia Plan, for example, where the construction industry was required to give priority to black applicants for employment, has upgraded the black construction worker in that area.

Regulation of wages, hours, and working conditions.   The Fair Labor Standards Act of 1938 provides for minimum hourly wages for the employees of most firms engaged in interstate commerce. The minimum hourly wage for all employees covered by this act, as amended in 1966, is $1.60. The act also requires employers to compensate employees at "time-and-a-half" for hours worked in excess of 40 per

[5] See Irving Kovarsky, "The Harlequinesque Motorola Decision and Its Implications," *Boston College Industrial and Commercial Review* 7 (Spring 1966): 535–47.

[6] As noted above, however, decisions of the EOCC are not binding.

[7] See Irving Kovarsky, "Apprentice Training Programs and Racial Discrimination," *Iowa Law Review* 50 (Spring 1965): 755–76.

week. It is noted that the law does *not* specify maximum working hours; the intent is merely to keep working hours from rising much above the 40-per-week "norm" by making the overtime hours relatively expensive to the employer.

It is also important for the small businessman to note that under certain terms of an agreement with their employees' representatives they may be exempted from the overtime provision of the act. For example, the parties may agree that up to a limit of 1,040 working hours in a 26-week period there will be no overtime penalty; this is an important provision of the law for those firms in highly seasonal industries. The law also waives the overtime provision for employers who sign labor agreements in which they guarantee the number of working hours per year (within a range of 1,840 to 2,240 hours).

Not all firms engaged in interstate commerce, nor all employees of such firms, are covered by the federal Fair Labor Standards Act. Those not covered include the employees of retail stores and service establishments with an annual gross volume of sales or receipts less than $250,000; outside salesmen; and executive, administrative, and professional personnel. It is estimated that in 1972, these persons numbered more than 7 million.

However, small businessmen who accept government supply contracts must comply with provisions of the 1936 Walsh-Healy Act. Unlike the Fair Labor Standards Act, in which the minimum wage is fixed by the terms of the law for all covered establishments and employees, the Walsh-Healy Act requires that firms with government supply contracts in excess of $10,000 must pay "prevailing wage rates"; thus the minimum wage varies from industry to industry and from locality to locality. The Walsh-Healy Act further provides for payment of time-and-a-half for hours worked in excess of 8 per day or 40 per week, whichever yields the higher compensation.

Those small businesses which are not covered by the federal Fair Labor Standards Act will most likely be subject to the same minimum-wage requirements in their respective states. As of 1972, 41 states plus Puerto Rico and the District of Columbia had minimum-wage laws, and these come very close to meeting federal minimum-wage standards. Unlike the federal government, however, only 24 states attempt to regulate the number of working hours by imposing overtime wage premiums. Most state laws limit the number of working hours for women and children and for male workers in hazardous occupations. A recent development is the enactment of time-off-for-voting laws; as of 1972 there were 30 states with such laws, in addition to Puerto Rico. All but two of these statutes provide for *paid* time, particularly in cases where there is insufficient time for employees to vote before or after work.

The various states have also attempted to regulate working conditions. Most of the state regulations deal with industrial health and safety. No comparable legislation exists at the federal level.

Protective legislation for women and children.   The federal Fair Labor Standards Act limits the employment of children in the following ways:

1. Children between sixteen and eighteen years of age may not be employed in occupations defined as "hazardous" by the Department of Labor.

2. A child under sixteen years of age is not permitted to work *unless* (a) he is employed by a parent or guardian in an industry other than mining and manufacturing or one defined (above) as being "hazardous"; and (b) he is at least fourteen years of age and has a temporary permit to work issued by the Department of Labor.

These limitations, of course, apply only to those firms engaged in interstate commerce. However, *all* of the states also have enacted child labor laws which, with only slight variations, impose the same limitations on firms engaged in intrastate commerce.

Protective legislation for women employees is of three types: (1) laws requiring special working conditions; (2) "equal pay for equal work" laws; and (3) "equal opportunity" laws. Laws of the first type have been enacted at the state level only. In general they require the provision of special facilities and the regulation of night work and industrial "home work."

By 1972, "equal pay" laws had been enacted in 43 states and the District of Columbia. (State employees only, however, are covered by the Delaware law). In 1963 Congress followed the lead of the state lawmaking bodies by passing the Equal Pay Act (an amendment to the Fair Labor Standards Act), which requires employers "to pay equal wages within an establishment to men and women doing equal work on jobs requiring equal skill, effort, and responsibility which are performed under similar working conditions." Wage differentials between classified male-female jobs are permissible only if there are demonstrable differences in job content.

Also, under the federal Civil Rights Act of 1964 and comparable state enactments, merit increases and promotions cannot be denied on the basis of sex alone.

Economic-security legislation. "Economic-security" legislation is designed to minimize losses in employee income resulting from industrial accidents, occupational diseases, and involuntary unemployment, and to provide workers with hospital and medical care and at least a minimal income after retirement.

Protection of workers from income loss resulting from industrial accidents and occupational diseases is afforded by the various state workmen's compensation laws. Since 1948 there has been no state which has not passed such legislation. Legislation at the federal level covers civil service employees only. Since the provisions of the laws vary from state to state, the small businessman should consult local sources for information and, in any event, seek the advice of competent counsel.

Unemployment benefits are provided by legislation at both the state and federal levels. Under the federal Social Security Act of 1935 and the Employment Security Amendments of 1970, all states have been encouraged to enact unemployment compensation laws. The act provides that if a state law is enacted which meets certain requirements, the state can retain approximately 85 percent of the tax levied on employers. As of 1972 the permissible upper limit of the tax had been set at 3.2 percent of each employee's annual wages up to $4,200 (of which 2.7 percent is the state's share). Prior to 1972 this tax was levied only on firms employing four or more persons, which effectively excluded many small businesses. The new amendments to the federal law now require that this tax be paid by any firm who employs one or more persons in each of 20 days in a year, each day being in a different week, or who has a payroll of at least $1,500 in a calendar quarter.

Most states, however, have a merit-rating or experience-rating system which provides that employers who have maintained a low labor turnover rate may pay a progressively lower tax. Also, the Social Security Act permits a state to use a tax base which is higher than $4,200 per year, and some states have taken advantage of this provision of the law.

Although very few states have old-age pension plans, public pensions for most workers who have reached retirement age are provided by legislation at the federal level only. Another provision of the Social Security Act is for retirement, survivors', and disability insurance (RSDI). Up to 1955, only those in dependent employment were covered by this provision of the act; since then, self-employed farmers, businessmen, and professional persons have also been covered.

RSDI is financed by a tax, in equal amounts on both the employer and employee, on the first $9,000 earned by the employee in a calendar year; the tax on this amount for the self-employed is approximately one-and-one-half times the tax he would pay as either an employer or a dependent employee.

Both the tax rates and tax base have increased as Congress has increased RSDI benefits and as a larger proportion of the population has become eligible for these benefits. Prior to 1972, the tax base was $7,800; since then it has been $9,000. Legislation in force for 1973–1975 set the tax on both the employer and the employee at 5 percent, and 7 percent on those who are self-employed; beginning in 1976, the employer-employee tax rate is increased to 5.15 percent, the tax on the self-employed remaining at 7 percent.

In addition to the payment of taxes for retirement, survivors', and disability insurance benefits, the Social Security Act (as amended in 1970) establishes a *separate* payroll calculation (on income up to $9,000) to finance the federal government's program of hospital and medical insurance for people sixty-five years of age and older. Contributions to this "Medicare" program go into a separate trust fund in the Treasury Department. The contribution rate schedule, which applies to employers, employees, and the self-employed alike, is as follows:

Calendar Year	Tax Rate (%)
1973–1975	.65
1976–1979	.7
1980–1986	.8
1987 and after	.9

To the small businessman we offer this counsel concerning his obligations under the federal Social Security program:

Whether or not you hire anyone, and even if you are an employee yourself, you *must* pay a Social Security tax and make an annual report. You file and pay your self-employment tax with your federal income tax, using schedule C in form 1040. This must be done even if you have no income tax liability. If you are both employee and employer, consider your wages first; if you were paid at least $9,000 in a covered occupation from which Social Security taxes were deducted, then you have earned your maximum credit in any one year and you do not report and pay on your self-employment income. If you received $7,000 in wages and earned $1,000 in self-employment, you must pay tax and report on the $1,000 of self-employment income. (Self-employed persons with net earnings of less than $400 during the taxable year need not report this income.)

You must also have a Social Security account number. If you had previously received one as a dependent employee, use the same number in making your report as a self-employed person; if it has been lost, apply for a duplicate of the old number. (This is not to be confused with your identification number as an employer.[8] In a nutshell, you have two roles to play: as an employer who is taxed for his employees' welfare; and as a self-employed person who is taxed for his own welfare.)

For Social Security purposes payroll records must show the following: the employee's name; his occupation, address, and Social Security number;[9] the amount of each payment to him (including any amount withheld); the date of each payment; the period of employment covered by each payment; and the amount of Social Security tax deducted from the wages paid. If the employee's tax is deducted at any time other than when the wages are paid, the date of deduction must be recorded. If all or any part of the wage payment is not taxable, the reason must be included in your records.[10]

If your type of business involves tips, such as in a restaurant, employees receiving cash tips of $20 or more in a month must report these tips to you before the tenth day of the following month. You then deduct (withhold) the employee's Social Security and income tax on this amount from the wages due him. However, you are required to match only the Social Security taxes deducted from the employee's *wages*; you need not match the employee's tax liability on the amount earned in tips.

From each payment of wages the employees' share is deducted up to a total of $9,000 in any one year. Four times a year these deductions are reported and payment is made for them together with the employer's matching share to the district director of the Internal Revenue Service. Each employee must be given a receipt for his payment. It is also necessary for the nonfarm self-employed to estimate their personal Social Security contributions (in their capacity as individual taxpayers and beneficiaries) and pay the estimated taxes in advance in quarterly installments.

Restrictions and Permits

Some state laws restrict business activity (1) by permitting only licensed practitioners to engage in particular occupations, such as pharmacy, barber shop or beauty parlor operation, and public accounting, and (2) by requiring the

---

[8] Every employer of one or more persons in covered employment must have an identification number. Application for such a number is made by filing form SS-4 with the nearest office of the Social Security Administration. The assigned identification number must appear on all Social Security records, correspondence, and tax returns.

[9] A new employee who has not been previously assigned a Social Security number should be asked to apply for one, using form SS-5.

[10] Some income may be subject to income taxes but not to Social Security taxes, and vice versa.

maintenance of prescribed standards in equipment and processes for protection of the health and safety of employees and the public. However, in general, most regulation of this sort is local, defined by city ordinance and enforced under the community's police powers.

A license is a permit granted by the governmental power to a person or company to pursue some business, subject to regulation under the police power. Licensing is used both to regulate business and as a source of revenue for the government granting the license. For example, plumbers, electricians, pawnbrokers, and auctioneers, as well as dance halls, taxi companies, hotels, amusement places, and food service and drinking places, are usually licensed and frequently inspected or supervised to see that regulations for protection of the public health, safety, and morals are observed. Other businesses, such as retail stores, may not be required to have a license but are subject to regulations necessary to reduce fire hazards. On both state and local levels, license requirements and regulatory taxes have been expanding.

In many cities licensing is used to enforce zoning restrictions. Licenses will be granted to operate a given type of business only in areas where zoning regulations permit this type of business. For example, a retail store will not be licensed to operate in a district zoned exclusively for residences. Similarly, a dry cleaning *store* may get a license to operate in a retail shopping district but the dry cleaning *plant* using certain dangerous fluids will be licensed to operate only in the industrial district.

Licensing is also used to restrict competition, as when itinerant vendors selling from temporary quarters, on the sidewalk, or from house to house are required to pay a relatively heavy license fee. Some regulation of this class of merchant is considered desirable to protect the public from "con artists" and fly-by-night peddlers. It is often difficult to draw the line between licensing for necessary customer protection and that designed to lessen competition for the local merchants. For example, "Green River ordinances" that prohibit all house-to-house solicitation except by personal invitation of the householder obviously not only protect local merchants from competition with outside sellers, but also relieve families from any annoying interruptions and from some swindling schemes. Another viewpoint, however, is that such ordinances place serious limitations on aggressive selling, especially the launching of new products and other innovations, which often can be done most effectively through such personal contact.

Many other regulations and restrictions are enforced locally, such as those pertaining to use of the business premises, alleys, adjoining sidewalks, parking spaces, store signs, wiring, plumbing, heating, delivery equipment, and similar matters. In addition, the small businessman will usually find among the established businessmen certain social controls relating to store hours, acceptable types of advertising, "going" rates of pay, pricing, and expected community services. Although these lack the compulsion of actual laws, they are nonetheless effective.

Bankruptcy and Court-approved Debt Settlements

As noted in Chapter 2, many new business ventures end in failure, particularly during the first few years of operation. So also do many business firms — successful or not — have customers who are unable to pay their debts. In either case, the small business owner should be familiar with the options available to him under federal and state bankruptcy laws.

A bankrupt is a person (including a fictitious "person," or corporation) who has been declared by a court of law as being unable to pay his debts. Bankruptcy proceedings may be initiated by the debtor himself (*voluntary* bankruptcy), or by one or more creditors (*involuntary* bankruptcy). In either case there is a "hearing" on the petition, and if the judge (or court-appointed *referee*) declares the debtor bankrupt, his property is placed in the hands of a *receiver* for liquidation. The proceeds from the sale of the property are then used to pay, first, secured claims (such as a mortgage), and then wage claims. Remaining proceeds (after the payment of taxes) are then divided among the unsecured creditors on a pro rata basis according to the amounts of their claims. For example, if a bankrupt owed $50,000 and the sale of his property netted $25,000 after all costs and prior claims were paid, each creditor would receive one-half the amount owed him, or "50 cents on the dollar." The bankrupt is *discharged* from further liability for existing debts.

There is, of course, a stigma attached to being declared a bankrupt — whether the debtor is a dependently employed consumer or a small businessman — and bankruptcy proceedings should be initiated only as a last resort. Thus section XI of the federal Bankruptcy Act provides for "compositions" and "extensions" wherein the debtor is called a *debtor* and not a bankrupt. An *extension* is a court-approved plan, proposed by the debtor, wherein the debtor is allowed to delay payment of his debts for a stipulated period of time, thus providing him with an opportunity to meet his financial obligations in full out of future earnings. If full cash settlement out of future earnings appears unlikely, or if this imposes an unreasonable burden on the debtor, then a *composition* may be approved by the court, wherein the creditors accept the debtor's plan for a pro rata cash settlement as payment in full.

Either an extension or a composition under section XI of the Bankruptcy Act must be initiated by the debtor. If the plan is accepted by at least half of the creditors to whom at least half of the debts are owed, the plan becomes binding on all the creditors. In this way, a businessman avoids the stigma of a legal bankrupt and his business (which might otherwise become prosperous) is not forced into liquidation. However, the court usually appoints a receiver to manage the business until such time as the extension or composition settlement is consummated.

TAXES

In addition to the Social Security taxes, previously discussed, the prospective small businessman will be confronted with a multitude of other taxes. At the federal level, the one which looms most important for any type of business is the income tax. Certain types of business will encounter special taxes, including manufacturers' and retailers' excise taxes, admissions taxes, and taxes on specific products such as tobacco and liquor. Also, a corporation often pays taxes in addition to those of a proprietorship or partnership, such as an accumulated earnings tax.

Some of the taxes that may be expected in most states are income taxes, sales taxes, and workmen's compensation and unemployment taxes. A corporation will usually have to pay a capital stock tax, as well as a "foreign" tax if it operates in states other than the one in which it is incorporated. At the county or city level, most businesses will also be required to pay real and personal property taxes. Before going into business one should check with the managers of a few stores and service establishments in the community in which he expects to locate, and find out what state and local taxes he may expect to encounter and what the filing requirements are.

A few of the more important tax provisions at the federal and state levels (other than Social Security taxes) are discussed below.

Federal Income Taxes

Federal income tax rates and provisions change almost every year. It would seem to be of little value, therefore, for us to consider the procedure by which the small businessman computes his taxable income. Rather, our purpose in this section is to discuss the basic provisions relating to the filing of income tax returns, and such related matters as the withholding of employees' taxes and the filing of information returns.

The kind of income tax return the firm must file with the Internal Revenue Service depends on the firm's legal form of organization. If a person is in business for himself as a sole proprietorship, and has an annual gross income from this source amounting to $400 or more, he files an "Individual Income Tax Return" (form 1040), reporting his business income and expenses on schedule C of that form.

If the firm is a partnership it files form 1065. (Only the signature of one of the partners is required.) The "Partnership Income Tax Return" is filed for information purposes only, since the partnership is not taxable as an entity. Its purpose is merely to report the business income that should be included on the partners' individual tax returns.

Individual proprietors and partners are required to put their federal income tax and self-employment tax liability on a "pay-as-you-go" basis. They do this by filing a "Declaration of Estimated Tax" (form 1040 ES) on April 15 each year, based on expected income and exemptions. Payments on the estimate are made over a period of nine months, the first payment being due on April 15. Additional payments become due on June 15, September 15, and January 15. At the time of each payment, adjustments to the estimate can be made.

A corporation, unlike a partnership, is a legal entity endowed with the rights and responsibilities of a person, and hence pays a tax just like any other "person." Its income is reported on form 1120 ("Corporation Income Tax Return"). The corporate entity pays a normal tax (currently 22 percent) on all taxable income, and a surtax (currently 26 percent) on the taxable income over $25,000.

As noted in Chapter 11, certain corporations can elect to be taxed as though they were partnerships (thereby avoiding the double tax on dividends). Their manner of reporting income is similar to that of partnerships, previously discussed, and the "Small Business Corporation Income Tax Return" (form 1120-S) is also for information purposes only, reporting the corporate income that must be included on the stockholders' individual tax returns.

Income tax returns may be prepared on a calendar- or fiscal-year basis. If the tax liability of the business is calculated on a calendar-year basis, the tax return must be filed with the Internal Revenue Service no later than April 15 each year. Most businesses, however, find it more convenient to report their income on a fiscal-year cycle; in this case, the tax return of the firm (or its proprietor or partners) is due on the fifteenth day of the fourth month following the end of the taxable year.

Withholding of tax.   In addition to his responsibilities as a taxpayer, the small businessman must also serve as a tax collector. The amount of the "pay-as-you-go tax" he is required to withhold from the wages of each of his employees is determined in the following manner:

First, he ascertains the amount of "taxable wages" earned by the employee during the payroll period. This is done by subtracting from the gross wage the value of the withholding exemptions claimed by the employee. The "value" of one withholding exemption is $14.40 per week. Thus an employee who earns $200 a week, and who has claimed five withholding exemptions, has taxable wages of $128, calculated as follows: $200 − ($14.40 × 5) = $128.

The employer's next step in the procedure is to apply the appropriate tax percentage to the amount of the employee's taxable wages. This percentage is on a sliding basis, varying with both the amount of the taxable wage and marriage status of the employee. Reproduced below is the IRS's percentage table for a weekly payroll period, based on tax rates for 1972. (Similar tables have been prepared for biweekly, monthly, semimonthly, annual, and other payroll periods.)

WEEKLY Payroll Period

(a) SINGLE person —

If the amount of wages is:		The amount of income tax to be withheld shall be:	
Not over $11		0	
Over—	But not over—		of excess over—
$11	−$35	14%	−$11
$35	−$73	$3.36 plus 18%	−$35
$73	−$202	$10.20 plus 21%	−$73
$202	−$231	$37.29 plus 23%	−$202
$231	−$269	$43.96 plus 27%	−$231
$269	−$333	$54.22 plus 31%	−$269
$333	. . . .	$74.06 plus 35%	−$333

(b) MARRIED person—

If the amount of wages is:		The amount of income tax to be withheld shall be:	
Not over $11		0	
Over—	But not over—		of excess over—
$11	−$39	14%	−$11
$39	−$167	$3.92 plus 16%	−$39
$167	−$207	$24.40 plus 20%	−$167
$207	−$324	$32.40 plus 24%	−$207
$324	−$409	$60.48 plus 28%	−$324
$409	−$486	$84.28 plus 32%	−$409
$486	. . . .	$108.92 plus 36%	−$486

Thus for a married employee with a weekly taxable wage of $128, the employer would withhold a tax of $18.16, calculated as follows: $3.92 + .16($128 − $39) = $18.16.

Detailed computations such as these for each employee following every payroll period are tedious and time-consuming. For convenience of the employers, the IRS provides wage-bracket withholding tables which give approximately the same results.

The employer is not permitted to grant withholding exemptions unless the employee has listed the number of his exemptions on form W-4. These exemption certificates are valid until amended by the employee; however, before December 1 of each year the employer is required to *ask* his employees to file new certificates if there have been changes in the number of dependents they had previously claimed.

The total amount of income taxes withheld are reported on form 941 each calendar quarter. This report also shows the amount of Social Security taxes withheld (as previously discussed).

When the fourth quarterly report is filed (at the end of the calendar year), the employer must also file the district director's copy of each employee's withholding statement (form W-2), showing the total amount of tax withheld during the year. Two copies of form W-2 must also be given to each employee on or before January 31 of each year. In addition, the employer is required to file a statement reconciling the amounts withheld as shown on the quarterly statements with the amounts shown on the annual statements. This reconciliation statement is known as form W 3.

Remitting withheld taxes. Taxes collected for the government (withheld from employees) must be deposited periodically with the district Federal Reserve Bank or with a commercial bank that is authorized to accept tax deposits. How often this must be done depends on the individual businessman's tax liability. If he withheld less than $200 in taxes during any month of a calendar quarter, as reported on form 941, the amount collected during that month is not due until the last day of the month following the close of the quarter. If the amount of tax withheld during any month is $200 or more (up to $2,000), the businessman must deposit this sum within 15 days after the close of such month except for the last month of a quarter. If the businessman withheld a total of more than $2,500 in taxes for any month of a calendar quarter, he must make semimonthly deposits − within three banking days after the seventh, fifteenth, twenty-second, and last day of each month of the quarter.

Information returns. By an "information" return is meant the reporting of income payments which are taxable to others. IRS's purpose here, obviously, is to "match" reported income payments with the reports of income received on individual income tax returns.

There are two types of information returns. One is the reporting of payments made in the course of trade or business totaling $400 or more during the calendar year, such as wages, royalties, rent, interest, and fees for attorneys, public accountants, business consultants, and other "outside staff" personnel. This report is made on form 1099. The other type of information return is the reporting of dividend payments to stockholders, or interest payments (or credits) by savings and insurance institutions to depositors or policyholders, totaling $10 or more during the calendar year. This report is also made on form 1099. Copies of these reports must be sent to the persons whose incomes are reported.

The Self-Employed Individuals Tax Retirement Act. It was noted in Chapter 11 that in the corporate form of organization the small businessman, for federal income tax purposes, can deduct his contributions to pension and profit-sharing plans in which he as well as his employees participate. Prior to the enactment of the Self-Employed Individuals Tax Retirement Act in 1962, small business proprietors or partners were not permitted to participate in such tax-favored plans because they were not "employees." The effect of this act is to make sole proprietors and partners employees for purposes of employee pension and profit-sharing plans; a sole proprietor is treated as his own employer, and a partnership is treated as the employer of each partner who has earned income.

The major provisions of this law are as follows:

1. A plan providing benefits to a self-employed individual must be a definite written program and arrangement setting forth all required provisions to qualify at the time the plan is established. Even though the self-employed individual happens to be the only person covered by the plan initially, the plan must still include all the provisions relating to the participation of employees who may become eligible in the future.

2. A plan in which the owner-employee participates must also provide benefits for all full-time employees who have worked for the company for three or more years.

3. The maximum annual contribution which may be made to a plan for the benefit of an owner-employee is $2,500 or 10 percent of his earned income for the year, whichever is smaller. For tax purposes, the owner-employee may deduct his *entire* contribution (up to the stated maximum).

4. If an owner-employee is covered by the plan, his employees' rights under the plan must be nonforfeitable at the time the contributions are made for their benefit.

5. Distributions under the plan are not permitted until the participant reaches age fifty-nine years and six months, is disabled, or dies, and must commence no later than age seventy years and six months.

Several methods of funding are authorized under certain conditions and the law should be checked carefully on these.

The extent to which contributions and deductions are limited may be illustrated by an example: During the year, let us assume that Mr. Doe has net earnings of $20,000 from his small retail store. He may contribute as much as $2,000 toward his retirement plan (10 percent of $20,000), and if he does he will be entitled to an income tax deduction of $2,000. During the following year, Mr. Doe's earnings increase to $30,000; in this case, his contribution is limited to $2,500 and his tax deduction may not exceed $2,500.

Summary. The federal income tax laws make it necessary for the employer to keep records sufficient to show not only his own tax liability but that of each of his employees. So far as his own tax liability is concerned, he should maintain accurate and complete depreciation records. Records should also be maintained in such form as to permit him to claim allowable deductions for such things as research and development work, bad-debt losses, gifts to charitable institutions, and contributions to pension and profit-sharing plans. If he keeps his records in good shape throughout the year and prepares a standard profit-and-loss statement at the end of the year, it will be a simple matter to copy the figures from the profit-and-loss statement onto his income tax return.

The employer also has certain obligations so far as his employees' tax liability is concerned. The information of the greatest importance that his records should show in connection with the withholding tax is: (1) number of persons employed during the year, (2) amount of wages paid to each person subject to withholding; (3) periods of employment of each person; and (4) amounts and dates of wage and salary payments and withholding tax deductions therefrom. In addition to these records, he must keep in a safe place copies of all withholding exemption certificates and notices of changes in exemptions for all employees.

There are three different reports that must be filed with the IRS district director in connection with the withholding tax procedure (relating to both Social Security and income taxes). These are:

1. Quarterly return of taxes withheld on wages (form 941)
2. Annual statement of taxes withheld on wages (form W-2)
3. Reconciliation of quarterly returns of taxes withheld with annual statement of taxes withheld (form W-3)

The employer must also file annually an "information" return (form 1099), showing (1) income payments to individuals in the course of trade or business totaling $600 or more during the calendar year; and (2) interest and dividend payments to individuals totalling $10 or more during the calendar year.

As a final note we wish to stress that in a book such as this only the more important of the federal income tax rules and regulations can be discussed. For other legal requirements, for penalties and definitions of terms, and for further elaboration of the regulations presented above, see subtitle A of the Internal Revenue Code.[11]

Federal Excise Taxes

Some business enterprises will find it necessary to keep records of the sales of certain items that are subject to federal excise taxes. Where a business is liable for such taxes, quarterly returns on form 720 must be filed, similar to those required in the case of Social Security and income taxes withheld from employees. If the monthly excise tax liability during a calendar quarter, as reported on form 720, is less than $100, quarterly deposits must be made; if $100 or more, but not more than $2,000, the deposits must be made monthly. Semimonthly deposits are required if the excise tax liability of the business is greater than $2,000 for any month during the previous quarter.

In regard to the computation of the tax on an article, the amount of the federal excise tax is not considered to be a part of the sales price of the article before tax. In other words, if the price the retailer wants to get for himself is $2.00 and the

---

[11] For further information concerning federal income and withholding taxes our readers are also referred to the *Prentice-Hall Federal Tax Service* (Englewood Cliffs, N.J.: Prentice-Hall, Inc.).

federal tax is 10 percent, the sale price will be $2.20. The Revenue Act may provide, however, that any retailer who represents to his customers that he is absorbing the tax (not charging it to them) shall be liable to penalty. Thus if a seller does not charge the tax to his customers as a separate amount, he must not make any written or oral statements that will cause any person to believe that the price of the article does not include the tax.

When a state or community retail sales tax is imposed on an article subject to the federal excise tax and billed as a separate item, it may be excluded from the taxable price. Thus in our previous example, a 5 percent state or local tax would raise the price to the consumer to $2.30, not to $2.31 — as it would if the 10 percent tax were figured on the retail price including the state sales tax. Whenever such a state or local sales tax is excluded from the taxable sales price of the article, the merchant must retain a copy of the invoice or other record of sale rendered to the purchaser that will prove to the IRS district director that the retail sales tax so excluded was stated as a separate item.

A retailer may be allowed a credit or refund of a tax paid on an article when the price on which the tax is based is later readjusted as a result of return or repossession of the article, or by a bona fide discount, rebate, or allowance. The allowable credit or refund is limited to the overpayment of the tax when calculated on the adjusted price. For example, if a $2.00 article subject to the 10 percent federal excise tax is sold for $2.20 and later a discount or allowance of $1.00 is made (plus $0.10 excise tax), the retailer is allowed a credit for the $0.10 tax that was refunded.

If in a business the owner is liable for the collection of excise taxes, it will be necessary for him to make provision in his accounting system for an adequate record of taxable sales or of the actual amount of tax collected from customers so that his records will be in order for inspection by federal officials at any time.

State and Local Sales Taxes

The sales tax is another type of tax about which a businessman will need to secure information. Various states and cities levy such taxes, with the rate varying from place to place. One should contact the state or local revenue office for information that will acquaint him with the applicable law; having done so, he can adapt his records to the requirements.[12]

If such taxes were levied on all sales, they would present no appreciable difficulty. But in almost all of the states or localities having retail sales taxes there are specific exemptions, either on a certain class (or classes) of merchandise, or a particular group of customers. In most states the applicable road tax on gasoline does not apply to fuel used by farmers in their tractors. In many instances cigars, cigarettes, and tobacco are exempt from the sales tax because a specific tax already has been levied upon them. Because of such exemptions, in keeping his records a

---

[12] Information concerning state and local taxes may also be found in the *Prentice-Hall State and Local Tax Service* (Englewood Cliffs, N.J.: Prentice-Hall, Inc.).

manager will need to devise some type of control by which he can distinguish tax-exempt sales that will be deducted from his total sales at the end of the taxable period.

In most cases there will be certain other items that may be deducted from gross sales after tax-exempt sales have been subtracted. Some of these are:

1. Cash discounts to customers and refunds for returned goods
2. Bad debts charged off
3. Finance and interest charges
4. Allowances on trade-ins
5. Freight and transportation charges

The small businessman should be sure to study carefully the deductions allowed by the particular state and/or city in which his business is located in order to prevent the overpayment of sales taxes.

SUMMARY AND CONCLUSIONS

The regulation of business by government through laws, licenses, and taxation is probably as old as business and government. Law constitutes the organized body of rules of conduct enforceable by government agencies. We have two important levels of legal authority (federal and state) as well as many minor levels (city, county, and other political subdivisions). Certain legal areas have developed general principles, such as the law of agency and the law of contracts. Although a great many legal documents are in use, a relatively small number are of great importance to most businessmen; among them are contracts, bills of sale, mortgages, and negotiable instruments.

With reasonable effort the small businessman can gain an understanding of the more important laws and legal documents that affect his business. He can also gain familiarity with the major forms of taxation.[13] However, both law and taxation are complex fields requiring extensive specialized training and experience. *In all important cases it is well to see competent counsel on legal and tax matters.*

Often tax savings are possible, or penalties may be avoided, by an alertness to changes in taxes and regulations, such as longer carry-backs or carry-forwards of losses, accelerated depreciation, modifications of the IRS code on retained earnings penalties, and modifications in state and local regulations. If possible, an enterpriser

---

[13]See *Tax Guide for Small Business*, IRS Publication 334 (Washington, D.C.: G.P.O., published annually). This booklet informs businessmen on Social Security, federal income tax, and withholding tax problems incident to conducting a business, and supplies needed information concerning the starting of an enterprise, acquiring a going business, and selling a business. The IRS has also prepared an information kit on tax procedures and requirements expecially for the new businessman; entitled *Mr. Businessman's Kit*, it is available free of charge through local IRS offices. Another good source of information is the latest edition of the *Retailers' Manual of Taxes and Regulations* (New York: Institute of Distribution); this manual covers up-to-date federal and state laws concerning retailers.

should subscribe to a good tax reporting service, such as that of Prentice-Hall, and have his attorney or accountant keep him posted on all significant developments.

REVIEW QUESTIONS

1. Why is it considered more important to secure competent counsel on legal and tax matters than for other problems facing the small businessman?

2. Of what significance is the fact that many of the recently enacted laws governing business are administrative regulations?

3. What is the Uniform Commercial Code?

4. Distinguish between an "agreement" and a "contract." What are the essential characteristics of a valid contract?

5. Under what conditions would a written contract be more desirable than an oral one? Explain.

6. When might a small businessman deal with an agent? Why should the extent of an agent's authority be determined before dealing with him?

7. What are some of the major provisions of the Uniform Commercial Code relating to sales?

8. May a merchant or manufacturer refuse to sell to any prospective purchaser at his discretion? What is the purpose of title II of the Civil Rights Act of 1964? What kinds of business are explicitly covered in title II?

9. What are the essential characteristics of a "negotiable instrument"?

10. Differentiate between "promissory notes" and "bills of exchange." Cite several varieties of each of these two types of negotiable instruments.

11. Discuss the different approaches taken by the Sherman and Clayton Acts toward the regulation of competition. What are some of the laws passed by Congress for the purpose of "cleaning up competition"?

12. What is "price fixing"? "Price discrimination"? Discuss some of the "indirect" methods of price fixing and price discrimination.

13. Why is a buyer held liable under the Robinson-Patman Act for knowingly accepting discriminatory low prices?

14. What is a "loss leader"? How common is this practice? What is a "fair" markup?

15. What is "resale-price maintenance"? Why has it been found difficult to enforce "fair-trade" laws? Do such laws aid the small businessman?

16. What are some of the more important regulations relating to the product itself? Discuss.

17. What are some of the more important regulations relating to the advertising of products and services and the terms of credit?

18. What provisions of the Wagner Act did the Taft-Hartley Act attempt to modify? How does the Landrum-Griffin Act affect the union member?

19. What do the authors regard as one of the most important developments in labor law in the past quarter-century? Why do they think so?

20. What are the salient features of the 1964 Civil Rights Act regarding fair employment practices?

21. Discuss the provisions of the Walsh-Healy Act and the Fair Labor Standards Act and their major points of difference. When, or under what conditions, is a small business subject to the provisions of these laws?

22. What kinds of protective legislation for women and children have been passed by the federal government and the various states? Discuss.

23. Discuss the various types of "economic-security" legislation at the federal and state levels.

24. For Social Security purposes, what information must be shown on an employee's payroll record? What is an employer's Social Security tax liability so far as "tips" earned by his employees are concerned?

25. After working from January through August 1972, at a salary of $500 per month in a covered occupation, Tom Jones became a partner in a business from which his share of profits or self-employed income for the balance of the year was $4,000. What were his total Social Security taxes for the year?

26. In what ways do some state laws restrict business activity?

27. Why should a small businessman be familiar with the provisions of the federal and state bankruptcy laws, even though he himself is not likely to petition for bankruptcy? Discuss fully.

28. (*a*) What are the major reports that a small businessman must file with the district director of the Internal Revenue Service in connection with the income and Social Security taxes he deducts from the wages of his employees? How often must these reports be filed? (*b*) How and when does he remit the taxes he collects for the government? Does he ever "withhold" his own income and Social Security taxes? Explain.

29. What are the major provisions of the Self-Employed Individuals Tax Retirement Act?

30. What is meant by an "information" tax return? Cite some examples.

31. How and when does the small businessman remit the federal excise taxes he has collected on the goods he sells?

32. Why is the collection of state and local sales taxes particularly troublesome for the businessman?

DISCUSSION QUESTIONS

1. If business is based on mutual trust and confidence, then why do we need so many laws relating to business?

2. What nongovernmental agencies are active in enforcing laws relating to business? In imposing restrictions on unfair competition or unethical business practices? Discuss.

SUPPLEMENTARY READINGS

Alyea, Paul E. *Impact of Overlapping Sales Taxes on Small Business*. Small Business Management Research Report prepared for the Small Business Administration. University, Ala.: University of Alabama, 1961. A study of the effect of local sales taxes on the operations of a small business. Concludes that such taxes cause some firms to employ additional clerical-bookkeeping help.

Journal of Small Business Management, vol. 10. (April 1972). The central theme of this issue is "Small Business Taxation." The incidence of business taxes on small firms and the development of a tax philosophy by the smaller business organization are among the topics covered.

Records To Be Kept by Employers. Wage and Hour and Public Contracts Division publication. Washington, D.C.: U.S. Department of Labor; reprinted from the Federal Register, July 1, 1967. Describes those records which, by regulation, must be kept by employers under the Fair Labor Standards Act.

Tax Guide for Small Business. Washington, D.C.: Internal Revenue Service, Department of the Treasury, published annually. Written in a nontechnical style, this booklet explains how the various federal taxes apply to sole proprietorships, partnerships, and corporations.

25

Simplified
record systems

Good record keeping, a constant and detailed knowledge of expenses, income, and profit or loss, is the first step toward profitable management of any business.

Many of the records needed for the profitable management of any business have already been discussed in other parts of this book. Certain information provided by the accounting records, for example, is used in profit planning and expense control, and the interpretation of financial statements was discussed in Chapter 23. Likewise, balance-of-stores ledgers, bin cards, and other records necessary for inventory control were discussed in Chapter 21. Similarly, tax records were discussed in Chapter 24, and production records in Chapter 22. The importance of complete and accurate credit records, particularly in the light of recent consumer credit legislation, was emphasized in Chapter 20. There is little need to elaborate on the superiority of factual information over rule of thumb or guessing. Mistakes in judgment, when based on the best obtainable facts, will be less serious and less costly than errors resulting from ignorance.

Some enterprisers believe record keeping takes more time than it is worth; others avoid it because of a dislike for "figure work," a feeling that other duties are currently of greater importance, or a lack of knowledge as to the information needed and how it may be obtained. Since facts must be secured for purposes of taxation and regulation, and additional data are often needed for intelligent operations, a certain amount of record keeping is absolutely necessary. Fortunately, there are many ways of simplifying these records. A major objective of this chapter is to explain how the small firm's records can be maintained with a minimum of effort.

ACCOUNTING RECORDS

Any experienced businessman knows that it is just common sense to keep an accurate, written record of every transaction. The man who has no oil pressure gauge on his automobile would have no way of knowing whether his motor was being properly lubricated until a knock in the motor or the mechanical failure of some moving part showed that it was not. Similarly, the lack of proper accounting and record keeping in the business concern makes it impossible for the manager to know how his enterprise is functioning, and in the majority of cases the first indication that something is wrong comes too late. Failure is already upon him. In addition, some have suffered losses in overpayment of income taxes due to the lack of adequate records. For the small businessman there can be no wiser expenditure than money spent to maintain accurate and complete records.

An adequate record-keeping system will either provide the required information or will assist the small-firm operator in obtaining answers to such basic questions as the following:

1. What was my income last year? What were my expenses?

2. How do the income and expense trends in my firm compare with those in similar businesses? How do they compare with my own operations during previous years? Does the present trend of my sales justify an increase or decrease in any of these items, such as advertising?

3. In what ways can I cut down or eliminate some of my last year's expenses?

4. What are my assets, liabilities, and net worth? How much money do I actually have invested in my business, and what rate of profit am I earning on my investment? What is my rate of profit after taxes?

5. Am I carrying too large or too small an inventory?

6. What is the current value of my building, delivery equipment, and other fixed assets after deduction of depreciation allowances?

7. How much cash business do I have? How much credit business?

8. How much do my charge customers owe me now? How much of this is overdue, and how long overdue? When does the remainder fall due? Am I extending too much credit or could I stand some more accounts? How much did I lose last year from bad debts?

9. How much ready cash do I have with which to meet my obligations? Will my income during the next 30, 60, or 90 days be sufficient to take care of obligations I have assumed?

10. Am I meeting delivery promises to my customers satisfactorily?

11. Which production orders, if any, are behind schedule? How much available machine capacity do I have in my shop for the handling of additional orders?

These and other questions, and many of the relevant records, have been discussed elsewhere in this book. Except for simplified accounting systems, only the additional records of value to the small businessman will be considered in this chapter.

Sales Records

Properly kept sales records are necessary for successful business management. Such records provide the means for measuring the efficiency of individual selling departments and sales clerks. Which department in my store, for example, is making the most profit? Which department operates on the closest margin? Should I hold a clearance sale or do some type of special advertising to close out slow-selling articles? Which of my salesclerks is making the most sales? How do their individual selling records compare with their wages? The answers to all these questions are easily found in the sales records if they have been properly made and preserved.

Daily sales figures may be obtained in one of several ways: by totaling the sales slips which are made out for each sale, by taking the total as recorded by the cash register, or by having salesclerks keep individual records of sales on a form designed for that purpose. The total daily sales of each department can be checked by using individual sales slips for each department, by using departmental keys on the cash register, or by keeping an individual cash register in each department. Sales of each clerk can be kept separate by requiring the clerks to initial their sales slips or to use the identifying letters assigned to them when ringing up sales on the cash register. In some businesses it might be practical to assign an individual cash register to each clerk; some registers have a key for charge sales.

Both cash and charge sales are recorded daily from the sales slips in stores that use the sales slip system. Credit sales may be posted from cash register totals by having the customer sign the register slip retained by the store, or by posting charge sales from the sales slips. Totals of individual sales slips are posted daily to the customers' ledger sheets in the customers' ledger. Many small retailers have found that an easier way to maintain the customers' ledger is to purchase a filing device designed especially for filing sales slips. One device has a number of hinged shelves that contain spring clips to hold the sales slips in place. When the clerk makes a sale on credit, he merely itemizes the articles on the sales slip and files the slip away in the special file. Many small business managers require the customer to sign the sales slip as evidence of his having received the goods, but this is a matter of the individual store's policy. All subsequent sales to the same customer are handled in the same way, all sales slips being pinned together. When the account is paid, the slips are given to the customer and his charge account file is empty. If merchandise is returned for credit, a credit memorandum is issued and a duplicate is filed in the customer's file at the close of the day. With this system it is unnecessary to maintain a separate accounts receivable ledger for charge customers, since the file is in itself an accounts receivable ledger, and much bookkeeping detail is eliminated.

Accounting for Cash Payments

One of the best methods of accounting for cash disbursements and receipts in modern business is to deposit to a checking account in the bank all money taken in and to write a check for each and every expenditure, except for very small items (costing, say, $2 or less) like postage, window cleaning, or express charges. The bank helps to keep the firm's records, because canceled checks furnish a complete record of each disbursement.

The matter of small cash disbursements is easily taken care of through what is known as a "petty-cash fund." A small fund of from $10 to $50, depending upon the need, is set aside to cover minor expenses. Each time an expenditure is made, a petty cash form is filled out for the amount of the expenditure in order to provide information for charging it to the proper expense account. When the fund is exhausted, a reimbursement check is drawn on the checking account, with the expense accounts being charged as indicated upon the petty-cash forms. The manner of recording expenditures in the "one-book" system will be explained later.

Purchase Records

Almost all small businesses do a certain amount of buying on credit. It is more convenient than having to pay for merchandise when ordered, because the owner can make his purchases as often as needed during the month and settle for all purchases at one time at the end of the month. This eliminates the detail involved in paying for each purchase individually, and it permits the manager to check the merchandise for quantity and quality before paying for it. Another advantage of credit is that it actually amounts to an addition to working capital during the credit period. When the businessman buys on credit, he can make purchases that he could not have made if it had been necessary for him to pay cash, and usually by the time the account becomes due he has sold enough of the merchandise to pay the bill.

Since credit is such an important asset, it is important that it be diligently safeguarded at all times. Invoices must be paid promptly when they become due. A good plan to insure prompt payment is to keep an invoice file with a section for each day of the month. As invoices come in, they should be filed under the date upon which they fall due or when they should be paid to secure cash discounts if these are offered. It then becomes a relatively easy matter to check this file daily and make payment on all matured invoices. After payment, each invoice is filed in an alphabetical file under the name of the company concerned. In the case of payments for which no invoices are available, a memorandum invoice should be prepared, giving the name of the person, the amount, the date, and the article purchased or service rendered. In this manner, a complete record of all purchases is made instantly available at all times. Invoices should always be marked with the check number and date of payment in order to eliminate the possibility of duplicate payment. Credit memorandums should be attached to relevant invoices upon receipt so that they will be deducted from the invoices before payment is made.

Equipment Records

Regardless of the type or size of business operated, the owner will need a certain amount of equipment. In many cases he will have to purchase new equipment each year in order to keep up with competitors and with the trends in his type of business. Many times this equipment will be rather expensive and its use will raise operating expenses, but if it brings in enough additional business at a gross margin greater than the increase in expenses, it will prove to be a good investment.

Equipment records should be maintained on all equipment owned by the business. These records may be kept in book form or on cards in a card file. On a separate sheet or card for each piece of permanent equipment should be shown the following:

Cost of equipment
Amount of down payment
Monthly payments
Balance due
Yearly depreciation

Each time a payment is made on a piece of equipment, it should be entered on the equipment record card. Also, at the end of each year depreciation should be computed and entered on the card. This depreciation is an expense of the business, just as much as rent, utilities, or salaries. The simplest and most practical method of computing depreciation is the straight-line method, an example of which follows:

Original cost of equipment	$500.00
Estimated trade-in or scrap value	50.00
Amount to be depreciated	$450.00
Yearly depreciation (estimated life: 10 years)	$ 45.00

The declining-balance method should be used whenever quicker recovery of the investment is desirable. Under this method the equipment is depreciated by a certain percentage of the balance each year. However, for tax-paying purposes, the Internal Revenue Service will not allow the rate of depreciation under this method to be greater than double the straight-line rate. Thus over a ten-year period of amortization, the equipment would be depreciated at an annual rate of 20 percent (rather than 10 percent). Using the above equipment as an example, depreciation under the double-declining-balance method is computed as follows:

Year	Depreciation (20% of remaining value)	Remaining Value
0	—	$500
1	$100	400
2	80	320
3	64	256
4	51	205
5	41	164
6	33	131
7	26	105
8	21	84
9	17	67
10	13	54

The declining-balance method permits the businessman to take heavy depreciation in the early years of the equipment's life. This is particularly desirable when the equipment has a high rate of obsolescence and its market value consequently decreases rapidly. When the equipment is scrapped at the end of the amortization period, its remaining value will be close to its estimated salvage value; in the above case, it is slightly higher ($54). The reader will note that under this method of depreciation the remaining value approaches but never reaches zero. In practice, therefore, the small business owner should switch to straight-line depreciation near the end of the asset's useful life.[1]

[1] In the example as given, the asset would probably be depreciated $17 each of the final two years.

One-Book Accounting Systems

Refined accounting methods as developed for large corporations may be unduly cumbersome for many small enterprises. Especially since labor and other costs of paper work have increased so greatly, many small businessmen have sought and found simplified systems which are adequate for their needs. Many of these operate on the one-book principle, thus avoiding much duplication of writing.

The adequacy of simplified systems, especially those prepared by commercial agencies or by the businessman himself, is a controversial subject. Accountants understandably prefer a system tailor-make by themselves to fit each enterprise, whereas the commercial agencies claim that their extensive experience makes possible the design of forms and systems which are as satisfactory as, if not superior to, those prepared by local accountants. The small businessman, of course, should withhold judgment on this matter until he has made a careful investigation of his specific needs.

Considerable misunderstanding exists regarding one-book systems. They *are* based on approved double-entry accounting in spite of the one-book designation often used. Students are often confused on this point, and relatively few are familiar with the systems available or those that can be self-designed.

Several commercial agencies produce simplified one-book systems that may be purchased in most office supply stores. In addition, most stationery stores carry ruled blank forms that may be adapted to a firm's record-keeping needs. In many cases, however, the best solution to a firm's need is to adopt, with possible adaptations, the record-keeping system prepared by the trade association in the field.

The systems prepared by trade associations and by leading commercial agencies embody the double-entry principle of checks and balances and are based on other sound accounting principles. If the small businessman decides to design his own one-book system, he should be especially careful to avoid an oversimplified single-entry system lacking accurate checks and balances. In addition, he should make certain that his system will furnish in easily accessible, usable form all information required for purposes of taxation and insurance, as well as the data actually needed for intelligent operations.

One of the most complete lines of simplified bookkeeping and tax record systems on the market is the Johnson system. Other well-known systems are the Blackbourn system and the Ideal system. All three of these organizations have designed records to meet the needs of specific types of small business. These books are available in standard sizes and at moderate prices. Each is a complete one-book system, and instructions are included.[2]

If investigation of record and tax systems available shows none to be suited to an enterpriser's needs, or if for other valid reasons he prefers to design his own system, it would be a relatively easy matter to purchase ruled columnar sheets in blank and

[2] Further information about any of these systems may be obtained by writing to The Johnson Systems, 828 N. Broadway, Milwaukee, Wisc. 53202; Blackbourn Binding, Inc., 1750 Thomas Avenue, St. Paul, Minn. 55104; or The Ideal Systems, 6 Church Street, New York, N.Y. 10006.

supply his own headings. By doing this, he could make his records as simple or as complex as desired. The following form, for instance, represents utter simplicity:

		Cash Receipts		Cash Payments			
		Cash Sales		Mdse.		Other Payments	
Date	Remarks	and Rec'd on Acc't	Other Income	for Resale	Operating Expenses	Account	Am't
(a)	(b)	(c)	(d)	(e)	(f)	(g)	(h)

These columns would be used as follows:

(a) Enter the date on which the transaction took place.

(b) Write a brief description of the transaction.

(c) Enter total cash receipts from cash sales and customers' payments on account. This could be entered as one total for the day's transactions on one line, or, if desired, individual entries could be made on separate lines under the same date.

(d) Enter any other cash receipts in this column.

(e) Enter total amount (or individual amounts) spent during the day by cash or by bank check for merchandise for resale.

(f) Enter total payments (cash or check) for expenses.

(g) Write in this column the nature of any other payment made which could not be classified under (e) or (f).

(h) Enter amounts of items listed in column (g).

This simple record, if well kept, would provide the small operator with general information and would be better than no records at all. However, it has serious limitations, for it lacks columns that an owner will need from time to time to record other transactions. For example, if he extends credit, it will be necessary for him to have two columns in the journal for customers' accounts, one for charges and one for credits. Otherwise, this information will need to be laboriously abstracted from the customers' tickets each time he needs to know his total accounts receivable. Similarly, a column should be provided for creditors' accounts payable — that is, accounts representing bills owed but not yet paid by the firm.

Following is a description of a one-book system designed by Harry W. Ketchum, formerly of the U.S. Department of Commerce. Though originally designed for a small retail store, it can be easily adapted to other types of small business. The principal parts of the system include:

1. A daily cash report to provide a check on cash receipts and payments and a summary and classification of cash received and paid out for entry into the cumulative one-book summary (see Figure 25-1.)

2. A cumulative one-book summary covering cash transactions, credit transactions, and payments by check to provide most of the information necessary to prepare statements of profit and loss and required tax reports (see Figure 25-2.)

Figure 25-1. Daily Cash Report

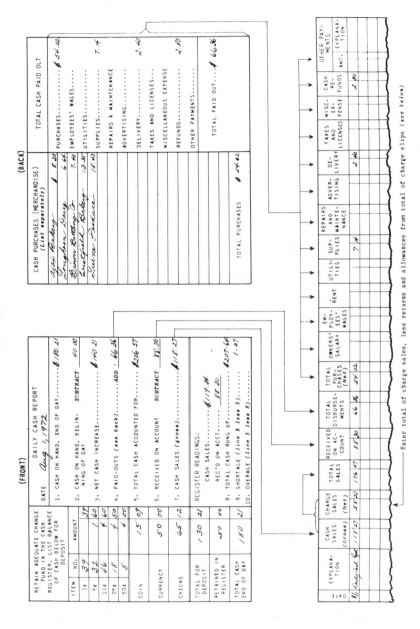

DAILY CASH REPORT

Figure 25-2. Cumulative One-Book Summary

CUMULATIVE ONE-BOOK SUMMARY

Aug. 1972

DATE	EXPLANATION	CHECK NO.	(A) CASH SALES (Gross)	(B) CHARGE SALES (Net)	(C) TOTAL SALES	(D) CASH RECEIVED ON ACCOUNT	(E) TOTAL DISBURSE-MENTS	(F) PUR-CHASES (Net)	(G) OWN-ER'S SALARY	(H) EMPLO-YEE'S WAGES	(I) RENT	(J) UTILI-TIES	(K) SUP-PLIES	(L) REPAIRS AND MAIN-TE-NANCE	(M) ADVER-TISING	(N) DE-LIVERY	(O) TAXES AND LI-CENSES	(P) MISC. EXPEN-SES	(Q) CASH RE-FUNDS	(R) OTHER PAYMENTS AMT.	EXPLA-NATION	LINE NO.
1	Daily Cash Rept.	X	118.27	58.20	176.47																	1
1	Wholesale Supply	46				88.20	66.36	59.02					7.14			.70		2.80			2
1	C.G. Electric Co.	47					10.14					10.14									3
2	Daily Cash Rept.	X	81.74	45.89	127.63	112.60	117.70	110.20						4.50	3.00						4
2	John Doe	48					50.00												50.00 Compensation (additional)	5
2	Acc. Storage	49					12.50								12.50					6
2	Dixon Property	50					116.50	116.50												7
3	Daily Cash Rept.	X	93.19	69.27	162.46	237.10	100.76	94.76			4.60						2.00			8
3	City Oil Co.	51					9.62	9.62												9
3	Grain Realty	52					80.00			80.00										10
3	Sylva Co.	53					60.00									60.00 County Supply		11
4	Daily Cash Rept.	X	132.96	79.20	212.16	321.92	126.07	109.27				3.27	5.20	5.00	5.00		1.60			12
4	John Doe	54					75.00		75.00											13
4	Smith Poultry	55					32.46	32.46												14
4	First Nat'l Bank	56					10.3.00										3.80		100.00 Note Payment	15
4	Out of State	57					10.00													16
5	Daily Cash Rept.	X	121.91	109.19	331.16	135.65	211.44	127.82		76.30						10.00		4.00		17
5	Jones Bros.	58					85.14	85.14												18
5	Out of State Co.	59					20.40			10.40						10.40				19
5	Out of State Co.	60					37.50			37.50										20
7	Etc.																				21
																					22
31	Total, Aug.		3,531.93	1,945.38	5,477.31	1,685.27	5,569.03	4,064.65	300.00	566.10	80.00	19.76	23.65	17.65	10.00	552.60	20.40	8.64	12.20	20.00		80
			(A)	(B)	(C)	(D)	(E)	(F)	(G)	(H)	(I)	(J)	(K)	(L)	(M)	(N)	(O)	(P)	(Q)	(R)		

NOTE. To insure accuracy of entries and additions the column totals should be cross-checked as follows: Column (C) should equal Column (A) plus Column (B). Column (B) should equal the total of columns (F) to (R), inclusive.

523

These records replace all journals and ledgers except accounts receivable, employee records, and records of fixed assets.

The daily cash report items which are entered in the cumulative one-book summary are indicated by the arrows (see Figures 25-1 and 25-2). At the time this information is entered in the one-book summary, total charge sales, less returns and allowances, should be entered on the same line. If the cash register provides sufficient keys and totals, charge sales can also be rung up and included in the daily report. Otherwise, information must be obtained from the charge slips, or from a separate listing of charge sales. If the cash register does not provide a separate key and total covering cash received on account, a separate record of such receipts must be maintained.

The daily cash report form may be mimeographed on an 8 1/2" X 11" sheet, and punched for filing in a ring binder or printed on the front and back of a manila envelope. All supporting papers, including paid-out receipts, cash register tapes, and carbons of deposit slips, should be attached or inserted, and the reports filed by day for future reference.

A one-book summary will supply a cumulative record of all cash transactions (including payments by check) and of all charge sales. The monthly (or quarterly) totals will provide almost all of the information necessary for the preparation of a profit-and-loss statement. The totals may be transferred to an annual summary, in the same form, to obtain totals for the annual profit-and-loss statement and income tax return.

Any number of columns may be used in the summary with any expense breakdown desired. It should conform with the classification to be used in the profit-and-loss statements. Expenses paid infrequently may be grouped in one column to reduce the number of columns required. However, in this case separate totals must be obtained for use in the profit-and-loss statement. If no credit sales are made, columns (*a*), (*b*), and (*d*) should be omitted. If operations are recorded on a departmental basis, additional columns for purchases and sales should be inserted.

None of the items listed in column (*r*) – other payments – are used in the profit-and-loss statement. This column, with space for explanations, is included for recording payments which are for neither purchase of merchandise nor operating expenses. Such payments include owner's cash withdrawals, repayments of loans, and pruchase of assets.

Pegboard Accounting

Another approach towards the simplification of accounting records has been the development, in recent years, of "pegboard accounting." Like the one-book method, the pegboard system is designed for firms which keep their books by hand; this, of course, includes most small businesses.

Under the pegboard system a business transaction need only be recorded *once,* the original entry of data being recorded on all relevant records *simultaneously.* This is achieved by the use of a board with a flat hard surface and carbon papers or carbonless carbon forms. All records requiring an entry are placed upon the board so as to lie one on top of the other. Proper alignment is determined by pegs that are affixed to the board. After each posting the records are advanced on the board one notch.

The distinct advantages of pegboard accounting are readily apparent. The entry of a business transaction on all relevant records is done in one writing, thereby reducing records-handling time and eliminating errors in transcription. Thus it provides far greater control than with an ordinary manual bookkeeping system. In short, it provides many of the advantages of machine bookkeeping without the high initial cost.[3]

SERVICE RECORDS

Another type of record system may be illustrated by the records needed for a repair service. Many businesses, in addition to the service establishments whose primary function may be to repair, must maintain a repair service for customers. Manufacturers may have their products returned to the factory for repair, or in certain cases may furnish repair service at the customers' locations. Merchants handling items like household appliances, television sets, furniture, and jewelry must make provisions for necessary repairs after the product has been sold. The need may arise either before or after a guarantee period has expired. If the former, repair costs will be borne by the merchant or charged to the manufacturer. Where and by whom such repairs are made is a matter of policy and agreement with the manufacturer. In any case, whether repair be a primary or subsidiary function, records are needed to handle the transactions efficiently, to prevent loss of goods, and to assure collection from the customer or manufacturer.

The sale or installation date usually determines the status of a guarantee, and this in turn determines who is to bear the cost of repairs. This information is also useful to a merchant who may be called upon to repair or service goods purchased from him without any specific guarantee. Most retailers want to stand behind their merchandise, but should not be expected to provide maintenance against normal wear and tear.

A complete record should be kept of each service call or of all work done on articles brought in for repair.

An adequate supply of essential repair parts is necessary to render efficient service. A simple bin card will help maintain this inventory. When parts are added to the bin stock, the amount is added to the bin tag, and the process is reversed as parts are removed.

It is a good practice to establish standard repair charges for as many run-of-the-mill repair jobs as possible. This will not only establish a fair profit basis for the repair work, but will help the bookkeeping department and increase customers' confidence in the fairness of the service charges.

Dealers and merchants rendering repair service on most kinds of mechanical products may secure from the manufacturer suggested customer charges for recurring types of repair jobs. Whether followed exactly or not, these lists are useful guides.

---

[3] Further information concerning pegboard (or one-writing) accounting systems may be obtained by writing to one of the following companies which provide such services: McBee Systems, 80 Greenwich Ave., Greenwich, Conn. 06830; The Burroughs Corporation, Todd Div., 1150 University Ave., Rochester, N.Y. 14607; The Master-Craft Corporation, Kalamazoo, Mich. 49001; and the Reynolds & Reynolds Company, Dayton, Ohio 49001.

MISCELLANEOUS RECORDS

A small retail lumber dealer has for many years maintained records of contractors and of carpenters in his area in such a way as to be able to tell at any time what each one is doing. For example, he knows that contractor Smith has just started construction on a duplex apartment house and will be needing eight or ten carpenters in about two weeks. From past experience he knows that Smith will soon be asking him where he can find them. When this time comes, he can immediately refer to his carpenter file and learn which ones are ready to start to work at once and when each employed man will be available. Most of the men now take the initiative in informing him of their status. By making his office a clearing house for employment, this service has built up goodwill with both groups; and by keeping construction moving forward at a more regular rate, it has helped to increase sales.

A small-job printer solved many of his problems by maintaining efficiency and activity records of each machine and of each employee. In this way he has instituted a miniature production control and costing system which enables him to plan jobs well in advance, make more accurate bids on competitive jobs, go after additional work whenever needed to keep his plant busy, and thus maintain greater stability of output and employment.

A small animal-and-poultry-feed distributor secures published crop forecasts and prepares his own charts to help in planning and timing his buying. From his sales records he prepares a daily commodity breakdown to show buying trends. By analyzing past sales to each customer, many of whom are large farmers and poultry and stock raisers, he has a record of the seasonal buying habits of each regular customer. These records are used in buying, sales promotion, and inventory control.

A small dress factory selling through agents to retail stores maintains a customer record card for each store showing the date and types and quantities of each purchase. These records are useful in planning production, in checking on the agents' solicitation of repeat business, and as a follow-up on the success of styles previously made and sold.

An insurance agent keeps records of all customers' policies, present and lapsed, showing renewal dates, reasons for changes, and similar data. By watching current news items, he sometimes secures reinstatement of a lapsed policy when circumstances have changed for a former customer. Naturally, customers are reminded of renewal dates, but this agent also studies each client's current needs and suggests changes to provide policy coverage better suited to present conditions. He also maintains records on prospective customers that are used for solicitation of new business.

These are just a few examples of particular small businessmen who have made effective use of records other than the standard accounting ones or those used in rendering repair services. In any small business a judiciously selected set of records will make possible increased sales, more regular and improved operations, and better customer and public relations.

PAPERWORK AND OFFICE PROCEDURES

When the small businessman first starts his own business, he will always have some paperwork, whether his office is merely a table top and a letter file or a separate, well-equipped room. It is necessary to have some organization of the paper work to be performed, such as the writing of business letters, filing of records, opening and sending out of mail, and filling out of orders and invoices. Perhaps the owner-manager will do all of this work himself. If so, he will need to have this paperwork so organized so that it will not interfere with his obligation to serve his customers. The small businessman who sits back at his desk in the rear of the store checking invoices, writing orders, and so forth during business hours while his customers stand around waiting is sacrificing goodwill for the sake of work that should be done either during slack periods of the day or after business hours.

In the organization of office procedures, no single important activity that should be performed daily can safely be neglected. Letters must be answered promptly, accounting records must be kept up to date, and all records necessary for carrying on the business should be filed daily.

Records must be arranged so that they will be available when they are needed for reference. The plan for filing each kind of record will depend upon the needs of the business. Correspondence, for example, may be filed alphabetically by name, location, or subject; the most practical method for the small businessman would probably be alphabetically by name.

Printed or typed material containing useful information from trade journals, trade associations, or suppliers should be kept for future reference. This material should not be piled on a desk or in a drawer in the hope that it can be found when needed, but should be filed by subject or name.

Sales records should be filed at first by customer's name and later, when the business is large enough, by territories. Purchase and pricing records, as well as quotations, should be filed alphabetically by commodity. Catalog indexes should be filed by commodity for easy reference. Mailing lists for advertising pieces should be filed by location.

Personnel records should be kept whether employees number one or fifty. These should be filed alphabetically by name, with such material as application letters, letters of reference, Social Security records, and the like in each employee's folder. When an employee leaves a firm, a notation of his reason for doing so should be made.

When a letter or paper might be filed in one of several possible places, the material should be filed in the most likely place and cross-reference sheets, like the sample one shown below, should be filed in the other locations. By this simple method of cross-referencing, the location of papers can be greatly facilitated.

```
                        CROSS-REFERENCE SHEET


    Name or
    Subject:  Joe Doakes              Date: 8/25/72


    Regarding:  Complaint


    SEE

    Name or
    Subject: New Supply Company
```

After the small businessman has been in business for a year or two, his files will begin to grow out of bounds. For the small business, once a year will be often enough to transfer records to inactive files. Deciding to retain all records may be expensive over a period of years, for adequate storage boxes and storage space must be made available. Where storage space is limited, the permanent records of the firm may be microfilmed. The more general practice for small business firms is to destroy certain material every year. Some general factors have an influence in determining what material should be immediately destroyed and what should be stored. The Commissioner of Internal Revenue has ruled that, in general, records bearing on income taxes must be kept for at least five years. The statutes of limitations in the various states, relating to the period during which suits may be brought, have much to do with deciding how long to keep records and correspondence concerned with contractual relations. Any record that may be involved in a case of fraud should not be destroyed. Generally speaking, the test of the advisability of transferring or destroying material is the number of references to past material and the need of protection in legal and tax matters.[4]

In a small office it is often advisable to send certain work out to agencies, particularly large-volume duplication work that cannot be performed economically by the small office staff. There are so-called letter-service companies that specialize in typing letters or in mimeographing, multigraphing, or printing material for small concerns that do not have the necessary equipment to do their own work. Prices for a particular type of service can be obtained from several agencies and may then be compared with the probable cost of doing the work in one's own office.

SUMMARY AND CONCLUSIONS

Modern business must be operated on the basis of adequate records. Financial records are necessary to determine *profit or loss, return on investment, owner's equity, assets, liabilities, and other pertinent facts. In addition, good accounting is an important tool of management.* Information obtained from records furnishes the basis for managerial decisions ranging in scope and importance from policy formation or revision down to day-to-day decisions regarding routine operations.

Financial and other related records are also required for tax and regulatory purposes. Often federal or state laws require that certain records be kept and that reports based on these records be made. Penalties are imposed for failure to comply with these statutes.

Keeping the necessary records for a small business need be neither complicated nor time-consuming. Simplified record systems, such as the one-book and pegboard systems described in this chapter, have been developed for recording essential accounting information. Whenever certain transactions occur frequently, as do sales in a retail store or service calls in a repair shop, the necessary recording can be reduced to a simple system. When the transaction is common to other businesses in the field, prepared record-keeping systems are usually available from trade associations or from local stationers.

[4] *The Guide to Record Retention Requirements* (Washington, D.C.: National Archives and Records Service, General Services Administration, published annually) details the retention requirements for the many types of records required to be kept by businessmen and others under federal laws and regulations.

Many small businessmen fail to keep accurate and complete records. The small business owner is reminded, however, that *in the long run time spent in keeping adequate records actually saves time* that would otherwise be necessary to secure essential information required for measuring progress, paying taxes, and making critical policy decisions. The results will be more accurate and the efficiency and profitableness of the business will tend to increase when decisions are based on reliable information that is available only through a system of adequate records.

REVIEW QUESTIONS

1. Why is record keeping not merely desirable but absolutely necessary in modern business?
2. What records would be most useful to you in deciding whether or not to buy a particular business that is offered for sale? How, if at all, could you verify the accuracy of these records? Discuss.
3. What kinds of records are necessitated by the requirements or provisions of various federal and state laws? Would all these records be unnecessary if these laws were repealed? Explain and discuss.
4. If you were called in to assist a small business that was getting into financial difficulties, explain how you would use records and recordkeeping.
5. What important records are needed in the small factory but not in the retail store? In the retail store but not in the factory? In either of these but not in the service business?
6. Explain how a simplified one-book system applies the double-entry principle. Illustrate.
7. What is meant by "pegboard accounting"?

DISCUSSION QUESTIONS

1. Visit a local stationery and office supply store to find out what simplified record systems are available. What systems are designed for such special purposes as keeping certain tax records, records of production control in the factory, and identification of each customer's goods in the service establishment? What conclusions do you draw from your investigations?
2. Bill had a minor in accounting for his degree in business. After serving two years as his own accountant for his own enterprise, he felt his time could be used better for top management duties. His firm makes a line of products sold directly to retailers and to customers. Most sales to retailers are on open account, those to consumers are for cash. All purchases are for cash. Bill wants to install a simple but adequate record-keeping system that will relieve him of all routine paperwork. What should he do, and why?

SUPPLEMENTARY READINGS

Ragan, Robert C. *Financial Recordkeeping for Small Stores*. Small Business Management Series no. 32. Washington, D.C.: Small Business Administration, 1966. Designed primarily for prospective and present small-store owners whose business doesn't justify hiring a trained, full-time bookkeeper, this booklet describes basic record-keeping systems. It also gives a number of suggestions for handling special situations as well as explaining how the record-keeping information can be applied in the day-to-day management of the business.

Recordkeeping Systems – Small Store and Service Trade. Small Business Bibliography 15. Washington, D.C.: Small Business Administration, 1966. Contains a concise description of record-keeping systems which can be used by operators of small retail and service-trade establishments.

PART FOUR
New Directions

- SMALL BUSINESS AND THE FUTURE
- SMALL BUSINESS INTERNATIONAL

26

Small business and the future

The future of American small business has never been more encouraging. A growing recognition of the importance of small business to our economy has been accompanied by a growing effort to secure more facts about independent enterprisers and their problems and needs. One result of the increasing number of studies on entrepreneurship and new-enterprise formation has been to expand training opportunities for small business owner-management. Another has been to make various public and private agencies in our society more aware of the symbiotic nature of all business, and particularly of their responsibilities to present and prospective small businessmen. Governmental assistance to small business was described in Chapter 2 and elsewhere throughout this book. It is interesting to note, also, the increasing emphasis given to entrepreneurship and small business management in our collegiate schools of business.

Predictions are hazardous at best and are especially difficult to make for specific periods of time. It is not our intention in this chapter to forecast the position of small business for the next year or for any other particular time. We are concerned with long-range trends and with an examination of fundamental factors that will continue to influence the position of small business, regardless of what conditions may develop.

The best approach seems to be to review briefly certain points about small business developed in this book and then to examine the probable effects on small business of different conditions that may appear at some time in the future. Finally, we hope to show that the surest way to insure an enduring place for small business is through continued study and application of the ideas and methods suggested throughout this book.

THE PROBLEMS OF SMALL BUSINESS — A COMPENDIUM

We have seen that small business occupies an important and unique place in our economy. Not only was every important big business of today started as a small enterprise, but also over 95 percent of all businesses are still properly classified as small. That this situation will continue in spite of conflicting and often confusing trends is the accepted belief of all well-informed observers.

Small business is unique in many respects. It has advantages, limitations, and problems that differ from those of large concerns. It is necessary to have a large number of small enterprises if true competition is to exist, if freedom of initiative and business enterprise is to be maintained, and if we are to continue our progress in extending more goods and services to an ever-increasing number of people. Big business alone cannot provide these things.

Of course, many limitations and problems accrue to certain enterprises merely because of their small size. Inability to operate in the fields of mass production where heavy investment in machinery is required is one of these. Particularly in the field of manufacturing, a given industry usually achieves maturity only by developing machinery and the subdivision of labor to an extent that seriously limits the opportunities for small-scale enterprise.

In general, the fields of natural monopolies are not for the small enterprise. The so-called heavy industries are represented by large concerns, although many small firms operate in service and facilitating capacities as well as in the distribution of some of these industries' products. Although a small enterprise can operate successfully in the vast majority of business areas, in most of these fields branches of large concerns may also be operated. It is principally when the potential volume is too small to be of interest to big business that the little fellow has the field to himself.

Of the many problems of small business, probably the most important are: (1) limited time of the owner-manager; (2) wide range of managerial ability demanded of one or a few men; (3) difficulty in making effective use of research; and (4) the problem of securing access to adequate financial resources. Some of the other problems, as we have seen, arise principally because of the type of individual normally attracted to business ownership; others plague a business of any size but seem to bear more heavily on the little fellow.

One advantage of a study of *small* business is that the recognition of its special problems stimulates efforts to solve them. We have seen many ways in which the independent businessman can adapt to his own needs some of the ideas and modern practices developed in the larger firms. He may, for example, share managerial duties with a partner or a few well-chosen members of a closed corporation. In certain retail fields he may affiliate with a voluntary chain organization and thus secure the benefits of specialized management knowledge. An ambitious beginner may find one of the expanding franchise plans, which would furnish "know-how" along with a well-publicized product or service, suited to his needs. And finally, for certain functions of management, he may utilize the "outside staff" discussed in Chapter 14.

Financing is commonly recognized as one of the most important problems of small business. However, as noted on several occasions in this text, the agreement seems to be pretty general among bankers and others concerned with the financial needs of small business that the real need is for management counsel. Given good management, most of the financial problems of small business become of minor importance, because (1) good management includes efficient handling of finances; and (2) lenders are usually anxious to invest money in a well-managed business.

There are, however, three other types of financial problems confronting small business for which it is not so easy to suggest solutions:

1. Small-scale financing is always more expensive per dollar than large-scale financing. Whether the lending or investing process can be simplified and organized

in such a way as to overcome this handicap remains to be seen. Several interesting but as yet untried proposals have been made. One approach involves separating the various cost elements, such as risk bearing, investigation, negotiation, paperwork, and contact, and reducing the cost of each of these elements to a minimum through use of whatever plan is appropriate. For example, the principles of underwriting and insurance might be applied to risk bearing. This has been done in reducing the cost of financing home ownership through the FHA, as well as the cost of temporary unemployment to the worker through unemployment insurance. The principle of guided self-declaration used in American income tax procedure, with appropriate penalties for falsification, might be applied to reduce the cost of investigation. Costs of paperwork and of contact could probably be reduced by centralization and use of machine methods.

2. A second problem is whether small businesses should be financed through loan capital or investment capital. Is it better to seek loans from private or government agencies, or to share the ownership and profits with those who can provide the necessary capital? Recently established SBICs (small business investment companies) combine both methods of financing by making their debentures convertible into stock of the small company. Too often, creative imagination (or "brains") and adequate capital do not go together, at least at the inception stage of a new idea. There may be ten to a hundred freak ideas launched by hopeful enterprisers that fail for one that succeeds, but who can pick the successful one at the start? In a given market that appears to be overcrowded with businesses of a particular kind, the right individual can succeed when scores around him are failing. This aspect of entrepreneurship affects both the availability of capital and the small businessman's preference of funds available.

3. Finally, it is difficult to build and maintain adequate financial reserves. Not only is the initial capital needed to start a business usually the hardest to get, but the effects of both the business cycle and our tax system lay additional financial burdens upon the beginning small business. Heavy taxes on personal incomes in the lower brackets affect the typical small business, which is usually a proprietorship or partnership, although they have no serious effect on larger corporate units. Also, whenever the tax system imposes heavy rates on low-business-profit brackets, the effects are more serious for small than for large business units.

The effects of the business cycle, especially when on the downswing, bear more heavily on the capital structure of small than of large businesses. However, small business has some compensating advantages, especially greater flexibility and relatively lower fixed overhead expenses. Also, the very nature of the recession period of the business cycle — a period of contracting overexpanded business facilities at current prices — may make this pressure on many small businesses desirable. Being more flexible than their large competitors, they may be able to reduce costs and prices to justify continuing operations. If this is not possible, and the ability to stay in business depends upon using accumulated capital, small business may actually take a lesser loss by retiring early in the recession period of a prolonged business depression. In some cases it may even be possible to make a second start later at bargain prices. This resembles the procedure of going through a reorganization of the capital structure, as big firms sometimes do.

The small business has special needs and problems that differ from those of big business when economic activity is changing, either for better or for worse. The fact that limited capital makes it harder for the little fellow to withstand a decline in business activity is not always an unmixed evil; but it also restricts his ability to expand rapidly to capitalize fully on opportunities resulting from an upswing in the business cycle. Once we appreciate this and other needs and problems characteristic of small business, we see the importance of profiting by the experience and methods of big business. Adequate reserves, well-formulated policies governing expansion and contraction, proper timing, the use of options instead of long-term commitments, and various other methods could be mentioned. The fundamental facts remain the same. Only the "dress" changes with different stages of the business cycle.

THE "PERMANENCE" OF SMALL BUSINESS

Our examination of small business in each of the three major areas of economic activity — merchandising, manufacturing, and service — has established that (1) the problems of independent business operation are sufficiently important and distinctive to warrant special study of small business as such; and (2) any business, large or small, can profit by the experience and methods developed in other concerns regardless of their size or field of operations. The former is the justification, the latter the major thesis of this book. The two belong together. The interdependence of all business has been stressed and illustrated throughout the book. Our purpose has been to study the small enterprise, not as an isolated segment, but as a part of the entire interrelated and interdependent business structure. Not only is the little fellow a part of the whole economic system, but he learns from and contributes to the entire field of economic activity.

These two points are important when we consider the future of small business. Economic conditions change; also, international conditions vary and influence national policies and business activities. In this respect change is the only constant factor. However, regardless of economic and international conditions, small business will continue as an important part of our economy. Each of the two types of changes mentioned affects both the immediate or temporary position of small business and its long-run or permanent position.

The long-range trend in American business history has been favorable to small business, especially in terms of new opportunities and the number of concerns. Each new industry, although it may eventually be dominated by large concerns, brings in new opportunities for small firms and results in a great increase in the total number of establishments. Electronics and semiconductors are recent examples. In wholesaling, the trend has been toward a larger number of small concerns. Nearly the entire field of service businesses was unknown a century ago. Only in farming has there been a decline in the number of small enterprisers relative to either population or the total number of businesses in operation. In fact, it is primarily the rise of many large industries and a steady increase in the use of capital goods and modern technology that have made it possible for us to have an ever-increasing number of small business units in operation.

Probably one reason for confused thinking on this point is the failure to compare similar periods of the business cycle. Naturally, the number of small businesses will be smaller during the depression stage than during the preceding boom stage, and usually small units represent a smaller percentage of the total number of firms in operation during hard times than during good times. However, if successive years of boom or of depression times are compared separately, the long-term upward swing in favor of small business is evident. Economic conditions cause the number and kinds of small businesses needed at particular times to vary but do not change the long-run trends of the increasing number and importance of small independent operators.

More small firms are in operation today than ever before in a similar period of our history. Many of them were launched hastily, often by persons who were not well prepared. Certain fields appear to be overcrowded and readjustments are needed. The more obvious opportunities for starting a small business have been discussed. Prospecting and seeking out new and justifiable opportunities will require increasing attention by entrepreneurs of the future. These conditions all point to the ever-greater importance of a careful study of small business organization and operation such as that suggested in this text.

Since the rise of our industrial economy, developments in the international situation have always affected small business as well as other areas of our economic activity. However, they have never lessened the ultimate importance of the individual enterpriser nor invalidated the fundamental principles relating to small business. Simply the emphasis as to type of needs and problems is shifted.

The point is that the study of small business is justifiable in its own right at all times. It should not be viewed opportunistically as something of importance only during a period of rapid business expansion or "easy going." Small business has certain advantages, limitations, problems, and opportunities that shift in emphasis with changing conditions, but remain surprisingly constant in fundamentals regardless of economic conditions.

And finally, if certain economic or international situations enforce a delay in starting the kind of business an individual ultimately hopes to own, the result may be actually to strengthen the business when it is finally started. Several examples of such semivoluntary delay have been cited in the book; it has been pointed out, for instance, that prospective retailers often work for years to secure a particular location before starting on their own. In other cases individuals with one type of know-how, such as technical training, have deliberately planned several years of business experience or training in management before launching their own enterprises. Usually the interval between deciding to enter business and starting the enterprise can be used profitably in planning, accumulating capital, and developing trade connections.

A long-range view of any type of business should include consideration of its probable status under changing conditions. Small business, in spite of ups and downs, has stood the test of operating under various economic conditions and is stronger today than ever before. The long-range future prospects seem bright, regardless of temporary setbacks that will probably appear from time to time.

IMPROVING THE OUTLOOK

That the future prospects of small business can be improved is implied in every effort to study the field, in every proposal to solve some of the problems of the little fellow, and in the growing recognition of the importance of this segment of our economy. Self-improvement is usually the most desirable. In general, the plan recommended in this book stresses self-improvement by present and prospective small businessmen as the surest road to future progress.

Self-improvement of the small, independent businessman is also the primary objective of two unique organizations which have come into existence in recent years. One is the National Council for Small Business Management Development, whose membership is composed of management educators, businessmen, and government executives interested in the development of research and educational programs for small business owners and managers. This group also publishes the only professional journal oriented exclusively to small business and the small businessman – the *Journal of Small Business Management.* The other is CIM-SAM (Council of Independent Managers, Society for the Advancement of Management), an association of independent businessmen whose primary objective is to educate themselves through a sharing of experiences and with the assistance of outside management specialists.

We have suggested that a potential business owner should first determine if he is better suited to being his own boss rather than someone else's employee. After selecting the kind of business to enter, he should determine the requisites for success in the chosen field and acquire as many as possible of the ones he lacks before actually starting the business. Questions of when to launch the business, where to locate, and how to formulate sound policies complete the "getting started" stage. Once safely launched, the new business can be reasonably sure of success if the modern management methods discussed throughout this book are applied.

No better concluding advice could be given to the small businessman, present or prospective, than to seek and use information available from his trade association, local banker, and other "outside staff."

SMALL BUSINESSES FOR OLDER PEOPLE

Looking toward the future should include some consideration of self-employment for people past their prime of life and those approaching the traditional retirement age of sixty-five. In 1970 we had over 20 million people sixty-five and older, or one out of ten, and five times as many as we had 50 years earlier. Life expectancy at sixty-five is double what is was a generation ago and is likely to continue increasing as more attention is devoted to the needs and problems of the older persons. But the earning years of employed people have been shortened because of longer periods of formal schooling, defense needs, and military obligations at the beginning of their careers, and earlier retirement. In addition, older employees often receive lower salaries and wages for some years before actual retirement. Thus the average employed person has a relatively short period to prepare for his retirement years through savings made on a regular and substantial basis. Also, long-range saving often is postponed until a family is raised.

Older men who are already self-employed have income security to a much greater extent than do employees, and their position is more flexible. They can delegate increasing responsibility or even sell the enterprise and start a smaller one better suited to their abilities and needs. Our primary concern, then, is for those who work for others. The long-range decline in the value of the dollar, the steady rise in our standard of living that makes correspondingly greater demands for larger consumer expenditures both before and after retirement, and the tendency to undervalue future benefits relative to more immediate ones all affect the position of a retired employee. A realistic calculation – of possible savings during the working years and anticipated expenditures during retirement – shows that few can adequately provide for their older years entirely from current savings.

Three general solutions to the problem of the older worker have been widely discussed: (1) increased employment of older men; (2) larger Social Security and other pension benefits;[1] and (3) directing energies, interests, and abilities of retired persons into community activities, hobbies, and other endeavors to keep them occupied as well as to give them a sense of usefulness, and possibly to provide society with some benefits.[2] The last would probably be of no help to the financial needs of retired people. Our aim now is to consider another alternative – namely, self-employment – suitable to older people.

A well-selected small business venture may easily mean the difference between happiness and despair, between longevity and premature death. But three points warrant major emphasis: (1) not all older people should attempt self-employment; (2) financial risks are more serious because of the irreplaceable nature of invested capital in the event of failure; and (3) advance planning and preparation are prerequisites to success.

Independent enterprisers may continue in business to suit their own convenience and conditions. In addition, the wide range of self-employment opportunities makes it possible to select one to suit almost any set of needs, and as his own boss the self-employed person can set his own pace. What he might be unable to do as a full-time dependent employee he can often do on his own. The fact that his major goals are moderate supplemental income, purposeful activity, and an increased feeling of security, rather than an ambition for large and increasing income, puts the older enterpriser in an entirely different category from younger ones.

A retired person with 20 to 40 years of successful employment behind him should seek to capitalize on his training and experience. A former executive in charge of some major function in big business, such as personnel, production, sales, or research might seek opportunities to make direct application of his experience in self-employment by applying his specific knowledge of business to a more general business situation. One formerly in charge of a branch plant, warehouse, or chain store may be able to shift to self-employment in the same or a closely related field.

Older people seeking self-employment opportunities often need counsel and advice more than do younger people. The latter are more likely to be better informed on the latest developments that open up opportunities for independent enterprisers. Records of the Small Business Administration show hundreds of cases in which consultation with older people contemplating self-employment has resulted in the discovery of small business opportunities which were more appropriate to their situations than were their original selections.

In general, the older person should follow recommended practices discussed throughout this text, but give special consideration to his peculiar needs and

---

[1] See p. 501 for a discussion of "Medicare" and the RSDI program.

[2] See p. 274 for a discussion of SCORE (Service Corps of Retired Executives).

interests because of his age, possible limitations not characteristic of younger men, his much broader background to draw upon, and the greater probability that if he fails he is less likely than a younger person to have a second chance.

SUMMARY AND CONCLUSIONS

Independent small businesses play an important role in the economy of America. The competition they provide, to each other and to big business, accounts for much of America's remarkable economic growth. A small business can respond more readily to changing conditions. It can experiment with new ideas. Opportunity for the energetic and dynamic entrepreneur is limited only by the limits he places on himself. Success brings economic and personal rewards which are his in full measure.

A growing recognition of the importance of small business to our economy, and a recognition of some of the problems which small businessmen face, is bringing increasing support for him from government, educational institutions, and large businesses.

An alternative to dependence or employment at low salaries for those over sixty-five is self-employment during the later years. Opportunities change continuously and vary according to the individual situation.

Challenging and interesting small business opportunities exist in foreign countries for the enterprising adventurer, as noted in the following chapter. Equally good opportunities exist in America for the person who is willing to prepare himself adequately, work hard, and apply initiative and good judgment to the task at hand. Hopefully, this book may assist him in this undertaking.

REVIEW QUESTIONS

1. Why have the authors concluded that the long-range trend in American industry has been favorable to small business?
2. How can the future prospects for small business be improved? Discuss some of the efforts that have been made in this direction.
3. Discuss self-employment as a possible solution to the problem of the older worker. Why is it likely that in the future more older people will go into business for themselves?

DISCUSSION QUESTIONS

1. What industries composed largely of small units today are most likely to be dominated by big businesses in the next few decades? Why do you think so?
2. What factors do you regard as significant in determining the role of small business in the future? Discuss.

SUPPLEMENTARY READINGS

Charlesworth, Harold K. "The Uncertain Future of Small Business: Can This Picture Be Changed?" *Business Topics,* Spring 1970, pp. 13-20. Analyzes past growth and forecasts future growth of small business, with particular emphasis on the number of old business discontinuances and new business starts.

Hollander, Edward D., et al. *The Future of Small Business.* New York: Frederick A. Praeger, 1967. This study, prepared by Robert R. Nathan Associates for the Small Business Administration, identifies the growth areas for small business in various sectors of the economy, and suggests that small businessmen can improve their chances for survival in these industries by entering into franchise arrangements.

"Small Business – A Look Ahead." *Small Business Reporter,* vol. 8, no. 1. San Francisco: Small Business Advisory Service, Bank of America, 1967. Presents the results of a national survey among those most knowledgeable about small business, concerning their thoughts and opinions about the future of small business.

U.S. Senate, Select Committee on Small Business. *Status and Future of Small Business.* Washington, D.C.: G.P.O., 1967. Report on hearings to review the present status of small business in the American economy, and to make reasonable projections for its future prospects

27

Small business international

A fortunate combination of circumstances makes the present a unique period in world history in opportunities and challenges for independent enterprise. For the first time the less developed countries of the free world believe they can improve their lot. Most of them are actively seeking to do so. But they need the managerial experience, technical know-how, and capital available only from the leading industrial countries, chiefly the United States.

The phenomenal rebuilding of Western Europe following World War II as a result of Marshall Plan technical and financial assistance is well known. Less well appreciated is the great contrast between these countries and the underdeveloped ones regarding education, training, and industrial experience. Also, many of the new and underdeveloped nations have had unpleasant experiences with colonialism and other forms of foreign intervention. They have seen the rapid industrialization of the Soviet Union under communism, and heard fantastic boasts of progress from Red China. The Communist-bloc countries are pursuing aggressive export policies. But the Soviets particularly have declared an economic war on the free world, as part of their "cold war" strategy, and there is evidence that they will go to any length to establish trade with the new, developing nations. Senator William Proxmire, for example, cites the personal experience that one small businessman related to him concerning a vicious price war that was being waged against American and Canadian exports. "[Their] products," he wrote the senator, "are of a superior quality and, I might add, of such a ridiculously low price level as to insure no competition whatsoever with certain products from the United States and Canada. It seems that they are willing to go to such measures as offering these same products at less than cost to attract business and start trade with these countries, so as to undermine trade with us." Few of these underdeveloped countries are in a position to appreciate the terrific social cost of these trade ventures. As Senator Proxmire has warned, "Communist economic assistance [directly, or through unfair foreign trade practices] comes with strings attached — economic dependence is the first step toward political takeover."[1]

[1] William Proxmire, *Can Small Business Survive?* (Chicago: Henry Regnery Co., 1964), pp. 171–72.

542

Private enterprise thus faces challenges as well as opportunities. In view of conditions such as these it is not surprising to find that in most other countries the government plays a more dominant role than in the United States, and that safeguards to protect nationals and natural resources are widespread. Although big business continues its participation in this free world struggle, there are many opportunities for small business to make its contribution within the framework of private enterprise.

At least three factors account for the growing importance of the international aspects of small business: (1) greater profit potentials; (2) the trend toward globalism; and (3) the cold war — especially its economic and related aspects. It is fitting that a comprehensive small business text give attention to this increasingly important interest in international business.

Scope and Emphasis

Small business international divides itself logically into two distinct areas: (1) international marketing — both importing and exporting; and (2) establishing a business in a foreign country. A common problem in each of these areas of international business is that of foreign exchange or a country's balance of payments.

Within a huge monetary area such as the United States, this problem has not been present in recent times. But international business — both trade and entrepreneurship — even when the United States is one of the parties involved, has in post-World War II years had to contend with this problem of the availability of foreign exchange to carry out the project. Thus a U.S. importer from Pakistan, Italy, Japan, or France should have no difficulty in making payment, because dollar exchange is in short supply throughout the world, but a U.S. exporter to any of these and all other countries would be limited by the respective importer's ability to obtain dollar exchange.

In establishing a business in a foreign country it is also the shortage of dollar exchange that plays a dominant role. For a foreigner to launch a business in the United States it is primarily a problem of converting his local money into dollars. For almost all other countries of the world it is also the impact of the proposed venture on the host country's balance of payments. Thus an American with sufficient capital to establish a business in some foreign country, even if he has the nonfinancial requirements, and even if the country stands to gain by the proposed venture, must still contend with certain aspects of the country's foreign exchange situation. These are mainly two: (1) the need to import equipment, materials, and supplies from countries where foreign exchange is in short supply; and (2) the ability of the proposed enterprise to generate, through exports, foreign exchange needed or desired by the host country.

Our emphasis on foreign exchange difficulties as an introduction to our subject has been deliberate because it is a universal problem of international business, but one not too familiar to Americans. Also, by stressing this problem at the beginning we may avoid repetition in later discussion. We have also assumed familiarity with terms commonly used in international business for the sake of space economy. Selected references cited at the end of this chapter should be consulted by readers who need the basic foundation of terms, principles, and practices of international business.

INTERNATIONAL MARKETING

Increasingly, the marketplace is becoming worldwide. One reason for this, obviously, is the rapid development of instantaneous communications. Another, more important reason is the breakdown in national tariff barriers and the development of multinational trading areas, such as the European Common Market and the Latin American Free Trade Zone. These developments are of utmost importance to the small businessman engaging in either importing or exporting activities.

Importing

Many small businessmen import products for domestic distribution. These include automobiles; electrical, electronic, and other mechanical articles; wearing apparel of either distinctive design or economy appeal; gifts, novelties, and other impulse items; foods; and others. A few small producers import some of their raw materials or parts. Although many of these goods are purchased from importers or wholesalers, other methods are common. Some retailers have friends abroad with whom they deal directly. Many make initial contact with foreign vendors through responding to international advertising either in mass media or direct mail. Others buy from foreign representatives present at trade fairs or exhibits. And some are solicited by foreign producers seeking distribution in different countries. The last is common where franchised dealers merchandise and service products such as automobiles and sewing machines.

A small businessman importing direct may engage a customs broker and freight forwarder to handle technical details and expedite the shipment. Governmental agencies, such as the Bureau of International Commerce and the Small Business Administration — as well as trade associations, many banks, and others — can also assist the importer. International marketing is often complex and should not be undertaken lightly by the uninformed or inexperienced.

Exporting

A small business engaged in exporting is likely to be a manufacturer or other producer. There are several avenues of distribution available to him. He may (1) set up his own export department, including foreign distributorships; (2) license (franchise) the manufacture of his product to a foreign producer; (3) employ export agents or commission houses; or (4) sell to export firms. The latter two methods of distribution are usually the simplest and most feasible for most small firms. Export *agencies* assume responsibility for proper packaging, insurance, marking, and meeting all legal requirements; arranging transportation and credit; billing; and collecting payments on invoices. Export *firms*, on the other hand, buy outright the products of domestic producers and then resell them in foreign markets; thus they assume all the risks as well as the "headaches" associated with foreign trade. These are topics covered adequately in standard references on foreign trade and need not be elaborated on here. One topic, however, warrants special comment: merchandising to the foreign market.

As used here, "merchandising" refers to adapting the product to each market – with regard to their functional design primarily, and to some extent to their packaging, trademarks, and other symbols, and even their coloration. In many countries, for example, the people have beliefs and preferences regarding certain colors and symbols. Important ones are known to the authorities on each country. Through inquiries they can be ascertained. Other features of the product may be less obvious but should be determined before foreign marketing is undertaken.

While it would be an endless task to detail all features about every product for all countries, a few suggestions as to what to investigate are in order. If some seem obvious, it is well to remember that the obvious often accounts for failures in foreign marketing.

For mechanical and electrical goods, sources and kinds of power available are important: American 110-volt electrical goods are unsuited to countries where 220-volt current is standard. Electrically powered products may be unsuited to regions where electric current is not available, too expensive, or unreliable. Gasoline-powered products may be unsuited in areas where gasoline is very difficult to obtain or too expensive.

Availability of repair and maintenance service as well as of repair parts and supplies are important for most mechanical products. If proper installation and instructions on use and care are relevant, they should be provided. In many countries potential customers may not be able to read or understand even simple printed instructions. Tools required for repair and maintenance may not be available. What we take for granted in industrialized countries may be nonexistent elsewhere. Even many industrialized countries have not yet adopted international standards for such common necessities as bolts, nuts, and screws.

The nature of user or consumer may be important. Does the foreign consumer have the strength, intelligence, or adaptability to use the product? Will normal hazards be recognized or cautions observed? Will beliefs or even prejudices prevent or hamper proper use? Wide differences in beliefs, superstitions, and prejudices exist in many parts of the world. Although these may at times seem silly to an exporter, and actually run counter to well-founded scientific knowledge, he cannot safely disregard them. Similar conditions still exist in many technically advanced nations, not excluding the United States.

For satisfactory consumer use certain products depend upon local factors such as character of the water supply, climate, and temperature. At one time European furniture was found to be unable to survive overheated stuffy American apartments. Pumps and other products may function efficiently with soft water, but poorly with hard water, and hardly at all with sea or heavily saline water. Additional conditions that may hamper a product's proper functioning include: humidity, sand, dust or other air pollution, excessive temperatures, terrain, and many others. Relevant ones for each product should be investigated.

The postwar economic revival of West Germany and Japan, as well as the growth of the European Common Market, has provided considerable competitive pressure on American producers in foreign trade, and in recent years the United States has been suffering chronic balance-of-payments difficulties. To encourage the export of American-made goods to these and other areas of the world, Congress in 1962 passed the Trade Expansion Act, giving the president authority to lower U.S. tariffs as much as 50 percent on most goods in return for similar trade concessions from other countries. The result has been a significant increase in foreign-trade potential for American producers, both large and small.

For the small manufacturer interested in exporting his product, the federal government provides assistance in numerous ways, primarily by means of (1) various publications and programs relating to international marketing, (2) the export financing programs of the Export-Import Bank, and (3) cooperation with private insurers in offering credit insurance to exporters.

Government foreign-trade publications.   Among the periodicals and other publications of the federal government that are related to international marketing is the monthly *Foreign Trade Report* prepared by the Bureau of the Census. These reports provide statistics, on a country-by-country basis, on the amounts and kinds of goods purchased from American firms. Other publications are available from the Bureau of International Commerce, as follows:

1. *Commerce Today* — a bi-weekly devoted in part to developments in world trade, changes in trade regulations, and trade opportunities
2. *Overseas Business Reports* (by country) — analysis of trading regulations in a particular country (as well as information about starting a business in that country), published annually for more than 100 countries
3. *Trade Lists* (by country) —listing names and addresses of principal manufacturers, wholesalers, and distributors' agents, by commodity groups
4. *World Trade Directory Reports* — providing credit information on specific foreign customers
5. Series of pamphlets on preparing shipments to specific countries — summarizing import regulations, rules for labeling and marking, and customs procedures

Also available from the Bureau of International Commerce, for those small businesses wishing to enter world markets for the first time, is an excellent handbook, *Exporting: How to Get Started.*

Government foreign-trade programs.   The federal government, through the Bureau of International Commerce, assists the small exporter in a number of other ways, by

1. maintaining the *American International Traders Index* — an automated file of information on American firms that are active in, or interested in, international trade (or investment); commercial officers in American embassies and consulates refer to this index when answering inquiries from prospective foreign purchasers, and small firms seeking to find overseas buyers for their products should request to be registered on this index;
2. maintaining the *Agency Index* — an auxiliary service for American firms that already have agents abroad; State Department commercial officers refer to this Index to find local sources of American products for interested overseas customers;
3. assisting American firms in finding overseas agents to handle their products in a specific country; such *trade contact surveys* cost $50 each;
4. Organizing or sponsoring overseas *trade missions* and *trade fairs;*

5. maintaining permanent *trade centers* in Milan, Stockholm, Tokyo, Paris, Sydney, London, and other central marketing areas where the sales potential for American products is high (smaller, regional trade centers have also been established in Bangkok and Buenos Aires); the American exhibitor pays a nominal fee for space occupied at these trade centers; and

6. sponsoring a *"Piggyback"* program for those firms desiring to export on a cooperative basis.

The Export-Import Bank.   The Export-Import Bank of the United States, familiarly known as *Eximbank,* is actively engaged in financing American foreign trade. Recognizing that credit availability is as important a competitive tool as price, quality, or service, Eximbank is determined that no American exporter will lose a sale for lack of credit, if the sale is sound. If credit facilities for American exporters are at least as good as those made available to exporters in other countries by their governments, then they are free to compete in world markets solely on the basis of their products, their prices, their salesmanship, and their service. To this end Eximbank offers 12 different export financing programs, as follows:[2]

1. Making direct or participation loans to borrowers outside the United States for purchases of American goods and services.

2. Guaranteeing loans made by American financial institutions to purchasers in other countries of American goods and services.

3. Guaranteeing loans made by financial institutions outside the United States to importers of American goods and services.

4. Assisting exporters in obtaining local cost financing. Increasingly, American suppliers are being required to meet foreign competition by providing financing for a portion of the local costs as well as the costs associated with major projects overseas. "Local costs" are those expenses incurred by the buyer of American goods and services for the purchase in his own country of goods and services associated with the transaction, such as engineering services, public utility connections, locally available construction materials, labor, and equipment installation.

5. Drafting preliminary commitments outlining the terms and conditions of the financial assistance it would extend to purchasers of American goods and services. This program is particularly useful to exporters when submitting proposals in response to bid invitations requiring plans for financing. Preliminary commitments are issued by Eximbank without charge and in no way obligates the American exporter.

6. Extending lines of credit (or relending credits) to foreign financial institutions. On the basis of these direct lines of credit, a bank or other financial institution in another country can make subloans, or "relends," to importers for financing purchases of American goods and services.

7. Financing small importers of American goods and services jointly with selected foreign financial institutions. This program is intended principally for use in financing those transactions requiring repayment terms of one to five years.

[2] Summarized from the third edition of the Eximbank brochure, *U. S. Export Financing Programs* (Dec. 1970). For detailed information concerning any of these programs and how to apply for loans and financial guarantees, write to Export-Import Bank of the U.S., 811 Vermont Ave. NW, Washington, D.C. 20571.

8. Lending to U.S. commercial banks up to 100 percent of the bank's export-debt obligations. In addition to such loans, Eximbank may purchase (discount), on a case-by-case basis, the underlying export-debt obligation.

9. Guaranteeing repayment of export-debt obligations acquired by U.S. banking institutions from American exporters. It is becoming increasingly essential for American exporters to grant appropriate credit terms on their sales in world markets in order to meet the financing offered by their foreign competitors. Thus the purpose of this program is to encourage and assist greater participation by commercial banks in the support of American exporters who must provide credit terms on their sales.

10. Guaranteeing payment of a lessee under contract to a lessor of U.S. equipment outside the United States.

11. Financing the costs involved in the preparation, by American engineering firms, of planning and feasibility studies for their foreign clients on large capital projects. Historically, the export sale of goods and services has generally followed the nationality of the feasibility-study contractor. By assisting American engineering firms to obtain foreign client-sponsored studies, it is anticipated that an increased number of design and construction contracts for large projects will be signed with American firms.

12. Providing political risks–guarantee coverage on American equipment used by American contractors in their performance on contracts abroad. The program covers uncompensated losses occurring as a result of war, rebellion, revolution, insurrection, or civil commotion; and requisition, expropriation, or confiscation of the equipment by a governmental authority.

Export credit insurance. Eximbank also cooperates with the Foreign Credit Insurance Association in offering export credit insurance to American exporters. The Foreign Credit Insurance Association (FCIA) is a consortium of 50 stock and mutual insurance companies. Backed by the resources and experience of its member companies, as well as the resources of Eximbank, FCIA endeavors to match competitive terms quoted by foreign suppliers who have long operated under their government-supported insurance and financing programs. Not only is a policyholder insured against loss resulting from failure of its buyers to pay for commercial or political reasons, but also he is normally able to arrange favorable financing of export receivables because of the security and collateral afforded by the insurance.

Several types of FCIA credit insurance policies are available to exporters, including a "Small Business Policy." For businesses which are newcomers in export trade and for exporters having modest sales volume, this policy provides comprehensive coverage up to 90 percent for short- and medium-term sales. Eligibility is limited to businesses with average annual export sales over the preceding three years of not more than $200,000. The policy may remain in force for a period not to exceed two years or until the exporter has insured $500,000 aggregate contract value of exports, whichever occurs first. A deductible clause may be required, and the exporter may request the FCIA insurer to obtain data to show the creditworthiness of buyers in lieu of obtaining this information from his own sources.[3]

---

[3] For premium rates and for further information concerning this small business export credit insurance policy, write to the FCIA home office, 250 Broadway, New York, N.Y. 10007, or to one of its regional offices located in Chicago, Cleveland, Houston, Los Angeles, and San Francisco.

ESTABLISHING SMALL BUSINESSES IN FOREIGN COUNTRIES

In recent years there have been increasing opportunities for American enterprisers to establish small businesses in foreign countries. In some cases, particularly in the underdeveloped or nonindustrialized areas, special inducements are offered the foreign investor, such as tax exemption, provision of land and buildings, and government loans on favorable terms. Among the "overseas business reports" ("OBR") published by the U.S. Bureau of International Commerce, previously mentioned, are those providing information on the establishment of businesses in 41 different countries, as follows:[4]

Argentina	France	Kuwait	Pakistan
Australia	West Germany	Lebanon	Singapore
Austria	Ghana	Liberia	Republic of South Africa
Denmark	Greece	Libya	Spain
East Africa	Hong Kong	Luxembourg	Switzerland
(Kenya,	India	Mexico	Taiwan
Uganda, and	Iran	Morocco	Thailand
Tanzania)	Israel	Netherlands	Turkey
Ethiopia	Ivory Coast	New Zealand	United Kingdom
Finland	Japan	Nigeria	Venezuela
		Norway	Zambia

Each of the above OBR provides the basic information needed by anyone contemplating the establishment of a business in that particular country, including the government's expansion policy as well as its business regulations and tax laws. The following is a typical "table of contents" which provides an overall perspective of these publications:

Government Policy on Investment
Regulations, Laws, Development Plans — Government Monopolies and Businesses — Foreign Ownership of a Business Entity — Foreign Ownership of Real Property — Expropriation

Entry and Repatriation of Capital
Screening Procedure and Criteria — Exchange Controls — Industrial Investment Guaranties

Trade Factors
Tariff and Trade Concessions — Advantages of Location in [name of country]

Business Organization
Types of Business Organization — Laws and Regulations Governing Business Enterprises — Organization of Foreign Firms — Organization Costs — Patent Licensing — Accounting and Correspondence

Regulations Affecting Employment
Employment of Aliens — Labor Legislation — Social Insurance Legislation

Taxation
Income Taxes — Real Estate Taxes — Stamp Taxes

Tax Agreement with United States

[4] Single copies of the report for any of the countries listed may be obtained for 15 cents from the Superintendent of Documents, U.S. Government Printing Office, Washington, D.C. 20402.

There are many reasons why a person may want to establish a business in a foreign country — for some they are personal reasons, for others economic, and for yet others they are social, humanitarian, or political motives. Some reasons are based on first-hand experience, such as travel or temporary residence abroad. Others may be founded on reading or hearsay. First-hand experience offers the best basis, but it should be supported by sound background knowledge.

Personal reasons for going into business in a foreign country include liking its climate, scenery, and the tempo or pattern of living of its residents. Many ex-servicemen and other Americans have returned from France, Germany, Italy, Japan, or some country in Latin America with such a liking for the place and people that they want to return to live there. If they are the "own business" type, establishing their own enterprise is a "natural." In most countries it is also easier than securing dependent employment.

Sometimes, also, a person's occupation may be crowded at home but in strong demand abroad. Many skilled technicians from Germany, France, Great Britain, and Switzerland, for example, have opened successful businesses in the United States and other countries. A man may believe in some idea or innovation that would be difficult to make the basis for an enterprise at home but very welcome in other countries.

Similarly, a desire to escape onerous conditions in one country has caused many people to emigrate and establish a business in the host country. Forces causing such migrations may be religious and racial discrimination or other forms of oppression. Mass migrations in world history are familiar examples: displaced persons and those escaping from Communist-dominated countries, for example.

Social, huminatarian, and political motives have also accounted for an unknown, but appreciable, number of enterprises established abroad. Social and humanitarian reasons appear most often in fields associated with health and medical care. They may or may not be partially subsidized. Political reasons are likely to be prompted by espionage and world-conquest ambitions of the two giant Communist countries. Our concern is less with these groups than with traditional private-enterprise ventures.

Economic reasons account for most big business operations abroad, often in spite of some difficulties. Since an increasing number of large corporations in the leading industrial nations have been expanding their foreign operations in recent years, they must have faith in the profit prospects. In many cases it may be the only feasible way to be competitive in promising markets protected by tariffs and similar barriers. This has been true of companies opening branch plants in one of the European Common Market countries, and to some extent elsewhere. For most prospective small businessmen the decision will involve starting with a single establishment in a foreign country rather than opening a branch, although the latter is possible. When a branch, franchise, or royalty agreement is under consideration, the possibility of taking profits or fees out of the country needs careful study. Whereas Mexico and a few other countries do not at present restrict such movements, most countries do. Thus investment may be for the distant future. While the enterprise may be profitable and expanded from profits, it may be years before any money can be withdrawn. In the typical case, however, the entrepreneur plans to live in the country and to operate the business himself, and therefore will have little need to withdraw funds from the country.

Faith in the growth prospects of a country is another reason for establishing a business there. An enterpriser with managerial ability, experience, and capital may also anticipate a greater excess of profit over his living expenses than he could at home. This tends to be true because of higher profits and lower living costs in many foreign countries. Sometimes a favorable exchange rate may give the prospective enterpriser greater purchasing power for his capital when it is transferred abroad. In addition, a business may be launched successfully with less capital in some countries than in others. Sometimes special financial incentives are offered, such as tax exemption, provision of land and buildings, or government loans on favorable terms. This seems to have been partly responsible for the phenomenal industrial expansion in Puerto Rico in recent years. Some men with military pensions or other continuing incomes from U. S. sources believe they can supplement these payments with a business in a foreign country of their liking better than they could at home.

Another economic reason is to process some local raw material for the domestic market, or possibly to cushion the wide price fluctuations characteristic of the world market for many raw materials. Underdeveloped countries often export raw material and import products made from them.

A foreign branch of a large American company sometimes needs parts or services they experience difficulty in securing. Either foreign exchange is not available for importing or local sources are unsatisfactory. A competent person from an industrialized country willing to establish a local business may be the answer. For the enterpriser, having an established demand may give him an assured start for a business that may later be expanded. Some countries permit this only when the authorities are convinced that nationals cannot furnish the materials or services needed. On the other hand, in most countries where such a situation is likely to develop, the host country welcomes the establishment of a new business, but may require that nationals be employed in positions below the management level.

Taxes, especially avoidance of double taxation, may also be an important consideration in establishing a business abroad when the enterpriser does not plan to seek naturalization. The United States has concluded treaties on this point with many countries, and others are in progress.

It is well to remember that in establishing a business abroad the entrepreneur becomes the foreigner. He must abide by the laws of the host country and generally conform to local customs. In some countries, such as Argentina, aliens may own land. In others, such as Mexico, land ownership is restricted to nationals. However, in many cases foreigners are permitted to own land and buildings if they agree to act as nationals and not to invoke their native government in case of disputes. Complete naturalization is the extreme, although not unusual. In many countries, such as West Germany, nationals and aliens have the same legal rights and privileges.

Mexico and several other countries reserve certain rights for the federal or provincial governments. These usually include the nationalization of transportation, mass communications, extraction of petroleum, and sometimes electric power. Under license such countries frequently permit exploration for oil deposits.

Except in these restricted fields most countries permit alien ownership or top management, but tend to emphasize employment of nationals at lower levels, especially in nonindustrialized countries, where underemployment tends to be high. A common provision is that no alien may be employed if local talent is available. Industrial countries vary in this respect — from West Germany with no restrictions, to Japan with some. For underdeveloped countries a major reason for welcoming businesses established by aliens may be as much to provide employment for nationals as it is to develop foreign exchange and promote a country's industrialization. Competent managerial ability among nationals is scarce or nonexistent.

Labor laws in many countries, especially in Latin America and some Asiatic countries, tend to stress continuity or employment. Mexico requires dismissal compensation of three months' pay plus 20 days for each year of employment. In some countries it is almost impossible to dismiss an employee for any cause after ten years of employment. Even when dismissal is legally allowed, local disapproval may cause a company to prefer to lose business during periods of peak demand rather than to add temporary employees; such is often the case in Japan and other Asiatic countries.

One aspect of the labor provisions in many of the lesser developed countries requires the employer to provide suitable housing for his employees if the plant is located away from population centers.

In the majority of countries permission must be secured before a business is established. Important considerations in granting such permission are (1) the contribution the alien business is expected to make to the economy in terms of local employment; (2) its appropriateness to the country's expansion goals; and (3) its effects on the country's foreign exchange. Most countries welcome a *new* industry if it does not impose a burden on their foreign exchange or threaten to deplete scarce natural resources. Some governments have published lists of desired industries; such lists are available from the Bureau of International Commerce.

SUMMARY AND CONCLUSIONS

A small businessman may be interested in the international aspects of business for one or both of two reasons: (1) He may be engaged in foreign trade — as an importer, an exporter, or both; or (2) he may want to establish a business in a foreign country. In either case he is most likely to be a manufacturer or other producer, and valuable government assistance is available to him. The financing programs of the U.S. Export-Import Bank and the publications and programs of the Bureau of International Commerce are particularly helpful to those small businessmen who wish to export their products and services. Export credit insurance is also readily available.

Though the establishment of a business in a foreign country is becoming increasingly attractive in terms of the prospective rate of return on investment, it may be undesirable from other points of view. For example, most countries restrict the outflow of profits and other funds. In nonindustrialized countries under-employment tends to be high, and great stress is placed on the employment of nationals. In some countries, such as Argentina, aliens may own land. In others, such as Mexico, land ownership is restricted to nationals. However, in many cases foreigners are permitted to own land and buildings if they agree to act as nationals and not to invoke their native government in case of disputes. The overseas business reports (OBR) referred to in this chapter are an invaluable source of information for those who contemplate establishing a small business in a foreign country.

REVIEW QUESTIONS

1. Why is government control over business greater in most countries than in the United States?
2. What are the two distinct areas of international business discussed in this chapter?
3. Why is foreign exchange a problem when an alien wishes to launch a business?
4. When is a small businessman most likely to import products? How may he go about it?
5. What methods of distribution are available to the small businessman who wishes to export his products? Discuss.
6. What are some of the factors a small businessman should take into consideration in merchandising for foreign consumption? Discuss.
7. In what ways does the federal government provide assistance to the small manufacturer who wishes to engage in export trade? Discuss the financing programs of Eximbank, and the variety of foreign-trade publications and programs of the Bureau of International Commerce.
8. What is the Foreign Credit Insurance Association? For what purpose was it formed? Discuss.
9. What are some of the reasons why a small businessman may wish to establish a business in a foreign country? What are some of the advantages that might accrue?

DISCUSSION QUESTIONS

1. During his military stint abroad Bob spent considerable time in Spain and acquired a mastery of spoken and written Spanish. He has $15,000 which he would like to use to start a business in Venezuela because he has heard of its potential for expansion and its beautiful scenery. What would you advise him to do and why?
2. Secure the latest OBR for one of the countries listed on page 549. On the basis of the information contained in this report, relate how you would go about establishing a business in that country.

SUPPLEMENTARY READINGS

Dichter, Ernest. "The World Customer." *Harvard Business Review* 40 (July-August 1962): 113–22. Emphasizing the importance of understanding the culture and psychology of customers in foreign lands, the author discusses ways to study the characteristics of the market.

International Marketing Institute. *Export Marketing for Smaller Firms.* 2nd ed. Washington, D.C.: Small Business Administration, 1966. Sets forth a practical, low-cost, self-administered system of market research to enable small business concerns to determine appropriate means for entry into, or expansion of, export operations.

McDonald, John G. "Minimizing the Risks of Moving Abroad." *Business Horizons* 4 (Spring 1961): 87–94. Discusses in detail the reasons why companies establish businesses in foreign countries, and the problems that face them.

PART FIVE
Short Cases

Arthur Adams—Owner or Renter?

Arthur Adams rents an entire building for $350 per month. His dry cleaning and laundry service occupies the first floor, but he sublets the second floor to a real estate broker who pays him $150 a month. The owner of the building has just approached Mr. Adams, offering him the building for $45,000. Mr. Adams can borrow $35,000 at 7 percent from the bank, and can spare $10,000 from the business if he needs it.

The building is in a good location, in fair condition. The area is at a standstill economically, but is not declining. The income level of the area is actually increasing, and much new building, both residential and commercial, is expected by city planners. Taxes on the property are $780 per year, insurance $400. Upkeep should cost about $1,500–$2,000 per year, Arthur believes. In a year or so, he had planned to ask the owner for considerable renovation, which would of course increase the rent.

Arthur is forty-five years of age and has a son in high school who, when he is graduated from college, expects to enter the business with his father. In the meantime, Arthur is considering the establishment of branch units of his business, one to the northeast, the other in the southern part of the city. This, too, will take money. Hence, the question of whether he should continue to rent or should buy this building is related to other plans.

If Arthur Adams should buy the building, what would his annual costs be? Should he buy it or continue renting? Can you draw up a recommendation addressed to him, explaining your viewpoint and reasoning?

Bonny's Bon Bons

While Bernice Brevoort, widow and former school teacher, was ill one spring and needed some added income, she remembered an unusual candy her mother used to make. After locating the recipe and experimenting a few times, she packaged some and took it to a friend's gift shop. It became very popular, and eventually she took over a section of the shop for her candy business. Later she arranged to sell it on consignment through other friends in various spots and after a few errors developed seven dependable outlets. Selling on consignment permitted her to replace older stock.

Her candy was high-priced, but was of exceptional quality and came in a variety of appealing flavors. She called her package "Bonny's Bon Bon Assortment" originally, but later put it out in smaller packages of single flavors. In the meantime her manufacturing and sales facilities had required considerable expansion. Yet she was making money at an increasing rate.

One day the president of the largest local department store asked her if she would mind coming to see him; so, in a few days she did so. He surprised her by suggesting that her candy was good enough to carry the store name, and that he was willing to place a substantial order under those conditions. This order was several times the monthly sales of any of her outlets, and almost as much as her total sales had been until recently. But the payment offered per pound was considerably lower than she was being paid by her "retailers" at this point. However, the order would not be on consignment.

About this same time a drugstore chain, locally represented but with its main offices elsewhere, sent a representative to see Bernice. He complimented her on her success, then said he was authorized to place an order for a year's supply at about the same price and amount per month as the department store offer. In this case, however, the "Bonny's Bon Bons" label was to remain; when questioned, the representative indicated that it would be sold in the drugstores often as a "special," at a price considerably lower than Bernice's other outlets had been getting.

Bernice is now considerably upset and confused, but nevertheless excited. Jokingly, she says, "All I can expect now is to be asked into a conglomerate." Yet it is satisfying and challenging to be so in demand. Her health is now excellent, and she is only approaching "middle age," so could operate the business whichever way she decides. However, she has some misgivings about making any move that would cause her to depart from the pattern which has become so successful thus far.

How would you approach a solution of the problem facing Bernice Brevoort? What factors and people are involved in each decision, and what situations might arise, favorable and unfavorable, as a result? Assume prices and amounts, based on conversations with stores, if it will help to make the problem clearer.

Credit Where Due

In the past five years, John Spangler's old "crossroads store" at Cox Corners, now under the operation of his son David, has become an important auto service center. The Spanglers sell the gasoline and oils of a small regional oil company. In addition to oil, fuel, tires, and batteries, they now install mufflers, brakes, and other replacement parts. Despite discount-house tire and major oil-company competition, their business grows because of their location, their reputation, and their low prices.

Most of the business has been on a cash basis, except for their local oil company's credit-card trade.

Currently, transient customers and those who buy gas and oil elsewhere are increasingly requesting credit. The transient customers, particularly, now present BankAmericard, Master Charge, American Express, and even major oil-company cards for credit. These visitors insist that many such businesses across the country honor almost any such cards. David Spangler and his father are concerned with this development. They are anxious to expand their businesses in any way possible, hoping to add a motel-restaurant eventually. Friends suggest that they take on another line of gasoline. However, the brand is locally very well known and is responsible for some of their best trade; more than that, the oil company owns the land on which their business is located. They have a lease for the next 18 years, but the oil company also owns a plot almost next door. The mutual but unwritten agreement between the two parties, who are old friends, is that the Spanglers will handle this line alone and that the oil company will not permit a competitor nearby. Yet the problem of credit remains, if the Spanglers are to achieve their full potential.

Here is a firm which wants to extend credit along modern lines. The older Spangler suggests simply that they extend their own line of credit. David replies that this would serve local people only, and would involve difficult clerical work. The father then suggests American Express. Only recently, also, the local bank approached them about Master Charge. At the moment they are puzzled and a little confused.

What would you do? Any bank will be willing to provide the student with factual data on most such arrangements.

The Fairview Grocery

Joe and Mary Farran, aged thirty-six and thirty-three respectively, have two children, a boy eight and a girl five. They live in a city of 45,000. Both are employed — Joe as an assistant bank cashier, Mary as secretary in a high school. Their combined income totals $12,500 per year. When not in school, the children are cared for by Mary's father (a retired teacher) and mother, who live nearby. Mary takes over this responsibility during her vacations. Joe's father (a retired railroad man) and mother live in another part of the state.

Through his banking connections, Joe has learned that a successful neighborhood grocery (Fairview Food Store) is for sale in his neighborhood, an older, established part of town having a high income level. The business has long been operated by the same owner and his wife, who are now retiring and will leave the area. They own the building, and are willing to rent it at a rate which seems reasonable as compared with downtown rentals.

The store did a total business of $110,000 last year, and net profits have averaged 9.5 percent of sales. The merchandise inventory, appraised at $15,000, appears to be fresh stock. Fixtures, old but acceptable, are appraised at $6,500. Outstanding customer credit accounts total about $5,000. Other expenses will include licenses, insurance, equipment, utilities, maintenance items, etc., in standard proportions.

Joe and Mary, according to their estimates, will need about $20,000 to get title to the inventory and equipment and to use as "starting expenses" for such items as advance rent, insurance, advertising costs, and credit extension. Personnel expenses have been limited by the present owner to an older man who is also caretaker and provides emergency delivery and stock pickup services. A high school student sometimes helps on Saturdays.

With this information, review the personal factors involved (for this discussion, ignore the business operations aspects of the decision):

1. Who are the people involved in the decision, and why are they involved?
2. What further information would you want about each? What would be desirable? What would be undesirable?

3. In summary, what must Joe and Mary be assured of in order to make a decision to take over this business?

Frankelson's Franchise

Morton Frankelson, a recent college graduate, has considered various career opportunities, but as yet has found nothing really challenging. Employed in a service station for two years after high school, after three years in the service he went to one of the state universities where he got his degree in business and economics. He is now married, has no children, and no great preference as to where he lives. He has a few thousand dollars saved, and his wife is an experienced medical technician.

Right now he is faced with what he considers an important decision. Two franchising opportunities and a chance to purchase a going firm face him. One is a new coin-operated laundry and dry cleaning business, location to be selected. The other is an old, established, well-known gift shop chain. The former is novel in many respects, the founder having left a franchising chain in order to have more freedom of action with his own ideas. The gift shop people, who have long specialized in hotel and motel lobby locations, are slowly but steadily growing. A third possibility exists at the service station of his former employer, who wants a partner to help him with the growing business. Mort has been approached on this.

The coin-machine operation requires the least investment. Desirable locations at low rents appear to be available in almost any well-populated neighborhood. Equipment is readily financed or leased by its manufacturers, supplies are inexpensive, and a direct original investment of only $5,000 is required. The representative apparently has the right connections, and will follow the contract pattern of his former employers. The gift shop chain is a little more difficult to negotiate. They have rigid requirements for their franchises, and Mort knows they are "checking him out." Both franchisors cite the records of past franchises, both promise management assistance.

The coin-machine man promises promotional aids, as well as regular counseling on the operation.

The gift shop representative offers little promotional aid, but will give assistance in finding a location and insists on selecting merchandise to be sold — at least at the start. Mort has visited some of these shops, and finds their business depends largely on traffic flow and merchandise appeal. This investment would take most of his savings, for he must take title to the inventory and pay two months rent in advance. Both franchisors collect a percentage of sales as royalty and both provide counseling and supervision. Both offer the opportunity to open added shops as they prove themselves capable. Both place restrictions on the franchisee's opening a similar business in the same location should the contract be terminated. All parties seem to be urging Mort to make a decision, and he wants to get started as soon as possible.

What aspects of these opportunities must Mort consider before deciding? What are the most important, and how would you rate them? What suggestions have you as to a step-by-step procedure for Mort to follow?

✓ Gambling in the Snow?

Alfred Cummins and Roy Page have operated a farm supply store near Green Creek for several years. They are experienced businessmen, both in their early thirties. Al is a born mechanic, and Roy an excellent manager. Both have many friends in the rural area around Green Creek. Their business consists of stock feed and farm seeds, hand garden tools, and more recently a line of powered garden equipment such as tractors and mowers. In connection with the last line they have an increasingly busy repair shop. They also rent garden equipment to the public.

A new development has taken place recently. Green Creek is in a semi-mountainous area, with enough snow in winter to encourage skiers. In fact, a ski run is being set up almost next door to their business and will no doubt attract skiers from major cities nearby. The owners of the run are friends and neighbors of Cummins and Page, and have suggested that the men contract to operate the ski lift and to rent snowmobiles to the public – in other words, to handle these mechanical aspects of the lift's operation. The wooded 80-acre area adjacent to the ski lift is large enough to permit snowmobile use.

The two men are fascinated by the whole idea. It should be a profitable and exciting year-round business. At a bridge party the other night, however, a neighbor, a lawyer who works in the city nearby, asked Al, "How much more insurance would that call for?" Al answered, "We already have standard liability insurance for the store and shop – what else would we need?" The lawyer replied, "You may have enough, or you may have been very lucky up till now – better check into it."

Check into it. List the kinds of insurance that might be required. Any casualty insurance man will be happy to help the student.

✓ Good Business: Ethics or Expediency?

Mrs. Helen Sparks, retired teacher, active in one of the local church organizations, came to Alliance Appliances, Inc., seeking a used dishwasher for use in one of the interchurch centers. This center was interdenominational and offered teenagers and other groups a place to gather for social affairs. Cooking and serving and most of the maintenance work was done by teams of volunteers from the different churches, at times assigned to them and for which they were responsible. Equipment was owned jointly by the churches. Mrs. Sparks had recommended trying a dishwashing unit and had authority to buy – but to pay no more than $100 for the appliance, installed. She hoped to find a good used one, and had bought other appliances in this store. She was approached by Jay Russell, a salesman.

Jay Russell's employer, Ray Dawson, was out of town when Mrs. Sparks came in. Jay's first thought was of a large dishwasher that had been taken in trade over a year ago, but which they had been unable to sell because it was so large and because it was a very old model. Yet despite its age it looked good, for it had not been mistreated in use. It would probably serve Mrs. Sparks's purpose. The major problem, if it did break down, would be finding replacement parts. Jay felt that if used with care, it should last two years at least.

As they discussed the group's need, the amount of money available, and the machine, Jay explained that it was of a good brand name, "a good big unit" that had been carefully used, and that it should last "a long time" if used with care. He did not say how old it was, but did give the name of the well-to-do family who had owned it. As Jay was about to close the sale, Mrs. Sparks said, "Well, I think I'll take it, but would you mind waiting until tomorrow, when Mr. Dawson comes back, so that I can talk with him?" Jay agreed to this and Mrs. Sparks left the store.

The next morning, when Mr. Dawson did return, Jay's first remark was, "Well, I think I sold the old Crescent unit at last. Some woman came in, wanted a cheap machine for some church group. Mrs. Sparks, of Maple Street, she said."

Mr. Dawson was greatly dismayed, although he did not say anything to Jay. He was worried about the possible consequences of selling this particular unit to this particular group. Mrs. Sparks, whom he knew rather well, would not return again until after lunch. In the meantime, he must decide how to handle the situation.

What worries might Mr. Dawson have in this situation? What should Mr. Dawson do, and how should he go about any changes he might wish to make?

Herndon's Home Restaurant

At a regional restaurant association meeting in a small college community in the northern part of the state, Jim Herndon was fascinated by a new restaurant he visited. Specializing in home-type foods, its appeals were quality and quantity at a low price of "volume operation." The decor was simple, fixtures inexpensive, and there was much self-service. Only beer was served in addition to the regular menu.

Jim had worked in restaurants, full or part time, for over six years. Most recently his employer, an older man, had come to depend on Jim for pricing of meals, kitchen supervision, and some buying of provisions. The restaurant was well located downtown in a city of 150,000 and enjoyed a brisk and profitable breakfast and luncheon trade but a declining evening business. It was conservative, medium-priced, "homelike" in atmosphere, had been successful for many years, and had a loyal following of patrons.

Jim felt that locations away from the center of town were more likely to succeed in the coming years. He felt particularly that students, "young marrieds," and others seeking "just good food" in an informal, inexpensive atmosphere were a good market.

As to location, there were three possibilities: (1) near the growing new junior college in a relatively undeveloped area; (2) in a well-established shopping center in a middle-income area; (3) outside town, near a thruway intersection, where various new businesses were emerging. There were no eating facilities near the college campus, not even dormitories. In the shopping center, at least one deluxe restaurant lounge had failed two years ago. The thruway spot offered a good choice as to markets, in Jim's opinion.

Financing might be difficult but not impossible. Jim had about $8,000 saved, his family was well known, and his personal business record good. He also had in mind taking in an older man, with more money, as a partner; or, he felt, he could possibly interest a franchising operation in his idea, if one could be located which seemed to fit into his own thinking as to the kind of restaurant he wanted to operate. As a last resort, of course, he might be able to buy out his present employer in a few years.

The problem here is to select a proper location for the type of restaurant Jim has in mind.

1. What would an ideal location be? How would you evaluate any location?

2. Establish standards for the location's selection and evaluate each possibility in A, B, and C ratings, with A being the most favorable and C being the least favorable.

How Gro-Green Didn't Grow

A few years ago, three young men – one a chemist, one a salesman, and the third an accountant – learned of a formula for a liquid fertilizer having unique characteristics. A 5/10/5 formula, (5 percent nitrogen, 10 percent phosphoric acid, 5 percent potash), the fertilizer also contained certain trace elements more or less standard for garden and lawn use. It was considered suitable for greenhouses, for home gardens, and for truck gardeners, and found some acceptance among growers of tobacco and tomatoes, who used it in the starting of small plants. It was also valuable for house plants during the winter time. It was not difficult to handle, it had no odor, and it "went to work at once." The cost of manufacture was negligible, and the chemicals were easily available. At the time, the idea of liquid fertilizer was relatively new, and there was no competition in the field except for the standard, dry, bulky fertilizers and a few dry-chemical fertilizers which could be mixed with water to make a liquid similar to that offered by this group.

The men proceeded to arrange to package the liquid in bottles, jugs, and drums for consumer, farm, and greenhouse use, allowing adequate discounts for dealers, yet making its price (cost) to users about the same as the conventional products. It was advertised as Gro-Green in local newspapers, and the men themselves did the selling, to get "the feel of the market" as well as to reduce expense.

Considerable sales resistance was encountered in contacts with both household consumers and with the florists, hardware stores, and feed stores. It was thought at one time that wholesalers might be employed to take the line, but wholesalers did not accept it readily because it had no record of sales. After a number of hardware merchants, feed-and-seed stores, and nursery outlets had purchased small quantities of the product in the various sizes, second calls were made in an effort to see how the product was moving and to see if any reorders were available. The partners in the manufacturing company found that it had not moved, that either through lack of effort on the part of the sales people in the places where it was available, or perhaps through an obstacle in the minds of possible users, it was not being readily accepted.

Feeling that the product needed something to go along with it to make a combination "deal" or to make it appear more easily used from the consumer's standpoint, an arrangement was made with a company making a product called the Hozer, which when attached to a garden hose drew the liquid from an attached bottle. They tried also to sell it as a "package" with garden seeds, but this called for an investment in seeds or practically giving the product away to the seed company.

An effort toward cooperative advertising was made, whereby the Gro-Green Company would pay merchants 50 percent of local newspaper advertising costs up to a maximum of 10 percent of their orders. Since most orders were in two-and three-dozen lots of various sizes, seldom amounting to more than $50, the advertising allowance was seldom more than $5. An effort to acquaint the public with the product was made by taking a booth at the local Home and Garden Show, which occurred in the early spring in a larger city nearby. This got some reaction, but it was not lasting. These men also considered sale or licensing of the formula to some larger concern under a better-known name. Yet the product could easily be duplicated through analysis.

After almost two years of effort and expense, these young men "threw in the towel" and closed out their business. Less than a year later, a major manufacturer of garden supplies put a liquid fertilizer on the market, and after a slow start, it succeeded. Currently there are several brands on the market, and makers of farm and garden equipment are doing well in marketing products for the application of liquid fertilizers of various types, some in combination with weed killers or insecticides.

Why did this enterprise fail? List basic reasons and explain each briefly.

How Should This Woman Pay?

Sylvia Simms has been employed by her uncle, a Chicago greeting card manufacturer, for the seven years since she left college. Becoming a little restless on her job and impatient with her uncle, she recently got his permission to represent the firm on the West Coast, with offices in Los Angeles. The firm has had distributors and occasionally one of its own salesmen out there, but efforts have not been rewarding in any sense. Sylvia believes that with a company-sponsored distribution center she can do a more effective job of serving and expanding the firm's market. Eventually, she hopes to operate independently of the firm.

Among her first problems as she surveys the new assignment is that of designing a sales compensation plan. She finds that prospective salesmen differ as to preference for straight salary vs. straight commission, and that most of them would welcome some combination of the two. Generally, newcomers seem to prefer the security of a straight salary, while veteran salesmen want the opportunity the straight commission provides to make "real money" in proportion to talent and effort. There is great variety of methods in the industry locally.

Miss Simms believes that a beginning salesman will be well satisfied with $8,000–$10,000 a year, but that experienced men demand $12,000–$15,000 if they "produce." She believes that she can afford 5 percent of sales, and that, since the line is well advertised, this should be sufficient. This means that a man would sell $200,000 annually to earn $10,000 in straight commissions. If on straight salary he sold that much, Sylvia's 5 percent requirement would be met. If he sold more, her sales-cost percentage would decline; if less, it would increase.

1. Which method of compensation should Sylvia adopt? Why?

2. Assume that her costs can (or must) be increased to 6 percent. What salary would be earned for $200,000 sales? What commission for $150,000 sales? What salary, and what commission, for $300,000 sales?
3. What arrangement might be made whereby the new salesmen could start with straight salary and go on straight commission later?
4. Can you suggest a combination of salary and commission which might be useful?

"Mice" for Machines

Malcolm McGruder, an office supplies salesman, has developed a combination leveler-silencer for office equipment which can be placed under the legs of duplicators, keypunch machines, accounting equipment, etc. It permits leveling on uneven floors and reduces machine vibration and noise. It is easily attached, except that because of the varieties of leg construction and weight of equipment, it is best done by someone accustomed to working with such things. People in offices where it has been used agree that it makes for greater calm and quiet and may improve equipment performance and prolong its life. A patent has been applied for.

Thus far, "Mac" has produced a few hundred units only, in three sizes. Production is relatively simple, consisting mostly of standard hardware store items, with one "special" component only, made on a simple metal-forming press Mac bought from a used-machinery distributor. Currently he can make them for 42¢ to 56¢ each and has sold them for $1.65 to $1.87 each. He is certain that in quantity he could reduce costs and prices substantially.

Before he goes much farther, Mac must decide how best to market his "Mice," as he calls them now. Currently, he sells them to his own regular customers and helps install them. Could he sell them to other distributors like his employers? Could he sell them to equipment manufacturers as part of the new units? Would direct mail do the job? How about getting them properly installed? Right now, Mac is confused. He knows he has a good thing, but how does he get it out into the world of business?

A Plumbing and Heating Business

Two young men, Arthur Steele and John Hubbard, plan to establish a plumbing–heating–air-conditioning business. Steele is an experienced plumber and tinner, having worked with his father for many years in another community. Hubbard has some engineering training, and has successfully sold supplies to the heating and air-conditioning trade. They propose to take over an old shop which was closed when its owner died and which has remained closed while the estate was settled. It is in a good location and has basic equipment and plenty of room.

They believe, at this point, that they can raise enough capital to lease the shop and buy existing equipment, buy a truck and adequate new equipment, establish an inventory of parts and materials, renovate the showroom, and get a few floor samples of products for display. Hubbard is confident that several good product lines are available, and does not feel the local area is now being properly served, particularly as to heating and air-conditioning requirements. He is certain, he says, that much can be done in working with contractors on new buildings. Much of this work is now being handled by representatives from cities some distance away.

As to nontechnical personnel, they will have a stenographer–clerk–office manager, and an accountant on a part-time basis. To start, they will need at least one plumber–heating man and one helper-truckdriver. Steele intends to work both in and out of the shop. Hubbard expects to make sales calls, build goodwill with contractors, and generally supervise the office.

As to the capital requirements, Steele will provide $18,000 and Hubbard $12,000. The remainder will be borrowed from the bank, with the building equipment, etc., as security. Both men have excellent credit and financial records.

These two men plan to sit down together this evening and put their ideas as to organization on paper. Not only must they be clear in their own minds as to individual rights and responsibilities, but their creditors and the bank will have some questions to ask. Briefly outline, hypothetically, the duties and responsibilities of each man. Suggest a type of organization that will satisfy all concerned.

Premier Stampings, Inc.

John Proctor, experienced accountant with a CPA firm, found himself specializing in costing problems, particularly those of smaller metalworking plants. With the larger firms it was a matter of aiding them in improved methods they knew they needed and wanted, but the typical small firm had little or no idea as to the breakdown of costs on past or present contracts nor an interest in such costing. This lack was often expensive in bidding for new work; sometimes the question of profit on a contract could not be answered until long after the work was completed. Since many of these small firms got as few as 5 percent of the jobs they bid on, as low man they often took a loss.

After working with many such operators, John concluded that their needs for accounting systems – for cost accounting particularly – were often greater than their need for operating expertise: the best technician could not make money on unprofitable sales. In talking with Karl Schmidt, the depressed owner of Premier Stampings one day, the suggestion was made by John that he become a partner, with the understanding that he would keep the books and eventually do some selling, while Mr. Schmidt ran the shop. After considerable discussion, they decided to give it a try. A contract was drawn up, the firm was incorporated, and John Proctor invested a very reasonable $16,000 for a half-interest.

After a six months' study of past job costs and their composition as to processes and materials involved, John developed a process-costing formula for the firm. They went slowly with the new idea at first, lost a "job" or two, but made money on those they got. John found in his talks with potential customers (and even with some competitors) that they preferred to deal with a firm which knew its costs. Too often, they had found themselves signing a contract with a firm that suddenly found itself financially embarrassed because of a series of losing contracts. This meant delays, and sometimes even advance payments by the buyer to get the work completed.

The business has doubled and tripled over the past four years. The annual volume now approaches $500,000; Mr. Schmidt and John can confidently anticipate, in good years, combined personal income of around 10 percent of sales.

They are receiving more and more invitations to bid, and their customers are increasingly loyal. They are less and less dependent on a few customers for whom they were often almost forced to price themselves out of existence.

The above case provides examples of benefits resulting from sound business practices. Can you suggest, as you review the firm's various outside business relationships, other benefits which might accrue as a result of its improved costing methods?

A Profit Insurance Program?

Alonzo Billings operates a small printing plant in a medium-sized midwestern city. His wife, father-in-law, one salesman, and one press operator are the entire staff, except for a number of housewives living nearby who are on call to come in and help with sorting, assembling, addressing, and stuffing of direct mail and similar jobs when needed. Mr. Billings also does much of the selling. This is an old, well-established, and reasonably prosperous firm. They handle all kinds of small printing jobs, and have not specialized in serving any particular industry such as banking, retailing, or manufacturers, or in performing any kind of work such as stationery, brochures, direct mail, or business forms.

Much work brought in by salesmen is on a bidding basis. Sometimes Mr. Billings is forced to accept jobs (to hold a customer or keep the plant busy) that he must do at a price which does not permit him to produce the quality of work he really prefers in his shop. There is, of course, much "repeat business," jobs which come from old customers and with which the employees are all familiar — to the point that the type may remain set up for years with little alteration from order to order. This is not often very profitable work, but it is, he feels, desirable for the firm because it is "dependable." It also builds and holds goodwill, he believes.

Mr. Billings knows that he does not get all the business of all of his present customers. He also knows that there are potential customers in the community who give him no business at all, simply because neither he nor his salesman have had time to call on them.

He also knows that he can do some kinds of printing better than others. Furthermore, various new printing processes are competing for some of his business. Business is good, but not improving. Recently he said, "How can I develop a plan or program that will get me the kind of business I do best at a profit?"

At a printers' convention seminar a few weeks ago, he heard a panel discussion concerning "Planning for Profit." The general theme was that by classifying customers' past records as to types of jobs done for them, and then classifying these types of jobs as to profitability, it is possible to concentrate on quality business at a profit. This sounds good, but Mr. Billings' father-in-law is afraid it would offend many customers, would take too long, and would be an expensive experiment for such a well-known firm as theirs. Furthermore, Mr. Billings' salesman, also an older man, wants no interference with his established routine and familiar contacts. Mr.

Billings knows, too, that any such change in policy might call for new equipment.

Assume that you are Mr. Billings and that you have decided to go ahead, at least in a small way. Draw up a pattern for analysis of work done, in terms of what you think you want to achieve.

A Sporting Chance?

The sporting goods store of Harris and Harris is operated by William and Edwin Harris in a fairly remote college town. It started ten years ago when the two brothers became campus representatives for a wholesaler in the nearest large city. The business has grown with the local college and with the expansion of other educational facilities in the area. New golf courses and athletic activities connected with new industrial plants within the 50-mile radius they serve have also helped in their growth.

Generally, the two young men have prospered, although frequently in the early days they agreed that they were better athletes than businessmen. They have kept the firm's business evenly balanced, not having entered any particular branch of athletics. Rather, they have responded to demand as it has developed. In fact, most of their business has "come to them," although they do make sales calls and do the usual goodwill-building things such as holding contests and giving awards to student athletes.

Recently they have seen some serious competition developing, as mail-order houses, department stores, discounters, and others (in larger cities some distance away) are advertising, by direct mail and by newspaper, TV, and radio, in their markets. Some of the items advertised are "loss leaders," the brothers believe. Others are closeouts, some apparently rejects or "seconds." The brothers know that these competitors are trying to get customers into their stores so that while there they will buy not only sporting goods, but home appliances, automotive accessories, and other offerings.

Will and Ed are worried but not discouraged. They feel that there must be some way of combating this invasion of their market. Their profits have been satisfactory. They have a markup varying from $33\frac{1}{3}$ to 50 percent of the sales price, often as suggested by the manufacturer. Now they fear they will have to reduce prices on certain highly competitive items. If they do this, they might have to raise prices on other goods. The trouble is that they do not know what their price-cutting competitors will do next. Nor do they know which items or supplies bring in the most profit during any given period.

Something must be done — not necessarily abruptly or all at once. How would you go about establishing a policy that will insure the permanence of their business over a reasonable period in the future?

✓ "Sweetaters" and the Law

Mrs. Doris Munson recently developed a means of making sweet potato chips, and has applied for a copyright on the name "Sweetaters." She expects them to serve as a snack, especially attractive to children, but also for adults, good with beverages. She has secured adequate financial backing through the Small Business Administration. A marketing consultant has been called in, and a program involving several possibilities has been laid out for consideration.

Packaging will be in transparent plastic bags appropriately printed. For distance shipping, she favors tins carrying the same label and descriptions. She will also have special cartons for shelf display in stores, and some in-store banners for use particularly at times of introduction into a new store or community. She will also advertise to the public in newspapers and over radio and TV. She will sell through wholesalers to retail stores.

Her consultant suggests also that, since her plant will be located in a store front near a shopping center and school, she establish a small retail store of her own there, to keep "in touch with the consumer" and adjust her product and programs as she sees fit. Also, she might wish to offer related food or grocery items in the store to build up her offerings and to compare them with her own product. Later she may wish to open other stores of her own.

This program, though obviously ambitious, will proceed one step at a time, probably slowly. Mrs. Munson and her business, which will probably become a corporation eventually, must bear in mind various federal, state, and local laws affecting a business of this type. She has asked her lawyer for a list of these and an explanation of the reasons why she will need to adhere to them. Can you prepare such a list?

⌐ Three People—Three Opportunities

1. Jerry Hausman was graduated from a prestigious university in the East seven years ago. Since then he has been employed by his father as cashier's assistant in the bank where his father is a senior officer. Jerry appears to be successful as a fledgling banker. He had worked in the bank in various capacities during summer vacations when a student in high school and college. His family assumes that he will make banking a career. Jerry, however, is becoming restless; as a result of contacts made at the bank, several ideas have occurred to him.

One possibility is a partnership with Sam Snively, a successful local golf "pro," in the establishment of a "chain" of pro shops now existing or to be located in selected country clubs. This arrangement would, according to the pro, be welcomed by pro shop owners and club members, for it should increase and standardize the shops' offerings and reduce some of the problems of management. Assistance of some manufacturers of golf equipment is assured – in the areas of inventory selection and control, and in management methods generally. Investment requirements would be substantial.

2. George Hawkins is an accomplished craftsman in woodworking, and has operated successfully as a cabinetmaker for many years. His work has earned him an excellent reputation in the area, and many fine homes, restaurants, and offices show his handiwork.

George was approached recently by a younger man, Joe Ward, a recent arrival in the community and a competitor, who has found the mobile-home industry a good means of income — requiring built-in baths, kitchens, dinettes, etc. Joe has been able to develop enough standardization and other cost-cutting methods to merit the approval of the firms employing him. He believes that the industry has a glowing future, and wants George to join him, forming a team to service mobile-homemakers and eventually, possibly, to manufacture complete mobile-home units.

George has enough money saved to afford the risks involved, and the younger man is convinced he could get bank support for financing the cabinetmaking venture or even the manufacturing firm. He is very enthusiastic about the prospects.

3. Josephine Jones is an accomplished typist-secretary-stenographer employed by a large, long-established real estate firm in a medium-sized city. She makes an unusually good salary and is highly respected by her employers and by the real estate community. Her prospects of holding her current position with the firm appear to be excellent, with normal salary increases from time to time as before. She is unmarried at thirty-eight, and is the sole support of her aging father and mother and an invalid brother.

"Joe" feels that she is not saving enough money, and for a year or more has been alert to some opportunity for larger income. She has recently heard that a large stenographic-duplicating service is for sale due to the owner's death six months ago. The firm had always been very successful, but has suffered recently for lack of direction and, to some degree, lack of modern equipment. The staff is made up largely of older, quite mature workers. The price asked is reasonable in terms of past performance.

Sources of business for Joe would be smaller real estate and other offices too small to have their own staffs and equipment, and occasionally larger firms at their peak periods of business. She has talked with a banker who will lend her a small amount without collateral — or more, if required, through a home mortgage.

These three cases, taken from observation, represent typical problems faced by persons contemplating entrance into business for themselves. Information given is not sufficient to permit a suggested decision in any case; additional information is required.

1. What further information would you seek in each case?
2. Under what conditions should each person go ahead?
3. What possible major strength or weakness does each situation reveal?

What Price Family Name?

Howard Menser comes from a long line of successful delicatessen owners in a large city. The family store is located centrally, and for decades has enjoyed a prestige trade, attracting people from all over the area when certain specialty items are desired. Business shows some signs of decline now, however, as downtown offices have moved to outlying areas and chain supermarkets have established their own "gourmet" facilities or lease such departments to independent operators.

Howard is thirty-three years old, the oldest of three brothers. Their father will soon retire, but they are beginning to worry as to whether the business can support all three families. Joe, the youngest, and just out of college, suggests a chain of gourmet shops, the new ones to be located in key shopping centers. The second brother wants to continue the present downtown store and lease departments in supermarkets. Most of these national organizations will not permit the use of any name other than their own on such departments.

The brothers recognize their need for growth, and have a great desire to maintain and exploit the good reputation of the family business. All of them enjoy it and have worked together with their father since childhood. They have, through the business and their father, ample funds. The father, being naturally conservative, is cautious but cooperative.

The question is: How can the three men and their business grow, to their best long-run advantage?

Mail-Order Marmalade?

Young's Hickory Haven is a well-known quality restaurant in the Ozark Mountains of southern Missouri. Founded at the turn of the century, it has always attracted a large year-round following, but has been particularly popular with summer vacationers, who come from all parts of the Middle West to enjoy the fishing, boating, and general "woodsiness" of the area. A state park, developed in recent years, has aided Hickory Haven in its growth.

Dallas Young, a recent college graduate, represents the third generation of the family in the business. In addition to a degree from Vanderbilt, he has taken special courses in restaurant operation at Cornell, and has served in various restaurant and hotel jobs on a part-time basis while in college. His family is confident that he will be able to carry on the business with great success. Dallas has now been back with the restaurant for almost five years. His father still "runs the show," but permits Dallas great freedom of action and welcomes his more modern ideas.

Over the years, restaurant customers have been particularly pleased with the pickles, preserves, and bakery items prepared in the Haven kitchens. Often they have asked for recipes, for small jars of some items, and for ready-mixed flours used in the baked goods.

Dallas is convinced that the restaurant is sufficiently well-known to its following to assure sales success of such products if they were packaged, labeled, and sold – either by direct mail or in selected stores. He has observed success of such gourmet items in restaurants, delicatessens, specialty food shops, and even in department stores and supermarkets, and is encouraged to "give it a try."

His current problems have to do with marketing – whether to establish a mail-order business, to sell through grocery wholesalers, or both. The family has adequate capital, but Dallas feels that he should use a minimum of such funds, preferring to "go to the bank." Although the family and restaurant are well-known there, Dallas wants to establish this part of the business on his own.

On his first call at the bank, its representatives appeared to be interested in the project. Their recommendation to him was in substance: "Go back and work out a specific program. Decide, with your father's help, what you want to do and how you want to do it — or, if you face alternatives, come back to us and perhaps we can help you with your plans. But next time, have your plans developed as far as you can go."

Dallas Young has a few things to decide, a few things to do, a few elements in his plan to be crystallized, before he goes back for the bankers' advice. How would you start? What steps would you follow? Could you develop a plan that would appeal to the bank at the next meeting?

Lost Shirts or "Lost Shirt"?

One of the top men's wear shops in Peoria, Illinois, was recently bought by Norman Schultz with funds he had accumulated as a professional hockey player. Established forty years before, it was known for good assortments of current styles at reasonable prices. Upon retiring, the former owner gave Mr. Schultz a generally good price and worked with him for three months following his retirement.

Yesterday, on a buying trip to Chicago, Norman was approached by a shirt salesman, who offered him eight dozen shirts at an attractive price. Usually priced at $36.00 per dozen or more to sell at $4.95, these were available at $29.50 per dozen, and thus could be sold for as low as $3.95. The styles were somewhat mixed, but generally good for this season, which is now almost half over.

An inventory of the shirts as to sizes in the assortment is presented below in numbers of shirts in each size:

	14	14^2	15	15^2	16	16^2	17	17^2	Total
White, plain	6	9	3	6	3	6	3	6	42
Colors,									
mixed, plain	3	9	—	3	6	—	6	3	30
Novelty stripes	3	6	6	—	—	3	9	3	30
Novelty prints	9	6	3	—	6	—	3	9	36
Mod collars,									
mixed patterns	—	6	9	3	—	3	3	—	24
Semiformal	3	3	6	9	6	3	3	6	39
Totals	24	39	27	21	21	15	27	27	201

Shirts are in boxes of three; sleeve lengths tend to be appropriate to neck sizes, color assortments are well-balanced.

Norman was definitely interested in this opportunity. His stocks were low, particularly in the more popular sizes and styles. The former owner had left him a basic model-stock, which he had followed for many years, that looked somewhat like this:

	14	14^2	15	15^2	16	16^2	17	17^2
Whites (%)	8	10	18	24	15	12	8	5
Colors (%)	8	12	20	24	15	10	6	5
Novelties (%)	6	12	21	22	18	10	8	3

Norman has studied the inventory of the assortment offered, has looked at the percentages recommended in the model, and now must let the shirt salesman know if he wants to buy the shirts. While he respects the former owner's judgment, he feels that the price offered is attractive and that the price he could offer his customers would bring him the business he needs. In many ways, his predecessor was an old-fashioned and conservative buyer. Norman feels that a more aggressive and youthful approach will appeal to his hockey fan customers and other admirers.

Norman Schultz must make a decision now. If you were in his situation, what would be today's decision and why? Any alternatives?

An Added Line Offers Profit?

Barry Bates is a manufacturers' agent, representing eight different manufacturers, who sells various items to laundries and dry cleaners including hangers, plastic bags, and laundry or dry cleaning tickets. His items are related but noncompeting. His area is upstate New York, where the business of any one of the lines is not enough to support a full-time salesman. Selling them together is economically profitable for his principals and for himself. He keeps busy and is making money as the business grows.

Recently he was approached by a former employer — The Fire-Stop Corporation — who has developed a new pre-alarm fire extinguisher that is attached to the electrical system of a building. When a fire occurs, not only does an alarm sound but a harmless foamy substance is sprayed into the area, quenching the fire. It is endorsed by fire prevention authorities. The costs of the equipment and of installation are relatively high, but justifiable in terms of increased security and reduced insurance rates.

Fire-Stop wants Barry to add this item to his line, to sell it not only to his present customers but to offices, stores, banks, and gas stations (as well as laundries and cleaners) in the towns he visits. They assure him that after the first few sales are made, local people can be trained to install and service the units. They argue that since he is in a town anyway, he might just as well sell a few Fire-Stop units. The commission is good — better even than that of his regular lines. He would, however, have to take a training course at the factory before selling Fire-Stop units.

Mr. Bates is tempted to "give it a try." While he can keep busy developing his regular business, he feels that this added product would give him a change of pace and possibilities for added personal growth. If you were in his shoes, how would you analyze the situation; what factors would you weigh; what further facts would you need; and what is your first general advice to him?

Appendices

A

Sources of information on organizing and operating specific types of small business (indexed) *

Apparel Manufacturing (*see also* Manufacturing)
- "Apparel Manufacturing," *Small Business Reporter*, Vol. 10, No. 3
- "Contract Dress Manufacturing," *Urban Business Profile*, 87 T

Apparel Store
- "Apparel and Accessories for Women, Misses, and Children," *Small Business Bibliography No. 50*
- "Apparel Retailing," *Small Business Reporter*, Vol 8, No. 3
- "Children's and Infants' Wear," *Urban Business Profile*, 81 T
- "Men's and Boys' Wear Stores," *Small Business Bibliography No. 45*
- "Women's Apparel Stores," *Small Business Reporter*, Vol. 5, No. 12

Automatic Food Vending (*see* Foodservice; *see also* Vending Machines)

Automotive Parts and Accessories Store
- "Auto Parts and Accessory Stores," *Small Business Reporter*, Vol. 8, No. 12

Automotive Service (*see also* Repair Services)
- "Independent Automotive Services," *Small Business Reporter*, Vol. 6, No. 8

Bantam Food Store (*see* Grocery Store)

Bar (*see* Cocktail Lounge)

*SBA's *Small Business Bibliographies* are freely available by writing to the Small Business Administration, 1441 "L" St., Washington, D.C. 20008, or to one of its field offices; however there is a small charge for individual publications in the *Starting and Managing Series.* Issues of the *Small Business Reporter* (published by the Bank of America, P.O. Box 37000, San Francisco, California 94137) are available free of charge to individuals and businesses in the state of California; out-of-state requests for single copies will be honored, within limits of supply, if accompanied by a postpaid, self-addressed envelope. *Urban Business Profiles,* published by the U.S. Department of Commerce, are available at nominal cost (20¢–30¢ each) and may be ordered from the Government Printing Office, Washington, D.C.

Beauty Salon
- "Beauty Salons," *Small Business Reporter,* Vol. 9, No. 2
- "Beauty Shops," *Urban Business Profile,* 77 T

Billiard Parlor
- "Family Billiard Centers," *Small Business Reporter,* Vol. 6, No. 6

Bookkeeping Service
- "Starting and Managing a Small Bookkeeping Service," *Starting and Managing Series No. 4*

Bookstore
- "Bookstores," *Small Business Bibliography No. 42*

Bowling Alley
- "Bowling Alleys," *Urban Business Profile,* 85 T
- "Bowling Centers," *Small Business Reporter,* Vol. 6, No. 7

Boys' Wear (*see* Apparel Store)

Building Contractor
- "Building Contractors," *Small Business Reporter,* Vol. 10, No. 1
- "Starting and Managing a Small Building Business," *Starting and Managing Series No. 5*

Building Service Contracting
- "Building Service Contracting," *Urban Business Profile,* 88 T

Cafeteria (*see* Foodservice)

Camera Shop
- "Photographic Dealers and Studios," *Small Business Bibliography No. 64*
- "Starting and Managing a Small Camera Shop," *Starting and Managing Series No. 17*

Car Wash
- "Coin-Operated Car Washes," *Small Business Reporter,* Vol. 7, No. 3
- "Starting and Managing a Carwash," *Starting and Managing Series No. 14*

Card Shop (*see* Greeting Card Store)

Carpenter Shop (*see* Woodworking Shop)

Catering (*see also* Foodservice)
- "Mobile Catering," *Urban Business Profile,* 80 T
- "Restaurants and Catering," *Small Business Bibliography No. 17*

Children's Wear (*see* Apparel Store)

Cocktail Lounge
- "Bars and Cocktail Lounges," *Small Business Reporter,* Vol. 5, No. 8

Coffee Shop (*see* Restaurant)

Consignment Sale Shop (*see* Swap Shop)

Contract Construction (*see also* Building Contractor)
- "Contract Construction," *Urban Business Profile,* 76 T

Convenience Food Store (*see* Grocery Store)

Dairy Store
- "Soft-Frozen Dessert Stands," *Small Business Bibliography No. 47*

Day Nursery
- "Day Nurseries for Preschoolers," *Small Business Reporter,* Vol. 8, No. 10

Discount Store
- "Discount Retailing," *Small Business Bibliography No. 68*

Drive-In Restaurant (*see* Foodservice)

Drugstore
- "Drugstores," *Small Business Bibliography No. 33*
- "Independent Drug Stores," *Small Business Reporter,* Vol. 9, No. 12
- "Starting and Managing a Small Retail Drugstore," *Starting and Managing Series No. 11*

Dry Cleaning
- "Coin-Operated Dry Cleaning," *Small Business Reporter,* Vol. 8, No. 7
- "Dry Cleaning " *Urban Business Profile,* 86 T
- "Laundry and Dry Cleaning," *Small Business Bibliography No. 22*
- "Starting and Managing a Small Dry Cleaning Business," *Starting and Managing Series No. 12*

Equipment Rental
- "Equipment Rental Business," *Small Business Reporter,* Vol. 10, No. 6

Florist Shop (*see also* Retail Nursery)
- "Retail Florist," *Small Business Bibliography No. 74*
- "Starting and Managing a Retail Flower Shop," *Starting and Managing Series No. 18*

Foodservice (*see also* Restaurant and Catering)
- "The Foodservice Business," *Small Business Reporter,* Vol. 8, No. 2

Food Store (*see* Grocery Store)

Furniture Store
- "Furniture Retailing," *Small Business Bibliography No. 48*
- "Furniture Stores," *Urban Business Profile,* 75 T

Garage (*see* Automotive Service)

Garden Store (*see* Florist Shop)

Gas Station (*see* Service Station)

Gift Store
- "Gift Stores," *Small Business Reporter,* Vol. 9, No. 4

Girls' Wear (*see* Apparel Store)

Greeting Card Store
- "Greeting Card Stores," *Small Business Reporter,* Vol. 7, No. 9

Grocery Store
- "Convenience Food Stores," *Small Business Reporter,* Vol. 9, No. 6
- "Convenience Stores," *Urban Business Profile,* 90 T
- "Food Stores," *Small Business Bibliography No. 24*

Handicraft Home Business
- "Handicrafts and Home Business," *Small Business Bibliography No. 1*
- "The Handcraft Business," *Small Business Reporter,* Vol. 10, No. 8

Hardware Store
- "Hardware Retailing," *Small Business Bibliography No. 35*
- "The Hardware Business," National Retail Hardware Association, located at 964 North Pennsylvania St., Indianapolis, Ind. 46204
- "Starting and Managing a Small Retail Hardware Store," *Starting and Managing Series No. 10*

Heating and Air-Conditioning (*see* Plumbing Shop)

Hobby Shop
- "Hobby Shops," *Small Business Bibliography No. 53*

Hotel (*see also* Motel)
- *The Hotel and Restaurant Business,* by Donald E. Lundberg (Chicago, III.: Institutions/Volume Feeding Magazine, 1971)

Ice Cream Store (*see* Dairy Store)

Industrial Laundry
- "Industrial Launderers and Linen Supply," *Urban Business Profile,* 78 T

Interior Decorating Shop
- "Interior Decorating," *Small Business Bibliography No. 54*
- "Painting and Wall Decorating," *Small Business Bibliography No. 60*

Janitorial Services, Contract (*see* Building Service Contracting)

Jewelry Store
- "Jewelry Retailing," *Small Business Bibliography No. 36*
- "Starting and Managing a Small Retail Jewelry Store," *Starting and Managing Series No. 21*

Laundry (*see also* Industrial Laundry)
- "Coin-Operated Laundries," *Small Business Reporter,* Vol. 8, No. 6
- "Laundry and Dry Cleaning," *Small Business Bibliography No. 22*

Linen Supply Service
- "Industrial Launderers and Linen Supply," *Urban Business Profile,* 78 T

Liquor Store
- "The Liquor Store," *Small Business Reporter,* Vol. 7, No. 2

Machine Shop (*see also* Repair Services)
- "Machine Shop – Job Type," *Small Business Bibliography No. 69*
- "Machine Shop Job Work," *Urban Business Profile,* 79 T

Manufacturing (*see also* Apparel Manufacturing)
- "Custom Plastics Industries," *Urban Business Profile,* 84 T
- "Manufacturing," *Small Business Reporter,* Vol. 9, No. 3

Men's Wear (*see* Apparel Store)

Mobile Home Dealer
- "Mobile Home and Recreational Dealers," *Small Business Reporter,* Vol. 9, No. 11
- "Mobile Homes and Parks," *Small Business Bibliography No. 41*

Mobile Home Park
- "How to Build and Operate a Mobile Home Park," Home Manufacturers Association, 1625 "L" St., N.W., Washington, D.C. 20036
- "Mobile Home Parks," *Small Business Reporter,* Vol. 9, No. 7
- "Mobile Homes and Parks," *Small Business Bibliography No. 41*

Motel
- "Motels," *Small Business Bibliography No. 66*
- "Motels," *Small Business Reporter,* Vol. 7, No. 6
- "Starting and Managing a Small Motel," *Starting and Managing Series No. 7*

Music Store
- "Starting and Managing a Small Retail Music Store," *Starting and Managing Series No. 20*

Nursery (*see* Day Nursery *or* Retail Nursery)

Painting and Wall Decorating (*see* Interior Decorating Shop)

Pet Shop
- "Independent Pet Shops," *Small Business Reporter,* Vol. 10, No. 2
- "Pet Shops," *Small Business Bibliography No. 76*
- "Pet Shops", *Urban Business Profile,* 91 T
- "Starting and Managing a Pet Shop," *Starting and Managing Series No. 19*

Photography Shop (*see* Camera Shop)

Photography Studio
- "Photographic Dealers and Studios," Small Business Bibliography No. 64
- "Photographic Studios", Urban Business Profile, 89 T

Plumbing Shop
- "Plumbing, Heating, and Air Conditioning Job Shop, Small Business Bibliography No. 43

Printing Shop
- "Job Printing Shop," Small Business Bibliography No. 44
- "Small Job Printing," Small Business Reporter, Vol. 9, No. 5

Real Estate Broker
- "Real Estate Brokerage," Urban Business Profile, 74 T
- "Real Estate Business," Small Business Bibliography No. 65

Rental, Equipment (see Equipment Rental)

Repair Services
- "Repair Services," Small Business Reporter, Vol. 10, No. 9

Restaurant (see also Foodservice)
- The Hotel and Restaurant Business, by Donald E. Lundberg (Chicago, Ill.: Institutions/ Volume Feeding Magazine, 1971)
- "Restaurants and Catering," Small Business Bibliography No. 17
- "Starting and Managing a Small Restaurant," Starting and Managing Series No. 9

Retail Nursery (see also Florist Shop)
- "The Nursery Business," Small Business Bibliography No. 14
- "Retail Nurseries," Small Business Reporter, Vol. 0, No. 10

Retailing
- "Retailing," Small Business Bibliography No. 10
- "Retailing," Small Business Reporter, Vol. 8, No. 4

Service Station
- "Service Stations," Small Business Reporter, Vol. 10, No. 7
- "Starting and Managing a Service Station," Starting and Managing Series No. 3

Shoe Repair Shop (see also Repair Services)
- "Starting and Managing a Small Shoe Service Shop," Starting and Managing Series No. 16

Snack Bar (see Foodservice)

Soft-Frozen Dessert Stand (see Dairy Store)

Sporting Goods Store
- "Independent Sporting Goods Stores," Small Business Reporter, Vol. 10, No. 11
- "Sporting Goods," Small Business Bibliography No. 62

Swap Shop
- "Starting and Managing a Swap Shop or Consignment Sale Shop," Starting and Managing Series No. 15

Tax Service (see Bookkeeping Service)

Trailer Court (see Mobile Home Park)

Trucking Service
- "Trucking and Cartage," Small Business Bibliography No. 51

Variety Store
- "Independent Variety Stores," Small Business Reporter, Vol. 7, No. 8
- "Variety Stores," Small Business Bibliography No. 21

B

Checklist for organizing and operating a small business

The following checklist should be completed satisfactorily before any person is ready to enter business for himself. It follows the general plan and recommended procedures of this text. An important consideration for any prospective business owner is to plan carefully and to work out every major requirement for success *before actually starting the business.* It is not enough merely to read the text and to have good intentions of applying its recommendations as each need arises. Not only is there danger that some important matters will be overlooked unless this checklist is followed seriously, but once the business is in operation the pressure of daily work greatly reduces the likelihood that the best practices will be adopted and the best decisions made on all important questions.

The plan of the checklist is simple. Each topic is presented as a question intended to stimulate analysis concerning some important point. The question should be considered carefully and answered honestly and realistically. An affirmative answer to a question means that the topic has been considered and provided for to the best of the enterpriser's ability. When further attention to a topic is needed, an attempt to answer the question should convince the prospective businessman of this need and also suggest what further action is called for. Requirements thus discovered should be recorded and checked off as completed.

TOPIC QUESTIONS

I. The Decision for Self-Employment

1. Have you rated yourself and had some acquaintances rate you on the personal qualities necessary for success as your own boss, such as leadership, organizing ability, perseverance, and physical energy?

2. Have you taken steps to improve yourself in those qualities in which you are weak but which are needed for success?

583

3. Have you saved money, made business contacts, taken special courses, or read particular books for the purpose of preparing yourself for business ownership?

4. Have you had training or experience in your proposed line of business or in one similar to it?

5. Are you (a) good at managing your own time and energy? (b) not easily discouraged? (c) willing to work harder in your own business than as an employee?

6. Have you estimated the net income from sales or services you can reasonably expect in the crucial "first two years"?

7. Have you compared this income with what you could make working for someone else?

8. Are you willing to risk the uncertainty or irregularity of your self-employment income during the early years of the enterprise?

9. Would you worry less as an employee than you would as the owner of your own business?

10. Have you carefully considered and enumerated the reasons why you want to enter business on your own?

II. Buying a Going Concern

1. Have you checked the proposition against the specific warnings issued by Better Business Bureaus and other authorities as discussed in Chapter 5?

2. Are the physical facilities in satisfactory condition?

3. Are the accounts receivable, inventory, and goodwill fairly valued?

4. Have you determined why the present owner wants to sell?

5. Have you compared what it would take to start a similar business of your own with the price asked for the business you are considering buying?

6. Has your lawyer checked to see that the title is good, that there are no liens against the business and no past due taxes or public utility bills?

7. Have you compared several independent appraisals of the business, arrived at by different methods?

8. If it is a bulk sale, has the bulk sale provisions of the Uniform Commercial Code been complied with?

9. Have you investigated possible developments, such as those discussed in Chapter 5, that might affect the business adversely?

III. Justifying a New Business

1. Have you analyzed the recent trend of business conditions?

2. Have you analyzed conditions in the line of business you are planning to enter?

3. If your business will be based on an entirely new idea, have you attempted to secure actual contracts or commitments from potential customers instead of merely getting their polite approval of your idea?

4. Have you discussed your proposition with competent advisors who are in different occupations or who have different viewpoints?

IV. Acquiring a Franchise

1. Have you viewed the franchise offer in the light of the material presented in Chapters 6 and 7?

2. Have you contacted personally several of the company's franchise holders to see how they like the deal?
3. Have you asked for a business responsibility report on the franchise promoter from your local Better Business Bureau or Chamber of Commerce?
4. Have you engaged the services of a lawyer to go over all provisions of the franchise contract?

V. Selecting the Profitable Location

1. Did you compare several different locations before making your final choice?
2. Did you use one or more detailed checklists to guide your selection?
3. Have you arranged for legal counsel before signing the lease and any similar contracts?
4. Are you, and the members of your family affected, satisfied that the community in which you plan to locate will be a desirable place in which to live and rear your children?
5. If your proposed location is not wholly suitable, are there sound reasons (not merely your impatience to get started) why you should not wait and try to secure a more nearly ideal location?

VI. Building and Layout

1. Have you studied your proposed building with function, construction, and modernization in mind?
2. Have you made a personal inspection of the physical plant of other successful businesses similar to the one you plan to start, including both independents and the branches of large organizations?
3. Have you made a scaled layout drawing of your store or shop?
4. If the proposed building does not meet all of your important needs, are there any *good* reasons for deciding to use it?

VII. Financing and Organizing the Business

1. Have you written down a complete, itemized list of all capital needs for starting your kind of business, including a fair allowance for operating expenses and your own living expenses until the business is able to support itself *and* provide a substantial reserve for the "one serious error" most businessmen make during their first year of operation?
2. Have you discussed this financial prospectus with a banker and a successful businessman in your proposed field?
3. Have you used as a guide the standard operating ratios for your business in calculating your capital requirements?
4. Have you considered all the factors for and against each legal form of organization?
5. If you plan to secure much of your initial capital from friends or relatives, are you *certain* that your business will remain free of "friendly" domination?

VIII. Establishing the Business Policies

1. Have you made an objective investigation of the probable success of your proposed policies?
2. Have you written down the main provisions of your general and major policies?

3. Have you discussed your proposed policies with competent advisors to counteract the beginner's tendency to offer what *he* likes and wants instead of what his potential *customers* like and want?

4. Have you written down an adequate statement of the reputation you want your business to acquire with customers, suppliers, and competitors?

5. Have you made adequate provisions to insure that your policies will be understood and enforced and that you will receive ample warning of the need for policy adjustments?

IX. Management and Leadership

1. Have you considered the way you will organize duties and responsibilities?

2. Have you made up a tentative plan or schedule to guide the distribution of your own time and effort?

3. Have you thought about how you would go about preparing standards, budgets, schedules, and other management aids as discussed in the text?

4. Have you provided some check on your own actions to insure that you do adequate management planning before making commitments or important decisions covering future activities of the business?

5. Have you arranged to use periodically some checklist covering detailed activities regarding customer relations, maintenance, safety, or whatever type of activity will require close attention to details in your particular business?

X. Insurance and Risk Management

1. Have you evaluated all the hazards to which your business will be exposed?

2. Have you determined the hazards for which you should provide insurance coverage?

3. Have you determined how much of each kind of insurance you should purchase, and the costs of this insurance?

4. Have you made allowances in your budget of estimated expenses for losses resulting from predictable, uninsured risks (such as shoplifting and bad debts)?

5. Have you considered the nature of the protective devices and precautionary control measures you will need to reduce the business risks you will face?

XI. Personnel and Employee Relations

1. Will you be able to hire employees, locally, who possess the requisite skills?

2. Have you prepared your wage structure, and are your wage rates in line with prevailing wage rates?

3. If you plan to employ friends and relatives, are you sure you have determined their qualifications objectively?

4. Have you planned working conditions to be as desirable and practical as possible?

5. Are you certain the employee incentives you plan to use represent the workers' viewpoint rather than what *you* think they want?

6. Have you planned your employment, induction, and training procedures?

XII. Procurement and Supplier Relations

1. Have you considered each of the desirable objectives in choosing a particular supplier, as discussed in Chapter 17, before selecting the companies you plan to deal with?
2. Have you carefully analyzed the points for and against concentrating your purchases with one or a few vendors, taking into account your personal skill and ability as well as conditions in your line of business?
3. Have you given adequate attention to each of the fundamentals of buying, as discussed in Chapter 17, in making your plans for this function?
4. Have you investigated your field of business with reference to the existence of cooperative buying groups, and the advantages of affiliating with one of these groups?

XIII. Pricing for Profit

1. Have you thought through the advantages and disadvantages of acquiring the price reputation you plan for your business?
2. Have you considered the probable reaction of competitors to your pricing practices?
3. Have you compared the relative importance in your business of each major marketing instrument, including price?
4. Have you investigated possible legal limitations on your pricing plans?
5. Have you considered possible applications of price-lining to your business?
6. Have you decided on the formula or method you will use in pricing each class of goods and services?
7. Have you decided how and to what extent you will meet probable price competition?

XIV. Advertising and Sales Promotion

1. Have you analyzed your probable competition in connection with the direct and indirect sales promotional methods you plan to use?
2. Have you planned definite ways to build and maintain superior customer relations?
3. Have you defined your potential customers so precisely that you could describe them in writing?
4. Have you decided how you can measure and record the degree of success achieved with each sales promotion so that you can repeat the "hits" and avoid the "duds"?
5. Have you considered different features of your business that would be appropriate for special promotions timed to your customers' needs and interests?
6. Have you made a list of all the media suitable for advertising *your* business, with some evaluation of each?
7. Have you selected the most promising reasons why people should patronize your business, and have you incorporated them in plans for your opening advertising?
8. Have you made use of all appropriate sources in the preparation of a good initial mailing list?
9. Have you given careful thought to the advertising value of the proposed names for your firm, products, and services?
10. Have you made plans for some unusual gesture of welcome and appreciation for all customers during the opening days of your business?
11. Have you planned how you can measure the effectiveness of your advertising?

XV. Credit and Collections

1. Have you carefully investigated the need for credit extension by your business?
2. Have you planned specifically the various ways you will secure and use information obtainable from your charge account customers?
3. Have you made a personal investigation of the services and costs of affiliating with the local credit bureau?
4. Have you planned the basic procedures you will *always* follow before extending credit to any applicant?
5. Have you formulated plans to *control* all credit accounts?

XVI. Inventory Control

1. Have you determined carefully what constitutes a *balanced* inventory for your business?
2. Have you recorded on paper the exact information you will need for effective inventory control?
3. Have you planned the best methods for securing this information?
4. Have you selected the most appropriate inventory control *system* to use?
5. Have you planned the best procedures to use for stock or stores keeping?
6. Have you listed the purposes and uses of the information you plan to secure from your inventory control system?

XVII. Production Control

1. Have you prepared a production control routine or "system" suitable to your manufacturing processes?
2. Have you anticipated future production requirements, and have you made plans for increasing the capacity of the plant as needed?

XVIII. Profit Planning and Expense Control

1. Do you know what your "break-even" volume is?
2. Have you made an estimate of what your volume is likely to be during the early years of your business?
3. Have you investigated the standard systems of expense classifications used in your type of business and selected the most appropriate one for your use?
4. Have you determined what are usually the largest items of expense for your type of business and made definite plans for controlling these expenses from the very beginning of the business?
5. Have you determined which, if any, expense items, though normally small for your type of business, very easily become excessively large unless carefully controlled *at all times?*
6. Have you prepared on paper a *flexible* expense budget for two or three different probable amounts of volume of business, including provisions for frequent operating expense reports to be compared with planned figures in your budget?
7. Have you determined the standard operating ratios for your field that you plan to use as guides?
8. Have you compared the expense of "farming out," or having certain activities of the business done by outside agencies, with what it would cost you to do the work yourself?

XIX. Regulations and Taxes

1. Have you ascertained from reliable sources all regulations that must be complied with in your business?
2. Have you provided for an adequate system of record keeping that will furnish essential information for all taxation purposes?
3. Have you checked the police, health, fire, and other safety regulations that apply to your business?
4. Have you provided for securing all information from employees required by law?
5. Have you obtained a Social Security number?
6. Have you complied with regulations governing the use of a firm or trade name, brand names, or trademarks?

XX. Records

1. Have you decided what records will be adequate for each division and need of your business?
2. Have you secured the necessary forms to enable you to start keeping adequate records from the first day of operation of the business?
3. Have you planned your record system so that appropriate use will be made of standard operating ratios?
4. Have you investigated the possibilities of using simplified record-keeping systems for some of your needs?
5. Have you considered applications of the "one-book" system to your business?
6. Have you decided by whom each record needed will be kept?
7. Have you investigated the record-keeping system recommended by the trade association in your field?

C

SBA management and marketing reading "aids" (classified by chapter subject)

Individual copies of the following "Aids" are available free of charge from field offices and Washington headquarters of the Small Business Administration *if they are in stock.* Otherwise, they are reprinted in their respective "Annuals" (listed below), which are available at nominal cost from the Superintendent of Documents, Washington, D.C., or from the U.S. Department of Commerce field offices.

Management Aids	Marketing Aids
Annual No. 1 (Aids 1–31)	Annual No. 1 (Aids 1–13)
Annual No. 2 (Aids 32–52)	Annual No. 2 (Aids 14–24)
Annual No. 3 (Aids 53–63)	Annual No. 3 (Aids 25–33)
Annual No. 4 (Aids 64–74)	Annual No. 4 (Aids 34–45)
Annual No. 5 (Aids 75–85)	Annual No. 5 (Aids 46–57)
Annual No. 6 (Aids 86–95)	Annual No. 6 (Aids 58–68)
Annual No. 7 (Aids 96–104)	Annual No. 7 (Aids 69–80)
Annual No. 8 (Aids 105–116)	Annual No. 8 (Aids 81–92)
Annual No. 9 (Aids 117–126)	Annual No. 9 (Aids 93–103)
Annual No. 10 (Aids 127–129, 134, 141)	
Annual No. 11 (Aids 130–133, 142–153)	
Annual No. 12 (Aids 154–165)	
Annual No. 13 (Aids 166–176)	

CHAPTER 4: THE DECISION FOR SELF-EMPLOYMENT

Management Aids
208. Problems in Managing a Family-Owned Business

Small Marketers' Aids
46. Essential Personal Qualities for Small Store Managers
145. Personal Qualities Needed to Manage a Store

CHAPTER 5: BUYING A GOING CONCERN

CHAPTER 6: JUSTIFYING A NEW BUSINESS

CHAPTER 7: ACQUIRING A FRANCHISE

CHAPTER 8: SELECTING THE MERCHANDISING OR SERVICE LOCATION

CHAPTER 9: SELECTING THE INDUSTRIAL LOCATION

CHAPTER 10: PROVIDING PHYSICAL FACILITIES

CHAPTER 11: FINANCING AND ORGANIZING THE BUSINESS

CHAPTER 12: POLICIES — THE BUSINESS PERSONALITY

CHAPTER 13: MANAGEMENT AND LEADERSHIP

CHAPTER 15: INSURANCE AND RISK MANAGEMENT

CHAPTER 16: PERSONNEL AND EMPLOYEE RELATIONS

CHAPTER 17: PROCUREMENT AND SUPPLIER RELATIONS

CHAPTER 18: PRICING FOR PROFIT

CHAPTER 19: ADVERTISING AND SALES PROMOTION

CHAPTER 20: CREDIT — A SALES TOOL

CHAPTER 21: INVENTORY CONTROL

CHAPTER 22:   PRODUCTION CONTROL IN THE SMALL PLANT

CHAPTER 23: PROFIT PLANNING AND COST CONTROL

CHAPTER 24: REGULATIONS AND TAXES

CHAPTER 25: SIMPLIFIED RECORD SYSTEMS

CHAPTER 27: SMALL BUSINESS INTERNATIONAL

Index